The Macmillan Guide to Writing Research Papers

THE MACMILLAN GUIDE TO WRITING RESEARCH PAPERS

William Coyle
FLORIDA ATLANTIC UNIVERSITY

MACMILLAN PUBLISHING COMPANY
NEW YORK

Editor: Barbara A. Heinssen
Production Supervisor: Eric Newman
Production Manager: Pamela Kennedy Oborski
Text and Cover Designer: Robert Freese
Cover photograph: Preston Lyon
Special thanks to Brooklyn College.

This book was set in Palatino
by Publication Services, Inc., and printed and bound by
R. R. Donnelley & Sons Company/Crawfordsville. The cover was printed by
The Lehigh Press, Inc.

Macmillan Publishing Company
866 Third Avenue, New York, New York 10022

LIBRARY OF CONGRESS CATALOGING-IN-PUBLICATION DATA

Coyle, William.
    The Macmillan guide to writing research papers / William Coyle.
        p.   cm.
    Includes index.
    ISBN 0-02-325291-X
    1. Report writing—Handbooks, manuals, etc.   2. Research—
Handbooks, manuals, etc.   I. Title.
    LB2369.C646 1990
    808'.02—dc19   89-30794
                                                         CIP

Printing: 1 2 3 4 5 6 7   Year: 0 1 2 3 4 5 6

ACKNOWLEDGMENTS

Excerpts from "Dance, the Art of" in *Encyclopaedia Britannica*, 15th ed. (1985), reproduced
    by permission of Encyclopaedia Britannica, Inc.
Excerpts from *Books in Print* and *Magazines for Libraries* reproduced by permission of
    R. R. Bowker Company.
Essay and General Literature Index, 1986, Copyright © 1986 by The H. W. Wilson Company.
    Material reproduced by permission of the publisher.
Database citations reproduced with permission of Dialog Information Services, Inc., and
    searches conducted via the DIALOG* Information Retrieval Service (*Service mark Reg.
    US Pat. & TM Off.) and with permission of the American Psychological Association,
    publisher of *Psychological Abstracts* and the PsycINFO Database (Copyright © 1967–
    1988 by the American Psychological Association), not to be reproduced without its
    prior permission.
(Acknowledgments continue on facing page, which constitutes a continuation of the
    copyright page.)

Introduction: To the Instructor

The Macmillan Guide to Writing Research Papers is designed primarily for use in freshman composition classes, but it has been made as inclusive as possible so that it can also be useful to students in their future courses. The coverage of various styles of documentation in Chapters 5 and 6 and the listings of reference works (pages 59–65 and 234–57) should be particularly helpful in any courses involving research. Although many students dispose of textbooks immediately after completing a course, as Naval Academy graduates fling their caps into the air, they should be encouraged to retain *The Macmillan Guide* for future use.

The Writing Process

The Macmillan Guide is adaptable to whatever degree of supervision you consider appropriate for a class. Students who have written research papers previously may need little classroom discussion of research techniques and can use this book on their own as a "self-pacing" reference, supplemented by individual consultations with you. If, on the other hand, your students need considerable explanation of research procedures, *The Macmillan Guide* follows the preparation of a paper from the search for a topic to the final proofreading and is organized in sections that can be assigned on a day-to-day basis.

There is some danger that the word *process* and the step-by-step procedure of investigating and developing a topic may give students the impression that writing is a stereotyped sequence of mechanical steps. Each student should be encouraged to develop a personal but sensible and orderly method of writing a paper. Too many students approach a writing assignment in a haphazard manner, and following a systematic procedure in writing their research papers should make them better writers and, perhaps, better students as well.

Getting a paper underway is often the most difficult stage of the writing process. Chapter 1 suggests such preliminary techniques as keeping a research log, brainstorming, and freewriting. Also discussed are two considerations often overlooked: determining the purpose of a paper and identifying the audience for which it is intended.

The use of word processors, which is rapidly increasing on campuses and in society at large, is described in Appendix A. Students who compose on a word processor sometimes neglect revision, for which the word processor is especially well suited, perhaps because the text produced by the printer looks so neat and attractive.

Library Procedure

Students are often bewildered by their first encounter with an academic library, and recent technological innovations may heighten their bewilderment. Chapter 2 discusses new services such as online catalogs, InfoTrac, and computer searching of databases. Most students when they come to college are familiar with *Readers' Guide to Periodical Literature* and its subject–author organization, and they find many specialized indexes organized in the same way. They should also, however, become familiar with indexes following a different system, such as the ERIC indexes, the *Citation Indexes* published by the Institute for Scientific Information, and the *Monthly Catalog of U.S. Government Publications*. Chapter 2 and Appendix B contain listings of nearly 500 basic reference works as well as databases for twenty academic fields.

Writing the Paper

Chapters 3 and 4 discuss methods of gathering and organizing material as well as the actual writing of a paper. Students sometimes rely solely on books and periodicals; a listing of twelve kinds of supplementary sources may direct them to usable information elsewhere. The kinds of notes and methods of note-taking are discussed in Chapter 3. A successful research paper smoothly blends quotations with the text; methods of incorporating quotations into the text are described in Chapter 4. Students should rely on their handbooks for general mechanics, but a discussion of punctuation marks used with quotations (pages 120–22) should be convenient for quick reference.

Two sample papers in Chapter 5 and one in Chapter 6 illustrate different styles of documentation as well as the treatment of different kinds of subjects. You might consider asking students to read all three at the outset of their research for a general impression of content, structure, and style.

Documentation, MLA Style

The MLA style of documentation, as toastmasters often say of obscure speakers, "needs no introduction." Progress toward simplicity and uniformity in documentation procedures began in 1951 with publication of *The MLA Style Sheet* (2nd ed., 1970), which recommended the use of footnotes. A new, much-expanded book, *MLA Handbook for Writers of Research Papers* (1977), emphasized endnotes. After being tried out in *PMLA* for two years, a new style—in-text citation keyed to a list of works cited—was introduced in a second edition of *MLA Handbook* (1984). A third edition (1988) contains discussions of computer searching and online library catalogs and additional examples of bibliographic forms but retains the basic in-text system. Throughout *The Macmillan Guide,* recommended documentation forms and practices follow this latest edition. They are illustrated by a sample paper. The practice of citing references within the text and keying citations to a list of sources is easy to master, and students quickly come to appreciate the simplicity and efficiency of this procedure. Some students' styles improve because in-text citation facilitates the blending of quotations with their text. It is possible as well that because a citation in parentheses is so much easier to write than a footnote or endnote, the incidence of plagiarism may be reduced.

Although endnotes are rapidly following footnotes into oblivion, students will encounter them in their research and should be able to interpret them. Therefore, the use of endnotes is described in Chapter 5 and is illustrated by the second sample paper.

Unless your slogan is "All the Way with MLA," you may wish to modify some recommendations. Many instructors, for example, prefer that a paper have a title page and an outline page, neither of which is recommended by MLA. Some also prefer that block quotations, explanation and reference notes, and bibliographic entries of more than one line be single-spaced, because double-spacing is mainly a convenience to typesetters when a manuscript is to be printed.

Documentation, APA Style

APA style, recommended by the American Psychological Association, is described in Chapter 6 and is illustrated by a sample paper there and by another in the instructor's manual. Variations of APA style predominate in education and in most of the social sciences. If your students plan to major in these fields, you may want them to document their papers in APA style. At least they will need to be able to interpret it during their research. Actually, MLA and APA styles are similar enough that a student who masters one can readily adapt to the other. Variant styles in nine other disciplines are discussed briefly and are illustrated in Chapter 6.

Instructor's Manual

An instructor's manual, printed in an 8-1/2 × 11'' format to facilitate photocopying, contains suggestions and supplementary exercises for each chapter. The exercises can be used as in-class or as take-home assignments. The manual also includes three annotated papers: a short contrast-of-sources paper using endnotes, a short critical paper using in-text citations, and a longer paper illustrating both APA and MLA styles. Facing pages display the same text but different methods of documentation. Any of these papers could be photocopied and distributed to students, or they could be analyzed in class by means of an overhead projector.

Acknowledgments ⸻⸻⸻⸻⸻⸻⸻⸻⸻⸻⸻⸻⸻⸻⸻⸻⸻⸻

I wish to express my gratitude to Barbara A. Heinssen, English editor, Macmillan Publishing Company, who has been involved with this book from its conception and whose guidance has been most helpful, and Eric Newman, production supervisor, whose painstaking editing and suggestions regarding both style and format have been extremely valuable. I would also like to thank the following persons for their thoughtful comments and suggestions: Donna Alden, New Mexico State University; Linda Blackwell Billingsley, University of Louisville; Diana Y. Dreyer, Slippery Rock University; Donella Eberle, Mesa Community College, Philip H. Kelly, Gannon University; Daniel Lynch, LaGuardia Community College, CUNY; Lois Rosen, University of Michigan at Flint; and Linda Wiler, Florida Atlantic University. The calligraphy in the intructor's manual was produced by Lawrence Pitts and Shawn Tennell of the Florida Atlantic University Graphics Division. I am especially grateful to William Miller, director of Florida Atlantic University Libraries, who scrutinized not only the original version of the library chapter but also a revision. His insightful suggestions did much to enhance the usefulness of that chapter. Any surviving omissions, inaccuracies, or other errors, are, of course, my responsibility.

WILLIAM COYLE

Introduction: To the Student

Research paper . . . library paper . . . source paper . . . term paper . . . investigative theme—whatever it is called, producing one may not rank very high on your list of enjoyable pastimes. Nevertheless, research writing can be a rewarding experience if you choose a topic that arouses your curiosity and stirs your imagination. It can also be a valuable introduction to procedures and skills that you will need in future courses. In any field you can expect to be required to use the library efficiently, to interpret and organize ideas, and to document borrowed materials. Because *The Macmillan Guide to Writing Research Papers* is designed to be useful to you throughout your college career, it contains more examples of documentation form and of reference sources than you will need for a single paper. It has been made as complete as possible so that it can be used as a reference guide in advanced courses. Even though, like many students, you sell your textbooks back to the bookstore (at considerable loss) when a course is over, you would be wise to keep this one on your bookshelf.

Documentation (listing the sources used in a paper and crediting a source for each piece of borrowed information) seems a mighty maze to some students and distracts them from more important matters like organizing material logically and writing clearly and effectively. The system of documentation stressed in this book is that of the Modern Language Association (MLA style). It is simple and easy to use. If you master the basic forms for a book and for a periodical, you can adapt them to the variant forms that are illustrated in Chapter 5. The other system in widespread use is that of the American Psychological Association (APA style), which is described in Chapter 6. If you major in education or in one of the social sciences, you will need to become familiar with this style. Actually, MLA and APA styles are similar enough that if you master one, you can easily adapt to the other. The intricacies of documentation are not as important as finding relevant support for a suitable topic and writing the results in a pleasing and appropriate style.

The ability to gather, interpret, and organize information is a valuable skill in college and in almost any business or profession. The purpose of this book is to help you attain and use that skill.

W. C.

Brief Contents

Detailed Contents

CHAPTER 4   Writing Your Paper   97

CHAPTER 5   Documenting Borrowed Material:
MLA Style   129

*The Macmillan
Guide to Writing
Research Papers*

Getting Started

When a research paper is assigned, your first reaction may be a groan or a shudder, after which you can follow one of three courses of action. You may give it the Scarlett O'Hara treatment and "think about it tomorrow"; you may head straight for the library and begin searching for books and periodicals; or you may take some time to consider the problem and plan your strategy. One purpose of this chapter is to encourage you to choose the third possibility.

A number of steps that you can follow during the early stages of your research are suggested in the following paragraphs. In a sense, the orderly sequence of steps is misleading because writing is a recursive, not a linear, procedure. That is, it is not a step-by-step process that follows a straight line to a completed paper; instead, it inevitably involves false starts, dead ends, and changes of direction. Before beginning your concentrated research, you need to identify your audience, determine your purpose,

1

settle on a narrow topic, formulate a thesis, and begin setting up a tentative plan. A few problems will seem to solve themselves; others will require both trial-and-error experimentation and hard thinking. Some decisions will be made simultaneously, and others will be made in an order different from what is suggested here.

A number of procedures that other students have found helpful are suggested in this chapter. Try those that seem suited to your work habits and remember the ones that are successful. They will help you develop a research-writing strategy that you can use in future courses.

Using Research

If you shudder a bit when a research paper is assigned, perhaps the term *research* puts you off. It may bring to mind a pale, bespectacled student surrounded by stacks of dusty volumes in a library carrel or a grim-looking scientist in a white coat peering intently at a test tube in an antiseptic-looking laboratory. Actually, research is something you have done informally all your life. Have you ever compared two cereals to see which one you preferred, admired a quarterback and collected his passing statistics, enjoyed a movie and then read reviews to see what critics thought of it, compared brochures to select a summer camp, computed the calories in a dinner menu, joined a family discussion of what model new car to buy, examined catalogs and visited campuses to choose a college? If you answered yes to any of these questions, you have done research, which simply means a more or less systematic search for information.

Although textbooks, including this one, refer to a "research process," the term may be misleading; it suggests a formalized sequence of steps to be followed as in assembling a motor or baking a cake. Preparing a research paper is less systematic than the term *process* suggests, but in general your work goes through these stages:

1. You begin with a broad subject area and a general idea (a hypothesis) about that subject.
2. As you read and think about the subject and consider your prospective audience, you restrict the subject to a specific *topic* and determine what you hope to accomplish in developing it.
3. You narrow your hypothesis to a definite idea about your topic—a thesis.
4. You investigate your topic by reading and by exploring any other appropriate sources of information, looking for material that will support your thesis.
5. You organize your supporting material in a logical plan.
6. You write the results of your research in an orderly essay, crediting the sources of all borrowed facts and opinions.

Of course, the actual preparation of a paper is not as simple as these steps suggest. There are certain to be false starts, changes of direction, and searches for material that cannot be found. But this general procedure describes the nature of your task. Furthermore, it is a procedure that you are likely to follow in other courses.

In a history class, for example, you may be asked to write a term paper on the Yalta Conference or the Berlin airlift, in an economics class a paper on the Laffer Curve or options trading, in a philosophy class a paper on Alfred North Whitehead's philosophy of organism, or in a literature class a paper on urban imagery in Theodore Dreiser's *Sister Carrie*. You can expect a similar assignment in almost any field. In the social sciences, you may be asked to write a case study, conduct and analyze a poll, or review research on a current issue. In the natural sciences, you may write reports of experiments, a paper on an issue like air pollution, or a review of research. In any of these fields, some of the procedures you follow while writing your research paper should prove useful.

Research does not come to an end when you accept your diploma and step off the stage. The basic procedure of focusing on a topic from a particular point of view and collecting information about it is followed by a politician studying public opinion polls, by a broker predicting the future price of pork bellies, by a lawyer searching casebooks for precedents, by a football coach scouting his next opponent, by a reporter investigating an election fraud, by a department store buyer trying to determine what fashions will be popular, by a physician reading reports of a new drug, and by a garden club member preparing a talk on the uses of compost.

Setting a Work Schedule

A research paper is always assigned several weeks in advance. You will need to consider the phases of the project and budget your time accordingly. If your instructor suggests dates when various phases should be completed, try to stay ahead of that schedule or at least keep up with it. Otherwise, draw up your own schedule. In your notebook, list the major phases of the research process:

> Topic
> Thesis
> Main headings
> Bibliography cards
> Note cards
> Working outline
> Rough draft
> Revision
> Final copy

Estimate the number of hours you will need for each stage of the process, correlate the times with your study and work schedules, and set a date for completing each of them. Meeting or beating a deadline can be a minor satisfaction that will give you a psychological lift.

Start work as soon as possible. If the due date for the paper is several weeks away, it is easy to procrastinate, postpone the choice of a topic, and turn your attention to other matters. A paper turned out on the weekend before it is due will almost certainly not represent your best work. A successful research paper is not written in a day or two. Collecting and organizing the material will take longer than you expect, and the more time you have for thoughtful revision, the better. Consequently, you should begin considering possible topics as soon as the paper is assigned.

The human mind functions in mysterious ways. While a subject lies dormant, an incubation process can occur, and an idea may flash into your awareness like the light bulb above a character's head in an old-time comic strip. Even though you are not consciously pondering a topic, your mind may subconsciously refine it, add to it, or narrow it so that when you begin reading and note-taking, your ideas fall into place more readily than you expected. Obviously you cannot rely too heavily on this sort of subconscious action, but you lose the benefits of a mental gestation period if you try to turn out a paper the night before it is due.

Trying Preliminary Strategies

Just as a pianist does finger exercises or a baseball pitcher warms up in the bullpen, you can benefit from a limbering-up process in the early stages of your research writing. Some strategic techniques can serve as a kind of reconnaissance that will assist you in finding a suitable topic and purpose, evaluating material, and devising a workable plan. They can also be helpful after you begin to write, especially if you reach an impasse and your imagination seems to be blocked. Consider the following suggestions and try those that sound useful.

1. *Taking a mental inventory.* Because some students think of their assignment as a "library paper," they rush to the catalog or the stacks and neglect an important source of information—what they already know. You are not likely to choose a topic that is totally unfamiliar to you, and so you should assess what is already in your mind. Tom Graham, the writer of the first sample paper (pages 168–81), heard a class lecture on the California gold rush that mentioned the transportation problems it created, and he had read a discussion in his textbook. Rita Hogan, writer of the second sample paper (pages 191–203), had just read *Pride and Prejudice*. Both students, therefore, were able to consider their own ideas before reading historical accounts, criticism, or other secondary sources.

2. *Keeping a log or journal.* In the early stages of your research, note cards may seem formal and forbiddingly businesslike. Use your notebook as a running diary in which you jot down possible topics, ideas, questions, sources to look for, main headings for the outline, and reminders of various kinds. Your research log can begin with the mental inventory described in step #1. After listing what you know about your topic, jot down reminders of what you do not know—information you must search out to support your thesis. These notes are entirely for your own use and will contain abbreviations, your personal shorthand, and other shortcuts. All that matters is that they be meaningful to you. A daily record of your research will help keep your efforts focused on your purpose and may also prod your conscience if you let several days elapse with no work on your project. Following are some rough notes made for the stagecoach paper:

Tues.

Use Moody for desc. of coach -- make cards.

Not too much on Calif. history

Where can I type in Library?

Look for _Am. Heritage_.

How much was fare? How comfortable was coach?

Include movies? Yes

Where are books on movies?

When was John Ford film made?

Look for movie reviews and story film was based on.

Wed.

Wasted day!

Thur.

What is a thoroughbrace?

Stagecoach = frontier ingenuity
(use in thesis?)
Hank Monk in __DAB__?
Include a map?
__Am. Merc.__ on microfilm (Jan. 1950)
Paintings? Best Remington painting
   to use?
Use Twain for drivers, station
   agents.

3. *Brainstorming.* Our minds and imaginations do not function like well-oiled machines but dart about as one idea suggests another. Shift your mind into cruise control and let it drift within a broad subject. Free association often will bring up more ideas than you expect. Many, of course, will be irrelevant trivia, but others will be fresh insights that you can use in your paper. The important thing is to set your mind and imagination in motion. Use your research log to record the results of a brainstorming session. After crossing out items that obviously do not belong, you can simply rearrange facts and ideas in a running outline (see pages 20–24). Some students find it helpful to "cluster" ideas by making a topical map like the one on page 24. You begin by encircling a key term in the middle of a sheet of paper and then writing ideas that radiate from it. Clustering might be described as controlled brainstorming.

Brainstorming can be useful throughout the preparation of a paper. After a note-taking session in the library, spend a few minutes ranging mentally over what you have read and jot down usable ideas. Sometimes a new aspect of your topic or a turn of phrase will pop into your mind when you least expect it.

4. *Freewriting.* To prospect for ideas and to put your mind and imagination in a writing mode before you start your rough draft, you might spend ten or fifteen minutes in nonstop automatic writing, disregarding logic, spelling, commas, and other niceties. Freewriting is a discovery technique intended to generate ideas. You simply allow your mind to hover around a subject, and you set down whatever occurs to you. The result will be an indiscriminate listing of words, phrases, and brief questions. Reading over your freewriting a day or two later may suggest a fresh approach to your topic. Just the physical act of writing may unblock your imagination. This technique works best with a typewriter or a word processor because writing with a pen or pencil often lapses into mere doodling.

After reading *Pride and Prejudice*, Rita Hogan typed some random thoughts about the novel. Her brainstorming soon led her to the variety of marriages in the story, and this became her topic. She crossed out unusable ideas and kept the freewriting in her journal for future reference. In the following example, the abbreviations and other shortcuts are permissible because such notes will be seen by no one else.

```
JA's comic style . . . What makes it comic? . . .

Do I know enough about language? . . . Is opening

sentence ironic? . . . Mr. Bennet's cruel humor

. . . Humor in JA's comments and in characters'

speeches

The Bennet sisters--how alike and how different?

Lydia = an irresponsible teenager . . . How do

sisters resemble their parents?

JA's use of letters

Mrs. Bennet as a mother . . . Her concern to marry

off her daughters . . .

Mr. and Mrs. Bennet = an unsuitable marriage . . .

the Gardiners = an ideal couple . . .

Dancing as courtship . . . How many dances in the

novel?

Elizabeth . . . What if she had accepted Mr.

Collins? . . . Would she have become bitter like

her father?
```

```
Compare Darcy and Wickham

Elizabeth and Darcy = an ideal couple?

Why is marriage so important to JA? . . . How many

marriages in the novel? . . . How many happy?

Barriers between Elizabeth and Darcy . . . What

breaks down her resistance? . . . Pemberley?
```

In reading over these rough notes, Rita noticed the predominance of marriage in her thinking, and this became her topic.

Identifying Your Audience

During the early stages of your research, you will need to consider three basic questions:

> Who will be my readers?
> What do I want to accomplish?
> What shall I write about?

Determining your audience, your purpose, and your topic are interrelated decisions that may be made more or less simultaneously. Unfortunately, the first two are often ignored or not considered thoughtfully enough.

All communication is a two-way process involving a speaker or writer and listeners or readers (the audience). In written communication, because the audience is invisible or imaginary, it is easy to ignore this element in the process. However, the kind of audience you write for determines both what and how you write. In describing the World Series to a British reader, you would need to supply definitions, explanations, and facts that an American reader would not require. Similarly, if you write about cricket for an American audience, you would need to include much elementary information. If you wrote about the commodities market for your economics class, your language and your facts would be more technical than in a paper written for readers with little knowledge of the subject. A discussion of acid rain written for an audience of environmentalists would be quite different from one written for factory owners.

While choosing a topic, you should determine your audience and ask yourself how much prior knowledge your readers have, what opinions they hold, and how their interest can be aroused and sustained. It is usually not a good idea to write for an audience of specialists. Assume that your readers have a general knowledge of your subject and that they are thoughtful, open-minded, and perceptive. Keep your audience in mind during every phase of the research process.

In actuality, of course, your instructor will be your primary reader, but it is sometimes unwise to choose a subject in which he or she is an expert. Some teachers suggest writing for one's classmates, and an audience of your peers is especially advisable when final papers are read aloud in class or are circulated and read by other students. It is often best to create a *persona*—an implied reader who is approximately as familiar with your topic as you are when you begin your research. Thus you can determine which terms need to be defined and how much factual support is required for your ideas. Adapting your style and your material to this reader's interest and knowledge will help you maintain a consistent tone and point of view throughout your paper.

Defining Your Purpose

People write for an endless number of reasons—to describe, to amuse, to protest, to inform, to interpret, to diagnose, to define, to clarify, to criticize, and so on. In your research paper, your reason for writing or purpose will be to explain, to analyze, or to persuade. These purposes—explanation, analysis, and argumentation—may all be found in the same paper, but one will be dominant. Considering who your audience will be and what purpose you hope to accomplish will help you focus on a narrow topic and formulate a meaningful thesis.

The explanatory paper is written to inform or clarify, to acquaint the reader with a body of material. Essentially it is an expository report. The most common fault in explanatory papers is the lack of a meaningful thesis. The paper should do more than simply record information; it should relate the content to a unifying idea. Such a paper, for example, might describe the techniques used by shoplifters; the thesis might be simply to show the ingenuity and deception involved in their operations.

Analysis means dividing something into its component parts and examining their relationships. An analytical paper considers separate aspects of a topic in order to support an overall judgment or thesis. These aspects become the major steps in the plan. Inaccurate or incomplete analysis is probably the most common fault because it is sometimes easy to overlook an important aspect of a topic. Such a paper might categorize shoplifters by age and by sex and analyze the motives or the methods of each group.

An argumentative paper attempts to persuade your audience to accept your judgment on an issue and, perhaps, to take some action. Because topics for such papers are often controversial, it is important that you are not swayed by your personal bias or preconceived ideas. Avoid an emotional topic like abortion or animal rights if you cannot objectively present both sides of the issue. To convince your audience, you need to be objective and fair-minded. Such a paper usually presents both pro and con arguments. An argumentative paper on shoplifters might advocate improved security in department stores and stricter penalties for offenders.

As indicated in the foregoing paragraphs, these purposes may be combined in the same paper, but one will dominate. The first sample paper (pages 168–81) is primarily an explanation of the construction and operation of frontier stagecoaches, but it also analyzes the stagecoach as a symbol in popular culture. The second paper (pages 191–203), like many papers on literary, artistic, or musical topics, is analytical; it examines the marriages in *Pride and Prejudice* in relation to their effect on the marriage of the main characters. The third paper (pages 218–28) analyzes types of elder abuse and also argues that improved social services and legislation to protect the elderly are needed.

Reducing a Subject to a Topic

The term *subject* refers to a broad field of knowledge; *topic* denotes a limited aspect of a subject that can be examined with some thoroughness and developed in a paper. A subject is a stretch of open country ten miles square; a topic is a half-acre lot on which you will erect a house. If your instructor assigns the entire class a general subject like "politics" or "popular culture," your task will be to settle on a narrow topic within that field. If the assignment is open-ended, you will need to survey a subject that interests you in search of a usable topic.

Evaluating Possible Topics

In the early stages of your research, no decision is as important as the choice of a topic. Devote some time to searching for one that interests you and that meets the requirements of the assignment. Considering the following characteristics of a suitable topic may help you make a choice.

1. *It should be narrow enough to be developed fully.* Because a research paper is relatively long, there is a natural tendency to choose a broad topic. But if the assignment is a 2,000-word paper, it will be eight or nine pages long, about the length of a column and a half in a newspaper. It is impossible to cover "The Operas of Wagner" or "The Life of Lincoln" in that much space. Biographical papers are often unsatisfactory, in fact, because they attempt to cover the subject's entire life. If you write about an individual, focus on one aspect of that person's career.

2. *It should require research.* A subjective notion or attitude that cannot be supported by facts and opinions from printed sources is an unsuitable topic. It would be impossible to find supporting material in the library for "Why I Go to Church" or "My Parents."

3. *It should be a topic that you can consider objectively.* A controversial question may motivate your research, but if you have strong preconceptions concerning it, they may distort your judgment. Also, reliable information may be unobtainable; charges and countercharges may frustrate your attempt to sift the true from the false. The role of the CIA in Central America, the right-to-life movement, and supply-side economics are potentially satisfactory subjects, but they may be too controversial or too complex for a relatively short paper.

4. *It should be a topic that you are curious about but not thoroughly familiar with.* A research paper should take you into new territory. Work in the library should produce a thrill of discovery, not bored recognition of the already known. If, for example, you are an expert on nutrition, collecting information on junk food would soon become tedious. Unless you clear it with your instructor, do not write on a topic you have already investigated in another course. Above all, do not hand in a paper previously written for another course. The first action is foolish because retracing familiar ground soon becomes tiresome; the second is dishonest and would probably result in a failing grade.

5. *It should be within your scope.* Whether a topic is too technical for you to investigate will depend on your background and your interests. A paper on "Free-electron Lasers" would not be suitable for a student untrained in science. "The Great Vowel Shift" would not do for a student with no knowledge of linguistics. In general, avoid subjects involving totally unfamiliar concepts and baffling technical terminology.

Scanning Listings in Reference Works

Any work that subdivides a subject into categories can be helpful in reducing a subject to a topic. Joseph Walsh, writer of the third sample paper (pages 218–28), was assigned a short research paper in his social psychology class. He first scanned the table of contents in his textbook, sometimes a good source of potential subjects. A chapter entitled "Problems of Aging" caught his eye, but he soon found the subject much more complex than he expected. In *Social Sciences Index* for 1987 there were six pages of articles listed under "Aged." To see how much had been published in popular magazines, he looked in *Readers' Guide* for 1986, where he found seventeen "see also" references, thirteen general articles, and many additional articles listed under forty subheadings. He had noted a subheading, "Abuse of the aged," in *Social Sciences Index*, and he considered a paper with three main sections: abuse by family members, by nursing home personnel, and by criminals such as muggers or street gangs. Skimming two articles convinced him that his subject was still too broad, and so he limited it to abuse by relatives. As he continued reading, he realized that abuse of the elderly had been ignored until recently and still seemed a problem with no solution. He made this idea the focus of his paper and included it in his title: "Abuse of the Elderly: An Overlooked Form of Family Violence." Just before falling asleep one night (a productive time for generating ideas, provided that they can be recalled the next day), he thought of five main points for his paper:

1. Extent of abuse
2. Kinds of abuse
3. Abusers
4. Victims
5. Possible ways of dealing with the problem

The "getting started" phase of his project was completed, and he was ready to begin taking notes and thinking of a rough draft. He later decided that "Victims" would fit more naturally after "Kinds of abuse"; otherwise, he developed the skeleton outline shown above. By examination of indexes and some articles and by thoughtful analysis, he had reduced an enormous subject to a manageable topic.

Although you cannot base an entire paper on encyclopedias, they can be very useful when you are surveying a subject in search of a topic and looking for basic sources. A student considering a paper on some aspect of dancing found a long (thirty-four page) article in *Britannica Macropaedia*. It begins with an outline of the discussion:

Sample entry from *Brittanica Macropaedia*.

The forms of dance 986	Historical development 993
Origins and functions of the	Origins in the Renaissance
dance 986	17th century
Primitive beginnings	18th century
From antiquity to the Renaissance	Romantic and classical traditions
The East	in the 19th century
The Renaissance	Early 20th century
Post-Renaissance developments	Ballet since Diaghilev
Components of the dance 987	Modern dance 1000
The dancer	Principles underlying modern
The choreographer	dance 1000
Accompaniments to the dance	Ballet and modern dance
Theatrical effects	Intellectual and artistic influence
Narrative methods and materials	Historical development 1001
Kinds of dance 989	Pioneers
Natural, or untutored, dance	The late 1920s and after
Solo and group dance	Renewed searches for new forms
Ethnic dance	Further development
Folk dance	Choreography and dance

Court dance	notation 1005
Ballroom dance	Choreography 1005
Theatrical dance	Elements and principles
Ballet 991	of composition
The aesthetics of ballet 991	Formal training
Dancers	Dance notation 1005
Composers	20th century
Librettists	Personal use of notation
Designers	by choreographers
Choreographers	

At the close of the article, an annotated bibliography lists several sources.

BIBLIOGRAPHY. CURT SACHS, *Eine Weltgeschichte des Tanzes* (1933; Eng. trans., *A World History of the Dance*, 1937, reprinted 1963), the most comprehensive, systematic, and factual history of dance in all its epochs and forms, with special emphasis on its earliest beginnings and close attention to dance accompaniment; W.F. RAFFE, *Dictionary of the Dance* (1965), detailed descriptions of the particular dances, their background, and history; ANATOLE CHUJOY and P.W. MANCHESTER (eds.), *The Dance Encyclopedia*, rev. ed. (1967), a collection of articles on all forms of dancing—particularly detailed in its coverage of ballet, including entries on specific productions, artistic biographies, and histories of ballet in various countries; LINCOLN KIRSTEIN, *Dance: A Short History of Classic Theatrical Dancing* (1942, reprinted 1969), a very thorough book on the pre-balletic forms of dance as well as classic theatrical dance; WALTER SORELL, *The Dance Through the Ages* (1967), a general, readable survey of the worldwide dance scene from prehistoric times through today, with superb pictures of ancient and modern dance; A.H. FRANKS, *Social Dance: A Short History (1963),* the first attempt at relating the origins and developments of the most important social dance forms to their social environment; FRANCES RUST, *Dance in Society* (1969), a study giving documentary evidence of the social dances and their relationships to the changing structures of society, with emphasis on the English scene and the teen-age explosion in dance during the 1960s; MARY CLARKE and CLEMENT CRISP, *The History of Dance* (1981), well-written, illustrated, and indexed survey.

(H.Ko.)

Annotated bibliography from *Brittanica Macropaedia.*

Permuterm Subject Index (see pages 45–46) is an example of extensive subdivision. The 1984 volume for social sciences lists under the general term "Aging" more than six columns of terms, from "Abroad" to "Years." Another work that can help you limit a subject is *Library of Congress Subject Headings,* two large volumes bound in red that will probably be found near the catalog in your school library. This work indicates the call numbers used for a broad subject and lists key terms or descriptors under which titles are filed in the library catalog. The same terms are used by various periodical indexes and other specialized reference works. The general term "Aged" is subdivided, and there are cross-references to related terms such as "Life care communities" or "Age and employment." The general terms under "Aged" are as follows:

Aged	*(Indirect) (Geriatrics, RC952-954.6;* *Public welfare, HV1450-1493;* *Sociology, HQ1060-1064)* Here and with local subdivision are en- tered works on the conditions of the aged in general and in particular places. Works on the discipline of gerontology are entered under Ger- ontology.
sa	Aged, Killing of the Aging Centenarians Children and the aged Church work with the aged Day care centers for the aged Developmentally disabled aged Gardening for the aged Gerontocracy Indians of North America—Aged Life span, Productive Minority aged Old age assistance Parents, Aged Police services for the aged Retirement income Rural aged Sex instruction for the aged Social case work with the aged Social work with the aged Television and the aged

Sample entry from *Library of Congress Subject Headings.*

The "see also" (*sa*) subheadings may start your mind moving toward a topic. The classification numbers tell you where to look in the stacks for books on the subject.

Any listing that subdivides a general subject into categories or proceeds from the general to the specific can jog your imagination, put your mind in a reductive mode, and assist you in finding a narrow topic.

Exploratory Reading in General Sources

During the preliminary stages of your research, besides scanning lists of topics, you will probably need to read one or two general discussions of a subject, looking not for information but for a phase of the subject that stirs your interest. Encyclopedias, textbooks, handbooks, and general magazines are best for this type of reading. Skimming a brief encyclopedia article on meat-packing, for example, supplied a student with the following topics:

Early cattle drives
Chicago as a packing center
Cincinnati as "Porkopolis" in the nineteenth century
Use of the by-products
Classification of beef by quality
The Jungle by Upton Sinclair
The career of Philip D. Armour
Ingredients of frankfurters
Government regulations
Humane killing procedures

Further reading and thinking would enable the student to choose one of these topics for investigation.

Your paper should not duplicate work done for another course; but one of your classes, especially one in your major field, may lead you to a rewarding topic. A remark in your American history class about the Zouaves, colorful volunteer troops during the Civil War, might send you to the library to look for more information. Be alert in class lectures and in conversations with your friends for references that spark your imagination: the campaign to impeach Chief Justice Earl Warren, the Black Sox scandal of 1919, the race to the South Pole by Robert Scott and Roald Amundsen, the rediscovery of F. Scott Fitzgerald's fiction in the late 1940s, compact discs and information retrieval, the antipolio vaccines discovered by Dr. Jonas Salk and Dr. Albert Sabin. When such a subject arouses your interest, skim a general account of it to determine its possibilities.

The Art of Skimming

A by-product of your research project may be improvement of your reading skill—especially your ability to skim efficiently. An experienced driver can control an automobile at any speed and knows what speed is appropriate to a given situation; a novice driver chugs along at the same speed under all conditions. Similarly, a skillful reader adjusts reading speed to the purpose of the reading and the nature of the material; an unskillful reader plods along at the same rate, often reading word-for-word. Gathering material for a research paper should make you a more proficient reader by expanding the range of your reading rate.

Exploratory reading requires intelligent skimming. Skimming an article in a journal or a chapter in a book is a skill that can be developed through practice. It does not mean skipping alternate pages or reading the first three lines on each page but reading at your most rapid rate, hitting the high spots in search of an author's main ideas. Concentrate on the first and last sentences of paragraphs and on opening and closing paragraphs. Many articles open with reviews of previous research; these reviews may furnish leads to other sources. The close of an article can also be useful because the major ideas will probably be summarized there; reading it carefully will enable you to judge whether the body of the article will furnish support for your thesis. If the author's summation sounds promising, write yourself a reminder to return to it when you begin taking notes.

Browsing in the Library Stacks

Browsing, like skimming, is sometimes dismissed unfavorably, probably because it is casual and does not follow a clear plan to a fixed objective. Nevertheless, some of the major discoveries in human history were made by accident, and if you are lucky a minor discovery may occur for you as you browse in the library stacks.

Tom Graham, writer of the first sample paper (pages 168–81), began with a vague intention of finding a topic related to history, his major field. A class lecture made reference to the unique problems created by the discovery of gold in California; people, freight, and mail had to be transported across 1,500 miles of sparsely populated country. Tom considered the sea voyage that many took, the land routes, the stagecoach, the Pony Express, and the Union Pacific Railroad. Browsing in the library stacks, he thumbed through a pictorial history of the West, where a full-color picture of a Concord stage caught his eye. This became his topic. As he read accounts of Western history and recalled television westerns, he realized that the stagecoach was an essential part of frontier history and legend. This idea became his thesis. His preliminary searching had moved in descending order:

1. American history
2. The West
3. The gold rush
4. Need for efficient transportation
5. Types of transportation
6. Stagecoaches, construction and operation
7. Stagecoaches in legend

Some of this narrowing was automatic. No one would seriously consider writing on the first three subjects, and the next two are also hopelessly general. The sixth topic, actual stagecoaches, turned out to be too limited, and so Tom expanded it to include the role of stagecoaches in popular culture. In the Library Media Center, he was able to view the 1939 John Ford film *Stagecoach*, and a discussion of this classic movie became the climax and the final paragraph of his paper.

It is crucial that you find a narrow topic that meets your instructor's specifications and is also interesting to you. Even after you are satisfied with your topic, however, taking notes would be a waste of time until you are committed to a thesis.

Formulating a Thesis

Your thesis is an assumption about your topic, an approach to it, a proposition to be supported, a purpose for writing, the controlling idea that determines what kind of material you will look for. However it is defined, a thesis narrows your topic further and assures that it is manageable.

In form a thesis is a single sentence, usually with the topic of the paper as the grammatical subject. Sometimes it suggests the main divisions of the basic plan of the paper. It often is the most difficult sentence in the paper to compose. You will probably need to try several versions before you arrive at a satisfactory statement. Keep revising until the sentence clearly expresses your topic and your central idea. Avoid overly obvious statements like "The purpose of this paper is . . ." or "This paper will discuss . . . ". Also avoid vague omnibus terms like *interesting* and *important*. If, after conscientious effort, you are absolutely unable to write a satisfactory thesis statement, you probably should look for a different topic or for a new approach to the topic you have.

The student considering the general subject of meat-packing considered several possible theses:

> Federal laws control every aspect of meat-packing from the purchase of live animals to the packaging of meat products.

> The vivid descriptions of the Chicago stockyards in *The Jungle* by Upton Sinclair shocked the public and led to the enactment of food inspection laws.

> Philip D. Armour succeeded because he organized his packing plant efficiently, reduced waste, and found uses for all parts of slaughtered animals.

Any of these statements could be developed in a paper of 2,000 to 2,500 words.

You are on your way to a thesis when you begin asking *Why?* during your exploratory reading. Consider as well the other questions traditionally asked by journalists: *Who?, What?, Where?, When?,* and *How?* Asking yourself questions is, in fact, a good method of arriving at a thesis. During his exploratory reading on stagecoaches, Tom Graham jotted the following questions in his notebook:

How did American coaches differ from British coaches?

What were the major problems confronting travelers in the West?

How were stagecoach lines organized?

How were coaches constructed?

What did Mark Twain write about stagecoaches?

Why have stagecoaches appealed to the public's imagination?

How accurate is the John Ford film?

Some of these questions were too general to be very meaningful, but they helped Tom formulate his thesis. Questions are useful, but in its final form, a thesis must be a declarative statement that requires amplification.

A thesis often is derived from a cause–effect relationship, one of our most common and most productive modes of thinking:

> The stagecoach was well adapted to frontier needs because . . .

> The stagecoach has appealed to writers and artists because . . .

When he finished his exploratory reading, Tom devised a tentative thesis:

> The stagecoach was important in the opening of
> the West, and it shows how pioneers adapted to new
> conditions and special problems, and it also is a
> part of Western legend.

This sentence contained Tom's key ideas but sounded awkward, largely because of the overuse of *and*. After some verbal changes and some shifting of sentence parts, he came up with an improved version:

```
The stagecoach not only illustrates frontier

ingenuity in adapting to difficult conditions but

also has become a colorful part of the legendary

West.
```

Do not regard your thesis as a total commitment. Your ideas may change as you delve deeper into a subject. It is important to have a meaningful thesis to guide your research, but it is just as important to keep an open mind and be willing to revise it as you learn more and think more about your topic.

Considering Methods of Development _____

Any topic can be developed in more than one way. Sometimes reviewing possible methods can help you devise a thesis. For example, when an instructor assigned the general subject "Nominating Presidential Candidates," a student considered the following possible methods:

1. *Enumeration.* Simply specifying the common procedures (caucus, state primary, regional primary, state convention, and national convention) might be the method used in one or two paragraphs, but it would not be feasible for an entire paper because no meaningful thesis seems possible.

2. *Definition.* Another method likely to be used in a single paragraph, definition puts a term in a general class and then differentiates it from other terms in that class; for example: "A caucus is a conference of political leaders to decide policies or select candidates."

3. *Analysis.* Separating a process into its parts (for example, the stages of a national convention from approval of a platform to the acceptance speech of the nominee) also seems more likely to be the method for a paragraph than for an entire paper. It might, however, supply the basic plan for a paper with an argumentative thesis, for example: "Much that happens at a convention is meaningless play-acting arranged for newspapers and television."

4. *Example.* Having heard stories of political maneuvering in smoke-filled rooms, the student investigated the nomination of Warren G. Harding and came up with the following thesis: "The nomination of Harding in 1920 was arranged through political deals by some of his fellow senators after the convention was hopelessly deadlocked."

5. *Cause/effect.*   A possible thesis is the following: "State primaries extending over several months [*cause*] enable voters to become thoroughly familiar with the candidates [*effect*]."

6. *Comparison/contrast.*   Discussing ways in which a caucus and a primary are alike and ways in which they differ would probably produce a thesis advocating one method or the other.

7. *Argument.*   Evaluating pros and cons can produce a thesis; for example, "Advantages of state primaries outweigh the disadvantages and make them the most effective method of choosing a presidential candidate."

Of course, even though one method would probably dominate, a combination of methods would be used. Reviewing possible ways of treating a topic can help you decide on a thesis.

Selecting Main Points _____

After you narrow your topic and formulate a tentative thesis, brainstorming can become more purposeful. While reading and thinking for several days about the Western stagecoach, Tom Graham compiled a running outline in his notebook:

```
 1. effect of gold rush

 2. Sutter's Mill

 3. demand for mail and freight

 4. sea route

 5. dispute over land routes

 6. North vs. South

 7. pressure on Congress

 8. arrival of first stage in San Francisco

 9. the Concord coach

10. top-heavy British coaches

11. egg-shaped body

12. wide tires
```

13. decoration

14. artist, John Burgum

15. John Butterfield

16. Ben Holladay

17. Russell, Majors, and Waddell

18. Yankee ingenuity

19. arrangement of seats

20. organization of stage lines

21. division 200-250 miles long

22. stations 10-15 miles apart

23. changing horses

24. Pony Express

25. drivers

26. Charlie Parkhurst

27. reining

28. accuracy with whip

29. stagecoaches in media

30. dime novels

31. Frederic Remington

32. Buffalo Bill's Wild West Show

33. Mark Twain's trip in 1861

34. use of his brother's journal

35. written in Elmira, 1871

36. John Ford film, 1939

37. remake with Bing Crosby

38. John Wayne

39. mixed group of passengers

40. speed, excitement

As the running outline grew, Tom began grouping ideas, and the major topics gradually emerged:

    I. Effect of gold rush

   II. The Concord coach

  III. Stagecoach operators

   IV. Organization

    V. Drivers

   VI. Media

He thus had six main topics, each of which would be developed in one or more paragraphs. He evaluated the items in his running outline in relation to these main topics, labeled them with outline symbols, and wrote a zero after those that should be eliminated as irrelevant. He would add to the list as he continued his research and would probably need to recopy it more than once, but he was on his way to the working outline he would follow in writing his rough draft. His evaluation of his first running outline looked like this:

1. effect of gold rush   I

2. Sutter's Mill   O

3. demand for mail and freight   I

4. sea route   O

5. dispute over land routes ⎫
6. North vs. South   ⎬ I
7. pressure on Congress   ⎭

8. arrival of first stage in San Francisco   O

9. the Concord coach   II

10. top-heavy British coaches   O

11. egg-shaped body

12. wide tires

13. decoration   } II

14. artist, John Burgum

15. John Butterfield

16. Ben Holladay   } III

17. Russell, Majors, and Waddell

18. Yankee ingenuity   ) II

19. arrangement of seats

20. organization of stage lines

21. division 200-250 miles long   } IV

22. stations 10-15 miles apart

23. changing horses   O

24. Pony Express   O

25. drivers

26. Charlie Parkhurst

27. reining   } V

28. accuracy with whip

29. stagecoaches in media

30. dime novels

31. Frederic Remington   } VI

32. Buffalo Bill's Wild West Show

33. Mark Twain's trip in 1861   *?*

34. use of his brother's journal   *0*

35. written in Elmira, 1871   *0*

36. John Ford film, 1939   *VI*

37. remake with Bing Crosby   *0*

38. John Wayne   *0*

39. mixed group of passengers   } *VI*

40. speed, excitement

Another method of refining main topics, a bit more sophisticated than a running outline, is a version of brainstorming that produces a topical map like the one shown here, which Rita Hogan put together for her paper on *Pride and Prejudice*. Write your main topic in the center of a page, let free association take over, write related topics around the main topic, and connect them with lines. You will undoubtedly make several versions before arriving at a satisfactory set of topics. This technique encourages you to see relationships among ideas.

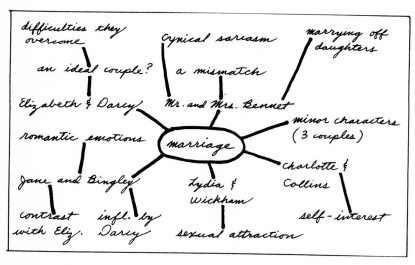

Topical map.

As Rita added topics to this cluster, she saw Elizabeth and Darcy as more and more important, and their marriage became the focal point of her paper. Her first attempt at a thesis was far too general:

> Marriage is Jane Austen's primary concern in
>
> Pride and Prejudice.

Her second version of a thesis was simply a narrative statement that would require little research:

> In Pride and Prejudice, Elizabeth and Darcy
>
> are finally married after overcoming a series of
>
> misunderstandings.

In considering the cluster of ideas, Rita observed that most of the other marriages are unsatisfactory in some way, and yet all of them help bring about the eventual marriage of Elizabeth and Darcy. This observation resulted in a workable thesis:

> In Pride and Prejudice, the examples of eight
>
> other marriages, most of them less than harmonious,
>
> contribute to the eventual union of Elizabeth and
>
> Darcy.

Rita decided to discuss each married couple separately. The arrangement of the paragraphs was her next problem. After juggling various possibilities, she decided to start with the ideal marriage of Elizabeth and Darcy, discuss the minor characters briefly, and then arrange the other marriages from the least to the most satisfactory. The main topics in her working outline looked like this:

> Thesis: In Pride and Prejudice, the examples of
>
> eight other marriages, most of them less than
>
> harmonious, contribute to the eventual union of
>
> Elizabeth and Darcy.
>
> I. Elizabeth and Darcy
>
> II. Minor characters
>
> III. Mr. and Mrs. Bennet

```
   IV. Lydia and Wickham

    V. Charlotte Lucas and Mr. Collins

   VI. The Gardiners

  VII. Jane and Bingley
```

In a preliminary outline like this, leave space under each main topic so that you can write in possible subdivisions and other notes.

Unless you have a highly disciplined and logical mind and are also very fortunate, you cannot expect to set down a detailed outline at this stage. Your outline will develop gradually as your reading becomes more purposeful and you begin taking notes.

Beginning to Collect Possible Sources ⎯⎯⎯⎯⎯

At the close of your paper, on a page headed Works Cited, you will list the sources you have used. By the time you have scanned sources in the library and decided on a topic and a thesis, you will almost certainly have encountered some books and articles that look useful. You should, therefore, begin compiling a working bibliography—a card file of potential sources. For this purpose, 3 × 5 index cards are most suitable. Write only one source on a card so that they can be alphabetized readily later on. If a source contains nothing useful when you examine it more closely, do not throw the card away but write "No help," "Zilch," or some other code term on it so that you will not waste time returning to that source later. It may turn out to be useful if you revise your topic or your thesis.

Include on each card the information that belongs in the list of works cited. Arranging and punctuating the items in standard bibliographic form will reduce the possibility of omissions or transcription errors later on. Standard forms for a book, a quarterly journal, and a monthly magazine are shown in the accompanying illustrations. Additional examples of cards appear in Chapter 2 (pages 66–71), and a full array of variant bibliographic forms is given in Chapter 5 (pages 132–53). Consult the checklist on pages 131–32.

Recording the call number of a book or the location of a periodical and a brief note on the content or how you plan to use it will also prove helpful. These notes are for your own guidance, of course, and do not appear in the list of works cited. Be sure to include all bibliographic information even though you are not absolutely certain you will use the source. It is depressing, to say the least, to discover while typing the final draft of a paper that a publisher's name or the subtitle of a book is missing. Such discoveries are usually made late at night, when the library is closed.

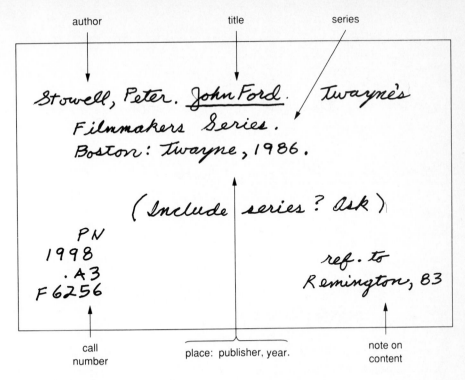

author   title   series

Stowell, Peter. *John Ford.* / Twayne's
Filmmakers Series.
Boston: Twayne, 1986.

(Include series ? Ask)

PN
1998
.A3
F6256

ref. to
Remington, 83

call number   place: publisher, year.   note on content

Bibliography card for a book.

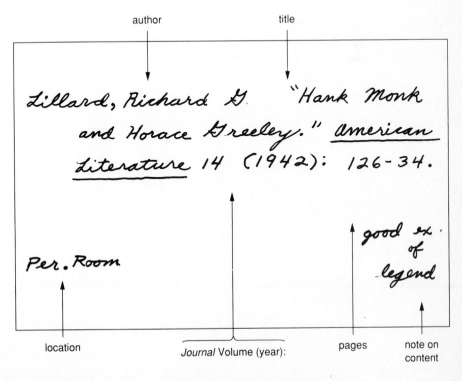

author   title

Lillard, Richard G. "Hank Monk
and Horace Greeley." *American
Literature* 14 (1942): 126-34.

Per. Room

good ex.
of
legend

location   *Journal* Volume (year):   pages   note on content

Bibliography card for a journal continuously paged.

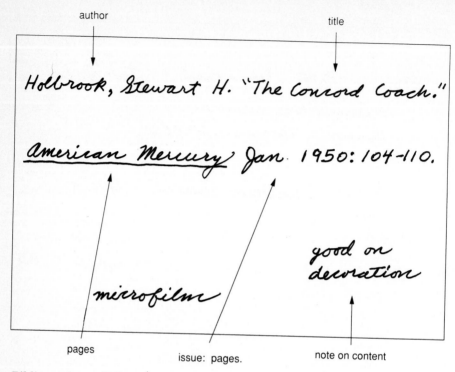

author

title

Holbrook, Stewart H. "The Concord Coach."

American Mercury Jan. 1950: 104-110.

*good on
decoration*

microfilm

pages

issue: pages.

note on content

Bibliography card for a monthly magazine.

Exploring the Library

At the very beginning of your search for a topic, you may notice an intriguing title in a bookstore display, on a newsstand, or on a friend's bookshelf. As suggested at the close of Chapter 1, it is wise to record such a source on a bibliography card. Likewise, when you begin your systematic search for material in the library, filling out a bibliography card is the first step after you find a relevant book or article. This chapter contains examples of bibliography cards (pages 66–71) that you can use as models for cards that you will compile as you discover sources in the catalogs and indexes you use during your exploration of the library.

Learning Your Way Around _____

Despite the compelling attraction of the student union, the gymnasium, or the computer center, the library is the most important building on campus. Perhaps you have already discovered its value as a place to meet friends or, more important, as a quiet spot for day-to-day studying with reference books conveniently at hand, as a collection of books and magazines for leisure reading, and as a source of reference materials for reports and term papers. To prepare a satisfactory research paper, you must be able to use library resources efficiently. Your first research experience will inevitably involve confusion, frustration, false starts, and wheel-spinning. However, as you become familiar with the catalog, indexes, and other tools of research, you will develop a research strategy that will make future papers easier to write.

If you are not accustomed to using a large library, your first visit to your school library may be as bewildering as arrival in a strange city. Asking directions and noting major landmarks, however, will help you get oriented. The sooner you feel at home in the library, the better. Libraries differ in various ways, of course, but basic procedures are similar enough that if you become familiar with your school's library, you can quickly adapt to any other you may visit. As you work in the library, observe what other students are doing, and ask questions of librarians, you will encounter terms and abbreviations that relate to library procedures; some of the more common ones are listed in Appendix C (pages 259–61). Perhaps as a new student you have taken an orientation tour. You should follow this with your own exploration. An excellent way to familiarize yourself with the library is to draw a simple floor plan in your notebook. The main features will include the following:

1. *Information desk.*   In large libraries someone is usually stationed near the main entrance to answer general questions and direct visitors.

2. *Circulation desk.*   The circulation desk is the nerve center of the library. Here books are charged out and returned. Some of your questions will be answered here. If you are required to have a card or some other form of identification, you can learn about it here.

3. *Catalog.*   A card catalog or an online catalog is an alphabetized listing by author, title, and subject of all books in the library. It is the single most important tool for most research.

4. *Stacks.*   The shelved books are sometimes not open to undergraduates. Even if you have access to the stacks, a search of the shelves may be misleading because important books may be on loan, in special collections, or on reserve. Browsing in the stacks, however, can result in some fortunate discoveries.

5. *Reference room.*   Reference books are collections of information that are designed to be consulted rather than read consecutively. A reference librarian is trained especially to assist with research problems and can save you time-wasting errors. Don't hesitate to ask for assistance, but first take a moment or two to compose a clear statement of your problem. General works like encyclopedias and dictionaries (see pages 59–65) are more or less useful in all fields; specialized works of all kinds are available in every field (see Appendix B, pages 234–57). Get to know the basic general works as well as the specialized ones in your major field of study.

6. *Reserve section.* Books to be used in the library or withdrawn only for brief periods are placed on reserve by faculty members. A notation in the catalog will indicate that a book is on reserve, and a file or a computer listing of reserve books is usually available.

7. *Periodicals section.* Current periodicals are usually arranged alphabetically in a reading room or another central location. After they have been bound, the volumes may be shelved alphabetically, or they may be assigned call numbers and shelved according to their subject matter. If they have been discarded and replaced by microforms, that fact will be noted in the library's listing of its periodical holdings and in the catalog.

8. *Microform readers and computer terminals.* Readers for microfilm and other microforms are usually located in a special room. Large libraries are rapidly expanding computer services with access to public and commercial databases (see pages 41–44). To use these facilities for the first time, you are almost certain to need assistance from a librarian. *At Ref. Desk*

9. *Union catalog.* Your library may have a union catalog that lists holdings of other libraries. You may find that a book you need is available in a nearby library. *In Current Period -*

10. *Media center.* In some libraries, films, slides, recordings, video-tapes, and similar materials are located in a special department. *write Citations*

11. *Photocopiers.* Copying machines are usually located throughout a library. Look for them first in the vicinity of the periodicals section.

Searching for Books _____

To find books dealing with your topic, you will need to consult the catalog as well as indexes and bibliographies.

Classification of Books

A library catalog, whether it is a card file or an online database, is an enormous bibliography. It is a record of all the books in the library and may also include entries for other materials such as periodicals, cassettes, films, and microforms. In a large library of a million or more volumes, some foolproof system for locating each book is necessary. For this reason, each book is assigned a specific code symbol or call number, consisting of numbers and letters. It will be found on the spine of a book and on all catalog entries for that book.

Call Numbers. The first part of a call number (usually the top two lines) is the classification number, which will be uniform in all libraries using the same system. Below it is the author number (known to librarians as the "Cutter number"), a combination of the initial letter of the author's last name, code numbers, sometimes the first letter of the title, and sometimes the year of publication. The larger the library, the more symbols will be required in an author number. For example, in a library using the Library of Congress system, three critical studies of Jane Austen by Margaret Kirkham, Jane Nardin, and K. C. Phillipps have the same classification number: PR 4038. The author numbers differ, however, and the books are shelved as follows:

F44 K57   Kirkham
R4 N3   Nardin
L3 P5   Phillipps

The two classification systems in general use are the Dewey Decimal and the Library of Congress. You should become familiar with the system used by your school library as well as with the specific categories related to your major field of study.

The Dewey Decimal System. The Dewey Decimal system of classification, as its name suggests, is based on numbers divisible by ten. The various fields of knowledge are divided into these ten general categories:

000–099	General Works	**600–699**	Applied Arts and Sciences
100–199	Philosophy	**700–799**	Fine Arts, Recreation
200–299	Religion	**800–899**	Literature
300–399	Social Sciences	**900–999**	History, Geography, Travel, Biography
400–499	Philology		
500–599	Pure Science		

Each general category is subdivided by tens. For example:

500–509	Pure Science	**550–559**	Geology
510–519	Mathematics	**560–569**	Paleontology
520–529	Astronomy	**570–579**	Biology
530–539	Physics	**580–589**	Botany
540–549	Chemistry	**590–599**	Zoology

Each of these fields is also subdivided. For example:

510	Mathematics	**515**	Descriptive geometry
511	Arithmetic	**516**	Analytic geometry
512	Algebra	**517**	Calculus
513	Geometry	**518**	Unassigned
514	Trigonometry	**519**	Probabilities

Each specific category is subdivided further by adding numbers after the decimal point. For example:

511	Arithmetic	**511.5**	Analysis
511.1	Systems	**511.6**	Proportion
511.2	Numeration	**511.7**	Involution, evolution
511.3	Prime numbers	**511.8**	Mercantile rules
511.4	Fractions	**511.9**	Problems and tables

A weakness of the Dewey Decimal system is that since it was devised in the 1870s, the vast expansion of knowledge in Social Science (the 300s) and Pure Science (the 500s) has made these categories inadequate. Classification numbers are often long and cumbersome. The Dewey Decimal system is most likely to be found in relatively small academic libraries and in many public libraries.

The Library of Congress System. The Library of Congress system, which is based on letters, is preferred by most large libraries. Because there are twenty-one main categories instead of only ten, classification requires fewer symbols. The letters *I, O, W, X,* and *Y* are not used. The major categories are as follows:

A	General works, Polygraphy
B	Philosophy, Religion
C	History, Auxiliary Sciences
D	History, Topography (except America)
E	America (general), United States (general)
F	United States (local), America (except the United States)
G	Geography, Anthropology
H	Social Sciences (general), Statistics, Economics, Sociology
J	Political Science
K	Law
L	Education
M	Music
N	Fine Arts
P	Language and Literature
Q	Science
R	Medicine
S	Agriculture
T	Technology
U	Military Science
V	Naval Science
Z	Bibliography, Library Science

Further subdivision is accomplished by adding a letter, one or more numbers, and the author number. For example, the principal subdivisions of category S (Agriculture) are as follows:

S	General agriculture, soils, fertilizers, implements
SB	General plant culture, horticulture, parks, pests
SD	Forestry
SF	Animal culture, veterinary medicine
SH	Fish culture, fisheries
SK	Hunting, game protection

Classification number + the author number = the call number. No two books have precisely the same number. For example, these two similar books in the "S" category have distinctively different call numbers:

Sprague, Howard B., ed. *Grassland of the United States.*   **SB**
193
S68

Sellers, G. Archer, and Clarence E. Bunch. *The American Grass Book.*   **SB**
197
A66

A call number functions like the address of your home: the city, the ZIP code, the street, and the house number are progressively more specific; and the total address designates your home and no other.

The Card Catalog

A card catalog is designed to enable you to find a book even though you have only partial information. In gathering material for a paper on women writers, for example, you might recall the names Sandra M. Gilbert and Susan Gubar. Under "Gilbert" and also under "Gubar," you would find author cards for their book *The Madwoman in the Attic.* Perhaps, on the other hand, you remember only the title; you could find a title card filed under "Madwoman." If you knew neither the authors nor the title, you could try subject headings. The large category "English Literature" is subdivided, and you would find the book filed under "Women Authors, History and Criticism." By examining other cards in this category, you could find other books on the same subject. The book would probably also be filed under names of authors who are discussed in detail, for example, Emily Dickinson.

Library of Congress Subject Headings. *LC Subject Headings,* discussed in Chapter 1 (pages 13–14), can be very useful when you are searching a catalog. It lists alphabetically all of the subject headings or descriptors under which cards are filed. It is usually located near the catalog and can be consulted much more easily than a half-dozen separate file drawers. Some of the descriptors may not be the terms you would expect. If you look under "Film," for example, you will be referred to "Moving Pictures." If you look under "Stagecoach," you will not find that term or a cross-reference; but relevant headings are listed under "Coaching." In using any index like this one, have several related terms in mind and look under each of them—for example, *Aged, Aging, Elderly, Geriatrics, Gerontology, Seniors.*

Alphabetization Practices. A catalog in a large library may contain several million entries. Such an enormous collection of data obviously requires uniform procedures of arrangement and alphabetization. Some library practices useful to remember are described here.

1. Works by a person are listed first; works about that person follow. This sequence is especially significant in a large library. In the Library of Congress, for example, Shakespeare cards take up seventeen file drawers.

2. Numerals are alphabetized as though spelled out in full. For example, *2001: A Space Odyssey* is filed under *T*.

3. Abbreviations are usually filed as though the first letter were a word (the practice followed in telephone books). For example, UNESCO will be at the beginning of the *U*'s. This practice is not consistent, however; you should check all possibilities and, if necessary, consult a librarian.

4. Names beginning with *Mc* or *M'* are filed as though spelled *Mac*.

5. In titles, prefixes like *de* or *von* and the articles *a, an,* and *the* as well as articles in a foreign language are disregarded. In authors' names, however, some libraries consider a prefix as part of the word. For example, cards for the poet Walter De la Mare may be filed as though the name were spelled Delamare. If you do not find a card filed where you expect it to be, ask a librarian about any special alphabetization practices that may help you locate it.

6. Most libraries alphabetize word by word (a practice sometimes described as "short before long") as is done in *Encyclopedia Americana*, rather than letter by letter as is done in *Encyclopaedia Britannica* and in telephone books. For example:

WORD BY WORD	LETTER BY LETTER
West Point	Western Union
Western Union	Westminster Abbey
Westminster Abbey	West Point

7. If the same word is used for a person, a place, and a title, the cards are filed in that order. For example:

London, Jack
London, England
"London" [a poem by Samuel Johnson]

Author Cards. The author card is the basic form or "main entry." Library catalogers make title and subject cards by typing above the author's name a book's title or its subject in full capitals, sometimes in red. All other information is the same. The sample author card that follows illustrates the information found in a card catalog. Most of the facts below the fourth line are technical data for librarians. Notice, however, the tracing: the subject headings and other entries under which cards for that book are filed. They may help you "trace" other books on the same subject.

Most cards in your school library will resemble the example on page 36. New cards, however, repeat the author's name after the title and use

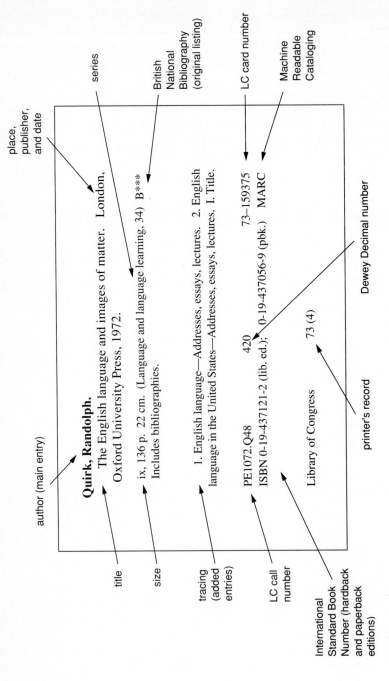

author (main entry)

Quirk, Randolph.
The English language and images of matter. London,
Oxford University Press, 1972.

ix, 136 p. 22 cm. (Language and language learning, 34) B***
Includes bibliographies.

1. English language—Addresses, essays, lectures. 2. English
language in the United States—Addresses, essays, lectures. I. Title.

PE1072.Q48   420   73–159375
ISBN 0-19-437121-2 (lib. ed.);   0-19-437056-9 (pbk.)   MARC

Library of Congress   73 (4)

series

place,
publisher,
and date

British
National
Bibliography
(original listing)

LC card number

Machine
Readable
Cataloging

title

size

tracing
(added
entries)

LC call
number

International
Standard Book
Number (hardback
and paperback
editions)

printer's record

Dewey Decimal number

Author card.

somewhat different punctuation, as shown in the second example. The basic information is the same. The purpose of the revised form is to facilitate computerization.

Stanton, Michael N.
English literary journals, 1900-1950 : a guide to information sources / Michael N. Stanton. — Detroit, Mich. : Gale Research Co., c1982.

xvi, 119 p. : 23 cm. — (Gale information guide library, American literature, English literature, and world literatures in English ; v. 32)

Includes indexes.
ISBN 0-8103-1359-6 : $36.00

1. English literature—Periodicals—Bibliography. I. Title. II. Series.
Z2005.S73   1982   016.82'08—dc19   74-32504
[PR1]   AACR 2 MARC

Library of Congress   81

New-style author card.

The Online Catalog

Your school library will probably make a drastic revision of its cataloging procedures soon, if it has not already done so. Most large libraries have begun or are considering representing their holdings in an online catalog. The Library of Congress, which sets the pace for American libraries, has added no new cards to its catalog since 1980; computer terminals are located around the perimeter of the Reading Room. The New York Public Library has eliminated its card catalog altogether, recorded its present holdings in dictionary catalogs, and installed computer terminals for new and future acquisitions. Some computer catalogs are also linked to regional or national databases so that information on books in other libraries is available.

The first time you use an online catalog, you may need assistance from a librarian; but when you press the "Enter" key, instructions will appear on the screen, and they are relatively simple. The commands will vary depending on the make of the computer, but the general procedures are standardized. In a typical situation, you can type the author symbol (a =)

and an author's name to call up a list of that author's works. Be sure to invert the author's name and spell it correctly. Here is a portion of the listing that would appear if you typed a= Austen, Jane:

```
LUIS SEARCH REQUEST: A=AUSTEN JANE
 AUTHOR/TITLE INDEX — 20 ENTRIES FOUND, 2 - 18
    DISPLAYED
  2 FA:AUSTEN JANE +I JANE AUSTEN A RE CREATION IN RIME
    ROYAL
  3 FA:AUSTEN JANE +JANE AUSTENS LETTERS TO HER SISTER
    CASSANDRA
  4 FA:AUSTEN JANE +LETTERS 1796 1817 <1955
  5 FA:AUSTEN JANE +MANSFIELD PARK <1934
  6 FA:AUSTEN JANE +NORTHANGER ABBEY <1934
```

"LUIS" is an abbreviation for "Library User Information System." Titles 2 and 3 have been shortened.

Typing a "4" would bring up the following information concerning the fourth title:

```
LUIS SEARCH REQUEST: A=AUSTEN JANE
BIBLIOGRAPHIC RECORD — NO. 4 OF 20 ENTRIES FOUND

Austen, Jane, 1775-1817.
 Letters, 1796-1817, selected and edited by R. W.
    Chapman.
Oxford University Press <1978>
 x, 226 p. 16 cm. (The World's classics, 549)
 Chiefly letters to her sister Cassandra.

 LOCATION: Main
 CALL NUMBER: PR4036 .A57 1978
```

The above printout includes the essential information that would be found on a printed author card.

The procedure just described is the simplest way of using an online catalog. You can also begin by typing the title symbol (t=) and the title of the book you want. Or you can type the symbol for subject headings (s=) and the subject to call up a numbered list of titles. Typing the appropriate number will call up catalog information on whatever title interests you. Unless the subject heading is precise, you are likely to have a bewildering list of titles. Use *LC Subject Headings* to find viable headings.

A card catalog and an online catalog are alike in purpose and in content. Only the method of use has changed. A few minutes' practice should familiarize you with the procedures and reduce the time you would spend searching the catalog.

Books in Print

If you choose an offbeat topic and find few books in the library catalog, you might examine *Books in Print*, annual author, title, and subject listings of currently available books. The subject volumes are minutely indexed and cross-referenced and can be extremely helpful. If a book listed there is not in your library, it may be obtainable through Interlibrary Loan. If, for example, you wanted to write about soilless agriculture, a cross-reference under that heading would direct you to "Hydroponics," where you would find twenty-one titles listed in the form illustrated here.

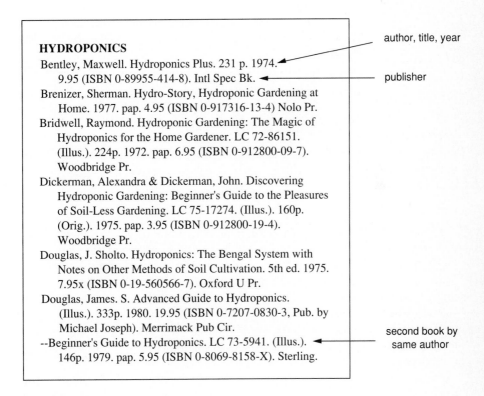

HYDROPONICS
Bentley, Maxwell. Hydroponics Plus. 231 p. 1974.
    9.95 (ISBN 0-89955-414-8). Intl Spec Bk. ◄——————— *author, title, year* / *publisher*
Brenizer, Sherman. Hydro-Story, Hydroponic Gardening at
    Home. 1977. pap. 4.95 (ISBN 0-917316-13-4) Nolo Pr.
Bridwell, Raymond. Hydroponic Gardening: The Magic of
    Hydroponics for the Home Gardener. LC 72-86151.
    (Illus.). 224p. 1972. pap. 6.95 (ISBN 0-912800-09-7).
    Woodbridge Pr.
Dickerman, Alexandra & Dickerman, John. Discovering
    Hydroponic Gardening: Beginner's Guide to the Pleasures
    of Soil-Less Gardening. LC 75-17274. (Illus.). 160p.
    (Orig.). 1975. pap. 3.95 (ISBN 0-912800-19-4).
    Woodbridge Pr.
Douglas, J. Sholto. Hydroponics: The Bengal System with
    Notes on Other Methods of Soil Cultivation. 5th ed. 1975.
    7.95x (ISBN 0-19-560566-7). Oxford U Pr.
Douglas, James. S. Advanced Guide to Hydroponics.
    (Illus.). 333p. 1980. 19.95 (ISBN 0-7207-0830-3, Pub. by
    Michael Joseph). Merrimack Pub Cir.
--Beginner's Guide to Hydroponics. LC 73-5941. (Illus.). ◄——— *second book by*
    146p. 1979. pap. 5.95 (ISBN 0-8069-8158-X). Sterling.   *same author*

Sample entry from *Books in Print.*

Essay and General Literature Index

The *Essay and General Literature Index* is another useful supplement to the catalog. It is an author and subject index to anthologies, collections of essays, and other composite volumes. It covers all fields in the humanities and social sciences, but the emphasis is on literary figures. The books that are indexed are listed in an appendix in case you need publication data.

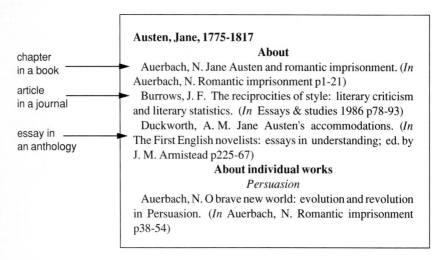

chapter in a book

article in a journal

essay in an anthology

> **Austen, Jane, 1775-1817**
> **About**
> Auerbach, N. Jane Austen and romantic imprisonment. (*In* Auerbach, N. Romantic imprisonment p1-21)
> Burrows, J. F. The reciprocities of style: literary criticism and literary statistics. (*In* Essays & studies 1986 p78-93)
> Duckworth, A. M. Jane Austen's accommodations. (*In* The First English novelists: essays in understanding; ed. by J. M. Armistead p225-67)
> **About individual works**
> *Persuasion*
> Auerbach, N. O brave new world: evolution and revolution in Persuasion. (*In* Auerbach, N. Romantic imprisonment p38-54)

Sample entry from *Essay and General Literature Index.*

Guarding Against Oversights

Five practical suggestions may save you some time and annoyance when you begin looking for books:

1. Many libraries post charts that indicate the location of basic reference works as well as the various categories of books.

2. Be alert for sources indirectly related to your topic. When you are investigating something, its importance becomes distorted for you. You feel that any book pertaining to your particular interest should be listed in the catalog under that heading. Sometimes a useful discussion of your topic will be found on a single page of a book on a different, though related subject. Use *LC Subject Headings*, "see also" cards, and your imagination to discover relevant sources. If you were writing a paper on poltergeists, you might not find any title cards under that heading, but you might find cross-references to "Apparitions" and "Demonology." Consulting *LC Subject Headings* and using your ingenuity, you would also look in the catalog under "Ghosts," "Spirits," "Invisible World," and "Psychical Research."

3. When you find a promising title in the catalog, copy its call number accurately. Omitting or changing one letter or numeral may make it impossible to find the book. Include the call number on your bibliography card.

4. When you find a book in the stacks, look at the books on either side of it. They will be related in subject matter even though you did not find them when searching the catalog. If a book or an article is especially useful, check the catalog and periodical indexes for other works by the same author.

5. If the book you want is not on the shelves, it probably has been checked out, but it may have been misshelved. Look at the shelves above and below, and look behind the books to make sure that it has not been accidentally pushed out of sight. Occasionally the book you need will be found on the cart holding books to be reshelved or near the photocopiers. Library research may give you a new appreciation of the word *serendipity*.

Computer Searching _____

Computers have not only revolutionized methods of cataloging books, they have also introduced a new means of locating articles and other source material—access to online databases that store many basic references formerly accessible only in printed sources. Although computer searching may not be practical for a short research paper, you should be aware of its availability for more extensive research that you will do in advanced courses.

From an information service that stores and supplies databases, you can obtain three kinds of material:

1. Citations of sources related to your topic
2. Abstracts (brief summaries) of any or all of the sources
3. The full text of a source not available in your library.

Technological advances, especially the development of CD ROM ("compact disc, read only memory"), are reducing retrieval time to microseconds and are also reducing the cost of the service.

If you have access to a personal computer equipped with a modem (a device that transmits data over a telephone circuit), you can subscribe to an information service and conduct a search yourself. If you request a search at a library, it will be conducted by a librarian. Some large newspapers also provide computer-searching service for a fee. The services most widely used by academic libraries are BRS (Bibliographic Retrieval Service) and DIALOG; the latter includes more than 250 databases. Each offers a service at reduced rates in the evening and on weekends; BRS service is After Dark, and the DIALOG service is Knowledge Index. Most basic research tools (for example, *ERIC, MLA International Bibliography,* and *New York Times Index*) are accessible through an information service. *Readers' Guide* and seven other H. W. Wilson Co. indexes are stored on WILSONLINE; indexing begins with 1983.

A computer terminal is linked by a modem with an information service through a telecommunications network such as TELENET, TYMNET, DIALNET, or WATS. The operator "logs on" (initiates) the search by means of an assigned password and then types descriptors or search terms that relate to the subject, the database to be searched, and the time span to be covered.

It is possible to request a search for a single term. For example, through DIALOG the incidence of the term *parole* in titles was requested. The database accessed ˈ ˈas NCJRS (National Criminal Justice Reference Service), and the time·spɑn was 1980–88. In less than two minutes, the computer reported thaˈ the term *parole* appeared in 1,254 titles. This was an impressive but not very encouraging total. A sample citation looked like this:

```
108209
New Jersey Department of Corrections, Division of
    Policy and Planning, Bureau of Parole: Annual
    Report, 1984-1985
New Jersey Bureau of Parole, Trenton, NJ 08628
1985  45 p
United States
```

Except by calling up every title, there was no way of determining which sources might be relevant. It would be necessary to add terms in order to restrict the limits of the search.

It is far more efficient to use a cluster of search terms (usually three). They must be carefully chosen. Some databases provide a listing of search terms. *Thesaurus of Psychological Index Terms* supplied the information that discussions of abuse of the elderly by relatives could be accessed by using the search terms *family, violence,* and *aged.* Two databases provided by the American Psychological Association were accessed. PsycALFRT indexes 1300 journals and provides bibliographic information. When an article is abstracted in PsycINFO, it is dropped from this database; PsycALERT is, therefore, an up-to-date bibliography. It supplied titles like the following:

```
2009878
708973006
When the elderly are abused: Characteristics and
    intervention.
Powell, Sharon; Berg, Robert C.
The Counseling Ctr, Arlington, TX
Educational Gerontology,
1987 Vol 13(1) 71-83
```

2015312
715226001
Violence in the home: II. Battered parents and the
    battered elderly.
Goodstein, Richard K.; Johnson, Robert W.
Carrier Foundation, Belle Mead, NJ
Carrier Foundation Letter,
1987 Jun Vol 126 4 p
Languages: ENGLISH
DOC TYPE: JOURNAL ARTICLE

PsycINFO covers 1,300 journals, monographs, and dissertations. Each entry contains a brief summary of the item's content. For example:

Elder abuse & neglect.
Quinn, Mary J.
Superior Court of California, San Francisco
Generations, 1985 Win Vol 10(2) 22–25 ISSN: 07387806
Journal Announcement: 7411
Language: ENGLISH Document Type: JOURNAL ARTICLE
Discusses the ethical and legal conflicts experienced
    by practitioners of all disciplines who are
    involved with abuse and neglect of the elderly. The
    issues of freedom vs safety, nonconsenting clients,
    and access to a home are addressed. (PsycINFO
    Database Copyright 1987 American Psychological
    Assn, all rights reserved)
Descriptors: PROFESSIONAL ETHICS (40720); LEGAL
    PROCESSES (28110); CRISIS INTERVENTION (12510);
    FAMILY VIOLENCE (19294); AGED (01370)

If the sources listed were in your library, your reliance on DIALOG would be at an end and you could "log off." If you wanted a source that was not in your library, you could order the full text, but it would be much more economical to do this by mail (offline). You might first try obtaining the text through Interlibrary Loan.

The chief advantages of computer searching are speed and thoroughness. You can receive information in a minute or two that would require hours of manual searching. Also, a database includes recent citations that may not appear in printed bibliographies for at least a year. At present, three considerations should be kept in mind:

1. Your instructor may prefer that you have firsthand experience with printed bibliographies and indexes. Be sure to obtain advance approval for the use of an information service.

2. Most databases began in the late 1960s when technology for storing bibliographic files was perfected. If you need materials published before 1970, you should consult printed sources.

3. In most libraries, computer searching is conducted at the patron's expense. You can stipulate limits on the time and the scope of a search, but a routine search may cost ten dollars or more. The cost of searching is declining, and the number of available databases is expanding. Computer searching may not be practical for a short paper, but you should keep the possibility in mind when you write longer papers for advanced courses. As computer technology improves, it will undoubtedly revolutionize research techniques in the future.

The most recent technological breakthrough is the development of CD ROM, which is making databases more accessible and reducing retrieval time. One of the services made possible by the new technology is Info-Trac, a computerized index that provides up-to-date access to more than 1,100 periodicals. A single disc covers three years. Coverage of most files begins with 1982. InfoTrac originally specialized in law, business, management, and technology; but it has added titles in the social sciences and humanities and is continuing to expand. It is even simpler to operate than a computer catalog. The keys are clearly labeled, and instructions can be called up on the screen. After typing the "Start" key and the "Subject Guide," you simply type in your search term, and a listing of articles appears on the screen. You can copy references that look promising, or you can ask the machine to print them.

Searching for Articles _____

For some topics, articles will provide the most useful material. However, because they are parts of larger units, articles can be more difficult to locate than books. Therefore, indexes like those described in the following paragraphs are indispensable in most research. Some of them index books as well as journals, but they are primarily used to locate articles. After you begin compiling your bibliography, you will be amazed at how many articles are published each year and at how many ways there are of locating them.

A possible first step in searching for articles would be to consult *Standard Periodical Directory*, 10th edition (New York: Oxbridge, 1987). Thousands of periodicals are listed in a subject index. You would find, for example, over four pages of titles under "Gerontology." Even more useful is *Magazines for Libraries*, 5th ed. (New York: Bowker, 1986). This work, edited by Bill Katz and Linda Sternberg Katz, not only lists periodicals by subject but also evaluates each one. See the example at the top of the next page.

50 Plus (Formerly: *Retirement Living*). 1960 m. $15. Bard Lindeman. Retirement Living, 850 Third Ave., New York, NY 10022. Subs. to: 50 Plus, 99 Garden St., Marion, OH 43302. Illus., index, adv. Circ: 290,000. Sample. Vol. ends: Dec. Microform: B&H, UMI.

Indexed: RG. *Aud:* Ga.

A popular choice for public libraries, this is an upbeat, "newsy" magazine for the general reader, similar both in format and content to *Modern Maturity* and *Dynamic Years*. A wide range of subjects of interest to today's seniors is covered, ranging from "What Makes Couples Happy" to age discrimination, adult fitness, entertainment, politics, money management, food, health, travel, biography, retirement planning, and changing life-styles. These issues are presented in a lightweight, informally "chatty" style, and provide informative, lively, undemanding recreational reading for today's active senior.

Sample entry from *Magazines for Libraries*.

Citation Indexes

Most indexes to periodicals are organized in the same basic way—an alphabetical listing of author and subject headings. A different principle is followed in three computer-produced indexes: *Science Citation Index* (covers more than 3,000 journals), *Social Sciences Citation Index* (covers about 1,500 journals), and *Arts & Humanities Citation Index* (covers about 1,300 journals). All of them also index some books. The way you use these indexes is similar to the way you would conduct a computer search. In fact, each of them is available online as well as in print. Because they are based on key words (permuterms) from the titles of articles rather than on general subject headings, they offer more accurate retrieval of titles, but they are also more complex than most indexes.

Each index consists of three separate parts, each with a distinctive function. Because they index sources by different methods, the same reference may be listed a dozen or more times. They are designed to enable you to find a source even though you have only partial information. You can "enter" (begin using) the indexes with any of the three volumes, but you would probably start with the *Permuterm Subject Index*.

Permuterm Subject Index. *Permuterm Subject Index* lists alphabetically primary terms from the titles of articles; other words from a title are *co-terms* or *subheadings*. Look carefully for variants of the same permuterm; in the 1986 Humanities volume, for example, thirty-nine co-terms are listed under "Austen" and fifty-four co-terms are listed under "Austen, Jane." If you were writing on the family theatricals in Austen's *Mansfield Park*, you would note the Litvak article in the example. Other co-terms in this listing that name Litvak are *infection, Mansfield,* and *theatrical* (all taken from the title of his article). Each of these would appear elsewhere as a primary term.

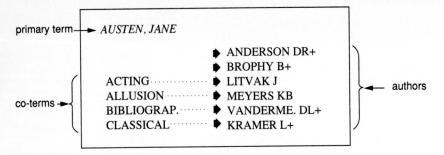

Sample entry from *Permuterm Subject Index*.

Permuterm Subject Index directs you to names of authors who have written about a particular subject, but it can also help you narrow a subject. As you scan a list of co-terms, you can sometimes arrive at a narrow topic for your paper.

Source Index. *Source Index*, which is arranged alphabetically by authors' names, enables you to locate articles that you discovered in *Permuterm Subject Index*. Here you would find a full description of the Litvak article plus a condensed listing of thirty books and articles cited therein. These references can be a means of expanding your bibliography. Only the first eight references are shown in the example.

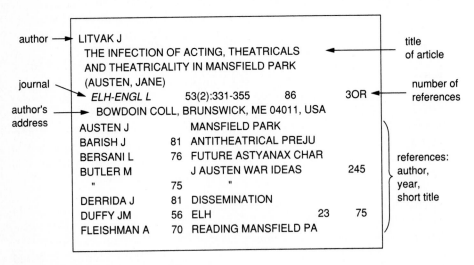

Sample entry from *Source Index*.

The extreme condensation necessary in such a massive work can create some problems. When you found the article, you would discover the author to be *Joseph* Litvak, and that is how the name should appear on your Works Cited page.

Citation Index. *Citation Index* is more likely to be used by specialists or by professional scholars curious as to how often their work has been cited by others. It is arranged alphabetically by the names of authors who are cited. It can be useful in the humanities because an author or an artist will, of course, be cited in a discussion of that person's work. Under "Austen, Jane," you would find that *Mansfield Park* was cited by nine authors, including J. Litvak. If you use *Citation Index* at all, it will primarily be as a means of expanding your bibliography. The example lists authors who cited *Mansfield Park*.

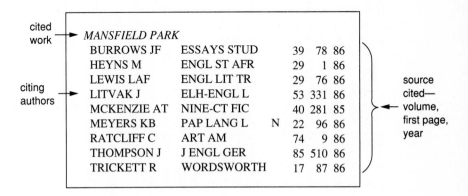

Sample entry from *Citation Index*.

Citation indexes can be rather intimidating because the volumes contain such enormous quantities of information (literally millions of items), because the type is so small that you may need a magnifying glass, and because the condensed form of the entries can be confusing. However, these indexes can direct you to many sources that you might otherwise overlook. With a little practice you can master the basic procedures, and you will find these reference works very helpful.

ERIC

Another computer-oriented program is Educational Resources Information Center (*ERIC*), a federally funded project that indexes both published articles and unpublished papers, reports, and other documents. It is available in print, online (DIALOG and BRS), and through InfoTrac. Many students overlook this reference because they assume that it is designed only for research in Education. Actually it covers a broad range of topics.

Current Index to Journals in Education. Published articles are listed in *Current Index to Journals in Education (CIJE)*. Monthly issues are cumulated twice a year. The monthly and semiannual indexes follow the same arrangement. If you looked in the Subject Index, you would find

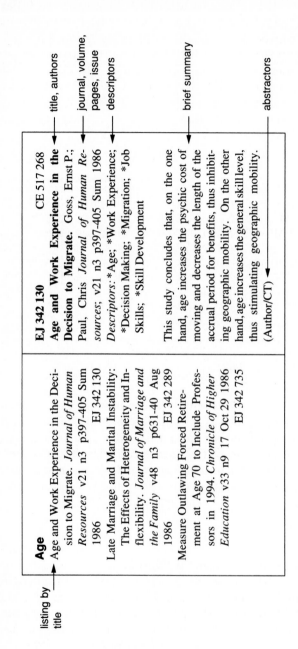

listing by title → **Age**
Age and Work Experience in the Decision to Migrate. *Journal of Human Resources* v21 n3 p397-405 Sum 1986   EJ 342 130
Late Marriage and Marital Instability: The Effects of Heterogeneity and Inflexibility. *Journal of Marriage and the Family* v48 n3 p631-40 Aug 1986   EJ 342 289
Measure Outlawing Forced Retirement at Age 70 to Include Professors in 1994. *Chronicle of Higher Education* v33 n9 17 Oct 29 1986   EJ 342 735

EJ 342 130   CE 517 268
Age and Work Experience in the Decision to Migrate. Goss, Ernst P.; Paul, Chris *Journal of Human Resources*; v21 n3 p397-405 Sum 1986
Descriptors: *Age; *Work Experience; *Decision Making; *Migration; *Job Skills; *Skill Development

This study concludes that, on the one hand, age increases the psychic cost of moving and decreases the length of the accrual period for benefits, thus inhibiting geographic mobility. On the other hand, age increases the general skill level, thus stimulating geographic mobility. (Author/CT)

title, authors

journal, volume, pages, issue

descriptors

brief summary

abstractors

Sample entries from *Current Index to Journals in Education.*

48

articles listed by title, as shown in the left-hand portion of the example on page 48. Turning to the Main Entry section at the beginning of the volume, you would find the article listed by its accession number (EJ 342 130). The number given at the far right (CE 517 268) designates the clearinghouse that classifies the article by its content. Note the descriptors, other terms under which the article is listed; looking under those headings would lead you to additional articles. As the examples show, summaries of articles in *CIJE* are quite brief.

Resources in Education. The arrangement of *Resources in Education (RIE)*, which indexes unpublished materials, is similar to that used in *CIJE* but not identical. In the Subject Index you would find items listed by subject and indentified by ED ("*ERIC* Document") numbers. Articles are not summarized in the semiannual volumes. To find an abstract or "document resume" of ED 276 902, listed in the example on the left on page 50, you would need to look at the spines of monthly numbers, where you would learn that this ED number is in the May 1987 issue. There you would find the description and the abstract shown on the right. Obviously, abstracts in *RIE* are considerably longer than those in *CIJE*.

If your school library subscribes to the complete *ERIC* service, you could find the paper reproduced on microfiche and indexed under ED 276 902. Your library probably has a machine that will print a copy from a microfiche for a few cents a page. You can also purchase many papers, including this one, from *ERIC* Reproduction Service (P.O. Box 190, Arlington, VA, 22210), but sending for it may take more time than you have available.

Another useful reference is *Thesaurus of ERIC Descriptors*, a listing of terms under which items are indexed. Though designed primarily to assist you in using the indexes, it can also help you narrow a subject. For example, if you were planning to write on some aspect of public park areas, you would find twenty-three terms from "Athletic Fields" to "Zoos" listed under "Recreational Facilities."

Readers' Guide

Other than the catalog, the most widely used research tool in the library is probably *Readers' Guide to Periodical Literature*, an index to nearly two hundred general periodicals, ranging in a recent volume from *Aging* to *The Writer*. Many students learn to use *Readers' Guide* in high school and thus find it fairly easy to use the specialized indexes that are similarly organized. In an enormous index like this, space must be conserved whenever possible, and so there are many abbreviations. Some may confuse you at first, so you will need to consult the key at the beginning of a volume. Author and subject entries resemble those in a card catalog; an article is listed under the author's name and under at least one subject heading. Titles of articles are seldom main entries, but short stories and plays are listed by title. Since it would be impossible for anyone to examine two

Nursing Homes

Cops, Consultants, and Goldfish: Variations in Nursing Home Regulation.
ED 276 902

Family Involvement in Nursing Home Care.
ED 277 926

Four Percent Fallacy Revisited: Urban and Rural Differences.

ED 276 902 CG 019 517

Gardiner, John A. ◄——————— author

Cops, Consultants, and Goldfish: Variations in Nursing Home Regulation. ◄——— title

Spons Agency—Retirement Research Foundation.

Pub Date—Nov 86

Note—30p.; Paper presented at the Annual Scientific Meeting of the Gerontological Society (39th, Chicago, IL, November 19-23, 1986). ◄——— descriptive note

Pub Type—Reports - Research (143) — Speeches/Meeting Papers (150)

EDRS Price - MF01/PC02 Plus Postage. ◄——— microfiche or paper copy

Descriptors — *Agency Role, *Certification, *Government Role, *Nursing Homes, *Punishment, *Standards

Nursing home regulatory agencies are ◄——— abstract subjected to a variety of pressures. Nursing home residents' families and friends want the agencies to "get tough" while the nursing home industry wants agencies to act as consultants rather than cops. The task of regulating nursing homes in the United States is primarily carried out by units of state government, operating under Medicaid certification guidelines and procedures set by the Health Care Financing Administration. State agencies in fact have enormous discretion as to how the guidelines will be interpreted, what level of compliance will be expected, and when and how non-compliance will be penalized. Data on the imposition of penalties by the states show enormous variations in which penalties (fines, decertification, etc.) are used, and what proportion of facilities are penalized. The states with more facilities are more likely to use penalties; few other correlations appear. (An appendix details the lack of reliable data on regulatory enforcement and the reasons why available data do not permit comparisons of states' enforcement policies.) (Author/ ◄——— abstractors ABL)

Sample entries from *Resources in Education.*

hundred magazines even for one month, indexes like *Readers' Guide* are indispensable.

If you were writing a paper on "Doonesbury" and looked under the artist's name, you would find two entries in the 1986 volume. As in a card catalog, works by a writer come first, and discussions of the writer follow. Other features of *Readers' Guide* are illustrated in the accompanying excerpt.

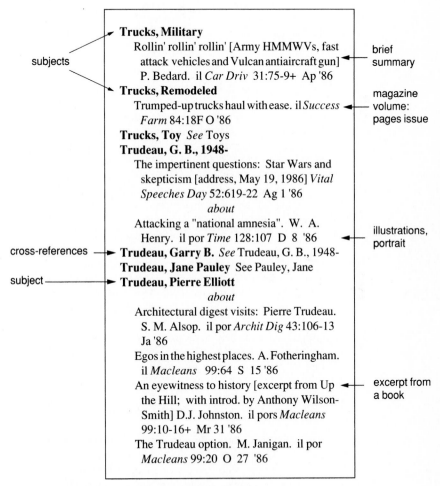

Sample entries from *Readers' Guide to Periodical Literature.*

Book Review Digest

Book Review Digest indexes and excerpts reviews of more than six thousand books a year. Entries are arranged alphabetically by author. To locate a book, the essential information is the year of publication, which you can learn from the title page of the book, from the catalog, or from *Books in*

►**HUTCHEON, LINDA, 1947-**. A theory of parody; the teachings of twentieth-century art forms. 143p il $25; pa $10.95 1985 Methuen

700 1. Parody 2. Art, Modern—1900-1999 (20th century)

► ISBN 0-416-37080-2; 0-416-37090-X (pa)

► LC 84-14856

In her "discussion of parody as 'repetition with difference,' Hutcheon drops [what she considers to be] the pejorative cast of traditional definitions arguing against the perspectives of 'trans-historical' theories and for the 'teachings' of works of literature, music, visual art, and architecture; her purpose is to examine the nature and range of parosodic intertextuality in 20th-century art." (Choice) Bibliography. Index.

summary

"Literature is central in Hutcheon's consideration (as indicated in her bibliography), with musical and visual examples generally used to illustrate tendencies parallel to the literary. The inclusion of some reproductions is gratuitous. Hutcheon's functional model for describing the interrelation of parody and satire reveals that the writer is more meta-critic than critic. Her book bristles with provocative generalizations about parody in 20th-century art, but surely the 'teachings' of modernism and postmodernism are more distinct than what she conveys."

excerpt from a review

►*Choice* 23:592 D '85. W.B. Holmes (180w) ◄

journal volume: page issue

reviewer (length of review)

"[This] is a rare achievement—a work of critical theory that is accessible to the non-theorist. It analyses complex issues clearly, has copious examples from 20th-century literature, film, music, art, and architecture, and includes an extensive bibliography . . . . Hutcheon raises a number of interesting, and ultimately unresolved, issues. What are the relationships of reader, text, and author? What happens if a reader does not recognize that a work is meant to be parody? Is it in fact still parody? Who, then, is more powerful, reader or author?"

Quill Quire 51:46 O '85. Anne Russell (310w)

"Linda Hutcheon's thoughtful engagement with the theory of parody picks its way meticulously through this conceptual minefield, to emerge with a convincing map of the terrain which admirably complements her previous account of the nature of artistic self-reflection, Narcissistic Narrative."

Times Lit Suppl p1075 S 27 '85. Terence Hawkes (1200w)

Sample entry from *Book Review Digest.*

Print. Reviews of an important work may continue to appear for several years after publication, and so you should consult more than one annual volume.

Though used primarily to locate reviews, *Book Review Digest* also contains a useful, though often overlooked, feature—a subject–title index that can help you compile a bibliography. In a single alphabetization, titles are listed individually and under appropriate subject headings. For example, if you were writing on apartheid and looked in the 1986 volume under "South Africa," you would find the subheading "Race Relations" and a listing of eleven titles. You could quickly scan the reviews of any that sounded promising and make bibliography cards. Similarly, if you were writing on parody and looked under that term, you would be referred to the entry on page 52. Excerpts from three reviews suggest that the book would be very useful. You might also want to find the 1,200-word review in the (London) *Times Literary Supplement*.

Biography Index

A guide to biographical information on persons both living and dead, *Biography Index* covers books and more than three thousand periodicals.

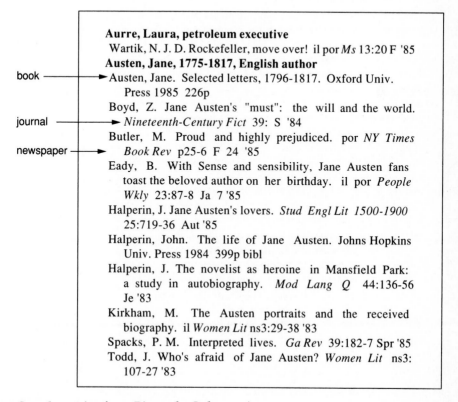

Aurre, Laura, petroleum executive
Wartik, N. J. D. Rockefeller, move over! il por *Ms* 13:20 F '85
Austen, Jane, 1775-1817, English author
book ——▶ Austen, Jane. Selected letters, 1796-1817. Oxford Univ. Press 1985 226p
Boyd, Z. Jane Austen's "must": the will and the world.
journal ——▶ *Nineteenth-Century Fict* 39: S '84
Butler, M. Proud and highly prejudiced. por *NY Times*
newspaper ——▶ *Book Rev* p25-6 F 24 '85
Eady, B. With Sense and sensibility, Jane Austen fans toast the beloved author on her birthday. il por *People Wkly* 23:87-8 Ja 7 '85
Halperin, J. Jane Austen's lovers. *Stud Engl Lit 1500-1900* 25:719-36 Aut '85
Halperin, John. The life of Jane Austen. Johns Hopkins Univ. Press 1984 399p bibl
Halperin, J. The novelist as heroine in Mansfield Park: a study in autobiography. *Mod Lang Q* 44:136-56 Je '83
Kirkham, M. The Austen portraits and the received biography. il *Women Lit* ns3:29-38 '83
Spacks, P. M. Interpreted lives. *Ga Rev* 39:182-7 Spr '85
Todd, J. Who's afraid of Jane Austen? *Women Lit* ns3: 107-27 '83

Sample entries from *Biography Index*.

It is especially useful for locating information in collective biographies and for incidental material in nonbiographical sources like critical studies, diaries, letters, biographical novels, poems, and obituaries. Persons are listed alphabetically; in an appendix they are listed by profession or occupation. The example on page 53 shows several typical entries from the index.

MLA International Bibliography

For literary topics, the most useful reference is the *MLA International Bibliography* published annually by the Modern Language Association. The arrangement of entries proceeds from the geographical (British literature) to the chronological (1800–1899) to the individual author (Jane Austen) to particular works (*Pride and Prejudice*). Volumes before 1981 are less convenient to use because listings of most authors' works were not subdivided. If no year is cited in an entry, you can assume that the work was published in the year covered by the bibliography—in the example,

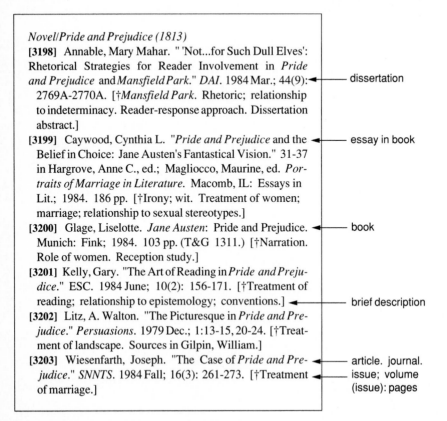

Novel/Pride and Prejudice (1813)

[3198] Annable, Mary Mahar. " 'Not...for Such Dull Elves': Rhetorical Strategies for Reader Involvement in *Pride and Prejudice* and *Mansfield Park.*" *DAI.* 1984 Mar.; 44(9): — dissertation 2769A-2770A. [†*Mansfield Park.* Rhetoric; relationship to indeterminacy. Reader-response approach. Dissertation abstract.]

[3199] Caywood, Cynthia L. "*Pride and Prejudice* and the — essay in book Belief in Choice: Jane Austen's Fantastical Vision." 31-37 in Hargrove, Anne C., ed.; Magliocco, Maurine, ed. *Portraits of Marriage in Literature.* Macomb, IL: Essays in Lit.; 1984. 186 pp. [†Irony; wit. Treatment of women; marriage; relationship to sexual stereotypes.]

[3200] Glage, Liselotte. *Jane Austen*: Pride and Prejudice. — book Munich: Fink; 1984. 103 pp. (T&G 1311.) [†Narration. Role of women. Reception study.]

[3201] Kelly, Gary. "The Art of Reading in *Pride and Prejudice.*" ESC. 1984 June; 10(2): 156-171. [†Treatment of reading; relationship to epistemology; conventions.] — brief description

[3202] Litz, A. Walton. "The Picturesque in *Pride and Prejudice.*" *Persuasions.* 1979 Dec.; 1:13-15, 20-24. [†Treatment of landscape. Sources in Gilpin, William.]

[3203] Wiesenfarth, Joseph. "The Case of *Pride and Prejudice.*" *SNNTS.* 1984 Fall; 16(3): 261-273. [†Treatment of marriage.] — article. journal. issue; volume (issue): pages

Sample entry from *MLA International Bibliography.*

1984. Abbreviations like "ESC" and "SNNTS" are identified at the beginning of each volume.

Humanities Index

The *Humanities Index* covers about three hundred journals in classical studies, literature, philosophy, religion, and similar fields. Rather unexpectedly, perhaps, archeology and history are also covered.

Ausonius, Decimus Magnus, d. 395
about
Still waters run deep: a new study of the professores of Bordeaux. R. P. H. Green. Classical Q ns35 no2:491-506 '85
Austen, Jane, 1775-1817
about
Austen's Emma. R. Creese. *Explicator* 44:21-3 Wint '86
The derivation and distribution of "consequence" in Mansfield Park. A. T. McKenzie. *Nineteenth-Century Fict* 40:281-96 D '85 ◄——— journal volume: pages issue
Female family romances and the "old dream of symmetry". M. Hirsch. *Lit Psychol* 32 no 4:37-47 '86
The fools in Austen's Emma. M. A. Stewart. *Nineteenth-Century Lit* 41:72-86 Je '86
The infection of acting: theatricals and theatricality in Mansfield Park. J. Litvak. *ELH* 53:331-55 Summ '86
Jane Austen and the limits of language. J. Thompson. *J Engl Ger Philol* 85:510-31 O '86
Jane Austen's miniatures: painting, drawing, and the novels. L. Bertelsen. *Mod Lang Q* 45:350-72 D '84

Sample entry from *Humanities Index*.

Social Sciences Index

Social Sciences Index covers about three hundred journals in anthropology, economics, geography, political science, psychology, and related fields. Note the extensive cross-referencing in the excerpt from the index (page 56).

Public Affairs Information Bulletin (PAIS)

Public Affairs Information Bulletin—or *PAIS*, as it is generally referred to—is an extremely useful index to articles, government documents, and some books that relate to public affairs. It is particularly useful in the social sciences. (See page 57.)

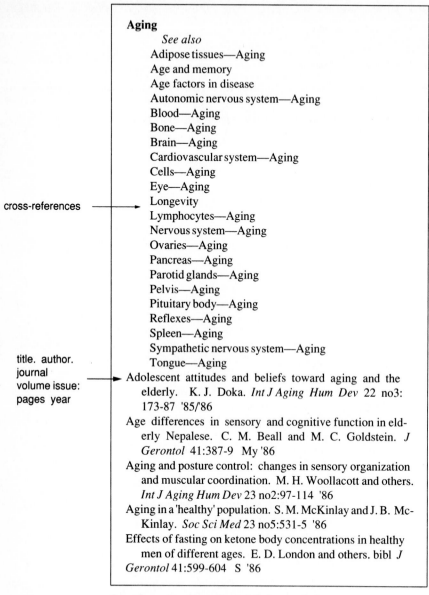

cross-references

title. author.
journal
volume issue:
pages year

Aging
　　See also
　　Adipose tissues—Aging
　　Age and memory
　　Age factors in disease
　　Autonomic nervous system—Aging
　　Blood—Aging
　　Bone—Aging
　　Brain—Aging
　　Cardiovascular system—Aging
　　Cells—Aging
　　Eye—Aging
　　Longevity
　　Lymphocytes—Aging
　　Nervous system—Aging
　　Ovaries—Aging
　　Pancreas—Aging
　　Parotid glands—Aging
　　Pelvis—Aging
　　Pituitary body—Aging
　　Reflexes—Aging
　　Spleen—Aging
　　Sympathetic nervous system—Aging
　　Tongue—Aging
Adolescent attitudes and beliefs toward aging and the
　　elderly. K. J. Doka. *Int J Aging Hum Dev* 22 no3:
　　173-87 '85/'86
Age differences in sensory and cognitive function in eld-
　　erly Nepalese. C. M. Beall and M. C. Goldstein. *J
　　Gerontol* 41:387-9 My '86
Aging and posture control: changes in sensory organization
　　and muscular coordination. M. H. Woollacott and others.
　　Int J Aging Hum Dev 23 no2:97-114 '86
Aging in a 'healthy' population. S. M. McKinlay and J. B. Mc-
　　Kinlay. *Soc Sci Med* 23 no5:531-5 '86
Effects of fasting on ketone body concentrations in healthy
　　men of different ages. E. D. London and others. bibl *J
　　Gerontol* 41:599-604 S '86

Sample entry from *Social Sciences Index.*

Abstracts

An abstract is a capsule version of a work that summarizes its thesis and major supporting ideas. It can save you considerable time by enabling you to judge whether an article would be relevant to your topic and your thesis. Many scholarly journals print an abstract with each article, and in most fields collections of abstracts are published on a regular basis (see the listings of specialized reference works in Appendix B, pages 234–57). The example on page 57 is from *Abstracts of English Studies.*

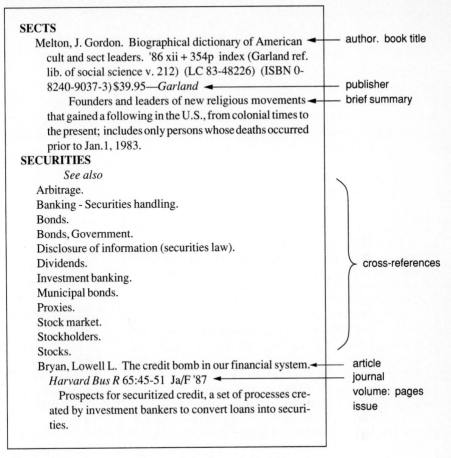

Sample entries from *Public Affairs Information Bulletin.*

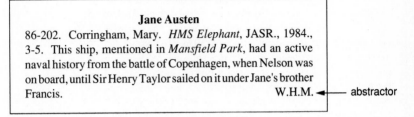

Sample abstract from *Abstracts of English Studies.*

New York Times Index

Useful for locating news stories and for dating events, the *New York Times Index* is arranged by subject. Stories within a category are arranged chronologically. It is lavishly cross-referenced. Under the general heading "Aged" in the 1986 volume, there are cross-references to seventy-six other topics, from "Accidents" to "Women." As the following excerpt indicates, you can surmise the relevance of an article from the summary of its content. Be sure to include on your bibliography card the full date, including the year.

> Manufacturers are finding profit in making products that mean improved care, greater independence and increased self-esteem for elderly (M), S 1, I, 40:2 ◀─────
>
> Claire Gerber article on enjoying growing old; drawing (M), S 14, XI, 27:1
>
> Corporations are beginning to offer programs to their employees on problem of caring for elderly relatives; programs begun by Pepsico and Ciba-Geigy, Westchester County, NY, discussed; photo (M), S 14, XXII, 27:1
>
> Rep John McCain of Arizona, running for Senate, makes humorous remarks about state's reputation as haven for retirees, and some older people are not amused (S), O 5, I, 34:6
>
> National Center for Health Statistics reports that one in five elderly people visit centers or use other facilities or services designed for them, and women are more likely than men to avail themselves of the programs (S), O 8, III, 15:1
>
> Dr. Charles Longino Jr, researcher into problems of the aged, comments on senior citizens who return to New Jersey after living in Florida, usually because they have grown older and need more assistance from families (S), O 12, XI, 30:3
>
> Article on day-care and clinical care programs for elderly on Long Island, one at Jewish Institute for Geriactic Care in New Hyde Park and one at Nesconset Nursing Center; centers provide full range of medical services to 50 to 60 patients a day in day-care setting; health-care experts say such facilities are growing trend because of shortage of nursing home beds and because many families are having difficult time coping with needs of the frail elderly at home; photos (M), O 19, XXI, 6:3
>
> Relationships column discusses problems of adult children caught in midst of quarrels between elderly parents (S), O 20, II, 18:1

Sept. 1, section I
page 40: column 2

summary

length of story
(*L* = over 2 cols.;
M = 1/2 to 2 cols.;
S = less than
1/2 col.)

Sample entries from *New York Times Index.*

General Reference Works —————————————

You are most likely to use general reference works like those listed in this section to get an overview of a subject in the early stages of your research or to verify factual information after you begin reading purposively and taking notes. General reference works are ordinarily shelved in a special room and must be used there. Be certain that the work you consult is suited to your purpose; that is, you would not find General Robert E. Lee in *Current Biography* or the population of Spain in *National Atlas of the United States*. A reference librarian can be extremely helpful in directing you to sources of information. Make your request as specific as possible.

The listing that follows represents less than one percent of the wealth of reference materials available, but it includes the sources most frequently used. Specialized reference works in twenty disciplines are listed in Appendix B (pages 234–57). If you do not find a reference you need in any of these listings or if you simply want to see what a range of material is available, take a look at Eugene P. Sheehy, *Guide to Reference Books*, 10th edition (Chicago: ALA, 1986). This enormous bibliography is arranged according to subject categories, but you will find it more convenient to use the author–title–subject index at the back of the volume.

A dash after a year (1981–) indicates continuing publication, usually on an annual basis. Titles of edited works rather than the editors' names are cited first because you are likely to look for these books by title. The editors may change when new editions are published, but the titles usually remain constant. Brief comments in parentheses describe special features of some works and include cross-references to discussions elsewhere in this chapter.

Atlases and Gazetteers

For information about places, you should turn to an atlas (a collection of maps) or a gazetteer (a dictionary of places). Check the copyright year of these sources to be certain that their information is up-to-date.

> *Columbia Lippincott Gazetteer of the World*. Ed. Leon E. Seltzer. 2nd ed. New York: Columbia UP, 1962.
> *Goode's World Atlas*. Ed. Edward B. Epenshade, Jr. 16th ed. Chicago: Rand, 1983.
> *Hammond World Atlas*. Maplewood, NJ: Hammond, 1984.
> *National Atlas of the United States*. Washington: GPO, 1970.
> *National Geographic Atlas of the World*. 5th ed. Washington: National Geographic Soc., 1981.
> *The New Atlas of the Universe*. Ed. Patrick Moore. 2nd rev. ed. New York: Crown, 1984.
> *New International Atlas*. Rev. ed. Chicago: Rand, 1986.
> *Rand McNally Atlas of the United States*. Chicago: Rand, 1983.
> *Rand McNally Commercial Atlas and Marketing Guide*. New York: Rand, 1876–. (Annually.)

The Times Atlas of the World. 7th ed. New York: Times Books, 1985.
Webster's New Geographical Dictionary. Rev. ed. Springfield: Merriam, 1984.

Biographical Dictionaries

For a complete account of a person's life, use full-length biographies, but for checking biographical facts, reference works like those in the following list are more convenient to use. The wide range of specialized biographical dictionaries is illustrated by the fact that in Sheehy's *Guide to Reference Books*, there are 122 titles beginning with the words *Who's Who.*

American Men and Women of Science. 16th ed. 8 vols. New York: Bowker, 1986.

Biographical Dictionaries: Master Index. 3 vols. Detroit: Gale, 1975. (An index to biographical information in more than fifty sources. Two supplementary volumes, 1979–80.)

Biography Index. New York: Wilson, 1947–. (Quarterly. Cumulated annually and every three years. An index to books and articles about living and nonliving persons. See pages 53–54.)

Chambers Biographical Dictionary. Ed. J. O. Thorne and T. C. Collocott. Rev. ed. Cambridge: Cambridge UP, 1986.

Current Biography. New York: Wilson, 1940–. (Monthly except August. Annual cumulations. Articles about living persons. Especially useful for current celebrities. Index in each annual volume covers preceding years of the decade.)

Dictionary of American Biography. 20 vols. New York: Scribner's, 1928–. (Reissued in 11 volumes, 1974. Supplements.) Authoritative articles on Americans no longer living who made significant contributions to American life.)

Dictionary of National Biography. 63 vols. London: Smith, 1985–. (Supplements. The basic source of information on British notables no longer living.)

Dictionary of Scientific Biography. 16 vols. New York: Scribner's, 1970–80.

The McGraw-Hill Encyclopedia of World Biography. 12 vols. New York: McGraw, 1973.

National Cyclopaedia of American Biography. 76+ vols. New York: White, 1892–. (Supplements. Includes living and deceased persons. Not alphabetized; consult index in each volume or general index.)

Webster's Biographical Dictionary. 3rd ed. Springfield: Merriam, 1976.

Who's Who. London: Black, 1849–. (Annually. *Who Was Who* reprints discontinued entries.)

Who's Who in America. Chicago: Marquis, 1899–. (Biennially. *Who Was Who in America* reprints discontinued entries.)

Dictionaries

For spelling, capitalization, and similar information, you can use any standard desk dictionary. For a listing of related words that can serve as a word-finder, use a thesaurus. For precise shades of meaning and a wide range of synonyms, use an unabridged dictionary. For the semantic history of a word with dated quotations illustrating changes in meaning, use a historical dictionary (*OED* or *DAE*).

> *A Dictionary of American English on Historical Principles.* Ed. William A. Craigie and James R. Hulbert. 4 vols. Chicago: U of Chicago P, 1936–44. (*DAE.* A historical dictionary of American words and meanings modeled after the *OED.*)
>
> *Dictionary of American Regional English.* Ed. Frederic G. Cassidy. Vol. 1. Cambridge: Harvard UP, 1985–. (Four more volumes will complete this authoritative record of American speech. Maps show the distribution of many terms.)
>
> *Funk & Wagnalls New Standard Dictionary of the English Language.* New York: Funk, 1964.
>
> *McGraw-Hill Dictionary of Scientific and Technical Terms.* Ed. Sybil P. Parker, 3rd ed. New York: McGraw, 1984.
>
> *Oxford English Dictionary.* 13 vols. Oxford: Clarendon, 1933. (*OED.* Originally published as *A New English Dictionary on Historical Principles* (*NED*), 1884–; retitled in 1933. Four-volume supplement, 1972–86. Dated illustrative quotations trace the history of a word's meanings. New edition in 20 vols. published 1989.)
>
> *Random House Dictionary of the English Language.* New York: Random, 1987.
>
> *Roget's International Thesaurus.* Rev. Robert L. Canfield. 4th ed. New York: Harper, 1977. (Several other editions available.)
>
> *Webster's Third New International Dictionary of the English Language.* Springfield: Merriam, 1961. (Often referred to as *W. 3.*)

Dictionaries of Quotations

Works like those listed here are useful if you want to find a suitable quotation for your paper (sometimes as an introductory device), to discover the source of a quotation, or to verify its precise wording. Because methods of organization vary, you should look over the preface before using one of these works.

> *Bartlett's Familiar Quotations.* Ed. Emily Morison Beck. 15th ed. Boston: Little, 1980. (Arranged chronologically by author. Key-word index.)
>
> *Dictionary of Quotations.* Ed. Bergen Evans. New York: Delacorte, 1968. (Arranged alphabetically by subject.)
>
> *The Home Book of Quotations, Classical and Modern.* Ed. Burton E. Stevenson. 10th ed. New York: Dodd, 1984. (Arranged by subject. Key-word index.)
>
> *The International Thesaurus of Quotations.* Ed. Rhoda T. Tripp. New York: Crowell, 1970. (Entries arranged in "idea groups.")
>
> *New Cyclopedia of Practical Quotations.* Ed. Jehiel K. Hoyt. Rev. ed. New York: Somerset, 1947. (Arranged by subject. Index.)
>
> *A New Dictionary of Quotations.* Ed. Henry L. Mencken. New York: Knopf, 1942. (Arranged by subject. No index.)

> *Oxford Dictionary of Quotations.* 3rd ed. New York: Oxford UP, 1979.
> (Arranged alphabetically by author.)
> *Quotations in Black.* Ed. Anita King. Westport: Greenwood, 1981.
> (Quotations from black writers. Includes a section on proverbs.)
> *What They Said.* Beverly Hills: Monitor, 1970–. (Annual collections of
> statements by prominent persons.)

Encyclopedias

Encyclopedias are especially useful for narrowing a topic during your exploratory reading and for verifying factual information while you are writing your paper. Major articles often include useful bibliographies. Because some encyclopedias are in a process of "continuous revision," they are usually identified by year (1988 ed.) rather than by number (15th ed.).

> *Academic American Encyclopedia.* 21 vols. Danbury: Grolier, 1982.
> (Available in print and online through DIALOG and BRS.)
> *Collier's Encyclopedia.* 24 vols. New York: Macmillan, 1984. (Designed
> for high school and college use. Supplement, *Collier's Encyclo-
> pedia Yearbook.*)
> *Encyclopaedia Britannica.* 30 vols. 15th ed. Chicago: Encyclopaedia Bri-
> tannica, 1984. (In 1974, the *Britannica* was completely restruc-
> tured into three parts: *Micropaedia*, 10 volumes containing short
> factual articles; *Macropaedia*, 19 volumes containing over 4,000 in-
> depth articles; and *Propaedia*, an outline of knowledge serving
> as an index to the other 29 volumes. The 14th edition is also
> still available in many libraries. Traditionally strong in history
> and literature. Supplement, *Britannica Book of the Year.*)
> *Encyclopedia Americana.* 30 vols. New York: Americana, 1984.
> (Especially strong in science and technology. Supplement, *Amer-
> icana Annual.*)
> *International Encyclopedia of the Social Sciences.* Ed. David L. Sills. 18
> vols. New York: Macmillan, 1968–80.
> *McGraw-Hill Encyclopedia of Science and Technology.* 5th ed. 15 vols. New
> York: McGraw, 1982.
> *The New Columbia Encyclopedia.* Ed. William H. Harris and Judith S.
> Levey. 4th ed. New York: Columbia UP, 1975.
> *Van Nostrand's Scientific Encyclopedia.* Ed. Douglas M. Considine. 6th
> ed. 2 vols. New York: Van Nostrand, 1982. (Useful for defini-
> tions and basic information in all science-related fields.)

Government Publications

The vast number and the variety of materials published by the national, state, and local governments make reference works like the following indispensable. Some libraries maintain a separate catalog and filing system for government documents, in which case you may need the assistance of a reference librarian to locate what you need.

American Statistics Index. Washington: CIS, 1973–. (Annually. Monthly supplements. Index and abstracts of all federal government publications containing statistical data.)

Congressional Information Service Index to Publications of the United States Congress. Washington: CIS, 1970–. (Useful for hearings and other activities of Congressional committees. Brief abstracts. Monthly. Annual cumulations. Usually referred to as *CIS/Index*.)

Guide to U.S. Government Publications. McLean, VA: Documents Index, 1973–. (Annually. Quarterly supplements.)

Index to U.S. Government Periodicals. Chicago: Infordata, 1970–. (Author–subject index to periodicals published by the federal government. Quarterly. Annual cumulations.)

Jackson, Ellen. *Subject Guide to Major United States Government Publications*. Chicago: ALA, 1968.

Leidy, W. Philip. *A Popular Guide to Government Publications*. 4th ed. New York: Columbia UP, 1976.

Monthly Catalog of U.S. Government Publications. Washington: GPO, 1895–. (Monthly. Semiannual and annual cumulations. Index. See pages 78–79.)

Monthly Checklist of State Publications. Washington: GPO, 1910–. (Monthly. Annual cumulations.)

Schmeckbier, Laurence F., and Roy B. Eastin. *Government Publications and Their Use*. 2nd rev. ed. Washington: Brookings Institute, 1969.

Schwarzkopf, LeRoy C. *A Guide to Popular Government Publications*. Littleton, CO: Libraries Unlimited, 1986.

Statistical Abstract of the United States. Washington: GPO, 1879–. (Annual summaries of statistics on many subjects.)

Statistical Reference Index. Washington: CIS, 1980–. (Monthly abstracts of statistical publications from private organizations and state governments.)

U.S. Congress. HR. *How Our Laws Are Made*. Washington: GPO, 1981. (A useful summary of the legislative process.)

Vertical File Index. New York: Wilson, 1935–. (Monthly except August. Lists pamphlets and booklets by subject. Annual index of titles.)

Indexes

Just as the index of a book does not discuss a subject but indicates where a discussion can be found, a reference work called an index will direct you to sources. Indexes to periodicals are especially useful. Most follow the basic format of *Readers' Guide* (see pages 49, 51).

Applied Science and Technology Index. New York: Wilson, 1958–. (Formerly *Industrial Arts Index*, 1913–57. Subject index. Monthly except July. Quarterly and annual cumulations.)

Arts & Humanities Citation Index. Philadelphia: Institute for Scientific Information, 1978–. (Indexes periodicals and books. Two "interim volumes" a year, annual and five-year cumulations. See pages 45–47.)

Bibliographic Index. New York: Wilson, 1938–. (A subject index to bibliographies in books and journals. Semiannual issues. Annual cumulations.)

Book Review Digest. New York: Wilson, 1905–. (Digests of many book reviews and citations of others. Title and subject index. Monthly except February and July. Annual cumulations. See pages 51–53.)

British Humanities Index. London: Library Assoc., 1962–. (Index to British periodicals. Quarterly. Annual cumulations.)

Essay and General Literature Index. New York: Wilson, 1934–. (Author–subject index of books. Especially useful for anthologies. Semiannually. Annual and five-year cumulations. The first volume covers 1900–33. See pages 39–40.)

General Science Index. New York: Wilson, 1978–. (Monthly except June and December. Annual cumulations.)

Humanities Index. New York: Wilson, 1974–. (Quarterly. Annual cumulations. Supersedes *International Index*, 1907–65, and *Science & Humanities Index*, 1965–74. See page 55.)

Index to Book Reviews in the Humanities. Detroit: Thomson, 1960–. (Quarterly. Annual cumulations.)

Magazine Index. Menlo Park, CA: Information Access, 1976–. (Monthly index recently expanded to cover more than 1,100 magazines. Available on microfilm, online through DIALOG and BRS, and on InfoTrac. See page 44.)

National Newspaper Index. Menlo Park, CA: Information Access, 1976–. (Indexes *New York Times, Christian Science Monitor, Wall Street Journal, Los Angeles Times*, and *Washington Post*. Available on microfilm and online through DIALOG and BRS. Individual indexes available in print.)

Newspaper Index. Wooster, OH: Bell, 1972–. (Indexes *Washington Post, Chicago Tribune, Los Angeles Times*, and *New Orleans Picayune*. Each newspaper is also indexed separately.)

New York Times Index. New York: *New York Times,* 1913–. (Subject index. Summaries of news items. Useful for dating events even when newspaper is not available. Semimonthly. Annual cumulations. Quarterly cumulations since 1978. See page 58.)

Nineteenth Century Readers' Guide. 2 vols. New York: Wilson, 1944. (Indexes periodicals from 1890 to 1899 and includes entries omitted from *Readers' Guide*, 1900–22.)

Poole's Index to Periodical Literature. 6 vols. Boston: Houghton, 1888–1908. (Subject index. Stories and poems are listed by title. Indexes periodicals from 1802 and 1906. Reissued by P. Smith, 1963.)

Popular Periodicals Index. Camden: Botoroff, 1973–. Subject index to periodicals not covered in *Readers' Guide*. Semiannually.)

Public Affairs Information Service. New York: *PAIS,* 1915–. (Subject index to periodicals, pamphlets, and some books. Semimonthly. Quarterly and annual cumulations. See pages 55, 57).

Readers' Guide to Periodical Literature. New York: Wilson, 1905–. (Semimonthly, monthly in July and August. Quarterly, annual, and biennial cumulations. Indexes general interest periodicals from 1900 to the present. See pages 49, 51.)

Science Citation Index. Philadelphia: Institute for Scientific Information, 1961–. (Index to periodicals and some books. Bimonthly volumes, annual and five-year cumulations. See pages 45–47.)

Social Sciences Citation Index. Philadelphia: Institute for Scientific Information, 1972–. (Index to periodicals and some books. Bimonthly volumes, annual and five-year cumulations. See pages 45–47.)

Social Sciences Index. New York: Wilson, 1974–. (Quarterly. Annual cumulations. Supersedes *Social Sciences and Humanities Index*, 1965–74. See pages 55–56.)

Technical Book Review Index. Pittsburgh: Carnegie Library, 1917–29; 1935–. (Monthly except July and August. Annual cumulations.)

Yearbooks

Yearbooks, almanacs, and handbooks are useful sources of statistics and similar factual data.

An Almanack. London: Whitaker, 1869–. (Usually referred to as *Whitaker's Almanac*.)

Annual Register of World Events: A Review of the Year. New York: St. Martin's, 1758–. (Various publishers. Summaries of news events.)

Europa Year Book. 2 vols. London: Europa, 1946–. (Factual data on European countries in first volume, on other countries in the second.)

Facts on File. New York: Facts on File, 1940–. (Weekly news digests. Annual cumulations.)

Guinness Book of World Records. New York: Sterling, 1962–. (Annual compilations of records in almost every human activity.)

Information Please Almanac. New York: Simon, 1947–.

Keesing's Contemporary Archives. London: Keesing's, 1931–83. (Weekly news digests. Biennial cumulations. Published monthly by Longman since 1983.)

Statesman's Year-Book. New York: St. Martin's, 1864–. (A British handbook. Useful for information on governments and international organizations.)

The World Almanac and Book of Facts. New York: Newspaper Enterprise Assn., 1868–.

Sample Bibliography Cards _____

Bibliography cards for books and articles listed in some of the reference works discussed in this chapter are illustrated on the following pages. Indexes often shorten authors' given names, print titles in lower case, and abbreviate names of journals. Revise or expand your card when you use the actual book or article. A brief notation of the index where you found an article listed will enable you to recheck a listing if necessary. Address other reminders to yourself at the bottom of the card.

Quirk, Randolph. _The English Language and Images of Matter_. London: Oxford UP, 1972.

PE
1072
Q48
See ch. 3.

Bibliography card for a book in the card catalog (see page 36).

Brenizer, Sherman. _Hydro-Story: Hydroponic Gardening at Home_. Berkeley: Nolo Press, 1977.

BIP 85-86
check bookstores or order from publisher.

Bibliography card for a book in _Books in Print_ (see page 39).

Litvak, J. "The Infection
of Acting: Theatricals
and Theatricality in
<u>Mansfield Park</u>."
ELH 53 (1986): 331-55.

<u>Source Ind</u>. 1986
author's first name?

Bibliography card for an article in *Source Index* (see page 46).

Goss, Ernst P., and Chris Paul.
"Age and Work Experience
in the Decision to
Migrate." <u>Journal of
Human Resources</u> 21 (1986):
397-405.

<u>CIJE</u> Jan.-June 1987, p. 79

Bibliography card for an article in *Current Index to Journals in Education* (see pages 47–49).

Henry, W. A. "Attacking a
'National Amnesia'."
<u>time</u> 8 Dec. 1986: 107.

(Check author's name; vol. no.
    not necessary)
RG 1986

Bibliography card for an article in *Readers' Guide to Periodical Literature* (see pages 49, 51).

Hutcheon, Linda. <u>A Theory
of Parody: the Teachings
of Twentieth - Century
Art Forms.</u>
New York: Methuen, 1985.

BRD 1986

Bibliography card for a book in *Book Review Digest* (see pages 51–53).

Holmes, W. B. Rev. of *a Theory of Parody: the Teachings of Twentieth - Century art Forms*, by Linda Hutcheon. *Choice* Dec. 1985: 592.

BRD 1986
author's full name?

Bibliography card for a book in *Book Review Digest* (see pages 51–53).

Halperin, John. "Jane Austen's Lovers." *Studies in English Literature 1500–1900.* 25 (1985): 719–36.

Biog. Ind. 1984–86

Bibliography card for an article in *Biography Index* (see pages 53–54).

Kelly, Gary. "The Art of Reading
    in *Pride and Prejudice*."
English Studies in Canada
10 (1984): 156–71

MLA Bibl. 1984

Bibliography card for an article in *MLA International Bibliography* (see pages 54–55).

Hirsch, Marianne. "Female
    Family Romances and
    the 'Old Dream of
    Symmetry.'" *Literature
    and Psychology* 32.4
    (1986): 37–47

Hum. Ind. 1986–87

Bibliography card for an article in *Humanities Index* (see page 55).

Doka, K. J. " Adolescent Attitudes
and Beliefs Toward
Aging and the Elderly."
International Journal
of Aging and Human
Development 22
(1985-1986): 173-87.

55 Ind. vol. 13
author's full name?

Bibliography card for an article in *Social Sciences Index* (see pages 55–56).

Bryan, Lowell L. "The Credit
Bomb in Our Financial
System." Harvard
Business Review 65
(1987): 45-51.

PAIS, Mar. 1987

Bibliography card for an article in *Public Affairs Information Bulletin* (see pages 55, 57).

Finding Material and Taking Notes

Being able to find books and periodicals in the library is a valuable skill, but it will not guarantee a successful research paper. You must also be able to discriminate among sources, read efficiently, select material that supports your thesis, interpret it perceptively, and take usable notes.

Criteria for Evaluating Sources

Perhaps because they are accustomed to relying so heavily on textbooks, some students have excessive reverence for whatever they find in print. Yet it is obvious that being printed does not make a fact accurate or an opinion valid. Composing a research paper should improve your ability to judge the reliability of sources and evaluate their content.

Only a specialist can judge a source with finality. You may hesitate to accept or reject a work on the basis of your own judgment, but the following points are significant when you try to decide whether a source is trustworthy.

1. *Author.* An author's professional qualifications can usually be checked in a biographical reference like *Who's Who in America* or *Directory of American Scholars*. Also, in scholarship, as in sports or entertainment, there are acknowledged stars, and as you investigate a particular subject, you soon learn to recognize respected names.

2. *Publisher.* You will also come to recognize names of respected publishers. Generally, you can assume that their publications are trustworthy. In the same way, the reputation of a periodical may attest to the reliability of an article. Most scholarly associations publish at least one journal, and a journal published by a national association or by a major university can be assumed to be reliable. Brief evaluations of many periodicals can be found in Katz and Katz, *Magazines for Libraries* (see pages 44–45). You should keep in mind that popular magazines usually reflect a particular editorial viewpoint. You would not look for pro-labor articles in *Fortune* or for a pro-feminism statement in *Hustler*. Magazines are more likely than scholarly journals to shift their editorial philosophy. An editorial in *New Republic* today would probably be more conservative than an editorial in the same magazine thirty years ago. If you are in doubt regarding a journal or the author of an article, consult a faculty member in the field served by that journal.

3. *Title.* The full title of a book often indicates its content and purpose. If you were investigating the Battle of Tarawa, you might easily overlook *Eagle against the Sun* by Ronald H. Spector unless you noticed the subtitle: *The American War against Japan.*

4. *Publication date.* The copyright year (on the reverse of the title page) will tell you how recent a book is. This is especially important with social or scientific subjects. An article on women's liberation or moon landings written before 1965 would probably not be very useful. An article on Patrick Henry or Westminster Abbey, on the other hand, will not suffer so much from the passage of time.

5. *Preface.* Many readers automatically skip over introductory material, but an author's preface may be a valuable overview of the content and purpose of the book.

6. *Table of contents.* The chapter titles tell you the major subjects treated in a book, and one of them may suggest a more narrow topic for your paper.

7. *Abstract.* Many scholarly journals preface an article with a brief summary of its content (see page 56). In some books, an abstract precedes each chapter.

8. *Illustrations.*   Paging through a book will show you whether there are pictures, maps, diagrams, or other graphic materials that might be useful.

9. *Documentation.*   An author's notes and bibliography are an indication, though not proof, of reliability. Furthermore, the bibliography may direct you to other treatments of the same subject.

10. *Index.*   The alphabetical listing of topics covered in a book does not indicate its reliability, but it can be very useful in determining its relevance. Students sometimes waste hours paging through books in search of information when a glance at the index would tell them whether their topic was discussed. In collecting material on the early history of the Mormon Church, you could in a few minutes scan the indexes of twenty or more histories and biographies looking for listings of *Mormon, Moroni, Joseph Smith, Palmyra, gold plates, Latter Day Saints*, and a few other related topics. To avoid missing any, make an alphabetical list of your key topics. If you are writing on a literary work, be sure to determine the indexing system that is followed. Some indexes alphabetize each work separately by its title, and some list all works under the author's name.

11. *Glossary.*   A technical book may include in an appendix a useful list of terms with brief definitions.

12. *Reviews.*   It may be helpful to examine reviews of a book. Consult the volume of *Book Review Digest* covering the year when the book was published (see pages 51–53). Sometimes a review itself may prove to be a valuable source.

13. *Expert opinion.*   For many subjects you could consult a faculty member or some other specialist regarding authorities in the field you are investigating.

Primary and Secondary Sources _____

Besides judging the probable usefulness and reliability of a source, you should consider whether it is primary or secondary. The distinction is not as vital in a freshman research paper as in advanced work, but it is significant.

Primary sources are firsthand materials, such as original documents, letters, or diaries. For the paper on stagecoaches that appears in Chapter 5 (pages 168–81), the script and the film of *Stagecoach* would be primary sources. For the paper in Chapter 5 on *Pride and Prejudice* (pages 191–203), the novel itself or one of Jane Austen's letters would be a primary source.

Secondary sources are discussions of a subject after the fact. A history of California and a biography of John Ford would be secondary sources. A biography of Jane Austen or a critique of her novel would likewise be secondary.

PRIMARY SOURCES	SECONDARY SOURCES
the text of *Hamlet*	a critical article
a performance of the play	a review, an actor's memoirs
An Autobiography by Anthony Trollope	*Trollope: His Life and Art* by C. P. Snow
election results	a television commentary on the election
photographs of homeless persons on a city street	the mayor's call for action
a laboratory report on the effects of "passive smoking"	an editorial advocating a smoking ban in restaurants
the diary of a Civil War soldier	a chapter in a history book

Primary source is an impressive term, but some primary sources, especially manuscripts, must be used with caution because they are inaccurate or incomplete. You could base a paper on a diary kept by your grandfather during World War II, but you would need to consult secondary sources for factual background.

A balanced mixture of primary and secondary sources, carefully chosen for their relevance to your thesis, may be desirable, but many successful student papers are based entirely on secondary sources.

Fact and Opinion

Material that you find while reading will be of two general kinds: fact and opinion.

A *fact* denotes something that actually exists; it can be verified or proved. For example, the number of divorces in 1989, the amount of rainfall in 1988, and the date of the next election are verifiable facts. You use facts to support your opinions. A thesis statement cannot be wholly factual, for it would not require development in an essay.

An *opinion* is an idea about a fact or about another opinion. It is an interpretation, a deduction, a supposition. The reasons for a high number of divorces, the effect of rainfall on grain prices, and the probable outcome of the next election are opinions. Opinions taken from your sources can supply supplemental support but not absolute proof of your ideas.

In the following passage from *The Unembarrassed Muse* by Russel B. Nye, the names, dates, publishers, circulation figures, and the story line of *Superman* are all facts. Speculation regarding the popularity of the story is opinion.

Jerry Siegel and Joe Shuster, who invented Superman while high school students in Cleveland, failed to sell him to the comic strips and after several years of disappointment, finally sold the idea to *Action Comics*. When circulation doubled within a few months, it was clear that Superman was a winner. The McClure Syndicate bought the strip and began publishing it in January, 1939; Superman went on the air in February, 1940, and shortly after into movies and movie cartoons. By 1941 the semimonthly comic book devoted entirely to his adventures reached a circulation of 1,400,000, while the comic strip version reached a combined newpaper audience of 20,000,000 daily. No other comic book, and few strips, ever attained such popularity.

In retrospect, it is easy to see why, for "Superman" put together (either accidentally or by shrewd design) most of the salient features of science fiction, adventure, gangster, and police comics with the appeal of fairy-tale fantasy. A migrant from the lost planet Krypton, sole survivor of a superrace possessed of infinite strength, unlimited knowledge, X-ray vision, and the power of flight, Superman enforced law, redressed wrongs, and defeated the forces of evil at home, abroad, and in space. Disguised as Clark Kent, a mild-mannered, chicken-hearted newspaperman, permanently subjected to the jibes of his girlfriend Lois Lane, Superman satisfied everyman's dream of showing off.

A weakness of many students' papers is that they record material from their reading but do not venture opinions of their own. They are so intent on climbing the tree that they never go out on a limb. Their papers are heavy with borrowed opinions but light on original ones. Taking notes from printed sources can benumb the mind, but stay alert and infer conclusions from what you read. You may need to qualify your inferences with words like *may, perhaps,* or *probably,* but do not hesitate to express opinions if they are supported by evidence. Look again at the quotation from *The Unembarrassed Muse* and then consider the four statements that follow. The first two contain inaccurate information ("on the air" in 1940 meant radio, not television). The last two are sound opinions justified by the quotation.

Superman was first written for high school students in Cleveland.

Soon after Superman succeeded as a comic strip, it was made into a television series.

Clark Kent's heroic deeds as Superman probably appealed to the Walter Mittys of the world,

```
mild-mannered persons who dream of daring

adventures.

        Superman's effortless conquest of the forces

of evil may have been appealing in wartime when the

evil of Nazi Germany seemed unconquerable.
```

Supplementary Sources _____

Most of the supporting material for your research paper will come from books and periodicals in your school library, but you should not overlook other possibilities.

   1. *Government publications.* The federal government is a prolific publisher of pamphlets and reports on all kinds of subjects. The Government Printing Office (GPO) produces more than one million copies of various publications each year, most of which are distributed by the Superintendent of Documents. To learn what is available, consult *Monthly Catalog of U.S. Government Publications*; monthly issues are cumulated twice a year. Both monthly and semiannual issues index publications by author, title, subject, issuing agency, and key words. The key-word index and the subject index are easiest to use. They assign each document an entry number that enables you to find the listing in the main section of the catalog, where documents are listed in numerical order. In the example on page 79, the entry number is on the left; the center number is the classification number, which is used to order the document. The listing indicates that the book by John L. Frisbee contains illustrations and a bibliography and can be ordered from the Superintendent of Documents, GPO.

   After finding one or more titles, you have two options:

   a. Look for them in your school library or in nearby libraries. In each congressional district, there are two depository libraries entitled to receive copies of government publications. Your school may be one of them. You may need to ask a librarian for assistance, because most libraries file government publications by their entry numbers rather than by Dewey Decimal or Library of Congress classification numbers.

   b. Order them from the GPO or from the agency that issued them. Congressional committees are listed in *Congressional Directory*; agencies of the executive branch are listed in *United States Government Organization Manual*. Sometimes (especially in an election year) a letter to your congressperson may expedite the response.

87-17852

D 301.96:M 28

Makers of the United States Air Force / edited by John L.
  Frisbee. — Washington, D.C. : Office of Air Force History,
  U.S. Air Force : For sale by the Supt. of Doca, U.S. G.P.O.,
  1987.
    xv, 347 p. : ill., ports. ; 25 cm. — (USAF warrior studies)
  Shipping list no.: 87-516-P. Includes bibliographies and
  index. •Item 422-M-1 S/N 008-070-00593-0 @ GPO ISBN
  0-9127-9942- ISBN 0-9127-9941—(pbk.) $13.00
    1. Aeronautics, Military — United States — Biography.
    2. United States. Air Force — Biography. I. Frisbee, John
  L., 1916- II. United States. Air Force. Office of Air Force
  History. III. Series. UG626.M35 1987 87-600206 358.4/
  0092/2 [B]/19 OCLC 16004834

Sample entry from *Monthly Catalog of U.S. Government Publications.*

2. *Corporate publications.* Many companies publish pamphlets and brochures of various kinds in addition to their annual reports. A clear, courteous request will usually bring whatever materials are available. However, such publications must be used with caution because they are promotional in nature.

3. *Organizations. Encyclopedia of Associations,* consisting of four volumes (Detroit: Gale, 1956–), lists thousands of societies of every conceivable type; for example, there are nine organizations related to the ballet and ten related to pigeon fanciers. This work, which is revised every two years, classifies organizations in seventeen categories; by scanning the appropriate listing, you can identify any that seem pertinent to your topic. A letter to the secretary of an organization may bring you useful information.

4. *Special collections.* The latest edition of *American Library Directory* (New York: Bowker, 1923–) will direct you to special collections. Since it is arranged geographically, you can easily check listings for nearby libraries as well as for your school library.

5. *Clippings.* Many libraries maintain a file of newspaper and magazine clippings, especially on subjects of local interest. Such files are not always listed in the catalog and can be located only by consulting a librarian.

6. *Reproductions.* In recent years many books and periodicals have been reproduced on microforms. Because such reproductions are often listed in a separate file, you may overlook a wealth of material unless you consult a librarian.

7. *Interlibrary loans.* Sometimes a book or a copy of an article not available in your library can be procured from another library. This service, which usually takes a week or more, is not always available to undergraduates. When you submit a request, you will probably be asked to identify the source of the reference. Make a brief note on your bibliography card—for example, MLA Bibl. 1986 102.

8. *Interviews.* A specialist in the field you are investigating can sometimes supply useful information. A paper on alimony awards, for example, might be enhanced by a conversation with an attorney or a marriage counselor. However, you should not invade the office of a total stranger without arranging an appointment in advance; your informant will undoubtedly be busy. Devise thoughtful, specific questions beforehand. Take notes unobtrusively and expand on them as soon as possible after the interview. A tape recorder will be very useful if your informant approves. Interviews should not be abused, but if conducted tactfully, they can be a valuable source of firsthand information. As a courtesy to your informant, send a brief thank-you note after the interview.

9. *Lectures.* Watch the calendar of events being offered at your school. If you are fortunate, an outside lecturer may be discussing a topic relevant to your research. With some topics you might also find it helpful to attend a class lecture even though you are not registered for the course. Ask the professor for permission in advance.

10. *Correspondence.* You should refrain from pestering busy specialists by requesting information that could be obtained from a reference book. You should also avoid vague requests for "all the information about" a subject. Sometimes, however, valuable facts and opinions can be acquired by correspondence. Make your letter courteous and concise. If your topic involves a foreign country, you might write to the United Nations Delegation (see a Manhattan telephone directory). Address your letter to the Public Information Officer. Some countries maintain tourist bureaus in major cities; consult a telephone directory and address your letter to the Director of the Bureau.

11. *Observation.* Some topics require and others permit that you visit a government office, a battlefield, a flood control project, or some other site. Take notes on the spot or as soon as possible after leaving.

12. *Telephone call.* Sometimes information can be obtained by a telephone call in lieu of a letter or a personal interview. Identify yourself as a student, state the information you need, and ask to speak with the person who can supply it.

Ingenuity and imagination in seeking material to supplement library research will often improve a paper.

Purposeful Reading ————————————————

Writing skill is essential in preparing a research paper, but your success will also depend on your ability to read carefully and take notes efficiently. By exploratory browsing, reading at your most rapid rate, you choose a narrow topic. By analysis that is both thoughtful and imaginative, you decide on a tentative thesis and possible main points. You are then ready to begin taking notes and shaping your working outline.

Reading Proficiency

Any topic will involve a few key words or names. With a little practice, you can train your eyes to spot these words on a page. To a certain extent they serve the way descriptors function in a computer search. For example, if you were writing about telescopes, you would be alert for references to *Galileo, Herschel, Mt. Palomar, Lick Observatory, reflector, refractor*, and a few other terms. If your eye picked up one of these terms on a page, you would examine the passage more closely to see if it related to your thesis.

Misinterpreting an author's language is a major cause of inefficient reading. You cannot interrupt your reading every few minutes to consult a dictionary, so make a note of any word you are uncertain about and check its meaning before using the passage in your paper. A fairly common word usually has more than one meaning. In the following sentences, the words in boldface type could be misunderstood by a hasty reader:

> Everyone was charmed by her **artless** manner. (*simple and natural, not inartistic*)

> He was accused of **misprision** of treason. (*concealment, not avoiding jail*)

> As a result of his studying in Paris, he was **conversant** with major French authors. (*familiar with, not talking to or about*)

> At her throat a **carbuncle** gleamed red from a silver chain. (*a garnet, not a severe boil*)

> **Disgruntled** after being dropped from the team, he stopped attending classes. (*disappointed, not making guttural noises*)

A more subtle type of misunderstanding is failing to recognize an allusion, a kind of symbolic shorthand through which an author suggests whatever emotional or intellectual connotation is associated with the reference. History, mythology, literature, and the Bible are especially prolific sources. If an allusion occurs in a passage you intend to use, check an appropriate reference book to make certain the passage is suited to your purpose. The following sentences contain allusions to mythology, the Bible, Shakespeare, American painting, and popular culture:

Problems facing the new chairperson made the labors of Hercules look like simple tasks.

The first sentence of *Moby Dick*, "Call me Ishmael," implies that the narrator, like the son of Hagar and Abraham, is an outcast and a wanderer.

He was as welcome in our group as Banquo at Macbeth's table.

After thirty years of marriage, the Prentices describe themselves as urban American Gothic.

Longfellow has become the Rodney Dangerfield of nineteenth-century American poetry.

In each sentence, the allusion carries implications that affect the meaning. You will become more responsive to allusions as your reading skill improves. The important consideration in a research paper is to avoid quoting an unfamiliar allusion that is inconsistent with your purpose.

Do not be intimidated by long sentences. If necessary read them through a second time, focusing on the main clause and relating other sentence elements to it. Reading long sentences aloud is often helpful as well. The following sentence by Matthew Arnold contains 121 words (about five times the length of most sentences), but its basic meaning is clear:

When one looks, for instance, at the English Divorce Court—an institution which perhaps has its practical conveniences, but which in the ideal sphere is so hideous; an institution which neither makes divorce impossible nor makes it decent, which allows a man to get rid of his wife, or a wife of her husband, but makes them drag one another first, for the public edification, through a mire of unutterable infamy—when one looks at this charming institution, I say, with its crowded trials, its newspaper reports, and its money compensations, this institution in which the gross, unregenerate British Philistine has indeed stamped an image of himself—one may be permitted to find the marriage theory of Catholicism refreshing and elevating. ("The Function of Criticism at the Present Time")

Keep in mind the author's purpose and attitude, often suggested by the tone of a passage. Be alert for irony; authors may say the opposite of what they really mean in order to stress a point. In the preceding sentence, words like *hideous* and *infamy* and the allusion to the Philistines suggest Arnold's actual attitude; he did not really mean that British divorce laws were "charming" or that Catholic restrictions on divorce were "refreshing." Knowing something of an author's general viewpoint can be helpful. You should be especially alert for ironic implications in the works of such diverse writers as Jonathan Swift, Thorstein Veblen, and Tom Wolfe.

There is no quick and easy road to efficient reading, but the requirements of a research paper, in which you are continually evaluating authors' ideas in relation to your thesis, should be useful practice and help make you a more attentive, more critical reader.

Keeping Track of Usable Material

Do not consider yourself fortunate if you find several books devoted solely to your topic; it may mean that you are trying to cover too much in a short paper. Fairly brief passages in books and journals will probably be more useful than entire works. You can discover relevant passages by checking the index of a book or by skimming an article.

In using an article or a portion of a book, skim it first and then return to passages that seem pertinent. It is difficult, if not impossible, to follow an author's train of thought if you interrupt your reading every few minutes to take notes. Devise a system for recording passages that look useful and then take notes after you have examined the entire work.

If you own the book or periodical, the simplest procedure is to star or underline a passage to which you expect to return. Do not underline a passage unless you are fairly certain of using it. Any kind of marking is unsuitable, of course, when you are using library sources.

Another procedure is to insert cards or slips of paper in the work as you read. After completing your reading, you can turn back to your starting point and make notes from the pages where you left bookmarks.

A third method is to keep track of usable passages on a piece of scratch paper. This is done most efficiently by using a decimal system for locating a passage on a page. For example, a sentence halfway down page 267 would be recorded as 267.5. A notation of content is often useful. For a paper on Thoreau's relationship with Emerson, you might record the following from a biography of Emerson:

```
64.1      Th a handyman at E's home

94.6      E buying Walden Pond land

102.8     attitudes toward slavery

127.3     E's eulogy at Th's funeral
```

The abbreviations are an acceptable time-saver.

Always keep your thesis uppermost in your mind and use it to judge the relevance of material. If a fact or an opinion pertains to your thesis, it may belong in your paper. Take care to record it on a note card. Although you are not certain of its pertinence, it will be prudent to make a note card because the source may be gone if you return to look for it later. Purposeful reading is more selective than exploratory reading, and it requires the taking of notes as your outline evolves.

No matter how systematic and thorough your purposeful reading and note-taking have been, once you start writing you are almost certain to discover gaps that must be filled. One reason for setting aside several days to write the paper is the likelihood of your needing to return to the library for additional research.

Expanding Your Working Outline _____

By this time, your working outline should be taking shape. Your note cards and the running outline you compiled in your notebook while doing the exploratory reading (see pages 15–17) should have helped you to decide on your main topics and to group related ideas in subtopics. Consider the most logical order in which these elements can be arranged; standard outline symbols can help to show the relationships among ideas. Leave space for reminders to yourself, revisions, and details. You will probably try several versions of a plan before finding a satisfactory one. Here is Tom Graham's first attempt at planning the opening of his paper on stagecoaches, which appears in Chapter 5:

Gold rush created transportation problems.   **I**

People poured into California.   **– Part of A**

Demand for mail and goods from the East   **A**

Dispute over routes   **C**

Pressure on Congress   **B**

Difficult travel conditions   **– use in D or II**

Need for a durable vehicle   **D**

Petition for better mail service in 1856   **use in B**

Do not worry about parallelism or other niceties at this stage. A working outline is solely for your own use.

The chief danger is regarding a preliminary outline as final. Keep an open mind and make revisions as your research progresses. You may decide to change the order of topics, eliminate a topic, expand a subheading to a main topic, or reduce a main topic to a subheading. Outlining is a logical process, and few of us can arrive at the most sensible pattern of ideas on our first attempt.

Outlining is not an exercise in making diagrams or a form of penance inflicted on students; it is a mode of thinking. Having an outline in mind as you search for material will help you produce a coherent essay. Some students insist that they cannot construct an outline and so postpone the task until they have written the paper, but making an outline after a paper has been completed is as futile as charting your route *after* taking a trip. Keep an open mind and add, delete, or rearrange entries as your familiarity with your topic increases. An outline is a tool, not a shackle. Your working outline should be regarded as tentative until the paper is completed. The final outline that accompanies the paper will undoubtedly be shorter than the working outline that evolves as you do your research. A final outline is like the blueprint for a house; the blueprint shows the location of a wall but does not show the number of nails used or the color it will be painted.

Taking Notes

A research paper cannot be written from memory. While doing the purposive reading, you collect facts and opinions that support your thesis. Collecting material takes longer than the actual writing; therefore, purposive reading and note-taking should begin as soon as possible. However, taking notes before you have narrowed your topic and formulated a thesis is risky; you may be tempted to keep your topic broad so that you can use all of your notes. With experience you will become more proficient in determining what notes to take and how to take them.

Note-Taking Techniques

From the time you begin taking notes, you should realize that you are obligated to acknowledge the exact sources of all borrowed facts and opinions whether you quote an author's exact words or paraphrase them. Of course, facts that are common knowledge need not be cited. You would not credit a source with the fact that Shakespeare wrote *Macbeth*, but you would cite an author who maintained that Francis Bacon wrote the play. You would not cite the fact that Ronald Reagan was elected president in 1980 and reelected in 1984 or that Topeka is the capital of Kansas. Usually your sense of obligation to a source will be clear-cut. Occasionally, however, you will be confronted with an ethical question: "Is information found only in one source, is it general knowledge, or is it the product of my own thinking?" Careful note-taking and an honest intention to give credit for borrowed facts and opinions will ensure adequate documentation and avoid any suggestion of plagiarism (see pages 97–98).

When you first decide to use a source, make out a bibliography card (see pages 26–28 and 65–71) that includes the author's name, the title, and the publication data. If you find a source listed in a bibliography or a periodical index, where authors' names and titles are often shortened, compare your card with the actual book or article to make certain that your card is complete and accurate. Take bibliographic information from the title page of a book, not from the cover or the spine. Since you have your bibliography card for reference, you will need to write only a code word (usually the author's last name) and the page number on each note card. Identify the source at the top of the card before writing your note. While you are working in the library, either scholarly zeal or careless haste may cause you to take notes rapidly; after filling one card you immediately begin another. It is dangerously easy, therefore, to forget to record the source and the page number at the bottom of a card. Few activities are as depressing as having to search through a five-hundred-page volume to locate a passage you neglected to record.

It is also helpful to label each card in the upper right-hand corner with a word or phrase (sometimes called a "slug") indicating its content. If your outline has taken shape, you can use the appropriate outline symbol or a key word from the outline. When you are ready to write your first draft, you can glance at each label and sort the cards into related groups. Otherwise, you would need to read each card to decide where it belongs. To some extent, the habit of labeling note cards will make you a more selective note-taker because it will compel you to consider the function of each note and to keep your thesis and your plan clearly in mind.

The Mechanics of Quoting

After summarizing material from a source, compare your notes with the original to be certain that you have not inadvertently echoed key passages that should be in quotation marks.

Copy a quotation exactly as it appears in the source. After copying it, compare your note with the printed text to be certain that you have copied it accurately. Doing this habitually will prevent transcription errors, which are perilously easy to make. If a quotation contains anything out of the ordinary, such as the use of & or the omission of an accent mark, make a note at the bottom of the card so that you will reproduce the original accurately. Should there be an obvious error in the source, insert *sic* (thus) in brackets. It is generally not underlined. Do not use [sic] after a British spelling like *colour* or *centre* or after an alternative spelling like *judgement*. Students are sometimes eager to use [sic], but the occasion seldom arises; if a passage contains an error, you are not likely to use it. You should know what the word means when you encounter it in your reading. Do not use [sic] sarcastically to indicate disagreement, and do not follow it with an exclamation point.

Although you cannot change the wording of a quoted passage, you can omit words from it. As long as you do not distort the meaning, you can omit a phrase or several sentences. The omission must be indicated by an ellipsis (. . .), three spaced periods—a legitimate, though often misused, punctuation mark. To facilitate the blending of a short quotation into your own sentence (often a mark of a skillfully written paper), you may omit the ellipsis from the beginning or the close of a quotation if the meaning of the passage is not altered in any way. An ellipsis is always needed, of course, when words are deleted *within* a quotation. It is even possible to combine quotations from two paragraphs. In this case, *four* spaced periods indicate where sentences have been deleted. Complete sentences should precede and follow the elision. Such extensive elision seldom occurs in student papers. It is dangerously easy to distort the original context, and, in addition, students are not encouraged to quote lengthy passages.

Frequently judicious pruning of a quotation will enable you to blend it more smoothly into the text of your essay (see page 116). Also, a word or a brief phrase within brackets may clarify a passage so that less of the original must be quoted. For example:

```
"Living in a home where there is no love,

Quentin [Caddy's daughter] is the unhappiest of the

Compsons."

    "Inspired by the Transcendentalist philosophy

of Emerson and others, the president of Harvard

[Charles W. Eliot] introduced the elective system

into American higher education."
```

If your typewriter is not equipped with square brackets, draw them in as neatly as possible. Hand-drawn brackets, ⌐ ⌐ , are preferable to those made with the typewriter slash and the underline: ⌐ ⌐.

Note Cards

Like most professional scholars, students usually find that material can be recorded most efficiently on *note cards*. Each card should contain material relating to the same point. Ordinarily all material on a card will be taken from the same source, but sometimes brief notes from two different sources can be written on the same card if they are closely related and are certain to be used together in the paper. Be careful to identify the source of each quotation accurately.

The reason for using note cards is that they can be manipulated and rearranged as often as necessary. Notes taken in a notebook are frozen in a single order and are difficult to organize. You may find yourself following one source too closely or overlooking important points. If you make the mistake of taking notes in a notebook and writing on both sides of the page, your only recourse may be to photocopy the pages, front and back, and cut them into slips so that you can arrange them in the sequence they will follow in your paper.

By experimenting you can find what type of card is best suited to your writing habits. Memo pads are satisfactory in size, but the sheets tend to stick together. A 3 × 5-inch index card is too small for some notes; a 5 × 8-inch index card is too large and invites the inclusion of too much material on one card. The 4 × 6-inch index card is just right. Most of your notes will not be long enough to fill more than one side, but there is no really good reason for not writing on both sides of a card when necessary; if you spread a note over two cards, you run the risk of losing or misplacing one of them. To make certain that you do not overlook the reverse side, write OVER at the bottom of the card. Because penciled notes tend to smudge, it is advisable to take notes in ink or on a typewriter. The number of notes you will need depends on your topic and the kind of material it entails. For a 2,000-word paper, you might expect to need from fifty to a hundred cards.

Note Sheets

Despite universal advocacy of note cards in handbooks like this one, some students prefer not to use them. If note cards are not required by your instructor and if you have a strong aversion to using them, you can take notes on *sheets of paper*. A legal-sized pad is most suitable. Do not take all the notes from a source on the same sheet, because you are almost certain to overlook some items when you write the first draft. Take notes topically; write notes pertaining to the same point on the same sheet. Space them generously so that you can use arrows, numbers, and other notations as you plan how to use the notes in your paper. See the sample note sheet on page 89. When you begin to write, you may want to cut the sheets into separate slips so that you can arrange them in order. Note cards are strongly recommended, but if you follow some other method, make certain that it is practicable.

Photocopies

The widespread availability of copying machines has revolutionized note-taking techniques for some students and professional scholars. After selecting passages that you plan to use, you can take your books and journals and a roll of coins to a photocopier and in a few minutes duplicate each page. Before leaving the library, write the source at the top of each copy and be certain that each page has been reproduced legibly, including the page number.

The major advantage of photocopying is that it reduces the possibility of transcription errors. A major disadvantage, besides the expense, is that you may find the photocopied pages unwieldy and difficult to manage. Essentially, after you have copied forty pages and taken them to your room you have just what you had in the library—forty pages of printed material. You still must decide what to quote, what to summarize, and what to omit. Cards are still useful. It may be advisable to write summary notes on cards and to clip out passages that you expect to quote and tape or paste them to cards. Do not omit the reference at the top of each card. Another possibility is to encircle or underline useful-looking passages and

Construction

Moody

11 English coaches top-heavy   omit?
   steel springs = uncomfortable ride

12 Yankee builders used leather
   thoroughbraces — coach
   rocked like a cradle

12 egg-shaped body = less
   wind resistance

15 " built to withstand the
   most severe road and weather
   conditions imaginable"   introd?

Hollon 29-30

   tires 5 inches wide, set far
   apart to reduce danger of
   tipping

Holbrook 107-09

   107 British artist, John
       Burgum, was "chief
       ornamenter"

   109 landscape or portrait on
       each door

Sample note sheet.

to write marginal comments indicating how you expect to use the material (see the example below).

Taking notes by using photocopies is not always as efficient as it appears, and it may be wise to adopt it gradually as you acquire greater skill in evaluating material and in composing a research paper.

Nye 259

who pub?

employee of agency

Dashiell Hammett began to develop the character of his private detective, the Continental Op, for *Black Mask* and in 1929 wrote him into a novel, *Red Harvest*, serialized in the magazine. The Op, a more complicated character than most of his companions, fortyish, a bit fat, and very tough-appeared again the same year in *The Dain Curse*, but in *The Maltese Falcon* (1930) Sam Spade replaced him. The investigator of *The Glass Key* (1931) was not a detective but Ned Beaumont, a racketeer's bodyguard. A study of character and brutality, it remains the most complex of Hammett's novels. The *Thin Man (1934)* shifted to Nick Charles, an exdetective who wanted only to be left alone to enjoy his bourbon and his pretty wife but who got involved in murder over his protest. the heart of Hammett's work lies in his first four novels, his three Sam Spade stories, and his early Continental Op series.

independent detective

omit

former detective

The Op, Spade, and Beaumont-Hammett's three versions of the tough hero-have similiarities and differences. The Op is (a professional, doing well what he is paid to do.) He is scrupulously honest, not because of any ethical commitments but because his job demands it. He cleans up a corrupt city in *Red Harvest* because a man hired him to do it; that is will be just as corrupt five years hence matters not at all. "Emotions are nuisances during business hours," so he has none. Sex, hate, and anger divert the attention and impair efficiency; there is, he says, "hard skin over what's left of my soul ... after twenty years of messing around with crime." His closest approach to introspection occurs in *Red Harvest*.

quote

(Each detective less professional than the one before)

Sample of notes made on a photocopied passage.

Types of Notes

The notes that you take will be direct quotations, various types of summary, combinations of quotation and summary, and reminders to yourself.

1. *Quotation note.* Although student papers are often overloaded with quotations, this cannot be said of their note cards. If you are not sure whether you will use an author's actual words, take down the quotation. When you write your first draft, you can convert a quotation to a summary, but you cannot replace a summary with a quotation except by returning to the original source. There are four general reasons for using a direct quotation:

   a. *Accuracy*: when the precise language of the original is crucial.
   b. *Authority*: when the exact words of a source carry more weight than a summary.
   c. *Conciseness*: when a quotation states an idea in fewer words than a summary would require.
   d. *Vividness*: when the language is more colorful or more descriptive than a summary would be.

If you cannot justify the use of a quotation by one or more of these reasons, you probably should summarize it in your own words. A citation will still be necessary, of course. Remember, too, that a quotation must be copied exactly as it appears in the original source and must be enclosed in quotation marks. Doublecheck quotation marks, ellipses, underlining, hyphens, and apostrophes in your notes, and write them legibly.

Twain 30   *division agents*

"It was not absolutely necessary that the division-agent should be a gentleman, and occasionally he wasn't. But he was always a general in administrative ability, and a bull-dog in courage and determination."

Quotation note.

2. *Paraphrase / summary note.* A *paraphrase* restates an author's ideas in different words. Its purpose is to clarify or interpret a passage, and it may not be much shorter than the original. The term *summary* suggests a more extreme reduction of a passage. In any type of condensation, it is essential that you doublecheck your note to make certain that you have not echoed the style of the original. Unintentional plagiarism can be as serious as any other kind.

Compare the use and the misuse of summary in the two note cards on page 93 based on the first four sentences of the quotation from *The Unembarrassed Muse* on page 90. The first card uses the content of the original but does not borrow its language. It also properly credits the source with a page reference in the upper left-hand corner. The second card, however, is an example of the most serious form of plagiarism. Phrases are altered slightly (e.g., "rather fat" for "a bit fat"), not enough to constitute legitimate paraphrase. Be certain not to include key phrases from the original unless you place them within quotation marks. (See also the example on page 94 of a paraphrase/summary note card prepared by Tom Graham, author of one of the sample papers that appear in Chapter 5.)

3. *Outline note.* When only factual information is taken from a source, rough notes in *outline* form may be sufficient (see page 94). Abbreviations and other time-saving devices, which are not used in quotation notes, are permissible in outline notes. However, overuse of outline notes often causes a writer to follow one source too closely.

4. *Combination note.* A *combination note* contains both quotation and summary (see page 95). For the experienced writer of research papers, this type of note is particularly useful because it encourages the blending of quoted material with the writer's own words. In a sense, when you write a combination note, you are beginning to compose your essay. It is especially important to be meticulous in the use of quotation marks. Be careful to close quotations. Try to quote brief passages rather than long blocks of material. Merge quotations with your own sentences.

5. *Personal note.* If your memory is sometimes untrustworthy, it may be prudent to record in *personal notes* things you will want to remember when writing the rough draft. As the example on page 95 shows, the personal note serves as a safeguard against memory lapses.

Nye 259

Dashiell Hammett created three detectives:
the Continental Op (1929), Sam Spade
(1930), and Nick Charles (1934). Nick
is a retired detective who un-
willingly becomes involved in a
murder investigation. Each detective
is less professional than the one
before.

Proper use of summary.

Nye 259
Dashiell Hammett's Continental Op
is a complicated man, about forty
years old, rather fat, and very
tough. He was followed in
Hammett's fiction by Sam Spade,
Ned Beaumont, and Nick Charles.

Improper use of summary.

Moody 17-18   seating

Nine passengers could ride inside the
coach — three on a rear seat facing
forward, three on a front seat facing
back, and three on a middle seat facing
forward. A broad leather belt suspended
from the ceiling served as a backrest for
the middle seat. The place of honor was beside the driver, and it usually went to a
man of importance or a charming young lady.

Paraphrase/summary note.

Hollon 29   construction
3000 lbs.
capacity 2 tons
cost $1400.
used finest white ash, oak, elm, basswood
broad iron tires, wheels set wide apart
Colt revolver & stagecoach = 2 Yankee
contributions to frontier legend

Outline note.

Haugood 249   "stagecoach kings"

The businessmen who drew up stage
routes and competed for government
contracts in the 1850s were "men
of great ability and much ruthlessness."

Combination note.

construction

Yankee ingenuity in adapting to new and
difficult conditions

egg-shaped body, thoroughbrace, wide
tires, etc.

Personal note.

Writing Your Paper

After you have spent days compiling a list of sources, taking notes, and projecting an outline, the actual writing of the paper may seem anticlimactic; but it is the most important phase of your research project because your work will be judged on the basis of what you set down on paper. This chapter suggests some procedures to follow, but writing is an individualistic activity that cannot be reduced to a series of formal steps. Suggestions in this chapter are not prescribed as mechanical steps in a formula. Try them and adopt those that work well for you.

Avoiding the Perils of Plagiarism

A research paper can be marred by various imperfections—lack of a meaningful thesis, an illogical plan, monotonous sentences, inaccurate or inappropriate diction, careless documentation, and mechanical errors. The most serious fault that can damage a paper, however, is *plagiarism*. Plagiarism (derived from a Latin word for kidnapper) means using another person's language or ideas without acknowledgment. *Random House Dictionary* defines it as the "unauthorized use or close imitation of the language and thoughts of another author and the representation of them as one's own original work." In plain English, it is theft.

Intentional plagiarism is a serious act of dishonesty that always carries a heavy penalty—failure of the paper, failure in the course, or even expulsion from school. It is regarded just as seriously in professional life; every few weeks, it seems, newspapers report that an author, a public official, or a business executive has been accused of presenting as original work something written by someone else. The result is often disgrace and personal tragedy that may never be overcome. In college papers, deliberate copying from an encyclopedia, a book, or a journal is relatively rare, but the penalty is always severe. Readymade papers purchased from a "research service" are probably the most blatant kind of academic dishonesty. Plagiarism can also be unintentional when a student omits citations, fails to use quotation marks, or thoughtlessly echoes the language of a source. Careless note-taking (see Chapter 3) can also result in plagiarism. Unfortunately, the penalty for unintentional plagiarism can be as severe as for flagrant cribbing from a book or a periodical.

When you begin a research project, you may feel that you will need a great many citations; but because you do not credit to a single source facts that are common knowledge or opinions that are generally known and accepted, you will probably need fewer than you expect. Many facts and ideas that are new to you will appear in most discussions of your topic. If you express them in your own words, you ordinarily do not need to cite them. But a fact or an opinion derived from one source requires citation. MLA style makes the citation of sources so simple that it should reduce the incidence of careless plagiarism. From the time you start taking notes, you should recognize your obligation to acknowledge borrowed material. Careful note-taking and an understanding of how to document sources (see Chapter 5) will keep you from the reality and the appearance of plagiarism. The use and misuse of a source are shown in the two examples that follow, each of which is based on this passage from page 34 of *Adolescent Suicidal Behavior* by David K. Curran (Washington: Hemisphere, 1987):

> Things change quickly in our time. Rapid and continuous adaptation is being demanded of our young at younger and younger ages. While our society and technology may indeed have advanced in impressive ways, it is not at all clear that the human organism has changed all that much in recent years, or that it is capable of standing up to these demands. It is not surprising that increasing numbers of teens may respond by hunkering down, turning to drugs or alcohol, and waiting for all this to pass, electing not to jump on the merry-go-round. Some who have ridden the dizzying ride to exhaustion may risk themselves by simply jumping off.

1. Society and technology have advanced

   impressively, but the human organism has

not changed very much. Teenagers respond by

turning to drugs or alcohol and electing

not to jump on the merry-go-round (Curran 34).

2. Rapid changes in society have not been

matched by changes in human beings. Many

teenagers find it difficult to adapt to this

situation and turn to drugs or alcohol,

"electing not to jump on the merry-go-round"

(Curran 34).

Example 1 uses phrases from the original without quotation marks. This kind of haphazard paraphrase is more common than intentional word-for-word copying, but it is just as serious. Actually, the perpetrator of such blatant plagiarism probably would not even cite the source. Example 2 summarizes the original without using any key phrases except the last one, which is properly quoted.

Here are two more examples, based on an excerpt from an article by Erdwin H. Pfuhl, Jr., "Computer Abuse: Problems of Instrumental Control," *Deviant Behavior* 8 (1987): 123:

> Still another factor helping to shape people's consciousness of computer offenses is that they are almost always directed against corporations—banks, railroads, utilities, manufacturers—and other bureaucracies. . . . Popular antagonism toward corporate bureaucracies often leads these acts and the offenders to be less subject to stigmatization than in cases of garden-variety thuggery.

1. Computer offenses are less subject to

stigmatization than garden-variety crimes

because they are usually directed against

corporations, banks, and railroads, which

many people regard with antagonism.

2. Many people are more tolerant of computer

offenders than of other criminals because

```
computer offenses are usually committed

against bureaucratic institutions, which

are resented by the general public

(Pfuhl 123).
```

Example 1 purloins phrases without using quotation marks and without citing the source. Flagrant plagiarism like this invariably results in a failing paper. Example 2 is an intelligent summary of the original that expresses its basic meaning without echoing any of its key phrases.

To avoid any suggestion of plagiarism, copy a quotation with meticulous care, enclose it in quotation marks, and compare it word by word with the source. Write a summary or an outline note from memory. Then compare it with the source to make certain that you have not unintentionally echoed the style of the source and that any borrowed phrasing is enclosed in quotation marks. Careful note-taking is essential, but you must be equally careful when writing your paper. It is all too easy to omit or misplace quotation marks.

Starting Your Rough Draft

Collecting material for your paper will take time, but it should not be prolonged unduly. If you feel reluctant to begin the actual writing, filling stacks of note cards in the library may be a way of postponing the task—procrastination disguised by a false sense of accomplishment. At any rate, there is a point of diminishing returns in research, and when you have investigated your topic thoroughly, you should begin to write.

It is impossible to judge your material while it exists only in your mind and on note cards. When you have set it down in a rough draft, you will have something tangible that you can evaluate and revise. Do not attempt to write the final version of your paper from your note cards. Only a few professional writers are capable of writing acceptable prose without making at least one preliminary draft. The number of drafts you write will depend on your work habits. Writing is not an easy task, and professional writers as well as serious students may turn out a half-dozen drafts before producing an acceptable version of an essay. Typically, a student writes a rough draft, an intermediate copy that is drastically revised, and the final copy. A word processor (see Appendix A) will reduce the amount of time needed to revise and recopy your paper.

Before beginning to write your rough draft, read through your log or journal to recall any notations made during the early stages of your research that may have faded from your memory. Also read through your note cards to determine the order in which your supporting ideas should be presented. A journal entry or a note card may jog your imagination and suggest a relevant point or an effective phrase. Reading and note-taking can become rather mechanical tasks in which your creative imagination is put on hold. Free writing and brainstorming (see pages 6–7) can be useful at this stage as a means of loosening up your imagination and also of gaining an overview of your material. Suspend your critical sense and just set down words and phrases as they come to mind without attempting to analyze them. Then examine your listing with your audience and purpose in mind. Such a free-wheeling review of your topic will help you evaluate your ideas and may also suggest fresh ideas or turns of phrase.

There are no ideal conditions for writing, but your job will be easier if you can find a place where you can work without interruption or distraction. Try to allot several hours to the rough draft so that you can get it on paper in a single sitting. Resist the temptation to postpone writing until another day. Do not lose your momentum by lingering over the choice of words. If you find an idea difficult to express, leave enough space for it and go on. As you write, keep looking ahead in your notes to anticipate transitions that will connect your ideas effectively. Also, do not attempt to cram as many words as possible on a single page or write on both sides. Crowded pages are impossible to revise. Writing on a legal pad or on oversize paper (e.g., 11 × 17 inches) may encourage you to leave ample space for revision. Leave wide margins on both sides and triple-space so that you can add, change, or move material.

For many students the most difficult portion of a paper to write is the opening. Just as a speaker may devote several minutes to throat-clearing and foot-shuffling, a student may devote three or four pages to a roundabout approach to a topic. For example, a student investigating modern funeral practices might open the paper with a summary of encyclopedia information on Egyptian, Sumerian, and Roman burial customs. This kind of introduction may be a form of freewriting, a useful way of warming up your creative engine. After you have written such an indirect warm-up introduction, delete it and try to introduce your topic and your thesis in one clear, crisp paragraph. Look for an opening gambit that will capture the reader's attention. For example, here are some possible openings for a paper on the discovery of penicillin.

An anecdote:

```
In the fall of 1928, Dr. Alexander Fleming

noticed that a culture plate exposed to the air

developed a nontoxic mold that combated certain

bacteria.
```

A quotation:

> George Santayana's definition of miracles as
> "propitious accidents" accurately describes the
> discovery of penicillin by Sir Alexander Fleming.

Contradiction of a widely accepted idea:

> Although the discovery of penicillin is often
> described as an accident, Sir Alexander Fleming
> began studying wound infections during World War I,
> and he was actively looking for an agent to combat
> bacteria when he made his discovery.

Statement of significance:

> The discovery of penicillin marked the
> beginning of the antibiotic era in medicine.

Origin, definition, or meaning of a term:

> The word "penicillin" comes from the Latin
> word for paintbrush; Sir Alexander Fleming chose
> this term because the mold from which the
> antibiotic was developed resembled tufts on a
> painter's brush.

Any of these ideas could be made the nucleus of an opening paragraph.
   At some point during the writing of the rough draft, you should attempt to write an abstract or a summary of no more than 150 words. Condensing your paper without omitting any major ideas will enable you to judge the unity of the paper and to identify any inadvertent digressions. If you find it impossible to fit an idea in the abstract, it may not belong in the paper.

Revise your rough draft frequently and do not worry much about neatness. Even if it is to be submitted with the final paper, a rough draft is not expected to be a thing of beauty.

Organizing Your Material _____

Sorting the Note Cards

When you begin composing your first draft, the value of taking notes on cards should become apparent. On a tabletop or on the floor if necessary, spread out the cards and sort them into piles that correspond to the main headings of your working outline. If you have labeled each card, this sorting process will be simplified. In classifying your note cards, you must be reconciled to two grim facts:

1. *Some note cards will be eliminated.* Anyone writing a research paper takes some notes on speculation. You should discard those that are clearly unrelated to your thesis and put doubtful ones in a special pile for later consideration. In any construction, some waste is inevitable, and a research paper is no exception. Trying to squeeze in all of your notes merely to justify the time and energy spent in recording them will destroy the unity of your paper.

2. *Some additional reading may be necessary.* As you work out the detailed structure of your paper, you are likely to find weak spots that need to be reinforced. You may have to return to some of your sources to obtain additional material or to check your citations. You may also have to find new sources to supplement your notes. If possible, complete your rough draft, leaving space for the additional material. Interrupting your writing to visit the library may be simply another form of disguised procrastination.

The Working Outline

As you begin writing your rough draft, you should consider the final outline if one is to be included with the paper. *MLA Handbook* does not recommend outlines with research papers, but many instructors require them. Look over the working outline in your notebook. Check its main points to be certain that they all pertain to your thesis and that they follow a logical order. Then look through the cards supporting your first main point to determine the most logical arrangement of the material.

Try to vary the development of your paragraphs. If one is arranged chronologically, try to follow a different arrangement in the next. It may be helpful to copy your working outline on a large sheet of paper and attach it to the wall above your typewriter table. You might also tape together the note cards for your first paragraph and place them beside the working outline.

The Formal Outline

The working outline that has developed gradually as you have investigated your topic is solely for your own guidance; the *formal outline* is in
tended for your readers. The purpose of a formal outline is to show graph-
ically the order, the unity, and the relative importance of the components
of the essay. It does this by using certain conventional devices.

1. Values are shown by symbols. The most common system is simple:

      I.

    II.

        A.

        B.

          1.
          2.

            a.
            b.

To subdivide further, you merely alternate arabic numerals and lowercase
letters. But if you subdivide to that extent, you have probably included too
many details or have omitted a necessary main heading. You will seldom
deal with a set of ideas on five or six levels of importance. Symbols are an
important way of showing relative values because all items with the same
kind of symbol are assumed to be of approximately the same importance.
Something is probably wrong with an outline in which A represents a
paragraph and B represents only a single sentence. Items below the second
rank (capital letters) are usually single-spaced. Note that roman numerals
are aligned on the period.

2. Indentation is another means of showing values. All headings on the
same margin are assumed to be of approximately the same importance.

3. Parallelism, also a way of showing values, means in an outline just
what it means in connected prose: Ideas of equal importance are given
equal or like expression. In a *topic outline* every item should be a word
or phrase; in a *sentence outline* every item should be a sentence. It is not
necessary, however, that every item contain the same number of words;
headings are parallel when they are in the same grammatical form. For
a simple example of parallelism, see the headings listed at the beginning
of this chapter: *Avoiding, Starting, Organizing, Writing, Managing,* and

Preparing. Nonparallel items are the most common violation of outlining conventions.

4. In a topic outline every heading should be a noun or a noun-equivalent (a gerund or, possibly, an infinitive). Most nonparallel items can easily be converted to nouns, and the revised form is usually more precise. For example:

> Very strong = Great strength
> In prison = Imprisonment
> Destroyed the temple = Destruction of the temple
> Delilah betrayed him. = Betrayal by Delilah

5. The extent to which topics are subdivided should be consistent. Ordinarily, for a research paper the subdivisions of each paragraph are represented in the outline. Occasionally, of course, a short paragraph will not be subdivided. In most outlines you will be tempted at least once to list minor details simply because they are so obvious. But if one roman numeral is subdivided into capital letters, and the next roman numeral is subdivided as far as lowercase letters, the outline is probably faulty.

6. Single division is a logical error in a formal outline. A single symbol, therefore, is a danger signal. When you indent and begin a set of subordinate symbols, you are dividing ideas. Since nothing can divide into one part, you must have two or more subdivisions or none at all.

7. Avoid using general terms like "Introduction," "Conclusion," "Example," and "Summary." A heading should signify the content of a portion of an essay, not its purpose or its method.

8. To conform to the last two conventions (no single divisions and no omnibus headings), write the thesis at the top of the outline page and then begin the outline proper. If the paper's central idea appears in the outline as item I, no other idea can rank with it, and adding a II with a vague heading like "Development" or "Body" would merely complicate the outline. Writing the thesis separately is also a test of your mastery of the topic. If you cannot formulate a thesis sentence, you probably need to narrow your topic or reconsider your objective.

9. The conclusion that will appear in the paper need not be included in the outline because it will be substantially similar to the thesis.

Three kinds of formal outline—*sentence, topic,* and *combination*—are discussed and illustrated on the following pages. Compare the sentence outline with Tom Graham's sample paper in Chapter 5 (pages 168–81), and compare the topic outline with Rita Hogan's paper, also in Chapter 5 (pages 191–203). Note the outlining conventions used in the sample outlines as well as the division and arrangement of ideas.

Sentence Outline. The *sentence outline* is more informative than the topic outline, but it tends to encourage the writing of similar short sentences—a common fault in mediocre prose.

The Frontier Stagecoach

Thesis: The stagecoach not only represents frontier ingenuity in adapting to difficult conditions but also has become a colorful part of the legendary West.

I. The discovery of gold in California created transportation problems.

A. New arrivals wanted goods and mail from the East.

B. Agitation for improved mail service increased after California became a state in 1850.

C. The choice of a route caused bitter disputes between the North and the South.

D. It was also necessary to develop a durable vehicle.

II. The Concord coach was an ideal vehicle to cope with frontier conditions.

A. The construction was adapted to rough travel and resulted in an indestructible vehicle.

B. The coaches were attractively decorated.

C. Passengers and freight were accommodated efficiently.

III. Competition for government contracts and for passengers was fierce.

A. John Butterfield operated stages on the southern route.

B. Russell, Majors, and Waddell operated freight wagons, stagecoaches, and the Pony Express on the central route.

C. Ben Holladay took over the lines and made service much more efficient.

IV. John Butterfield devised the organization that was adopted by his successors.

A. The basic unit was the division.

B. A division was divided into stations.

V. The driver was the most glamorous of stagecoach employees.

A. He was admired by passengers and by other employees.

B. His prestige was due to his skill with reins and whip.

VI. Two drivers became famous as individuals.

    A. Charlie Parkhurst, respected as a fast, safe driver, was actually a woman.

    B. Hank Monk was the hero of an anecdote involving Horace Greeley.

VII. The stagecoach is a familiar sight in imaginative treatments of the old West.

    A. Stage robberies occur frequently in dime novels.

    B. Buffalo Bill included an attack on a stage in his Wild West Show.

    C. Frederic Remington painted action pictures involving stagecoaches.

VIII. The most famous use of the legendary stagecoach by the media is John Ford's film Stagecoach.

    A. The exciting action centers on the high speed of the coach to escape attacking Apaches.

    B. The diversity of the passengers suggests the democratic mixing that occurred on the frontier.

Topic Outline. The *topic outline* shows the structure of a paper but little of its substance. A topic outline is the skeleton of an essay.

Marriage in <u>Pride and Prejudice</u>

Thesis: The examples of eight other marriages, most of them less than harmonious, contribute to the eventual union of Elizabeth and Darcy.

I. Elizabeth and Darcy

    A. Pride

    B. Prejudice

    C. "Approach and rejection"

II. Minor characters

    A. Mr. and Mrs. Hurst

    B. Sir William and Lady Lucas

    C. Mr. and Mrs. Phillips

III. Mr. and Mrs. Bennet

    A. Mr. Bennet

    B. Mrs. Bennet

    C. Effect on Elizabeth

IV. Lydia and Wickham

    A. Elopement

    B. Relation to the plot

V. Mr. Collins and Charlotte Lucas

    A. Mr. Collins

    B. Charlotte

    C. Effect on Elizabeth

VI. The Gardiners

    A. Gentility and dignity

    B. Darcy's admiration

VII. Jane and Bingley

    A. Pliability

    B. Jane's good nature

    C. Effect on Elizabeth and Darcy

Combination Outline. The *combination outline* combines the best aspects of sentence and topic outlines—its main headings are sentences and its subheadings are topics. The first main segment of each outline illustrates the combination form.

I. The discovery of gold in California created transportation problems.

    A. Demand for goods and mail

    B. Pressure on Congress

    C. Choice of a route

    D. Developing a durable vehicle

I. Though well suited to one another, Elizabeth and Darcy are kept apart by circumstances and by their own personalities.

    A. Pride

    B. Prejudice

    C. "Approach and rejection"

Writing a sentence for each main topic can help you identify the central idea unifying that portion of the paper. Similarly, writing the subtopics as phrases enables you to reevaluate their arrangement.

The form of an outline is not as important as its inherent logic. If you

have a free choice of forms, use the one that seems most efficie
certain to adhere consistently to the form you choose.

Providing Adequate Transitions

Although you need a clear, logical plan that is represented by a formal
outline, you also need to articulate that plan coherently in your paper.
Coherence is achieved by adhering to a sensible plan and by providing
adequate *transitions* between paragraphs, between subtopics within a paragraph, and between sentences. You will probably need more transitional
material than you expect. As the writer of a paper, you are like a driver on
a familiar highway who does not need to watch for signs or landmarks,
but your reader is like a driver on a strange highway who needs direc-
tional markers. You are so familiar with the material that you know what
is coming next, and it is easy to underestimate the amount of guidance
your readers will need. It is better to be overobvious than to be obscure.

The most effective transitions are organic ones that derive from the
material itself. Sometimes making an outline enables you to see how material can be rearranged so that one topic links up more smoothly with
the next. The most obvious way to link ideas, however, is through *transitional elements*—words and phrases that indicate relationships between
ideas. Following is a list of some kinds of relationships and the transitional
elements that express them.

agreement/comparison   correspondingly, in like manner, in
the same way, just as, like, similarly

cause/reason   as a consequence, because, consequently, due
to, owing to, since, therefore, whereas

condition   although, at any rate, even though, if, in case,
nevertheless, nonetheless, on condition that, provided that

continuation/addition   accordingly, again, along with, also,
and, as well as, besides, first, second (not firstly or secondly,
now chiefly reserved for sermons), further, furthermore, in
addition, last, likewise, moreover, next, too

effect/result   accordingly, as a result, consequently, hence,
then, therefore, thus

opposition/contrast   but, conversely, however, in contrast, on
the contrary, on the other hand, otherwise, yet

place   above, adjacent to, below, beyond, here, near, nearby,
there, where, wherever

purpose   in order to, so that

qualification   almost, however, nearly, perhaps, probably,
somewhat

summary   in conclusion, in short, in summary, to sum up

time   after, afterward, always, during, hereafter, in the meantime, later, meanwhile, never, next, now, since, sometimes,
soon, then, when, whereupon, while

Although the transitional elements in each grouping are similar in meaning, no two are identical. Two often-confused transitional words are *therefore* (for this reason) and *thus* (in this way). Sensitivity to nuances of meaning and the ability to choose appropriate transitional elements can be developed by attentive reading and by practice in writing.

Writing in an Appropriate Style _____

Your instructor will undoubtedly specify the level of formality appropriate for your paper, but this will also depend on your topic (e.g., a paper on the Beatles will have a less serious tone than one on Pope John Paul). In a highly formal style, most contractions and the pronouns *I* and *you* are usually considered inappropriate, yet referring to yourself as "the writer" or "this researcher" often sounds clumsy. Extreme formality may also encourage overuse of the passive voice.

Avoiding the Passive Voice

Passive verbs may suggest a tone of objectivity, but they also tend to be wordy, indirect, and awkward.

Passive: It was indicated by higher gold prices that inflation was imminent.
Active: Higher gold prices indicated that inflation was imminent.

Passive: *Innocents Abroad* was written by Mark Twain after returning from an excursion to Europe and the Holy Land.
Active: Mark Twain wrote *Innocents Abroad* after returning from an excursion to Europe and the Holy Land.

To some extent, your style will reflect your attitude toward your paper. If you are bored by your topic, your style is likely to be boring and lifeless—a major reason for choosing an interesting topic.

Avoiding "Buzz Words"

A research paper will almost always involve terms that are not part of your everyday vocabulary. Be certain to use them accurately. At any given time, some terms ("buzz words") are fashionable in the academic world, and because they are used so often, they are sometimes used loosely. If you use words like *charisma, continuum, counterproductive, optimize, parameters, rationale, scenario, supportive,* or *viable*, be sure that they express the meanings you intend. Avoid computerese like *ergonomic, input, interface,* and *undelete*. In general, do not use a word because you think it will impress your readers. Consult a thesaurus for a listing of related words from which you can choose the one that best fits your meaning; refer to your dictionary when you are in doubt about the precise meaning of a word. Avoid using *hopefully* as a sentence modifier; *thrust* as a noun; *contact, impact, implement,* and *program* as verbs; and the innumerable combinations that result from attaching words to the prefix *mini-* or to the suffix *-wise.* Sometimes writing a research paper will tempt students to elevate their vocabularies unduly: a prison becomes a correctional facility, a door becomes a means of egress, and a classroom becomes the setting for intellectual enlightenment. Your style should be somewhat more formal than usual, but it also should be simple and natural.

Eliminating Wordiness

Wordiness is a common fault in research papers, partly because students feel pressure to attain a certain number of words. When revising your paper, substitute specific words for general ones. Concentrate on the nouns and verbs; if they are exact, fewer modifiers will be needed. Try to eliminate all unnecessary words, especially bloated expressions like the following:

> at no time = never
> at the conclusion of = after
> at the time that = when
> at this point in time = now
> due to the fact that = because
> during the time that = while
> for the reason that = because
> in a short time = soon
> in all likelihood = probably
> in spite of = despite
> in spite of the fact that = although
> in the event that = if
> in the place that = where
> on or about = approximately
> on the local level = locally
> prior to the time that = before

Varying Sentence Length and Arrangement

Revise your sentences for clarity and correctness and especially for variety. There is a tendency in research papers to write sentences that are monotonously similar. Try to vary your sentences in structure, arrangement, and length. Sentence beginnings are especially important because there is a natural inclination to start every sentence with the subject. Moving a phrase or a subordinate clause to the beginning often improves the clarity as well as the sound of a sentence. Avoid, however, starting too many sentences with transitional elements. They should be submerged within the sentence if possible, especially between the subject and the verb or between the verb and its object. Like buttons, hooks and eyes, or zippers in clothing, transitional elements should join parts firmly but should be inconspicuous.

Reading Your Paper Aloud

Your style will improve if you can develop the knack of *hearing* a sentence as you are writing it. Also, at least once during the revision process, read your paper aloud. It may be helpful to read to someone if you can recruit a listener. Using a tape recorder will enable you to judge an oral version of your prose. When you read silently something as familiar as your paper will be by this time, your eyes have a tendency to glide over words uncritically. Reading aloud slows your eye movement and enables you to identify clumsy constructions and other weaknesses that you might overlook in silent reading. If you find a sentence difficult to read, perhaps it should be recast.

Using Nondiscriminatory Language

Your writing should be sensitive to the effect of words that imply prejudice based on ethnic, sexual, or racial differences. Although most of these types of expressions are more likely to occur in speech than in writing, they represent the fallacy of ascribing a particular trait to an entire class of persons.

A problem that may arise in your research paper is the form that should be used for titles and names. In general, do not use a title like *Mr.*, *Ms.*, *Dr.*, or *Professor* with a proper name; but there are exceptions for which usage has made the title seem natural: Sir Walter Raleigh, Dr. Johnson, Madame Curie. Give a person's full name on the first use, and afterward use the surname alone. A combination like *Scott and Jane Austen* or *Whitman and Emily Dickinson* may suggest a sexist bias, as would referring to Dickinson as *Emily* or as *Miss Dickinson*. In writing about a literary work, however, you should follow the characters' names used by the author—for example, Elizabeth and Darcy, Mr. Collins and Charlotte in the second sample paper.

Much attention has focused in recent years on sexist language. *Sexist*, a fairly new word, was coined by analogy with *racist* and has taken on the same unpleasant connotation. Sexist language stereotypes men and women in terms of outdated roles. *A lady lawyer* implies that it is unusual for a woman to be a lawyer; *Dr. Edward King and his wife, Susie*, suggests a dignified male professional accompanied by his wife, an immature but probably decorative appendage. Most nouns formed with *-ess* are offensive to women: for example, *ambassadoress, authoress, murderess, poetess, songstress*. Substitute expressions should be used for terms that imply sexist bias:

chairman = chair/chairperson
congressman = representative
mailman = letter carrier
mankind = humanity
manmade = artificial
the man on the street = the average person
a man-sized job = a demanding job
newsman = reporter
policeman = police officer
salesman = sales clerk/salesperson
weatherman = forecaster/meteorologist

That English has always been a male-oriented language is indicated by the fact that *he, him,* and *his* have been used in the past to refer to nouns that could be either masculine or feminine. Sentences like the following suggest sexual stereotyping:

> A broker must keep *his* customers informed of investment opportunities.

> A kindergarten teacher must know each of *her* pupils by name.

> Everyone planning to attend the banquet should make *his* reservation by Friday.

> A student pilot is always terrified when *he* solos for the first time.

> A serious scholar always keeps an accurate record of *his* sources in case *he* needs to consult them again.

Various methods of correcting or avoiding such sentences have been suggested:

1. The use of *he or she* or *he/she* is correct but can be awkward and monotonous if overused.
2. An ingenious suggestion of using *s/he* will work only for the subjective case and creates a pronunciation problem if one reads a sentence aloud.
3. Some writers advocate using *he* in one instance and *she* in the next, alternating *he* and *she* throughout an essay.
4. Use of the gender-neutral *their* to refer to a singular word like *everyone* is becoming more acceptable: "*Everyone* planning to attend the banquet should make *their* reservations before Friday." Some readers, however, object to the faulty pronoun agreement.

Recasting a sentence so that a sexist pronoun is unnecessary is usually the best procedure. English is a rich language, and there are always several ways of expressing an idea. Many sentences can be revised so that no pronoun is necessary. Changing a noun to plural number is sometimes

...e simplest correction. Since *they* is a unisex pronoun, it can replace *he* and eliminate the problem. Various methods of revision are shown here:

> A broker must keep all customers informed of investment opportunities.

> A kindergarten teacher must know each pupil by name.

> All persons planning to attend the banquet should make their reservations by Friday.

> A student pilot is always terrified on a first solo flight.

> Serious scholars should keep accurate records of their sources in case they need to consult them again.

Behavior, of course, is more important than words, but language is a basic element of human experience, and as language habits change, behavior tends to follow. Consciously avoiding the language of prejudice encourages the avoidance of behavior based on prejudice.

Managing Quotations, Basic Conventions ____

Be meticulous about copying quotations exactly as they appear on your note cards, about checking the wording of each quotation against the original source, and about the placement of quotation marks and ellipses. If you have a fairly long quotation, clip or tape the card to the page at the spot where it will be used. Copying and recopying it would just multiply the chances of errors creeping in.

If you are using footnotes or endnotes (see pages 182–83), it is unnecessary and perhaps unwise to write them in your rough draft. When you revise your draft, you can easily overlook or misplace a citation or include one that is no longer necessary. The simplest procedure is to write a brief citation in parentheses: (Winther 57). When you prepare your final draft, use your bibliography cards to expand such citations into footnotes or endnotes. If you use in-text citations (see pages 154–61), such parenthetical citations can be transferred to your final copy with little or no change — one of the time-saving aspects of MLA style. Have your list of works cited or your bibliography cards visible while you are writing so that you can cite sources readily.

A poor research paper is often a scissors-and-paste collection of quotations looming up at intervals in student prose. One of the marks of a superior paper is that quotations are gracefully blended into the text instead of standing alone with no clear connection to what precedes or to what follows. A major advantage of MLA style is that it facilitates the incorporation of brief quotations within the text of a paper. The merging of quoted material with the text is chiefly a concern during revision, but a beginning can be made in the rough draft. One reason for awkwardness with quotations may be uncertainty about mechanics. Following are the basic conventions (some of which are also discussed in Chapter 3, pages 86–87).

Single and Double Quotation Marks

A quotation within the text of a paper is enclosed in double quotation marks. A quotation within a quotation is enclosed in single quotation marks. If you quote a passage that contains double quotation marks, change them to singles and use doubles to enclose the passage. Some publishers, especially in England, enclose quotations in single marks— the opposite of general American practice. For the sake of consistency, it is permissible to change the singles to doubles.

Ways of Introducing Quotations

The colon is a common but formal device for introducing a quotation. A verb like *said* or *wrote* introducing a quotation is ordinarily followed by a comma. Some students erroneously extend this rule and place a comma before every quotation. When a quotation is an integral part of your own sentence (usually a subject or direct object), a comma is not needed. Also, when the word *that* precedes a quotation, a comma is seldom necessary. Any quotation can be introduced in more than one way. Variety is highly important; it is easy to get in a rut and overuse one construction. Several ways of introducing a short quotation are shown here:

```
Emerson bluntly stated his faith in

self-reliant individuals as follows: "An

institution is the lengthened shadow of one

man" (154).

Emerson wrote, "An institution is the

lengthened shadow of one man" (154).

According to Emerson, "An institution is the

lengthened shadow of one man" (154).

"An institution," according to Emerson, "is

the lengthened shadow of one man" (154).
```

```
    Emerson maintained that "an institution is the

lengthened shadow of one man"(154).
```

Block Quotation

A quotation of four or more lines is usually written in *block* or display form. Do not indent the first line, but if you quote more than one paragraph (seldom advisable), indent the first line of each paragraph three spaces. The entire quotation is indented ten spaces on the left but is not indented on the right. No quotation marks are needed unless they appear in the original. *MLA Handbook* recommends that block quotations be double-spaced, but you should determine whether your instructor prefers single- or double-spacing. At the close of the quotation, space twice and type the citation *after* the period. If there is not enough space for the citation, type it on the next line so that it ends flush with the right margin (set your typewriter at the right margin and backspace the number of characters in the citation). Block quotations are shown in the first two sample papers on pages 174, 175, 195, 196, and 199–200. See also page 164. The block form calls attention to a quotation, but too many lengthy block quotations will clog the flow of your prose and should be avoided.

The following example of a block quotation is taken from *The Theory of the Leisure Class* by Thorstein Veblen and is part of his ironic argument that social prestige is attained by "conspicuous consumption":

```
        The dog has advantages in the way of

        uselessness as well as in special gifts of

        temperament. He is often spoken of . . . as

        the friend of man, and his intelligence and

        fidelity are praised. The meaning of this is

        that the dog is man's servant and that he has

        the gift of an unquestioning subservience

        and a slave's quickness in guessing his

        master's mood. . . . He is the filthiest of

        the domestic animals in his person and the

        nastiest in his habits. For this he makes up
```

```
in a servile, fawning attitude toward his

master and a readiness to inflict damage and

discomfort on all else. The dog, then,

commends himself to our favour by affording

play to our propensity for mastery, and as

he is also an item of expense and commonly

serves no industrial purpose, he holds a

well-assured place in man's regard as a thing

of good repute. The dog is at the same time

associated in our imagination with the chase

--a meritorious employment and an expression

of the honourable predatory impulse.
```

```
                                    (Veblen 141)
```

Blending Quotations with Your Text

A quotation must be an exact reproduction of the original, but if the meaning and the emphasis are not distorted, the following exceptions—all intended to facilitate blending quotations with your text—are permissible:

1. Words may be omitted if the omission is signalled by an ellipsis, three spaced periods (see the preceding block quotation). Do *not* use three asterisks or dashes. If the ellipsis occurs at the end of your sentence, a fourth period is necessary.
2. A short phrase may be quoted with no ellipsis before or after it. If an ellipsis occurs at the close of your sentence, the period closing your sentence is placed after the citation:

```
The dog satisfies man's "propensity for

mastery"; furthermore, according to Veblen, "he is

also an item of expense, and commonly serves no

industrial purpose . . ." (141).
```

3. An initial capital letter can be reduced to lowercase if only a portion of the sentence is quoted:

```
    Thorstein Veblen argued ironically that the

dog is valued although "he is the filthiest of the

domestic animals" (141).
```

4. A word or a brief phrase enclosed in brackets may be inserted in a quotation.

```
    "The dog is . . . associated in our

imagination with the chase [hunting]--a meritorious

employment and an expression of the honourable

predatory impulse" (Veblen 141).
```

Punctuation in Quotations

Besides quotation marks, most other forms of punctuation are involved in writing and documenting quotations.

Period (.). Space twice after a *period* at the end of a sentence or after a period in a bibliographic entry. Space once after initials in a proper name. Place a period inside quotation marks except when the quotation is followed by a citation in parentheses.

```
    T. S. Eliot portrayed an old man spiritually

dead but longing for faith in his 1920 poem

"Gerontion."

    "The unflinching honesty of this confession

redeems it from utter hopelessness, for without

such honesty no faith will be possible"

(Williamson 113).
```

Comma (,). Space once after a *comma*. Place a comma inside a quotation mark except when the quotation is followed by a parenthetical citation.

Robert Browning never used the term "dramatic
monologue," but critics have found it a useful way
of describing many of his poems.

Greek mythology created a "humanized world"
(Hamilton 11), for it made life less frightening by
transforming forces of nature into men and women.

Semicolon (;). Space once after a *semicolon*. Place a semicolon outside
a closing quotation mark.

Theodore Roosevelt described the Presidency as
"a bully pulpit"; throughout his administration his
speeches and his actions kept him constantly in the
public eye.

Colon (:). Space once after a *colon* and place it outside a closing quotation
mark. A somewhat formal introductory mark, a colon normally follows a
statement that is grammatically complete.

A common type of settlement in early America
was the "single-minded community": e.g., Pilgrims,
Mennonites, Shakers, and Mormons.

Dash (--). Type a *dash* as two hyphens, leaving no space before or after.
Never use a dash with a comma as was frequently done in nineteenth-
century printing. Use one dash to indicate an abrupt break in the structure
of a sentence and two dashes to enclose parenthetical material. Do not
overwork either use.

Frank Lloyd Wright, America's greatest
architect, built only one skyscraper--Price Tower
in Bartlesville, Oklahoma.

"Surf talk was--and is--the hip slang of

California's youth"(McCrum, Cran, and MacNeil 348).

Brackets ([ ]). Within a quotation enclose a comment or an identification in square *brackets* (see page 87). If you change the capitalization of an initial letter, you can enclose the changed letter in brackets. However, this convention is not universally followed; consult your instructor.

"American tourists were astounded and

sometimes shocked by open prostitution as practiced

on 'Pig Alley' [the Place Pigalle] in Paris"

(Davenport 73).

Thorstein Veblen maintained that the dog is

valued even though "[h]e is the filthiest of the

domestic animals"(141).

Ellipsis (. . .). An *ellipsis* is used to indicate omission of words from a quotation (see pages 86–87). Space before, between, and after the periods.

"Edward Bok's <u>Ladies' Home Journal</u> . . . urged

young women to take more exercise and think kind,

happy thoughts that would make them look pleasant"

(Carson 226).

Slash (/). Use a *slash* (also called a diagonal, a solidus, or a virgule) to separate two or three lines of poetry written consecutively. Space before and after a slash in this use but not when one is used in prose. Try to avoid using the "and/or" construction.

The tradition-bound old farmer in Robert

Frost's "Mending Wall" is described as "Bringing a

stone grasped firmly by the top / In each hand

like an old stone-savage armed."

Preparing the Final Copy ————————

Whether you have copied and recopied your draft on a typewriter or have subjected it to the continual revision that a word processor makes possible, the time inevitably arrives when you must prepare the final copy for submission to your instructor.

Revision

Revision, which literally means to look back at, is a highly important but often neglected step in the writing process. It is a special skill that involves a kind of double perspective: You examine and evaluate small units—words, phrases, and sentences—but at the same time you must keep in mind overall aspects of your paper—the thesis, the plan, and the stylistic tone. Once again, it is a good idea to read your paper aloud at least once (see page 114). Too many students, when asked to revise a paper, assume that they are expected to recopy it neatly, add a few commas, and correct any spelling errors. Actually, revision can be just as creative as the initial act of writing.

To revise a paper effectively, you must keep your audience in mind. Remember that the test of a statement is not whether you understand or agree with it but whether a reader will be able to do so. In reading over your paper, try to assume the role of an uninformed, semireluctant reader whose interest must be aroused and whose attention must be held. Also, if time permits, put your draft aside for a few days before revising it. Immediately after finishing writing, your mind is so filled with what you wanted to say that you are a poor judge of what you actually said. A cooling-off period will enable you to judge your work more objectively.

Unlike the rough draft, which should be written in one sitting if possible, the final version should be revised a page or two at a time. The advantage of piecemeal revision is that you can concentrate on details. Carry the draft in your notebook and write in changes or additions as they occur to you. An elusive word or an effective combination of unwieldy sentence elements may pop into your mind unexpectedly. One of the ironies of composition is that such flashes of inspiration quickly fade away.

If you want to add a lengthy passage, do not recopy the entire page. Instead, write the new material on a separate sheet, assign it a code letter, and indicate where it belongs in the paper: Insert A. This technique and others are shown in the following portion of Rita Hogan's rough draft. The changes involve addition of details, rearrangement of sentence elements, substitution of more accurate language for general phrasing, and proofreading punctuation and spelling errors. Compare the revised draft with the opening paragraph of the final version in Chapter 5 (page 191).

Marriage is the main concern of Jane Austen's novels, the plot of all of them is based on the main character's having various dissappointments before eventually being married to a suitable husband. The union of Elizabeth Bennet and Darcy in Pride and Prejudice seems like an ideal match, but it comes about only after a series of difficulties. Tony Tanner writes, "everything tends toward the acheiving of satisfactory marriages, but few of the marriages are really satisfactory. Seven other marriages in the novel are all different from one another; most are unsatisfactory in some way but still survive; but all of them in one way or another influence the eventual coming together of Elizabeth and Darcy.

In revision, check each paragraph to make certain it is unified around a single idea and that the ideas are presented in a logical sequence. Make certain that the order of ideas corresponds to your outline.

Proofreading

Proofreading is to revision as washing dishes is to gourmet cooking—a humdrum, mechanical, but essential chore. Revision and proofreading are not separate processes but are performed simultaneously. Your concerns in revision are style and structure; in proofreading they are typographical errors, misspellings, errors in punctuation and capitalization, and similar slips. Consult your handbook when necessary. Be certain that all titles of books and journals are underlined. An error that occurs surprisingly often is the omission of a word. Although it is a purely mechanical error, it can distort or destroy the meaning of a sentence. Another minor error is improper word division at the end of a line. Words should be broken only between syllables; when in doubt, consult your dictionary. Yet should not divide words unless it is absolutely necessary; a somewhat irregular right margin is preferable to numerous hyphenated words.

Correct errors as neatly as possible, writing corrections above the line and indicating the insertion of material with a caret (   ). If a page contains several corrections and looks messy, you should recopy it. If you type the paper yourself, scan each page before removing it from the typewriter. Using correction tape or white correction fluid, you can easily correct errors without having to realign the page. If you use a word processor, call up the text on the monitor and read it carefully before printing it.

Manuscript Form

Although a research paper is evaluated primarily on its content, its overall appearance is also important. Your instructor will undoubtedly specify some aspects of the format required, and the following suggestions should be modified to fit those specifications.

Your paper should be typed. If possible, type the final copy yourself. In addition to the expense of hiring a typist, there are two other disadvantages to having a paper typed by someone else. First, you lose the benefit of last-minute inspiration. The psychological pressure of preparing the final version is sometimes beneficial; problems of expression seem to solve themselves, and disjointed sentence elements fall into their proper places. Second, you place yourself in a kind of double jeopardy: You are responsible for your own errors as well as those made by the typist. However, if you are unable to type the final copy, read and correct your written copy before giving it to the typist and again after it has been typed.

Use a good quality, 8-1/2 × 11-inch bond paper. Material typed on onionskin paper is difficult to read, and typing on "erasable" paper tends to smudge.

MLA Handbook does not recommend a title page or an outline page, but many instructors require both. The title of your paper should be brief but accurate. It should not be enclosed in quotation marks or underlined. Center the title and below it type your name, your section, your instructor's name, and the date. Since college papers receive no special credit for decoration, it is futile to waste your time on ribbons, pictures, or fancy lettering. A title page should be neat but not gaudy.

If an outline is required, it should follow the title page. In addition to reviewing its logic, parallelism, and general neatness, check the symbols, indentation, and other outlining conventions. Use one of the sample outlines shown earlier in the chapter (pages 106–110) as a model.

If your paper has a title page, type your last name and the page number (Graham 1) as a running head. It should be one-half inch (three spaces) from the top of the page and should end flush with the right margin. Double space, center your title, double space again, and begin your first paragraph.

If there is no title page, type a running head as described in the preceding paragraph. On the left, one inch (six spaces) from the top of the page, type your name, your instructor's name, your class designation, and the date your paper is handed in:

Tom Graham

Professor Scott

ENG. 11 C

4 May 1990

Double space, center your title, double space again, and begin your first paragraph.

Leave margins of one inch at the top and bottom and on both sides of a page.

Indent each paragraph five spaces. If a sentence closes in the last line of a page, be sure to continue with the next sentence unless it is the end of a paragraph.

If your paper is regarded as copy suitable for printing, block quotations, notes, and bibliographic entries should all be double-spaced as recommended by MLA. If, however, your paper is considered a finished product intended to resemble printed research, you can single-space block quotations, notes, and bibliographic entries. Double-space between notes and between entries in the bibliography. Be sure to get your instructor's approval if you plan to single-space.

Before typing the list of works cited, be certain that your bibliography cards are in alphabetical order. You should also compare your citations with your bibliography cards to make certain that every source cited is included in your listing. Hanging indentation is customary because it facilitates location of an item in an alphabetical list; the first line is flush with the margin, and every additional line is indented five spaces.

Be certain that the pages of your paper are in the proper order and that each page is numbered sequentially in the upper right-hand corner. Do not use the abbreviation *p.* or any form of punctuation with a page number. Including your last name as a running head on each page is a safeguard against pages' being mislaid or lost.

Fasten the pages with a paper clip rather than stapling them together. Often an instructor will want to detach the Works Cited page in order to refer to it while reading the paper.

Make a copy of your paper before submitting it. Since you may be asked to authenticate a citation or to rewrite a portion of your paper, you should keep your note cards until the paper has been returned.

Checklist

Before submitting your paper, read it through a final time with the following questions in mind.

1. If your paper includes an outline:
   a. Is the thesis statement clear and accurate?
   b. Is the thesis a complete sentence?
   c. Are the proper symbols used (i.e., roman numeral/capital letter/arabic numeral/lowercase letter)?
   d. Are subordinate entries indented properly?
   e. Are related entries parallel in form?
   f. Are all entries represented in the paper?
2. In revision:
   a. Is the thesis or essay-idea stated clearly in the first paragraph?
   b. Do all paragraph topics relate to the thesis?
   c. Is every paragraph unified by a topic sentence?
   d. Can any superfluous words be cut?
   e. Can any general phrasing be made more specific?
   f. Will the opening arouse a reader's interest?
   g. Are paragraphs linked by clear transitions?
   h. Does the close summarize the major ideas of the paper?
3. In proofreading:
   a. Are punctuation marks, especially commas and quotation marks, used correctly?
   b. Are there any doubtful-looking spellings that should be checked in a dictionary?
4. In manuscript form:
   a. Are the margins even and approximately one inch on all four sides?
   b. Is each paragraph indented five spaces?
   c. Should any pages be recopied because of messy erasures and corrections?
5. In documentation:
   a. Is all borrowed material cited?
   b. Do all citations include page numbers?
   c. Is all borrowed language enclosed in quotation marks?
   d. Is all cited material included in Works Cited?
   e. Are entries in Works Cited arranged in alphabetical order?
   f. Does every entry follow basic bibliographical order (Author. *Title*. Publication facts.)?
   g. Are all book and periodical titles underlined?
   h. Are titles of articles and other portions of published works enclosed in quotation marks?
   i. Are publication facts for a book (Place: Publisher, year) arranged correctly?
   j. Is the correct form used for a quarterly (*Journal* volume (year): pages)?

CHAPTER 5

Documenting Borrowed Material: MLA Style

Types of Documentation _____

In writing your research paper, you will use facts and opinions found in books, periodicals, and nonprint sources. You can use the actual language or you can summarize the borrowed material in your own words. In either case, you are obligated to document what you borrow. *Documentation*—acknowledgment of indebtedness to a source—is of two general types:

1. A list of the sources used in a paper, which serves as a general acknowledgment of indebtedness to each. It is headed Works Cited and follows the final page of the text.
2. Separate citation of each borrowed fact or opinion. The source and the page number are enclosed in parentheses following the borrowed material: (Stone 196). The same purpose can be served by *footnotes* or *endnotes* (see pages 182–83).

Consistency

Two facts about the forms of documentation should be recognized: they are not foolproof, and they are not absolute. In almost every paper, a few problems arise that are not covered by standard forms and require sensible improvisation. Improvised forms should be consistent with your practice elsewhere in the paper. The form and the content of documentation are covered by conventions, not by rigid rules. Possibilities for variation, therefore, are almost limitless. So many minor variations are possible that documentation can become a nitpicker's nightmare and distract your attention from more important matters like content, organization, and style.

The list of works cited and the citations in a paper are intended to enable readers to retrieve further information from the sources; they should be simple, concise, and functional. Because there are several methods of punctuating and arranging bibliographic listings and citations, your practice should be consistent throughout a paper. For example, it is permissible to abbreviate names of states in the list of works cited; but if you write "Penna." in one citation, "Pa." in another, and "PA" in a third, two of the three must be considered faulty. It is sometimes better to be consistently wrong than to be right only part of the time.

Determine the basic style preferred by your instructor and adhere to it throughout your paper. Do not hesitate to ask for assistance when you are confronted by a perplexing, out-of-the-ordinary source. Next to simple carelessness, inconsistency is the most common fault in documentation.

Listing Sources as Works Cited

Sources from which material has been borrowed are listed alphabetically on the final page or pages of a paper. Various headings can be used for this listing—Bibliography, Literature Cited, References, Sources,—but Works Cited is recommended. Bibliography, formerly in general use, is not altogether accurate because the word literally means "writing about books," and most research papers involve periodicals and other nonbook sources. If you have an unusually large number of sources, you can divide them into separately alphabetized sections, such as Books and Periodicals or Primary Sources and Secondary Sources. You can also list under the heading Works Consulted titles of sources that you examined but did not actually cite in the paper. In short research papers, however, a single alphabetized list is usually all that is required.

Many of the books and articles that you consult while gathering material will contain bibliographies, and these will often direct you to useful discussions of your topic in other sources. The listings will vary widely in form, and so you will need to convert a reference to the form you are following in your paper. As recommended in Chapter 1, you should create a bibliography card before taking notes from a source. It will save time and trouble if you record the source in the form you will follow in your paper.

To make in-text citations while writing your rough draft, you will need to consult your list of works cited. Either make a rough draft of the Works Cited page or arrange your bibliography cards in alphabetical order and tape them to the wall above your worktable.

Do not be intimidated by the number of examples that follow. If you master the standard forms for books and periodicals (Examples 1 and 2), you can adapt them to special situations as they arise.

An entry for a book or a periodical consists of three basic elements in the following format—Author. Title. Publication data. They are separated by periods and two spaces. A word processor that justifies (makes even) the right margin will sometimes reduce or lengthen the space after a period; therefore, if you use a word processor, you should turn off the justification command so that the period-plus-two-spaces rule will be observed. Most of the variables, especially for periodicals, occur in the publication data. You should have little difficulty in devising sensible forms for unusual sources if you maintain the same sequence of items, omit what is not available, and add in the appropriate place supplementary information like an editor's name or the title of a series. Such information is also followed by a period and two spaces.

Checklist of Basic Forms

The numbered examples in the following checklist illustrate most of the problems you may encounter, and they can serve as models. When you make out a bibliography card for a source that is somehow out of the ordinary, use the checklist to find an example that resembles your source. In a second checklist some miscellaneous problems are keyed to the same examples.

1. Book, standard form
2. Periodical, standard form
3. Anonymous work
4. Anthology
5. Cartoon
6. Collaborator
7. Computer software
8. Computerized material
9. Corporate author
10. Edition

11. Editor
12. Film
13. Filmstrip/videotape/ cassette
14. Government publication
15. Interview
16. Introduction
17. Lecture
18. Legal reference
19. Letter, personal
20. Letter, published
21. Manuscript material
22. Map/chart
23. Microform
24. Multiple authors/editors
25. Multivolume work

26. Musical composition
27. Newspaper
28. Pamphlet
29. Performance
30. Pseudonym
31. Recording
32. Reference work
33. Republished work
34. Review
35. Selection in anthology
36. Television/radio program
37. Title within a title
38. Translation
39. Untitled article
40. Work of art
41. Works by the same author

Checklist of Special Problems

Some special problems that may prove troublesome are listed below. Each is keyed to the example where it is briefly explained.

Book published before 1900   1
Condensed page numbers   15
Cross-reference   35
Dictionary   32
Dissertation   19
Editorial   25
Encyclopedia   32
Foreword/Preface/ Afterword   16
Identifying term   5
Incomplete publication data   26
Journal continuously paged   2

Journal paged separately in each issue   2
Journal with no volume number   15
Monthly magazine   2
Public document   14
Publisher's imprint   3
Quotation marks for titles   2
Series   4
Subtitle   1
Underlining titles   1
Unpaged source   16
Unpublished work   19
Volume number   23
Weekly magazine   2

Sample MLA-Style Forms

1. Book, Standard Forms

```
Stone, I. F. The Trial of Socrates. Boston: Little,

    1988.
```

```
Lubben, Richard T. Just-in-Time Manufacturing: An

    Aggressive Manufacturing Strategy. New York:

    McGraw, 1988.

Harris, Kenneth Marc. Hypocrisy and Self-Deception

    in Hawthorne's Fiction. Charlottesville: UP

    of Virginia, 1988.

DuChaillu, Paul. Wild Life under the Equator. New

    York, 1872.
```

a. Reverse, or hanging, indentation (five spaces) makes it easier for readers to locate items in an alphabetized list.

b. The author's name is inverted for alphabetization. It should be written as it appears on the title page: "White, E. B.," not "White, Elwyn Brooks." The name is followed by a period and two spaces.

c. Copy the title from the title page, not from the cover or the spine of a book. The title of a book (or of any work published as a unit) is underlined—the equivalent of italics in print. Underlining word by word (A Tale of Two Cities) is sometimes recommended—perhaps because it is more trouble—but continuous underlining (A Tale of Two Cities) is more sensible. Most word processors underline each word separately, but if you type your paper, continuous underlining is simpler. What really matters is that your practice be consistent throughout a paper. Omitted underlining is such a common fault in papers that it might be advisable to underline a title immediately after typing it instead of waiting until you finish a sentence. The title is followed by a period and two spaces.

d. A subtitle is also underlined (see the Lubben example). It is separated from the main title by a colon even if no colon appears in the original.

e. If more than one city is listed on the title page, cite the first one. Include the state or country only when necessary to identify a city. A university press, even if it is located in a small town, does not require the designation of a state. In Works Cited, but not in the text of a paper, postal abbreviations for states (see Appendix D, page 266) are acceptable.

f. Publishers' names are shortened (see Appendix D, pages 266–68). University Press is abbreviated UP (no periods). The letters are placed where they occur in the official name of the press.

g. It is not necessary to cite the publisher of a work published before 1900 like the DuChaillu example.

h. Cite the year of publication from the title page if one appears there. Otherwise, look on the reverse side of the title page (the copyright page), where you may find a confusing jumble of years. If there are several copyright years, use the most recent one. If there have been several printings of the edition you are using, cite the earliest one.

2. *Periodical, Standard Forms*

Kehes, John. "Understanding Evil." <u>American</u>

<u>Philosophical Quarterly</u> 25 (1988): 13-24.

Tong, T. K. "Temporary Absolutism Versus Hereditary

Autocracy." <u>Chinese Studies in History</u> 21.3

(1988): 3-22.

Langdon, Philip. "A Good Place to Live." <u>Atlantic</u>

Mar. 1988: 39-60.

McIntyre, Robert S. "The Populist Tax Act of 1989."

<u>Nation</u> 2 Apr. 1988: 445+.

a. The preceding examples illustrate entries for quarterly, monthly, and weekly periodicals. Although the form differs somewhat, the basic order is the same for each: Author. Title. Publication data.

b. The title of an article (like all *portions* of published units) is enclosed in quotation marks. Subtitles are treated the same as in the listing of a book.

c. An initial "The" as in *Atlantic* and *Nation* can be dropped. (This is not done with book titles.) The name of a periodical is underlined; no punctuation follows.

d. Most quarterlies are paged continuously throughout a volume, as in the preceding Kehes example. In this case, cite the volume number (an arabic numeral without the abbreviation "vol."), enclose the year of publication in parentheses, follow it with a colon, and give the inclusive page numbers (not just the pages used in your paper).

e. For a quarterly that is paged separately in each issue, follow the same form but add a period and the issue number after the volume number, leaving no space between them (see the preceding entry for Tong). The issue is usually identified on the cover of a journal or on its contents page.

f. For a monthly or a weekly magazine, give the date immediately after the name of the magazine. Follow it with a colon and the page numbers. (See the Langdon example.)

g. The abbreviations "p." and "pp." are not used; it is assumed that numbers to the right of a colon are page numbers.

h. If an article is not printed consecutively, type a plus sign after the page number or numbers to indicate a continuation elsewhere in the same issue. (See the McIntyre example.)

3. Anonymous Work

A Critical Fable. Boston: Houghton, 1922.

The 1986 Baseball Encyclopedia Update. New York:

Collier-Macmillan, 1986.

"Sound Effects." New Yorker 21 Mar. 1988: 27-28.

When a work is published anonymously (without an author's name) begin the entry with the title. If you wish to identify the author, do so in the text of your paper. You can also place the author's name in brackets before the title, but the work should be alphabetized according to its title. Do not use "Anonymous" unless the word appears on the title page. If the name of a publisher's imprint (a subsidiary of the main publisher) appears on the title page, as in the second example, cite the imprint first, follow it with a hyphen, and cite the publisher (e.g., Anchor-Doubleday, Belknap–Harvard UP, Mentor-NAL).

4. Anthology

Yanarella, Ernest J., and Lee Sigelman, eds.

Political Mythology and Popular Fiction.

Contributions in Political Science. New York:

Greenwood, 1988.

DeMott, Benjamin, ed. Close Imagining: An

Introduction to Literature. New York:

St. Martin's, 1988.

Begin the citation of an anthology or any similar compilation with the name of the editor. (To cite a selection from an anthology, see example 35.) Note in the first example that the name of a series follows the title of a book and is not underlined.

5. *Cartoon*

> Herblock. "Nice Timing." Cartoon. Washington Post.
>
>   23 Mar. 1988: A26.
>
> Steig, William. "New Neighbors." Cartoon. New
>
>   Yorker 7 Mar. 1988: 35.

Cite a cartoon with the artist's name, which may be incomplete on the drawing; the caption or title, if any; and the identifying term Cartoon. The rest of the entry follows standard form for a newspaper or magazine (see example 27). Identifying terms like Cartoon, Letter, Lecture, and Review are not quoted or underlined.

6. *Collaborator*

> Makeba, Miriam. Makeba: My Story. With James Hall.
>
>   New York: NAL, 1987.

Autobiographical books by nonliterary celebrities are often produced with professional help, which is acknowledged, if at all, by *with, as told to,* or a similar phrase. Cite the collaborator by using the phrase that appears on the title page.

7. *Computer Software*

> Investment Tax Analyst. Computer software. New
>
>   York: Wiley, 1984. IBM, 128K, Visicalc 1.1.
>
> Kusmiak, Gene. Bank Street Writer. Computer
>
>   software and manual. San Rafael, CA:
>
>   Brodenbund, 1983. IBM, 64K. 1.1 or 2.0.

Methods of citing the great variety of commercial computer programs have not been completely standardized. In general, an entry should show the writer of the program, if known; the title, underlined; the identifying term Computer software; the publisher or distributor; and the year. At the close of the entry, add relevant information such as the type of computer for which the program is designed, the number of kilobytes (units of memory), and the operating system. These items are separated by commas.

8. Computerized Material

Quinn, Mary J. "Elder Abuse and Neglect."

Generations 10 (1985): 22-25. DIALOG file 1,

item 74-31920.

Gardiner, John A. "Cops, Consultants, and Goldfish:

Variations in Nursing Home Regulation." ERIC,

1986. ED 276 902.

Material obtained through an information service like DIALOG is cited like any printed material; but at the close of the entry, cite the name of the service, the file number, and the accession number. If material from a service like ERIC has not been published, cite the service as the publisher. For ERIC, include the ED number (see page 49). No place of publication is cited for ERIC because different types of material are published by sixteen clearinghouses in various locations.

9. Corporate Author

National Commission on Space. Pioneering the Space

Frontier. New York: Bantam, 1986.

American Diabetes Association. Diabetes in the

Family. Rev. ed. New York: Prentice, 1987.

When an institution, a committee, or some other group is designated as author on the title page of a book, it is cited in the author position even if the same group is also the publisher.

10. Edition

Ginsburg, Herbert P., and Sylvia Opper. Piaget's

Theory of Intellectual Development. 3rd ed.

Englewood Cliffs: Prentice, 1988.

```
Douglas, Marjory Stoneman. The Everglades: River

    of Grass. Rev. ed. Sarasota: Pineapple Press,

    1988.
```

Cite the designation (2nd ed., Abr. ed., Rev. ed., and so on) that appears on the title page.

11. Editor

```
Spender, Stephen. Journals 1938-1983. Ed. John

    Goldsmith. New York: Random, 1986.

Magee, Rosemary, ed. Conversations with Flannery

    O'Connor. Jackson: UP of Mississippi, 1987.
```

The editor of an anthology (a collection of stories, poems, or essays by different authors) is cited first; "ed." after the name means "editor," and "eds." is used if there are two or more editors (see example 24). The editor of a work by a single author is cited after the title. "Ed." means "edited by" and is not made plural if there are two or more editors.

12. Film

```
Radio Days. Dir. Woody Allen. Prod. Robert

    Greenhut. With Julie Kavner, Michael Tucker,

    Seth Green, and Renee Lippin. Orion, 1987.

Allen, Woody, dir. Radio Days. Prod. Robert

    Greenhut. With Julie Kavner, Michael Tucker,

    Seth Green, and Renee Lippin. Orion, 1987.
```

A film is ordinarily cited in the order followed in the first example: title, director, producer, major performers, distributor, and year. If a paper concerns the work of an individual, that person's name can be cited first.

13. Filmstrip/Videotape/Cassette

```
Mythology Lives! Filmstrip. Mount Kisco, NY: Center

    for Humanities, 1983.
```

"The Lottery" by Shirley Jackson. Disc. James

    Durbio. Videotape, Chicago: Britannica Films,

    nd. Nos. 47757, 47758.

The identifying term for the medium follows the title. Depending on the nature of the material, the rest of the citation follows the form for a book or a film entry.

14. *Government Publication*

United States. Department of Labor. Bureau of Labor

    Statistics. BIS Measures of Compensation.

    Washington: GPO, 1986.

---. Department of State. Patterns of Global

    Terrorism: 1984. Washington: GPO, 1985.

---. HR. Committee on Ways and Means. Hearings on

    Comprehensive Tax Reform. 99th Cong. 1st sess.

    9 vols. Washington: GPO, 1986.

Florida. Department of Transportation. Standard

    Specifications for Road and Bridge

    Construction. Tallahassee: Dept. of

    Transportation, 1986.

Cong. Rec. 30 Apr. 1986: S5123-24. Daniel

    Moynihan. "American Policy toward the United

    Nations."

Cong. Rec. 128, Pt. 5, 29 Mar. 1982: 5624-32.

Federal, state, county, and city governments issue an enormous variety of documents, including bills, statutes, reports, regulations, statistics, reports of hearings, proceedings, executive orders, and speeches. Because these publications vary greatly in form, documenting them is often complicated. The government and the agency issuing the document are ordinarily cited first. The title is underlined. A congressional publication includes the number and the session of Congress, the house, and the type of document (including its number if it has one). For the use of three hyphens in the second and third citations, see example 41. Abbreviations are used freely; for example:

Cong. Rec.	*Congressional Record*
Doc.	Document
GPO	Government Printing Office
HR	House of Representatives
Res.	Resolution
S	Senate

Reports of congressional hearings often contain valuable information, but searching it out requires patience. Reports of lengthy hearings are published piecemeal in pamphlets, which are collected in bound volumes after the hearings are completed. Use the bound volumes whenever possible because libraries store or discard the pamphlets after receiving the bound volumes.

The *Congressional Record* illustrates some of the inconsistencies that create problems when you use public documents. It is a record of Congressional proceedings augmented by any material that a member requests be "read into the record." It is published each day that Congress is in session and then is republished in bound volumes that, inconveniently, do not correspond to the original issue in content or in pagination. The page numbers given in the preceding examples indicate the enormous scope of this source. A practical way of using it is to determine the date of a speech or a debate by consulting *New York Times Index* and then to examine the issue for that date. Because of the bulk of the annual volumes, many libraries now have the *Congressional Record* only on microfilm.

15. *Interview*

Fowles, John. "A Conversation with John Fowles."

    Interviewer: Robert Faulke. Salmagundi No.

    68-69 (1985-86): 367-84.

Buckley, William F. Interview. Larry King Show.

    Mutual. WIOD, Miami. 21 Apr. 1986.

Martin, Chester, President Tubular Steel Corp.

    Telephone Interview. 17 Apr. 1989.

```
Norris, Emily. Personal Interview. Pittsburgh.

     14 Feb. 1989.
```

Interviews in a printed source and on radio or television are listed like the first two examples. The person interviewed is cited first. The title, if any, is enclosed in quotation marks. If there is no title, use the identifying term Interview. The name of the interviewer, if known, follows the title and is introduced the way it appears in the source (often "by" or "with"). The rest of the entry follows the form appropriate to the kind of source. Numerals above 100 are condensed (367–84). Note in the first example that a journal with no volume number is cited by the number of the issue; this example is a double issue. For an interview conducted by yourself, give the name of the person interviewed, the type of interview, and the date. The subject's official title can be included if it is relevant.

16. Introduction

```
Hall, N. John. Introduction. The Illustrated

     Zuleika Dobson. By Max Beerbohm. New Haven:

     Yale UP, 1985. N. pag.

Burgess, Anthony. Introduction. Augustus Carp, Esq.

     By Himself: Being the Autobiography of a

     Really Good Man. 1924. Woodbridge, Suffolk:

     Bookmaster-Boydell, 1985. v-viii.
```

The preceding form is used when only the introduction is cited rather than the main text. Give the author of the introduction first. Use the identifying term (Introduction, Foreword, Preface, Afterword) that is used in the book. Give the author of the book after the title, preceding it with "By." "N. pag." in the first example means that there is no pagination; for the citation of unpaged material, see page 187. The second example illustrates several minor variations: an anonymous work, a republished work, a publisher's imprint, and the use of lowercase roman numerals for pages (used only when they appear in the source).

17. Lecture

```
Moore, John T. Class lecture. Economics 312.

     Westminster College. 10 Nov. 1987.
```

```
Spacks, Patricia Meyer. "Female Resources:

    Epistles, Plot, and Power." Jane Austen

    Society. New York City, 10 Oct. 1987.
```

The speaker's name, the title (if any) in quotation marks, the occasion and the sponsoring organization (if any), and the place and date are the basic facts. If there is no title, use an identifying term as in the first example.

18. *Legal Reference*

```
Railroad Retirement Act of 1937. 10 USC. Title 45.

    Secs. 228a-228z. Washington: GPO, 1971.

Brown v. General Services Administration et al. 425

    U.S. Reports. No. 74-768. U.S. Sup. Ct. 1976.
```

Laws and legal cases are even more varied and more formidably complicated than government publications. The system of abbreviations used by attorneys and legal writers seems like a secret code to most laypersons. In documentation, these abbreviations should be expanded as needed for clarity. In citing a law, give the title, the volume number and title of the statute book (*USC* is the standard abbreviation for *U.S. Code*), the title number and the sections, and the publisher. For a legal case, cite the parties to the suit, the volume number, the title and pages of the source, the name of the court, and the year in which the case was decided. A minor oddity is that names of cases are underlined in the text of a paper but not in the documentation. Titles of laws or legislative acts are never underlined or enclosed in quotation marks. If you are using a number of legal references, consult the latest edition of *A Uniform System of Citation* (Cambridge: Harvard Law Rev. Assn.).

19. *Letter, Personal*

```
Pynchon, Thomas. Personal letter. 6 May 1988.
```

A personal letter can also be identified as "Letter to the author," which in the preceding example would be slightly ambiguous.

20. *Letter, Published*

```
Selected Letters of William Faulkner. Ed. Joseph

    Blotner. New York: Random, 1957.
```

Thomas, Dylan. Letter to John Malcolm Brinnin.

18 Mar. 1953. The Collected Letters. Ed.

Paul Ferris. New York: Macmillan, 1985.

878-80.

Rocha, Mark William. Letter. "James as Playwright."

PMLA 103 (1988): 175.

If you use more than one letter from a collection, cite the book and identify individual letters by in-text citations. If you use only one letter, cite it like a selection in an anthology (see example 35). A letter in a periodical usually has a heading that functions as a title. The identifying term "Letter" is still necessary.

21. *Manuscript Material*

Faulkner, William. Letter to Morton Goldman. 18

July 1935. Arents Coll. New York Public

Library.

Melville, Herman. Journal for August 1860. Papers

and Library of the Melville Family. Harvard

Library.

Worthie, Peleg. Diary 1862-1865. Two manuscript

notebooks owned by the Worthie family,

Newton, OH.

Sommer, Robert F. "The Masks of Henry Adams." Diss.

Duke U. 1985.

Clark, Virgina Martha. "Aldous Huxley and Film."

DAI 44 (1984): 3069A. U. of Maryland.

In a short research paper, you are not likely to use unpublished letters, diaries, or other manuscript materials; but if you do, the entries should conform as closely as possible to standard bibliographic form. Your basic purpose is to identify the source and its location. Include any special designations used by the repository of the material (e.g., Folder 5, Drawer A, Notebook 7).

The last two examples are the only ones with actual titles. The title of any unpublished work, regardless of its length, is enclosed in quotation marks. If you use a published dissertation, cite it like a book but add Diss. (not quoted or underlined), the university, and the year after the title. If you use an abstract from *Dissertation Abstracts International (DAI)*, include the identification number after the year and close the citation with the name of the university granting the degree.

22. Map/Chart

West Indies and Central America. Map. Washington:

   National Geographic Soc., 1981.

23. Microform

Mitchell, D. H. "Mushrooms." Microfiche. Mycology.

   No. 1. Denver: Poisindex, 1974.

Follow the appropriate form for a book or an article and identify the medium (microfiche, microfilm, microcard) after the title.

24. Multiple Authors/Editors

Abramson, Jill, and Barbara Franklin. Where Are

   They Now: The Story of the Women of Harvard

   Law 1974. Garden City: Doubleday, 1986.

McMahon, Elizabeth, Robert Funk, and Susan Day. The

   Elements of Writing about Literature and Film

   New York: Macmillan, 1988.

Elliot, Emory, et al., eds. Columbia Literary

   History of the United States. New York:

   Columbia UP, 1988.

If a work has two or three authors or editors, cite them all in the order in which they are listed on the title page. Invert only the first name; follow it with a comma. If there are more than three names (the third example has six), cite only the name that appears first on the title page and follow it with et al. (and others).

25. Multivolume Work

Edel, Leon. <u>Henry James</u>. 5 vols. Philadelphia:

    Lippincott, 1953-72.

Edel, Leon. <u>The Middle Years: 1882-1895</u>. Vol. 3 of

    <u>Henry James</u>. 5 vols. Philadelphia: Lippincott,

    1953-72.

Blotner, Joseph. <u>Faulkner: A Biography</u>. 2 vols. New

    York: Random, 1974. Vol. 2.

Whether or not you use all the volumes of a multivolume work, give the total number of volumes immediately after the title. If you use only one volume, give its number at the close of the entry, as in the third example. If each volume has a separate title, as in the second example, give the title of the one you are using, the volume number followed by "of," and the title of the complete work. If you use more than one volume, list the entire work, as in the first example. If a work has been published at intervals, give the inclusive years. This type of citation is one of the rare occasions when the abbreviation "vol." is still used.

26. Musical Composition

Mozart, Wolfgang Amadeus. Concerto in D Major for

    Flute and Piano. San Antonio: Southern Music

    Co., n.d.

Bach, Johann Sebastian. <u>Brandenburg Concerti</u>. New

    York: Broude, n.d.

A published musical score is cited like a book. The title of a musical work is underlined, but an instrumental composition identified only by form, number, and key is not underlined or quoted. The year of publication for musical scores is often unobtainable.

27. Newspaper

Chicago Tribune. 21 Mar. 1988. Sports Final: 6.

DeVault, Russ. "Of Time and the Riverman." Atlanta

Constitution 18 Mar. 1988: 1+.

Porter, Sylvia. "Why Should You Buy Credit Life

Insurance." Evening Sun [Baltimore] 21 Mar.

1988: C11.

"Slow Down." Editorial. Detroit Free Press 27 Mar.

1988: A8.

Material that can be cited from a newspaper varies greatly. The preceding examples illustrate respectively, an unsigned, untitled news story, a signed feature story that is not paged consecutively, a syndicated column, and an editorial. Cite the name of a newspaper as it appears on the masthead but omit an initial "The." If the city is not part of the name, add it in brackets, as in the third example. If the newspaper is divided in sections, cite the section before the page number; follow the form used in the newspaper. If a specific edition is identified on the front page, cite the edition (as in the first example) because other editions may be paged differently. An editorial is identified as such after its title.

28. Pamphlet

Dickman, Irving R. Behavior Modification. New York:

Public Affairs Comm., 1976.

Dittrich, Kathinka, and Henry Marx, eds. Cultural

Guide for Berlin. n.p.: n.p., n.d.

As the preceding examples show, publication data for a pamphlet can range from all to none. Follow the normal order for a book and omit whatever is unavailable. The abbreviation "n.p." means "no place of publication" when it appears on the left side of the colon and "no publisher" when it appears on the right side; "n.d." means "no date."

29. *Performance*

Burn This. By Lanford Wilson. Dir. Marshall Mason.

With John Malkovich. Plymouth, New York. 21

Mar. 1988.

Bartlett, Eric. Cello recital. Kaufman Concert

Hall, New York. 22 Mar. 1986.

Leinsdorf, Erich, cond. Philadelphia Orchestra.

Concert. Carnegie Hall, New York. 15 Mar.

1988.

The listing of a performance begins with the title, if any, underlined; cites key names involved in production and performance; and closes with the theatre or concert hall, the city, and the date. The theatre and city are separated by a comma; all other elements are separated by periods. If a paper focuses on an individual, that person's name can be placed before the title. An identifying term like "Concert" or "Recital" is sometimes needed. Data for performances vary so widely that some improvisation is often required.

30. *Pseudonym*

Nasby, Petroleum V. [David Ross Locke]. The Nasby

Papers. Indianapolis, 1864.

A pseudonym should be treated like an ordinary name. If you identify the author's real name, enclose it in brackets, but this is unnecessary if it is identified in the text of your paper. Never identify a well-known pseudonym like Mark Twain or O. Henry. If you need to learn the real name of a pseudonymous author, you can find it in the library catalog or in a dictionary of pseudonyms. The publisher is not cited in the preceding example because the book was published before 1900.

31. *Recording*

Mahler, Gustav. Symphony No. 1 in D Major. Cond.

Erich Leinsdorf. Royal Philharmonic Orchestra.

London Records, SMAS 94801, 1972.

Halbreich, Harry. Jacket Notes. Symphony No. 1 in

D Major. By Gustav Mahler. Cond. Erich

Leinsdorf. Royal Philharmonic Orchestra.

London Records, SMAS 94801, 1972.

Eliot, T. S. "The Wasteland." Caedmon Treasury of

Modern Poets. Caedmon, TC2006, n.d.

Gaines, Ernest. A Gathering of Old Men. American

Audio Prose Library, 6051. 1986.

The citation of a recording can begin with the composer, conductor, or performer, depending on the emphasis in your paper. Jacket notes are cited as illustrated in the second example. Underline the title of a record, but musical compositions identified by form, number, and key are not underlined or quoted. Give the manufacturer, the catalog number, and the year, separated by commas.

32. Reference Work

Budden, Julian Medforth. "Beethoven." Encyclopaedia

Britannica: Macropaedia. 1985 ed.

"Easter Island." The New Columbia Encyclopedia.

4th ed.

"Filariasis." Encyclopaedia of Papua and New

Guinea. Ed. Peter Ryan. Melbourne, Australia:

Melbourne UP, 1972.

"Tyler, Anne." Who's Who of American Women. 15th

ed. 1987-1988.

"Gerontocracy." Webster's Third New International

Dictionary. 1965.

If an encyclopedia article is signed, cite the author's name. Major articles in the *Americana* are signed in full; articles in the *Macropaedia* volumes of *Britannica III* are signed with initials, which are identified in the index volume (*Propaedia*). An unsigned article is listed by its title. Publication facts are not cited for standard reference works. Identify the year of the edition you use and the number of the edition, if any. If a dictionary is used for more than one definition, only the title of the dictionary is cited. Page references are usually not necessary in a work that it alphabetically arranged.

33. *Republished Work*

Pynchon, Thomas. The Crying of Lot 49. 1966. New

York: Perennial-Harper, 1986.

Wyman, David S. Paper Walls: America and the

Refugee Crisis 1938-1941. 1968. New York:

Pantheon, 1985.

For a book reissued by a different publisher (usually a paperback version of a clothbound original), give the date of the original edition after the title, follow it with a period and two spaces, and then cite the publication facts for the edition you are using.

34. *Review*

Hecht, Anthony. "Portraits by Lowell." Rev. of

Robert Lowell: Collected Prose. Ed. Robert

Giroux. New York Review of Books 3 Mar. 1988:

11-17.

Olson, Steven E. Rev. of The Western Lands, by

William S. Burroughs. Antioch Review 46

(1988): 110.

Nightingale, Benedict. Rev. of Brighton Beach

Memoirs, by Neil Simon. Lyttleton Theatre,

London. <u>New Statesman</u> 7 Mar. 1986: 30-31.

Milnes, Rodney. "Hankie Time." Rev. of <u>Hansel and</u>

<u>Gretel</u>, by Engelbert Humperdinck. Coliseum,

London. <u>The Spectator</u> 2 Jan. 1988: 32.

Rev. of <u>The Dead</u>. <u>New Yorker</u> 14 Mar. 1988: 20.

If full information is available, begin with the reviewer's name and the title of the review in quotation marks. Follow the title with "Rev. of," the title of the work (underlined), a comma, "by," and the author's name. If a review is unsigned and untitled, as in the last example, begin with "Rev. of" but alphabetize the entry under the first word of the title of the work being reviewed. The preceding examples illustrate, respectively, two books, a play, an opera, and a film. The same basic form can be used for a review of a concert, a recital, a dance program, or any other type of performance.

35. *Selection in an Anthology*

Shevory, Thomas C. "Winning Isn't Everything:

Sports Fiction As a Genre of Political

Criticism." <u>Political Mythology and Popular</u>

<u>Fiction</u>. Ed. Ernest J. Yanarella and Lee

Sigelman. Contributions in Political Science.

New York: Greenwood, 1988. 61-79.

Jackson, Shirley. "The Lottery." DeMott 786-94.

Malamud, Bernard. "The Magic Barrel." DeMott

836-52.

Miller, Arthur, <u>Death of a Salesman</u>. DeMott

1290-1374.

To cite one selection from an anthology or a similar collection, give the author and the title of the selection, then the title of the anthology, the editor, the publication data, and inclusive page numbers, as in the first example. If you use two or more selections, cite the anthology in its proper alphabetical position and make a cross-reference to that entry, citing merely the editor's name and inclusive page numbers. Enclose the title of a selection in quotation marks unless it was originally published in book form, as is true of the last example.

36. Television/Radio Program

"Alaska: The Great Land." Nature. PBS. WPBT, Miami.

3 April 1988.

This Week with David Brinkley. ABC. WPLG, Miami.

5 June 1988.

Cosi Fan Tutti. By Wolfgang Amadeus Mozart. Cond.

James Levine. Metropolitan Opera Orchestra

and Chorus. WTMI, Miami. 3 April 1988.

The basic items of information are the name of the program, the network, the local station, and the date. A comma separates the station and the city; periods separate all other items. Individuals such as writers, narrators, or producers are included after the name of the program if they are relevant to the paper. Programs vary so widely in format that some improvisation may be necessary.

37. Title Within a Title

Kurtz, Elizabeth Carney. "Faulkner's 'A Rose for

Emily.'" Explicator 44.3 (1986): 52-54.

Novak, Frank G., Jr. "Crisis and Discovery in

The Professor's House." Colby Library

Quarterly 22 (1986): 327-45.

Hamilton, David Mike. "The Tools of My Trade":

Annotated Books in Jack London's Library.

Seattle: U of Washington P, 1987.

Bishop, John. <u>Joyce's Book of the Dead</u>: Finnegans

Wake. Madison: UP of Wisconsin, 1986.

The preceding examples show the various combinations in which one title can appear within another title. When the title of an article contains a title or a quotation in double quotation marks, change them to singles and use doubles to enclose the title of the article. When the title of an article contains a book title, the book title is underlined. When the title of a book contains a quoted title or a quotation, the quotation marks are retained. When the title of a book contains a book title, as in the last example, the shorter title is not underlined.

38. *Translation*

Machado, Antonio. <u>Selected Poems</u>. Trans. Alan S.

Trueblood. Cambridge: Harvard UP, 1988.

Márquez, Gabriel García. "Pentecost Sunday." Trans.

Edith Grossman. <u>New Yorker</u> 28 Mar. 1988:

24-50.

Euripides. <u>Helen</u>. Trans. Robert Emmet Meagher.

Amherst: U of Massachusetts P, 1986.

Lattimore, Richard, trans. <u>The Iliad of Homer</u>.

Chicago: U of Chicago P, 1962.

The name of a translator follows the title of the work except when the translation is your major concern or when you wish to designate a particular version of a classic that has been translated many times (as in the third example).

39. *Untitled Article*

<u>Time</u> 8 Feb. 1988: 61.

Articles without some type of title are uncommon, but if you cite one, you should follow the basic form of a periodical and omit whatever is not available. The preceding item is from the "People" section of <u>Time</u>.

40. *Work of Art*

Peale, Charles Willson. Staircase Group.

Philadelphia Museum of Art. Philadelphia.

Greenough, Horatio. George Washington. National

Museum of American History, Washington. Illus.

73 in 19th Century Sculpture. By H. W. Janson.

New York: Abrams, 1985.

Homer, Winslow. Snap the Whip. Butler Institute,

Youngstown. Slide PB 590. New York: Sandak,

n.d.

In listing a work of art, give the artist's name, the title of the work (underlined), the museum followed by a comma, and the city. If you use a reproduction, identify the museum or other repository immediately after the title of the work; identify the number of the illustration or slide; give the title of the book, the author, and the publication data or the company that produced the slide.

41. *Works by the Same Author*

Irving, John. The Cider House Rules. New York:

Morrow, 1985.

---. The Hotel New Hampshire. New York: Dutton,

1981.

---. The World According to Garp. New York: Dutton,

1978.

When you list two or more works by the same author or editor, the name is necessary only in the first entry. After the first entry, type three hyphens, a period, and two spaces. The works should be listed alphabetically.

In-text Citation

The most revolutionary change involved in MLA style of documentation is *in-text*, or *parenthetical*, *citation*. It is also the most efficient time-saver. To identify a source, the first main word in the list of works cited (usually the author's last name) and the page reference are cited in parentheses immediately after the borrowed material. Thus, a reader can easily identify a source by glancing at the Works Cited page. If an entire work is cited in the text, no parenthetical citation is necessary; the work will, of course, be listed in Works Cited. A citation should be placed where there is a pause, preferably at the close of a sentence. It follows the borrowed material and precedes your own punctuation.

Facts that are common knowledge—such as the chemical components of water, Robert Frost's middle name, or the capital of Oregon—need not be cited even though you have not known them before. Otherwise, you are obligated to acknowledge material taken from any source other than your own mind or imagination, whether it is a direct quotation, a summary of an author's opinion, or a factual statement. If you are in doubt as to whether a citation is needed, it is best to include one. An in-text citation is so much simpler to write than an endnote or a footnote that MLA style probably reduces the possibility of unintentional plagiarism, which sometimes destroys an otherwise good paper.

Sample Citations

The kinds of sources most likely to be cited are illustrated on the following pages. They are keyed by number to the sample Works Cited entries on pages 132–53, so that you can compare each citation with its bibliographic counterpart. No examples are given for the following nonprint sources, which are usually cited in the text (see pages 162-63):

Cartoon (5)	Musical composition (24)
Film (12)	Performance (27)
Filmstrip/videotape/	Recording (31)
cassette (13)	Television/radio program (36)
Lecture (17)	Work of art (40)
Letter, personal (19)	

The following print sources are not illustrated because they follow normal form for a book or an article:

Collaborator (6)	Microform (23)
Computer software (7)	Pamphlet (28)
Computerized material (8)	Pseudonym (30)
Edition (10)	Republished work (33)
Editor (11)	Title within a title (37)
Legal reference (18)	Translation (38)
Map/chart (22)	

Book (1)

Author and page number in parentheses:

"In Japan, project planning occupies 90% of the total time, and implementation requires the remaining 10%. In western countries, project planning requires only 10%, and the implementation requires the other 90%" (Lubben 15).

Author cited in text, page number in parentheses:

According to I. F. Stone, Plato did not follow his own mystical view of death after the death of Socrates but fled from Athens "lest he be caught in a wave of repression" (196).

Entire work cited in text:

Kenneth Marc Harris relates Hawthorne's fascination with self-deceiving hypocrites to his study of Puritan psychology.

Periodical (2)

Author and page in parentheses:

The belief that evil actions are signs of corruption is based on the assumption that purity and goodness are dominant in human nature but can be corrupted by evil (Kehes 13).

Author cited in text, page in parentheses:

According to Robert S. McIntyre, in the last decade federal taxes have risen for 95% of American families (462).

Entire work cited in text:

> Philip Langdon argues that nontraditionalist
> architects and planners are rejecting planned
> developments and are turning to building styles of
> the past.

Anonymous Work (3)

> In A Critical Fable, published anonymously by Amy
> Lowell, she satirized Robert Frost as "a foggy
> benignity wandering in space / With a stray wisp of
> moonlight just touching his face" (21).

> Books are being turned into audiocassettes that use
> sound effects originally developed for radio plays
> ("Sound Effects" 27-28).

In the first example, note that a slash separating two lines of poetry is preceded and followed by a space. When an anonymous work is not identified in the text, as in the second example, the title is included in the citation.

Anthology (4)

> Close Imagining emphasizes "active reading" as the
> reader is encouraged to collaborate with the author
> (DeMott 1).

For the citation of a selection from an anthology, see example 35.

Corporate Author (9)

> Over eleven million Americans have diabetes, and
> the number is increasing because it usually
> develops in later life and people today live longer

(American Diabetes Association 12).

The American Diabetes Association reports that over

eleven million Americans have diabetes and that

the number is increasing because it usually develops

in later life and people today live longer (12).

Both of these forms are acceptable, but the second one is preferable. If the name of a corporate author is so long that it results in a cumbersome citation, it should be identified in the text.

Government Publication (14)

Senator Moynihan reviewed the history of America's

commitment to the United Nations (Cong. Rec. 30

Apr. 1986: S5624-32).

Interview (15)

"The difference between the historian and the

novelist is analogous to the difference between the

photographer and the painter" (Fowles 367).

A personal interview can be cited most readily in the text.

Introduction (16)

Anthony Burgess ranks Augustus Carp, Esq. as "one

of the comic novels of the twentieth century"

(Introduction v).

Note that the indentifying term is included in the citation.

Letter, Published (20)

In a letter to Robert K. Haas, Faulkner suggested

several possible titles for Intruder in the Dust

(Blotner, Selected Letters 265).

Mark William Rocha denies that James was a total failure as a playwright and argues that his "logic of delegation" theme was developed first in his plays (175).

Multiple Authors/ Editors (24)

Several women who intended to become "storefront lawyers" later decided that they would be more comfortable in the establishment (Abramson and Franklin 71-120).

In his directing style, Alfred Hitchcock "reflects paranoia and anxiety to make his thrillers more thoroughly frightening" (McMahon, Funk, and Day 60).

Multivolume Work (25)

It required much persuasion by Faulkner's family and friends to convince him that he should go to Stockholm to accept the Nobel Prize (Blotner, Faulkner 2: 1341-49).

When The Bostonians was published in Century, the editors complained that "they had never published a serial which had encountered such an awesome silence" (Edel 3: 137).

The volume and page numbers are separated by a colon. The title is included in the first example because two books by Blotner are listed in Works Cited.

Newspaper (27)

> A London shopkeeper is reported to be selling
>
> "do-it-yourself" caskets (<u>Chicago Tribune</u> 6).

> According to Sylvia Porter, insurance rates on
>
> consumer loans vary widely from state to state and
>
> are lowest in Maine and New York (C11).

> An editorial in the <u>Detroit Free Press</u> calls for
>
> legislation to outlaw radar detectors or "fuzz
>
> busters" (A8).

The name of the newspaper is not necessary in the second example because the author is identified in the text; in the third example, the newspaper is identified in the text.

Reference Work (32)

> "For Beethoven, the piano sonata was the vehicle
>
> for his most bold and inward thoughts" (Budden,
>
> <u>Britannica</u> 14:621).

> Chile, which annexed Easter Island in 1888, does
>
> not consider it a colony but regards the natives as
>
> citizens of Chile ("Easter Island").

> More liberal retirement provisions might prevent
>
> our government from becoming a gerontocracy,
>
> defined by Webster as a society in which "a group
>
> of old men or a council of elders dominates or
>
> exercises control" (Gerontocracy).

When citing reference works give enough information to enable your reader to locate the source. The page is cited in the first example because the *Britannica* article is eight pages long. The title of the article is sufficient in the second example.

Review (34)

> Robert Giroux describes Lowell's "Antebellum
>
> Boston" as "perhaps the best prose memoir written
>
> by an American" (17).

> William Burroughs "questions the sordid ironies of
>
> the human condition with indefatigable imagination,
>
> humor, and candor" (Olson 110).

> "Working in a mood of tranquil exuberance, the
>
> eighty-year-old John Huston made a great, warm,
>
> funny movie out of James Joyce's story" (New Yorker
>
> 20).

Selection in an Anthology (35)

> "Baseball pastorals" are a conservative critique of
>
> American culture and represent "a failed attempt to
>
> restore lost tradition" (Shevory 61).

> In Arthur Miller's Death of a Salesman, Willy
>
> Loman's wife pleads with her sons to be tolerant of
>
> their father: "He's not the finest character who
>
> ever lived. But he's a human being and a terrible
>
> thing is happening to him. So attention must be
>
> paid" (1320).

Untitled Article (39)

> Arnold Schwarzenegger was voted the Most Violent
>
> Actor and Whoopi Goldberg the Most Violent Actress
>
> (Time 61).

Articles without some kind of title are rare, but if you cite one, give the name of the periodical and the page. The preceding example is from the "People" section of *Time*.

Works by the Same Author (41)

> "If Garp could have been granted one vast and naive
>
> wish, it would have been that he could make the
>
> world safe. For children and for grownups" (Irving,
>
> World 199).

If you use two or more works by the same author or editor, you must include the title in a citation, as in the example. Author and title are separated by a comma. A long title can be shortened to a key word or phrase. Generally, the first word is used, but in the example, *Garp* would have served as well as *World*.

Special Situations _____

Several variant methods of quoting or citing material are illustrated in the following examples: graphic materials, indirect citations, nonprint sources, quotation of poetry, shortened titles, citation of two sources, unpaged sources, and works with numbered divisions.

Graphic Materials

A paper should not be overloaded with illustrative materials like pictures, maps, tables, and graphs, but if you use any, make certain that they are relevant to your thesis, not just window dressing. If your paper contains several illustrations, you can place them in an appendix and refer to them in the text of your paper as "Fig. 3," "Table 1," and so on.

A statistical table is labeled Table and assigned a number; the label and a brief title are typed *above* the table. A graph, a map, or some other form of illustration is labeled Figure (Fig.) and assigned a number; the label and a brief title are typed *below* the illustration.

The examples on page 163 are taken from Douglas A. Hibbs, Jr., *The American Political Economy* (Cambridge: Harvard UP, 1987). The table appears on page 201 in Hibbs's text, the figure on page 140. If you reproduced the table, for example, you would include the book in Works Cited and type a caption, "Photocopied from Hibbs 201," below the table.

Indirect Citation

```
Clifton Fadiman called Absalom, Absalom! "the most

consistently boring novel by a reputable writer to

come my way during the last decade" (qtd. in

Blotner, Faulkner 2: 948-49).
```

To identify the original source of a quotation that occurs in the source you are using, identify the writer or speaker, follow the name with "qtd. in," and cite your source. Your first thought in such a situation, however, should be to look for the original source because it may contain other usable material.

Nonprint Source

```
Professor Moore told his Economics class that a

cycle of boom and bust is inevitable in the

American economy.

Woody Allen does not appear in Radio Days, which is

based on his boyhood memories, but he is heard in

voice-over narration and commentary.

Peale's Staircase Group is so lifelike that viewers

sometimes step back to allow the young men to enter

the room.
```

Because no page reference is possible, nonprint sources like those in the preceding examples are usually cited within the text. They are, of

Table 6.3 Issues underlying support for Reagan in the 1980 and
1984 elections

Issues most important in affecting the vote for Reagan	Percentage of voters who cited in—	
	1980	1984
The economy (inflation, jobs, unemployment)	60	44
Federal taxes, spending	13	32
Federal budget deficit	26	20
Foreign relations and U.S. prestige	19	28
Crisis in Iran	9	—
Arms control	—	6
ERA and abortion	5	5

Sources: For 1980, *New York Times*/CBS News Election Day Poll, reported in the *National Journal*, November 8, 1980, p. 1877. For 1984, *Los Angeles Times* exit polls, reported in the *National Journal*, November 10, 1984, p. 2131.

Photocopied from Hibbs 201.

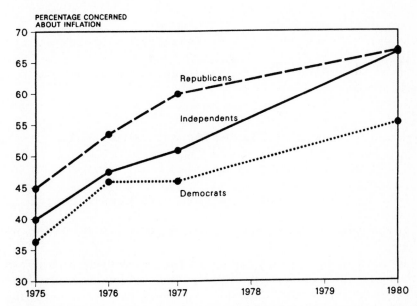

Figure 4.7 Concern about inflation versus unemployment among partisan groups.

Photocopied from Hibbs 140.

course, included in the list of works cited. Nonprint sources are listed on page 154.

Quoting Poetry

A. E. Housman poignantly describes those who live on after their fame has died: "Runners whom renown outran / And the name died before the man" ("To an Athlete Dying Young" 19-20).

Milton's attitude toward women is suggested in his description of the temptation of Adam:

> In recompense (for such compliance bad
> Such recompense best merits), from the
>   bough
> She gave him of that fair enticing fruit
> With liberal hand; he scrupled not to
>   eat,
> Against his better knowledge, not
>   deceived,
> But fondly overcome with female charm.
>
> PL 9.994-99

Two or three lines of poetry can be written consecutively with a slash separating the lines. A longer passage is written in block or display form (see pages 118-19). A block quotation is indented ten spaces and is not enclosed in quotation marks. Space twice and type the citation after the closing punctuation mark. If there is not enough space, as is true in the preceding example, the citation should be typed two spaces down and flush with the right margin (set the typewriter at the right margin and backspace the number of characters in the citation). The numerals in the example mean Book 9, lines 994–99 (see pages 165-66).

Shortened Titles

When a work is referred to a number of times in a paper, the title can be abbreviated or reduced to a key word. This is done most simply by designating the short title the first time the work is mentioned in the paper:

In Paradise Lost (PL), Milton announced that he

would "justify the ways of God to man."

Two Sources in a Citation

Emily Dickinson's father, Edward Dickinson, was a

lawyer, a congressman, and a leading citizen of

Amherst for forty years. To his family he was stern

and remote, but she often referred to him as a

rather comic figure (Sewall 1: 51-65; Cody 56-67).

If you need to acknowledge two sources in the same citation, separate the references by a semicolon. If the resulting citation is so long that it interrupts the flow of your sentences, write it as an endnote (see page 182).

Unpaged Source

Max Beerbohm spent thirteen years writing Zuleika

Dobson but illustrated a copy for his own amusement

in two months right after it was published (N. John

Hall, introduction [2-3]).

A short selection without page numbers can be cited by its title alone, but because the selection cited in the example is sixteen pages long, page numbers are included as a courtesy to the reader. The brackets indicate that the page numbers are not in the original.

Works with Numbered Divisions

In his despair Hamlet describes the world as "an

unweeded garden / That grows to seed" (1.2.135-36).

> After the death of Arthur Hallam, Tennyson found
>
> partial escape in poetry: "In words, like weeds,
>
> I'll wrap me o'er, / Like coarsest clothes against
>
> the cold" (IM 5.9-10).
>
> Those who quote "of making books there is no end"
>
> usually do not complete the quotation: "much study
>
> is a weariness of the flesh" (Eccles. 12.12).

A play, a long poem, the Bible, or any other work divided into numbered sections can be cited like the preceding examples. For a play, upper- and lowercase roman numerals are sometimes preferred: (I.ii.135-36). The numerals are separated by unspaced periods. Avoid abbreviating the words *line* or *lines* as "*l.*" or "*ll.*" because of the confusing similarity to the numbers one and eleven. "IM" in the second example means *In Memoriam*, poem number 5. Books of the Bible are usually abbreviated (see pages 268–69) and are not underlined.

Explanation and Reference Notes _____

The chief use of notes is citation—identifying the sources of borrowed material. As you have no doubt observed during your research, however, notes can serve two other functions: They supply additional information (*explanation notes*), and they suggest additional sources (*reference notes*). Many students ignore such notes when doing research, but they can be very helpful. They may contain facts or opinions that relate to your thesis, or they may furnish useful leads to other sources.

1. *Explanation notes* contain information that pertains to some aspect of the paper's topic but is not directly relevant to the thesis. They should be used sparingly in student papers because, in general, if something does not support the thesis, it should not be included. If you are inclined to include an amusing or interesting sidelight on your topic, consider putting it in an explanation note. Such notes can also be a convenient way of identifying individuals or events and of defining terms.

2. *Reference notes* direct the reader to another page of your paper or, more often, to another source that either supports or contradicts a statement. They are usually introduced by *See also* or *Compare* and may include a brief comment on the source.

Often the two types of notes are combined: A note contains a comment and also cites one or more sources. If you use material from a source, include it in Works Cited. If you merely mention a work, you need not include it. For examples of such notes, see the first sample paper (page 179).

To write a note of either kind, type a numeral (a superscript) in the text a half space above the line; a corresponding numeral, elevated a half space and followed by a space, precedes the note. In the text a note number follows any punctuation mark except a dash. The procedure is described more fully in the next section and is illustrated in the second sample paper (pages 191–203). Notes can be written at the bottom of the page as footnotes or, preferably, on a separate page headed Notes and placed after the text but before the Works Cited page. A brief reference (see Stone 46) can be made in the text, but if the reference is long enough to impede the sentence flow, it should be written as a reference note. Many students' papers contain neither explanation nor reference notes.

Sample Paper: In-text Citation _____

Like the other two sample papers, this one has been revised somewhat in order to illustrate as many aspects of research writing as possible. The three papers are not models of perfection, of course, but they represent superior student writing and may suggest ways in which your own paper can be improved. To conserve space, title pages and outline pages are not included, but outlines of the first two papers will be found on pages 106–10.

Brief marginal comments in the first paper point out transitional devices, techniques of documentation, and other aspects of structure and style. If you are following MLA style in your own paper, read this paper through a second time to note the form of the citations and of the sources listed in Works Cited.

The paper that follows has a dual thesis—examining the history of stagecoaching and analyzing some of the legends that became part of popular culture. Both aspects of the thesis involve numerous temptations to digress—the discovery of gold, the types of people who poured into California, outlaws who specialized in stage robberies, the Pony Express, Mark Twain's stay in Nevada, the building of the railroad, the life of Frederic Remington, the popular appeal of John Wayne. The writer managed to avoid or delete such digressions and adhered to his main purpose—discussing the stagecoach in history and in legend.

Tom Graham

Professor Scott

ENG 11C

4 May 1990

The Frontier Stagecoach

thesis expanded
into a short
paragraph

    The familiar stagecoach that lumbers across prairies and hurtles down mountain slopes on television and movie screens is a colorful part of the legendary Old West. It was also of great practical importance because it was the most efficient means of transporting passengers and mail before the railroad. The construction of the coach and the way stagecoach lines were organized and operated illustrate frontier ingenuity in adapting to new and difficult situations.

"situation"
= echo
of previous
paragraph

citation
of book
(author pages)

    One example of an unprecedented situation is the discovery of gold in California, which quickly resulted in a large population separated from the East by a vast stretch of unpopulated territory. The United States had never faced a transportation problem of this magnitude. People heading for the gold fields were in a hurry to get there, and after they arrived they wanted mail and goods. Stagecoaches, wagons, and pack mules were traveling from Sacramento and San Francisco to the mines by the fall of 1849 (Winther 5-7), but the East must have seemed impossibly remote. After California became

a state in 1850, its Senators began agitation for improved

service, and in 1856 Congress received a petition signed by

75,000 Californians demanding through mail (Moody 68-71).

Most members of Congress agreed that overland service was

necessary, but selecting the route it should follow caused

bitter dispute because the North and the South both realized

that the favored route would probably be used for the first

transcontinental railroad. Several routes were surveyed, but

debate centered on two: the southern "oxbow" route and the

northern route used by many emigrants.[1] Each had advantages

and disadvantages, and both involved rough terrain, bad

weather, and long distances. The choice of a route was

important, but the development of a suitable vehicle was

even more vital. Covered wagons and freight wagons were slow

and uncomfortable; ordinary wagons and buggies were not

sturdy enough. A vehicle was required that combined speed

with some degree of comfort and that was durable enough to

survive "twenty-five days of constant jolting over washboard

roads, mudholes, deserts, and swollen streams" (Hollon 28).

    The ideal vehicle to cope with such conditions was the

famous Concord coach manufactured by the Abbott-Downing

Company of Concord, New Hampshire. On rough roads passengers

"such conditions" = link to close of previous paragraph

and mail might be transferred to "celerity wagons," smaller

coaches, usually drawn by mules, but the Concord coach was

preferred. Yankee ingenuity adapted it to frontier

conditions. Its body was egg-shaped to reduce wind

resistance, and it was sealed to be as watertight as possible

so that it could ford streams. Instead of stiff steel springs,

thick leather belts called thoroughbraces gave the coach a

citation of a summary

rocking motion (Moody 12-13). Some passengers compared the

motion to that of a ship, and Mark Twain described the stage

author named in text; only page number cited

in which he traveled to Nevada as a "cradle on wheels" (7).

Wheels and other parts were handmade of seasoned ash,

basswood, and white oak. The iron tires were five inches

wide so that they would not sink into soft sand, and the

wheels were set wide apart to reduce the danger of tipping

(Hollon 29-30). Careful workmanship produced a coach that was

virtually indestructible. In California, for example, a

Concord coach that rolled three hundred feet down a steep

slope and landed in Greenhorn Creek was only slightly damaged

(Holbrook 109). Most coaches were painted red or green with

yellow trim, and the interiors were lined with russet leather

(Hollon 29). A young English artist, John Burgum, served

Abbott-Downing as "chief ornamenter," and he made each coach

as attractive as possible (Holbrook 107). The outside was

Graham 4

decorated with gold-leaf scrolls, and a landscape or a

portrait was painted on each door panel (Holbrook 109).

Thanks to western movies, the interior of coaches is as

familiar as the outer appearance. Nine passengers could

ride inside, three facing forward and three facing the rear,

and if necessary three more on a removable bench across

the center. Freight was carried on the roof and in the

"boot," a leather-covered rack suspended from the rear roof.

The back and both sides of the roof were enclosed by an iron

railing, and passengers could perch there if the coach was

crowded. Only two feet below the roof was the driver's seat,

six and a half feet above the ground. In good weather this

was a seat of honor, and a prominent citizen might be

invited to sit between the driver and the messenger-guard or

conductor (Moody 17-18).

Competition for passenger travel and for mail contracts

was fierce, and more fortunes were lost than were made by the

competitors, "men of great ability and much ruthlessness"

(Hawgood 249). In 1857, a contract for semiweekly service

with a subsidy of $600,000 a year was awarded to John

Butterfield, a friend of President Buchanan (Winther 113).

Although he was a New Yorker, Butterfield favored the

southern route. He devoted a year to preparations, spending

transition by comparison: interior with exterior

appositive useful for brief definitions

spell out fractions

numbers in one
or two words
spelled out;
numbers in
more than two
words written
in figures

nearly a million dollars marking a road and establishing

stations; buying 1,800 horses and mules, wagons, harness,

and coaches; and hiring agents, drivers, blacksmiths,

hostlers, and other workers. Service began on 15 September

1858 (Hollon 28-29). Butterfield's main rival, the firm of

Russell, Majors, and Waddell, operated freight wagons

profitably over the central route; but one of the partners,

William H. Russell, coveted the government subsidies awarded

Butterfield. To demonstrate that the central route was faster

than the southern, he persuaded his partners to start a

stagecoach line and to carry mail by the famous Pony Express.

Both enterprises lost money, and the Central Overland

California and Pike's Peak Express became known as Clean Out

of Cash and Poor Pay (Hawgood 251-53). Ironically, the

company went bankrupt just when the Civil War forced the

shift of mail service to the central route. On 21 March 1862,

the assets of the COC and PPE were taken over by the most

successful of the stage operators, Ben Holladay. He bought

new coaches, hired more reliable drivers, and kept his

coaches on schedule. Twice a year he made an inspection trip

over his line in a specially designed coach, and he once

made a record trip from San Francisco to Atchison in twelve

days and two hours (Winther 141). Holladay's prestige on the

Graham 6

frontier is illustrated by Mark Twain's anecdote about the

young man touring the Holy Land who was told that Moses led

the Israelites through the desert. The young man exclaimed,

"Forty years? Only three hundred miles? Humph! Ben Holliday

[sic] would have fetched them through in thirty-six hours!"   [sic] =
                                                                      a misspelling
(33). In 1866, Holladay foresaw the completion of a   in the source

transcontinental railroad and sold his holdings to Wells Fargo

(Winther 144). The railroad eliminated cross-country coach

lines, but stagecoaches continued to be used on short runs

for many years.

    Ben Holladay perfected the organization that John   names = link
                                                                      to previous
Butterfield had devised. Its basic unit was the division,   paragraph

a stretch of 200-250 miles supervised by a division

agent. According to Twain, an agent "was always a general

in administrative ability and a bull-dog in courage and

determination" (30). He expressed even more admiration for

the conductor, who rode beside the driver over the entire

length of the division and was responsible for passengers,

mail, and freight. A division was broken into stations ten to

twenty miles apart. At each station the horses were changed,

an operation requiring no more than four minutes; twice a day

a stage stopped forty minutes for a meal at a "home station"

(Dick 320-28). The station-keepers, stock-tenders, and other

Graham 7

employees were described by Twain as "low, rough characters"
who were often wanted by the law (31).

Much more glamorous than other stagecoach employees

was the driver, described by Lucius Beebe as "the synthesis

of everything enviable . . . remote as an earl and

unapproachable as a god" (10). Mark Twain noted the attitude

of station employees:

> How admiringly they would gaze up at him in his
>
> high seat as he gloved himself with lingering
>
> deliberation, while some happy hostler held the
>
> bunch of reins aloft, and waited patiently for him
>
> to take it! And how they would bombard him with
>
> glorifying ejaculations as he cracked his long whip
>
> and went careering away. (19)

The prestige of a driver or "jehu"[2] was largely due

to his driving skill. New England drivers had developed a

technique of "reining," which required great dexterity. The

reins for each pair of horses were held between different

fingers, and by merely twitching a finger a driver could

control the horses (Moody 23). He was also skillful with his

long whip and might boast that he could flick a fly from the

ear of one of the leaders without touching a hair (Dick 326).

Stage drivers were usually known only by nicknames like

Whisky Jack, Rowdy Pete, or Long Slim; but two are identified in frontier history as individuals: Charlie Parkhurst and Hank Monk. Parkhurst is a mysterious figure who began driving in California in 1851 and "won the reputation of being one of the fastest and safest stagecoach drivers in California." After Parkhurst died in 1879, it was discovered that the famous driver was a woman and had once borne a child (Moody 320-22). An even more famous driver was Hank Monk. According to a popular anecdote, apparently invented by Artemus Ward, Monk drove Horace Greeley from Folsom to Placerville for a lecture while Greeley was touring the West. Eager to deliver his famous passenger on time, Monk ignored Greeley's pleas to slow down and assured him, "Keep your seat, Horace, and I'll get you there on time!" In some versions of the story, Greeley bounced so high that his head was protruding from the roof when the stage arrived (Lillard 130). Mark Twain complained that he heard the story 481 times (106). Greeley always resented the fact that Monk had made him look ridiculous (Beebe 12-13). On 6 March 1883, in the Virginia City _Enterprise_, Monk's obituary appeared, written in appropriate stagecoaching language:

> The famous stage driver is dead. He has been on the
> downgrade for some time. On Wednesday his foot lost

Graham 9

its final hold on the brake and his coach could

not be stopped until battered and broken on the

sharp turn, it went over into the canyon, black and

deep, which we call death. (Lillard 132)

echo of
previous
paragraph

Although Charlie Parkhurst and Hank Monk were actual

persons, they illustrate the kind of legends that the

stagecoach inspired. In all of the media treating Western

themes, the stagecoach has played an important part. For

example, in a bibliography of dime novels, the phrase "usual

stage holdup" is used numerous times to describe a plot

citation of an
entire work

(Johannsen). Typical titles of dime novels are Black John,

the Road Agent and Bison Bill, the Prince of the Reins.

William F. Cody (Buffalo Bill), who was the hero of many

dime novels, originated his Wild West Show in 1883. One of

the most popular acts, which was imitated by other showmen,

was "The Startling and Soul-Stirring Attack upon the Deadwood

Mail Coach" (Russell 298). Indians pursued the coach as it was

driven at full speed, and at the last desperate moment

Buffalo Bill led a group of cowboys to the rescue (Russell

332). The same kind of exciting action is found in the

paintings by Frederic Remington, the most popular western

painter. A typical picture is Mixed-Up: six galloping horses

are raising clouds of dust, the guard and a passenger are

firing at shadowy figures on a bluff, and the driver is

gripping the reins and kicking the brake (101 Drawings 105).[3]

Since John Ford admired Remington's paintings and used

details from them in She Wore a Yellow Ribbon (Stowell 83),

it seems probable that he also borrowed from Remington while

creating Stagecoach in 1939. This film, which has been

described by André Bazin as "the ideal example of the

maturity of a style brought to classic perfection"(qtd. in

Stowell 23), embodies several aspects of the legendary

stagecoach. The driver (Andy Devine) is loud and boisterous.

He yells at the horses and flicks pebbles at them to keep

them moving. Actual stagecoaches averaged 120 miles or less

in twenty-four hours (Hollon 30), but John Ford's coach

hurtles along at twice that speed. The high speed is

necessary because the Apaches are on the warpath; but, of

course, after an exciting chase the cavalry arrives to save

the passengers from Geronimo's braves. The passengers include

an army officer's pregnant wife, a suave gambler formerly

acquainted with her, an absconding banker, a whisky salesman,

a drunken doctor, a prostitute, the Ringo Kid (John Wayne)

who has been falsely accused of a crime, and a marshal.[4] When

the stage stops so that the baby can be born, it suggests the

way life continued on the frontier despite adversity and

Remington = link with previous paragraph

indirect citation

danger. The diversity of this group and the changes in their

relationships under stress may also symbolize the democratic

mixing that occurred on the frontier.

summarizing
final paragraph

  From a practical standpoint, the stagecoach was vital

in the settlement of the West. It served as a stopgap until

the Union Pacific was completed, and for several years it

was the chief link between the West and the East. Actual

stagecoaches are in museums today. The legendary

stagecoaches, representing speed, efficiency, adaptation,

danger, excitement, and human diversity, still clatter across

movie and television screens at breakneck speed while

outlaws or Indians gallop in pursuit.

Notes

[1] Southern route: St. Louis-Tipton-Fort Smith-El Paso-Tucson-Fort Yuma-Los Angeles-San Francisco.

Northern route: St. Joseph-Fort Laramie-Salt Lake City-Carson City-Sacramento.

See maps in Moody 92-93; 102-103.

[2] Travelers and journalists sometimes referred to a stage driver as a jehu from a portion of a Biblical verse: "the driving is like the driving of Jehu the son of Nimshi; for he driveth furiously" (2 Kings 9.20).

[3] Equally famous and equally action-packed is Downing the Nigh Leader. In this painting Indians are attacking the lead team while the driver saws on the reins and two men fire rifles from the roof of the stage.

[4] In 1986, Bodie Thoene described a remake of the film for television with country singers in the leading male roles: Johnny Cash as the marshal, Willie Nelson as Doc, Waylon Jennings as the gambler, and Kris Kristofferson as the Ringo Kid.

supplementary information and sources

Graham 13

Works Cited

monthly
magazine

Beebe, Lucius. "King of the Stagecoach Drivers." <u>Holiday</u>

Sept. 1953: 10-13.

book:
standard form

Dick, Everett. <u>Vanguards of the Frontier</u>. New York: Appleton,

1941.

Hawgood, John A. <u>America's Western Frontiers</u>. New York:

Knopf, 1967.

Holbrook, Stewart H. "The Concord Coach." <u>American Mercury</u>

Jan. 1950: 104-10.

Hollon, W. Eugene. "Great Days of the Overland Stage."

<u>American Heritage</u> June 1957: 26-31+.

Johannsen, Albert. <u>The House of Beadle and Adams and Its Dime</u>

university press

<u>and Nickel Novels</u>. 3 vols. Norman: U of Oklahoma P,

1950.

Lillard, Richard G. "Hank Monk and Horace Greeley." <u>American</u>

<u>Literature</u> 14 (1942): 126-34.

Moody, Ralph. <u>Stagecoach West</u>. New York: Crowell, 1967.

numeral
alphabetized
as though
spelled out

<u>101 Frederic Remington Drawings of the Old West</u>. Ed. Irvin W.

Hanson. Willmar, MN: Color Press, 1968.

Russell, Don. <u>The Lives and Legends of Buffalo Bill</u>. Norman:

U of Oklahoma P, 1960.

film listed
by title

<u>Stagecoach</u>. Dir. John Ford. Prod. Walter Wanger. With Claire

Trevor, John Carradine, Thomas Mitchell, and John Wayne.

Graham 14

United Artists, 1939.

Stowell, Peter. <u>John Ford</u>. Twayne's Filmmakers Series.

    Boston: Twayne, 1986.

Thoene, Bodie. "<u>Stagecoach</u> a Legend: The Stage to Lordsburg

    Runs Again." <u>American West</u> May-June 1986: 38-47.

Twain, Mark. <u>Roughing It</u>. 1872. New York: Rinehart, 1953.

Winther, Oscar Osburn. <u>Via Western Express & Stagecoach</u>.

    Stanford: Stanford UP, 1945.

book in
a series

bimonthly
magazine

Citation in Notes _____

Borrowed material can be cited in notes rather than in the text. The basic procedure is the same as for explanation and reference notes (see page 167): A numeral (superscript), raised a half-space, is placed immediately *after* the borrowed material, and a corresponding numeral, also raised and followed by a space, precedes the note. Notes should be numbered consecutively throughout a paper. Endnotes, written on a separate page that follows the text of the paper, and footnotes, written at the bottom of each page, are identical in form except that an endnote of two or more lines is usually double-spaced whereas a footnote of two or more lines is single-spaced. The only other difference is their placement.

   A note contains the three basic elements of a bibliographic entry (author, title, and publication data) plus a specific page reference. Citing publication facts even though they appear in Works Cited is customary, though time-consuming. Note form differs from bibliographic form in the following ways:

1. Indentation is conventional (five spaces).
2. Authors' names are not inverted.
3. A comma followed by one space separates the author and the title.
4. Publication data are enclosed in parentheses. No punctuation precedes or follows.
5. Exact page references are cited.

Footnotes

Footnotes are a convenience for a reader but a nuisance for a writer. The main problem is estimating how much space will be required. It is discouraging, to say the least, after you have typed a neat and error-free page to discover that there is no room for the footnotes. If you use footnotes, make it a habit to look ahead in your rough draft before you insert a sheet of paper into your typewriter, determine how many footnotes will be needed, and make a light pencil mark where they should begin. Be a little generous in your estimate; extra space will look better than crowded notes. Never write two footnotes on the same line. Single-space a footnote of two or more lines, but double-space between footnotes. It is not necessary to separate your text and the notes by a line across the page; simply double-space twice between the text and the first footnote. The last few lines of a paper using footnotes would look like the example at the top of the next page.

Endnotes

By 1984 endnotes had superseded footnotes for most researchers, just as in-text citation is now superseding the use of endnotes. Listing notes in

At their first meeting Elizabeth and Darcy are both
guilty of the faults expressed in the title of the novel. He
is proud of his social position, and she is proud of her
"fallible perceptions"[3]--her faith in her ability to judge

[1] Mary Lascelles, Jane Austen and Her Art (Oxford:
Clarendon, 1963) 160.

[2] Tony Tanner, introduction, Pride and Prejudice, by Jane
Austen (New York: Viking Penguin, 1986) 8.

[3] Marilyn Butler, Jane Austen and the War of Ideas
(Oxford: Clarendon, 1975) 207.

sequence on a separate page is simpler than typing footnotes on each
page. The listing is headed Notes (not Footnotes or Endnotes); it follows
the last page of the text and precedes Works Cited.

Primary Notes. A *primary note* is the first citation of a source. It should
be complete enough to enable readers to locate the work readily. Following
are some standard primary notes for books and periodicals.

[1] I. F. Stone, The Trial of Socrates (Boston:
Little, 1988) 102.

[2] Richard T. Lubben, Just-in-Time
Manufacturing: An Aggressive Manufacturing Strategy
(New York: McGraw, 1988) 46.

[3] Paul DuChaillu, Wild Life under the Equator
(New York, 1872) 78.

[4] John Kehes, "Understanding Evil," American
Philosophical Quarterly 25 (1988): 18.

[5] T. K. Tong, "Temporary Absolutism Versus

Hereditary Aristocracy," <u>Chinese Studies in History</u>

21.3 (1988): 16.

6 Philis Langdon, "A Good Place to Live,"

<u>Atlantic</u> Mar. 1988: 56.

Many variations in the preceding forms are possible. Subtitles and publishers' names are sometimes omitted from notes in a short paper. If you vary the basic forms, be certain that your instructor approves. Note that a colon precedes a page reference to a periodical but not to a book. Note also that a publisher is not shown for a book published before 1900 (see note 3); the city and year are separated by a comma. For a journal that is paged separately in each issue (see note 5), the volume and issue numbers are separated by a period.

Secondary Notes. A basic principle of citation by notes is that the first reference to a work should be as complete as necessary to locate it easily, and subsequent references to the same work should be as brief as possible. The usual form of a secondary note is an author's last name and the page reference (not separated by a comma). If you use two or more sources by the same author, include a short form of the title as in note 7. If you have two authors with the same last name, include the given name (see note 8).

7 Stone, <u>Trial</u> 118.

8 Richard T. Lubben 143.

9 Kehes 14.

10 Langdon 42.

Sample Primary Note Forms

Sample primary notes for the kinds of sources you are most likely to cite are cross-referenced to the bibliographic examples in the discussion of works cited (pages 132–53). Nonprint sources like works of art or performances can usually be cited more gracefully within the text; they are, of course, listed in Works Cited.

Anonymous Work (3)

11 <u>A Critical Fable</u> (Boston: Houghton, 1922)

21.

12 "Sound Effects," New Yorker 21 Mar. 1988: 28.

Anthology (4)

13 Benjamin DeMott, ed., Close Imagining: An Introduction to Literature (New York: St. Martin's, 1988) 1-3.

Computerized Material (8)

14 Mary J. Quinn, "Elder Abuse and Neglect," Generations 10 (1985): 24 (DIALOG file 1, item 74-31920).

Corporate Author (9)

15 American Diabetes Association, Diabetes in the Family (New York: Prentice, 1987) 12.

Edition (10)

16 Marjory Stoneman Douglas, The Everglades: River of Grass, rev. ed. (Sarasota: Pineapple Press, 1988) 12.

Editor (11)

17 Stephen Spender, Journals 1938-1983, ed. John Goldsmith (New York: Random, 1986) 102.

Government Publication (14)

18 U.S. Department of State, Patterns of Global Terrorism: 1984 (Washington: GPO, 1985) 31.

19 U.S. Cong. Rec. 30 Apr. 1986: S5124.

Interview (15)

20 John Fowles, "A Conversation with John

Fowles," Interviewer: Robert Faulke, Salmagundi No.

68-69 (1985-86): 367.

21 Emily Norris, personal interview, 14 Feb.

1989.

A nonprint interview can often be acknowledged more gracefully in the text and in Works Cited.

Introduction (16)

22 Anthony Burgess, introduction, Augustus

Carp, Esq. By Himself: Being the Autobiography of a

Really Good Man (1924; Woodbridge, Suffolk:

Bookmaster-Boydell, 1985) v.

An identifying term like *introduction* is not capitalized when it follows a comma. The preceding example cites a republished book (see also note 37).

Legal Reference (18)

23 Brown vs General Services Administration

et al., 425 U.S. Reports No. 76 (U.S. Sup. Ct.

1976).

Laws and legal cases are often difficult to document. Supply whatever information is needed to locate the source. Entire cases are cited more often than specific pages.

Letter, Published (20)

24 Dylan Thomas, letter to John Malcolm

Brinnin, 18 Mar. 1953, The Collected Letters, ed.

Paul Ferris (New York: Macmillan, 1985) 879.

25 Mark William Rocha, letter, "James as Playwright," <u>PMLA</u> 103 (1988): 175.

Manuscript Material (21)

26 Peleg Worthie, Diary 1864-1865, Worthie Family papers, Newton OH, [9].

27 Robert F. Sommer, "The Masks of Henry Adams," diss., Duke U., 1985, 62.

The brackets in note 26 indicate that the writer has supplied the page number. The title of an unpublished dissertation is enclosed in quotation marks; the page number follows a comma (as in note 27).

Multiple Authors/Editors (24)

28 Jill Abramson and Barbara Franklin, <u>Where Are They Now: The Story of the Women of Harvard Law 1974</u> (Garden City: Doubleday, 1986) 71-120.

29 Elizabeth McMahon, Robert Funk, and Susan Day, <u>The Elements of Writing About Literature and Film</u> (New York: Macmillan, 1988) 60.

Multivolume Work (25)

30 Leon Edel, <u>Henry James</u>, 5 vols. (Philadelphia: Lippincott, 1953-72) 3: 137.

Volume and page numbers are separated by a colon.

Newspaper (27)

31 Russ DeVault, "Of Time and the Riverman," <u>Atlanta Constitution</u> 18 Mar. 1988: 3.

32 "Slow Down," editorial, <u>Detroit Free Press</u> 27 Mar. 1988: A8.

Pamphlet (28)

33 Irving R. Dickman, Behavior Modification

(New York: Public Affairs Comm., 1976) 27.

Pseudonym (30)

34 Petroleum V. Nasby, The Nasby Papers

(Indianapolis, 1864) 186.

Reference Work (32)

35 Julian Medforth Budden, "Beethoven,"

Encyclopaedia Britannica: Macropaedia. 1985 ed. 14:

621.

36 "Easter Island," The New Columbia

Encyclopedia. 4th ed.

Ordinarily, page references are not necessary for a reference book that is alphabetically arranged (see note 36). However, the *Britannica* essay in note 35 is eight pages long, and so citing the page number makes it easier for readers to locate the quotation.

Republished Work (33)

37 Thomas Pynchon, The Crying of Lot 49 (1966;

New York: Perennial-Harper, 1986) 58.

For a book republished by a second publisher (usually a paperback edition of a hardback original), include the year of the original publication, followed by a semicolon. In the preceding example, the publisher's imprint is included.

Review (34)

38 Anthony Hecht, "Portraits by Lowell," rev.

of Robert Lowell: Collected Prose, ed. Robert

Giroux, New York Review of Books 3 Mar. 1988: 17.

39 Steve E. Olson, rev. of The Western Lands,

by William Burroughs, <u>Antioch Review</u> 46 (1988):

110.

    40 Rev. of <u>The Dead</u>, <u>New Yorker</u> 14 Mar. 1988:

20.

Selection in an Anthology (35)

    41 Thomas C. Shevory, "Winning Isn't

Everything: Sports Fiction as a Genre of Political

Criticism," <u>Political Mythology and Popular Fiction</u>,

ed. Ernest J. Yanarella and Lee Sigelman,

Contributions in Political Science (New York:

Greenwood, 1988) 61.

    42 Arthur Miller, <u>Death of a Salesman</u>, <u>Close</u>

<u>Imagining</u>: An Introduction to Literature, ed.

Benjamin DeMott (New York: St. Martin's, 1988)

1320.

The title of the selection and the title of the anthology are separated by a comma.

Translation (38)

    43 Gabriel García Márquez, "Pentecost Sunday,"

trans. Edith Grossman, <u>New Yorker</u> 28 Mar. 1988: 46.

Untitled Article (39)

    44 <u>Time</u> 8 Feb. 1988: 61.

Sample Paper: Endnotes _____

Papers on literature often focus, as this one does, on a single aspect of a work—a character, a theme, or a recurring symbol—and analyze its relation to the work as a whole. Critics' opinions are used to substantiate your judgements. In this paper, marriage is both the controlling idea and the basis of the plan. Each marriage is discussed in terms of its effect on the relationship between Elizabeth and Darcy.

If the paper had a title page, the endorsement and the title would not be necessary on page 1. The student's last name would still be used as a running head on each page. An outline of the paper appears on pages 106–08. An outline page, if included, would follow the title page. Note that the title of the novel is underlined in the title of the paper.

There are nineteen endnotes in the paper, but there would be many more if *Pride and Prejudice* had not been cited in the text. When one work is referred to a number of times in a paper, in-text citation saves time and trouble. The usual procedure is to cite the work once in a conventional note and indicate that subsequent citations will be made within the text (see note 5 on page 11 of the paper). For a literary classic that has been reprinted many times, the page number alone will not be very useful to the reader, and so it may be advisable to include the chapter as well. Cite the page number, follow it with a semicolon and then cite the chapter: "(81; ch. 8)." For a play, cite the act, scene, and lines rather than the page: "(*Macbeth* 5.4.19-28)." Consult your instructor if you are in doubt about the citation of a literary work.

Comparing the Notes with Works Cited indicates considerable duplication of effort since publication data are included in each primary note and then are repeated in bibliographic entries in Works Cited. When publication facts are included in endnotes or footnotes, a bibliography is sometimes considered unnecessary. Consult your instructor, however, before deciding to omit a Works Cited page. In-text citation is more efficient than endnotes, but endnotes are more efficient than footnotes.

Rita Hogan

Professor Smart

ENG 102D

20 April 1990

Marriage in Pride and Prejudice

Matrimony is the central concern in Jane Austen's novels; the plot of each of them is based on the heroine's undergoing various disappointments and frustrations before eventually being married to a suitable husband. The union of Elizabeth Bennet and Fitzwilliam Darcy in Pride and Prejudice seems like an ideal match; but it comes about only after a long process of "diverging and converging lines, by the movement of two people who are impelled apart until they reach a climax of mutual hostility, and thereafter bend their courses toward mutual understanding and amity."[1] According to Tony Tanner, "everything tends towards the achieving of satisfactory marriages,"[2] but few of the marriages are really satisfactory. Eight other marriages in the novel are all different and represent different motives for marrying. Most are unsatisfactory in some way but still function, and all of them in one way or another influence the eventual coming together of Elizabeth and Darcy.

At their first meeting Elizabeth and Darcy are both

guilty of the faults expressed in the title of the novel. He is proud of his social position, and she is proud of her "fallible perceptions"[3]--her faith in her ability to judge a person on the basis of her first impressions (Jane Austen's original title for the novel). Darcy is prejudiced against the vulgarity of the Bennets and their neighbors, and Elizabeth is prejudiced against Darcy's arrogant rudeness. The remainder of the novel follows a pattern of "approach and rejection."[4]. Just when they seem about to reach a better understanding of one another, something occurs to force them farther apart. Finally, when Darcy proposes for the second time, Elizabeth's pride has been humbled and her prejudice has been overcome; she, therefore, replies that she will "receive with gratitude and pleasure, his present assurances."[5] "The moral and emotional revolutions that Darcy and Elizabeth experience by facing hard, unpleasant truths about themselves make them equal and complementary partners in marriage."[6]

Some of these "unpleasant truths" are revealed by other versions of matrimony they observe. Three marriages of minor characters are more or less harmonious, but only because the couples share the same deficiencies. Mr. and Mrs. Hurst are both shallow snobs; he lives "only to eat, drink, and

play at cards" (81; ch. 8), and his wife thinks only of
fashion and social niceties. They represent the artificial
world of high society to which Elizabeth assumes Darcy
belongs because they are in his company when she meets them.
Thus, she bases her animosity toward him on "a form of guilt
by association."[7] Sir William Lucas, whom Darcy despises as
much as Elizabeth despises the Hursts, made a small fortune
in trade and was knighted while mayor of Meryton. He bought a
country house and renamed it Lucas Lodge, "where he could
think with pleasure of his own importance, and . . . occupy
himself solely in being civil to all the world" (65; ch. 5).
His wife is "not too clever to be a valuable neighbour to Mrs.
Bennet" (65; ch. 5)--a suggestion that she is not very
bright. Mutual stupidity and social climbing are not an ideal
basis for a marriage, but the Lucases seem to live
comfortably together. Darcy is scornful of them, especially
when Sir William describes dancing as "one of the first
refinements of polished societies" and urges him to dance
with Elizabeth (72-73; ch. 6). Elizabeth's aunt has married
her father's law clerk, "broad-faced, stuffy uncle Phillips"
(120; ch. 16). Both of them are fond of gossip and the
society of militia officers. Mrs. Phillips is more vulgar
than Mrs. Bennet; she keeps a close eye on the street and

throws open the window to call down to her nieces (117;

ch. 15). Miss Bingley reminds Darcy of Elizabeth's "low"

connections: "Do let the portraits of your uncle and aunt

Phillips be placed in the gallery at Pemberley" (97; ch. 10).

The least satisfactory marriage in the novel is that of

Elizabeth's parents. Mr. and Mrs. Bennet are an extreme

example of a mismatched couple. Sexually attracted to a

beautiful young woman, Mr. Bennet married the daughter of an

attorney, below him in social class. His disappointment in

being married to a silly wife who has not given him a son

finds an outlet in cynical sarcasm. He has lost respect for

her and for himself, and his marriage offers him only "a kind

of grim entertainment."[8] When his wife and five daughters

become too much for him, he retreats to his library. His

detachment is an escape from "the familial miseries brought

about by his having married a sexually attractive but

unintelligent woman."[9] Although his sarcastic remarks to his

wife give him some satisfaction, she does not hear or does not

comprehend many of them. In twenty-three years, she has not

learned to understand her husband, but this does not trouble

her because "the business of her life was to get her daughters

married" (53; ch. 1). Elizabeth's father and mother have

given her an example of the unhappy result of a marriage

between social and intellectual unequals and have probably
made her skeptical about marriage in general. She sympathizes
with her father but disapproves of his detachment from his
family:

> She has learned from his example that a complex
> personality may yield to the pressure of sensuality;
> that marriages made by sex. . . represent, for the
> free individual, an abdication of choice, an
> irremediable self-degradation and defeat.[10]

Perhaps she fears that as Darcy's wife she would resort to
using her father's weapon--sarcastic wit.

Lydia Bennet, the youngest sister, "is a self-assured,
highly sexed, wholly amoral and unintellectual girl"[11] --
probably a vulgar version of what her mother was at fifteen.
When she elopes with George Wickham, her father is not as
indignant as might be expected, perhaps because he senses
that Wickham is duplicating his own mistake. Mrs. Bennet is
less ashamed of Lydia's living with Wickham for two weeks
before their marriage than of the fact that Lydia did not
have a new wardrobe for the wedding (324; ch. 50). Jane
Austen obviously does not foresee much happiness for the
marriage of a couple whose "passions were stronger than their
virtue" (325; ch. 50):

His affection for her soon sunk into indifference;
her's [sic] lasted a little longer; and in spite of
her youth and her manners, she retained all the
claims to reputation which her marriage had given
her. (395; ch. 61)

Lydia and Wickham serve the main plot in various ways.
Lydia's behavior repels Darcy, and Wickham feeds Elizabeth's
prejudice by telling her lies about Darcy. She is attracted
to his handsome appearance and his outgoing personality, but
as she comes to see through him, her opinion of Darcy changes
for the better. When she learns that Darcy found Wickham and
Lydia in London and arranged their marriage, her last traces
of prejudice are dispelled. That Darcy is willing to accept
Wickham as a brother-in-law proves the depth of his love:
"Having made the Bennet family worse than it was before, he
marries into it."[12]

The marriage of Mr. Collins and Charlotte Lucas is not
motivated by sexual attraction but by prudent self-interest.
He wants to marry because his patron, Lady Catherine de
Bourgh, has suggested that he should. He has great respect for
rank and status. He comes to Longbourne planning to marry
Jane, the eldest daughter; but he readily turns to Elizabeth,
the next eldest, when Mrs. Bennet tells him that Jane is

spoken for. When Elizabeth refuses his long-winded proposal,
he will not take no for an answer: "It is by no means certain
that another offer of marriage may ever be made you. Your
portion is unhappily so small that it will in all likelihood
undo the effects of your loveliness and amiable
qualifications" (150; ch. 19). Thus he both insults her and
recognizes the importance of marriage to young women and the
financial considerations that underlie many marriages. At the
age of twenty-seven, Charlotte Lucas is on the verge of
spinsterhood and is completely cynical about marriage:
"Happiness in marriage is entirely a matter of chance . . .
it is better to know as little as possible of the defects of
the person with whom you are to pass your life"(69-70;
ch. 6). Charlotte is "Austen's first complex portrait of
misused sense."[13] Because she considers herself objective and
practical, she makes the immoral decision to marry without
love. Her marriage is the most pathetic one in the novel
because she is intelligent but must pretend to be ignorant.[14]
Elizabeth "is appalled by Charlotte's loveless marriage for
financial security . . . [and] is equally shocked by Lydia's
reckless pursuit of passion."[15] Prudent marriages are not
always condemned, however; Darcy's cousin, Colonel
Fitzwilliam, an admirable character, freely admits that few

Hogan 8

younger sons "can afford to marry without some attention to money," and Elizabeth seems to agree (216; ch. 33). Charlotte's marriage advances the plot by giving Elizabeth a chance to see Darcy again. When she visits the Collinses in Kent, she finds Charlotte apparently contented. She encourages her husband to work in the garden to keep him out of the house and pretends not to hear his silliest remarks (192; ch. 28). She has chosen for herself a room at the back of the house, which her husband seldom visits because he watches the road for Lady Catherine's carriage (202; ch. 30).

In contrast, the Gardiners are an admirable, congenial couple. Mr. Gardiner is much more genteel and sensible than his sisters, Mrs. Phillips and Mrs. Bennet. His residence in London may have given him the bearing of a gentleman, but the influence of his wife has also been important. Mrs. Gardiner is a sensible woman who has been a motherly advisor to Elizabeth and Jane. The Gardiners are parents of well-behaved children who are far different from the three youngest Bennet sisters. Elizabeth's aunt and uncle furnish her with the example of a well-matched, happy couple. They also serve the plot by taking her to Pemberley, where she again meets Darcy. He is impressed by the dignity of the Gardiners and the way they contrast with "the clownish groveling of Mr. Collins and

Sir William Lucas."[16] Mr. Gardiner demonstrates to Darcy that a man can be in business without being vulgar or obsequious. The last sentence of the novel states that both Darcy and Elizabeth "really loved" the Gardiners.

Jane Bennet and Charles Bingley are another example of a well-matched couple, but they are drawn together by unthinking romantic emotion just as Wickham and Lydia are united by sensuality. Both are naive and easily led; Bingley allows Darcy to take him away from Netherfield, and Jane is immediately convinced that he does not care for her. After Bingley leaves and Charlotte accepts Mr. Collins, Elizabeth is bitter and sounds almost as cynical as her father: "There are few people whom I really love, and still fewer of whom I think well" (173; ch. 24). Her disillusionment is offset somewhat by Jane's "warmer vision" and her "prepossession to think well of people."[17] Because Jane thinks well of everyone, she exists in "a cocoon of ignorance,"[18] but it is a happy condition. In what amounts to a compliment coming from Mr. Bennet, he passes judgment on their marriage:

> "Your tempers are by no means unlike. You are
> each of you so complying that nothing will ever be
> resolved on; so easy, that every servant will cheat
> you; and so generous, that you will always exceed

your income." (358; ch. 55)

When Darcy brings Bingley back to Netherfield and encourages
him to propose to Jane, Elizabeth senses that her own marriage
to Darcy is not impossible. The love Jane and Bingley show
so openly for each other may inspire similar emotion in both
Elizabeth and Darcy. "Darcy and Elizabeth are kept apart by
the belief that a deep social rift lies between them. Bingley
and Jane illustrate how mistaken they are."[19] Thus, six more
or less unsuitable marriages and two happy ones serve in
various ways to bring Elizabeth and Darcy together.

It is true, as many critics point out, that Jane Austen
is primarily concerned with marriage in her novels,
but this is understandable as marriage was the primary
concern of middle-class young women of her day. She does not
falsify it as a "happy-ever-after" state. Six of the
marriages in Pride and Prejudice are less than admirable;
only the Gardiners and the Bingleys seem well suited to each
other. Nevertheless, all of the couples in some way influence
the coming together of Elizabeth and Darcy. They seem a
perfect couple, but their marriage is kept from being just a
romantic fairy tale by contrast with the other marriages that
helped bring about their union.

Notes

1 Mary Lascelles, Jane Austen and Her Art (Oxford: Clarendon, 1963) 160.

2 Tony Tanner, introduction, Pride and Prejudice, by Jane Austen (New York: Viking Penguin, 1986) 8.

3 Marilyn Butler, Jane Austen and the War of Ideas (Oxford: Clarendon, 1975) 207.

4 David Monaghan, Jane Austen: Structure and Social Vision (New York: Barnes, 1980) 71.

5 Jane Austen, Pride and Prejudice (New York: Viking Penguin, 1986) 375; ch. 58. Hereafter cited within the text.

6 Joseph Wiesenfarth, "The Case of Pride and Prejudice," Studies in the Novel 16 (1984): 269.

7 James Sherry, "Pride and Prejudice: The Limits of Society," Studies in English Literature 19 (1979): 613.

8 Sherry 618.

9 Tanner 27.

10 Marvin Mudrick, Jane Austen: Irony as Defense and Discovery (Princeton: Princeton UP, 1952) 115.

11 Mudrick 100.

12 Wiesenfarth 266.

13 Susan Morgan, In the Meantime: Character and Perception in Jane Austen's Fiction (Chicago: U of

Chicago P) 92.

[14] Joel Weinsheimer, "Chance and the Hierarchy of Marriages in Pride and Prejudice," ELH 39 (1972): 408.

[15] Butler 214.

[16] Monaghan 86.

[17] Morgan 98.

[18] Weinsheimer 411.

[19] Monaghan 80.

Hogan 13

Works Cited

Austen, Jane. Pride and Prejudice. 1813. New York: Viking

Penguin, 1986.

Butler, Marilyn. Jane Austen and the War of Ideas. Oxford:

Clarendon, 1975.

Lascelles, Mary. Jane Austen and Her Art. Oxford: Clarendon,

1963.

Monaghan, David. Jane Austen: Structure and Social Vision.

New York: Barnes, 1980.

Morgan, Susan. In the Meantime: Character and Perception in

Jane Austen's Fiction. Chicago: U of Chicago P, 1980.

Mudrick, Marvin. Jane Austen: Irony as Defense and Discovery.

Princeton: Princeton UP, 1952.

Sherry, James. "Pride and Prejudice: The Limits of Society."

Studies in English Literature 19 (1979): 609-22.

Tanner, Tony. Introduction. Pride and Prejudice. By Jane

Austen. New York: Viking Penguin, 1986.

Weinsheimer, Joel. "Chance and the Hierarchy of Marriages in

Pride and Prejudice." ELH 39 (1972): 404-19.

Wiesenfarth, Joseph. "The Case of Pride and Prejudice."

Studies in the Novel 16 (1984): 261-73.

6

Documenting Borrowed Material: Other Styles

In the research papers you write for your composition and literature classes, you will probably be asked to follow MLA style with in-text citations or, possibly, with endnotes. When you conduct research on almost any topic, you will encounter a wide variety of documentation styles that you will need to interpret. There is no academic discipline in which procedures are completely uniform. After mastering one style for your own use, you should have little difficulty interpreting other forms of documentation. If you choose a major in one of the natural or social sciences, papers that you write for advanced courses will probably involve a form of documentation similar to one of those described in this chapter.

The system most widely used outside the humanities is APA style, which is described in the *Publication Manual of the American Psychological Association*, 3rd ed. (Washington: APA, 1983). With some variations this style is followed in many journals in the social sciences. APA style is described in the following section and is illustrated in a sample paper at the close of the chapter. The number system of citation, which seems to be losing popularity, and the use of notes for bibliographical information are described briefly. Typical practices in nine disciplines are illustrated by examples from major journals.

APA Style

Listing References

In APA style, the sources used in a paper are listed alphabetically on a separate page headed References. If there are two or more works by the same author, they are listed chronologically; if published in the same year, they are assigned lowercase letters (e.g., 1989a, 1989b). So that APA and MLA styles can be compared, the following examples are keyed to the MLA-style examples in Chapter 5 (pages 132–53).

Book (1)

Lubben, R. T. (1988). Just-in-time manufacturing:

An aggressive manufacturing strategy. New York:

McGraw-Hill.

Harris, K. M. (1988). Hypocrisy and self-deception

in Hawthorne's fiction. Charlottesville:

University Press of Virginia.

Edition (10)

Douglas, M. S. (1988). The Everglades: River of

grass (rev. ed.). Sarasota, FL: Pineapple Press.

Multiple Authors/Editors (22)

McMahon, E., Funk, R., & Day, S. (1988). The

elements of writing about literature and film.

New York: Macmillan.

Selection in an Anthology (35)

Shevory, T. C. (1988). Winning isn't everything:

Sports fiction as a genre of political

criticism. In E. J. Yanarella & L. Sigelman(Eds.),

Political mythology and popular fiction

(pp. 61-79). New York: Greenwood.

Guidelines for Books

1. Each line after the first is indented *three* spaces (hanging indentation).

2. Authors' given names are reduced to initials. All names are inverted. An ampersand (&) joins the last two names. All authors are listed except when there are more than five, in which case et al. (and others) is used after the first name.

3. Because recency of research is important in the sciences, the date of publication, enclosed in parentheses, is the second element of the reference.

4. Only proper nouns and the first word of a title and of a subtitle are capitalized ("down style"). Titles of books are underlined.

5. An edition is designated in parentheses.

6. Editors' names are not inverted after a title. The abbreviations p. and pp. are used. Inclusive pages for a selection in an anthology or a similar compilation follow the title of the work.

7. Postal abbreviations for states are used when necessary. Publishers' names are shortened, but not as drastically as in MLA style. Names of university presses are written in full.

Periodicals. The following citations are also keyed to the examples of MLA style (pages 132–53).

Journal Paged Continuously (2)

Kehes, J. (1988). Understanding evil. American

Philosophical Quarterly, 25, 13-24.

Journal Paged Separately in Each Issue (2)

Tong, T. K. (1988). Temporary absolutism versus

hereditary autocracy. Chinese Studies in

History, 21(3), 3-22.

Weekly Magazine (2)

McIntyre, R. S. (1988, April 2). The populist tax

act of 1989. The Nation, pp. 445, 462-464.

Letter, Published (20)

Rocha, M. W. (1988). James as playwright [Letter].

PMLA, 103, 175.

Newspaper (25)

Porter, S. (1988, March 21). Why should you buy

credit life insurance. Baltimore Evening Sun,

p. C11.

Review (34)

Hecht, A. (1988, March 3). Portraits by Lowell.

[Review of Robert Lowell: Collected prose].

New York Review of Books, pp. 11-17.

Guidelines for Periodicals

1. The author and date are positioned the same as for a book. Months are not abbreviated. Military style is not used for dates (e.g., March 21, not 21 March).

2. The title of an article is not enclosed in quotation marks. Only proper nouns and the first word of a title or subtitle are capitalized.

3. Names of periodicals are underlined, are capitalized conventionally, and are not abbreviated.

4. The volume number of a quarterly is underlined. If a journal is paged separately in each issue, the issue number is given in parentheses. The abbreviations vol., p., and pp. are not used for a quarterly. Volume and page numbers are separated by a comma.

5. For a monthly, weekly, or daily periodical, p. or pp. is used for page numbers. Discontinuous pages are cited in full. Inclusive page numbers are not condensed (462–464, not 462–64).

6. Identifying terms like Letter or Review are enclosed in brackets.

If you use APA style, in compiling your list of references you can adapt other sources to the preceding forms.

Author–Date System in Citation

Authors using APA style of documentation cite entire works or large portions of works more often than specific pages, and direct quotation is relatively rare. The APA author–date system of citing sources resembles MLA style except that the citation includes the date and an abbreviation like p., pp., chap., or vol. is used.

A typical citation consists of the author's name and the year of publication:

```
Hawthorne's concern with hypocrisy can be

traced to Puritan psychology (Harris, 1988).


A recent study (Harris, 1988) concludes . . .
```

If the author is named in the text, only the year is cited:

```
According to Harris (1988) . . .
```

Specific page or chapter citations follow the year:

```
The Everglades received its name through a

misreading of River Glades on an early map

(Douglas, 1988, p. 12).
```

Other Styles

Besides MLA and APA styles, two other methods of documentation are in fairly widespread use: the *number system* and the use of *notes*.

The Number System of Citation

Some journals in biology, chemistry, computer science, mathematics, nursing, and physics use the *number system* of documentation, which assigns each source in the list of references a number. The sources are arranged either alphabetically or in the order of their appearance in the paper. Citation is accomplished within the text by inserting the appropriate numbers within parentheses. Multiple citation is common; for example:

```
Recent research (2, 6, 9) suggests . . .
```

Entire works are usually cited, but page references can be included:

```
Analysis of ionized gases (2, pp. 48-51)

suggests . . .
```

The cluster of numbers in this system can be confusing and inconvenient. It has recently been abandoned by major journals in chemistry and physics, and its use appears to be decreasing.

Documentation in Notes

Some journals place all bibliographical data in endnotes or footnotes and dispense with a list of works cited. (See the chemistry, history, and physics examples that follow.) This system is also used by many journals in art, music, philosophy, and religion. This style eliminates the repetition of publication data that occurs with the use of endnotes and a list of works cited. It is a sensible procedure and is especially appropriate in a short paper based on only a few sources, but you should use it only if your instructor gives prior approval.

Documentation in Other Disciplines _____

The documentation styles of nine academic fields are described on the following pages, and examples from major journals are shown. Yet even within the same discipline, journals may use different styles. A style manual or other source of guidelines is cited for each discipline. An authoritative guide that is not restricted to any particular field is *The Chicago Manual of Style*, 13th ed. (Chicago: U of Chicago P, 1982), which contains clear descriptions of the alternative methods of documentation. However, it is intended for professional authors, editors, and book designers and may be too technical for most student writing.

Most of the journals in the social sciences use a variation of APA style. In all fields, indentation of three spaces is standard in notes and bibliographies.

Biology (Bioscience)

```
Eickwort, G. C. 1981. Presocial insects. Pages

199-279 in H. R. Hermann, ed. Social Insects,

vol. II. Academic Press, New York.
```

Knapp, R., and T. M. Casey. 1986. Thermal

    ecology, behavior, and growth of gypsy moth

    and eastern tent caterpillars. <u>Ecology</u> 67:

    598-608.

Wilson, E. O. 1975. <u>Sociobiology: The New</u>

    <u>Synthesis</u>. Belknap Press, Cambridge, MA.

Documentation styles in biology vary greatly because there are so many subdivisions of the field, each with its own journals. The preceding forms resemble APA style with these minor variations:

1. Only the first author's name is inverted.
2. Dates are not enclosed in parentheses.
3. The publisher precedes the place of publication.
4. Volume and page numbers are separated by a colon.

The first example cites an article in an edited work. The method of citation is author–date. See Council of Biology Editors, Style Manual Committee, *CBE Style Manual: A Guide for Authors, Editors, and Publishers in the Biological Sciences*, 5th ed. (Bethesda: Council of Biology Editors, 1983).

Business (Journal of Business)

Amemiya, Takeshi. 1985. <u>Advanced Econometrics</u>.

    Cambridge, Mass.: Harvard University Press.

Donaldson, George. 1963. Financial goals:

    Management vs stockholders. <u>Harvard Business</u>

    <u>Review</u> 41 (May-June): 116-29.

McElroy, Katherine Maddox, and Siegfried, John J.

    1985. The effect of firm size and mergers on

    corporate philanthropy. <u>Quarterly Review of</u>

    <u>Economics and Business</u> 25, no. 2 (Summer):

    18-26.

The preceding forms resemble APA style with these minor variations:

1. Authors' given names are written in full, and the word *and* instead of an ampersand is used to join names.
2. Dates are not enclosed in parentheses.
3. Page numbers are preceded by a colon.

The author–date method is used for citation, and footnotes are used for explanation and reference notes. Several manuals on report-writing are available; for example, Raymond V. Lesikar, *Report Writing for Business*, 6th ed. (Homewood, IL: Irwin, 1981).

Chemistry *(American Chemical Society Journal)*

(1) Poliakoff, M.; Weitz, E. Adv. Organomet. Chem.

1986, 25, 277.

(2) Braterman, P. S. Metal Carbonyl Spectra,

Academic: New York, 1975.

(3) Conner, J. A. Top. Current Chem. 1977, 71, 71.

Articles in chemistry are written for specialists who speak the same language. Footnotes are used for citation, explanation, and reference. There is no list of works cited. Note the following space-saving shortcuts:

1. Authors' names are separated by a semicolon.
2. Titles of articles are not included; only the first page of an article is cited.
3. Names of journals are abbreviated. The year is printed in boldface type (indicated in a manuscript by a wavy line).
4. For a book, the place and year follow the name of the publisher.

See American Chemical Society, *ACS Style Guide* (Washington: American Chemical Soc., 1986).

Economics *(American Economic Review)*

Day, Theodore E., "Real Stock Returns and

Inflation," Journal of Finance, June 1984, 39,

493–502.

Jaffe, Jeffrey and Mandelker, Gershon, "The 'Fisher

Effect' for Risky Assets: An Empirical

Investigation," Journal of Finance, May 1976,

31, 447-58.

Varian, Hal R. Microeconomic Analysis, New York:

W. W. Norton, 1984.

Usage varies in economics but is basically conservative, as in business. In the preceding examples, note the following:

1. Titles of articles are quoted and are capitalized conventionally.
2. Authors' given names are written out. Joint authors are not separated by a comma.
3. A volume number for a periodical is underlined.

The author–date system is used for citation; footnotes are used for explanation and reference. See Conrad Berenson and Raymond Colton, *Research and Report Writing for Business and Economics* (New York: Random, 1971).

Education (American Educational Research Journal)

Bacharach, S. B., Conley, S., & Shedd J. (1986).

Beyond career ladders: Structuring teacher

career development systems. Teachers College

Record, 87, 563-574.

Boyer, E. L. (1983). High school: A report on

secondary education in America. New York: Harper

& Row.

DeLong, T. J. (1983, Winter). Career orientations

of rural educators: An investigation. The Rural

Educator, 12-16.

APA style predominates in education, but there are many exceptions because there are so many different types of journals. The method of citation is author–date. See National Education Association, *NEA Style Manual for Writers and Editors*, rev. ed. (Washington: National Education Assn., 1974).

History (American Historical Review)

[1] George R. Stewart, American Given Names: Their Origin and History in the Context of the English Language (New York, 1979), 29-31.

[2] Daniel Scott Smith, "Child-Naming Practices, Kinship Ties, and Change in Family Attitudes in Hingham, Massachusetts, 1641 to 1880," Journal of Social History, 18 (1985): 548.

[3] See Robert Fogel and Stanley Engerman, Time on the Cross: The Economics of American Negro Slavery, 2 vols. (Boston, 1974), 1: 126-57. Fogel and Engerman found acceptance by Afro-Americans of both a Protestant work ethic and a system of kin organization that emphasized the nuclear family. See also Genovese, Roll, Jordan, Roll, 162-63.

Because bibliographic information appears in notes, no list of works cited is necessary. Footnotes are used for citation, explanation, and reference. Combination notes are common (see note 3). After the first citation of a source, the author's last name and a short title are used (see the close of note 3). Some special features include the following:

1. Publishers' names are not included in the citation of a book.
2. In the citation of a journal, page numbers are preceded by a colon.

See Jacques Barzun and Henry F. Graff, *The Modern Researcher*, 4th ed. (New York: Harcourt, 1985).

Physics (American Journal of Physics)

[1] W. M. Hartmann, Am. J. Phys. 54, 28 (1986).

2 S. W. Shaw and P. J. Holmes, J. Sound Vib. 90,

129 (1983).

3 P. Hagedorn, <u>Non-Linear Oscillations</u>

(Clarendon, Oxford, 1981), pp. 35-43.

4 Reference 2, pp. 130-132.

As in chemistry, documentation in physics is highly condensed. Endnotes are used instead of footnotes, but the content is basically the same:

1. Titles of articles are not shown, and only the first page is cited.
2. Names of journals are abbreviated and are not underlined.
3. The volume number for a journal is in boldface (indicated by a wavy line).
4. Notes of two or more lines are not indented.
5. Secondary citations are rare, but when they occur they follow the form of note 4.

See American Institute of Physics, Publications Board, *Style Manual for Guidance in the Preparation of Papers,* 3rd ed. (New York: American Inst. of Physics, 1978).

Political Science (American Political Science Review)

Brams, Steven J. 1985. <u>Superpower Games</u>. New Haven:

Yale University Press.

Fudenberg, Drew, and Jean Tirole. 1983. Sequential

Bargaining with Incomplete Information. <u>Review</u>

<u>of Economic Studies</u> 50: 221-47.

Snyder, Glenn H. 1972. Crisis Bargaining. In

<u>International Crises</u>, ed. Charles Hermann. New

York: Free Press.

The preceding examples resemble APA style with these minor exceptions:

1. The ampersand is not used to join authors' names.
2. Dates are not enclosed in parentheses.
3. Titles of articles are not quoted but are capitalized conventionally.
4. Volume and page numbers are separated by a colon.

For a brief description of this style, which was recently adopted by the American Political Science Association, see "APSA Style Manual" in the Fall 1985 issue of *PS,* a journal published by the Association. It is also available in pamphlet form.

Sociology (American Sociological Review)

Featherman, David L. and Robert M. Hauser. 1978.

Opportunity and Change, Studies in Population.

New York: Academic Press.

Marini, Margaret Mooney. 1984a. "Age and Sequencing

Norms in the Transition to Adulthood." Social

Forces 63: 229-44.

- - -. 1984b. "The Order of Events in the

Transition to Adulthood." Sociology of Education

57: 63-84.

Documentation style in sociology has recently been revised somewhat and with minor exceptions resembles APA style:

1. Joint authors are not separated by a comma.
2. Titles of articles are quoted and capitalized conventionally.
3. Volume and page numbers are separated by a colon.

As the last two examples indicate, two or more works published in the same year by the same author are assigned lowercase letters and are arranged alphabetically. The method of citation is author–date. Basic conventions are summarized in each issue of *American Sociological Review.*

Sample Paper: APA Style _____

The paper that follows was written for a social psychology class and is documented in APA style. With minor variations this style is used in most of the social sciences, including education. Some special aspects of the documentation are noted in marginal comments. Comparing this paper with the other sample papers reveals some general differences from MLA style.

Many instructors in the social sciences require that a paper resemble as closely as possible a manuscript as it would be submitted to a journal. To assure that the writer is not identified by persons considering the paper, a word or two from the title is used as a running head above the page number. The full running head at the bottom of the title page would appear at the top of each page if the article were printed. An abstract is included as the second page of the paper. Direct quotation is used sparingly. Entire works are frequently cited instead of specific pages.

title page
numbered,
two spaces
below close of
running head

Abuse of the Elderly:

An Overlooked Form of Family Violence

Joseph Walsh

Social Psychology 212

4 May 1990

complete
running head
in full capitals

Running Head: ABUSE OF THE ELDERLY

Elder Abuse

2

Abstract

Until recently, abuse of the elderly has been ignored
by the public, by social workers, and by legislators.
Estimates of the incidence of abuse range from 500,000
to 2.5 million cases per year. Many are not reported because
the victims are more or less invisible and are not observed
by outsiders and because the victims are unwilling to report
mistreatment. They may feel ashamed of having raised an
abusive child, they often hesitate to make trouble for the
abuser, and they fear being placed in a nursing home. Typical
forms of mistreatment are physical, financial, and emotional
abuse and passive and active neglect. Women are victims more
often than men; the typical abused person is described as a
woman over 75, widowed, and physically or mentally impaired.
Researchers disagree, but most find daughters to be the most
frequent abusers. Various forms of counseling and oversight
are the measures most often suggested by social workers.
Legal or police intervention is usually resisted because it
often leads to institutionalization. Many states have no
effective adult protection laws. As the elderly population
increases, the problem will intensify unless ways of coping
with it are found.

An abstract
averages about
150 words; it
should include
all major ideas.

title included
even though
there is a title
page

Abuse of the Elderly:

An Overlooked Form of Family Violence

Newspapers, magazines, and police reports are filled
with accounts of mistreated children and battered wives, but
much less attention has been given to another form of family

author cited in
text; year and
page in
parentheses

violence--abuse of the elderly. According to Pagelow (1984,
p. 363), no scientific research was done before 1977, and
research since then has been limited to small samples. Most
writers cite an estimated range of 500,000 to 2.5 million

citation of an
entire work

cases a year. According to Gelles and Cornell (1985), many
cases are not reported because the victims are not involved
in school, employment, or shopping where their condition
could be observed by outsiders. Furthermore, the victims
themselves are unwilling to report abuse. Only one in four
cases is reported by a victim. An elderly parent may be
ashamed of having raised a violent child, may feel affection
for the abuser and not wish to cause trouble, or may fear
institutionalization. The latter fear is usually seen as the
chief reason for victims' silence about mistreatment.

reference
notes,
separated by
semicolons,
arranged
chronologically

There is disagreement on a definition of the kinds of
elder abuse, and researchers (Lau & Kosberg, 1979; Bookin &
Dunkle, 1985; Poertner, 1986; Sengstock & Barrett, 1986;

Elder Abuse

4

Valentine & Cash, 1986) propose somewhat different

categories. Most resemble those used by Powell and Berg

(1987):

    Physical abuse

    Financial abuse

    Emotional abuse

    Passive neglect

    Active neglect

Multiple abuse is common with physical, financial, and

emotional abuse as the most frequent combination.

    Pagelow (1984, p. 373) found deliberate physical abuse

in 15% to 19% of all cases. According to Poertner (1986), it

is often due to "caretaker stress." Middle-aged persons,

just when their children are becoming less dependent on them,

find their parents becoming more dependent. It is difficult

to adjust to this reversal of roles as the elderly parent

becomes more and more like a child. Taking an elderly person

into the home is often a financial burden, and it disrupts

family patterns. Resentment and frustration may be expressed

by slapping or pushing or by restraining the victim in a

chair or bed. Physical abuse, according to Eastman (1984), is

more likely to occur in a family where violence has been the

& used in citations, but not in text

author cited in text; year and page in parentheses

norm; abused children often grow up to be parent-abusers. However, stress alone would not account for a case cited by Valentine and Cash (1986, p. 25) of an 85-year-old man who was tied in his wheelchair, sexually molested, burned with cigarettes, and beaten with a stick by his nephew. Financial abuse involves an elderly person's money or property; it can range from appropriating a Social Security check to forcing the victim to sign over securities or the deed to a house. Sengstock and Barrett (1986) found this to be the most common type of abuse, but their study was based on data from a Detroit legal aid society, which would be concerned with such cases. Emotional abuse can consist of insults and ridicule, infantilization, or threats of placement in a nursing home. Passive neglect is often unintentional; it usually consists of ignoring signs of illness or mental deterioration. It may be due to the caretaker's other responsibilities or to the elderly person's wish to be independent. It is seldom reported. Active neglect is more sinister and may be motivated by a wish to hasten the death of the victim. It can involve withholding food or medicine, administering sedatives to keep the victim comatose, or refusing to dress or bathe the victim.

general
knowledge—
citation
unnecessary

Elder Abuse

6

For a number of reasons, women are more likely to be victims of abuse. They make up 61% of the population over 75, they live an average of eight years longer than men, and they are not likely to remarry. Most elderly men (77%) live with wives, but only 36% of elderly women live with husbands (Pagelow, 1984, p. 361). Pagelow describes the typical victim as a woman between 75 and 85, widowed, middle- to lower-middle class, Protestant, white, and suffering physical or mental impairment (p. 359). A survey of cases in Cleveland revealed that 51% of the elderly under treatment could not walk alone and 41% were partially or completely senile (Lau & Kosberg, 1979, p. 11). Most writers believe that the victims are dependent on the abusers for support and that dependency increases mistreatment. Pillemer (1985), however, contends that interviews with abused elders in Massachusetts, New York, and Rhode Island revealed that a majority of victims were abused by persons dependent on them for household tasks or financial assistance.

An abuser may be a neighbor or some other outsider, but it is usually a relative. Most studies indicate that daughters are the most frequent abusers. This is probably due to the fact that they are responsible for day-to-day care. Lau and

full citation: author, year, page

year in preceding citation

Elder Abuse

7

Numbers
under ten are
usually spelled
out, except
when they
occur in a series
with other
numbers.

Kosberg (1979) found that of 49 abusers, 13 were daughters, 6 were sons, and 6 were granddaughters. However, Powell and Berg (1987), in a survey of victims in Texas, found that 31.7% of the abusers were sons and only 13.3% were daughters.

The most discouraging aspect of elder abuse is that many situations seem almost hopeless. An abused child can be placed in a foster home. A battered wife can receive police protection, live in a safehouse, or obtain a divorce and start a new life. For the elderly, the possibilities are much more limited. The alternative to living with an abuser is moving to a nursing home, which they may not be able to afford and which many of the elderly dread. Fear of being abused more severely, affection for the abuser, the inability to speak clearly, as well as other special factors may prevent victims from reporting mistreatment.

Pagelow (1984) suggests improved social services: home visits, counseling of caretakers, in-home caretakers, homemaker services, community recreation, and hot lines for reporting abuse. According to Bookin and Dunkle (1985), the social work approach is not always effective because social workers concentrate on care-giving rather than abuse, and attempt to use the same methods with the elderly as with

Elder Abuse

8

abused children. According to Quinn (1985), intervention is sometimes seen as a violation of the victim's civil rights. As long as the elderly person is capable of choosing, he or she has the right to refuse treatment. The right of privacy is cherished by Americans, and social workers may find it difficult to enter a home where abuse is suspected. Legal agencies that deal with abuse tend to ignore the general family situation and try for a quick, immediate solution (Sengstock & Barrett, 1986, p. 60). Police intervention and removal of the victim is the least effective measure because it results in the loss of family ties and often causes rapid deterioration of the victim's health (Pratt, Koval, & Lloyd, 1983).

> citation of two authors

> three authors

Until recently, legislators have ignored the problem of elder abuse. All fifty states require mandatory reporting of child abuse, but only a few have a similar requirement regarding abuse of the elderly (Pratt, Koval, & Lloyd, 1983). About half the states have some kind of adult protection laws, but they differ widely and do not even agree on a definition of abuse. The problem is gradually being brought before the general public. Newsweek reported that a woman in Texas was found wearing only an old shirt, lying in filth,

> citation of a weekly magazine

and starving within a few feet of food that she could not reach. Her son, whose living quarters were neat and clean, was arrested but was set free. A police sergeant was quoted as follows: "We had all the elements for murder. . . . You can't let your children, your wife or your dog starve to death, but there's nothing in the general code that says you've got to feed your mother" (1985, September 23, p. 75). Shocking cases like this may eventually arouse public opinion to demand laws controlling the care of the elderly.

The problem of elder abuse will intensify as the older population increases. The number of people over 65 was 16.6 million in 1960 and 25.6 million in 1980. Persons 75 and older make up the fastest growing part of the population (Eastman, 1984, p. 30). According to Gelles and Cornell (1985, p. 101), of persons from 65 to 72, one in fifty needs long-term care, but of those 73 and older, one in fifteen needs it. As the elderly population increases, the problem of elder abuse will intensify. Unless the general public, social work agencies, and lawmakers become more aware of the extent of the problem and take measures to cope with it, the so-called "golden years" will be tarnished for more and more older Americans.

Elder Abuse

10

References

Abusing the elderly. (1985, September 23). Newsweek, *weekly magazine: p. or pp. used when there is no volume number*

pp. 76-77.

Bookin, D., & Dunkle, R. E. (1985). Elder abuse: *two authors joined by &; given names reduced to initials; volume number underlined*

Issues for the practitioner. Social Casework,

66, 3-12.

Eastman, P. (1984, January). Elders under siege. *monthly magazine*

Psychology Today, p. 30.

Gelles, R. J., & Cornell, C. P. (1985). Intimate *book*

violence in families. Beverly Hills: Sage.

Lau, E. E., & Kosberg, J. I. (1979, September-October). *bimonthly magazine*

Abuse of the elderly by informal care providers. Aging,

pp. 10-15.

Pagelow, M. D. (1984). Family violence. New York:

Praeger.

Pillemer, K. (1985). The dangers of dependency: New

findings on domestic violence against the elderly.

Social Problems, 33 146-158.

Poertner, J. (1986). Estimating the incidence of abused *journal paged separately in each issue; number of issue given in parentheses*

older persons. Journal of Gerontological Social Work,

9(3), 3-15.

Elder Abuse

11

Powell, S., & Berg, R. C. (1987). When the elderly are
    abused: Characteristics and intervention. Educational
    Gerontology, 13 71-83.

Pratt, C. C., Koval, J., & Lloyd, S. (1983). Service
    workers' responses to abuse of the elderly.
    Social Casework, 64, 147-153.

Quinn, M. J. (1985). Elder abuse & neglect raise new
    dilemmas. Generations, 10(2), 22-25.

Sengstock, M. C., & Barrett, S. (1986). Elderly victims
    of family abuse, neglect and maltreatment: Can legal
    assistance help? Journal of Gerontological Social Work,
    9(3), 43-61.

Valentine D., & Cash, T. (1986). A definitional discussion of
    elder maltreatment. Journal of Gerontological Social Work,
    9(3), 17-28.

& is part of
the title as
printed

Using a Word Processor

If you have learned how to use a word processor, you will probably prefer to compose your paper on a computer. If you have never used one, this would be a good time to learn, because some aspects of research writing are especially adaptable to word processing.

The use of computers and word processors by students and the general public is increasing rapidly. In some courses and in any job that involves writing, you will probably be expected to have basic computer and word-processing skills. To start, you will need two-finger typing ability, a few hours' practice to learn basic commands on the program you are using, and access to a computer. If you own a personal computer (*pc*), you can operate it in your own home, but as a beginner you will need someone to teach you basic techniques and to rescue you when the screen or *monitor* goes blank and you cannot find a command to return you to the *menu*. Perhaps your school has a computer center in which writing terminals are linked to a *mainframe computer*. The center will probably be crowded, especially at term paper time, and an appointment may be necessary; the advantage is that someone will be on duty there to answer questions and solve any problems that arise.

The simplest (and least efficient) way of using a computer is to handwrite or type a rough draft, transcribe it on a computer, and then revise the text that appears on the monitor. Another procedure is to lay out your working outline and note cards so that they are visible and type your rough draft on the computer. As you attain more expertise, you can compose an entire paper on the computer. Assign each main section of the paper a *filename* consisting of no more than eight characters and containing no numbers, spaces, or punctuation. For example, main sections of the stagecoach paper (pages 168–81) could be assigned the following filenames: *gold, coach, organiz, drivers, media*. You can type quotations, summaries, and your own comments in the appropriate files, thus creating your

229

personal database. Once enough material has been collected, you can call up each file, add, delete, or move material as necessary, and then merge the files. You can then add connective materials, smooth the blending of quotations with the text, sharpen the phrasing, and perform all other procedures of revision. You might label another file *Bibliog* and type bibliographic entries in it. Once you recorded all of your sources, you could arrange them in alphabetical order. Some programs will alphabetize lists automatically, but it is simple to move entries if your *software* does not have that capability.

For most students, a word processor is probably more useful in revising than in composing a paper. An unexpected problem is that a word-processed page is so neat in appearance that you may neglect to edit it carefully. You can add, delete, or move words simply by pressing the proper keys. Manipulating the text as it appears on the monitor is easier and more enjoyable than revising a manuscript by writing between the lines and crossing out passages. Computer keys are so sensitive to the touch that you will probably make some odd-looking typographical errors, but these are easy to correct. At first, you may prefer to print out a copy, revise it, and then type the revisions on the computer. As you become more skillful, you will be able to revise the text as it appears on the monitor. Some programs allow you to view two different files at the same time by *windowing*. For example, you could window your outline at the top of the monitor while you type your first draft.

A computer is exciting and efficient—a technological miracle. The immediacy of watching your words take shape on the screen stirs the creative imagination, as does the *cursor*, a flashing signal that indicates where you are on a line as it moves forward like the bouncing ball in a sing-along film. However, this most efficient tool must be used with care. The greatest hazard is the possibility of losing your text because you inadvertently press the wrong key or because of a power failure, a power surge, a faulty disk, or some other calamity. Magnetic scanning devices at a library exit can erase a disk, as can X-ray equipment at a security checkpoint in an airport. A safeguard against disaster is to type the command to save your text every two or three pages to ensure that it will not be lost. At the end of each writing session, it is also wise to print out what you have composed. Save the printout and your notes until the paper is completed. Another, more elaborate safeguard is to transfer your file to a back-up disk, which can be stored in a safe place and used in case something befalls the original.

Word-processing programs differ widely and new features are constantly being added by competitive manufacturers. The capabilities of machines are continually being expanded. Most programs have automatic *wraparound* or *word wrap*, which means that they will start a new line after a specified number of characters have been typed. A computer will center your title, start a new page when a specified number of lines have been typed, and number the pages. It will also *justify* (make even) the right margin by adjusting the spacing between words. Although a justified page looks attractive, it is advisable to type your research paper without justification so that proper spacing will follow punctuation marks.

In typing your first research paper, you will need practice to accustom yourself to the commands for underlining and for reference numbers. If you press the proper command before and after a title, it will be underlined when printed; but if you forget to take off the command, the printer will continue to underline until you can stop it. Similarly, if you press the *superscript* command before and after a reference number, it will be elevated a half-space and printed after the cited material. (One of the many ways MLA documentation style has simplified research writing is by eliminating most reference numbers.)

Different programs have many other capabilities. For example, if a particular expression has been used too often in the paper, you can use a *global command* to ask the computer how often it appears. The computer searches out each use of the phrase and displays them in what is called a *string*. You can then substitute other expressions in some of the sentences. The ability of some programs to search for designated expressions and replace them with other expressions is often abbreviated *SAR*. In more sophisticated software, a thesaurus offers a choice of synonyms for a general word and will automatically insert the one you prefer. Most programs can identify spelling errors, but they cannot detect misspelled proper names or homonyms like *cite-site-sight*. Techniques have been developed that can help you to identify punctuation errors. If contractions are not acceptable in your research paper, you can use the search function to find all apostrophes so that you can eliminate those that are not used with possessives. Some programs can count the number of words in each paragraph so that you can determine whether an idea has been developed fully enough. Some *style checkers* identify passive verbs, determine the ratio of monosyllabic to polysyllabic words, show the frequency of subordinate clauses, and compute the average length of sentences. You can also call up the first and last sentences of each paragraph to judge the effectiveness of the transitions used. Some programs can even create a bar graph or a pie chart from a set of numbers.

On many printers, paper is fed from a continuous roll. Perforated strips secure the paper to a *tractor*. Be sure to separate the sheets and tear off the tractor strips before submitting your paper. Some computer paper is of poor quality, but on most machines you can feed bond paper into the printer one sheet at a time. This does not take long and results in a more attractive paper. Most printers offer a choice of typefaces, but you should choose standard pica or elite type rather than Gothic script or some other fancy variety.

Despite the many ways in which a computer can facilitate composition, it cannot take the place of the writer. Vague generalities, inexact words, and awkward constructions are not improved or corrected by the computer. The ideas and language that you put into the machine are what really matter. The most important word processing, after all, takes place in your own mind.

B

Specialized Reference Works

Some basic reference works in twenty academic disciplines are listed on the following pages:

Art	Film	Political science
Biology	History	Psychology
Business	Literature	Religion
Chemistry	Music	Sociology and social
Criminal justice	Mythology and folk-	work
Ecology	lore	Women's studies
Economics	Philosophy	
Education	Physics	

Sources relevant to your topic can probably be found in at least one of these categories. Those listed for the field in which you plan to major should also be useful in future courses. When consulting any reference work, look first at the preface to determine its intended use and method of organization. Continuing publication of a work is indicated by a dash after the year, and edited works are listed by title rather than by the editor's name. Some representative databases available through DIALOG or BRS are listed for each discipline; but there are many more available, especially in business, current affairs, and the sciences. Periodicals are not included because there are literally thousands available—from special-topic newsletters to major journals. Most periodical researching is geared toward locating specific articles rather than entire journals. Articles related to your topic can be found more readily in the general periodical indexes described in Chapter 2 and the specialized indexes listed here.

Art

Arntzen, Etta Mae, and Robert Rainwater. *Guide to the Literature of Art History*. Chicago: ALA, 1981.

Art Index. New York: Wilson, 1929–. (Author–subject index to periodicals. Quarterly. Annual and biennial cumulations.)

Art Library Manual: A Guide to Resources and Practice. Ed. Philip Pacey. New York: Bowker, 1977.

Arts in America: A Bibliography. Ed. Bernard Karpel. 4 vols. Washington: Smithsonian Inst., 1979–80.

The Britannica Encyclopaedia of American Art. Chicago: Encyclopaedia Britannica, 1973.

Canaday, John. *Lives of the Painters*. 4 vols. New York: Norton, 1969.

Cheney, Sheldon. *Sculpture of the World: A History*. New York: Viking, 1969.

Dictionary of Contemporary Artists. Ed. Paul Cummings. 4th ed. New York: St. Martin's, 1982.

Dictionary of Women Artists: An International Dictionary of Women Artists Born before 1900. Ed. Chris Petteys et al. Boston: Hall, 1985.

Encyclopedia of World Art. 16 vols. New York: McGraw, 1959–83.

Gardner's Art through the Ages. 8th ed. 2 vols. New York: Harcourt, 1986. (A basic source. Revisions by various editors.)

Groce, George C., and David H. Wallace. *The New York Historical Society's Dictionary of Artists in America, 1564–1860*. New Haven: Yale UP, 1957.

Hamlin, Talbot Franklin. *Architecture through the Ages*. Rev. ed. New York: Putnam, 1953.

The Illustrated Dictionary of Art and Artists. Ed. David Piper. New York: Random, 1984.

Index of Twentieth Century Artists. 4 vols. New York: College Art Assn., 1933–37. (Rpt. Arno, 1970.)

Janson, Horst W., and Anthony Janson. *History of Art: A Survey of the Major Visual Arts from the Dawn of History to the Present Day*. 3rd ed. Englewood Cliffs: Prentice, 1986.

Jones, Lois S. *Art Research Methods and Resources: A Guide to Finding Art Information*. 2nd ed. Dubuque: Kendall/Hunt, 1984.

Larkin, Oliver W. *Art and Life in America*. Rev. ed. New York: Holt, 1960.

Lucas, Edna Louise. *Art Books: A Basic Bibliography on the Fine Arts*. Greenwich: New York Graphic Soc., 1968.

McGraw-Hill Dictionary of Art. Ed. Bernard S. Myers. 5 vols. New York: McGraw, 1969.

Macmillan Encyclopedia of Architects. Ed. Adolf K. Placzek. 4 vols. New York: Free, 1982.

Mayer, Ralph A. *A Dictionary of Art Terms and Techniques*. New York: Crowell, 1969. (Rpt. Barnes, 1981.)

Monro, Isabel S., and Kate M. Monro. *Index to Reproductions of American Paintings*. New York: Wilson, 1948. (Supplement, 1964.)

—. *Index to Reproductions of European Paintings*. New York: Wilson, 1956.

The Oxford Companion to Art. Ed. Harold Osborne. New York: Oxford UP, 1970.

Phaidon Dictionary of Twentieth Century Art. New York: Phaidon, 1973.

Praeger Encyclopedia of Art. 5 vols. New York: Praeger, 1971.

Robb, David M., and Jessie J. Garrison. *Art in the Western World*. 4th ed. New York: Harper, 1963.

Stierlin, Henri. *Encyclopedia of World Architecture*. 2nd ed. New York: Van Nostrand, 1982.

Sturgis, Russel. *A Dictionary of Architecture and Building*. 3 vols. New York: Macmillan, 1902. (Rpt. Gale, 1966.)

Walker, John Albert. *Glossary of Art, Architecture and Design Since 1945*. 2nd rev. ed. Hamden: Linnet, 1977.

Databases

ArtBibliographies Modern, DIALOG

Art Literature International (RILA), DIALOG

Arts and Humanities Search, BRS

Biology ⸻

Biological Abstracts. 1926–. (Semimonthly. Annual cumulations.)

Biological and Agricultural Index. New York: Wilson, 1964–. (Supersedes *Agricultural Index*, 1916–64. Subject index. Monthly, except August. Annual cumulations.)

Bottle, Robert T., and H. V. Wyatt. *The Use of Biological Literature*. 2nd ed. Hamden: Archon, 1971.

Davis, Elizabeth B. *Using the Biological Literature*. New York: Dekker, 1981.

A Dictionary of Birds. Ed. Bruce Campbell and Elizabeth Lack. Vermillion, SD: Buteo, 1985.

Dictionary of Life Sciences. Ed. Elizabeth A. Martin. 2nd ed. New York: Pica, 1983.

The Encyclopedia of the Biological Sciences. Ed. Peter Gray. 2nd ed. New York: Van Nostrand, 1970. (Rpt. Krieger, 1981).

Guide to the Literature of the Life Sciences. Ed. Roger Smith et al. 9th ed. Minneapolis: Burgess, 1980.

Henderson, Isabella F. *A Dictionary of Biological Terms*. 9th ed. New York: Van Nostrand, 1979.

Jaeger, Edmund C. *A Source-Book of Biological Names and Terms*. 3rd ed. Springfield, IL: Thomas, 1978.

Leftwich, A. W. *A Dictionary of Zoology*. 3rd ed. New York: Van Nostrand, 1973.

Smit, Pieter. *History of the Life Sciences: An Annotated Bibliography*. New York: Hafner, 1974.

Steen, Edwin B. *Dictionary of Biology*. New York: Barnes, 1971.

Walker's Mammals of the World. Ed. Ronald M. Nowak and John L. Paradiso. 4th ed. 2 vols. Baltimore: Johns Hopkins UP, 1975.

Willis, John C. *A Dictionary of Flowering Plants and Ferns*. 8th ed. New York: Cambridge UP, 1973.

Databases

Biosis Previews, DIALOG, BRS

Life Sciences Collection, DIALOG

Business

Accountant's Index. New York: American Inst. of CPA's 1921–. (Quarterly. Annual cumulations.)

Ammer, Christine, and Dean S. Ammer. *Dictionary of Business and Economics*. Rev. ed. New York: Free, 1986.

Bibliographic Guide to Business and Economics. Boston: Hall, 1975–. (Annual bibliographies.)

Brownstone, David M., and Gordon Carruth. *Where to Find Business Information*. 2nd ed. New York: Wiley, 1982.

Business and Economics Books, 1876–1983. New York: Bowker, 1983–.

Business Periodicals Index. New York: Wilson, 1958–. (Monthly except August. Annual cumulations.)

Commodity Year Book. New York: Commodity Research Bureau, 1939–. (Annual volumes except for 1943–47.)

Daniells, Lorna M. *Business Information Sources*. Rev. ed. Berkeley: U of California P, 1985.

Dictionary of Economics and Business. Ed. Erwin E. Nemmers. 4th ed. Totowa: Littlefield, 1978.

Encyclopedia of Business Information Sources. Ed. Paul Wasserman et al. 5th ed. Detroit: Gale, 1983.

Financial Handbook. Ed. Edward I. Altman. 5th ed. New York: Wiley, 1981.

Johannsen, Hano, and G. Terry Page. *International Dictionary of Business*. Englewood Cliffs: Prentice, 1981.

Kohler, Eric H. *Dictionary for Accountants*. Ed. W. W. Cooper and Yuji Ijiri. 6th ed. Englewood Cliffs: Prentice, 1981.

Munn, Glenn G. *Encyclopedia of Banking and Finance*. Ed. Ferdinand L. Garcia. 8th ed. Boston: Bankers, 1983.

Rice, Michael D. *Prentice-Hall Dictionary of Business, Finance and Law*. Englewood Cliffs: Prentice, 1983.

Rosenberg, Jerry M. *Dictionary of Banking and Financial Services*. 2nd ed. New York: Wiley, 1985.

Standard & Poor's Register of Corporations, Directors and Executives. New York: Standard, 1928–. (Annually.)

Wall Street Journal Index. New York: Dow, 1958–. (Monthly. Annual cumulations.)

Wyckoff, Peter. *The Language of Wall Street*. New York: Hopkinson, 1973.

Databases

Business & Industry News, DIALOG

Business Dateline, DIALOG

Harvard Business Review, DIALOG, BRS

Chemistry

Antony, Arthur. *Guide to Basic Information Sources in Chemistry.* New York: Wiley, 1979.

Chemical Abstracts. 1907–. (Semimonthly. Indexed annually and every ten years.)

The Condensed Chemical Dictionary. Ed. Gessner G. Hawley. 10th ed. New York: Van Nostrand, 1981.

Crane, Evan Jay, et al. *A Guide to the Literature of Chemistry.* 2nd ed. New York: Wiley, 1957.

Encyclopedia of Chemical Technology. Ed. Herman F. Mark et al. 3rd ed. 24 vols. New York: Wiley, 1978–84.

Handbook of Chemistry and Physics. Boca Raton, FL: CRC Press, 1913–. (Annual revisions.)

McGraw-Hill Encyclopedia of Chemistry. Ed. Sybil P. Parker. New York: McGraw, 1983.

Maizell, Robert E. *How to Find Chemical Information.* New York: Wiley, 1979.

Mellon, Melvin G. *Chemical Publications: Their Nature and Use.* New York: Wiley, 1979.

Perry's Chemical Engineers' Handbook. Ed. Don W. Green. 6th ed. New York: McGraw, 1984.

Thorpe, Jocelyn F., and M. A. Whiteley. *Thorpe's Dictionary of Applied Chemistry.* 4th ed. 12 vols. New York: Longman, 1937–56.

The Use of Chemical Literature. Ed. Robert T. Bottle. 3rd ed. Boston: Butterworth, 1979.

Woodburn, Henry M. *Using the Chemical Literature: A Practical Guide.* New York: Dekker, 1974.

Databases

Analytical Abstracts, DIALOG

CA Search, DIALOG, BRS

Heilbron, DIALOG

Criminal Justice _____

Cordasco, Francesco, and David N. Alloway. *Crime in America: Historical Patterns and Contemporary Realities. An Annotated Bibliography.* New York: Garland, 1985.

Crime and Punishment in America: An Historical Bibliography. Santa Barbara: CLIO, 1984.

Criminal Justice Abstracts. 1977–. (Quarterly.)

Criminal Justice Periodical Index. 1975–. (Three issues a year. Annual cumulations.)

Davis, Bruce L. *Criminological Bibliographies.* Westport: Greenwood, 1978.

DeSola, Ralph. *Crime Dictionary.* New York: Facts on File, 1982.

Encyclopedia of Crime and Justice. Ed. Sanford H. Kadish et al. 4 vols. New York: Free, 1983.

Felhenes, George T., and Harold K. Becker. *Law Enforcement: A Selected Bibliography.* 2nd ed. New York: Scarecrow, 1977.

Rush, George Eugene. *Dictionary of Criminal Justice.* Boston: Holbrook, 1977.

Wright, Morton. *Use of Criminology Literature.* Hamden: Archon, 1974.

Databases

Criminal Justice Periodical Index, DIALOG

NCJRS, DIALOG

Ecology _____

Air Pollution Abstracts. 1969–76. (No longer published.)

Allaby, Michael. *A Dictionary of the Environment.* New York: Van Nostrand, 1977.

Environment Abstracts. 1971–. (Monthly. Covers books, periodicals, films.)

Environment Index. New York: Environment Information Center, 1971–. (Annually.)

Handbook of Air Pollution Technology. Ed. Seymour Calvert and Harold M. Englund. New York: Wiley, 1984.

Harris, Cyril M. *Handbook of Noise Control*. 2nd ed. New York: McGraw, 1979.

Pollution Abstracts. 1970–. (Bimonthly.)

Water and Water Pollution Handbook. Ed. Leonard L. Ciaccio. 4 vols. New York: Dekker, 1971–73.

Databases

Environline, DIALOG

Environmental Bibliography, DIALOG

Pollution Abstracts, DIALOG, BRS

Economics _____

Amstutz, Mark R. *Economics and Foreign Policy: A Guide to Information Sources*. Detroit: Gale, 1977.

Bibliographic Guide to Business and Economics. Boston: Hall, 1975–. (Annually.)

The Dictionary of Modern Economics. Ed. David Pearce. 3rd ed. Cambridge: MIT, 1986.

Encyclopedia of American Economic History: Studies of the Principal Movements and Ideas. 3 vols. New York: Scribner's, 1980.

Encyclopedia of Economics. Ed. Douglas Greenwald. New York: McGraw, 1982.

Hanson, John L. *A Dictionary of Economics and Commerce*. 5th ed. Plymouth, Eng.: Macdonald, 1977.

Index of Economic Articles. 1961–. (Annually.)

Melnyk, Peter. *Economics: Bibliographic Guide to Reference Books and Information Sources*. Littleton, CO: Libraries Unlimited, 1971.

McGraw-Hill Dictionary of Modern Economics. Ed. Douglas Greenwald et al. 3rd ed. New York: McGraw, 1983.

Moffat, Donald W. *Economics Dictionary*. 2nd ed. New York: Elsevier, 1984.

The Money Encyclopedia. Ed. Harvey Rachlin. New York: Harper, 1984.

Databases

Chase Econometrics, DIALOG

Economic Literature Index, DIALOG

Education

Altbach, Philip G. *Comparative Higher Education Abroad: Bibliography and Analysis.* New York: Praeger, 1976.

Berry, Dorothea M. *A Bibliographical Guide to Educational Research.* 2nd ed. Metuchen: Scarecrow, 1980.

Best, John W., and James V. Kahn. *Research in Education.* 5th ed. Englewood Cliffs: Prentice, 1986.

Camp, William L., and Bryan L. Schwark. *Guide to Periodicals in Education and Its Academic Disciplines.* 2nd ed. Metuchen: Scarecrow, 1975.

Current Index to Journals in Education. Phoenix: Oryx, 1969–. (Monthly. Semiannual and annual indexes. Sponsored by ERIC. Various publishers. See pages 47–49.)

Dictionary of Education. Ed. Carter V. Good. 3rd ed. New York: McGraw, 1973.

Digest of Educational Statistics. Washington: GPO, 1962–. (Annually.)

Education Index. New York: Wilson, 1929–. (Author–subject index to periodicals. Monthly except July and August. Annual cumulations.)

Encyclopedia of Education. Ed. Lee C. Deighton. 10 vols. New York: Macmillan, 1971.

Encyclopedia of Educational Research. Ed. Harold E. Mitzel. 5th ed. 4 vols. New York: Macmillan, 1982.

International Dictionary of Education. Ed. G. Terry Page et al. New York: Nichols, 1977.

Kennedy, James R. *Library Research Guide to Education.* Ann Arbor: Pierian, 1979.

Leaders in Education. 5th ed. New York: Bowker, 1974.

Resources in Education. Washington: GPO, 1975–. (Entitled *Research in Education,* 1966–74. Sponsored by ERIC. Monthly indexes and abstracts. Indexes cumulated semiannually. See pages 49–50.)

Standard Education Almanac. Chicago: Marquis, 1968–. (Biennially.)

Woodbury, Marda. *A Guide to Sources of Educational Information.* 2nd ed. Washington: Information Resources, 1982.

Databases

A–V Online, DIALOG

ERIC, DIALOG, BRS

Exceptional Child Education Resources, DIALOG, BRS

Film

Armour, Robert A. *Film: A Reference Guide*. Westport: Greenwood, 1980.

Beaver, Frank E. *Dictionary of Film Terms*. New York: McGraw, 1983.

Bukalski, Peter J. *Film Research: A Critical Bibliography*. Boston: Hall, 1972.

Cowie, Peter. *Concise History of the Cinema*. 2 vols. New York: Barnes, 1971.

Film Literature Index. New York: Filmdex, 1973–. (Subject–author index. Quarterly. Annual cumulations.)

Film Review Digest. Millwood, NY: Kraus, 1975. (Quarterly. Annual cumulations.)

Geduld, Harry M., and Ronald Gottesman. *An Illustrated Glossary of Film Terms*. New York: Holt, 1973.

Halliwell, Leslie. *The Filmgoer's Companion*. 8th ed. New York: Scribner's, 1984.

International Encyclopedia of Film. Ed. Roger Manvell. New York: Crown, 1972.

International Index to Film Periodicals. Chicago: St. James, 1972–. (Annually.)

International Motion Picture Almanac. New York: Quigley, 1929–. (Annually.)

MacCann, Richard D., and Edward S. Perry. *The New Film Index: A Bibliography of Magazine Articles in English, 1930–1970*. New York: Dutton, 1975.

Manchel, Frank. *Film Study: A Resource Guide*. Rutherford: Fairleigh Dickinson UP, 1973.

New York Times Film Reviews 1913–1968. 10 vols. New York: New York Times and Arno, 1971–72. (Biennial supplements.)

The Oxford Companion to Film. Ed. Liz Anne Bawden. New York: Oxford UP, 1976.

Rehrauer, George. *The Macmillan Film Bibliography*. 2 vols. New York: Macmillan, 1982.

Sheehan, Eileen. *Moving Pictures*. South Brunswick: Barnes, 1979. (Annotated bibliography.)

Shipman, David. *The Great Movie Stars*. Rev. ed. 2 vols. New York: Hill, 1979–80.

Database

Magill's Survey of Cinema, DIALOG

History

The Almanac of American History. Ed. Arthur M. Schlesinger, Jr. New York: Putnam, 1983.

America: History and Life. 1964–. (Abstracts, book reviews, bibliographies. Quarterly. Annual cumulations.)

American Historical Association. *Guide to Historical Literature*. New York: Macmillan, 1961.

Barzun, Jacques, and Henry F. Graff. *The Modern Researcher*. 4th ed. San Diego: Harcourt, 1985.

Beers, Henry P. *Bibliographies in American History*. New York: Wilson, 1942. (Rpt. New York: Octagon, 1975. Two-volume supplement covering 1942–78, Woodbridge, CT: Research Publns., 1982.)

A Bibliography of Modern History. Ed. John Roach. New York: Cambridge UP, 1968.

Cambridge Ancient History. 12 vols. New York: Cambridge UP, 1923–39. (Revision in progress.)

Cambridge Medieval History. 8 vols. New York: Cambridge UP, 1911–36. (Revision in progress.)

Cartwright, William H., and Richard L. Watson, Jr. *The Reinterpretation of American History and Culture*. Washington: National Council for the Social Studies, 1973.

Cassara, Ernest. *History of the United States of America: A Guide to Information Sources*. Detroit: Gale, 1977.

Commager, Henry S. *Documents of American History*. 9th ed. 2 vols. New York: Appleton, 1973.

Cook, Chris. *Dictionary of Historical Terms*. London: Macmillan, 1983.

Day, Alan E. *History: A Reference Handbook*. Hamden, CT: Linnet, 1977.

Dictionary of American History. Rev. ed. 8 vols. New York: Scribner's, 1976.

A Guide to Historical Method. Ed. Robert J. Shafer. 3rd ed. Homewood, IL: Dorsey, 1980.

Harper Encyclopedia of the Modern World. New York: Harper, 1970.

Harvard Guide to American History. Ed. Frank Freidel and Richard K. Showman. Rev. ed. 2 vols. Cambridge: Harvard UP, 1982.

Historical Abstracts, 1775–1945. 1955–. (Quarterly. Cumulative index every five years.)

Historical Atlas of Britain. Ed. Malcolm Falkus and John Gillingham. New York: Continuum, 1981.

Index to Book Reviews in Historical Periodicals. Metuchen: Scarecrow, 1972–. (Annually.)

Morris, Richard B., and Jeffrey B. Morris. *Encyclopedia of American History.* 6th ed. New York: Harper, 1982.

New Cambridge Modern History. 14 vols. New York: Cambridge UP, 1957–79. (Revision of 1902–26 ed.)

The New Illustrated Encyclopedia of World History. Ed. William Langer. 2 vols. New York: Abrams, 1975.

Poulton, Helen J., and Marguerite S. Howland. *The Historian's Handbook: A Descriptive Guide to Reference Works.* Norman: U of Oklahoma P, 1972.

Recently Published Articles. 1976–. (Three issues a year.)

Shepherd, William Robert. *Shepherd's Historical Atlas.* 9th ed. New York: Barnes, 1980.

Steinberg's Dictionary of British History. Ed. Sigfrid H. Steinberg and I. H. Evans. 2nd ed. New York: St. Martin's, 1971.

Stephens, Lester D. *Historiography: A Bibliography.* Metuchen: Scarecrow, 1975.

The Times Atlas of World History. Ed. Geoffrey Barraclough. Rev. ed. Maplewood: Hammond, 1984.

Wager, W. Warren. *Books in World History: A Guide for Teachers and Students.* Bloomington: Indiana UP, 1973.

Databases

America: History and Life, DIALOG

Historical Abstracts, DIALOG

Literature

Abstracts of English Studies. 1958–. (Ten issues a year.)

Adelman, Irving, and Rita Dworkin. *The Contemporary Novel: A Checklist of Critical Literature on the British and American Novel Since 1915.* Metuchen: Scarecrow, 1972.

—.*Modern Drama: A Checklist of Critical Literature on 20th Century Plays.* Metuchen: Scarecrow, 1967.

American Authors, 1600–1900. Ed. Stanley J. Kunitz and Howard Haycraft. 8th ed. New York: Wilson, 1971.

American Literary Scholarship. Durham: Duke UP, 1963–. (Annually. Useful bibliographical essays.)

American Writers: A Collection of Literary Biographies. 4 vols. New York: Scribner's, 1974–81. (Supplements.)

Articles on American Literature, 1900–1950. Ed. Lewis G. Leary. Durham: Duke UP, 1954. (Two additional volumes cover 1950–75.)

Author Biographies Master Index. 2nd ed. 2 vols. Detroit: Gale, 1984. (Index of biographical dictionaries.)

Baker, Ernest A. *A History of the English Novel.* 11 vols. London: Witherby, 1924–39. (Rpt. Barnes, 1950.)

Baker, Nancy L. *A Research Guide for Undergraduate Students: English and American Literature.* 2nd ed. New York: MLA, 1985.

Barzun, Jacques, and Wendell Hertig. *A Catalogue of Crime.* New York: Harper, 1971. (Biographical and bibliographical information on detective fiction.)

Benet, William R. *The Reader's Encyclopedia.* 2nd ed. New York: Crowell, 1965.

Black American Writers, Past and Present: A Biographical and Bibliographical Dictionary. Ed. Theressa G. Rush et al. 2 vols. Metuchen: Scarecrow, 1975.

Black American Writers, 1773–1949: A Bibliography and Union List. Ed. Geraldine O. Matthews. Boston: Hall, 1975.

Blanck, Jacob N. *Bibliography of American Literature.* 7 vols. New Haven: Yale UP, 1955–83.

Briney, Robert E., and Edward Wood. *SF Bibliographies.* Chicago: Advent, 1972.

Cambridge History of American Literature. 4 vols. New York: Putnam, 1917–21. (Bibliography in each volume.)

Cambridge History of English Literature. 15 vols. New York: Putnam, 1907–33. (Bibliography in each volume.)

Cassis, A. F. *The Twentieth-Century English Novel: An Annotated Bibliography of General Criticism.* New York: Garland, 1977.

Columbia Dictionary of Modern European Literature. Ed. Jean-Albert Bede and William Edgerton. 2nd ed. New York: Columbia UP, 1980.

Columbia Literary History of the United States. Ed. Emory Elliot et al. New York: Columbia UP, 1988.

Contemporary Authors: A Bio-Bibliographical Guide to Current Authors and Their Works. Detroit: Gale, 1962–. (Annually.)

Contemporary Literary Criticism. Detroit: Gale, 1973. (Excerpts criticism of current books.)

Dictionary of Literary Biography. 48 vols. Detroit: Gale, 1978–. (In progress.)

Gohdes, Clarence, and Sanford E. Markovitz. *Bibliographical Guide to the Study of the Literature of the U.S.A.* 5th ed. Durham: Duke UP, 1984.

Hackett, Alice Payne, and James H. Burke. *80 Years of Best Sellers, 1895–1975.* New York: Bowker, 1977.

Holman, C. Hugh, and William Harmon. *A Handbook to Literature.* 5th ed. New York: Macmillan, 1986. (A standard reference since 1936. Originally edited by Thrall and Hibbard.)

Kuntz, Joseph M., and Nancy C. Martinez. *Poetry Explication: A Checklist of Interpretations Since 1925 of British and American Poems Past and Present.* Boston: Hall, 1980.

A Literary History of England. Ed. Albert C. Baugh. 2nd ed. New York: Appleton, 1967.

Literary History of the United States. Ed. Robert E. Spiller et al. 4th ed. 2 vols. New York: Macmillan, 1974.

MLA International Bibliography of Books and Articles on Modern Language and Literature. New York: MLA, 1921–. (The most complete bibliography. International coverage and the present title began in 1956. See pages 54–55.)

New Cambridge Bibliography of English Literature. Ed. George Watson. 5 vols. New York: Cambridge UP, 1969–77.

New Century Classical Handbook. Ed. C. Avery. New York: Appleton, 1962.

New York Times Theatre Reviews, 1870–1919. 6 vols. New York: New York Times and Arno, 1975.

New York Times Theatre Reviews, 1920–1970. 10 vols. New York: New York Times, 1971–. (Biennial supplements.)

The Oxford Companion to American Literature. Ed. James D. Hart. 5th ed. New York: Oxford UP, 1983.

The Oxford Companion to Classical Literature. Ed. Sir Paul Harvey. Rev. ed. New York: Oxford UP, 1966.

The Oxford Companion to English Literature. Ed. Margaret Drabble. 5th ed. New York: Oxford UP, 1985.

Oxford History of English Literature. 12 vols. New York: Oxford UP, 1945–. (In progress.)

Patterson, Margaret C. *Literary Research Guide.* 2nd ed. New York: MLA, 1983.

Princeton Encyclopedia of Poetry and Poetics. Ed. Alex Preminger et al. Princeton: Princeton UP, 1974.

Salem, James M. *A Guide to Critical Reviews.* 3rd ed. 5 vols. Metuchen: Scarecrow, 1984. (Index to reviews of plays and films.)

Schweik, Robert C., and Dieter Riesner. *Reference Sources in English and American Literature: An Annotated Bibliography.* New York: Norton, 1977.

Science Fiction Book Review Index, 1923–1973. Ed. Halbert W. Hall. Detroit: Gale, 1975. (A second volume covers 1974–79, and annual supplements are planned.)

The Science Fiction Encyclopedia. Ed. Peter Nicholls. Garden City: Doubleday, 1979.

Supernatural Fiction Writers: Fantasy and Horror. Ed. E. F. Bleiler. 2 vols. New York: Scribner's, 1985.

Twentieth-Century American Science Fiction Writers. Ed. David Cowart. 2 vols. Detroit: Gale, 1981.

Twentieth-Century Authors. Ed. Stanley J. Kunitz and Howard Haycraft. New York: Wilson, 1942. (Supplement, 1955.)

Twentieth-Century Short Story Explication. Ed. Warren S. Walker. 3rd ed. Hamden: Shoe String, 1977.

Databases

BIP (*Books in Print*), DIALOG, BRS

Book Review Digest, DIALOG

MLA Bibliography, DIALOG

Music _____

Abraham, Gerald. *The Concise Oxford History of Music*. New York: Oxford UP, 1979.

Anderson, Ruth. *Contemporary American Composers: A Biographical Dictionary*. 2nd ed. Boston: Hall, 1982.

Apel, Willi. *Harvard Dictionary of Music*. 2nd ed. Cambridge: Harvard UP, 1969.

Baker's Biographical Dictionary of Musicians. Ed. Nicolas Slonimsky. 7th ed. New York: Macmillan, 1984.

Barlow, Harold, and Sam Morgenstern. *A Dictionary of Musical Themes*. Rev. ed. New York: Crown, 1976.

Blom, Eric. *Everyman's Dictionary of Music*. 5th ed. New York: St. Martin's, 1971.

Davis, J. H. *Musicalia: Sources of Information in Music*. 2nd ed. Elmsford: Pergamon, 1969.

Druesedow, John F. *Library Research Guide to Music*. Ann Arbor: Pierian, 1982.

Duckles, Vincent H. *Music Reference and Research Materials: An Annotated Bibliography*. 3rd ed. New York: Free, 1974.

The Encyclopedia of Opera. Ed. Leslie Orrey. New York: Scribner's, 1976.

Fink, Robert, and Robert Ricci. *The Language of Twentieth Century Music: A Dictionary of Terms*. New York: Schirmer, 1975.

Fuld, James J. *The Book of World-Famous Music: Classical, Popular, and Folk*. Rev. and enl. ed. New York: Crown, 1971.

Grout, Donald Jay. *A History of Western Music*. 3rd ed. New York: Norton, 1980.

—.*A Short History of Opera*. 2nd ed. New York: Columbia UP, 1965.

The International Cyclopedia of Music and Musicians. Ed. Oscar Thompson. 11th ed. New York: Dodd, 1985.

Kinkle, Roger D. *The Complete Encyclopedia of Popular Music and Jazz 1900–1950*. 4 vols. New Rochelle: Arlington, 1974.

Meggett, Joan M. *Music Periodical Literature: An Annotated Bibliography of Indexes and Bibliographies*. Metuchen: Scarecrow, 1978.

Music Index. 1950–. (Monthly. Annual cumulations.)

New College Encyclopedia of Music. Ed. J. A. Westrup and F. L. Harrison. New York: Norton, 1976.

The New Grove Dictionary of Music and Musicians. Ed. Stanley Sadie. 6th ed. 20 vols. Washington: Grove's, 1980.

New Oxford Companion to Music. Ed. Denis Arnold. 2 vols. Oxford: Oxford UP, 1983.

New Oxford History of Music. Ed. Gerald Abraham et al. 10 vols. London: Oxford UP, 1957–. (In progress.)

Picerno, Vincent J. *Dictionary of Musical Terms.* Brooklyn: Haskell, 1976.

Sandburg, Larry, and Dick Weissman. *The Folk Music Sourcebook.* New York: Knopf, 1976.

Sears, Minnie E. *Song Index.* New York: Wilson, 1926. (Supplement, 1934.)

Stambler, Irwin, and Grelun Landon. *Encyclopedia of Folk, Country and Western Music.* 2nd ed. New York: St. Martin's, 1983.

Database

RILM Abstracts (*Repertoire Internationale de Litterata Musicale*), DIALOG

Mythology and Folklore ———————————

Abstracts of Folklore Studies. 1963–. (Quarterly.)

Bell, R. S. *Dictionary of Classical Mythology.* Santa Barbara: ABC–Clio, 1982.

Brunvand, Jan Harold. *The Study of American Folklore.* 3rd ed. New York: Norton, 1987.

Campbell, Joseph. *The Masks of God.* 4 vols. New York: Viking, 1959–68.

Cotterell, Arthur. *A Dictionary of World Mythology.* New York: Putnam, 1980.

Crowell's Handbook of Classical Mythology. Ed. Edward Tripp. New York: Crowell, 1970.

DeCaro, Francis A. *Women and Folklore: A Bibliographic Survey.* Westport: Greenwood, 1983.

Folklore and Literature in the United States: An Annotated Bibliography. Ed. Steven S. Jones. New York: Garland, 1984.

Diehl, Katherine S. *Religions, Mythologies, Folklores: An Annotated Bibliography.* 2nd ed. Metuchen: Scarecrow, 1962.

Frazer, Sir James. *The Golden Bough.* 3rd ed. 12 vols. New York: St. Martin's, 1955. (A basic source. Various editions and publishers.)

Funk & Wagnall's Standard Dictionary of Folklore, Mythology, and Legend. Ed. Maria Leach. New York: Funk, 1973. (Reissue of two-volume edition published 1949–50).

Gayley, Charles M. *The Classic Myths in English Literature and Art*. Rev. ed. Boston: Ginn, 1939.

Hamilton, Edith. *Mythology*. Boston: Little, 1942.

Handbook of American Folklore. Ed. Richard M. Dorson. Bloomington: Indiana UP, 1983.

Haywood, Charles. *A Bibliography of North American Folklore and Folksong*. 2nd ed. 2 vols. New York: Dover, 1961.

Mythology of All Races. 13 vols. New York: Cooper Square, 1964. (Rpt. of 1916–32 ed.)

Radford, Edwin, and Mona Radford *Encyclopedia of Superstitions*. Rev. ed. Chester Springs, PA: Dufour, 1969.

Thompson, Stith. *Motif-Index of Folk-Literature*. Rev. ed. 6 vols. Bloomington: Indiana UP, 1955–58.

Thorndike, Lynn. *A History of Magic and Experimental Science*. 8 vols. New York: Columbia UP, 1934–58.

Philosophy

Baldwin, James M. *Dictionary of Philosophy and Psychology*. 3 vols. New York: Macmillan, 1901–05. (Useful though out of date. Rpt. Gordon, 1977.)

Bertman, Martin A. *A Research Guide in Philosophy*. Morristown: General Learning, 1974.

The Concise Encyclopedia of Western Philosophy and Philosophers. Ed. James O. Urmson. 2nd ed. London: Hutchinson, 1975.

Copleston, Frederick. *A History of Philosophy*. 9 vols. Garden City: Doubleday, 1977.

Dictionary of the History of Ideas: Studies of Selected Pivotal Ideas. Ed. Philip P. Wiener et al. 5 vols. New York: Scribner's, 1973–74.

The Encyclopedia of Philosophy. 8 vols. New York: Macmillan, 1967.

Koren, Henry J. *Research in Philosophy: A Bibliographical Introduction*. Pittsburgh: Duquesne UP, 1966.

Lacey, Alan R. *A Dictionary of Philosophy*. London: Routledge, 1976.

New Dictionary of Existentialism. Ed. St. Elmo Nauman, Jr. New York: Philosophical Library, 1971.

Philosopher's Index. 1967–. (Quarterly author–subject index to periodicals. A three-volume supplement published in 1978 indexes U.S. periodicals from 1940.)

Tice, Terence N., and Thomas P. Slavens. *Research Guide to Philosophy.* Chicago: ALA, 1983.

Database

Philosopher's Index, DIALOG

Physics _____

Concise Dictionary of Physics and Related Subjects. New York: Oxford UP, 1986.

The Encyclopedia of Physics. Ed. Robert Besancon. 3rd ed. New York: Van Nostrand, 1985.

Encyclopedia of Physics. Ed. Rita G. Lerner and George L. Trigg. Reading, MA: Addison, 1981.

Handbook of Chemistry and Physics. Boca Raton, FL: CRC Press, 1913–. (Annual revisions.)

McGraw-Hill Dictionary of Physics and Mathematics. Ed. Daniel N. Lapedes. New York: McGraw, 1978.

A New Dictionary of Physics. Ed. Harold J. Gray and Alan Isaacs. New York: Longman, 1975.

Parke, Nathan G. *Guide to the Literature of Mathematics and Physics.* 2nd ed. New York: Dover, 1958.

Science Abstracts. London: Inst. of Electrical Engineers, 1898–. (Semimonthly. Semiannual author–subject index.)

Thewlis, James. *Encyclopaedic Dictionary of Physics.* 9 vols. Elmsford: Pergamon, 1961–64. (Supplements, 1966–75.)

Whitford, R. H. *Physics Literature: A Reference Manual.* 2nd ed. Metuchen: Scarecrow, 1968.

Databases

Inspec, DIALOG, BRS

SciSearch, DIALOG

SPIN (Searchable Physics Information Notices), DIALOG

Political Science

ABC Pol. Sci. Santa Barbara: ABC–Clio, 1969–. (Author–subject indexes to periodicals. Six issues a year.)

The Book of the States. Chicago: Council of State Governments, 1935–. (Biennially.)

Brock, Clifton. *The Literature of Political Science: A Guide for Students, Librarians and Teachers.* New York: Bowker, 1969.

Congressional Record. 1873–. (Daily. Cumulated for each session. See page 140.)

Day, Alan J., and Henry W. Degenhardt. *Political Parties of the World.* Detroit: Gale, 1984.

A Dictionary of Politics. Ed. Walter Z. Laqueur. Rev. ed. New York: Free, 1974.

Garson, G. David. *Handbook of Political Science Methods.* 2nd ed. Boston: Holbrook, 1976.

Greenstein, Fred I., and Nelson W. Polsby. *Handbook of Political Science.* 9 vols. Reading, MA: Addison, 1975. (Bibliographic essays.)

Holler, Frederick L. *The Information Sources of Political Science.* 4th ed. 5 vols. Santa Barbara: ABC–Clio, 1985.

LaBarr, Dorothy F., and Joel D. Singer. *The Study of International Politics: A Guide to the Sources for the Student, Teacher and Researcher.* Santa Barbara: ABC–Clio, 1976.

Municipal Year Book. Chicago: International City Managers Assn., 1934–.

Pfaltzgraff, Robert L., Jr. *The Study of International Relations: A Guide to Information Sources.* Detroit: Gale, 1977.

Plano, Jack C., and Milton Greenberg. *The American Political Dictionary.* 7th ed. New York: Holt, 1985.

Political Handbook of the World. New York: McGraw, 1975–. (Biennial revisions. Entitled *Political Handbook and Atlas of the World,* 1927–74.)

Smith, Edward C., and Arnold J. Zurcher. *Dictionary of American Politics.* 2nd ed. New York: Barnes, 1968.

Vose, Clement E. *A Guide to Library Sources in Political Science: American Government.* Washington: American Political Science Assn., 1975.

Yearbook of the United Nations. New York: United Nations, 1947–.

Databases

Congressional Record Abstracts, DIALOG

PAIS (Public Affairs Information Service) International, DIALOG, BRS

U.S. Political Science Documents, DIALOG

Washington Presstext, DIALOG

Psychology

Alexander, Franz G., and Sheldon T. Selsnick. *The History of Psychiatry: An Evaluation of Psychiatric Thought and Practice from Prehistoric Times to the Present.* New York: Harper, 1966.

American Handbook of Psychiatry. Ed. Silvano Arieti et al. 2nd ed. 8 vols. New York: Basic, 1974–86.

Annual Review of Psychology. Palo Alto: Annual Reviews, 1950–.

Bachrach, Arthur J. *Psychological Research: An Introduction.* 4th ed. New York: Random, 1981.

Bell, James E. *A Guide to Library Research in Psychology.* Dubuque: Brown, 1971.

Borchardt, Dietrich H., and R. D. Francis. *How to Find out in Psychology.* Elmsford: Pergamon, 1984.

Chaplin, James P. *Dictionary of Psychology.* Rev. ed. New York: Dell, 1985.

Dictionary of Behavioral Science. Ed. Benjamin B. Wolman. New York: Van Nostrand, 1974.

Drever, James A. *A Dictionary of Psychology.* Rev. ed. Baltimore: Penguin, 1964.

Encyclopedia of Mental Health. Ed. Albert Deutsch. 6 vols. New York: Watts, 1963.

Encyclopedia of Psychoanalysis. Ed. Ludwig Eidelberg. New York: Free, 1968.

Encyclopedia of Psychology. Ed. Hans J. Eysenck et al. 3 vols. New York: Herder, 1979.

Handbook of Abnormal Psychology. Ed. Hans J. Eysenck. San Diego: Knapp, 1973.

Harvard List of Books in Psychology. 4th ed. Cambridge: Harvard UP, 1971.

International Encyclopedia of Psychiatry, Psychology, Psychoanalysis, and Neurology. Ed. Benjamin B. Wolman. 12 vols. New York: Van Nostrand, 1977.

Longman Dictionary of Psychology and Psychiatry. Ed. Robert M. Goldenson. New York: Longman, 1984.

Loutitt, Chauncey M. *Handbook of Psychological Literature.* New York: Gordon, 1974.

McInnis, Raymond G. *Research Guide for Psychology.* Westport: Greenwood, 1982.

Nordby, Vernon J., and Calvin S. Hall. *A Guide to Psychologists and Their Concepts.* San Francisco: Freeman, 1974.

Psychological Abstracts. 1927–. (Monthly. Annual cumulations.)

Wilkening, Howard E. *The Psychology Almanac: A Handbook for Students.* Monterey: Brooks, 1973.

Zusne, Leonard. *Bibliographical Dictionary of Psychology.* Westport: Greenwood, 1984.

Databases

Mental Health Abstracts, DIALOG

PsycALERT, DIALOG, BRS

PsycINFO, DIALOG, BRS

Religion

Bach, Marcus. *Major Religions of the World: Their Origins, Basic Beliefs, and Development.* Nashville: Abingdon, 1977.

A Catholic Dictionary. 3rd ed. Ed. Donald Attwater. New York: Macmillan, 1958.

Catholic Periodical and Literature Index. New York: Catholic Library Assn., 1968–. (Bimonthly. Biennial cumulations.)

Dictionary of American Religious Biography. Ed. Henry W. Bowden. Westport: Greenwood, 1977.

A Dictionary of Comparative Religion. Ed. S. G. F. Brandon. New York: Scribner's, 1970.

Encyclopaedia Judaica. 16 vols. New York: Macmillan, 1972.

Gaustad, Edwin S. *Historical Atlas of Religion in America.* Rev. ed. New York: Harper, 1976.

Guide to Hindu Religion. Ed. David J. Dell et al. Boston: Hall, 1981.

Harper's Bible Dictionary. Ed. Paul W. Achtmeier, 2nd ed. New York: Harper, 1985.

Hastings, James. *Encyclopaedia of Religion and Ethics.* 2nd ed. 12 vols. New York: Scribner's, 1907–27.

The Interpreter's Dictionary of the Bible. Ed. George A. Buttrick and Keith R. Crim. 5 vols. Nashville: Abingdon, 1962–76.

Kennedy, James R. *Library Research Guide to Religion and Theology.* 2nd ed. Ann Arbor: Pierian, 1979.

Mead, Frank S. *Handbook of Denominations in the United States.* 8th ed. Nashville: Abingdon, 1985.

Nelson's Complete Concordance of the New American Bible. Nashville: Nelson, 1977.

New Catholic Encyclopedia. 17 vols. New York: McGraw, 1967–79.

New Schaff-Herzog Encyclopedia of Religious Knowledge. 13 vols. Grand Rapids: Baker, 1949–50. (Two-volume supplement, *Twentieth Century Encyclopedias of Religions,* 1955.)

New Standard Jewish Encyclopedia. Ed. Cecil Roth and Geoffrey Wigoder. 5th ed. Garden City: Doubleday, 1977.

Oxford Dictionary of the Christian Church. Ed. F. L. Cross and Elizabeth A. Livingstone. 2nd ed. New York: Oxford UP, 1974.

A Reader's Guide to the Great Religions. Ed. Charles J. Adams. 2nd ed. New York: Free, 1977. (Bibliographic essays.)

Reese, William L. *Dictionary of Philosophy and Religion, Eastern and Western Thought.* Atlantic Highland, NJ: Humanities, 1980.

Religious and Theological Abstracts. 1985–. (Quarterly.)

Rice, Edward. *Eastern Definitions: A Short Encyclopedia of Religions of the Orient.* Garden City: Doubleday, 1978.

Shorter Encyclopedia of Islam. Ed. H. A. Gibb and J. H. Kramers. Ithaca: Cornell UP, 1957.

Strong, James. *Exhaustive Concordance of the Bible.* London: Hodder, 1895. (Rev. ed., Abingdon, 1980.)

Wilson, J. F., and Thomas Slavens. *Research Guide to Religious Studies.* Chicago: ALA, 1982.

World Christian Encyclopedia: A Comparative Study of Churches and Religions in the Modern World, AD 1900–2000. Ed. David B. Barrett. Oxford: Oxford UP, 1982.

Yoo, Yushin. *Books in Buddhism: An Annotated Study Guide.* Metuchen: Scarecrow, 1976.

Database

Religion Index, DIALOG, BRS

Sociology and Social Work

Bart, Pauline, and Linda Frankel. *The Student Sociologist's Handbook.* 4th ed. New York: Random, 1986.

Dictionary of Sociology and Related Sciences. Ed. Henry Pratt Fairchild. Totowa: Littlefield, 1977.

Encyclopedia of Social Work. New York: National Assn. of Social Workers, 1965–. (Annually.)

Encyclopedia of Sociology. Rev. ed. Guilford, CT: DPG Reference, 1981.

The Harvard Encyclopedia of American Ethnic Groups. Ed. Stephan Thernstrom et al. Cambridge: Harvard UP, 1980.

International Encyclopedia of the Social Sciences. Ed. D. E. Sills. 18 vols. New York: Macmillan, 1968–80.

Reference Sources in Social Work: An Annotated Bibliography. Ed. James H. Conrad. Metuchen: Scarecrow, 1982.

Social Work Research and Abstracts. New York: National Assn. of Social Workers, 1977–. (Quarterly. Indexes cumulated annually. Supersedes *Abstracts for Social Workers,* 1965–77.)

Sociological Abstracts. 1952–. (Six issues a year.)

Sociology of America: A Guide to Information Sources. Ed. Charles Mark and Paula F. Mark. Detroit: Gale, 1976.

Databases

Child Abuse and Neglect, DIALOG

Family Resources, DIALOG, BRS

Population Bibliography, DIALOG

Sociological Abstracts, DIALOG, BRS

Women's Studies

Davis, Audrey B. *Bibliography on Women: With Special Emphasis on Their Roles in Science and Society.* New York: Science History, 1974.

Haber, Barbara. *Women in America: A Guide to Books, 1963–1975.* Urbana: U of Illinois P, 1981.

Hughes, Marija M. *The Sexual Barrier: Legal, Medical, Economic and Social Aspects of Sex Discrimination*. Washington: Hughes, 1977.

Lerner, Gerda. *Black Women in White America*. New York: Pantheon, 1972.

Macksey, Joan et al. *The Book of Women's Achievements*. New York: Stein, 1976.

Notable American Women, 1607–1950: A Biographical Dictionary. 3 vols. Ed. Edward T. James and Janet W. James. Cambridge: Harvard UP, 1971.

Notable American Women, the Modern Period: A Biographical Dictionary. Ed. Barbara Sicherman and Carol Hurd Green. Cambridge: Harvard UP, 1980.

Schwartz, Narda L. *Articles on Women Writers: A Bibliography*. Santa Barbara: ABC–Clio, 1977. (Covers 1960–75. 1985 Supplement covers 1976–84.)

Stineman, Esther, and Catherine Loeb. *Women's Studies: A Recommended Core Bibliography*. Littleton, CO: Libraries Unlimited, 1979.

Sullivan, Kaye. *Films for, by, and about Women*. Metuchen: Scarecrow, 1980.

Warren, Mary Anne, *The Nature of Women: An Encyclopedia and Guide to the Literature*. Inverness, CA: Edgepress, 1979.

Who's Who of American Women. Chicago: Marquis, 1958–. (Biennially.)

Williams, Ora. *American Black Women in the Arts and Social Sciences: A Bibliographic Survey*. Rev. ed. Metuchen: Scarecrow, 1978.

The Women's Rights Almanac. Bethesda: Stanton, 1974–.

The Women's Rights Movement in the Seventies. Ed. Albert Krichmar et al. Metuchen: Scarecrow, 1977.

The Women's Rights Movement in the United States, 1848–1970: A Bibliography and Sourcebook. Ed. Albert Krichmar. Metuchen: Scarecrow, 1972.

Women's Studies Abstracts. 1972–. (Quarterly. Annual index.)

Women's Studies: An Interdisciplinary Collection. Ed. Kathleen O. Blumhagen and Walter D. Johnson. Westport: Greenwood, 1978.

Women's Work and Women's Studies. New York: Barnard Coll., 1972–. (Annual bibliographies.)

Database

Catalyst Resources for Women, BRS

Library Terms and Abbreviations

Like all professionals, librarians have their own specialized vocabulary. Some of the more common library terms and abbreviations are defined here.

abstract A summary of the substance of a work. In some scholarly journals, an abstract precedes each article. Collections (e.g., *Psychological Abstracts*) enable you to estimate the potential usefulness of an article before looking for the original.

ALA American Library Association.

analytical entry A catalog card for a portion of a book (e.g., a play in an anthology).

annotated bibliography Identification and brief evaluation of each entry. Also called a *critical bibliography*.

BIP *Books in Print*. Annual author, title, and subject indexes of books currently available from publishers.

CBEL *Cambridge Bibliography of English Literature*. The revised edition is designated *NCBEL*.

CBI *Cumulative Book Index*. A monthly author, title, and subject listing of books published in English. Annual and biennial cumulations.

CIS Congressional Information Service, publisher of indexes and abstracts of government publications.

cumulation The recombination of entries from several issues of a serial into a single alphabetical arrangement.

DAB *Dictionary of American Biography*.

DAE *Dictionary of American English*.

database A collection of computerized data (often bibliographical) available through a public or a commercial computer service.

descriptor A reference word keyed to an entry in an index; for example, subject headings in a card catalog or key words in *Roget's Thesaurus*. The use of descriptors (also called *search terms, key words, primary terms,* or *permuterms*) is increasing rapidly, because they are essential to the retrieval of computerized data.

dictionary catalog A card catalog in which author, title, and subject cards are filed in a single alphabetization.

divided catalog A card catalog in which author, title, and subject cards are filed in separate alphabetizations. Sometimes title and subject cards are combined and author cards are filed separately.

DNB *Dictionary of National Biography*.

edition The bound copies of a book printed from a single setting of type. A new edition is presumably a revision.

ERIC Educational Resources Information Center (See pages 47–49).

f Folio, a book more than fifteen inches high. On a catalog card, "f" indicates that a book is large and is not shelved in accordance with its call number. Ask a librarian where oversized books are located. (See "q.")

Festschrift A collection of essays by several authors, published in a memorial volume to honor an event or a person, usually a scholar.

GPO Government Printing Office.

incunabula Books printed from movable type before 1501.

journal Used in two senses: (1) a publication like a newspaper or a weekly news magazine; (2) a periodical intended for specialists, often termed a *scholarly journal* (e.g., *Journal of Literary Semantics*).

LC Library of Congress.

LHUS *Literary History of the United States*.

magazine A weekly or monthly periodical of general interest. Most magazines are paged separately in each issue; most scholarly journals are paged continuously throughout a volume.

OED *Oxford English Dictionary*.

online A computer term indicating that information is accessible.

Per. Periodical. "Per." typed at the top of a catalog card indicates that a work is shelved in the Periodical Room.

Periodical A publication that appears at regular intervals. Generally used for magazines and journals: occasionally used for newspapers as well.

q Quarto, a book eleven to fifteen inches high. (See "f.")

quarterly A scholarly journal published four times a year (e.g. *Southern Folklore Quarterly*).

recto The front of a printed page, the right-hand page of an opened book (always odd-numbered).

Ref. Reference. On a catalog entry, "Ref." indicates that a work is shelved in the Reference Room.

review A journal devoted chiefly to criticism (e.g. *Sewanee Review*).

see A cross-reference from a heading that is not used to one that is used (viable).

see also A cross-reference from one viable heading to another viable heading. Sometimes abbreviated *sa*.

serial A general term for any publication issued in a consecutive, indefinitely continuing sequence; for example, periodicals, newspapers, yearbooks, installments of a long work published in successive issues of a periodical.

shelf list A library's holdings arranged by call numbers, often in the form of a computer printout.

TLS (London) *Times Literary Supplement*.

tracing Descriptors on a catalog card that indicate other headings under which the work is listed. Also called *added entries*.

ULS *Union List of Serials*. A listing of American magazines, their publishing history, and libraries where they can be found.

union catalog A card catalog of the holdings of a group of cooperating libraries. Useful for obtaining publication data as well as for locating books not in your school library.

verso The back of a printed page, the left-hand page of an opened book (always even-numbered).

vertical file Pamphlets, clippings, and similar material not listed in the card catalog may be assigned subject headings and filed in folders placed in a file drawer. (Termed a *vertical file* because items are filed standing on edge or vertically.)

Abbreviations and Reference Words

The use of *abbreviations* and *reference words* in documentation is acceptable; in the text of a research paper they should be enclosed in parentheses. Consistency and clarity are essential in the use of these forms. None should be used that do not save space and the reader's time. If you feel that an abbreviation might be misinterpreted, it is better to write it out in full.

Scholarly Forms _____

For some years there has been a trend away from the use of Latin forms in scholarly writing. *Vide* is an example of an unnecessary Latin reference word, for it contains one more letter than its English equivalent, *see*. You will probably find a few Latin forms useful in your paper, and you will need to know others that you will encounter in your reading. Latin words and abbreviations like *et al.* and *sic* that have been assimilated into English are usually not underlined. You should learn and follow the preference of

263

your instructor. Foreign words that have not been adopted into English should be underlined. If you are in doubt about the status of a word, consult a dictionary.

Abbreviations consisting of all capital letters are usually written without periods or spaces between the letters (e.g., AD, BC, GPO, MLA). However, periods are used in most abbreviations made up of lowercase letters (e.g., a.m., p.m., i.e., rpt., n.p.).

abbr.   abbreviated, abbreviation

abr.   abridged

AD   *anno Domini*, the year of the Lord (precedes numerals: AD 1989)

adapt.   adapted by, adaptation

aet.   *aetatis*, at the age of

ALS   autograph letter signed

anon.   anonymous

ante   before

app.   appendix

approx.   approximate, approximately

art.   article

assn.   association

b.   born

BC   before Christ (used after numerals: 421 BC)

bibliog.   bibliography, bibliographer

biog.   biography, biographer

bk.   book

bull.   bulletin

©   copyright (followed by the year)

c., ca.   *circa*, about (used with approximate dates: c. 1340)

cf.   *confer*, compare (used chiefly in reference notes to call attention to a contrasting opinion)

ch., chs.   chapter, chapters

col.   column

comp.   compiled by, compiler

Cong. Rec.   *Congressional Record*

cp.   compare

d.   died

dept.   department

dir.   directed by, director

diss.   dissertation

doc.   document

ed.   edited by, editor, edition

e.g.   *exempli gratia*, for example (preceded and followed by commas; do not confuse with i.e.)

enl.   enlarged

esp.   especially (as in "See Simpson, esp. ch. 3")

et al. *et alii*, and others (used for more than three authors in MLA style and for more than five authors in APA style)

et seq. *et sequens*, and the following

etc. *et cetera*, and so forth (avoid using whenever possible; never write *&c* or *and etc.*)

f., ff. and the following page, pages (used after a page number, but *31–38* is preferable to *31ff.*)

fig. figure

fl. *flourit*, flourished, lived (used when dates of birth and death are unknown: fl. 1182–1206)

front. frontispiece

ibid. *ibidem*, in the same place (used only in citation notes; never used in MLA style and seldom in any other)

idem the same as previously mentioned

i.e. *id est*, that is (preceded and followed by commas)

illus. illustrated by, illustrator, illustration

infra below

introd. introduced by, introduction

jour. journal

K, KB kilobytes (units of memory in a computer)

l., ll. line, lines (avoid using if it could be confused with the numbers one or eleven)

loc. cit. *loco citato*, in the place cited (an obsolete Latin term; used in the text to refer to a passage already cited)

mag. magazine

misc. miscellaneous

ms., mss. manuscript, manuscripts

n, nn note, notes ("118n" means a note on page 118)

narr. narrated by, narrative, narration

NB *nota bene*, mark well, take careful note (use is seldom advisable in student papers)

n.d. no date of publication

no. number

n.p. no place of publication, when used before the colon in a listing for a book; no publisher, when used after the colon

n. pag. no pagination

n.s. new series (used with periodicals published in more than one sequence of volumes)

NS New Style (used when necessary for a date after 1752 reckoned by the Gregorian calendar)

obs. obsolete

op. cit. *opere citato*, the work cited (used after an author's name in a secondary citation; never used in MLA style; virtually obsolete)

o.s. old series, original series (used with periodicals; cf. ns)

OS   Old Style (used when necessary for a date before 1752 reckoned by the Julian calendar)

p., pp.   page, pages (not used before page numbers in MLA style)

passim   here and there throughout a work (used for scattered references: Ch. 6 passim or 124–35 et passim)

per se   in or of itself (avoid using if possible)

post   after

pref.   preface

prod.   produced by, producer

pseud.   pseudonym

pt.   part

qtd.   quoted

q.v.   *quod vide,* which see (used for a cross-reference)

rev.   revised by, revised; reviewed by, review (write out if ambiguous)

rpm   revolutions per minute (used without periods in describing recordings)

rpt.   reprint, reprinted by

sc.   scene (not used when the act number is also shown: *Hamlet* 3.2)

scil.   *scilicet,* namely

ser.   series

sess.   session

sic   thus (written in brackets after an obvious errer [sic] in a quotation)

soc.   society

st.   stanza

sup.   *supra,* above

supp.   supplement

s.v.   *sub verbo,* under the word (used to refer to an item in an alphabetized listing)

TLS   typewritten letter signed

ts., tss.   typescript, typescripts

var.   variant

v., vid.   *vide,* see

v., vs.   *versus,* against (used in titles of legal cases)

viz.   *videlicit,* namely, that is

vol.   volume

Publishers' Names

The *MLA Handbook* recommends that short forms be used for publishers' names in bibliographic entries. If a name is usually abbreviated, the abbreviation is acceptable: for example, GPO (Government Printing

Office), MLA (Modern Language Association), UMI (University Microfilms International). The words *University Press* are abbreviated as *UP* (without periods) and are placed where they occur in the official name of the press:

Yale UP
U of Chicago P
State U of New York P

The short forms for some well-known commercial publishers are listed here. Other publishers' names can be shortened in similar fashion.

Abrams   Harry N. Abrams, Inc.
ALA   American Library Association
Allen   George Allen and Unwin Publishers, Inc.
Allyn   Allyn and Bacon, Inc.
Appleton   Appleton-Century-Crofts
Ballantine   Ballantine Books, Inc.
Bantam   Bantam Books, Inc.
Barnes   Barnes and Noble Books
Basic   Basic Books, Inc.
Beacon   Beacon Press, Inc.
Bowker   R. R. Bowker Co.
Dell   Dell Publishing Co., Inc.
Dodd   Dodd, Mead & Co.
Doubleday   Doubleday and Co., Inc.
Dover   Dover Publications, Inc.
Dutton   E. P. Dutton, Inc.
Farrar   Farrar, Straus, & Giroux, Inc.
Free   The Free Press
Funk   Funk and Wagnalls, Inc.
Gale   Gale Research Co.
Harcourt   Harcourt Brace Jovanovich, Inc.
Harper   Harper & Row, Publishers, Inc.
Heath   D. C. Heath and Co.
Holt   Holt, Rinehart & Winston, Inc.
Houghton   Houghton Mifflin Co.
Knopf   Alfred A. Knopf, Inc.
Lippincott   J. B. Lippincott Co.
Little   Little, Brown & Co.
Macmillan   Macmillan Publishing Company
McGraw   McGraw-Hill, Inc.
Merrill   Merrill Publishing Co.
Norton   W. W. Norton and Co., Inc.
Penguin   Penguin Books, Inc.
Pocket   Pocket Books
Prentice   Prentice-Hall, Inc.
Putnam's   G. P. Putnam's Sons

Rand Rand McNally and Co.
Random Random House, Inc.
St. Martin's St. Martin's Press, Inc.
Scott Scott, Foresman and Co.
Scribner's Charles Scribner's Sons
Simon Simon & Schuster, Inc.
Viking The Viking Press, Inc.

Months and States

Months of more than four letters are abbreviated in a citation but are written out in the text of a paper.

Jan.	May	Sept.
Feb.	June	Oct.
Mar.	July	Nov.
Apr.	Aug.	Dec.

Similarly, states are abbreviated after the name of a city in a citation; in the name of a university press and in most other instances, a state should be written out. The two-letter postal forms (written without periods) are recommended by MLA.

Alabama	AL	Kentucky	KY	North Dakota	ND
Alaska	AK	Louisiana	LA	Ohio	OH
Arizona	AZ	Maine	ME	Oklahoma	OK
Arkansas	AR	Maryland	MD	Oregon	OR
California	CA	Massachusetts	MA	Pennsylvania	PA
Colorado	CO	Michigan	MI	Rhode Island	RI
Connecticut	CT	Minnesota	MN	South Carolina	SC
Delaware	DE	Mississippi	MS	South Dakota	SD
District of		Missouri	MO	Tennessee	TN
Columbia	DC	Montana	MT	Texas	TX
Florida	FL	Nebraska	NE	Utah	UT
Georgia	GA	Nevada	NV	Vermont	VT
Hawaii	HI	New Hampshire	NH	Virginia	VA
Idaho	ID	New Jersey	NJ	Washington	WA
Illinois	IL	New Mexico	NM	West Virginia	WV
Indiana	IN	New York	NY	Wisconsin	WI
Iowa	IA	North Carolina	NC	Wyoming	WY
Kansas	KS				

Books of the Bible

The following abbreviations and words are used for books of the Bible. They are not underlined.

OLD TESTAMENT (OT)		*NEW TESTAMENT (NT)*	
Gen.	Genesis	Matt.	Matthew
Exod.	Exodus	Mark	Mark
Lev.	Leviticus	Luke	Luke
Num.	Numbers	John	John
Deut.	Deuteronomy	Acts	Acts
Josh.	Joshua	Rom.	Romans
Judg.	Judges	1 Cor.	First Corinthians
Ruth	Ruth	2 Cor.	Second Corinthians
1 Sam.	First Samuel	Gal.	Galatians
2 Sam.	Second Samuel	Eph.	Ephesians
1 Kings	First Kings	Phil.	Philippians
2 Kings	Second Kings	Col.	Colossians
1 Chron.	First Chronicles	1 Thess.	First Thessalonians
2 Chron.	Second Chronicles	2 Thess.	Second Thessalonians
Ezra	Ezra	1 Tim.	First Timothy
Neh.	Nehemiah	2 Tim.	Second Timothy
Esth.	Esther	Tit.	Titus
Job	Job	Philem.	Philemon
Ps.	Psalms	Heb.	Hebrews
Prov.	Proverbs	Jas.	James
Eccles.	Ecclesiastes	1 Pet.	First Peter
Song Sol.	Song of Solomon	2 Pet.	Second Peter
Isa.	Isaiah	1 John	First John
Jer.	Jeremiah	2 John	Second John
Lam.	Lamentations	3 John	Third John
Ezek.	Ezekiel	Jude	Jude
Dan.	Daniel	Rev.	Revelation
Hos.	Hosea		
Joel	Joel		
Amos	Amos		
Obad.	Obadiah		
Jon.	Jonah		
Mic.	Micah		
Nah.	Nahum		
Hab.	Habakkuk		
Zeph.	Zephaniah		
Hag.	Haggai		
Zech.	Zechariah		
Mal.	Malachi		

Index

Expanding the Frontier in Rural Finance
Financial Linkages and Strategic Alliances

Expanding the Frontier in Rural Finance
Financial Linkages and Strategic Alliances

Edited by
Maria E. Pagura

Published by Food and Agriculture Organization of the United Nations and
Intermediate Technology Publications Ltd
trading as Practical Action Publishing
Schumacher Centre for Technology and Development
Bourton on Dunsmore, Rugby
Warwickshire CV23 9QZ, UK
www.practicalactionpublishing.org

First published in 2008

ISBN 978 1 85339 666 3

A catalogue record for this book is available from the British Library.

The contributors have asserted their rights under the Copyright Designs and Patents
Act 1988 to be identified as authors of their respective contributions.

Since 1974, Practical Action Publishing has published and disseminated books and
information in support of international development work throughout the world.
Practical Action Publishing (formerly ITDG Publishing) is a trading name of
Intermediate Technology Publications Ltd (Company Reg. No. 1159018), the wholly
owned publishing company of Intermediate Technology Development Group Ltd
(working name Practical Action). Practical Action Publishing trades only in support
of its parent charity objectives and any profits are covenanted back to Practical
Action (Charity Reg. No. 247257, Group VAT Registration No. 880 9924 76).

The designations employed and the presentation of material in this publication do
not imply the expression of any opinion whatsoever on the part of the Food and
Agriculture Organization of the United Nations concerning the legal status of any
country, territory, city or area or of its authorities, or concerning the delimitation of
its frontiers or boundaries.

The designations 'developed' and 'developing' economies are intended for statistical
convenience and do not necessarily express a judgement about the stage reached by
a particular country, territory or area in the development process.

The views expressed herein are those of the authors and do not necessarily represent
those of the Food and Agriculture Organization of the United Nations.

Cover design by Mercer Online
Indexed by Indexing Specialists
Typeset by S.J.I. Services
Printed in UK

Contents

Preface

Today millions of poor people in developing countries have access to financial services. In 2004, the Consultative Group to Assist the Poor (CGAP) studied all types of 'alternative financial institutions' dedicated to serving people not normally served by banks. It estimated that these institutions held about 660 million small savings and loan accounts. However, when only loans were counted, the number of accounts fell to about 150 million loans outstanding, a much less impressive number compared to the millions that are estimated to demand small loans (Christen, Rosenberg, and Jayadeva, 2004). This problem exists in spite of the much acclaimed microfinance revolution in which thousands of specialized microfinance institutions (MFIs) have been created specifically to serve the poor with non-collateralized loans.

The poor in rural areas represent a particularly difficult target group to serve even for MFIs because of the high operating costs of reaching dispersed populations and in making small loans to farmers with risky enterprises and seasonal cash flows. Even though increased levels of competition are forcing MFIs to expand into new market niches, most tend to compete for non-farm clients located in densely populated rural and peri-urban areas.

This book reports on the study of one important strategy that innovative financial institutions are pursuing to help meet the challenge of sustainably serving additional poor clients in rural areas. This strategy involves the creation of linkages between two or more formal and informal institutions through which they expect to capture the comparative advantages that each possesses in offering financial services. The premise is that there are natural complementarities because of differences in access to information, creation of incentives and ability to enforce contracts so that together two institutions will be able to reduce costs and risks in ways that each would be unable to accomplish by itself. The expected benefits include a more rapid expansion, a broader variety, and a higher quality of products and services offered to clients.

An important strength of the research was that a common research framework was used by the authors to study eleven linkage cases selected for study in Africa, Asia and Latin America. Several of the findings were unexpected. For example, in spite of the heavy involvement of donors in microfinance, most of the linkages were driven more by market opportunities than donor interventions. Most of the linkages were more oriented to credit than to other services. Therefore, the most significant impact of these innovations has been to expand the rural outreach of loans, rather than improvements in the variety or quality of services offered. The country's economic and financial system affects the possibilities for establishing linkages, but the process has not been easy or costless for any of the cases studied. The lessons extracted from these linkages provide a rich variety of lessons for policy makers and donors, and for both formal and informal intermediaries.

The general conclusion is that in fact formal and informal institutions do have comparative advantages in supplying rural financial services, but tapping these advantages has not been easy. The book provides further evidence in support of the view that there is no simple silver bullet to solve the rural finance challenge.

Richard L. Meyer
Professor Emeritus
The Ohio State University

Reference

Christen, R. P., Rosenberg, R. and Jayadeva, V. (2004) 'Financial Institutions with a "Double Bottom Line": Implications for the Future of Microfinance,' *CGAP Occasional Paper* No. 8, Washington, DC.

Acknowledgements

The editor would like to thank the individuals from the financial institutions and supporting organizations that gave of their time freely for the case study interviews. A special note of gratitude goes to all of the clients of the institutions reviewed, especially for their openness and availability to meet with the researchers. The editor would like to acknowledge and express sincere gratitude to the case study researchers for all of their hard work and dedication to this study. Their knowledge, views and opinions significantly shaped the nature and outcome of this work. This study would not have been possible without the financial support of the Ford Foundation. For this, and for the technical and administrative support received from the Ford Foundation's Development Finance and Economic Security group in the Andean Region, the editor is greatly appreciative. The editor would also like to thank the following individuals for their insightful comments on this and earlier versions of the manuscript: Chet Aeschliman, John Conroy, Claudio Gonzalez-Vega, Douglas Graham, Malcolm Harper, Marié Kirsten, Jean-Paul Lacoste, Michael Marx, Richard Meyer, David Myhre, Gerda Piprek and Dieter Seibel. The editor would like to thank her colleagues from the Food and Agriculture Organization for their detailed comments and corrections during the final stage of the writing; in particular, appreciation goes to Doyle Baker, Ivana Gegenbauer, Calvin Miller, Ake Olofsson and Andrew Shepherd. A very special note of gratitude goes to Ivana Gegenbauer who ensured that all stylistic and text formatting was correct.

The views presented in this book are solely those of the contributors and not the organizations they represent. The designation employed and the presentation of material in this book do not imply the expression of any opinion whatsoever on the part of the Food and Agriculture Organization of the United Nations concerning the legal or development status of any country, territory, city or area or of its authorities, or concerning the delimitation of its frontiers or boundaries. The mention of specific firms and organizations does not imply that these have been endorsed or recommended by the Food and Agriculture Organization of the United Nations in preference to others of similar nature that are not mentioned.

Tables

Figures

Boxes

Acronyms and abbreviations

ACA	Academia de Centroamérica
ACORDE	Asociación Costarricense para Organizaciones de Desarrollo
ADA	Appui au Développement Autonome
ADB	Asian Development Bank
AFD	Agence Française de Développement
AFP	Administradora de fondos de pensiones
AGUADEFOR	Asociación guanacasteca de desarrollo forestal
AMPRO	Asociación de Microempresarios y Productores de Occidente
ANDI	Asociación Nacional de IndusTriales
APRACA	Asia–Pacific Rural and Agricultural Credit Association
ASAPROSAR	Asociación Salvadoreña Pro-Salud Rural
ASHI	Ahon Sa Hirap, Inc.
ASONOG	Asociación de organismos no gubernamentales
BANADESA	Banco Nacional de Desarrollo Agrícola
BANHPROVI	Banco Hondureño para la Producción y la Vivienda
BASIX	Bhartiya Samruddhi Financial Services
BCIE	Central American Bank for Economic Integration
BI	Bank of Indonesia
BIM	Banque Internationale pour le Mali
BISWA	Bharat Integrated Social Welfare Agency
BKD	Badan Kredit Desa
BKK	Badan Kredit Kecamatan
BKS-LPD	Badan Kerjasama LPD
BMB	Barangay Microenterprise Business
BMS	Banque Malienne de Solidarité
BMT	Baitul Mal Wat Tamwil
BNDA	Banque Nationale de Développement Agricole
BNR	Banque Nationale du Rwanda
BP	Banque populaire
BPD	Bank Pembangunan Daerah, Regional Development Bank (Indonesia)
BPR	Bank Perkreditan Rakyat
BRI	Bank Rakyat Indonesia
BRS	Banco Regional de Solidariedad
CAF	Corporación Andina de Fomento

CAFTA	Central American Free Trade Agreement
CARD	Centre for Agriculture and Rural Development
CAREC	Centre d'Appui au Réseau des Caisses d'Epargne et de Crédit
CAS/SFD	Cellule d'Appui et de Suivi des Systèmes Financiers Décentralisés
CCE	Communal credit enterprise
CCP	Certificados de contribucíon patrimonial
CDC	Comité de Développement Communautaire
CGAP	Consultative Group to Assist the Poor
CIA	Central Intelligence Agency
CICAL	Cooperativa Industrializadora de Alimentos Limitada
CIDA	Canadian International Development Agency
CIDR	Centre International de Développement et de Recherche
CINDE	Coalición Costarricense de Iniciativas de Desarrollo
CMDT	Companie Malienne de Développement des Textiles
CMEC/SAN	Caisse Mutuelle d'Epargne et de Crédit / SAN
CNBS	Comisión Nacional de Banca y Seguros
CODESPA	Fundación Cooperación al Desarrollo y Promoción de Actividades Asistenciales
CONADECO	Confederación Nacional de Asociaciones de Desarrollo Comunal
COOPEC	Cooperatives d'épargne et de crédit
COPEME	Consortium of private organizations to promote the development of small and micro enterprises
CPIP	Credit Policy Improvement Project
CRDB	Cooperative and Rural Development Bank
CREHO	Fundación Crédito Educativo Hondureño
CVECA	Caisses villageoises d'épargne et de crédit Autogerées
CVECA-ON	Caisses villageoises d'épargne et de crédit Autogerées – Office du Niger
DABANAS	National Private Commercial Bank Foundation
DANIDA	Danish International Development Agency
DEG	Deutsche Entwicklungs- und Investitionsgesellschaft, Cologne
DELSAR	Agency for the Development of Santa Rosa
DFID	Department for International Development
DKK	Danish krone
ECC	Employees Compensation Committee
ECLA	Economic Commission for Latin America and the Caribbean
ECOCOMF	Expanding Competitive Client-Oriented Microfinance
EDESA	Empresa para el Desarrollo S. A.
EDPYMEs	Entidad de Desarrollo de la Pequeña y Micro Empresa
EIB	European Investment Bank

ESAF	Enhanced Structural Adjustment Facility
FADES	Fundación para Alternativas de Desarrollo
FAO	Food and Agriculture Organization
FCRMD	Fédération des Caisses Rurales Mutualistes du Delta
FDC	Fonds de développement communautaire
FFP	Fondo Financiero Privado
FHIA	Honduran Foundation for Agricultural Research
FIDAGRO	Fideicomiso agropecuario
FIE	Centro de Fomento a Iniciativas Económicas
FINCA	Fundación Integral Campesina
FINRURAL	Asociación de Instituciones Financieras para el Desarrollo Rural
FINTRAC	Financial Transactions Reports Analysis Centre
FOMIN	Fondo Multilateral de Inversiones
FONADERS	National Fund for Sustainable Rural Development Project
FONAPROVI	Fondo Nacional para la Producción y la Vivienda
FONDESIF	Fondo de Desarrollo del Sistema Financiero y de Apoyo al Sector Productivo
FUNBANHCAFE	Fundación Banhcafé para el Desarrollo de las Comunidades Cafeteras de Honduras
FUNDASIN	Fundación Aquiles Samuel Izaguirre
GDP	Gross Domestic Product
GEMA PKM	Gerakan Bersama Pengembangan Keuangan Mikro
GFI	Government financial institutions
GSIS	Government Service Insurance Fund
GTZ	Deutsche Gesellschaft für Technische Zusammenarbeit (GTZ) GmbH
HDH	Hermandad de Honduras
IADB	Inter-American Development Bank
IFAD	International Fund for Agricultural Development
IGA	Income generating activities
IMAS	Instituto Mixto de Ayuda Social
IMF	International Monetary Fund
INCA	Empresa comercializadora
INEC	Instituto Nacional de Estadística y Censos
IRDA	Insurance Regulatory and Development Authority
ISI	Import substitution industrialization
JICATUYO	Fundacíon Jicatuyo
KfW	Kreditanstalt fuer Wiederaufbau
KPKM	Kredit Pengembangan Kelompok Mandiri
KSP	Kalimantan Sanggar Pusaka
KUD	Village cooperative unit
LBP	Land Bank of Philippines
LDKP	Lembaga Dana dan Kredit Pedesaan (Village credit fund institution)

LIC	Life Insurance Corporation of India
LKP	Lembaga Kredit Pedesaan
LPD	Lembaga Perkreditan Desa
MACS	Mutually aided cooperative societies
MAG/PIPA	Ministerio de Agricultura y Ganadería/Programa de Incremento a la Productividad Agropecuaria
MCPI	Microfinance Council of the Philippines
MDR	Ministère du Développement Rural
MFI	Microfinance institution
MFO	Microfinance organization
MMC	Microfinance mega centres
MOB	Microfinance-oriented banks
MOU	Memorandum of understanding
MSME	Micro small and medium enterprise
MYRADA	Mysore Rehabilitation and Development Association
NABARD	National Bank for Agriculture and Rural Development
NCC	National Credit Council
NCL	Non-collectible loan ratio
NEF	Near East Foundation
NGO	Non-governmental organization
NLSF	National Livelihood Support Fund
NMB	National Microfinance Bank
NOVIB	Dutch Organization for International Development Co-operation
NPL	Non-performing loans
NTB	Nusa Tenggara Barat
OIKOS	Dutch privately owned cooperative society
OIMC	Organización Internacional para el Desarrollo de las Microfinanzas Comunales
ON	Office du Niger
ONILH	National Organization of the Lenca Indians
OSU	The Ohio State University
PAAF	Pratica Administrativa da las Autoritads Federalas
PACCEM	Cereal Marketing Assistance Program
PAR	Portfolio at risk
PCFC	People's Credit and Finance Corporation
PDCD	Programme d'Appui au Développement des Communes Rurales du Cercle de Dioila
PDO	Private development financial organization
PERBANAS	Persatuan Perbankan Nasional
PILARH	Asociación Proyecto e Iniciativas Locales para el Autodesarrollo Regional de Honduras
PLBS	Project Linking Banks and Self Help Groups (Philippines)
PLPDK	Pusat LPD Kabupaten
PRBC	Producers Rural Banking Corporation

PRODAPEN	Proyecto de Desarrollo Agrícola de la Península de Nicoya
PRODEM	Promoción y Desarrollo de Microempresas (Promotion and Development of Microenterprises)
PROMICRO	Proyecto Centroamericano de Apoyo a Programas de Microempresa
PRONAMYPE	Programa Nacional de Apoyo a la Micro y Pequeña Empresa
PSS	Services for Progress Organization
PT HM Sampoerna	PT Hanjaya Mandala Sampoerna Tbk.
REDMICROH	Red de Instituciones de Microfinanzas de Honduras
RESAFI	Réseau d'Epargne Sans Frontière
RMFP	Rural Microenterprise Finance Project
ROA Kiruvi	Ruaha Outgrowers Association in Kiruvi
ROSCA	Rotating savings and credit association
Rp	Indonesian Rupiah
SACCO	Savings and credit cooperatives
SADESC	Sociedad para el Apoyo al Desarrollo Económico Social Comunitario
SANAA	Servicio Autonomo Nacional de Acueductos y Alcantarillados
SBEF	Superintendence of Banks and Financial Entities
SBS	Superintendence of Banks and Finance – Peru
SCA	Savings and credit associations
SCCULT	Savings and Credit Cooperative Union League of Tanzania
SEC	Securities and Exchange Commission
SELF	Small Entrepreneur Loan Facility
SEWA	Self-Employed Women's Association
SHG	Self-help group
SIDBI	Small Industries Development Bank of India
SIDESA	Sistema Descentralizado de Sanidad Agropecuaria
SME	Small and medium enterprise
SNV	Netherlands Volunteer Organization
SUGEF	Superintendencia General de Entidades Financieras – Cost Rica
SUP	Debt instruments
SYCREF	Systèmes de Crédit et d'Epargnes pour les Femmes
UBPR	Union of People's Banks in Rwanda
UMA	Unidades Municipales Ambientales
UNDP	United Nations Development Programme
UNHCR	United Nations High Commissioner for Refugees
USAID	United States Agency for International Development
USP	Unit Simpan Pinjam

Contributors

Chet Aeschliman is an Investment Officer for the Food and Agriculture Organization (FAO) Subregional Office for Africa, in Libreville, Gabon. Chet has 35 years of broad experience in rural and micro finance throughout the developing world, specializing in French-speaking Africa, and has worked in the rural finance arena in over thirty different African countries, including every West and Central African country but three. He previously carried out consultations for USAID, the World Bank, the French AFD, and was a Chief of Party for an MFI development project in Togo for seven years, an MFI adviser and microenterprise officer for 2 years in Mali, and adviser to an MFI network in Cameroon for 4 years. He has substantial experience in financial analysis, accounting and financial systems development, database design, project formulation, technical manual writing, and technical training, mastering all components of MS Office, including automation with Visual Basic for Applications. He has an MBA in Finance, from the University of Washington in Seattle and is fluent in English and French, with a working knowledge of Spanish, Continental/African Portuguese and certain African languages.

Iketut Budastra is an independent consultant. Born in 1961, he completed undergraduate study in Agricultural Economics at Mataram University in 1987, then proceeded to Master of Regional Planning from Cornell University in 1996 and to Doctor of Agribusiness from Queensland University in 2003. He has been a senior lecturer in Agribusiness Mataram University since 1987. He is also a senior researcher in several research centres within Mataram University.

John Conroy has been a development economist since 1968, with extensive periods of residence in Papua New Guinea and Indonesia, and field experience in much of South and East Asia. He is co-author of two books on linkages, *Banking with the Poor*, (FDC, 1992, republished by Verlag Breitenbach, 1993), and *Best Practice of Banking with the Poor*, (FDC, 1995). He co-authored a seven country comparative study, *Getting the Framework Right: policy and regulation for microfinance in Asia* (FDC, 1997) and a 12 country comparative study, *The Role of Central Banks in Microfinance* (ADB, 2000). He was consultant to the government of Mexico on microbanking during that country's chairing of the APEC process in 2002. More recently he has conducted studies for the World Bank in Fiji and post-conflict East Timor, and for FAO in Indonesia.

Mayra Falck is a Honduran macroeconomist specializing in development policies and rural development topics. Her broad experience includes work in applied research, teaching and project development. During nearly 30 years of professional life she has worked with universities and other public institutions and international bodies on agricultural and environmental projects at regional and national levels. Her areas of specialization include financial services, analysis of policy impact and design of markets for environmental services among others. She has carried out consultancies for various bilateral and multilateral organizations, such as the World Bank, GTZ, UNDP, FAO, European Union and has presented her work in meetings with the Governors of the IDB, at the Microcredit Summits and other international fora. Presently she is a teacher, researcher and director of the Carrera de Desarrollo Socioeconómico y Ambiente de Zamorano. She has been acknowledged for the Best Graduation Index of the Faculty of Economic Sciences from the UNAH, and she has been honoured by the Junta Interamericana de Agricultura for her contributions as a female researcher in rural development. She holds a Bachelors degree in Economics from the UNAH and a Masters degree in Agricultural and Rural Development Policies in Latin America and the Caribbean from the Rural Federal University of Rio de Janeiro and the University of Naples, Italy.

Claudio Gonzalez-Vega, economist and lawyer from Costa Rica, has been Professor of Agricultural, Environmental and Development Economics and Professor of Economics at OSU since 1982 and currently is Director of the Rural Finance Program, a centre of excellence in finance and development. With his colleagues at OSU, he received the Distinguished Policy Contribution award from the American Agricultural Economics Association in 1989. Over two decades of association with OSU as professor, researcher, and consultant have resulted in theoretical contributions and policy recommendations that have established him as one of the world leaders in the field. He has conducted pioneering research on rural financial markets, financial reform, and microenterprise finance in several countries. Recently, he has investigated issues related to rural poverty in Latin American countries. He has published extensively in the areas of finance and development, rural financial markets, microenterprises, macroeconomic management and commercial policy in developing countries.

Malcolm Harper was educated at Oxford University, the Harvard Business School and the University of Nairobi. He worked for nine years in a medium-sized household hardware manufacturing business in England, mainly in marketing. He then taught in Nairobi, from 1970 to 1974, before coming to Cranfield School of Management, where he was Professor of Enterprise Development. Since 1995 he has worked independently, mainly in India. He has published over twenty books and numerous articles on various aspects of self-employment, enterprise development and microfinance. His research and consultancy work has been supported by a wide range of national, international and non-government development agencies. He has advised and evaluated a number of enterprise development and microfinance programmes and institutions in India and in East and West Africa, Latin America and the Caribbean, the Middle East and Gulf area, South and South East Asia, as well as in the United Kingdom. From 1996 until 2006 he was Chairman of Basix Finance of Hyderabad, a leading 'new generation' micro-finance institution, and he is Chairman of M-CRIL of New Delhi, the pioneer of micro-finance credit rating in Asia. He was also the founding Editor-in-chief of the journal Small Enterprise Development, and is a director and trustee of a number of other institutions, including Homeless International, EDA (UK) Limited, APT Enterprise Development and Intermediate Technology Publications in the United Kingdom.

Marié Kirsten is the coordinator for the Institutional and Financial Programme in the Research Unit in the Development Bank of Southern Africa (DBSA). Marié is also on the Board of Directors of the Small Enterprise Foundation, South Africa's most successful and currently only sustainable microfinance NGO. Marié has a Masters degree in Economics from the University of Stellenbosch, and has worked at the DBSA for over 15 years. During this time she has been seconded to the United Nations FAO in Rome and to the South African Department of Trade and Industry. She specializes in microfinance and poverty related research.

Janina León is an Associate Professor and Director of the Masters Programme in Economics at Pontificia Universidad Católica del Perú. Her teaching areas include applied microeconomics, development and labour economics. She is an expert in the following research areas: microenterprise and microfinance; efficiency of microfinance institutions; poverty and labour markets. Besides short articles, her recent consultancy and publication work include: Incorporación de género en la investigación CIES: Balance y propuestas; Typology of Rural Microfinance Institutions: literature review; Evaluation of the National Programme for Microenterprises in Mexico Pronafim; Microfinance for Microenterprises: the state of the art; Cost Efficiency of Peruvian Municipal Banks.

Fiacre Murekezi is a financial accountant with 20 years of experience in the community-based development sector, including developing microfinance businesses with international and local organizations. He led the Rwandan Microfinance Network to promote and implement national policies of microfinance institutions in Rwanda. In this capacity he conducted microfinance studies, developed business tools and advised organizations. Recently, he has started a non-profit association, whose main work is to strengthen linkages between savings and credit groups and formal banks in Huye District, Southern Province of Rwanda.

Jean-Paul Ndoshoboye is an economist and certified trainer of CAPAF (Renforcement des Capacités des institutions de microfinance en Afrique Francophone/CGAP) in capacity-building of microfinance institutions. With a bachelors degree in economics, he has over seven years work experience in the microfinance sector. He coordinates the 'Family strengthening and poverty reduction program' for SOS Rwanda Foundation.

Maria Pagura is a Rural Finance Officer at the Food and Agriculture Organization in Rome, Italy. At FAO she helps design and review programmes and projects in rural finance. Currently she is working on financial products and services for agribusinesses and strengthening formal–informal financial sector linkages. She has over 14 years experience examining rural and micro finance and small enterprise development issues in Africa and Asia, with extensive experience in Mali. She has facilitated project evaluation training in South Africa and Uzbekistan and reviewed microfinance sectors in Bangladesh, India, Indonesia, Mali, Peru and Rwanda. She is fluent in French and holds a Masters in Economics and a PhD in Agricultural Economics from The Ohio State University.

Nilotpal Pathak was a senior analyst for M-CRIL Ltd, the local company employed to conduct the study on AVIVA Life Insurance in India.

Gerda Piprek is a Senior Specialist in enterprise development, micro- and rural finance at ECI *Africa* (Johannesburg). Other fields of specialization include research (micro and rural finance, benchmarking studies, impact studies) and financial education. She has successfully led and implemented multiple projects in these fields in Mozambique, Angola, Tanzania and South Africa. Ms Piprek was previously a Rural Finance Consultant in the Sustainable Development Division of the World Bank (Washington, D.C.) where she co-authored the publication, *Rural Finance: Issues, Design and Best Practices* (2007) with Jacon Yaron and McDonald Benjamin (jnr). Before shifting to microfinance, she worked for several years in commercial retail banking and insurance, where she focused on market research, product development, business and marketing strategy. Ms Piprek holds a Bachelor of Economics from the University of Stellenbosch (1984) and an MBA from Georgetown University (1995), Washington, D.C.

Benjamin Quiñones is presently the Chairman of the Coalition of Socially Responsible Small and Medium Enterprises in Asia (CSRSME Asia), an association of organizations from various Asian countries providing technical and consultancy services to SMEs (small and medium enterprises). CSRSME Asia is convenor of the Asian Forum for Solidarity Economy and it operates a financing programme that links socially responsible investments to socially responsible enterprises. Mr. Quiñones previously served as Secretary General (1986–92) of the Asia–Pacific Rural and Agricultural Credit Association (APRACA) in Bangkok, Thailand. He was instrumental in launching the APRACA Project Linking Banks and Self Help Groups. His published works on linkage banking and microfinance include Social Capital in Microfinance; Microfinance and Poverty Alleviation: Case Studies from Asia and the Pacific; Linkage Banking in

South Asia – The Experience of India, Nepal, and Bangladesh; and Linking Self Help Groups and Banks in Developing Countries.

Rodolfo Quirós is a Costa Rican economist, with degrees in Economics from the Universidad de Costa Rica and in Agricultural Economics from The Ohio State University. For over 19 years he has been conducting evaluations and research on rural finance and microfinance organizations and projects as well as analysing diverse issues in economic development. He has been a consultant in many Latin American countries for a multiplicity of international organizations, most recently conducting studies in rural finance, agricultural value chain finance, microenterprise technical assistance facilities and investment climate. Until 2004 he worked in Bolivia as development finance specialist and Deputy Director for SEFIR, a financial services project funded by USAID and implemented by DAI. Before and since his work in Bolivia, he has been associated with Academia de Centroamérica, a research institute based in Costa Rica.

Hans Dieter Seibel is emeritus professor at Cologne University and senior fellow at the Development Research Center (ZEF), University of Bonn. He specialized in rural and microfinance, agricultural development bank reform and SHG-bank linkages. From 1999 to 2001 he was Rural Finance Adviser at IFAD in Rome, and author of its Rural Finance Policy. From 1988 to 1991 at GTZ he was teamleader of 'Linking Banks and Self-Help Groups in Indonesia'.

CHAPTER 1

Introduction: Linkages between formal and informal financial institutions

Access to a broad range of rural financial services can have a significant impact on people's ability to weather economic shocks, make investments and build up financial and physical assets. But, supplying financial services in rural areas continues to be a formidable endeavour. Faced with high costs and risks of doing business in harsh economic and physical environments, most financial institutions are reluctant to enter rural markets. In their absence informal financial institutions emerge, but typically they are only able to offer a narrow range of financial services in a small geographic area. Through strategic partnering formal and informal financial institutions are finding new ways of establishing a presence in rural markets. As the cases presented in this book reveal, strategic partnerships and alliances allow them to surmount many of the cost and risk obstacles that preclude them from expanding financial services at and beyond the rural market frontier.[1] However, although conceptually valid, establishing and maintaining such linkages in practice may be harder than it looks.

In this book we examine eleven financial linkage cases from Africa, Asia and Latin America. The cases were funded by the Ford Foundation with additional contributions from the Food and Agriculture Organization (FAO) of the United Nations. Over a period of 18 months one country overview and 11 case studies were conducted from late 2004 to early 2006. The aim of the study was to evaluate the degree to which financial linkages increase the supply of a broad range of financial services, not just credit, in rural areas. We defined a 'financial linkage' as a mutually beneficial arrangement between formal (commercial, state, apex banks, etc) and semi and informal financial institutions (microfinance institutions, NGOs, credit cooperatives, village banks, self-help groups, etc.). The linkages were considered successful when based on market principles and resulting in sustainable expanded access to financial services for new segments of the rural population not traditionally served, broadening the variety of products and services already offered and/or creating quality improvements of current products through better terms and conditions.[2]

The rationale for linking is based on the premise that natural complementarities exist between the formal and informal financial sectors that, when joined, reduce the costs and risks in supplying services in rural areas. The complementarities principle is derived from modern economic theory that attempts to explain information, incentive and contract enforcement problems of credit markets and how they result in a mismatch of resources and abilities between formal and informal lenders (Armendáriz de Aghion and Morduch, 2005; Bell, 1990; Fuentes, 1996; and Varghese, 2005). On the one hand, formal financial institutions have extensive infrastructures and systems, access to funds and opportunities for portfolio diversification, permitting them to offer a wide range of services. However they are usually at a distance from rural clients, making obtaining adequate information and enforcing contracts difficult. In contrast, informal financial institutions operate close to rural clients, possess good information and enforcement mechanisms and are typically more flexible and innovative. However, constrained by regulation (e.g. not authorized to take deposits) and a lack of resources and infrastructure, informal financial institutions are only able to offer a narrow range of services in a small geographic area (Figure 1.1). In theory linkages between formal and informal financial institutions appear to have much potential in overcoming the persistent difficulties in supplying rural financial services.

A variety of institutions exists to enable the transmission of financial information and transactions (Johnson, 2005). According to Johnson all the institutions along this continuum represent 'solutions' to the problem of financial intermediation – how to match the supply and demand of funds. Not only the institutions, but the relationships between them as well are designed to address information asymmetries, resolve enforcement problems and reduce the cost associated with the transaction. In essence, linkages afford the players,

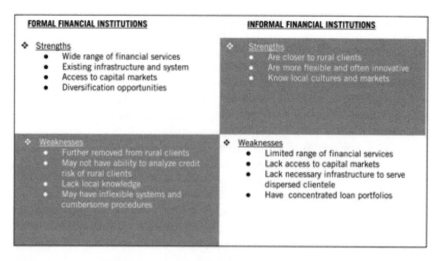

Figure 1.1 Complementarities of formal and informal financial institutions
Source: Adapted from Pearce, 2003.

both formal and informal, the opportunity to overcome a weakness in what they can achieve on their own.

Since a wide variety of formal, semi-formal, and informal financial institutions exists, the possible financial linkages between actors along the chain are numerous. In Figure 1.2 we have illustrated this concept as a continuum of formality, with more formal institutions on the left side of the diagram on down to those institutions that are less formal on the right side. It is helpful to conceptualize linkages using a continuum of formality principle, especially since the meaning of 'formal', 'semiformal' and 'informal' varies widely across countries. In this way, it is helpful to think of linkages as mutually beneficial partnerships between upstream (more formal) and downstream (less formal) institutions. This includes linkages between institutions that are more towards the centre of the continuum, as well as those at the extreme ends.[3]

Using case studies we employed a common research framework to answer the following questions below.

- What was the main motivation behind the development of the financial linkage?
- What were the main preconditions for the linkage to emerge, such as a senior management buy-in, shared vision on financial service provision, minimum levels of institutional capacity, etc?
- What were the key design factors and processes that led to the success of the linkage?
- How did linkages impact the financial organizations that were linked together?
- In what way did linkages improve access to rural financial services for rural small-holders and micro-entrepreneurs?
- In what ways did the legal and/or regulatory framework help or hinder the establishment of the financial linkage?

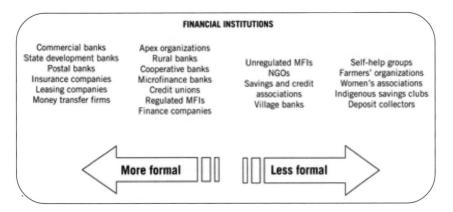

Figure 1.2 Continuum of formality

The case studies

In the following chapters, we present one country overview and eleven cases that met most of the following selection criteria:

- demonstrated success in expanding access to underserved rural market segments;
- were based on cost-covering principles, or had clear exit strategies if they were externally supported;
- had been in existence for two or more years;
- added to the diversity of linkage types reviewed.

The selected cases fell into four broad categories:

(i)   Cases that are strategic in nature and driven by the informal institution;
(ii) Cases that are strategic in nature and driven by formal bank/insurer;
(iii) Cases in which mentoring and/or capacity building of informal institutions is a key component;
(iv) Cases that are externally driven by a third party (e.g. donors, governments), but that demonstrated a certain level of formal sector openness to engage with the informal sector.

The cases under each category are highlighted below.

Strategic – informal sector driven linkage

Under this category we highlight two informal institutions that successfully established linkages with a range of financial and non-financial partners in order to expand their service offerings and/or to establish more stable sources of funds.

In Chapter 2, we present the case of Fundácion para Alternativas de Desarrollo (FADES), a Bolivian non-regulated MFI specializing in the supply of financial services with significant outreach in rural areas. This is an interesting story of an informal financial institution's explicit strategy of increasing its supply of a wide range of non-traditional financial services by establishing a 'multiplicity' of inter-institutional linkages with financial and non-financial partners. This story highlights several lessons learnt about the benefits and costs of establishing and maintaining a multiplicity of linkages. The authors end the Chapter with insightful recommendations on the importance of picking the right partners, persuading staff of new partnership benefits, and knowing how to manage a set of inter-institutional linkages.

In Chapter 10 we present the case of Confianza, a regulated MFI in Peru with significant outreach in rural areas. This is a story about a newly regulated MFI, formerly an NGO, and the impact of its new regulatory status on the ability to source funds from a range of commercial and non-commercial providers. Trade-offs emerge for the organization in choosing the right mix of partners that is most appropriate for its long-term strategic interests. However, the author questions the impact of the institution's new regulation and interaction with commercial partners on rural outreach. She considers the possibility that

Confianza, in an attempt to cut costs and meet prudential requirements, relies more on increasing financial services in urban rather than rural areas. The data presented for recent years supports this view.

Strategic – formal sector driven linkages

In this grouping we describe two commercial banks and one insurer using linkages to reach rural markets. What may have begun as acts of corporate social responsibility and/or a response to priority sector targets soon became absorbed for these commercial actors into their mainstream business and long term corporate strategies.

In Chapter 5 we present the case of a now well-known private bank in India, ICICI Bank. Motivated by an internal drive to 'be a leader in every field of banking' and a belief that new micro clients will grow into mainstream banking clients, ICICI developed a unique model to tap into rural markets. The case describes the innovative 'outsourcing' model and provides two 'linkages in action' sub cases depicting the spillover effects of the ICICI linkage on two partner organizations and their sponsored SHG (self-help group) members. Although the authors state that ICICI Bank is no doubt demonstrating its effectiveness in profitably serving the rural poor, they are cautiously optimistic about the future and highlight some concerns for consideration. In fact, in February 2007 after the completion of the field study, ICICI Bank had to temporarily suspend its main partnership model with microfinance institutions (MFIs) because the Reserve Bank of India said that it was not meeting the 'know your customer' requirements through the partnership model. Since the suspension, ICICI Bank has worked with its partners to overcome this challenge by upgrading data systems to enable them to meet the requirements, but many MFIs, especially those that depended heavily on ICICI Bank for their funds, are still feeling the pain of suspension.

In Chapter 6 we present a second case from India about Aviva, a large private life insurer, and its unique approach of responding to priority sector requirements of the Indian government. This is a unique story about a massive international insurer's effectiveness in supplying life insurance products in remote rural markets. As with ICICI Bank, serving the rural poor became a long-term corporate business strategy and not just a 'requirement'. The author provides a good overview of the insurance market in India, including an historical review of the Insurance Regulatory and Development Authority (IRDA) and its regulatory norms. He highlights the challenges and successes Aviva faces in setting up 'tailor made' business models with an MFI and a trade union. The first case demonstrates the numerous advantages of working with a well-qualified local partner while the second tells the story of Aviva's success in beating out the competition to win over the business of a large trade union with over 500,000 members.

In Chapter 13 we present the case of CRDB Bank, the fifth largest commercial bank in Tanzania, and its desire to do 'something positive' about the majority of

Tanzanians alienated from the commercial banking sector. The author describes CRDB's corporate vision to successfully serve the broader Tanzanian market commercially. Although this appears to be a story about CRDB's level of corporate social responsibility, it may have more to do with a smart, forward-thinking bank preparing for what they feel will eventually be a saturated urban banking market. The author describes CRDB's strategy of linking with Savings and Credit Cooperatives (SACCOs) as a way to cost-effectively increase the supply of financial services in the rural countryside.

Mentoring – capacity-building driven linkages

It is not surprising that in all of the cases that we studied formal actors met severe difficulties in partnering with local organizations because of their low level of institutional capacity. What is interesting, however, is the way in which formal actors chose to deal with this problem. The cases presented under this category exemplify a range of strategies that different formal actors have undertaken. We feel the contrasts among the cases are striking and provoke much reflection and debate on how to tackle what will continue to be a long-term challenge in our field.

In Chapter 3 we present a case about FINCA/Costa Rica, a non-financial NGO with linkages with local and regional financial NGOs operating in rural areas. Originally, FINCA/Costa Rica was established as a village banking programme with a resource intensive model of creating and funding village banks on a continual basis. In the late 1990s/early 2000s, faced with chronic problems of financial self-sufficiency, an inability to secure loanable funds and an inefficient MIS system, FINCA/Costa Rica made a radical decision to close its financial operations and specialize completely in the creation of incorporated village banks, otherwise known as communal credit enterprises (CCEs). The authors provide a wealth of information about FINCA/Costa Rica's institutional transformation that strengthened financial linkages and enhanced rural access to financial services. Anyone interested in a story about a courageous local organization willing to rethink and adjust an international programme's 'one size fits' all model should read this chapter. Lessons abound on the flexibility to adjust, the dangers of conditionality, the challenges of scaling up and the importance of institutional strengthening.

In Chapter 4 we illustrate a unique case about the José María Covelo Foundation in Honduras. This is an interesting story of the foundation's evolution from a typical second-tier organization providing capacity building training and funding to private development finance organizations (PDOs) to one of a highly sophisticated holding company offering financial, human resource management, administrative systems, marketing and organizational services to the six organizations in the holding group. The study focuses on a multiplicity of intra- and extra-group linkages with a range of financial and non-financial actors. The authors examine market-deepening linkages for rural finance and provide in-depth analysis of two local organizations and their linkages with Covelo Group among others. This case is rich in detail and at times complex, but for those interested in exploring a new way of building local capacity, it is essential reading.

In Chapter 7 we present the case of financial linkages between the Regional Development Bank (BPD) and village credit institutions (LPDs) in the province of Bali, Indonesia. This case demonstrates the impact of banking policies, regulation and supervision on the nature, and to a certain extent, the level of success, of formal and informal financial sector linkages. BPD, mandated by government decree, supervises and provides management training to LPDs in the provinces. Although other financial ties exist between the BPD and LPDs, the main purpose of the relationship appears to be the transfer of knowledge and assurance of good financial health. The case focuses on the linkage between the Regional Development Bank in Bali and its partner LPDs. The author claims this relationship to be a success but cautions against certain rigidities of the model, e.g. restrictions on an LPD having saving accounts with other financial institutions.

For readers not familiar with the Indonesian banking context, it may be helpful to review Conroy and Budastra's clear and concise overview of the variety of microfinance linkages in Indonesia as presented in Chapter 8. The authors provide a descriptive mapping of different linkage models that exist in Indonesia, and reflect on Indonesia's rich variety and wide range of financial institutions. The linkages are characterized by several small, regulated financial institutions engaging in chain relationships with major financial institutions and grassroots financial actors. Indonesia also has special apex institutions set up to create linkages, and linkages have an explicit role in a new 'banking architecture' being created by the central bank. The linkages are categorized based on a distinction between autonomous linkages and those occurring as the result of government or central bank initiative.

In Chapter 11 we describe the case of the People's Credit and Finance Corporation (PCFC), a government-initiated and donor-supported second-tier wholesale finance corporation in the Philippines. Created to fill the vacuum of financial services available to the poor in 1994, PCFC concentrated on building the capacity and outreach of local organizations through training and funding for on-lending. PCFC's strategy of lending only to the 'best of the crop' MFIs backed by accredited training options for weaker MFIs, permitted them to reach significant numbers of the poor substainably. The author provides a good historical overview of PCFC's development and evolution, highlighting the organization's willingness to adjust its lending technology requirements.

Donor driven – formal sector willing to engage with informal actors

To some this may seem like an odd title for this grouping of cases. However, we decided to make a fourth category to highlight an interesting contrast in the way two commercial banks engage with informal financial institutions. Both stories have to do with the way in which donors influence formal sector engagement.

In Chapter 9, we present the case of the Banque Nationale de Développement Agricole (BNDA) and its linkages with rural microfinance institutions in Mali. In addition to using its own resources for on-lending to MFIs, the bank has a long history of acting as an executing bank for donor funds targeted at priority cooperatives and groups. Almost half (47 per cent) of BNDA's loan portfolio with MFIs is covered through donor resources. The author compares two MFI recipients of BNDA wholesale lending and the striking difference in the way they link up with the bank; one to expand its portfolio and the other mainly for liquidity balancing. He questions the impact of the ample donor funding on local organizations' incentive to mobilize savings and BNDA's motivation to actively engage with the informal sector. The author concludes the case with an interesting reflection about the permanency versus the temporary nature of financial linkages in this context.

In contrast, in Chapter 12 we present a case in which the donors have a clear exit strategy in channelling funds to targeted recipients in Rwanda. The authors present the case of CARE/Rwanda's strategy of mobilizing rural poor into savings and credit associations and linking them to the Union of People's Banks in Rwanda (UBPR), a formal credit union with over 150 branches throughout the country, including rural areas. With a clear exit strategy in mind CARE/Rwanda sought buy-in from the UBPR to provide financial services to a non-traditional clientele, consisting mainly of rural women organized in informal savings and loan groups. At the heart of the strategy was the aim of gradually reducing the CARE credit fund provided to the bank, 50 per cent after the first year and 100 per cent after year two, to be replaced by the bank's internal funds. The authors highlight favourable indications of success based on the performance outcomes with the new clientele, provide initial lessons learnt and highlight future challenges.

In the next section of the book we present the case studies in Chapters 2–13, organized alphabetically by country for the reader's ease of reference. We conclude this book by summarizing the cases, with an attempt to draw out the key messages and lessons learnt from this exercise. The book ends with recommendations for formal and informal financial actors, practitioners, governments and donors on ways to strengthen sustainable financial linkages and partnerships in rural finance.

Notes

1   The title of this book was chosen to illustrate the potential role of formal and informal financial sector linkages in 'creating value at the frontier' as defined in Von Pischke (1991). In this sense the cases reviewed herein describe relationships between formal actors operating inside the frontier and those (informal actors) operating at or beyond the frontier.

2 Similarly, Gallardo, Goldberg and Randhawa (2006) examine strategic alliances and development partnerships in rural finance that introduce new services, expand existing services and/or improve outreach and institutional performance.

3 We recognize that the usage of formal and informal financial linkages may be confusing given the range of formality within and across countries. Therefore, one should bear in mind that by 'formal financial institutions' we mean those that have a banking charter and are prudentially regulated by the banking authority in their country. In this sense, regulated and non-regulated microfinance institutions are both considered 'informal' institutions.

References

Armendáriz de Aghion, B. and Morduch, J. (2005) *The Economics of Microfinance*, MIT Press, Cambridge, Massachusetts.

Bell, C. (1990) 'Interactions between institutional and informal credit agencies in rural India', in *The World Bank Economic Review*, **4** (3): 297–327.

Fuentes, G. A. (1996) 'The use of village agents in rural credit delivery', in *The Journal of Development Studies*, 33 (2): 188–210.

Gallardo, M., Goldberg, M. and Randhawa, B. (2006) 'Strategic alliances to scale up financial services in rural areas', *World Bank Working Paper*, number 76, Washington, D.C.

Johnson, S. (2005) 'Fragmentation and embeddedness: an alternative approach to the analysis of rural financial markets', in *Oxford Development Studies*, **33** (3 & 4): 357–375.

Pearce, D. (2003) 'Links between banks and non-banks to promote access to financial services for the poor', CGAP Presentation at the American Banking Association Annual Meeting, San Francisco, 10 August 2003.

Varghese, A. (2005) 'Bank-moneylender linkage as an alternative to bank competition in rural credit markets', in *Oxford Economic Papers*, **57** (2): 315–325.

Von Pischke, J.D. (1991) *Finance at the Frontier: Debt Capacity and the Role of Credit in the Private Economy*, The World Bank, Washington, D.C.

CHAPTER 2
Strategic alliances for scale and scope economies: lessons from FADES in Bolivia

Claudio Gonzalez-Vega and Rodolfo Quirós

Abstract

This study of the Fundación para Alternatives de Desarrollo (FADES) in Bolivia makes an interesting case for non-traditional financial linkages. FADES, a non-regulated NGO and the third largest MFI in Bolivia, decided to enter into strategic alliances with several public and private institutions, with the sole purpose of expanding its rural outreach, despite the existence of restrictive legislation and infrastructural constraints. These linkages resulted in new services becoming available to old and new clients, since the partnerships brought with them inherited clients. The new services range from additional financial services (e.g., remittances, deposit mobilization) to the payment of utilities and a social programme benefiting the elderly. This chapter introduces FADES' innovative range of diverse linkages, and shares initial results. We urge the readers to follow FADES' progress, and continue to learn from this interesting linkage 'laboratory'.

Introduction

The supply of financial services in rural areas of developing countries is not easy. Financial organizations that seek to establish a rural presence face numerous obstacles, including severe information, incentive and contract enforcement problems (Gonzalez-Vega, 2003) and difficulties associated with agriculture (Harper, 2005). Thus, the expansion of rural outreach is an uneven and slow process. Further, managerial, funding, and regulatory constraints keep many organizations from offering a wider range of services.

In addressing these challenges, some financial organizations take advantage of their greater proximity to rural clients, but typically they offer only a narrow range of services. In part, this is explained by their unregulated nature, which prevents them from engaging in deposit mobilization and other functions reserved for regulated entities. In part, it is explained by their inability to generate sufficient economies of scale, economies of scope, and portfolio diversification to lower operating costs and risks. The ability to increase rural outreach in a competitive environment is grounded on declining costs.

Bolivia is an interesting case for the analysis of these questions, given the pioneering role of many organizations in the development of microfinance, under a flexible but demanding framework of prudential regulation and supervision, which raised standards of performance and prepared the organizations for the difficult times the country has experienced. Moreover, substantial externalities and demonstration effects influenced the evolution of non-regulated financial organizations such that, as their regulated counterparts, they are among the best in the world.

There are two ways to address the difficulties. One is to develop a comprehensive, in-house structure to offer a whole range of services *à la* Promoción y Desarrollo de Microempresas (PRODEM), in Bolivia. The coordination and internal control challenges associated with this model are formidable and require superior managerial skills and supporting logistics. This approach frequently leads to transformation into a regulated entity. Another way is to create the equivalent of a 'planetary system' and supply a number of services through inter-institutional linkages, developed around a core programme. This is the approach followed by FADES.

This study focuses on FADES, a non-regulated NGO specializing in the supply of financial services, with 20 years of experience. In terms of rural outreach, FADES is one of the leading non-regulated microfinance institutions (MFIs) in Bolivia. In recent years, the numbers of clients and branches and the loan portfolio grew substantially. This growth forced its management to seek additional funding, while at the same time making sure that the organization remained financially self-sufficient and sustainable in the long run.

Both the motivations for expansion and its cost consequences persuaded FADES' management to seek strategic alliances for the supply of additional services. The approach is conceptually valid, but it has not been easy to apply in practice. The decision was made to supply a wide range of non-traditional financial services simply because they are valuable for clients. Given FADES' own limitations, however, this choice required strategic alliances with public and private organizations. The multiplicity of linkages is not, therefore, fortuitous or unintended. Rather, it is an intentional and central component of FADES' institutional strategy, consistent with its mission of supplying an integrated array of financial services to its target population.

The development of alliances has been deemed a necessary condition to address the burden of fixed costs that the extensive infrastructure of branches, needed for rural outreach, represents. The supply of additional services creates economies of scale and economies of scope at the branch level, facilitates liquidity management throughout the organization, and allows a diversification of FADES' sources of revenue. Because of the multiplicity of linkages, FADES has become a valuable laboratory for the testing of different schemes for offering services through strategic alliances and for understanding the institutional requirements for doing so efficiently.

Microfinance in Bolivia

With a rugged landscape covering over one million square kilometres and with less than nine million inhabitants, density of population is very low in Bolivia, except in a few urban centres. This creates high transaction costs for rural microfinance. In Latin America, only Haiti and Nicaragua have lower per capita GDP (US$960 in 2004). Hyperinflation in the early 1980s was followed by successful macroeconomic control, which required reduction of the public sector's size, privatization of state-owned enterprises, closing of public banks, and market-oriented policies. Price stability and rapid economic growth ensued, accompanied by the formation of a large informal sector. It was into this scenario that the Bolivian microfinance revolution emerged in the late 1980s.

Recently, Bolivia has again experienced macroeconomic difficulties, social disturbances, and political uncertainty. The crisis has induced financial disintermediation, with reductions of deposits and credit portfolios and higher default rates for all types of intermediaries. In contrast to banks, MFIs rapidly reacted to these challenges and the growth and health of their portfolios continued uninterrupted. Features of microfinance clients and the innovations of MFIs contributed to their superior performance (Gonzalez-Vega and Villafani-Ibarnegaray, 2004).

In recent years, a quarter (US$115 million) of the loan portfolio of MFIs has been disbursed in rural areas, to 130,000 clients. Given this outreach, bringing additional financial services to remote and dispersed rural communities will be costly. After the crisis, most MFIs reconsidered the timing of their rural expansion and focused on the consolidation of urban achievements.

The Superintendence of Banks and Financial Entities (SBEF) supported innovations in microfinance as desirable on social grounds and to promote financial stability. In 1993, it approved the licence for the first microfinance bank (BancoSol). By 1995, it created the charter of Fondo Financiero Privado (Private Financial Fund), thus allowing Caja Los Andes, Centro de Fomento a Iniciativas Económicas (Centre for the Development of Economic Initiatives – FIE), EcoFuturo and PRODEM to become regulated. SBEF regulations create options for inter-institutional linkages between regulated and non-regulated entities. 'Windows' are an outlet for specific services, such as tax collection and payment of utilities, which can be placed in public or private facilities (SBEF, 2005). 'External cash desks' include ATMs, offices in supermarkets and stores, and 'auto banks'. Correspondence creates a contract between regulated intermediaries and NGOs or associations, which operate on behalf of the former for a fee. These contracts allow the: collection of money from clients of the financial intermediary, to be transferred for final credit to the client's account; receipt of cash to be transferred to other offices of the regulated institution and acceptance of transfer payments and international remittances; payment of salaries of public employees and, tax collection. One of the first inter-institutional linkages was created, in 2002, by FFP FIE and the NGO Pro Mujer, which introduced external cash desks in nine centres of Pro Mujer. Another experience has been the linkage between FADES and Trapetrol, which led to a correspondence contract in April 2002.

The strategic transformation of FADES

FADES is among the most important organizations in Bolivia's rural microfinance landscape. Measured by the value of its rural portfolio (US$18.6 million), it is the largest financial NGO. FADES also built the second largest rural portfolio among all MFIs, regulated and non-regulated, only surpassed by PRODEM. From the perspectives of the number of rural clients (22,000), FADES is the third largest MFI in Bolivia. To underpin this breadth of rural outreach, FADES built the largest branch network among financial NGOs (74 offices), developed a large number of inter-institutional linkages and is co-owner of a regulated MFI (EcoFuturo). From rural origins, when created in 1986, FADES grew by offering services to clients in rural and peri-urban areas, based on its extensive branch network. As a pioneer in rural microfinance and agricultural credit, in particular, it developed credit products for its rural clientele.

Over the last several years, FADES has experienced important transformations (Rodríguez-Meza et al., 2003). One milestone was the decision to create EcoFuturo, in 1999, with three other non-regulated MFIs. FADES traded its least rural offices for shares of stock in EcoFuturo. The plan was segmentation, in terms of the rural–urban market niches served. The growing penetration of EcoFuturo into rural markets, however, questioned the simultaneous existence of FADES and EcoFuturo.

A second milestone was the change in strategy. A new Executive Director was appointed in February 2002 and implemented major revisions in approach that reflected changes in how the institutional mission is interpreted. While in 2000 the mission was described as supporting the development of the lowest-income groups, two years later it became a contribution to economic alternatives that benefit lower-income groups, with priority in rural areas (FADES, 2003). This must be complemented by efforts to achieve sustainability and make the organization viable in the long run.

After 1996, FADES rapidly expanded its loan portfolio. Most of it is rural but not necessarily agricultural, as loans are granted for trade, services and small-scale manufacturing. FADES used several sources of funds, showing interest in diversifying its liabilities. It was one of the first to borrow in Euros, from Oiko Credit in 1999, and was quick to pay in advance when this currency appreciated. Still, 55 per cent of its funding came from FONDESIF, a state-owned apex.

Between 2000 and 2004, the numbers of fixed and mobile branches and of employees increased three-fold and two-fold, respectively (Table 2.1). The contrast between increases both in the loan portfolio and number of branches and the stagnant behaviour in the number of clients is striking. The average portfolio per branch decreased almost by half and the number of clients per branch became one-third of the figure for four years earlier. This created pressures on

Table 2.1 FADES: general information, 2000–4

Variable	2000	2001	2002	2003	2004
Equity (million US$)	4.8	4.3	4.0	4.0	4.1
Assets (million US$)	17.7	20.4	21.5	21.0	20.5
Loan portfolio (million US$)	11.7	13.2	15.0	16.1	17.7
Rural portfolio (percentage)	n.a.	n.a.	94.7	93.0	92.0
Average loan size (US$)	518	631	737	751	791
Portfolio in arrears (percentage)	6.5	10.9	24.4	16.3	n.a.
Clients	22,582	20,929	20,344	21,436	22,387
Female clients (percentage)	n.a.	n.a.	35.0	35.0	33.5
Branches	24	35	55	65	66
Portfolio per branch (US$)	487,500	377,143	272,727	247,692	268,182
Clients per branch	941	598	368	330	339
Employees	102	120	154	186	211

Sources: FADES (2003), FINRURAL (2002, 2003 and 2004)

FADES, in general, and on each branch, in particular. The new management is aware of the dangers of this rapid growth in the numbers of branches.

Inter-institutional linkages are, therefore, a mechanism for supporting each branch's efforts in becoming self-sufficient, by generating economies of scale and of scope at the branch level. FADES offers multiple non-traditional financial services. These services did not result from isolated initiatives; they are part of a strategy based on an integrated vision of the promotion of rural development. FADES' non-regulated nature, however, restricts its operations and prevents it from mobilizing deposits. FADES thus established strategic alliances to supply financial services other than credit and transfer payments.

These alliances also require administrative efforts, including additional staff training, adequacy of software, acquisition of IT hardware, and periodic reports to each partner. To coordinate these efforts, FADES established a National Office of Auxiliary Financial Services. The staff of this office is, however, limited: only three, including the person in charge and two assistants, one in La Paz and another in Santa Cruz (who oversees the Trapetrol alliance).

Auxiliary services create positive and negative consequences. Questions to consider are: How profitable are they? What share of total revenues do they generate? What are the costs of administration? The flagship services are two of FADES' own products, currency exchanges and local transfers (*giros*), which account for over 50 per cent of the total revenue generated by auxiliary services. Non-traditional services still represent, however, a small proportion of total operating revenues (3 per cent), while the rest comes from the loan portfolio and stock investments. Some alliances were recently introduced, so it will take time for some products to be fully operational and, until then, it is difficult to determine how attractive they are for the organization and its clients.

FADES has information on the volume of operations and dollar amounts, for each service and branch, to calculate revenues. It does not have activity-based costing, so it lacks estimates of how much each product costs and ignores how profitable each one is, individually or per branch. The Financial Manager estimates that all products are globally profitable, but some are not in certain branches. The collection of payments of utilities levies the least administrative burden.

Up to 2002, there were no problems in transferring funds to the branches. Each branch collected money and sent it, every day, to the main office; when they needed funds, they received them from La Paz. With rapid growth, it became difficult to administer liquidity. Now, there are 74 branches, all over the country, with different patterns of collection and disbursements. The challenge of administering liquidity is closely linked to the supply of auxiliary financial services, because the latter provide FADES with funds to disburse loans at the branch level. This allows a more efficient management of its flows of funds but requires, however, sophisticated mechanisms of internal control.

Non-traditional services forced FADES to speed up steps to improve software adequacy, internal control and human resources. These reforms caused high levels of stress. The organization decided, however, to identify the potential ahead, continue growing, and establish reliable controls.

Inter-institutional linkages

By December 2004, FADES had developed an impressive set of inter-institutional linkages: 11 strategic alliances with private and public entities (Table 2.2). These linkages resulted in 20 new services, offered to three types of clients: its traditional clientele; inherited clients, coming from partner institutions and people in communities where FADES operates, who visit its offices looking for the new products. The linkages range from those that allow the organization to

Table 2.2 FADES: summary of strategic alliances, as of December 2004

Type of institution	Name and line of activity	Number of alliances*
1. Financial entities	a. Trapetrol/regulated credit union	
	b. Western Union/remittances	3
	c. AFP Previsión/private pension fund administrator	
2. Utilities	a. Entel/Fixed and mobile phone service	
	b. Elfec/Electric power	
	c. Cotel/Fixed phone service	4
	d. Nuevatel-Viva/Mobile phone service	
3. State programmes	a. Bonosol/benefits for the elderly	
	b. Fundaempresa/vendor of enterprise card, for bids for public projects	3
	c. Caja Nacional de Salud/social security	
4. Other	a. Folade/International NGO	1
Total		11

Source: Interviews with FADES' senior Management, December 2005.

offer additional financial services (e.g. remittances, deposit mobilization) to the payment of utilities and social programme benefits.

The services currently offered are not the only motivation; rather, a broader spectrum of products, available at partner institutions, might eventually be added. The range of alliances and other relationships are depicted in Figure 2.1. The resulting 'planetary model' illustrates a system of strategic alliances developed to overcome different types of restrictions, which keep FADES from directly offering services.

The diagram also depicts the influence of its founding members (namely, NGOs willing to offer an integrated set of products to the target clientele) and sources of funding (FONDESIF, by and large). It includes FADES' investments in two firms. These relationships (founders, financiers, investments) are institutional linkages, indeed, but are perceived as different. They are typical connections, compared to the more innovative strategic alliances. Their influence on FADES matters, but they are just typical lending or investment contracts. The description of the innovative inter-institutional linkages begins with Trapetrol, the most important alliance in terms of volume of operations, profitability, complexity, and lessons learned.

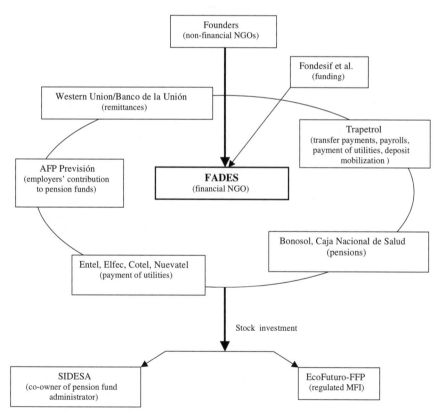

Figure 2.1 FADES: main institutional linkages

Trapetrol is a credit union regulated by the SBEF, based in Santa Cruz, where FADES has operated for many years. Regional rivalries make it difficult, however, for organizations from the highlands (*Altiplano*) to engage in alliances with entities from Santa Cruz. The inter-institutional linkage between FADES and Trapetrol matters, because it is one of the few and earliest attempts to establish an operational relationship between a regulated intermediary and a financial NGO.

The linkage began in April 2002. Achieving and keeping it alive required extensive support from Profin, the microfinance support programme of the Swiss Agency for Development and Cooperation (COSUDE). This donor played a key role in analysing and choosing the best legal option (correspondence), selecting Trapetrol from a shortlist of potential partners, and supervising the alliance (Campero, 2004). For some, the linkage would have never occurred without this support. The donor is a member of the Operations Committee, a board that oversees issues related to the linkage. At the time of the study, the Committee had not met for six months, despite a pressing agenda. This probably reflected the recent removal of managerial staff at Trapetrol, for reasons not related to the alliance.

Routine problems are resolved through local coordinators, one in each institution, who replaced the original general coordinator. This person was located in Trapetrol and, with time, practically became an employee of the credit union, working in activities unrelated to the alliance, and inclined to solve disputes in favour of Trapetrol. The nature of some difficulties (telecommunications, software, procedures) suggests the convenience of visits to branches, but few take place. A large number of offices of both organizations are involved: FADES has 16 branches, 10 fixed and 6 mobile, in Santa Cruz, while Trapetrol has 17 branches, 7 of them rural. The agreement prevents either organization from opening branches where the other already has one.

The alliance allows FADES to offer services in rural areas far away from the city of Santa Cruz. The furthest branch is seven hours away, by car, and it takes longer by public transport; in some cases, this option is only available once or twice a day. The linkage helps FADES in reaching this rural population with services that otherwise would have been unavailable or only accessible to some, at high transaction costs. This is a substantial benefit for clients, revealed by the large unsatisfied demand for these services.

Five services are offered by the FADES/Trapetrol alliance. First is the payment of public utilities (electricity, phone, and water bills). This service reduces the clients' transaction costs and, thereby, the total costs of these utilities; it also facilitates the collection of fees in distant communities, which would be too costly for utility providers, thereby encouraging them to develop services in remote and sparsely populated areas. Through this alliance FADES has contributed to a better public utilities infrastructure for these communities.

Second is the processing and payment of wages and benefits for public employees (teachers and social security beneficiaries). This matters for employees who work in communities far away from Santa Cruz, where their pay cheques must be cashed. Instead, they get their money at the nearest FADES branch, with a significant reduction in transaction costs. Each month, a FADES officer goes to the bank and cashes the cheques. Third, transfer payments sent (or received) by clients of Trapetrol and FADES are offered throughout the region. Fourth, Trapetrol loans are repaid at FADES, and Trapetrol collects payments on loans disbursed by FADES.

Deposit mobilization, the fifth and one of the most interesting dimensions of the alliance, is the least developed one. Several reasons explain this slow progress, including: lack of real-time connections between branches in distant rural communities and the regional office; low fees for FADES and the opportunistic behaviour of clients, who use savings accounts to transfer large amounts of money to Santa Cruz, thus avoiding transfer fees, explain the Regional Director's lack of interest.

FADES perceives three benefits from the linkage with Trapetrol. First, a service is offered that allows rural communities greater access to electricity, water and phone services, by reducing the operating costs of providers (increased supply) and saving the inconvenience of travelling to Santa Cruz to pay bills (increased demand). Local welfare effects are substantial. This matters, given FADES' institutional values of rural development. Second, representatives of partner institutions and other local organizations get acquainted with this financial NGO. They may deal directly with FADES, avoiding the intermediation of Trapetrol. Third, a steady flow of cash to the branch allows better liquidity management. FADES recognizes, however, that there are costs to sharing commissions with Trapetrol, as FADES could establish a direct relationship with the utilities.

Other linkages will be described only briefly. The main agent for Western Union in Bolivia is Banco de la Unión. FADES became the bank's agent, a linkage that took shape in June 2004. FADES participates only in the Bolivian portion of the transfer and receives a 12.5 per cent commission from the bank. International remittances arrive from Argentina, Spain, and the United States. The service is technically available in 45 of 47 fixed offices, because there are communications problems in two. It had operated only for five months at the time of the study and is expected to have great impact in rural areas. The link with Giros Folade, which has been established since 2003, offers international remittances from the United States, Europe and Costa Rica at the La Paz office.

AFP Previsión is one of two pension-fund administrators in Bolivia's private pension system. The linkage required the approval of the Superintendence, which at first rejected the plan arguing that FADES is not regulated. However, FADES was already disbursing benefits for the elderly (Bonosol), so the linkage was authorized. Branches become collection agents for contributions. This allows FADES to compete against regulated MFIs, which have a limited rural presence.

Entel, a major phone company, contacted FADES in 2003 to establish a linkage that has grown fast. ELFEC is an electric power company in Cochabamba. The linkage has been active since January 2003. The service lowers transaction costs for clients of the power company, who become potential clients for FADES. Cotel, a cooperative with the monopoly of fixed phone services in La Paz, was contacted by FADES. Service began in March 2004, demanded by clients and non-clients alike. If FADES does not offer it, some other MFI will. The linkage with Nuevatel-Viva, a mobile phone company, began in August 2004. Viva's phone cards are popular and FADES wants to capture a large share of the rural market.

Bonosol grants annual benefits (US$224) to Bolivians aged 65 years and older. The linkage, since 2003, has been between FADES and three organizations, Futuro, Previsión, and Datacom. The former two are pension-fund administrators; the latter selects organizations for disbursement of the benefits. FADES is the main provider of this service in rural areas. The private firm Fundaempresa won a public bid for the sale of the enterprise card, which allows small and medium producers to participate in bids for public sector projects. The Caja Nacional de Salud administers health and pension systems. For a few of these linkages, the volume of operations is low, which may justify termination. Finally, some alliances are recent, which makes it difficult to examine the full extent of their impact.

Lessons learned

The alliances developed by FADES have produced an invaluable laboratory for learning about a multiplicity of issues. The lessons are useful for negotiators, supervisors and coordinators of inter-institutional linkages. First, some services increasingly provided by financial NGOs, like payments of utilities, are sometimes ignored or criticized because of their presumed non-financial nature. Financial institutions all over the world, however, have broadened the scope of their services. In corporate banking, the largest share of revenues is generated by these products rather than by traditional credit and deposit services. Similar reasons are behind FADES' search for a broader array of services: the need to generate economies of scale and scope, lower costs, diversify risks, and obtain additional sources of revenue.

The multiplicity of linkages assures a volume of operations and financial sustainability that allow FADES an expansion of its rural network and operations, which would otherwise be unsustainable. FADES expects to be perceived as capable of managing these arrangements and as trustworthy, even if not regulated. In Santa Cruz, where closed local associations are dominant, linkages can be effective ways to bypass sometimes impenetrable shields.

Several reasons motivated FADES to develop inter-institutional linkages to allow clients (traditional and non-traditional) to pay for public utilities at their offices. These linkages generate important flows of people at the branch, and FADES hopes some may become traditional clients. Indeed, clients of non-traditional services inquire about other financial services, especially credit. Second, these services guarantee flows of funds at branch level that reduce the need for transfers within the network. Except for harvest seasons (when most loans are collected), the high costs of sending cash to branches, mainly due to insurance, are lowered, while staff exposure to theft risk is eliminated. Third, the fees charged are often high enough to pay for several expenses at the branch, such as the cashier's salary and electricity and water bills. Moreover, except for once a month, when utility bills are due, the cashier has plenty of time to spare. In smaller offices, sometimes he becomes a credit officer. In remote branches, however, valuable credit personnel are also used for activities different from those they were employed and trained for. The evidence suggests a positive net outcome, as only a few days a month someone has to devote time to non-traditional clients. This is, indirectly, a way of paying credit officers with the additional revenues.

A long list of linkages generates concerns about their cost–benefit. MFIs that develop a large set of services sometimes fail to see deficiencies in the supply of their original flagship products, in aspects like design and back-office support. Further, developing additional products is not costless. There is an analogue with institutional linkages. Rather than strengthening them, a large uncontrolled number of alliances may dilute consolidation efforts and sharply increase costs. Typical expenditures result from time and resources needed for internal control and to train personnel on the new services, although training often takes place through automated programmes, either in each computer (FADES), accessed through a main frame or by videoconference, all of which require minimum infrastructure.

In the best of cases, each product requires programming and adaptations, to include the service in the organization's software and enable the two systems (FADES and its partner) to 'talk' to each other. In the worst of cases, compatibility problems between the systems' platforms arise, which happened to FADES. Lack of compatibility forced FADES to run different programmes in more than one computer. Additional hardware must be purchased when computers are old and without capacity.

The alliances require a separate department to oversee day-to-day operations, coordinate with institutions, conduct periodic evaluations, prepare reports, and promote services among employees and clients. The National Office of Auxiliary Financial Services has a staff of three, which is not enough. During 2004, the person in charge was not able to visit branches. No formal evaluations of the linkages have been conducted, although a couple have had almost no activity. Aware of these limitations, FADES is considering creating a larger unit.

A multiplicity of linkages offers insights about key factors to consider when selecting a partner. Some are related to the institution's size, mission and formality. If the organizations have different lines of activity, it may not matter that one is a large enterprise and FADES a small NGO. This is the case of ELFEC, a large electric power company, because this firm needs FADES for its rural expansion. In contrast, when the partners have the same line of activity, large differences in size may present problems. FADES might be looked down on as a subordinate rather than a partner. One example was its experience in searching for a partner in Santa Cruz. The managers of Jesús Nazareno, the largest credit union in Bolivia, looked down on FADES. Next, at La Merced, a mid-size credit union, there was no interest because they were already operating in the same region. Finally, FADES visited Trapetrol, a relatively small credit union, and was greeted with interest, as an equal.

Once the potential partner is selected, institutional policies, mission and vision must be checked. Similarities help both during the negotiation and when problems begin to appear during implementation. In the FADES–Trapetrol alliance, the latter had mostly an urban outreach and had no idea of the difficulties of operating in rural areas. FADES, in turn, was concerned with information and telecommunication technology, as a consequence of the lack of minimum infrastructure where its branches are located.

Despite FADES' apprehension, the agreement was reached. Later on, when the linkage was implemented, Trapetrol demanded a quicker response from FADES in solving communication problems, but the issues were exogenous and beyond FADES' control.

Finding a potential partner of similar size and equal mission are ideal conditions but not sufficient to assure success. Due diligence is also necessary. In the case of Trapetrol, an analysis but not an in-depth evaluation of the organization was undertaken. FADES later on found out that Trapetrol lacked regulations, procedures and manuals. Many decisions (for authorizing expenses, for example) only required the general manager's approval. Surprisingly, FADES was a more formal institution than Trapetrol. This caused disagreement and led the credit union to frequently describe FADES as bureaucratic. Although regulated, Trapetrol's lack of formality was at the root of the institutional crisis it experienced, with replacement of most of its leaders. Unrelated to the linkage, this episode threatens its sustainability. One might conclude that the credit union was not the best institutional choice for a linkage, but there was little more to choose from in Santa Cruz. The best organizations were either too large or uninterested and the rest too small and weak.

Although problematic, alliances with state-owned entities are inevitable, given the far-reaching presence of the public sector in Bolivia. FADES has three of these linkages. They are seen as leverage for negotiating future linkages with the public sector. When agreements are discussed with private firms, a record of linkages with the state might be a valuable asset, particularly important for non-regulated entities. Complex and lengthy negotiations are typical, however, of agreements with the state, particularly because of transparency issues. A linkage between FADES and a public sector entity may expect a higher frequency of external audits than an alliance between two private organizations. Delays in payments of commissions are typical.

Another key factor in any alliance is for information to flow smoothly. Each organization should spread the news of the linkage, so all personnel are aware of it. In one of FADES' alliances, while the management staff knew all the details, mid-level personnel did not. Some problems can often be resolved between cashiers of both organizations, but this is not always the case, particularly when the rules of the game are not in writing or are ambiguous. In the FADES–Trapetrol case, the Operations Committee decided that each organization would name a coordinator responsible for the alliance, in charge of addressing communication problems. It is usual for the staff to be afraid of the excess work that the linkage may generate. These fears are often unfounded. Non-traditional services do not require much time, except on peak days. Before an alliance begins, the institutions involved should have a good internal communication strategy and incentives compatible with the goals of both the linkage and the organizations.

As in any legal document, linkage contracts should be clear and unambiguous. Wording of contracts that sequentially include several products requires special attention. In these cases, common practice is to prepare a general contract for the partnership and specific regulations for each service. Additional complications arise when a partner (Trapetrol) brings to the alliance a set of services that originate from a third party (payment of electric bills). Trapetrol had an agreement with the electric company, which included conditions on fees. When FADES and Trapetrol added the payment of bills to their alliance, the wording of clauses in the contract did not match the conditions that the electricity company expected. There was a verbal agreement with Trapetrol regarding fees. When the fees became high, the company stopped paying Trapetrol, arguing that the agreed fee was lower. Trapetrol, in turn, stopped paying the corresponding share to FADES.

Conclusions

Macroeconomic and political instability discouraged most Bolivian MFIs from expanding their rural outreach. FADES followed a counterintuitive path: a sharp increase in its number of branches, beyond its already important rural network. FADES also developed the largest set of strategic alliances among non-regulated MFIs. Many of the linkages are recent, so their impact is yet to be seen. Its multiplicity, however, allows some conclusions.

The multiplicity of linkages is not fortuitous. The board of founders mandated a consolidated approach in the provision of an integrated set of services, either purely financial (deposit mobilization, remittances) or less traditional (collection of utility payments and social security and pension contributions and cashing of salaries). Although the goal is for each branch to be self-sustainable through its credit portfolio, the additional services secure the viability of some branches. Otherwise, some branches should be closed. Several linkages have the potential of developing into major sources of revenue, thus contributing to FADES' overall sustainability. Some linkages have reduced client transaction costs and assisted in the development of markets and infrastructure. In other cases, the linkages have allowed FADES to bypass regulatory constraints, as in indirect deposit mobilization through regulated intermediaries.

Despite the justifications for an alliance, any NGO has to be careful with whom it develops one, particularly because it may be harder and costlier to break apart than create a linkage. Based on FADES' experience, it is important to look for organizations of similar size, if the partner also provides financial services. If the organization operates in a different sector, size does not matter much. An alliance between organizations with similar objectives is also recommended. A linkage with a firm with comparable mission and vision facilitates rapport and leads to better understanding of each other's difficulties in solving problems that the joint delivery of a service may introduce. Ideally, each organization should be able to conduct a due diligence evaluation of the other.

Managing the set of institutional linkages and defining adequate procedures for the implementation of each alliance are not trivial issues. Organizations with as many linkages as FADES require a separate unit for sound administration. This unit should prepare prompt reports, facilitate information for both internal and external clients, visit branches, coordinate administrative issues with counterparts, and perform evaluations of the linkages.

An important step in establishing a new alliance is to persuade branch-level personnel of the benefits, for the organization as a whole and for them in particular. A helpful practice is to write a procedure manual before the linkage is implemented. Another prerequisite is to have all the hardware, software and telecommunication devices needed for success in place. For complex linkages, it may be convenient to prepare a pilot programme.

In the end, both the sustainability of the linkages and their contribution to the sustainability of the organization matter. When installed capacity represents fixed costs and is not completely utilized, the new services generate economies of scale and help in diluting these costs with additional revenues. The joint production of several products creates economies of scope, through additional information and relationships that favour development of additional products. Client loyalty improves, as the value of the relationship increases, and opportunistic borrower behaviour declines. Some of the non-traditional services are not highly correlated with other local activities, so risk can be diversified. All these effects simultaneously enhance rural outreach and sustainability.

References

Campero, C. (2004) 'Alianzas estratégicas: Mecanismo para el desarrollo de las microfinanzas rurales', in *Yatiquaña*, (1), PROFIN/COSUDE, La Paz.

Fundación para Alternatives de Desarrollo (FADES) (2003) *Memoria*, La Paz.

FINRURAL (2002) *Boletín financiero*, La Paz.

FINRURAL (2003) *Boletín financiero*, La Paz.

FINRURAL (2004) *Boletín financiero*, La Paz.

Gonzalez-Vega, C. (2003) 'Deepening Rural Financial Markets. Macroeconomic, Policy and Political Dimensions', *Paving the Way Forward for Rural Finance, An International Conference on Best Practices*, USAID, Washington, D.C.

Gonzalez-Vega, C. and Villafani-Ibarnegaray, M. (2004) 'Las microfinanzas en el desarrollo financiero de Bolivia', PREMIER, La Paz, Bolivia.

Harper, M. (2005) 'Farm credit and micro-finance – is there a critical mismatch?", in *Small Enterprise Development*, 16 (3): 58–67.

Rodríguez-Meza, J., Gonzalez-Vega, C. and Quirós, R. (2003) 'La tecnología de crédito rural de FADES', in *Cuaderno de SEFIR 10*, La Paz.

Superintendencia de Bancos y Entidades Financieras de Bolivia (2005) http://www.sbef.gov.bo [accessed 25 October 2007].

.

CHAPTER 3

Institutional transformation to create linkages that enhance rural access to financial services: the case of the Fundación Integral Campesina in Costa Rica

Rodolfo Quirós and Claudio Gonzalez-Vega

Abstract

Today FINCA/Costa Rica, originally established in 1984 as a village banking programme with a resource intensive model of creating and funding village banks, has emerged as an organization highly specialized in the creation and linking of incorporated village banks with financial and non-financial actors in Costa Rica, El Salvador, Guatemala, Honduras and Nicaragua. The case study describes FINCA/ Costa Rica's revolutionary process of institutional innovations over the last 20 years culminating in the transformation from a financial apex organization to developer of the revolutionized village banks in order to improve opportunities for linkages that enhance rural access to financial services. The authors end the case with several lessons on the importance of organizational flexibility to adjust, strengthening institutional capacity to meet the growing needs of the organization especially as it pertains to personnel and MIS development and creating partnerships and alliances with both public and private entities. Caution is emphasized on the risks of conditionalities embedded into inter-institutional linkages and the ever- present risk of the state using the partnership for political purposes.

Introduction

Costa Rica is one of the countries where microfinance organizations (MFOs) were established first, during the early 1980s. Some of the non-governmental organizations (NGOs) created at that time were either pilot programmes or the first wave of expansion of well-known international microfinance networks, such as ACCION International and FINCA International. Towards the end of the decade and in the early 1990s, other important players arrived in Costa Rica, but of the select group of NGOs that received funding and technical assistance from these international sources, all but one disappeared. The only one still in operation is FINCA/Costa Rica, the focus of this case study. This has been among the best known of the programmes associated with FINCA International because of its multiple innovations, all of them revolutionary when they were introduced. It was the second FINCA programme ever created, right after the founder designed the original one in Bolivia, but it is no longer part of the network of FINCA International.

Established in 1984, FINCA/Costa Rica operates in the rural areas, currently under the framework of an advanced version of the village banking methodology, namely the communal credit enterprise (CCE), an incorporated village bank that represents its most significant innovation. During its two decades of operation, the organization has been constantly evolving, a process that culminated in the abandonment of the typical second-tier role of a village banking MFO. Today, the headquarters of the network is an organization committed to the creation of local capacity in rural communities, through the establishment of CCEs, to enable the provision to their members of financial services obtained from a diverse set of sources.

FINCA/Costa Rica has established multiple inter-institutional linkages. These linkages have included a recent international alliance with NGOs in four other countries, which is having a significant impact on the development of rural financial services through replication of the organizational innovations. It has also developed interesting alliances with a bank and with a communal development agency, which facilitate the graduation process of the CCEs and their direct access to formal finance. The organization has developed a number of additional linkages, current and past, with government agencies, the international donor community, and the private sector. In particular, the relationship between FINCA/Costa Rica and each one of the CCEs is in itself an extremely interesting alliance, with numerous potential positive externalities for the network.

The underlying assumptions for the case study have been that:

(i)   the specific organizational and legal innovations considered here will continue to pave the way for the CCEs, as a result of their legal status and features as formal enterprises, in allowing them to establish – directly and on their own – other linkages, additional to the existing alliance with FINCA/Costa Rica;

(ii)   these stronger CCEs, by abandoning the traditional village bank organizational approach of FINCA International, will have a greater capacity to address strategic issues, such as searching for additional sources of funds and establishing new linkages, to widen the range of services available to their members;

(iii)   the new organizational design of the headquarters of the MFO, with its focus on institution building, uses its comparative advantages to enhance the opportunities for individual CCEs to gain access to regular financial intermediaries on market terms. This creates a more efficient division of labour and valuable synergies between, on the one hand, the rural development organization (FINCA/Costa Rica) and, on the other, the sustainable financial intermediaries where the CCEs gain access to a broad supply of financial services.

Background

Costa Rica is a small, open economy, with a long-standing record of political and social stability, excellent education and health indicators, and a favourable geographic location. A number of policy reforms have spurred on continued structural change in the rural sector, which has evolved from a scenario mainly of a few traditional agricultural exports to one with a large number of traditional and non-traditional agricultural and non-agricultural products, sold in local and international markets. The country has not experienced macroeconomic or financial crises since the mid-1980s.

Country environment

The Costa Rican economy has shown a positive performance (Table 3.1), with annual growth rates of GDP per capita of around 2 per cent and relatively low unemployment rates. Exports are one of the most dynamic dimensions of the economy. After the policy reforms of the 1980s, the country abandoned import substitution and promoted exports and tourism. Today, Costa Rica ranks second in the Americas in terms of openness. Its social indicators show evidence of the investments Costa Rica made in education, health and infrastructure for improved access to drinking water and sanitation.

Costa Rica evolved from being dependent on the production and international prices of coffee and bananas to a diversified productive structure. The past 20 years have seen increases in agricultural productivity, orientation towards demanding markets, and focus on higher value added, while agritourism and environmental services are important sources of household income. Decades of investment in rural social infrastructure are reflected by indicators such as improved sanitary services and access to drinking water, at levels higher than in most developing countries.

Rural financial markets

Costa Rica has a long tradition of agricultural finance. Established in 1914, the Juntas Rurales de Crédito (rural credit boards) was among the first small farmer credit programmes in Latin America. Their record was impressive: during their first 50 years of operation, they disbursed millions of dollars through thousands of loans but less than 5 per cent of the clients defaulted (Gonzalez-Vega, 1973). Several country characteristics facilitated access to rural financial services, including its small size, well-developed communications infrastructure (as demonstrated by the density of public transportation, roads, and phone lines), and the widespread outreach of the branch network of formal financial

Table 3.1 Costa Rica: economic and social indicators, 2004 (%)

Sector	2004
Real	
GDP annual growth	4.2
GDP per capita (US$)	4,402
Export growth	3.0
Unemployment	6.5
Population growth	2.3
Financial	
Total credit/GDP	36.4
Money supply as M3/GDP	45.3
Prices	
Consumer price index - CPI (Dec. to Dec. change)	13.1
Devaluation rate (with respect to US$)	9.5
Social indicators	
Poverty (% population below poverty line)	20.3
Rural poverty	24.3
Adult literacy (as of 2000)	95.8
Education budget/total government budget	6.0
Life expectancy at birth (years)	78.0
Health expenses/GDP	10.5
Improved sanitary services (% total population)	93.0
Access to drinking water (% total population)	95.0

Sources: BCCR, INEC, ECLAC and UNDP [accessed August 2005].

intermediaries. The financial system has a well-developed physical infrastructure, with 540 branches of formal financial intermediaries located all over the country. The average of 7,400 persons per branch is low for developing countries. The participation of the state-owned banks is significant, given the late emergence of the private banks (1980s). They account for 60 per cent of the total assets and liabilities but only 45 per cent of the loan portfolio of the system (Table 3.2).

Table 3.2 Costa Rica: share of regulated financial organization, by category of the balance sheet, December 2004 (%)

Account	State-owned commercial banks	Other state-owned banks	Private banks	Credit unions	Rest of organizations[a]	Total
Assets	49	11	29	4	7	100
Loan portfolio	34	11	40	6	9	100
Liabilities	52	8	31	4	5	100
Capital	31	19	20	8	21	100
Number of organizations	3	2	12	26	6	49

[a]Private finance companies, *mutuales* (savings and loans), and currency exchange firms.
Source: Costa Rican Superintendence of Financial Entities, SUGEF, 2005.

By the 1980s, the Juntas Rurales de Crédito, managed by the state-owned Banco Nacional de Costa Rica, dwindled. The withering of this icon of small farmer credit resulted from reforms in its organizational design in the 1960s, which facilitated the politicization of the programme in the 1970s (Gonzalez Vega, 1973; Jiménez and Quirós, 1994). Nevertheless, the bank kept its role as the main lender to the agricultural sector and in 2001 introduced BN Desarrollo, a programme for micro, small and medium entrepreneurs. Credit unions are the sector with the largest number of organizations (26), but they lend only 6 per cent of the loan portfolio of the system. The 10 largest credit unions have their base in the rural areas, and a few manage a loan portfolio similar to the portfolio of the banks with operations in their regions of influence.

No current data are available on the overall degree of rural access to credit. The most recent research dates from the late 1980s, when a survey conducted in three rural areas revealed historical levels of access to formal sources of credit (that is, at least once in their lifetime) higher than 50 per cent of all rural households (Gonzalez-Vega et al., 1989). By that time, however, formal access had declined to just over 10 per cent of these households, while semiformal and informal sources of credit had increased their share of the market. There had been a 'de-formalization' of access to agricultural finance in Costa Rica, probably as a consequence of the severe economic crisis of the early 1980s (Quirós, 1991).

Financial transactions of non-regulated lenders with a strong presence in the rural areas include moneylenders, private finance companies, processing plants (e.g. dairy, sugar cane, poultry and grains), credit from input suppliers and procurement firms (e.g. supermarket chains), and the foreign loans obtained by large agricultural firms. There are also numerous public sector programmes with credit components, with an emphasis on crops.

Unlike other countries, microfinance organizations play a minor role in Costa Rica, not only in rural credit markets but also in the overall financial sector. They emerged after the financial crisis of the early 1980s, sponsored by international microfinance networks, as an option for those who had lost access to formal sources of credit. Their operations were mostly urban, but a few organizations targeted the rural population, particularly farmers. Among these exceptions, the only one that still operates in the rural areas is FINCA/Costa Rica, albeit with a different approach than 20 years earlier.

The near absence of MFOs in Costa Rica reflects a combination of factors, such as the:

(i)   heavy weight of the state-owned banks and a history of government intervention in financial markets where, over a long period, targeted subsidized credit was the norm, there was a crowding out of non-government intermediaries, and financial innovation was inhibited;

(ii) widespread network of branches of formal financial intermediaries, combined with a comparatively short distance between clients and institutions;

(iii)   highly developed social security system and other safety nets, which reduced the role of savings deposits and loans as risk management tools;

(iv)   relatively small size of the informal sector, in a country with unusually high shares of the labour force in salaried employment and with employment-related access to some kinds of financial services (e.g. employee associations such as *asociaciones solidaristas*);

(v)   widespread ownership of small rural properties, which makes it possible to pledge traditional collateral;

(vi)   absence of hundreds of thousands of microentrepreneurs, concentrated in large urban areas, as is the case in the Latin American cities where microfinance has flourished.

Despite the comparatively large outreach of rural finance in Costa Rica, important segments of the population still do not have access to efficient and sustainable financial services. This is particularly the case in rural areas outside the Central Valley.

FINCA/Costa Rica

In 1984, John Hatch and María Marta Padilla established FINCA/Costa Rica as a foundation. A year earlier, Rural Development Services, an international consulting firm managed by Hatch, had created a credit programme in Bolivia. He then went to Costa Rica, where he contacted Padilla, an agricultural economist with experience in managing grassroots organizations. The new Costa Rican NGO, Fundación Integral Campesina, would later be identified by the acronym FINCA, which John Hatch used for the international village-banking group – FINCA International – that he founded.

Characterized from the start by a brisk process of innovation, FINCA/Costa Rica rapidly left behind the lending technology inherited from its Bolivian counterpart. First, it abandoned loan payments in kind, introduced in Bolivia as a response to hyperinflation. Second, it adopted an exclusively rural focus and a mixed gender approach, unlike the affiliates of FINCA International, whose groups operate mostly in urban areas and work mainly, or exclusively, with women. Eventually, the most innovative adjustment was the introduction of shares of equity for the members of a village bank. Recently, FINCA/Costa Rica applied to itself the same principles of innovation and adaptation with which it always approached the village banking technology. Thus, it transformed itself from a financial apex organization to a developer of the revolutionized village banks in order to improve opportunities for linkages that enhance rural access to financial services.

Evolution: from payment in kind to financial services

The original lending technology used by FINCA/Costa Rica was borrowed from the Bolivian model during the first half of the 1980s. The programme's objective was to improve the welfare of rural people, and its main features were as follows (Jiménez et al., 1996):

(i) *Rapid group formation*. The methodology required field staff (namely, a promoter) to visit communities not yet familiar with the approach, explain the programme to farmers and, if interested, install a three-person executive committee (on the same day of the visit), and write the minutes.

(ii) *Instant loan disbursement*. Right after a village bank had been created, the loan amount would be determined (considering the quantity and price of specific crops to be grown), and immediate disbursement would follow.

(iii) *Five-year term*. The village bank had five years to repay the loan from FINCA/Costa Rica, amortizing 20 per cent of the principal each year. The final borrower had one year to repay the full amount of his individual loan.

(iv) *Payment in kind*. Both the individual loans and the debt of the group were repayable in kind and, in particular, in basic grains.

(v) *Interest rate*. There was no explicit interest rate. There was, nevertheless, implicit interest, which could be positive or negative depending on the variation in the price of the commodity.

(vi) *Mandatory savings*. Each member of the village bank was required to save each year an amount equal to 20 per cent of the loan they received, so that after five years they would have saved an amount equal to the loan received from FINCA/Costa Rica.

(vii) *Collateral* The members of the village banks offered FINCA/Costa Rica a joint liability guarantee. In the absence of any legal status that would make it possible to collect from the village bank in court, the guarantee was simply the willingness to pay of the members of the group.

After a few months of operation, Padilla noticed problems with the technology, regarding the:

(i) low level of commitment of the members and their lack of knowledge of basic administration principles, resulting from the hasty creation of the village banks;

(ii) fluctuations in prices and poor quality of the grains received in payment as well as the lack of comparative advantage of FINCA/Costa Rica's personnel in selling commodities;

(iii) lack of compliance with the savings principle; instead, each borrower was paying 20 per cent of the loan size per year and the term became, in practice, 5 years for both the village bank and the individual borrowers.

Less than a year after its creation, FINCA/Costa Rica adjusted the lending technology, thus separating the new programme from the Bolivian experience. Some changes introduced were:

(i) payments in cash;

(ii) interest rate charges;

(iii)   matching terms to maturity with agricultural cycles and harvests;
(iv)   strong emphasis on training, in areas such as basic accounting and the lending process;
(v)   adequate selection of the village bank's members.

A couple of years later, the process for obtaining legal recognition of the village banks as civil associations became an important adjustment to the model. In other countries, village banks lack any legal status. The absence of gender preferences and its rural focus further distanced FINCA/Costa Rica from the international network, leading to disassociation about a decade after its creation.

Revolution: incorporated village banks

After eight years of operation, FINCA/Costa Rica began a long-term evaluation of its programme through an alliance with The Ohio State University's Rural Finance Program (OSU) and its Costa Rican partner, Academia de Centroamérica (ACA), a private non-profit research institute. As part of the Financial Services Project funded by the United States Agency for International Development (USAID), OSU and ACA, investigators conducted surveys and examined various aspects of the village banks and the administration of FINCA/Costa Rica. The researchers raised concerns regarding the:
(i)   lack of long-term financial self-sufficiency of FINCA/Costa Rica;
(ii)   poor management information system (MIS);
(iii) risks associated with the operation of collective projects;
(iv)   weak sustainability of the village banks.

In particular, the researchers raised concerns about the limited potential for steady growth and sustainability of the village banks, given a design with attenuated property rights and a weak governance structure, especially as an outcome of the one person, one vote rule in an organization with both borrowers and savers (Chaves, 1996a).

Following recommendations of the OSU/ACA team, in 1995 FINCA/Costa Rica introduced adjustments in its operations. It asked the village banks to issue equity contribution certificates (*certificados de contribución patrimonial*, CCP). These were certificates of 5,000 colones each (US$24 at the time of their creation, but this amount is now equivalent to US$10). The certificates mimic the role of shares in a corporate firm; that is, the percentage of certificates owned determines each member's share of profits disbursed and their weight in the decision-making process. The CCP may be bought from the village bank or other members. The investment is not recovered unless the certificates are sold back to the organization, to another member, or to a non-member, given prior authorization by the village bank. The CCP were, nevertheless, only an imitation of equity, with a consequent lack of legal validity if tested in court.

FINCA/Costa Rica was worried, because the certificates were not solving all of the problems identified by the OSU/ACA team. Padilla decided to move forward with further adjustments and, in 1996, she introduced a fundamental innovation: the communal credit enterprise (CCE), namely an incorporated village bank. As a result, all new village banks were created as CCEs, while many of the old ones were transformed into CCEs. Nevertheless, some village banks kept operating as civil associations, still using the CCPs.

This innovative feature of village banks ? incorporation ? attempts to facilitate, even in the most deprived communities in the rural areas, the creation of sustainable financial organizations. The CCEs are legally established corporations. This allows them to develop their own linkages with other organizations and to engage directly in a broad range of transactions – that would have required an indirect channel, such as the headquarters of FINCA/ Costa Rica in its apex role.

Further, the CCEs belong to the local residents. This contributes to the accumulation and use of social capital, and it allows members to invest their savings in the equity of their own firm while, in exchange, they obtain the opportunity to receive loans from the enterprise. To gain a better understanding of the operation of CCEs and of village banks that still use the CCPs, the researchers visited two village banks of each type. Before their transformation, their number of members had declined, mostly because, given their earlier organizational design, the remaining members were reluctant to replace those who had left, as new members would not have contributed to the intangible assets that the group had accumulated, including their borrowing reputation, and would instead dilute the existing property rights. After the transformation, however, the membership has grown steadily, to reach between 35 and 111 shareholders in each of these four CCEs. Across them, average equity per shareholder ranges between US$334 and US$1,104, suggesting that low-income households are channelling important amounts of funds into the CCEs. In addition, deposits mobilized are substantial, with one individual account (the largest) of US$8,500. The CCEs finance their loan portfolios mostly from equity and deposits as well as external sources, such as regional development projects and commercial banks. Per CCE, average loan sizes range between US$426 and US$930. Their main competitors are the state-owned banks, which operate a large network of rural branches but ration credit strictly. Although the CCE interest rates are higher than at the banks, the members value the low transaction costs involved.

Culmination: institutional transformation

FINCA/Costa Rica continued its process of development and improvement of the new design. This has been accomplished through the establishment of new CCEs, both in Costa Rica and in four other Central American countries. The current methodology consists of 22 steps for the creation and initial strengthening of a CCE.

The first step – selection of a community – is itself a complete guide, with a set of 10 criteria. The next seven steps include an initial talk by the adviser and a series of training workshops in which the CCE members prepare several regulations. Future members sign an agreement with FINCA/Costa Rica, buy the stock, approve all regulations, elect a board of directors, and open the passbook savings accounts of the educational investment programme. These eight steps may take one week each or longer. Once all of these tasks have been undertaken, the group is ready for the inauguration. After the inauguration, a longer period of training follows.

This thorough process takes a minimum of five months, and it has an estimated cost of US$2,000 per CCE. Unlike traditional village banking technologies, FINCA/Costa Rica does not provide any funds – grants or loans – to the CCE nor does it obtain funds from other sources, during the implementation of the 22 steps. The enterprise must be created solely with the funds provided by the members and, in the beginning, the credit programme must be funded entirely with the initial equity.

In the late 1990s and early 2000s, FINCA/Costa Rica was involved in this resource-consuming process of creating dozens of CCEs in different regions of the country. Simultaneously, the organization was funding the village banks of the earlier generations and its Executive Director was supporting NGOs in Nicaragua and Honduras, in their efforts to replicate the new technology. This commitment as well as FINCA/Costa Rica's chronic problems with financial self-sufficiency, difficulties in obtaining loanable funds, and the lack of an efficient MIS forced the organization to make an important decision. It decided to close its financial operations and specialize solely in the creation of CCEs, as described in Figure 3.1.

The role of second-tier financial organization has been transferred to a newly created organization – EDESA (Empresa para le Desarollo S.A.), a firm owned by FINCA/Costa Rica and several village banks. The former Executive Director is now Director of its regional project, with a key task of transferring the new village bank design to several NGOs in Central America. At the same time, FINCA/Costa Rica continues to establish more CCEs in Costa Rica and to

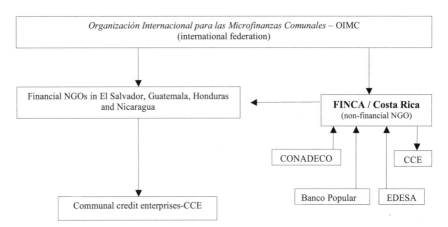

Figure 3.1 FINCA/Costa Rica: main institutional linkages
*Source:*Interviews and FINCA/Costa website, http://www.fic.or.cr (interviews held in June 2005)

consolidate recent ones, through an alliance with Banco Popular, a formal financial intermediary.

Inter-institutional alliances

A multiplicity of linkages has characterized the evolution of FINCA/Costa Rica (Table 3.3). There are currently 12 active alliances while historically there have been 59, if the connections with the village banks are excluded. These are linkages with organizations of varying nature, with emphasis on financial entities, state agencies, and private enterprises.

In 2003, FINCA/Costa Rica began its most complex and challenging strategic alliance, with impressive results after three years. It involves NGOs in four different countries and CODESPA, a Spanish NGO. Towards the end of 2003 FINCA/Costa Rica established a local network of multiple linkages, to facilitate and speed up the graduation of the CCEs, by linking them to a bank.

By continuing its traditional alliances with the private sector, FINCA/Costa Rica strengthened its specialization in non-financial services, while an alliance with a newly created financial NGO replaced FINCA's role as a financial apex for the village banks. The relationship between FINCA/Costa Rica and the CCEs it creates is atypical, involving autonomous village banks that are stronger than both its predecessors and typical village banks worldwide.

Multinational strategic alliance

FINCA/Costa Rica has enjoyed a long-term relationship with CODESPA, which began in 1988 with credit lines received through ACORDE (Asociación Costarricense para Organizaciones de Desarrollo), a Costa Rican financial apex. CODESPA funded the expansion to a second region, key from a risk diversification perspective. A more ambitious four-year project, implemented in 1999, included a small credit component and the consolidation of 120 CCEs. This project served the purpose of systematizing the CCE design that FINCA/Costa Rica had begun implementing in 1996. The technology was then transferred to a Nicaraguan NGO and a Honduran organization.

For many years, Padilla had visited other countries, to explain the methodology and find ways to facilitate its replication. The European Union suggested a regional project and CODESPA obtained the funding for it. This second stage started in 2003, when FINCA/Costa Rica and four other Central American NGOs set up a strategic alliance with CODESPA for the creation of a number of CCEs and for the establishment of a federation of organizations implementing the CCE design. FINCA/Costa Rica is the key player (technical advisor) in this international network of linkages (Figure 3.2). Its main responsibilities are threefold:

    (i)   *Creation and consolidation of CCEs.* FINCA/Costa Rica trained the technical staff of the NGOs in El Salvador, Guatemala, Honduras, and Nicaragua. This first involved an internship. Each NGO sent their staff

Table 3.3 FINCA/Costa Rica: summary of strategic alliances, as of September 2005

Type of institution	Name	Number
Current linkages/relationships		
1. Financial organizations	a. ASAPROSAR-El Salvador	
	b. Fundación del Centavo-Guatemala	
	c. FUNBANHCAFE-Honduras	
	d. SADESC-Nicaragua	
	e. BAC San Jose	
	f. Banco Cuscatlán	
	g. Banco Popular	
	h. EDESA	8
2. State organizations/programmes	a. CONADECO	
	b. IMAS	
	c. PRONAMYPE	3
3. International organizations	a. CODESPA	
4. Other	a. Communal credit enterprises	
Total		40
Previous linkages/relationships		
1. Financial organizations	a. ACORDE	
2. State organizations/programmes	a. AGUADEFOR	
	b. CINDE	
	c. Consejo Nacional de Producción	
	d. FIDAGRO	
	e. MAG/PIPA	
	f. PRODAPEN/MAG-IFAD	6
3. International organizations	a. Catholic Relief Services	
	b. Central American Bank for Economic Integration	
	c. FAO	
	d. European Union	
	e. Inter-American Development Bank	
	f. Inter-American Foundation	
	g. Office of the United Nations High Commissioner for Refugees (UNHCR)	
	h. PROMICRO/International Labor Organization (ILO)	
	i. The Resource Foundation	9
4. Other	a. Communal credit enterprises – 230	
	b. Private firms – 29	
	c. Research institutes – 2	261
Total		276

Sources: Interviews, held in June 2005 and FINCA/Costa Rica, http://www.fic.or.cr.

to Costa Rica, where they visited CCEs and interacted with their leaders. Workshops conducted by FINCA/Costa Rica's technical personnel complemented the visits. A second phase included several trips by Padilla to each country, where additional training took place. A hands-on approach emphasized learning-by-doing followed by immediate application of the new knowledge.

(ii) *Supervision and follow up.* Again, Padilla travelled to each country to visit the new CCEs, to verify their robustness. Members of the board of directors of several Costa Rican village banks helped in the supervision and technical assistance effort and trained their Central American counterparts.

(iii) *Creation of a federation.* The project culminated in the creation of an international organization to group the five village banking programmes supported by CODESPA, known as the International Organization for Communal Microfinance (OIMC). Established in 2004, its objective is to facilitate economies of scale in both fund-raising and technical assistance efforts.

The alliance had a target of 167 new village banks, to be established by the end of a three-year period (early 2006), namely 40 in Guatemala, 45 in Nicaragua, 37 in El Salvador, and 45 in Honduras. As of April 2005, there were 186 CCEs in operation, including some created earlier in Nicaragua (Table 3.4). Of the CCEs originally planned, some are still to be established in Guatemala and El Salvador.

If the Costa Rican CCEs are excluded from the computation (because they are much older), the remaining CCEs and members (186 and 5,173, respectively) have contributed over US$130,000 worth of equity, for an average of US$700 per CCE, US$25 per member, and 25 members per CCE. When the Costa Rican CCEs – created since 1996 – are included in the figure, equity per village bank

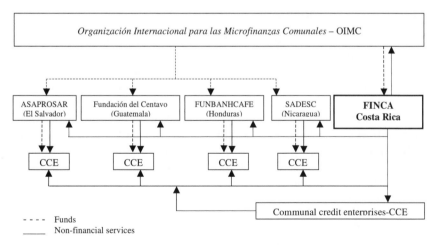

Figure 3.2 FINCA/Costa Rica: linkage with international federation of CCEs
Source: Interviews and FINCA/Costa website, http://www.fic.or.cr. Interviews held in June 2005.

Table 3.4 OIMC: results at CCE level, as of April 2005

Country	Number of CCEs	Equity (US$)	Members
Costa Rica	230	674,599	7,200
El Salvador	16	3,695	262
Guatemala	26	24,000	563
Honduras	44	29,958	1,153
Nicaragua	100	72,709	3,195
Total	416	804,961	12,373

Source: FINCA (2005).

increases to US$1,935, equity per member to US$65, and the number of members to 30. These amounts are not small for members in poor rural areas. Further, not only were all CCEs established in rural areas but also many are located in remote regions, where other lending technologies had been introduced by the same organizations with poor results.

Beyond these visible results of the international linkage, intangible but equally important outcomes have to do with the more autonomous operation of the village banks, as a result both of their greater institutional strength and their initial funding through equity. More importantly, these more robust local organizations – compared to traditional village banks – have addressed property rights weaknesses of typical NGOs, thereby increasing their potential creditworthiness with financial intermediaries and trustworthiness as enterprises capable of engaging in different types of linkages. The CCEs are village banks that have 'graduated' which allows the NGO headquarters to devote scarce resources to other strategic issues.

Alliance with a formal financial intermediary

Another institutional linkage involves three organizations, FINCA/Costa Rica, as the central player, a bank (Banco Popular), and the Confederación Nacional de Asociaciones de Desarrollo Comunal (CONADECO), a state agency that brings together communal development associations that operate in many of Costa Rica's 459 districts (Figure 3.3). FINCA/Costa Rica had already been, in its second-tier role, a client of Banco Popular, and this had given the financial intermediary an opportunity to perceive potential advantages from reaching these clienteles.

This agreement, implemented in November 2003, called for the establishment of 20 new CCEs. The Banco Popular initiative has had four objectives:
  (i)   reaching communities where the bank did not have a branch;
  (ii) attracting future clients;
  (iii) using the CCEs as windows for providing credit and credit card services;
  (iv) gathering information for feasibility studies for future branches.

Implementation began with the identification of potential communities, a responsibility of CONADECO. Despite their connections with the communal development boards, the staff of this state agency had to be trained by FINCA/ Costa Rica on the 10 rules for selecting a community. Once CONADECO identified towns with potential, FINCA began the process of creating CCEs. The linkage provided Banco Popular with an opportunity for expanding into the rural areas. It also facilitated the graduation of village banks, by establishing – from the very beginning – a linkage with a financial intermediary. Awareness of the achievements of the groups will induce the bank to finance them and, as in this case, it may even consider using them as windows for its own services.

FINCA/Costa Rica now creates CCEs only when there is an organization willing to finance all the costs. In this connection, the inter-institutional linkage with Banco Popular and CONADECO was an opportunity for grassroots

Table 3.5 FINCA/Costa Rica: results of linkage with Banco Popular, December 2003 and September 2005

Variable	December 2003	September 2005
1. Communal credit enterprises	21	21
2. Members	372	411
a. Women	240	243
b. Men	132	168
3. Children	226	94
4. Equity (US$)	4,525	15,827
5. Loan portfolio	—	17,930

Source: Interviews with FINCA/Costa Rica, June 2005.

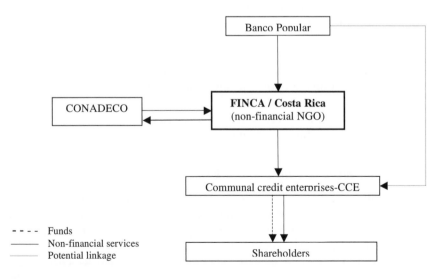

Figure 3.3 FINCA/Costa Rica: linkage with Banco Popular
Source: Interviews and FINCA/Costa Rica website, http://www.fic.or.cr. Interviews held in June 2005.

development, the creation of new village banks, and the development lending capacities otherwise not available. In the end, 21 CCEs were established. Further, for contractual reasons 12 CCEs initiated before signature of the agreement cannot be counted as part of the official list of enterprises created by the linkage.

Connection with the communal credit enterprises

The innovation of the incorporated communal credit enterprise has generated intangible dimensions not present in a traditional connection between a second-tier financial organization and the village banks in the network. There are two consequences of the atypical relationship between FINCA/Costa Rica and the CCEs. First, it has 'liberated' the apex from its commitment – and serious challenge – of satisfying the growing demands for credit from the village banks. This is not trivial, given the well-known difficulties that NGOs face in finding sources of funds. These troubles are worse because of their non-regulated nature, which constitutes both an impediment to mobilizing deposits and a repelling force for potential lenders, in general sceptical of the soundness of financial NGOs, and for local financial intermediaries willing to avoid high loan-loss provisions.

Second, the linkage between FINCA/Costa Rica and the CCEs has created several advantages:

(i)   creation of a virtuous circle, where the opportunity to establish a profitable and high-impact credit programme has become an effective mechanism – and incentive – for explicitly raising equity;

(ii) a legal status that has facilitated access to formal sources of credit and financial services in general;

(iii) more timely access to funding, given the more sound creditworthiness of the CCE;

(iv) direct access to financial services by the CCE rather than members of village banks borrowing or opening savings accounts on behalf of the organization but under their own name, with all the risks this practice involves.

These practices were observed in the four CCEs visited, including their own strategic alliances, sustainability, and consequences of being incorporated.

Strategic alliances of visited village banks

The four village banks visited showed an interesting set of institutional linkages. Their officers mentioned FINCA/Costa Rica as an important partner (past and present), a source of advice and, particularly, the mechanism through which they were created, strengthened and trained. Three of them have access to loans from several formal sources (Banco Crédito Agrícola de Cartago, Banco Nacional de Costa Rica, and Banco Popular) and one has been rejecting offers of credit from two financial intermediaries (Banco de Costa Rica and Banco Popular), evidence seldom observed in FINCA/Costa Rica's village banks of the early

1990s. Two are currently borrowing from EDESA. Their strategic alliances include financial agreements with regional development projects (funded by the Costa Rican Government and international donors), a processing plant, a producers' chamber, and a communal development association. These linkages involve technical assistance, training, institutional strengthening, and crop processing.

Several features of the CCEs, in areas such as administration, governance, and credit, favour their sustainability. These features include the growth in the number of members and their steady participation in the CCE's affairs, stability of the board of directors, growth in equity, limits on equity per shareholder, decision-making process based on the proportion of shares owned, distribution of profits according to ownership of equity, credit committees, sophisticated interest rate policies, different types of guarantees depending on loan size, limits on loan-size per shareholder, interest-rate spread, and the capitalization of profits. One of the village banks showed a hybrid governance structure; decisions are based on the one person-one vote rule, except for strategic issues, for which they use the one share-one vote criterion.

The CCEs have adopted a business approach. All of their permanent employees earn a salary, any project to be implemented has to be financially self-sufficient, and they are aware that, if the global operation is not profitable, their pockets will suffer, through a reduction in the value of their shares.

Representatives of the CCEs visited answered questions about the advantages or disadvantages of their incorporated nature. On the positive side, they mentioned that:

(i)   the sense of ownership induces additional commitment, greater interest, extra work, and more constructive criticism among the members;

(ii)   the initial equity finances a small administrative structure, a necessary condition in any organization;

(iii)   equity enables the creation of an independent credit fund;

(iv)   officers are accountable to shareholders, not to third parties;

(v)   CCEs avoid intrusion of the state (present in foundations) and politicians (usual in cooperatives);

(vi)   a business-oriented infrastructure increases opportunities;

(vii)   clearly-identified individual equity (through shares) can be sold;

(viii) distributions of profits based on ownership encourage capitalization;

(ix)   all work is remunerated, thus reducing free-riding.

Among the causes of the high mortality of traditional village banks, or their lack of growth, there are often problems of free-riding, uncertainty about asset ownership, and capture of the organization by the borrowers, with consequently high default rates, which are addressed successfully by the CCEs.

There were disadvantages of incorporation as well. The representatives mentioned:

(i)   CCEs are seen as capitalist enterprises rather than producer associations and thereby miss the chance of receiving government and international donor support;

(ii)   CCEs have fewer opportunities to receive grants than cooperatives or associations and do not enjoy tax exemptions, as is the case of cooperatives in Costa Rica.

One of the CCEs owns a supermarket, an example of the so-called 'collective projects'. These production projects, owned by all or most of the members and somewhat common in FINCA/Costa Rica's village banks of the early 1990s, were earlier criticized for seriously weakening village banks (Chaves, 1996(b)); their operation, under the new technology, should be examined.

Other linkages

As mentioned above, FINCA/Costa Rica has several other inter-institutional linkages, including:

1.   *EDESA*. Several village banks and FINCA/Costa Rica created this private financial firm. Their objective is for EDESA to undertake FINCA's former financing activities. Membership is open to any CCE or even private investors. As EDESA's major shareholder, FINCA/Costa Rica is a source of technical advice on administration and the lending business. The CCEs buy equity to reach the minimum amount that enables them to borrow. The threat from this dual role as owners and borrowers requires analysis.

2.   *Private sector*. Many private firms enthusiastically supported FINCA/Costa Rica from the beginning. Their contribution usually consisted of a grant for the creation of a number of village banks. This practice had the disadvantage, however, that it placed pressures on the organization, which had to figure out how to fund its lending activities. This is no longer the case, because each CCE is established with its own equity. Equity, leveraged by loans from financial intermediaries, funds their credit portfolio.

3.   *The Ohio State University/Academia de Centroamérica*. In the early 1990s, the OSU signed a four-year agreement with FINCA/Costa Rica, sponsored by USAID. The OSU's Rural Finance Program and ACA examined various aspects of the NGO's operation, conducted surveys, and disseminated findings on the technology. Concerns about FINCA/Costa Rica's weaknesses regarding self-sufficiency, MIS, compulsory savings and 'collective projects' as well as its problems with governance and property rights at the village bank level were raised, which induced fundamental changes in the operation of FINCA/Costa Rica.

In addition to these strategic alliances, other inter-institutional linkages developed throughout FINCA/Costa Rica's history are summarized in Table 3.3. Some just involved financing while others included institutional strengthening and research efforts.

Lessons learned

The multiple strategic alliances of FINCA/Costa Rica have been a rich source of lessons in the long run. Some of these lessons have been learned the hard way, while others have reflected important innovations that address traditional problems of village banking programmes.

Flexibility to adjust

Any process of institutional development should enjoy enough flexibility for the organization to adapt to changes in the environment and unexpected challenges. Such flexibility has characterized FINCA/Costa Rica throughout most of its history. Soon after its creation, the organization abandoned several key features of the original model of village banking that it had initially adopted, including the in-kind repayment of loans. The synchronization between repayment schedules and harvest cycles needed in lending to agriculture was absent in the original model, but FINCA/Costa Rica soon adopted it. Thus, in contrast to other village banking programmes, agricultural loans have been important in the portfolio of these atypical village banks. These and other revisions of the traditional methodology allowed the Costa Rican village banks to experience rapid growth and to begin thinking about the provision of other financial services.

In a second phase, FINCA/Costa Rica introduced the equity contribution certificates (CCPs) as a means to address the difficult governance and property rights issues that usually emerge at the village bank level. Later on, the organization consolidated this reform with the innovative creation of village banks as incorporated firms (that is, CCEs as *sociedades anónimas* – private companies).

Another important adjustment has been the transformation of the organization from a microfinance NGO – a role whose expansion presented many challenges in Costa Rica – to a rural development organization. This shift was motivated, in part, by challenges from the evolution of the environment. The conversion was also the result, however, of the NGO's inability to implement timely adjustments in areas such as staff selection and MIS. These shortcomings – which precisely reflected the limitations that many NGOs encounter in accomplishing this upgrade – had removed any credible ability to responsibly manage the growing credit component. Confronted with this, FINCA made the pragmatic (actually hard but brave and correct) decision of closing its credit programme at the second-tier level, before this component killed the organization. The design of the new type of village banks, the communal credit enterprises (CCE), has been among the new tasks of the organization.

Impact

The gradual creation by FINCA/Costa Rica of an international network of CCEs presents a unique opportunity to examine how the innovative design and a similar set of alliances perform in different social, economic, regulatory and institutional environments. This makes it possible to analyse the impact of diverse exogenous characteristics on the probability of success of the CCEs and the alliances that they have developed.

One interesting challenge has been the need to translate the materials from Spanish to various native languages, for the benefit of CCE members in several regions of Guatemala. Similarly, some teaching instruments had to be abandoned or modified, given the isolation of many communities without access to television. These circumstances are, nevertheless, evidence of the rurality and remoteness of the communities served by the NGOs linked to FINCA/Costa Rica. In the past, these Central American NGOs had unsuccessfully tried to implement credit programmes in these communities. Even in Costa Rica, with a much higher road density and easier access, there are communities that FINCA would not yet have served if it were not for the alliance it established last year with the Banco Popular. Because of this linkage, 21 CCEs were created, with a total equity of US$5,051 and 372 partners (not including members who are minors). As of September 2005, this equity had tripled (to US$15,563), there was a credit portfolio of US$17,000, and the number of partners had increased to 411.

Institutional strengthening

One of the hardest lessons learned by FINCA/Costa Rica has been that any organization that is growing needs to sufficiently strengthen all dimensions of its structure, be properly staffed (both in terms of numbers and qualifications), and have a good MIS. The NGO's weaknesses in these areas were already highlighted in the 1990s (Wenner, 1990; Chaves and Quirós, 1996). In particular, these observers noticed the lack of an adequate database, essential to provide the Executive Director with quick and reliable information about the operation and financial self-sufficiency of the NGO as well as the operation of the associated village banks. This problem was recently resolved, but only now that the credit programme has disappeared and that the requirements of information are probably less demanding. While these problems are common to many financial NGOs – except the most robust – the importance of information management highlights some of the challenges that these organizations may encounter, as they expand their range of activities and develop linkages that require timely information for relevant managerial decisions.

Similarly, FINCA/Costa Rica had a chronic problem with its personnel. The head of the organization now acknowledges that its older staff had enthusiasm in excess but that many of them lacked the skills or the training needed to carry out their responsibilities in a successful manner. The result was a concentration of the decision-making process in the hands of the Executive Director. Most of her time was frequently spent in tackling problems (of which there were never proper early warnings). As a result, the Executive Director could never dedicate enough time to the more productive and urgent strategic planning or fund-raising activities. This concentration on a prominent and irreplaceable head person is quite typical of this generation of NGOs, and it may spill over into inter-institutional linkages that are mostly based on personal relationships between such unique individuals.

Conditionality

The history of FINCA/Costa Rica reveals one of the most complete lists of requirements that emerge from the conditionality established by a wide range of organizations with which the NGO had or has established alliances. The most frequent stipulations were related to institutional linkages that included a credit component in the arrangement and that fixed the interest rates that FINCA could charge on its loans to the village banks and that the latter could charge on loans to the final clients. This requirement forced the NGO to disburse funds from lines of credit at different interest rates (depending on the source of the funds), with the corresponding cumbersome and costly administration. It also induced uneasiness among the members of the village banks, who complained about the different costs between one bank and another and who sometimes decided to remove a loan request until cheaper funds, from other source, became available.

A second source of conditionality in the agreements signed by FINCA was related to the selection of personnel and consulting firms and to items permissible for financing by the partner organization. In one case, the partner organization forced the selection of a particular firm for the development of FINCA/Costa Rica's MIS. The firm had great expertise in computer training for primary and high school students, but it was far from being an expert in developing business software. The project was a fiasco and a waste of scarce resources. This remained, sadly, precisely one of the weakest areas of the NGO, where much and timely support was needed.

Another example took place in the early 1990s, with a donor's insistence on the purchase of a computer for each village bank. The project was finally abandoned when FINCA convinced the donor's representative that many of the village bank 'offices' (namely, the kitchen table in the house of one of its members) did not have the conditions (for example, electricity was not available) for using a computer. As time went by, the village banks acquired a desk and a filing cabinet, and the larger ones even had a whole room to be used as an office. By the mid-1990s, several groups had acquired computers.

FINCA/Costa Rica was always aware of the negative consequences of these conditions. Nevertheless, it never used the prominent position and authority that it had acquired in local and international circles as leverage for negotiating better agreements with its partners in these alliances. This probably resulted from the great pressures the organization always encountered in funding its operations. Thus, FINCA/Costa Rica confronted a trade-off. It was desperate to obtain funds to respond to the growing demand for credit by a rapidly growing set of village banks, but it then ended up accepting the conditionality that accompanied the funding.

Nowadays, the traditional interest-rate conditionality is not that frequent, but it has not totally disappeared. Many well-established MFOs worldwide, regulated intermediaries and non-regulated NGOs, have successfully dealt with donor attempts to limit their flexibility with unnecessary and distorting conditions on the loans they disburse. The more subtle (yet equally damaging) conditions described above, however, should also be confronted with the same resolution and assertiveness.

Integrity of the technology

In the establishment of any strategic alliance not only should there be a clear understanding of the extent of the agreement but, in addition, the financial NGO should usually not allow the inclusion, as part of the negotiations, of a modification of its lending technology or changes in aspects that are inherent to its own operation, particularly if these features have been developed by the NGO and are working well before the agreement.

FINCA/Costa Rica has developed a technology that includes detailed guidelines for group creation and even for selecting a community. These procedures are the result of years of learning by doing, of trial and error. Such efforts should not be underestimated and, hence, the NGO should only modify the technology based on technical considerations and never in order to respond to transitory requests of the partner entity.

FINCA has surrendered to the temptation of modifying the procedures in order to obtain additional funding. Some of these mistakes had to do with:

(i) *Community selection.* There have been partners that have chosen communities, without following the 10 steps that FINCA/Costa Rica has established for this purpose. Either the groups have experienced problems soon after their creation, or FINCA has had to start the community selection process all over again.

(ii) *Creation versus strengthening.* Many organizations wanted partnerships with FINCA/Costa Rica so they could later say that they had sponsored the creation of a given number of groups, while the new village banks were presented as 'theirs'. This pushed the NGO into a dangerous race to create groups, with consequences not only for quality control but also in demands for loanable funds, a particularly serious challenge given the inevitable increases in loan size after each cycle. What FINCA/Costa Rica did not apply when it operated as an NGO it is now transmitting to the partners in the federation of CCEs: the need to reject demands from potential partners seeking only to create groups. Instead, FINCA/Costa Rica has urged partner NGOs to promote sponsorship of current CCEs. Moreover, in the technology for creating CCEs, the inauguration of the communal enterprise is the ninth step. The result is a stronger organization by the time of inauguration and a diminished temptation by donors to speed up the creation of groups, just for the sake of showing the accomplishment.

(iii)   *Staff training.* FINCA/Costa Rica has committed to train personnel from the partner organizations, so they can support the lengthy process of group formation. This creates local capacity at the partner organization and accumulates human capital. Moreover, it allows FINCA to undertake projects that it would have rejected because of the high cost of the 22 steps for creating a group.

Politics

One unrelenting risk in establishing alliances with the state is the abuse of the project for political purposes, either during the development of a project or afterwards, intentionally or as an unexpected outcome. Something that appears as a good opportunity may end up being counterproductive for the organization. FINCA/Costa Rica has suffered from this wheedling. One case was a linkage with an agency of the Ministry of Agriculture. The agency convinced FINCA/ Costa Rica to create dozens of village banks in a region were the NGO had never operated. In the end, the agency did not assume all of the technical assistance costs, and FINCA ended up with the obligation of finding loanable funds for all of the groups created. This was not possible and, many years after, the members of these groups complain, not against the state, the Ministry or the agency involved, but FINCA, who they claim left them alone.

Another incident resulted from an alliance with another state agency in charge of promoting agro-industrial projects, with funds from an international organization with an agricultural focus. The problems caused by the state agency were many, including: the selection of communities according to political priorities, thus ignoring the guidelines prepared by FINCA/Costa Rica; the involvement of the members of village banks in agroindustrial projects of dubious sustainability; and statements to the borrowers that they did not need to repay the loans, because the funding came from an international donor.

One recent case was a trust fund created by the state to purchase past due agricultural debt. FINCA decided to get rid of a few large borrowers that had stopped repaying. Many others, however, who were paying their loans on time, stopped doing so, because one of the conditions for being considered for write-off was to be behind in their payments.

In some of these examples, there were reasons to expect a bad outcome. In others, FINCA/Costa Rica could claim that the project seemed good but that, in the process, things went wrong. As a rule of thumb, organizations that are considering engaging in strategic alliances with the state should establish a linkage only when it is about a public service (for example, a utility), collecting or disbursing funds for an activity that reaches the entire country or a whole region. On the contrary, specific projects, targeted at particular groups with the same geographic location, may be better avoided, because they can easily be used politically, with potential negative externalities for the organization involved.

Incorporated village banks

The connection between FINCA/Costa Rica and the CCEs it creates has several innovative features:

(i)   establishing the CCEs is a comprehensive process that requires at least 22 weeks of technical assistance;

(ii) the basic initial requirements of the CCEs are funded only with liquid equity provided by shareholders;

(iii) no funds are transferred from FINCA/Costa Rica to the CCEs, either grants or loans;

(iv) the CCEs provide credit and deposit facilities to shareholders and non-shareholders;

(v)   the amounts of equity and deposits raised by the CCEs are relatively high, both in absolute terms and per individual, and are the primary source of funding for the credit programme;

(vi) the CCEs are business oriented: they permanently seek their financial self-sufficiency and everyone working for the enterprise receives either a salary or some type of remuneration;

(vii) the CCEs have developed their own network of strategic alliances, which includes formal financial intermediaries willing to lend to these village banks.

In short, this innovative design has induced what seems to be sustainable grass-roots development accompanied by a self-financed credit mechanism, facilitating direct financial layering by the CCEs. The evidence seems to confirm the research assumptions of the case study, namely that the organizational and legal innovations pave the way for the CCEs in establishing other linkages, beyond the existing one with FINCA/Costa Rica; and that this robust type of village banks allows the apex organization opportunities to address strategic issues.

Conclusions and recommendations

Costa Rica has never been associated with the microfinance world, and yet some of the earlier experiments of renowned microfinance networks took place in this country. Practically all of the MFOs established in Costa Rica in the 1980s with support from these international programmes have disappeared. Several reasons explain this outcome, including the availability of a wide network of branches of the formal financial sector, the small size of the country, good communication services (public transportation, road density, and phone lines), the relatively small informal microenterprise sector and the absence of a large concentration of microentrepreneurs in urban areas. The heavy presence of the state in financial markets has further inhibited the development of microfinance. These characteristics have resulted in a small ratio of the population per bank branch and relatively high levels of access to the services of formal financial intermediaries, thus crowding out the MFOs that dared to operate in this environment.

The exception to the high failure rate of MFOs in Costa Rica was Fundación Integral Campesina, established by John Hatch and María Marta Padilla in 1984. Survival was probably the result of this NGO's willingness to transform, regardless of the magnitude and consequences of the adjustments required. This flexible approach began a few months after FINCA/Costa Rica's creation, resulting in a very different model from the design Hatch began to introduce worldwide (FINCA International). The Costa Rican model became an exclusively rural village banking programme, without gender targets but with a 30 per cent participation of women and with payments in cash rather than in kind, careful selection of members and strong emphasis on training, and adaptation of the terms to maturity of the loans to crop cycles, resulting in mostly an agricultural portfolio. Several but not all of these innovations were later adopted by the international programme, a potential positive externality that has not been acknowledged.

A second stage of major adjustments arrived 10 years after its creation, motivated by an external evaluation (OSU) that highlighted governance problems at three levels:

(i)   for the headquarters of FINCA/Costa Rica, the usual NGO shortcomings were aggravated by the absence of efficient MIS and lack of concerns about financial self-sufficiency;

(ii)   for the village banks, their sustainability was threatened by lack of clarity about property rights;

(iii)   for the system, there were flaws in the overall dynamic relationship between the headquarters and the village banks.

The most influential outcome of the OSU assessment was the introduction of the patrimonial contribution certificates (CCPs), an instrument that attempted to reproduce the behaviour observed in corporations at the level of village banks legally established as civil associations.

Shortly after, in 1996, the innovation was consolidated by the creation of a new type of village banks and transformation of the older ones into incorporated firms, giving birth to the communal credit enterprises (CCEs). FINCA/Costa Rica's former general manager and now director of its regional project has been heavily involved in the dissemination of the CCE design, an effort that has taken the model to Venezuela, Ecuador, Panama, Nicaragua, Honduras, Guatemala and El Salvador, and will eventually take it to Colombia and Mexico.

The governance problems at the headquarters and system levels were never effectively confronted, however. The consequence was seen a decade later; in the early 2000s FINCA/Costa Rica reinvented itself, by specializing in the creation of CCEs, leaving behind the role of financial apex in its relationship with the village banks. FINCA/Costa Rica is now a rural development organization.

Despite its new focus, the organization still retains one characteristic: a multiplicity of linkages. FINCA/Costa Rica has a record of over 300 strategic alliances throughout its history, including the connection with the village banks in the network; excluding the latter, the number of linkages is still an impressive 59, with all sorts of partners. Moreover, after the elimination of the financial component, alliances have become more complex, involving FINCA/ Costa Rica, the village banks and sources of financial services.

Another positive point of FINCA/Costa Rica's strategic alliances is its key role in a regional project involving MFOs in Nicaragua, Honduras, Guatemala, and El Salvador. The result has been, in general, an extended and more sustainable rural outreach of financial services in these countries and, particularly, the creation of nearly 200 CCEs, with over 12,000 partners and US$130,000 in equity.

Numerous lessons learned and recommendations have emerged from these linkages, such as:

(i)   *Alliances with the state.* It is usual for NGOs to establish linkages with state agencies, both local and international (the donor community). It is important for the NGO to avoid conditionalities of the old type (interest rate restrictions, for example) as well as other requirements, such as the imposition of consultants, expansion into certain regions or adoption of unsustainable projects. The NGO should try to accept only those alliances with the state involving products that are widely offered, preferably if the service is shared with other organizations; this may work as a shield against the use of a certain service by the government's propaganda. International donors are natural allies, given their relatively good networking and access to state of the art technology.

(ii) *Flexibility to adapt.* MFOs should always try to keep their mission and values. The mechanisms for achieving this goal, however, may and should vary over time, in order to adapt well to changing circumstances, at three levels: the organization, the microfinance industry, and the environment (social, economic, regulatory). In other words, the organizations should be flexible and willing to change, no matter how difficult the adjustments may seem.

(iii) *Linkages with the private sector.* Private firms are willing to support development projects, an interest that has increased in recent years because of the work of social corporate responsibility movements. MFOs should take advantage of this, by establishing alliances with the private sector, particularly firms involved in value chain relationships with the village banks. This is the case of processing plants that buy the production of micro or small entrepreneurs or formal financial intermediaries that could supply financial services to the village banks. The NGO should be careful, however, not to surrender to the frequent pressures to create village banks beyond its ability to address all the short and medium terms demands for funds.

(iv) *Incorporated village banks.* The CCE model developed by FINCA/Costa Rica facilitates a self-sufficient internal credit mechanism, direct financial layering by the village banks and, in general, greater sustainability compared to its predecessors and most of its counterparts worldwide. This innovative model is smoothing the way for the CCEs to establish alliances with third parties and is allowing FINCA/Costa Rica to concentrate its energies on strategic issues rather than the day-to-day problems of the village banks. The incorporated village bank design addresses governance issues at two of the three levels of problems identified by OSU, namely the village bank and the system. The final impact on governance at the headquarters level will depend on the magnitude of two opposite effects. Alliances with stronger CCEs make it easier for the administration of the NGO to tackle old and new issues, thus reducing the strength of some of the threats. In turn, however, the linkages with the incorporated village banks may reduce the pressure (i.e. the incentive) the headquarters have for improving operations, MIS or fund-raising.

(v) *International dissemination of technology.* The creation of a regional network of CCEs presents a unique opportunity to examine similar alliances under different social, economic, regulatory, and institutional environments.

Future studies should address the consequences for the operation of EDESA of its governance structure: it is owned by village banks that at the same time are clients of the firm. Collective production projects should also be examined, to determine if the new incorporated status of the CCEs minimizes the property rights problems that these projects showed under the old village bank design.

References

Banco Central de Costa Rica: http://www.bccr.fi.cr/flat/bccr_flat.htm [accessed 25 October 2007]

Chaves, R. (1996a) 'Institutional design. The case of the bancomunales' in Gonzalez-Vega, C. Jiménez, R. and Quirós, R. *Financing rural microenterprises, FINCA Costa Rica*, The Ohio State University and Academia de Centroamérica, San Jose.

Chaves, R. (1996b) 'Property rights and collective projects. FINCA's bancomunales', in Gonzalez-Vega, C., Jiménez R. and Quirós, R. *Financing rural microenterprises: FINCA Costa Rica*, The Ohio State University and Academia de Centroamérica, San Jose.

Chaves, R. and Quirós, R. (1996) 'FINCA: financial analysis', in Gonzalez-Vega, C., Jiménez, R. and Quirós, R, *Financing rural microenterprises, FINCA Costa Rica*, The Ohio State University and Academia de Centroamérica, San José.

Comisión Económica para América Latina y el Caribe (ECLAC): http://www.eclac.org/estadisticas/ [accessed 25 October 2007]

FINCA/Costa Rica. Interviews held in June 2005 and website, http://www.fic.or.cr [accessed 25 October 2007]

Gonzalez-Vega, C. (1973) 'Small Farmer Credit in Costa Rica: the Juntas Rurales', in *Small Farmer Credit in Costa Rica*, AID Spring Review of Small Farmer Credit, Agency for International Development, Washington D.C.

Gonzalez-Vega, C., Jiménez R. and Mesalles L. (1989) 'Costa Rica: Fuentes de crédito para los agricultores', Academia de Centroamérica for USAID, San Jose.

El Instituto Nacional de Estádistica y Censo (INEC): http://www.inec.go.cr

Jiménez, R. et al. (1996) 'FINCA: Evolution of a methodology', in Gonzalez-Vega, C. Jiménez, R. and Quirós, R. *Financing rural microenterprises: FINCA Costa Rica*, The Ohio State University and Academia de Centroamérica, San Jose.

Jiménez, R. and Quirós, R. (1994) 'Las Juntas Rurales de Crédito' in Gonzalez-Vega, C. and Camacho, E. *Regulación, competencia y eficiencia en la banca costarricense*, The Ohio State University and Academia de Centroamerica, San Jose.

Quirós, R. (1991) 'Access to Agricultural Credit in Costa Rica. A Multinomial Logit Analysis', Master's Thesis, Ohio State University.

Superintendencia General de Entidades Financieras Costa Rica (SUGEF) (2005): http://www.sugef.fi.cr/

United Nations Development Programme (UNDP): http://www.undp.org/

Wenner, M. (1990) 'Group credit in Costa Rica. An econometric analysis of information transfer, repayment performance, and cost effectiveness', Paper presented at the annual meetings of the American Association of Agricultural Economists, Vancouver.

CHAPTER 4

Opportunities for the creation of linkages and alliances to expand the supply of rural financial services: The José María Covelo Foundation and its partners in Honduras

Mayra Falck, Rodolfo Quirós and Claudio Gonzalez-Vega

Abstract

The case of the José María Covelo Foundation in Honduras describes an interesting story of the foundation's evolution from a typical second-tier organization providing capacity building training and funding to private development finance organizations (PDOs) to one of a highly sophisticated holding company offering financial, human resource management, administrative, systems, marketing and organizational services to the six organizations in the holding group. The study focuses on a multiplicity of intra- and extra-group linkages with a range of financial and non-financial actors. The authors examine market-deepening linkages for rural finance and provide in-depth analysis of two local organizations and their linkages with Covelo Group among others. This case is rich in detail and at times complex, but provides many lessons for those interested in following a similar institutional development path.

Introduction

An expansion of the supply of financial services into the rural areas of developing countries is not an easy undertaking. Those financial entities that seek to establish a rural presence face numerous obstacles, including the high costs of overcoming the information, incentive and contract enforcement problems typically found in financial transactions, and the high systemic risks associated with operating in local markets. These obstacles make an increase in their rural outreach a slow process. There are, as well, managerial, funding, and regulatory constraints that frequently keep some organizations from offering a wider range of financial services to their actual and potential rural clientele.

In addressing these challenges, some organizations take advantage of their greater proximity (e.g. geographic, sectoral, cultural, ethnic) to particular classes of rural clients, but they can usually offer only a narrow range of financial services, given the constraints resulting from the local nature of their operations. These organizations may address the limitations either by:

- developing a comprehensive, in-house organizational structure – that is, by directly offering a whole range of financial services through a network of their own branches – *à la* PRODEM in Bolivia or;
- creating the equivalent of a planetary system – that is, by making a series of services available to their clientele through a number of institutional linkages and alliances, developed around a core programme activity.

This case study focuses on the activities of the group of organizations known as the Covelo Foundation, in Honduras, and of two non-governmental organizations (NGOs), namely Hermandad de Honduras (HDH) and the Asociación Proyecto e Iniciativas Locales para el Autodesarrollo Regional de Honduras (PILARH). Both NGOs offer financial services in rural areas and are part of the network of partners of the Covelo Foundation. The experience of these three organizations offers interesting lessons about strategic alliances, linkages, and relationships created to promote an expansion of the outreach of microfinance organizations into the rural areas of a poor country.

Despite the important achievements of some microfinance organizations, rural financial markets have been comparatively shallow in Honduras, and in the past most gains in outreach have not been sustainable. In addition, these markets have recently suffered important setbacks, mostly from the political interference that has accompanied legislated loan pardoning and has discouraged private bank intermediation. Moreover, in recent decades, very few, if any, of the numerous interventions and schemes designed to assist rural development in Honduras – including policies, projects and strategies for the promotion of formal and informal finance – have managed to trigger the kinds of organizational linkages and alliances that could reverse the productive, environmental, and social degradation that has characterized the country during this period. Instances of success have thus remained as isolated cases.

This case study shows, nevertheless, that linkages and alliances between second-tier institutions and financial organizations with an established presence in some agricultural regions have the potential to trigger positive local impacts among their clients. Indeed, the resulting access to these services seems to have contributed to the alleviation of poverty, chiefly by improving the borrowers' links to all types of markets and by thereby allowing a diversification of their sources of income towards non-farming activities. Some additional key questions to be addressed, however, are the following: Why, despite some successful experiences, has it not been possible to broadly replicate them in the rural areas of Honduras? Why, even when a first-tier organization has entered into an alliance with a second-tier institution and it has developed close bonds with its clients, is it unable to increase the scale of its operations? Why is the sustainability of this kind of organization so fragile? Answers to these, quite universal, questions may shed some light on preconditions for the robustness of linkages between financial organizations.

The rest of the chapter is structured into five sections. The following section summarizes the conceptual and methodological framework for the case study. The second section analyses the country context, including key economic and rural indicators, decisive events that have changed the country's rural development paradigm, and the policy and legal framework for rural financial intermediation. The third section explains the logical framework for the activities of the José María Covelo Foundation, as a private development organization involved in the financial services industry, and it highlights three main phases in its evolution. The fourth section analyses the specific linkages developed between the Covelo Foundation and HDH and PILARH, respectively, as well as the alliances developed by each of these NGOs on its own. The section highlights the vulnerability of these organizations, despite the linkages. The final section identifies lessons learned and conclusions.

Conceptual and methodological approach

The case study adopts several conceptual perspectives for analysis. First, it starts from the premise that the dynamics of development in the rural areas vary according to their agro-ecological, productive, and social conditions. In part by ignoring this, the public policies adopted to encourage rural development in Honduras have failed to promote the kinds of synergies that would have the potential to sustain rural financial market deepening. Because these synergies can be quite powerful, stronger linkages and alliances among market actors and development agents – at both the national and the rural levels – would not only allow local financial organizations to expand their outreach but also to develop lending technologies better adapted to specific local circumstances.

Thus, a 'territorial' approach is one of the conceptual frameworks used here as a platform for the analysis (and it is one that should be used for the implementation) of initiatives and policies at the rural level. This approach follows De Janvry and Sadoulet (2004), who have justified the differentiation between favourable rural areas and marginal rural areas and have suggested the use of this distinction as a guide in creating greater value added in the rural areas, in promoting linkages between urban and rural areas, and in incorporating the poor into markets for labour and products.

Second, the case study incorporates a concept of 'livelihoods' to highlight the complexity of farm-household strategies, particularly critical in examining the relationships of the local organizations with their clients. Third, following the recent contributions of Lederman (2005) and Jansen, Siegel, and Pichón (2005), the study stresses the importance of secure access to a bundle of 'assets' in promoting rural development. Fourth, the case study uses the distinction, introduced by North (1993), between 'institutions' – defined as the rules that constrain behaviour, including the governance of organizations – and 'organizations' – defined as the actual structures that allow various forms of collective action. Finally, the analysis makes use of concepts of horizontal organization, to evaluate alliances, linkages, and structures across organizations.

This case study examines the evolution of the Covelo Foundation, an organization with operations at both the first-tier and the second-tier in the provision of financial services. The 'profound-change' approach introduced by Senge et al. (2000) is used to study the development of the Foundation's linkages and alliances. This approach describes organizational change as a whole, combining internal modifications (values, approaches and aspirations) with external changes (strategies, practices and systems). The analysis of profound change at Covelo starts from the premise that various linkages and alliances have generated significant learning within the organization. The case study isolates and characterizes the various relationships and draws key lessons from these experiences.

Linkages are classified into two types. On the one hand, there are backward linkages, with organizations such as the National Commission on Banking and Insurance (CNBS), financial policymakers, including the Honduran National Congress (CN), and donors and other financial institutions. On the other hand, forward linkages are developed with first-tier organizations, such as HDH and PILARH.

HDH and PILARH concentrate their operations in three of seven agricultural regions, characterized by the mountains and valleys of the coffee-growing region of western Honduras and by the mountains and hills of southern Honduras, respectively. The linkages and alliances between each one of these two organizations and other formal and informal institutions beyond Covelo, as well as the bonds with their clients, are also considered. This makes it possible to cover the entire value chain of rural financial services in these three agricultural regions and to identify the connections of the chain with the policymaking processes.

The case study is based on a review of documentation and on interviews with Covelo managers, to evaluate the role of the linkages in relation to rural development and financial policies, at large, as well as on interviews with executives, the technical staff, and clients of both first-tier organizations. Further, executives and staff of Banco de Occidente, which keeps alliances with both HDH and PILARH, were also interviewed. Consequently, the case study reports their perceptions, evaluated in the light of a systematic review of documentation about trends in the economy, rurality, development policies, and organizations.

Country context

This section briefly discusses three dimensions of Honduras relevant to the case study: firstly, the characteristics of rurality, with special attention to the sector's diversity and processes of differentiation; secondly, main trends in the economy, with a comparison of the situation pre- and post-Hurricane Mitch; and, thirdly, a summary of the current legal framework for rural and financial matters.

The rural sector in the aggregate economy

Honduras is characterized by substantial rural diversity, accompanied by unstable economic growth, marked income inequality, and widespread poverty, particularly in the rural areas. Assorted environmental conditions, a varied territorial profile, and climate have favoured diversity in rural organization. This has resulted in the differentiation of seven agricultural regions, marked by deep regional inequalities. The availability of water has led to a pattern of land use centred on the so-called 'T of development' (*T del desarrollo*), which combines humid and dry tropics, and of which the Puerto Cortés-Choluteca corridor forms the stem and the Atlantic coast forms the top of the T. Sixty per cent of the Honduran population is concentrated in this area, which includes the country's main cities and the majority of its infrastructure of roads, telecommunications, airports, and electric supplies as well as the largest and most important valleys. Striking backwardness characterizes the rural areas excluded from the 'T of development' where, by and large, poverty is concentrated.

Policy reforms have not been sufficient to reverse the social and environmental degradation that compounds poverty, with losses in marginal areas from drought, soil erosion, and floods that increase each year. This unfavourable state of affairs has been exacerbated by the variability of coffee and oil prices, in augmenting agricultural risks and in putting pressure on the country's balance of payments (Falck, 2004).

Income per capita has grown slowly. The annual rates of growth of GDP averaged 3.4 and 2.8 per cent in the 1980s and 1990s, resulting in rates of growth of per capita GDP of 0.3 and 0.1 per cent, respectively. In recent years (2000–4), rates of growth of GDP ranged between 4.3 and 5.7 per cent, with a population growth rate of 2.6 per cent per year (1988–2002). Thus, per capita income was less than US$950 in 2002. According to the World Bank's classification of low income countries, in 2002 Honduras ranked 144th among 201 countries. In 2003, the UNDP Human Development Index was 0.657 for Honduras, below the Latin American and Caribbean average of 0.777, and the country ranked in 115th place out of 175 countries (Falck and Pino, 2003).

Agriculture's share in the GDP shrank, from 20 per cent in 1992 to less than 14 per cent in 2001 (Bustamante and Falck, 2005). Still, agriculture accounted for 34 per cent of total employment in 2000, compared to 39 per cent employed in the informal sector (Sauma, 2001). The contrast between the share of agriculture in employment and its contribution to the GDP is an indication of the low productivity of labour in agriculture. By 2004, about 55 per cent of the country's population lived, and 34 per cent of its labour force worked, in the rural areas (Instituto Nacional de Estadística, INE).

Despite their limited reliability, all sources agree that the incidence of poverty is concentrated in this rural sector. According to the Ministry of Agriculture, 75 per cent of the rural population was poor in 2004. INE confirmed that, in 2003, two out of every three Hondurans were poor and that three out of every four poor Hondurans were extremely poor. At the turn of the century, the Gini coefficient for the distribution of income was 0.564, with the poorest 40 per cent of the population earning only 12 per cent of total income, whereas the richest 10 per cent earned 37 per cent.

Decisive events

Three decisive events marked a return to a rural approach in Honduras, with a new vision of investing in the rural areas, in order to raise competitiveness. The new approach uses a value chain perspective and focuses on public interventions and policies that improve access to a package of what are assumed to be engines of economic growth and rural development, including rural finance and access to knowledge.

The first decisive event was Hurricane Mitch, which struck Honduras in 1998, with losses equivalent to at least 70 per cent of its GDP. This event marked a change in the country's development paradigm, by showing that the earlier anti-rural bias of policies and, especially, the polarization caused by targeted subsidies had resulted in great vulnerability, in terms both of environmental and social capital, thereby exacting high economic and social costs. Instead, rural areas with fragile ecosystems are now being considered as strategic in planning interventions and investments by the public sector, private development organizations, and international agencies. This paradigm change stemmed from three main factors: (i) the fragility of rural production systems (hillsides and valleys); (ii) rural depopulation, because of migration; and (iii) a reduction in forest cover, because of the expansion of livestock holdings (the *ganaderización* of agriculture). The new approach emphasizes local development, governance, microenterprises, and microfinance, in efforts to build human and social capital in the rural areas and reduce environmental and social vulnerability.

The second decisive event was the recent fall in coffee prices, which highlighted the vulnerability of the economy vis-à-vis international price fluctuations and concentration in a few export crops. This has called for a revamping of the country's trade strategies, which will have significant influence on the rural areas, where one out of every four farm producers is a coffee grower. These two events highlight the importance of mechanisms to address systemic risks, including the role of access to financial services (deposits and loans) for consumption smoothing and the potential role of indexed insurance.

The third decisive event has been the inclusion of Honduras in the Free Trade Agreement between the United States and Central America and the Dominican Republic (CAFTA/DR), with the opportunities that it creates and the concerns about the competitiveness of traditional agriculture that it raises (Monge-González et al., 2004; Lederman, 2005). Increased competitiveness has been identified as key for rural development. This has prompted several development agencies to use approaches centred on value chains. In turn, this has led to a debate on investment in education as a key factor in promoting change. All of this has culminated in the drafting of a National Competitiveness Plan in 2005, expected to assist in donor coordination.

The policy and legal framework for poverty reduction, rural development, and financial regulation

Prior to Hurricane Mitch, since the 1970s rural financial policies had been centred on the supply of subsidized credit by the state-owned agricultural development bank, BANADESA, which lacked transparency and encouraged political intrusion, resulting in high rates of delinquency. In the 1980s, macroeconomic instability resulted in the drying up of long-term finance, while the enactment of the Caribbean Basin Initiative led to the promotion of non-traditional exports using traditional rediscount lines of credit. In the 1990s, stabilization and structural adjustment policies led to a reduction of the preferential lines of credit and to the consolidation of FONAPROVI (the National Fund for Production and Housing), which channelled donor funds to the rural areas and other sectors. The United States Agency for International Development (USAID) and other donors promoted the formation of several microfinance organizations and networks, including Covelo.

A milestone in the promotion of rural financial deepening was the approval, in April of 1992, of the Law on the Modernization and Development of the Agricultural Sector. This legislation allowed the creation of rural savings and loan organizations (*cajas rurales de ahorro y crédito*). Throughout most of the 1990s, several projects, including those financed by the International Fund for Agricultural Development (IFAD), promoted the creation and operation of these *cajas rurales*. They were set up according to diverse operational models, at a time when the regulations governing their establishment and operation had not yet been approved.

After Hurricane Mitch, the goals of policy were redirected to respond to liberalization and deregulation, national reconstruction and transformation, and poverty reduction. The new policies defined visions and actions frequently at odds with each other, but with five main common objectives, namely: (i) poverty reduction, with a strong welfare flavour; (ii) development of the agrifood production sector, while ignoring non-agricultural activities; (iii) economic recovery; (iv) environmental sustainability; and (v) citizen involvement. All rural development and agrifood policies have identified credit as a key mechanism in launching productive activities. FONADERS (Sustainable Rural Development Fund) disburses project funds via three channels: (i) direct project financing; (ii) setting up trusts; and (iii) funds transferred by means of agreements and/or contracting. These channels are outside the regulated financial sector, creating distortions in the development of rural financial markets.

While there are no specific policies for the promotion of rural finance, the existing regulatory frameworks influence the provision of financial services for the rural sector through the categorization of a higher risk for farming activities, the legislated cancellation of agricultural debt, and the financing of production by state agencies.

Several features of the general policy framework and specific regulatory frameworks for finance, rural development, and the environment relate to the core theme of the study:

- The policies for the regulation of financial transactions have failed to take into consideration the specific requirements of rural areas.
- Rural development policies are centred on regulating structures and on creating a diverse range of offices, programmes and operational units at the central level, the operation of which lacks a proper territorial approach.
- Rather than a financial sector approach, the focus is on operating credit funds. This offers room to manoeuvre to programmes and projects that concentrate on channelling funds but that make very little effort to regulate transactions, in order to decrease risk and increase impact.
- Environmental policies have no operational links with financial policies.

Whereas aggregate financial policies are making significant progress in Honduras towards organizational linkages and harmonization, through the development of prudential regulation and the analysis of risk, rural development policies are consolidating the central management of structures, with a marked tendency to channel resources without regard for consistency with the requirements of financial development.

Debt cancellation trends

The Honduran financial system has been in crisis since Hurricane Mitch, because of low loan recovery rates resulting from substantial losses in the agricultural sector, moral hazard, and political economy forces. Agricultural loans represented 21 per cent of the credit portfolio in the formal banking system in 2000. Total delinquency rates rose from 17 per cent in 1998 to 24 per cent of the portfolio in 1999.

To address these problems, debt-relief mechanisms – chiefly for the agricultural sector – have been designed, including Velasteguí (2003):

- interest-rate relief, for reactivating and readjusting outstanding loans and transactions in default;
- relief on the borrowed principal;
- loan guarantees;
- establishment of a credit line in BANADESA;
- issue of bonds by FONAPROVI;
- constitution of a coffee trust;
- discount on the nominal value of loans acquired.

The banks have played a key role in operating these mechanisms, as they have powers to determine which producers to benefit. Many borrowers with past due transactions have had problems in obtaining new loans, as the banks have been reluctant to lend in cases of evident moral hazard. Already by 2002 there was a 66 per cent decline in the volume of new loans from the banking sector. According to the data analysed by Velasteguí, those who have benefited the most from the legislative decrees are producers with access to banking, which has excluded small-scale agricultural producers from these benefits. The debt cancellation process has had three main consequences: (i) there has been unfair competition with the recently regulated non-bank financial sector; (ii) the benefits of debt write-offs for certain groups have heavily undermined the overall willingness to repay; and (iii) lack of familiarity with the operating mechanisms has given rise to confusion.

José María Covelo Foundation

This section describes the set of linkages and alliances (financial and non-financial) forged by the José María Covelo Foundation between 1991 and today. The analysis distinguishes the following three phases:

Phase I: Start up by forging financial and non-financial linkages (1991–5)

This phase covered the period from 1991 to 1995, and it is characterized by the start-up of the Foundation and the forging of backward and forward links with an array of partners. With its origins as a micro small and medium enterprise (MSME) development support programme within the National Industry Association (Asociación Nacional de Industriales, ANDI), the José María Covelo Foundation was founded officially in March of 1991 by a group of entrepreneurs with the economic support of USAID as a second-tier financial organization. At the time of its creation there was no mechanism for providing specialized financial support to the MSME sector. Today strong affinity ties remain between the Foundation and the ANDI, as many of the Foundation's creators are members of this business association. In fact, today Covelo and the ANDI share the same office building in Tegucigalpa.

During this initial phase, Covelo established backward financial linkages with several international cooperation agencies. With the goal of developing a market for financial services for MSMEs, several donors channelled funds to eligible private development financial organizations (PDOs) through the Foundation's second-tier facility. Today, the Covelo Foundation has expanded its partner base by establishing financial linkages with several private Honduran and international banks as well as development cooperation agencies, which include: the Central American Bank for Economic Integration (BCIE), a regional bank for MSME funding; the Government of Finland, for the administration of a forest project fund; BANHPROVI, a second-tier government bank with rediscount lines of credit for PDOs; and four domestic banks.

In addition to successfully creating financial linkages with the international cooperation community to source funding during this early period, the Foundation created forward linkages (financial and non-financial) with first-tier organizations, PDOs. The Foundation focused its activities on building the institutional and business capacity of the major PDOs as well as providing them with bulk loans to expand their sources of funds. During this stage, the Foundation designed indicators of performance and encouraged PDOs to institute a programme of self-regulation in an effort to monitor and compare their progress vis-à-vis their peers. In essence through this process, the Covelo Foundation played the role of a substitute supervisory agency.

Over time, the Foundation's technical assistance and financial support connections grew from an initial 6 organizations in 1991 to 9 in 1995 and 18 organizations in 2003. The portfolio of loans to PDOs rose from US$6.1 million in 1995 to US$78.7 million in 2003. The evidence suggests a prudent initiation of the phase of second-tier activities, with a focus on first developing the PDO capacity to self-regulate, as a mechanism for ensuring that member organizations perceived themselves as operating in the financial services market and for getting away from earlier welfare-based visions and practices. Once this approach allowed a successful deepening of the market, Covelo's financial transactions began to grow more rapidly.

Phase II: Market deepening and regulation (1995–2003)

The second phase could be designated as one of financial market deepening and the achievement of formal microfinance regulation. During this phase, the market for the Foundation's second-tier financial services was deepened by significantly increasing the number of PDOs served and, consequently, the number of clients reached, the number of loans disbursed, and the size of their portfolios. Noteworthy was the significant female participation rate (over 71 per cent of the clients between 1995 and 2003). This represented an evolution from the original affinity linkage with the industrial sector towards a gender approach centred on female capabilities in the development of MSMEs. At the same time, the financial linkages grew, allowing an increasing trend in the total portfolio. By 2003, the number of clients and the credit portfolio had grown significantly since 1996 (Table 4.1).

Another factor that led to Covelo's financial market deepening to the MSME sector during this phase was the start-up of its direct credit programme – at the first-tier using the solidarity group methodology. The effort was geographically centred on the main markets of Tegucigalpa. As the programme was consolidated, the Foundation expanded its outreach to San Pedro Sula, the country's industrial city, as well as some medium-sized towns and gradually to less developed districts and neighbourhoods.

The numbers of clients linked to the first-tier transactions increased significantly, about 50-fold from 1993 to 2003. The value of the loans disbursed grew even faster during the period (Table 4.2). Given the Foundation's affinity, its branches have a major presence in the 'T of development' and its first-tier continues to be mostly an urban operation. From the perspective of its first-tier activities, therefore, Covelo has contributed little to rural financial deepening. The exceptions, of course, have been the second-tier operations of Covelo involving the rural NGOs HDH and PILARH.

Hurricane Mitch and the reconstruction efforts that followed influenced the Foundation's links with the international community and the Honduran government. Because of its well-established reputation in building sustainable

Table 4.1 Covelo: evolution in loans to PDOs

Breakdown	1996	1997	1998	1999	2000	2001	2002	2003	2004[a]
Active clients	33,011	43,576	52,319	65,914	66,313	74,701	122,411	119,371	119,753
Female clients	29,074	37,049	45,420	49,220	45,187	64,368	90,507	94,597	94,854
Male clients	3,937	6,527	6,899	16,694	21,126	10,333	31,904	24,774	24,899
Number of loans	55,029	70,577	113,932	121,444	25,420	120,224	211,510	250,239	70,399
Total loans[b]	10,015	14,669	23,576	223	255	42,089	26,274	78,656	23,705

Source: José María Covelo Foundation – FUNDASIN. 2005.
[a]As of April.
[b]Thousands of US dollars.

Table 4.2 Evolution of credit flows at the Fundación Microfinanciera Covelo (first-tier programme)

Characteristics	Year										
	1995	1996	1997	1998	1999	2000	2001	2002	2003	2004	2005[c]
Active clients	292	3,810	6,599	6,344	8,086	9,870	12,556	13,227	16,441	14,407	14,902
Male clients	32	1,829	2,990	2,874	2,537	2,723	3,706	3,952	4,684	4,022	NA
Women clients	260	1,981	3,609	3,470	5,549	7,147	8,850	9,275	11,757	10,385	NA
Number of active loans	70	730	1,230	1,600	3,541	3,097	6,105	6,820	9,550	8,410	8,403
Number of loans disbursed[a]	304	8,670	21,705	20,488	28,114	40,736	26,774	29,099	33,844	31,918	12,994
Value of loans disbursed[b]	83	3,630	5,355	8,161	9,645	12,210	15,580	16,186	17,413	14,878	6,893

Source: Aquiles Samuel Izaguirre Foundation. 2005. NA, not available.
[a]Annual total.
[b]Thousands of US$, annual total.
[c]As of June.

ties with first-tier PDOs, the government called upon Covelo to assist in its reconstruction efforts, especially in channelling funds to the MSME sector post-disaster. These circumstances led to a deepening of Covelo's relationships with the government, the international cooperation agencies, and the PDOs as well as directly with their clients via their first-tier operations. All indicators of portfolio growth and efficiency confirm an exceptionally dynamic performance through the first- and second-tier operations, as summarized in Table 4.2 and Table 4.3, respectively.

This influence and Covelo's linkages with international cooperation agencies, combined with the credibility of ANDI as a sectoral representative and its effectiveness in helping with post-Mitch reconstruction efforts, created a special relationship with the Honduran National Congress during this period. Building on this, the strategic governing bodies of the Foundation emphasized prudential regulation as a key mechanism for organizing the market, facilitating access to funds from the second-tier institutions and, primarily, guaranteeing lawfulness, transparency, and the security of transactions. Prudential supervision was seen as the key to strengthening the viability and sustainability of financial PDOs.

Using its reputational capital gained over the years, the Foundation effectively promoted the negotiation of a legal framework for prudential regulation, which culminated in the approval of the Law on Private Development Finance Organizations (Decree No. 229-2000, published in February 2001). Many observers describe the Foundation's role as a multiplier and impact disseminator and point out that this link with the National Congress can be characterized more accurately as a pro-regulation alliance. However, in the eyes of others, there was pressure on the PDOs to be regulated that did not spring from financial sustainability objectives. Rather, the proposed legal framework was seen as having mutated into an effort to promote the Foundation's second-tier role.

In summary, during the first two phases of its evolution, the Foundation underwent transformations in its linkages, which stemmed from internal questions about its operations, external demands from the PDOs in the Covelo Network, and challenges raised by the environment. Figure 4.1 summarizes the sources of change, the linkages, and the actors involved. The time came in 2003 (during the post-Mitch period) for rethinking and redesigning its structure by seeking a new institutional strategy.

Phase III: Organizational, reflection, investment and readjustment for change (January 2003–onwards)

Starting in 2003 (two years after the law on PDOs was approved), the Covelo Foundation began a period of organizational reflection and readjustment. The changes made were influenced by the following debates and initiatives that were occurring in the country at the time:

- the debate about the Poverty Reduction Strategy, which included a major microenterprise development component;

Table **4.3** Financial evolution in PDOs reached from the Covelo second-tier level (in thousands of US$)

Characteristics	1995	1996	1997	1998	1999	2000	2001	2002	2003	2004[a]
Total assets	6,287	8,038	10,392	14,085	16,434	18,913	27,123	48,833	43,295	39,860
Total portfolio	4,820	7,359	7,366	10,301	10,869	13,956	19,946	38,328	36,975	32,623
Total net worth	2,746	4,380	5,294	6,694	8,002	8,282	12,066	27,154	20,592	20,897
Operating income	1,286	2,409	3,257	4,416	5,211	6,018	5,967	15,874	15,368	5,466
Operating costs	1,354	2,466	2,769	3,905	5,013	6,043	5,746	13,744	13,728	4,689
Operating income	-68	-57	489	510	198	-25	221	2,130	1,640	777
Financial self-sufficiency (%)	95	97.7	117.6	113.1	104	114.4	103.1	115.7	111.8	116.6
Economic self-sufficiency (%)	93.1	74.3	99.6	94.0	93.9	107.7	95	101.7	102.7	102.8

Source: José Maria Covelo Foundation – FUNDASIN, 2005.

[a]As of April

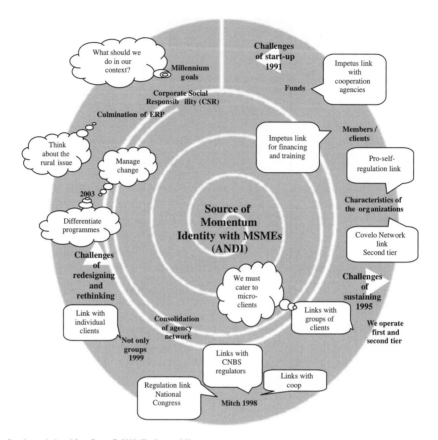

Based on and adapted from **Senge, P.** 2000. *The Dance of Change.*

Figure 4.1 Internal and external linkages of Grupo Financiero Covelo and connections to rural financial services

- an initiative of the Superintendence of Banks to empower and strengthen PDOs; and,
- a trend among international cooperation agencies to make rural sector development a top priority.

In an effort to better position itself to respond to these trends and to the needs of its partners and clients, the Covelo Foundation made the following major changes during this period:

- the transformation of the José María Covelo Foundation into a holding company in charge of defining the overall strategic vision of the Grupo Financiero Covelo, which includes six service organizations (see Figure 4.2);
- the separation of its first and second-tier operations, with the creation of the Fundación Microfinanciera Covelo at the first-tier and the Fundación Aquiles Samuel Izaguirre (FUNDASIN) at the second-tier;

- the uncoupling of the network of associated PDOs, giving the network its own identity, by creating the MICROH Network (a network of microfinance institutions in Honduras); and,
- the development of a special agricultural programme in an effort to deepen the supply of financial and non-financial services in rural areas.

Intra- and extra-group linkages cultivated throughout the three phases became an integral part of the Group's strategy for deepening financial markets for the MSME sector. In its current form, the Group's strategic vision is centred on intra-group linkages between the José María Covelo Foundation – which provides financial, human resources, administration, systems, marketing – and organizational services to the six service organizations of the Group. In addition, the second-tier level (FUNDASIN) offers technical assistance and funding to PDOs and carries out risk analysis and project administration activities. At the first-tier level, Fundación Microfinanciera Covelo is the most prominent organization, with financing activities implemented via regional management sub-boards, and is in charge of development of credit technologies, loan recovery, and risk management.

In addition, the Grupo Financiero Covelo has created extra-group linkages with multiple external actors that can be categorized as follows: market-deepening linkages (focusing especially on the rural sector), linkages for the management and channelling of funds, and policy-influence linkages.

(i) *Market-deepening linkages for rural finance.* The Grupo Financiero Covelo, in an effort to deepen the supply of services in the rural areas, has forged partnerships to develop a special agriculture programme through its first-tier operations. Alliances and linkages are being created with the Financial Transactions Reports Analysis Centre (FINTRAC), the

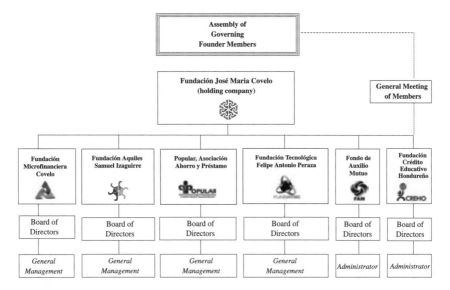

Figure 4.2 Structure of Grupo Microfinanciero Covelo

China/Taiwan Mission in Honduras, El Zamorano, the Honduran Foundation for Agricultural Research (FHIA), and a few agro-trading enterprises in an effort to extend technical assistance to clients (Gonzalez-Vega et al., 2006).

(ii)   In addition to this, Covelo via its first-tier operations has implemented a guarantee fund, contributed by USAID, to cover the risks associated with the agricultural sector. Microfinanciera Covelo provides technical assistance on the client's business plans and financial requirements. The programme is being operated in some rural areas as a pilot, with intentions to extend it to traditional livestock production areas. These linkages reveal a qualitative leap forward from the mostly urban approach of Covelo's first-tier operations in the past. It suggests cautious optimism about its potential for deepening rural financial markets. Figure 4.3 shows the gradual evolution of disbursements.

(iii)   *Funding linkages. The management and channelling of funds have resulted in the* Group's main forward and backward linkages. On the one hand, the organization mobilizes funds for on-lending to MSMEs through the linkages with international cooperation agencies and financial backers. On the other hand, the organization channels these funds through its linkages with first-tier organizations via FUNDASIN, which currently caters to 18 PDOs and exhibits a growing portfolio as shown previously in Table 4.1. Both HDH and PILARH participate in this programme. Their officers stated that this is an important linkage in the financing of their activities. They indicated that the flexibility of

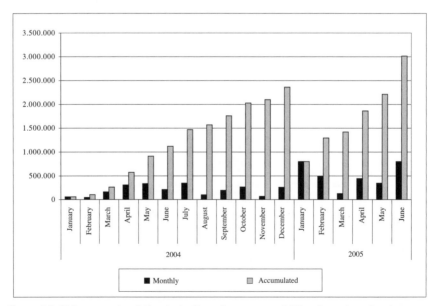

Figure 4.3 Disbursements of the Agriculture Programme of Microfinanciera Covelo (US$). *Source*: Fundación Microfinanciera Covelo. 2005.

the services assures them of sufficient funds to respond to the demand from their clients. These linkages are examined in detail in the next section of this chapter.

(iv) *Policy-influence linkages.* The strategic and management teams at Covelo have maintained close, continuing, and direct linkages with policymakers, with the objective of influencing decisions about microfinance issues. They have focused mostly on MSMEs and the access to assets required for their upgrading. The foundation for their strategy has been the desire to strengthen this segment of the financial system through regulation. Their most conspicuous achievement has been the value added in the process of negotiating the law on PDOs.

There have been, as well, doubts and objections about this role. Some observers, particularly among those especially concerned with rural development, have lamented a narrow financial perspective and would have liked to see the Foundation involved in promoting greater coherence between financial policies and policies for promoting the farming sector. The concerns are only partially valid. The emphasis on regulation has induced a healthy concern in meeting targets conducive to sustainability, through the implementation of information systems, management improvements, and internal linkages, to enable these PDOs to operate as financial entities. Thus, the majority, including the Foundation, have opted to separate their production support activities and have placed them in a parallel PDO. Some observers also fear that this distancing between production strategies and finance may perpetuate the contradictions responsible for backwardness in the rural areas in Honduras. Table 4.4 reports on some of the perceptions observed during the interviews with a broad range of actors.

The decision-makers interviewed see these policy-influence linkages as elements conducive to sustainability. However, for those at the first-tier level, Covelo's linkages with the policymakers are viewed with caution. They point out that the organization plays a dual role (with operations at the first-tier and the second-tier). That is, the Group is perceived as a competent authority and an able financier and, at the same time, as an agency in a position to influence jurisdiction issues. Thus, they claim that these linkages ensured that regulation be delegated to the Covelo Group. This dual role may complicate any strategy of expansion into rural financial markets, where Covelo would be competing with the PDOs.

Moreover, representatives of the first-tier level agree that Covelo's proactive role in encouraging regulation has not been accompanied by the development of a regulatory framework by the Superintendence of Banks, CNBS, that reflects appropriate knowledge of key features of the rural sector. At the same time, they feel that Covelo has not been sufficiently proactive in condemning legislation about debt cancellation in the agricultural sector, reflecting a focus on its mostly urban interests. However, at the Group level, there is a clear and widespread perception that this policy has undermined willingness to pay. Insufficient lobbying on this issue may have reflected a failure to gauge the implications for

Table 4.4 Decision-makers' perceptions of the role of Covelo

Issue	Perception
Actual impact	Covelo's steady and sustained effort is the key to its participation at the strategic levels of policymaking.
	Covelo and the Honduran National Congress formed an alliance and managed to push through legislation that not everyone supported.
	Covelo is the sector's political arm. Through its transformations, the Group has been strongly identified with the MSME sector. The Group is politically effective.
	Covelo is able to play a major role in legislation because it receives funds and assistance and influences where these resources are channelled.
Openness to the issue	Covelo is paving the way for non-profit organizations and inspires credibility and confidence.
	It is a strong institutional arm for international organizations, which see it as a trustworthy tenderer that can channel funds to the first-tier level.
	Although the Network is important, it has been demonstrated that it does not have to be housed in a second-tier organization.
	It represents a framework of reference for designing strategies and financial programmes targeted at the sector.
Rural financial services	The microfinance issues must be separated from rural financial services.
	The rural sector is the sector most penalized by policies.
	Covelo's aim was to pave the way in order to demonstrate that the first-tier is feasible and profitable. Now, it is attempting to do the same with the agricultural credit programme.

Source: Interviews with decision-makers from the National Congress, the Covelo Foundation, and the CNBS, June 2005.

the rural sector. With the new priorities on a 'return to a rural approach', their scant influence on rural policies is being felt.

Linkages with local rural operators: the case of HDH and PILARH

The Covelo Group currently maintains linkages – from the second tier (FUNDASIN) – with 18 organizations. Two of these organizations – HDH and PILARH – are involved in rural financial deepening, by offering services adapted to the areas in which they operate.

Linkages between Covelo and HDH

The linkage with Covelo began in 1990–1, when HDH sought to expand its portfolio toward microenterprises in manufacturing, commerce and agro-industry. The linkage provided funds and free training and created a win-win situation. Pressures from Covelo led to the adoption of self-regulation, which became a positive asset when HDH opted for prudential regulation in the 1990s. This self-regulation linkage involved the joint management of information and it led, in 1997, to the adoption of the solidarity group methodology.

One weakness in the initial linkage was the limitations of the Covelo advisers working in the region to effectively monitor and advise HDH. This was perhaps explained by the Foundation's tradition of working in urban areas, while its staff recruitment systems gave no special consideration to the rural sector. HDH's funding linkage with Covelo increased client outreach and the portfolio (Table 4.5). At the same time, Banco de Occidente, with its more flexible rural approach, has kept a line of credit open with HDH up to now.

Taking 2001 as the base year, there has been an increase in client outreach. The number of male clients has grown rapidly (60 per cent per year). The number of loans increased 123 per cent from 2001 to 2004, with microenterprise credit absorbing most of the funds, whereas the share of agriculture fell. The average loan amount declined from US$796 in 2001 to US$509 in 2004.

In the last two years a strong linkage has emerged with Banco de Occidente which, like HDH, operates in north-western Honduras. HDH has also received funding from donor agencies (one-fifth of the total). Net operating income switched from losses in 2001 to profits of US$191,600 in 2004, as a result of increases in the number of clients and the loan portfolio, with total income growing 21 per cent compared to 12 per cent per year for total expenditures (Table 4.6).

Table 4.5 Consolidated data: HDH

Variable	2001	2002	2003	2004
Members	2,028	2,863	4,657	7,085
% individual men	36	38	41	43
% individual women	64	62	59	57
% groups[1]	38	25	36	42
Depositors	2,028	2,863	4,657	7,085
Borrowers	2,028	2,863	4,657	7,085
Total assets (thousands of US$)	2,394	2,574	3,095	4,395
Bank deposits (thousands of US$)	319	78	103	322
Agricultural portfolio (percentages)	35	22	13	12
Microenterprise portfolio (percentages)	65	79	87	88
Donor funds	104	74	83	131
Bank indebtedness	N/A	N/A	184	625
Total loans	1,614	1,955	2,607	3,603
Return on assets (percentages)	7	9	9	12
Return on equity (percentages)	13	15	28	14

Source: Hermandad de Honduras, 2005. N/A, not applicable.
[1]The group percentage is out of the total number of clients.

Table 4.6 HDH: Statement of income and expenditures (thousands of US$)

Account	2001	2002	2003	2004
Income				
Income from interest and loan fees	520	563	745	975
Investment income	44	51	24	13
Total income	564	613	769	989
Expenditures				
Interest and loan charges	81	43	43	107
Provision for bad debts	126	131	94	72
Administrative costs: staff	266	281	318	439
Other administrative costs	124	117	171	221
Total expenditures	598	573	626	839
Net operating income	-35	40	143	192
Non-operating income	123	29	29	32
Non-operating expenses	70	55	14	15
Other non-operating revenues	210	232	238	311
Non-operating expenses	158	112	120	177
Consolidated earnings	70	134	277	302

Source: Hermandad de Honduras, 2005.

The main lessons learned from the linkage with Covelo Foundation are:

- The leverage of funds to secure technical assistance for institution building has been crucial, and in several cases participation in the Covelo Network opened the door to cooperation from USAID and the Inter-American Development Bank (IDB).
- The Foundation's influence on the law on PDOs has strengthened the MFO's position opposite the Superintendence of Banks.

Funding from the second-tier programme was crucial, especially during the pre-Mitch period, when it was difficult for MFOs to access funds. Now, with regulation, easier access to funds means that MFOs have sources alternative to FUNDASIN. Even though the Covelo linkage has been quite productive, there are a number of contradictions:

- The duality of its first and second-tier operations means that the Group handles client information and operates in the same area as the MFO partners of its second-tier operation, creating a certain level of competition between the two organizations.
- As FUNDASIN operates a line of credit with the Central American Bank of Economic Integration, the reports for this programme require a breakdown of clients. This may also create conflicts of interest and the possibility of double counting.
- The fact that HDH works with FUNDASIN, means that clients have difficulty understanding the different roles of the first-tier and second-tier operations of the Covelo Group.
- The Group uses information about the portfolios of the MFOs in its negotiations with external partners. This causes conflicts because, as a

regulated organization, HDH also seeks funds, sometimes from the same partners.

The issues related to information and the duality of the first and second-tier operations may introduce constraints on rural financial deepening. HDH views FUNDASIN as just another actor in its list of financial backers. As HDH is regulated, it feels that it can negotiate its own funding.

Forward alliances of HDH

HDH has as series of strategic alliances and relationships with grassroots groups, international donors, and formal financial intermediaries. This section focuses on the first type of alliances, given the direct impact and potential positive spillovers of the social interventions on the financial component of HDH.

(i)   *Cajas rurales.* The *cajas rurales* are small associations found frequently in rural Honduras, which finance communal development projects as well as individual ventures. They are a complement to public investment in areas such as health, education, strengthening of local organizations, enterprise development, and the funding of individual production projects. All have been legalized as *empresas asociativas campesinas* (peasant associative enterprises) and operate under the umbrella of the rural economic committees, a second-tier organization.

The *cajas* are created (or strengthened) by the social division of HDH and are funded by the microfinance unit. The objective is threefold: to promote grassroots development, improve infrastructure and living conditions in rural areas, and create a base of potential credit clients. This is achieved through integrated support consisting of institutional strengthening, technical assistance, and funding.

The *cajas* consist of groups of 12–34 members who receive, as seed capital, a loan from HDH, at zero interest rate and a five-year term. In some cases, the seed capital is not enough, so the *cajas* request working capital or loanable funds. This funding requires the member's joint liability or a mortgage.

As of December 2005, HDH had transactions with 56 *cajas rurales*, 20 established directly by Hermandad, and the remaining 36 strengthened by this organization. They had almost 1,000 members, the majority with agricultural activities, and others engaged in communal or collective projects such as grocery stores or agricultural and veterinary stores. The *cajas* are very rural, usually located in remote regions, accessible only by foot and reachable only during the dry season; 70 per cent have agricultural activities. There are *cajas* with only men, only women, or mixed membership; the latter reveal the best performance, for unknown reasons.

(ii)   PACTA. This is a land project, sponsored by the World Bank and implemented by FAO. It works with formal and informal organizations of farmers without access to arable land, who are contacted through the national organization of the Lenca Indians (ONILH), agro industrial cooperatives and municipal corporations. The project hires the social unit of HDH to empower farmers and provide technical assistance, including the preparation of feasibility studies for acquiring land.

The farmers negotiate directly with the owner of the land, and when a fair agreement is reached, the project is presented to a financial organization, which may be the financial unit of Hermandad, now that the two areas – social and financial – have been separated. HDH will fund up to 150 per cent of the cost of the land, for both investment and production purposes. The project has supported almost 200 farmers, with around US$2.5 million.

(iii) Alliances with indirect financial impacts. There are several strategic alliances in which HDH has been heavily involved, because of their overall positive impact on the communities and as a means to improve the creditworthiness of current and potential clients. Some of these linkages are:

(a) *UMA*. A new Reforestation Law was passed in 2000, as a consequence of hurricane Mitch, with heavy lobbying from HDH. One of its features is the creation of Unidades Municipales Ambientales (UMAs), in charge of fire control and reforestation. HDH has supported and actively promoted the creation and operation of UMAs in the five municipalities where it operates.

(b) *Health projects*. These are 'basic health packages' that reach 14 municipalities and 90 communities. HDH is involved in two municipalities, benefiting an estimated 28,000 people and improving the health conditions of its borrowers.

(c) *Adult education*. HDH's involvement in this project stems from the great difficulty in finding members of *cajas rurales* who can read and write, thus concentrating the participation in the boards of directors in a few people, who after some time abandon the group because of excessive work. The programme involves both adult and preschool education. The project currently operates in 30 different centres, with a total of 240 adults and 360 children.

(d) *CICAL*. This is a food security project, sponsored by the European Union. A food processing firm owned by 17 partners (mostly women) vacuum-packs fruits and vegetables. HDH helped to establish a value chain that includes production, processing, and marketing. CICAL was supported with training, legal advice, purchase of machinery and tools, greater physical infrastructure, permits, and patents.

(e) *SANAA*. To confront the local and central governments' budget restrictions for improving both drinking water and sanitation infrastructure, the state's water and sewer agency, SANAA, established a joint project with HDH and USAID.

(iv)   Financial relations. HDH has linkages with many financial organizations, ranging from private commercial banks (Banco de Occidente and Banco Mercantil) and international agencies (Inter-American Development Bank, Central American Bank for Economic Integration) to private financial organizations such as Covelo and Oiko Credit. Some of these relationships involve services other than credit, such as deposits, cash management and transfers, and, in a few cases, technical assistance and institutional strengthening.

HDH executives recommend, before an alliance is implemented, a clear understanding of the extent of the project, its costs and the resources each partner must invest – financial and non-financial. Even for the smallest linkage or joint project there should be a business or strategic plan.

HDH praises the results of the linkages in which it has been involved, many with the technical and financial support of the international donor community. These linkages have allowed it to organize and empower the target population and build social and production infrastructure. They lament that most assistance has been concentrated in areas directly impacted by hurricane Mitch, although all rural areas experienced indirect consequences of the natural disaster. Agencies located in the two largest cities – Tegucigalpa and San Pedro – are not always aware of the problems and challenges faced by isolated rural populations.

Linkages between Covelo and PILARH

Although initial efforts date back to 1999, the formal linkage between Covelo and PILARH began in 2001, resulting in the disbursement of funding in 2002.

Table 4.7 PILARH: consolidated data

Indicator	2001	2002	2003	2004
Members	1,622	3,000	4,007	3,785
Men (%)	61	69	71	70
Women (%)	39	31	29	30
Groups (%)	N/A	N/A	N/A	N/A
Borrowers	1,622	3,000	4,007	3,785
Total assets (thousands US$)	1,502	1,594	1,665	1,855
Bank deposits (thousands US$)	154	116	85	299
Loans outstanding (thousands US$)	610	8,470	1,011	959
Agricultural portfolio (%)	82	79	75	74
Microenterprise portfolio (%)	18	21	25	26
Bank indebtedness (thousands US$)	206	386	456	554
Total loans (thousands US$)	610	870	1,011	959
Donor funds (thousands US$)	1,061	999	969	923
Capital without donations (thousands US$)	441	474	695	932
Return on assets (%)	47	55	62	52
Return on equity (%)	69	60	60	52

Source: Interview with Executive Director, PILARH, August 2005. N/A, not applicable.

The delay called for a review of the self-regulation process, with monitoring to improve performance. The appeal of joining the Covelo Network was access to funding, although the trial period provided an opportunity to deepen the linkage in the areas of financial and organizational management. The funding linkage started with US$120,000, the current credit line is US$270,000. In addition, PILARH has credit lines from other entities for US$400,000.

Since 2001, linkages with clients have been deepened, with a 133 per cent increase in the number of clients by 2004, although this number declined in 2004. Male participation rose from 61 per cent in 2001 to 70 per cent in 2004. Average loan size fell from US$376 in 2001 to US$253 in 2004 (Table 4.7).

Funding increased at an average annual rate of 17 per cent, with funds from government projects taking the greatest share (72 per cent of the growth). Donor funds have declined gradually since 2001. PILARH is deepening its linkages with public agencies but not with the financial sector. The organization financial losses reflected the drop in the numbers of members and total loans in 2004 and high staff costs (PILARH spends US$0.51 for every dollar lent), Table 4.8.

In 2004, PILARH joined the MICROH Network, fearing that it would no longer have access to FUNDASIN's funding. The organization sees this linkage as a way of gaining prestige and national and international recognition. A policy of expansion calls for doubling the portfolio's growth rate, through increasing loan sizes. Each adviser will handle 350 clients, rather than 250 to 300. PILARH's confidence is based on its centralized accounting, risk management, and a collection system closely linked with AMPROs (Asociaciones de Microempresarios y Productores de Occidente – small self-help groups). It

Table 4.8 PILARH: statement of income and expenditures (thousands of US$)

Account	2004
Income	
Income from interest and loan fees	0.3
Income from other related financial services	3.4
Investment income	13.2
Total income	271.3
Expenditures	
Interest and loan charges	59.8
Provision for bad debts	8.9
Administrative costs: staff	490.0
Other administrative costs	6.7
Total expenditures	565.5
Net operating income	−294.2
Cash donations	278.0
Other non-operating income	218.9
Consolidated earnings	5.7

Source: Interview with Executive Director, PILARH, August 2005

hopes to strengthen ties with existing clients rather than to increase the breadth of outreach.

At first, PILARH perceived self-regulation as an excessive burden, but the process has become routine in the organization. Self-regulation parameters are still being revised and the Superintendence has developed a monitoring process for those willing to become eligible for self-regulation. The linkage with Covelo focuses on promoting regulation among unregulated organizations.

Forward alliances of PILARH

Despite its small size (compared to HDH), PILARH shows an interesting set of strategic alliances. The linkage with AMPROs matters because it is an effort developed and implemented by PILARH to promote empowerment and funding of production, which allows grassroots groups to participate in PILARH's decision-making process. Other alliances of PILARH have an indirect impact on its financial component.

(i) *AMPROs.* PILARH provides services to individual clients (basically credit) and to groups of clients (credit and non-financial services). In the five regions where it operates, it has created 230 groups, with approximately 4,000 members and an average of 17 associates per group – with outliers of 8 and 30. PILARH provides training, technical assistance, credit, and institutional strengthening. Each group has a board of directors and, in each region, the chairpersons constitute another AMPRO, which can be described as a federation of groups. Each AMPRO has legal status; five form one big AMPRO, also with a board of directors and participation in PILARH's Assembly. Indeed, of the 23 members of the Assembly, five represent AMPROs. The AMPROs have been established through the cooperation of Trias, a Belgian development organization. The current phase of the project aims at integrating the groups into processes of communal participation and policy dialogue.

(ii) *INCA.* In order to allow small coffee producers to lower their costs, PILARH and a private partner created this firm, which plans to supply as many services as possible along the value chain. It now includes an agricultural input supplier, a processing plant, a marketing operation, and it is adding a veterinary service. PILARH owns three-quarters of the firm and is hoping that the AMPRO buys-out the shares of the private partner.

(iii) *DELSAR.* The agency for the development of Santa Rosa (DELSAR) is a joint effort of local government and civil society. PILARH's involvement is through an IDB-sponsored project aimed at providing training and technical assistance to a group of 71 microentrepreneurs producing handicrafts (made out of leather, wood, and wrought iron), as well as textiles and traditional food. DELSAR and PILARH cover 30 per cent of the costs of the project.

(iv) *Escuela Agrícola Pompilio Ortega.* This technical high school and the Regional Centre of the Universidad Autónoma de Honduras have become valuable sources of personnel for PILARH, particularly facilitators working for the social component and credit officers. The NGO allows students to undertake their professional practice there, so it has the chance to test these potential employees before actually hiring them.

(v) *Other alliances.* There are several other linkages of PILARH that improve human capital, production opportunities and access to credit. The following stand out:

(a) *ASONOG.* This is an association with non-financial programmes supporting marginal clienteles.

(b) *JICATUYO.* This is a project sponsored by the European Union focused on coffee production. It supports groups of producers in their efforts to improve their production and marketing capabilities.

(c) *Scholarships.* As an incentive for children to stay in school, PILARH provides monthly scholarships of approximately US$17 to children of AMPRO members with a good academic record.

PILARH's executives believe that strategic alliances are positive as long as there is mutual understanding and good coordination and particularly transparency and trust. The objectives of the organizations involved must be similar, and there should be a complementarity of resources and actions in order to maximize the impact of the project. Coordination is not always easy, as a consequence of lack of personnel. The government does not provide much support, although the target population of the AMROs and, in general, the regions where PILARH operates, reveals the highest levels of poverty.

Impact of HDH and PILARH linkages with Covelo

Both organizations have deepened rural financial services significantly, judging by their link with 10,790 clients, representing 3.3 per cent of all producers nationwide and 5.7 per cent of producers in farming regions. There has been dynamism and growth in their portfolios during this decade. HDH has shown an average annual growth rate of 23 per cent in its portfolio and 34 per cent in the number of clients, with loans totalling US$2.5 million in 2004. PILARH had a smaller outreach of 3,785 clients in 2004, and the average annual growth rate of its portfolio was 13 per cent. Its loan portfolio ranged from US$609,648 to US$959,152, while average individual loan size was US$253 in 2004.

The linkages continue to have a weak impact on rural financial deepening. The levels of satisfaction and ownership of the linkage with the Covelo Group show that HDH and PILARH highly value the support received at the beginning, both funding and particularly the technical assistance and self-regulation programme. Further, they are enthusiastic about the new law sponsored by Covelo. Today, FUNDASIN is considered as one of the funding options, but not the only one. In addition, the functional dualism and overlapping of roles within the Group (first- and second-tier financing) makes both organizations cautious about providing information.

Lessons learned and conclusions

Several important lessons for rural financial deepening in Honduras have been learned.

- Factors in the relationship between the Covelo Group and first-tier organizations that explain the deepening of rural financial markets

The linkage with the Covelo Group originated from funding and self-regulation, based on a microenterprise approach, while the deepening of rural financial services by the organizations stems from their identification with the rural area and specifically with poor clients. The interviews did not show that the linkage had triggered rural deepening or incentives for it. What is clear, though, is that the linkage allowed the organizations to position themselves at the national and international level. Regulation now provides the organizations with direct access to other sources of funds, leading to lower transaction costs, which could allow interest rates to be lowered by eliminating a link in the chain.

The organizations have made major progress in opening up their portfolio of financial backers, which is why their linkage with the Group – and specifically with FUNDASIN – is currently centred on competition. Having become self-regulated (HDH), there is an opportunity to access funds directly. PILARH also considers this to be an added value factor of regulation, over and above the possibility of capturing savings.

- Risks or constraints the organizations encounter in their linkage with the Covelo Group

The main risk perceived by the organizations is the Group's dualism of first- and second-tier operations, which shows that its role of jurisdiction could come into conflict with the funding scheme. At the same time, the PDOs realized that the Covelo Group could conceivably be responsible for the regulation of the organizations, since this possibility was discussed during the process of negotiating the law on PDOs. This raises even greater concerns about Covelo, since this would give the Group the triple role of financial backer, competent authority and regulator, which in market terms would not promote a level playing field.

- Client's perception of the linkages with the organizations

The clients perceive the linkage of identity with the organizations from a central perspective, associated with three factors: flexibility, understanding, and respectful treatment. Thus, technical assistance may play a major role but, unlike in the past, this role would be to work with clients on the basis of their credit history and repayment record, rather than on the demand for credit.

PILARH claims to have learned the key lesson that transaction costs are considerably reduced when the producers are organized around a territorial approach and their organization participates in the institution's decision-making.

In HDH's case, heavy-handed monitoring, in order to set a precedent in cases of non-payment, is combined with a timely, flexible credit service and respectful treatment. Much of the technical assistance is provided by means of alliances with other actors specializing in this field.

The strategic alliances established with local organizations by HDH and PILARH may well be described as of a development nature. That is, they improve social and production infrastructure, at the same time as they increase human capital, production opportunities, creditworthiness and access to financial services by current and potential clients of the two NGOs. Given the high poverty levels and poor living conditions of the rural areas where they operate, the positive impact of these linkages is enormous.

- Regulation as an instrument for deepening rural financial markets, particularly in areas where livelihoods reflect high poverty levels

Regulation has contributed greatly to the organizations becoming specialized in financial services, and control has guaranteed the transformation of management, separating financial from non-financial transactions in each of the two organizations. Since both organizations sprang from a non-financial initiative, this proactive development contributes to deepening rural markets by providing a comprehensive service, including agricultural and microenterprise activities. Interestingly, both organizations have developed differentiated terms and programmes for the agricultural and non-agricultural sectors.

Regulation has not succeeded in linking their financial management approach with the financial system, as rural development policy hopes to promote. On the contrary, debt write-offs, used as instruments of rural development policy, have weakened the willingness to pay being promoted by the financial services of these organizations.

Conclusions

Linkages within the microfinance sector can play a role in poverty reduction by helping to improve the incomes of the poorest sectors, targeting the poorest and most vulnerable groups in the rural areas. This strategy involves three key elements. First, to play a major role, rural microfinance linkages must start to move away from just influencing overall regulation policies towards inclusive rural development policies that consider microfinance and its characteristics as policy instruments. They must begin to break with the mistakes of the past, where financial policies were structurally disconnected from rural development policies. This means that regulators should expand their vision of rural issues (without relaxing the supervision), and rural development policymakers should be linked operatively to a financial system that abandons the traditional welfare-based approach in favour of building stronger livelihoods.

Second, although improving incomes is the first direct and visible effect of microfinance, its additional and ultimate aim is to improve people's livelihoods, which means successfully triggering linkages and alliances that strengthen not only regulation but also a 'pro-rural' vision, which is more than agriculture and more than processing microenterprises.

Third, targeting involves studying the territoriality of rural poverty and, on that basis, determining means of operation, types of service, and activities to forge linkages with clients. Targeting calls for more than just widening the network of agencies in a rural area; instead, the aim should be to find the operational and financial means for deepening markets.

References

Bustamante, B. and Falck, M. (2005) *Análisis de las opciones de la gestión del desarrollo rural: el caso de Honduras*, COSUDE, Tegucigalpa.

De Janvry, A. and Sadoulet, E. (2004) 'Toward a Territorial Approach to Rural Development: International Experiences and Implications for Mexico's Microregions Strategy', Presentation at the 4th Regional Forum on Latin America and the Caribbean: Reaping Opportunities for Rural Development in the 21st Century, San Jose, Costa Rica, 19–21 October.

Falck, M. (2004) *Honduras: perfil de la situación socio-económica actual*, Escuela Agrícola Panamericana, Honduras.

Falck, M. and Pino, N.H. (2003) *Desarrollo rural y manejo de cuencas desde una perspectiva de medios de vida*, Edn. Guaymuras, Tegucigalpa.

Gonzalez-Vega, C. et al. (2006) 'Hortifruti in Central America: a case study about the influence of supermarkets on the development and evolution of creditworthiness among small and medium agricultural producers', USAID *microREPORT*, number 57.

Hermandad de Honduras (2005), *Memoria Annual 2004*, San Marcos Ocotepeque.

Instituto Nacional de Estadística, http://www.ine.es/ [accessed 28 October 2007]

Jansen, H., Siegel, P. and Pichón, F. (2005) 'Identificación de los conductores de crecimiento rural sostenible y reducción de la pobreza en Honduras', Documento de discusión, Washington, D.C.

Lederman, D. (2005) *Beyond the City: The Rural Contribution to Development*, The World Bank, Washington, D.C.

Monge-González, R., Loría, M. and Gonzalez-Vega, C. (2004) *Retos y oportunidades para los sectores agropecuarios y agroindustrial de Centroamérica ante el tratado de libre comercio con los Estados Unidos*, Academia de Centroamérica, San José.

North, D. (1993) *Instituciones, cambio institucional y desempeño económico*, Distrito Federal, Fondo de Cultura Económica, México.

PILARH, 'Internal Progress Reports, 2001–2004'.

Sauma, P. (2001) 'Desafíos de la equidad social' Insumo para el Informe de desarrollo humano, UNDP, San Jose.

Senge, P. et al. (2000) *La danza del cambio. Los retos de sostener el impulso en organizaciones abiertas al aprendizaje*, Grupo Editorial Norma, Bogotá.

Velástegui, M. (2003) 'Deuda agropecuaria en el sistema financiero formal: situación actual y perspectiva de solución en Honduras', Tesis de ingeniería, Escuela Agrícola Panamericana, Honduras.

CHAPTER 5
ICICI Bank partnership linkages in India

Malcolm Harper and Marié Kirsten

Abstract

Linking the formal financial sector with poor microfinance clients seemed impossible even a decade ago. Increasingly such linkages are emerging, either spontaneous or enforced, and it is crucial that we share the knowledge gained from these efforts. One of India's most innovative linkage models is ICICI Bank's recent 'facilitation' model with several MGO/MFIs. This approach is based on a partnership between ICICI Bank and selected NGOs/MFIs, according to which the latter takes the responsibility of monitoring and recovering loans from individuals and self-help groups, but the credit (and most of the risk) is directly between ICICI Bank and the SHG or individual clients. This chapter explains the model and provides two case study examples to illustrate this linkage methodology. Although there has been much enthusiasm about ICICI's linkage partnership and initial outcomes are encouraging, the future expansion and development of this type of model is vulnerable to current regulatory requirements as described in the postscript at the end of the chapter.

Introduction

This case study describes the MFI linkage model of ICICI Bank, India's second largest commercial bank. This bank has developed a unique partnership model to deliver small loans to the rural poor. The case focuses on two examples of ICICI Bank's microfinance facilitation links with microfinance intermediaries serving individuals and self-help groups (SHGs), one with BISWA (Bharat Integrated Social Welfare Agency), a Microfinance Institution (MFI) in Orissa and one with PSS (Services for Progress Organization), a smaller MFI working with self-help groups in the poorest parts of Warangal in Andhra Pradesh. The two cases were selected to demonstrate how a large commercial bank can use the strengths of local MFIs to link directly with large numbers of poor clients.

Microfinance in India

India's well-developed financial sector consists of 27 government-owned banks, more than 20 major private banks, of which ICICI Bank is by far the largest, and over 100,000 cooperative banks; the financial sector is strictly regulated and supervised. Government legislation requires all banks in India to lend at least

40 per cent of their credit (at an interest rate not more than 4 percentage points above their prime lending rate) to the so-called 'priority sector' which includes rural areas, small industries, exporting firms, housing and agriculture.

This policy and the general welfare objectives of India's public sector banks, the so-called 'new paradigm' microfinance, came very late to India. The government spent many years trying to alleviate poverty with large programmes of directed and subsidised credit. These programmes had limited success, were often hampered by the lack of technical banking skills of civil servants and resulted in credit going to the less poor. They did however occupy the 'institutional space', which might otherwise have been filled by micro-finance.

While these programmes helped some people, they also left long-term scars on the country's financial system. The cheap soft loans, often combined with subsidies, were distributed through the enormous network of over 150,000 bank branches, including rural cooperative banks. Recoveries were poor, often below 30 per cent, and default was further encouraged by local and even national loan waivers.

In the late 1980s the Mysore rehabilitation and development association (MYRADA) started to experiment with the formation of self-help groups (SHGs), based on traditional Southern Indian savings and credit groups. SHGs are effectively micro-banks, with between ten and 20 women forming a group, on their own initiative, or with the help of an NGO or other self-help group promoter. Each member saves a small regular amount and the group either use their accumulated savings as a pool to be lent out to those members who need it or they may open a savings account with a nearby commercial or co-operative bank. The Reserve Bank of India (RBI) has, since 1994, allowed unregistered groups to open savings accounts and to borrow from banks. So if an SHG needs to supplement their savings fund to make loans to their members, it can borrow from a bank. The members are free to set whatever interest rate they like on their loans and they often add on a substantial margin over what they pay to the bank, in order to build their own group equity.

In the early 1990s the National Bank for Agriculture and Rural Development (NABARD), the government's instrument for financial deepening in rural India, started to encourage the banks to accept SHGs as customers. NABARD refinances banks' loans to SHGs at 5.5 per cent. The banks have generally lent to SHGs at 12 per cent, and the resulting spread of 6.5 per cent was considered adequate to cover their transaction costs. SHGs became the dominant delivery channel for micro-finance in India and by the end of 2004, almost 1.5 million SHGs, with perhaps 20 million members, were said to have borrowed from banks. While this might include double counting, at least 20 per cent of India's one hundred million poor households probably have some access to formal financial services.

Motivation for ICICI's linkage plan

A number of factors worked together to convince ICICI Bank, India's second largest commercial bank, to enter the microfinance market in 2002. This decision was motivated by priority sector targets, as well as the internal drive to 'be a leader in every field of banking', and the belief that some of the new micro finance clients will eventually graduate into mainstream banking. In 2001 ICICI Bank purchased the privately owned Bank of Madura, in Southern India. The Madura Bank had a substantial portfolio of loans to 600 SHGs, and ICICI Bank had to integrate these accounts into its business model. The Bank of Madura staff had received extensive training (from NABARD) on the promotion of SHGs, and ICICI initially followed their model of lending direct to SHGs without any form of financial or management intermediation. However, the Bank of Madura approach was later abandoned in favour of a unique ICICI facilitation linkage model, described below.

By March 2005 ICICI Bank's exposure to the microfinance sector, through 27 partner MFIs, reached US$66 million. Motivated by this initial success, ICICI Bank is now extending its linkage model, to smaller MFIs, through a strategic partnership with CARE.

ICICI could meet its priority sector targets by lending directly to the 'weaker sections' or by lending equivalent amounts to public sector institutions such as NABARD or the Small Industries Development Bank of India (SIDBI), at 6 per cent or less, which these institutions then use for priority sector purposes. There are however very strong incentives, especially for private banks such as ICICI, to do a substantial amount of direct priority sector business and not to buy themselves out of their obligations with indirect investments. This played an important role in ICICI's decision to lend directly to self-help groups and individuals; the Bank also sees microfinance as a form of customer development.

Design of the linkage system

But how does a large commercial bank reach thousands of poor people with tiny loans? ICICI Bank have developed a unique linkage methodology, through which they are now reaching close to 300,000 clients in mainly rural areas, with direct loans. Furthermore, many of these clients are in the poorest regions of India, such as in Bihar and Uttar Pradesh, home to 37 per cent of India's poorest people. The Bank selects MFIs as partners who then act as managing agents for ICICI Bank. Most of these MFIs, such as PSS and BISWA which are described in this chapter, work through self-help groups (SHGs) which borrow direct and then on-lend to their individual members. A smaller number of the Bank's partners, however, are 'Grameen replicators', which follow the Bangladesh Grameen Bank's method of lending to individual clients; their groups facilitate and guarantee the loans for their members, but they do not themselves take loans.

The system or linkage works as follows: ICICI Bank carefully selects partner MFIs with substantial outreach and high quality microfinance portfolios. After a brief inspection of the MFI's loan accounting and monitoring systems, ICICI Bank staff visit a random sample of customers, to check the validity of the head office records and the quality of the SHGs' own records.

The Bank is quite clear that their intention is not to rate the strength of the MFI's own balance sheet, but its capacity to facilitate the relationships between the Bank and SHGs or other actual borrowers to whom the Bank will lend. The Bank rates the MFI's management capacity, the quality of its MIS and data reporting systems, the competence of its field staff and the quality of the training it provides to its SHGs and its own staff. Once an MFI's portfolio has been successfully 'screened' by ICICI Bank and the MFI has been recognized as an approved partner, it can start to distribute loans to SHGs or individuals on behalf of ICICI Bank, drawing the necessary funds from the nearest ICICI Bank branch. The MFI will be remunerated for originating and maintaining the accounts, and for recovering the loans. The MFI usually receives a percentage of the loan interest.

After the loans have been disbursed by the MFI, the accounts are monitored on a sample basis for the Bank by their own locally recruited contract staff and auditors. They follow a preset procedure to verify the monthly returns submitted by the MFIs. One full-time monitor is appointed for every partner whose portfolio exceeds one million dollars. These monitors are paid only about US$100 a month, but reliable and well educated people can be hired in India for this amount. They are trained to follow the required procedures and to observe obvious danger signals.

The final borrowers, in addition to ICICI Bank's interest charges, pay an additional service charge to the partner MFI. This means that the SHGs or individual clients actually pay, in total, similar rates to those they would pay if they were borrowing from the MFI (see the BISWA example later). However, their loan agreements state ICICI Bank's interest rates and do not include the MFIs' fees. Three officers of each SHG and every individual borrower from MFIs following the Grameen system sign loan agreements with ICICI Bank, not with the MFI. The agreements include photographs of the signatories, and proof of residence, such as a voter's or a ration card, although this may sometimes be replaced by signed approval of the whole group by a local village leader. This process is intended to ensure that the borrowers understand that they are customers of the Bank, and not of the MFI.

Risk reduction

ICICI Bank reduces its risk and ensures the commitment of the partner MFIs by taking first loss guarantees from the MFIs, which vary in amount according to the perceived quality of the loan portfolio, how long they have worked with the MFI and on the MFI's own preferences. One option is for the MFI to open a fixed deposit account for between 8 and 15 per cent of the total loaned, which cannot be withdrawn by the MFI until the loans have been repaid, but can be drawn down by ICICI Bank to cover any losses. Alternatively, the MFI may be given an overdraft limit with ICICI Bank up to the required amount, and the Bank can then require the MFI to use this to cover any losses. A third party can also deposit the necessary guarantee on behalf of the MFI. The Grameen Foundation of the USA has done this for ICICI Bank loans channelled through Cashpor and SHARE, India's largest Grameen replicators.

Such guarantees can be used to enhance the quality of securitized loans which the Bank may choose to sell on to other institutions, and thus to improve the price obtained by the Bank (see Box 5.1). Alternatively, the loans and the associated MFIs' obligations may be retained by ICICI Bank should it be decided not to package or sell on the assets arising from loans to a particular group of clients.

The Bank is aware that if an MFI collapsed they would have some difficulties in recovering all their dues, in spite of these precautions. However, they believe that their procedures would give them early warning of any serious problems, and the first loss guarantees provide some initial protection. As a last resort, they could perhaps sell the remaining balance of any remaining portfolio to another MFI, or could sub-contract the collection to a debt collection agency.

The first MFIs with which ICICI Bank formed partnerships of this kind, such as BISWA, were already directly involved in financial intermediation. They are using the Bank partnership to complement this activity and reach more clients without having themselves to access more funds for on-lending. Such MFIs may choose to continue to combine their own direct business with ICICI Bank partnerships, or, as they become financially stronger, and more bulk loans become available to them, or they become eligible to mobilize client deposits, they may replace the ICICI Bank funds with their own.

Alternatively, some smaller and financially weaker MFIs may choose to hand over the complete task of financial intermediation to the Bank and to focus on their 'core business' of community mobilization, loan origination and collection. Given the stringent requirements demanded by banks for bulk loans, and the very great difficulties in acquiring banking status, it is more likely that many if not most partners will choose this latter route.

Governance and cost considerations

ICICI Bank started its micro-finance activities under its Social Initiatives Group (SIG), a unit positioned somewhere between corporate responsibility and

---

Box 5.1 Securitization of loans

Securitization involves selling a package of loans to a third party. The seller, the originator of the loans, usually provides some sort of full or partial guarantee that they will be repaid and may be responsible for the collection. Securitization is used by banks such as ICICI Bank which tend not to mobilize enough savings deposits to finance their loan portfolios, and therefore need to acquire funds for on-lending before the loans they have made fall due.

ICICI Bank purchased one package of loans from Basix Finance, which is believed to have been the first securitization of microfinance loans in the world. The Bank has also done similar deals with other MFIs, but Basix have found the reporting requirements to be somewhat onerous and have therefore chosen instead to borrow directly from other large banks, such as ABN Amro and UTI Bank of India.

for-profit business. The bulk of the micro-finance activity has now been transferred to mainstream business. The five-member micro-finance team is located in the rural, micro-banking and agri-business group, within the wholesale banking division.

In early 2005 ICICI Bank's microfinance portfolio amounted to no more than a third of one per cent of the Bank's total assets, but it is growing much faster than most other areas, and is rather more profitable than the average for the Bank's business sectors. There is no need to justify the microfinance portfolio by reference to its social or public relations benefits or to view it as an investment in future client development. The spread on microfinance advances is as high, and the transaction costs are as low, as in other sections of the Bank's work, because the costs have been effectively out-sourced to specialist institutions. This is fundamentally consistent with the Bank's approach to any other business sector, such as housing or vehicle finance, and management are now confident that microfinance has been securely mainstreamed within the Bank.

Linkages in action

ICICI Bank and Services for Progress Organization (PSS)

PSS is one of the smaller MFIs whose customers have received loans from ICICI Bank. PSS works in the poorest parts of Warangal District of Andhra Pradesh, where three-quarters of the population earn their livelihoods from farming and related activities. Although it used to be relatively well off, the area has recently suffered heavily from drought. Cotton is the most popular crop, and this has led to problems not just because of the drought but also because of the high cost of seeds, fertiliser and pesticides.

PSS has an annual budget of around US$240,000 and is funded from Indian government and foreign sources. PSS has promoted over 1,250 SHGs, which have been grouped into 22 Mutually Aided Cooperative Societies (MACS), with about 20,000 members altogether. At the end of 2004, the SHG members owed about US$750,000 to their SHGs and the SHGs themselves owed about US$200,000 to various banks. The balance of the SHGs' funds was from their own savings, accumulated earnings and loans from PSS.

SHGs that have been promoted by PSS have now borrowed US$100,000 from the Bank, either directly or through their MACS and, under the ICICI Bank partnership model, in order to cover part of the risk of the US$100,000 that has been lent to PSS's self-help groups, ICICI Bank has required PSS to deposit with the Bank a sum equivalent to 15 per cent of the loans, as a first loss guarantee. This deposit earns the Bank's normal rate of 5.5 per cent interest, but the account cannot be closed until all the SHG loans have been repaid. Any defaults can be recovered from the deposit, before it is returned. While there has, to date, been no need to exercise this right, PSS is well aware of the possibility.

As a result of ICICI Bank's satisfactory experience with PSS, the State Bank of India and Corporation Bank, another large public sector bank, are becoming interested in lending to PSS' affiliated MACS and possibly to PSS itself.

The Jeevanajyothi MACS is one of the 19 MACS whose member SHGs have received loans from ICICI Bank, as a result of the linkage with PSS. The MACS has 76 member SHGs, which in turn have 722 members. All the SHG members are women and most are from the so-called 'scheduled' castes and tribes who have always been both socially and economically marginalized in India. The financial situation of the Jeevanajyothi MACS at the end of 2004 was as follows:

The SHG members realize that ICICI Bank loans are more expensive than loans from the nearest branch of the Kakatiya Rural Bank. They nevertheless prefer to borrow from their MACS, or from ICICI Bank, because:

- When the SHGs borrowed from the Kakatiya Bank, all the members of the group had to go to the branch, which cost them US$6 in bus fares, in addition to sixty cents each in lost wages. Two of their officers had to make two further visits to the branch, which cost the group US$2 for each trip.
- Loans from the Kakatiya bank were insufficient to enable the women to buy buffalos, which cost around US$100 each, or to make any other significant investment.
- The loans from ICICI Bank, in the same way as direct loans from their MACS, were more expensive than from the Kakatiya Bank, but part at least of the extra cost went to support the MACS, which was their own institution.

The women believe that it would be even better to borrow direct from their MACS, rather than from ICICI Bank, since MACS loans cost 18 per cent, as opposed to the effective rate of 24 per cent they pay for ICICI Bank loans, and they wish to develop their own institution. They appreciate, however, that it is difficult for the MACS to access more funds, and they are satisfied with the more expensive loans for the time being.

They have used their loans for a variety of purposes, including the purchase of goats and sheep, for sums as small as twenty to thirty dollars.

ICICI Bank and the Bharat Integrated Social Welfare Agency (BISWA)

BISWA, an NGO in Orissa, the poorest state in India, has promoted over 4,000 SHGs with about 64,000 mainly women members, in almost 2,000 villages.

ICICI Bank has lent a total of US$250,000 to SHGs promoted by BISWA and through them to 4,351 final borrowers. Prior to 2004 BISWA was funded by a number of organizations, enabling them to lend directly to 1,168 SHGs; the

Table 5.1 Financial situation of Jeevanajyothi MACS as of year-end 2004 (US$)

Assets / Use of Money		Liabilities / Sources of Money	
Loans outstanding with member SHGs	17,500	Members' savings	7,590
Fixed deposits	760	Loans from PSS	10,500
Cash at bank	1,460	Accumulated surplus	1,630
Total	19,720	Total	19,720

US$250,000 ICICI Bank loan went to a further 297 groups. BISWA also mobilizes savings from the SHGs and in early 2005 the balance of these savings amounted to US$10,500, earning 5 per cent interest. It is not strictly legal for an NGO such as BISWA to take savings, but as with many similar NGO/MFIs in India, the authorities turn a blind eye to the practice.

The ICICI Bank loan was disbursed into a special account opened at the ICICI Bank branch in the town of Sambalpur. The US$250 000 loan from ICICI Bank did not appear on BISWA's books, since the loan was distributed to the SHGs directly. The loans are repayable over eighteen months and the 297 SHGs that received ICICI Bank loans achieved 100 per cent on-time repayment. This is better than the average SHG on-time repayment rate of 98.6 per cent, partly because BISWA ensured that the selected SHGs were well established, with previous high repayment rates.

The SHGs pay a total of 18 per cent interest, plus a two dollar service charge to BISWA, and the members pay 24 per cent to their SHGs. The 6 per cent spread is retained by the SHGs to build their own funds or distributed to the members as a dividend, depending on the preference of each group. When borrowing from ICICI, the rate of 14.25 per cent that the SHGs pay includes the interest to ICICI Bank and the cost of BISWA's intermediation, and this is a considerable reduction in their costs. This reflects the general market situation of falling rates, where some banks are lending direct to SHGs at as low as 9 per cent. The SHGs are free to set their own on-lending rates, but most lend to their members at 2 per cent a month, or 24 per cent a year.

BISWA must carry the first risk of defaults on loans to the SHGs which it has introduced to ICICI Bank, by opening a guarantee deposit with ICICI Bank's branch in Sambalpur. The deposit required is for only 12 per cent of the loan amount since the ICICI Bank assessment concluded that the quality of BISWA's records and repayment performance was good. Nevertheless, this first loss guarantee deposit imposes a heavy burden on BISWA's limited cash resources and they hope that ICICI Bank will relax this requirement or replace it with an overdraft account, to be drawn down only if there are any defaults. This would not tie up any of the NGO's scarce cash resources.

The transaction with ICICI Bank was fairly simple and in many ways less difficult than the earlier bulk loans from other banks. The CARE representative who had worked with BISWA for some time made the initial introduction and only two further meetings were required, over a period of six weeks. BISWA estimate that the whole transaction, including setting up the necessary recording and reporting formats, and informing the SHGs of their obligations, took four days and cost approximately US$400 in staff time and expenses.

As a result of the ICICI Bank loans, BISWA has been able to retire some of its more expensive loans from banks and other sources. By January 2005, the ICICI Bank loan represented over half of the funds that were available to their SHGs. This has significantly reduced the cost of funds to the SHGs, since their BISWA loans cost 18 per cent whereas the ICICI Bank loan costs 3.75 per cent less.

Competition is increasing however and BISWA are being approached by other large foreign and Indian banks with highly competitive offers for bulk financing.

The SHG members themselves are also becoming more financially sophisticated and local bank branches are becoming more receptive to direct business with SHGs. BISWA can choose between bulk borrowing and the ICICI Bank partnership approach, and BISWA's client SHGs can also choose to place their business elsewhere. This diversity of sources of finance can only serve to benefit the SHG members.

The intermediation process between ICICI and BISWA is very streamlined and the transaction costs to BISWA are reasonable. Two hours after the 12 per cent deposit is received by ICICI, the funds are transferred to BISWA's special account in Sambalpur. BISWA then disburse the loans, in cash or by cheque, within a day or so. BISWA has every incentive to transfer the funds to the SHGs quickly, since interest is charged by ICICI to BISWA from the moment the funds are transferred.

In addition to more readily available funds, the main benefit to BISWA of the linkage arrangement with ICICI has been its enhanced credibility among Indian and foreign banks such as ABN-AMRO and State Bank of India. Many of these banks are keen to provide bulk loans to well-established institutions such as BISWA, at competitive interest rates.

ICICI Bank is willing to lend to any SHG that BISWA recommends. However, BISWA does not want their SHGs to become entirely dependent on ICICI Bank. The Bank might choose to exercise its right to securitize the loans and sell them to a less amenable partner. In fact BISWA prefers taking direct bulk loans from banks, since they can then exercise total control over the funds and the on-lending rate which they charge the SHGs. The 5 per cent management fee ICICI allow BISWA to add to the interest paid by the SHGs barely covers their costs, particularly if the opportunity cost of the first loss guarantee fund deposited with the Bank is accounted for. Ideally, BISWA would prefer to control the on-lending rate themselves.

Conclusions

ICICI Bank has designed and implemented a very innovative and apparently effective strategy to enter the microfinance market, despite the fact that the Bank has only 88 branches outside the major cities. The partnership model enables the Bank to use the expertise and networks of specialist institutions with long experience of social and financial intermediation, without taking on the risk of actually lending money to them. Many of these institutions are financially weak, poorly capitalized, and dependent on grant funds for their survival. ICICI is lending direct to SHGs or to individual micro-borrowers, whose aggregated credit risks have been shown to be very low. The intermediary institutions provide their services for a fee, which is bundled with the interest paid by the final borrowers.

From the MFI perspective, the linkage model has some disadvantages. The MFIs are simply loan agents, and, as illustrated in the BISWA case, they do not want their SHGs to become entirely dependant on ICICI Bank. Some MFIs are becoming financially stronger and some are already able to borrow bulk funds direct from ICICI Bank's competitors, such as ABN-AMRO Bank and others. It is likely that in the future many of ICICI Bank's best collaborators, and particularly those taking the larger sums, will prefer to take bulk loans themselves and to on-lend to their SHGs, thus enhancing their own status in the eyes of their clients. The ICICI Bank linkage will help them to do this, since ICICI approved MFIs gain status by being associated with the Bank, and the MFIs can use this to court other banks for bulk loans, in essence diversifying their partner base. Other MFIs, as has already been pointed out, may prefer to focus on their agency role, and to withdraw from direct financial intermediation.

ICICI's strategy is working well for the Bank also. The portfolio is growing, and the loans are profitable. By March 2005 ICICI Bank's exposure to the microfinance sector, through 27 partner MFIs, had reached US$66 million. Motivated by this initial success, ICICI Bank is now extending its linkage model, to smaller MFIs, through a strategic partnership with CARE. By dealing direct with microfinance clients, the Bank can satisfy the Reserve Bank requirements to lend to the so-called 'weaker sections' and it has created assets, which can be securitized and sold on to other financial institutions.

ICICI Bank acknowledges that a number of challenges remain. The Bank cannot yet offer savings products to its SHG clients. It is unlikely that they will succeed in persuading the regulators to allow deposit taking, in view of the long history of dishonest savings collectors. The threat is that ICICI clients might now go to their neighbouring bank branches for savings and may then take loans from them, which are available at 10 per cent or even less for strong SHGs.

Furthermore, the ICICI Bank loans are made to groups or to individuals and not to the MFIs. If the MFI's are unable to recover the loans, it is unclear if ICICI will be able to. The Bank has no presence in the areas where the clients live and has no staff of its own to collect repayments. Another possible threat for ICICI Banks' long-term success is that the SHG members will become more sophisticated. As their needs increase, they will start 'shopping around' for less expensive loans, at better rates.

Despite these concerns, ICICI Bank is demonstrating that an urban-based private bank can effectively and profitably reach the rural poor. This business is now a component of the Bank's mainstream operations and other Indian and foreign banks are appreciating that the rural poor can be valuable customers. A wider range of financial services is becoming available to hundreds of millions of people who have hitherto lacked access to any formal financial services at all. This experience shows that urban based banks, with few rural branches, can make use of the community contacts and experience of rural NGOs, so that both parties can cover their costs and do what they do best, for the benefit of their clients.

Postscript

In February 2007 the Reserve Bank of India (India's Central Bank) expressed some concern that ICICI Bank's loans under the partnership system did not conform to the 'know your customer' requirements, since all direct contact with microfinance clients was undertaken by the partner NGO or MFI, and not by the Bank itself. ICICI Bank was asked to refrain from future lending until the requirements could be satisfied. The Bank's management had already been aware of this problem, and they redoubled their efforts to assist their NGO/MFI partners to develop management information systems which would provide all the necessary information to the Bank.

It was informally suggested that the Reserve Bank was also concerned about the capital adequacy of the partner NGO/MFIs. The loans were of course on ICICI Bank's books, and their partners only carried the risk of the first guarantees. There had however in early 2006 been some cases of mass default on microfinance loans, stimulated by opportunist political agitation against the high rates of interest charged by some MFIs. If such defaults were to occur on ICICI Bank loans provided under the partnership system, it was not clear that all the NGO/MFIs would be able to honour their guarantees, and this could also lead to a 'snow-balling' effect, with defaults on these MFIs' other loans from different banks.

In the meantime, however, as loans managed by ICICI Bank's partner NGO/MFIs were repaid, they were not renewed. The NGO/MFIs had to identify alternative sources of finance in order to satisfy their clients' demands. Other banks, including the large nationalized commercial banks such as State Bank of India, had already started making bulk loans to some of the stronger MFIs. ICICI Bank's partners were not all financially strong, and the Bank had of course devised the partnership system in order to avoid lending large sums direct to weak institutions of this kind. Nevertheless, it appeared by mid-2007 that some of ICICI Bank's larger partners might be able to satisfy the Bank's 'know your customer' requirements, and that the others would be able either to access funds direct from commercial banks or to assist their clients to borrow direct from their local banks.

CHAPTER 6

A case study of AVIVA Life Insurance and its linkage with microfinance institutions

Nilotpal Pathak

Abstract

India has taken major steps over the last few years to provide basic financial services like banking and insurance to low income clients in the rural areas. Regulatory provisions have been put in place by the authorities to ensure coverage of insurance to disadvantaged sections of society. While initially, these provisions were viewed merely as regulatory compliances, insurance companies are increasingly seeing this market segment as an area of opportunity. AVIVA India, a leading global insurance company, has taken initiative and is developing linkages with some leading microfinance institutions (MFIs) to reach out to the rural market in a profitable manner. The study explores some of the nuances of these linkages and makes an attempt to underline the factors responsible for the success and failure of such relationships. Findings from the case study underline the need for a client focused and financially sustainable strategy for tapping this market. The need for investment to develop the market and understand the requirements of clients and intermediaries is also emphasized.

Introduction

A vast majority of India's 250 million poor live in rural areas. Very few of them have any access to insurance services. It is apparent that access to basic services in India is still very limited (Table 6.1). This is partly because of the high cost (high per unit transaction costs, travel costs) and risks (seasonality, price, production, correlated outcomes) associated with providing services in rural areas. The challenge of sustainable service provision is quite daunting. However, the Government of India issued a policy on insurance and set out a regulatory framework for access to insurance services in India, specifically for rural areas. This chapter explains how insurers in India are addressing the challenges and are meeting the regulatory conditions. AVIVA, an international insurance company, is providing insurance services in rural areas by linking up with strategic partners, especially those with a comparative advantage in effectively servicing rural clients, such as microfinance institutions (MFIs).

Table 6.1 Status of economy and development of India

Indicators	Status
Population (end 2004, millions)	1,091
Annual population growth (2002–4)	1.5%
Population density (persons/km^2)	332
Population below poverty line	25%
Life expectancy (2002, in years)	63.7
Infant mortality (2003, per thousand)	63
GDP growth rate (2003–4)	6.5%
Agriculture growth rate (2003–4)	0.6%
Industry growth rate (2003–4)	8.0%
Services growth rate (2003–4)	8.2%
Per capita gross national income (2003, US$)	530
Availability of phone lines (as % of population)	4.63
Availability of personal computers (as % of population)	0.72
Access to insurance coverage (as % of economically active workforce)	1.4
Rate of inflation (2003–4, %)	6.0%
Human development index (HDI) Value, 2002	0.595
Human development index ranking (2004)	127

Source: Asian Development Bank, August 2005.

This chapter, based on a longer case study completed as part of a global review on financial linkages implemented by the Food and Agriculture Organization (FAO) of the UN for the Ford Foundation, examines the main constraints to insurance service provision and identifies the important pre-conditions for this type of linkage to emerge. The chapter also identifies key design factors and processes of the linkage and, most importantly, evaluates the impacts of the financial linkage, particularly at the policy and institutional levels. Finally, the chapter endeavours to determine how that impact has resulted in significantly expanded access to financial and insurance services to rural clients.

Current state of insurance in India

For the first time in several decades, the insurance market in India is no longer a monopoly of the state insurers. There are 14 organizations in the life insurance market while there are another 13 in the general non-life insurance business. The market share of the former public sector monopoly, Life Insurance Corporation of India (LIC), has been in decline since the arrival of new private players, resulting in a greater range of products and an improvement in overall service quality in the insurance industry (Table 6.2).

Growth of the insurance business in rural areas is constrained by a number of factors. Notable among these are:

- *Lack of adequate insurance infrastructure.* In spite of the nearly 50-year-old presence of public sector companies in this market, insurance continues

Table 6.2 Market share of life insurance companies in India (30 June 2005)

Insurance company	Market share, premiums (%)	Market share, policies (%)
LIC	74.87	87.25
ICICI Prudential	7.53	2.91
BIRLA Sunlife	1.84	0.80
Bajaj Allianz	4.18	1.81
SBI Life	1.69	0.88
HDFC Standard	3.20	1.32
TATA AIG	1.93	1.57
Max New York	1.44	1.55
AVIVA	1.14	0.48
Om Kotak Mahindra	0.77	0.33
ING Vyasa	0.53	0.36
AMP Sanmar	0.47	0.27
Metlife	0.39	0.35
Sahara Life	0.02	0.14

Source: IRDA Monthly Journal, August 2005.

to be an urban phenomenon. The necessary infrastructure for insurance, such as a good health care system and a system to scrutinize claims, are yet to develop in rural areas. This puts a severe constraint on new entrants into the market.

- *Long gestation period of insurance coupled with uncertainties in the rural market.* In general, the risk of moral hazard runs very high in the insurance business. This risk is more pronounced in the rural areas as the presence of an insurance company is further removed. Apart from the risk of moral hazard, different parts of rural India also suffer from regular bouts of natural calamities such as drought, floods and disease epidemics. These uncertainties of environment, coupled with the lack of trust between insurers and clients, and the problem of moral hazard limit the insurance market in rural areas.

- *Lack of professional and trustworthy partners.* It might be very difficult for the new entrants into the insurance business to develop their own service delivery channels. They seek the help of non-governmental organizations (NGOs), cooperatives and other such organizations working in rural areas. Lack of understanding of the insurance business and professionalism among such partners often creates problems of coordination with the insurers.

- *Low profitability.* In spite of the business potential, insurance in rural areas is not considered a very profitable proposition. This can be attributed to the high costs associated with doing business in rural areas, lack of knowledge about the rural client, lack of technology and systems, lack of outlets to deliver and process the policies, and claims efficiently. However, part of the blame also lies with the insurance companies that have been less than innovative in their product design and processes.

In India, growth in the provision of insurance services to rural and social sectors is primarily regarded as a regulatory compliance rather than a serious market commitment, and for that reason is mainly driven by push factors. However, some of the insurance companies have taken the lead in looking at the rural market as a potential area of growth. Keen to explore new markets as the cream in the urban market is being squeezed because of fierce competition, these companies have tried to develop market channels and linkages in the rural areas. These methods include employment of direct selling agents for insurance in rural areas, employing corporate agents for the sale of insurance products and developing master policyholders to sell group insurance.

While most insurance companies view insurance in the rural areas as regulatory compliance (see below), some see it as a market with genuine potential. ICICI Prudential started in 2001 and has made serious forays into the rural market. They have developed a robust rural distribution model involving tied agents, brokers as well as referral arrangements with NGOs, microfinance institutions (MFIs) and companies. The operations of TATA-AIG Insurance Company Ltd in rural India involve partnerships with several NGOs, some of whom are also MFIs. It has also launched a project to provide insurance coverage to landless and daily-wage labourers in Andhra Pradesh, with funding support from the British Government's Department for International Development (DFID). The main features of the project are relevant and affordable long-tenure plans; livelihood creation through enlisting of women's community enterprises; mentoring and monitoring through rural organizations; and specialized promotional activity tuned to the requirements of the target market.

AVIVA Life Insurance Company India Private Limited, a relatively late entrant into the Indian insurance market, has also expanded into the rural market. It aims to capture the majority share of the Indian rural insurance market in the next 10 years. To accomplish this, AVIVA has developed partnerships with several NGO-MFIs, cooperative societies, banks and other rural voluntary organizations to provide insurance services in rural areas. As of 31 July 2005, it had 18 partners spread across the states of West Bengal, Andhra Pradesh, Gujarat, Tamil Nadu, Orissa and Uttar Pradesh. It has partnerships with some of the leading MFIs and women's organizations in India, such as Bhartiya Samruddhi Financial Services Limited (BASIX) and the Self-Employed Women's Association (SEWA). While BASIX is a MFI and commercially orientated, SEWA is registered as a trade union and provides a variety of services to its member women. Aviva's partnerships with these two organizations are explored in some detail below, following a brief discussion on the Indian life insurance sector.

Development of life insurance business in India

The business of life insurance in its existing form started in India in 1818 with the establishment of the Oriental Life Insurance Company in Calcutta. However, the recorded history of the insurance business in India began in 1914 when the Government of India started publishing returns of insurance companies in

India. The Indian Life Assurance Companies Act, 1912, was the first statutory measure to regulate this business. Some of the important milestones in the life insurance business in India are summarized in Table 6.3.

Insurance Regulatory and Development Authority

Reforms in the insurance sector started with the passage of the IRDA Bill in parliament in December 1999. The key objectives of IRDA were to promote competition to enhance customer satisfaction through increased consumer choice and lower premiums, while ensuring the financial security of the insurance market. The IRDA opened the market in August 2000 with an invitation of applications for registration. Foreign companies were allowed ownership up to 26 per cent.

In order to ensure the widespread coverage of insurance services especially to rural areas, the IRDA issued norms for coverage in the rural and social sectors to be met by both life and general insurance companies. To comply with this regulation, life insurance companies must cover at least 18 per cent of the number of lives in rural areas by the end of their sixth year of operation, starting from 7 per cent in the first year. For the general insurance companies the equivalent figures are 5 per cent by the end of the sixth year starting from at least 2 per cent in the first year (Table 6.4).

Similarly, the social sector requirement for both types of insurance companies is coverage of 20,000 policies by the end of 6 years starting from 5,000 policies in the first year. While the IRDA defines rural areas by population limits of the policyholder, the 'social sector' depends on the occupation of the policyholder. The IRDA defines the 'social sector' as: unorganized sector (self-employed

Table 6.3 Milestones in the history of life insurance in India

Year	Milestones
1912	The Indian Life Assurance Companies Act enacted as the first statute to regulate the life insurance business
1928	The Indian Insurance Companies Act enacted to enable the government to collect statistical information about both life and non-life insurance businesses
1938	Earlier legislation consolidated and amended by the Insurance Act with the objective of protecting the interests of the insuring public
1956	245 Indian and foreign insurers and provident societies taken over by the central government and nationalized. LIC formed by an Act of Parliament, viz. LIC Act, 1956, with a capital contribution of Rs50 million from the Government of India
1994	Malhotra Committee Report on the insurance sector reforms submitted to the Government. The report with contained revolutionary recommendations on the structure, competition, regulation and customer services obligations of the insurance sector
1999	IRDA (Insurance Regulatory and Development Authority) Act passed by the parliament

Table 6.4 Regulatory norms for life and general insurance companies

Year	1	2	3	4	5	6
Rural sector						
Life insurer (as % of total policies)	7	9	12	14	16	18
General insurer (as % of total policies)	2	3	5	5	5	5
Social sector						
All insurers	5,000	7,000	10,000	15,000	20,000	20,000

Source: IRDA, Final Regulation Rural Sector Obligations, 2002.

workers such as agricultural labourers, bidi workers, carpenters, cobblers, construction workers, fishermen, physically handicapped self-employed persons, primary milk producers); informal sector (small-scale, self-employed workers typically at a low level of organization and technology, with the primary objective of generating employment and income); economically vulnerable or backward classes, and other categories of persons, both in rural and urban areas. Similarly the rural area means any place with a population of less than 5,000 (as per the latest census in 2001), a population density of less than 400 per square kilometre; and more than 25 per cent of the male working population engaged in agricultural pursuits.

The linkage

AVIVA plc is the United Kingdom's largest and the world's sixth largest insurance group. It is one of the leading providers of life insurance and pension products to Europe and has substantial businesses elsewhere around the world. In India, AVIVA has a joint venture with Dabur, one of India's oldest and largest groups of manufacturing companies. A professionally managed company, Dabur is the country's leading producer of traditional health care products. In accordance with government regulations, AVIVA holds a 26 per cent stake in the joint venture and the Dabur group holds the remaining 74 per cent. AVIVA has developed institutional linkages with 18 different partners to provide insurance services in the rural areas. As part of the in-depth case study review on AVIVA, linkages with three of their partners, namely Bhartiya Samruddhi Finance Limited (BASIX), Village Welfare Society (VWS) and Self-Employed Women's Association (SEWA) were examined, and two of these, namely BASIX and SEWA are discussed below.

BASIX

BASIX – registered as a Public Limited Company (non-banking finance company) – was established in 1996 with the aim of providing sustainable financial services to the rural population for the promotion of livelihoods. An impact assessment study carried out by Indian Marketing Research Bureau (IMRB) in 2001 revealed that 23 per cent of BASIX's clients reported an effective decline in their earnings.

The reasons for this decline related to the productivity and risks associated with small enterprises. Based on the findings of the impact study, BASIX developed a livelihood triode. Access to various financial services was an essential part of this triode. Rural people need a comprehensive set of financial services, including savings, credit and insurance. BASIX has the vision of providing all poor households, especially those of its clients, with access to risk-management services covering their lives and livelihoods together with insurance companies that provide these services willingly on a financially sustainable basis.

In striving to carry out its new livelihood strategy, BASIX began an initiative to deliver insurance services in 2001, coinciding with the opening up of the Indian insurance sector. Since the beginning, BASIX has actively collaborated with multiple insurance companies to design insurance products for rural customers. BASIX initially worked with ICICI Prudential to deliver life insurance to their clients but later shifted to AVIVA Life Insurance Company (October 2002) because they were more willing to experiment and pilot new products. In 2003, BASIX received a corporate agency license from IRDA to distribute retail life insurance products from AVIVA. BASIX is also actively working with other insurers in designing suitable health insurance products for its rural clients. BASIX's model for microinsurance delivery and its partnerships is best illustrated as follows:

As stated, BASIX entered the life insurance business in 2001 by linking with ICICI Prudential. At the start of the relationship, ICICI Prudential offered a basic product, with a coverage of Rs10,000 (US$21) at an annual premium of just Rs100 (US$2.10). A year later BASIX asked ICICI Prudential for coverage of more clients as well as further investment in experimentation. As a newcomer to the microinsurance market and still testing the waters, ICICI Prudential was reluctant to invest in new product design and piloting. In the end, this reluctance resulted in the termination of the partnership. Apparently, ICICI Prudential was not quite ready for investment in research and design of product at that point in time. As it turned out, the long-term commitment of BASIX was incompatible with ICICI Prudential's short-sighted strategy of regulatory compliance.

AVIVA had a different approach to the rural and social sector. In contrast to ICICI Prudential's short-term strategy of meeting the rural and social sector regulatory requirement, AVIVA viewed the market with a long-term perspective. AVIVA was willing to experiment with the products and valued BASIX's expertise in community understanding. In essence, they chose a 'tailor made' approach to collaborating with MFIs and various organizations rather than a 'one model fits all' approach. In fact, this 'tailor made' approach is the way AVIVA runs all of

Figure 6.1 BASIX insurance linkage model

its partnerships, whether partners are big or small, urban or rural, corporate or non-corporate.

In October 2002 – after co-designing a life insurance product and getting it approved by IRDA – AVIVA and BASIX entered into a master policy agreement. According to this agreement, all BASIX clients were to be brought under insurance coverage. The policy with each of the members is renewed each month upon payment of the premium as part of the equated monthly instalment (EMI) that clients pay against their loan from BASIX. This product is called 'Credit Plus'. In December 2003, BASIX signed a corporate agency agreement with AVIVA to sell the life insurance product to rural customers outside the purview of Credit Plus. Under this arrangement, the unit offices of BASIX with the help of its customer service agents are functioning as retail outlets that sell AVIVA insurance products to clients and non-clients of BASIX. Table 6.5 outlines the life insurance products offered by BASIX.

Table 6.6 presents BASIX's coverage of life insurance with details on premium collection, total policies, number of lives covered and the number of claims

Table 6.5 BASIX's life insurance products

Parameters	Credit Plus	Jan Suraksha	Amar Suraksha	Anmol Suraksha
Eligibility	Credit clients, Age 18–45 yrs	Rural dweller, Age 18–45 yrs	Rural dweller, Age 18–45 yrs	Rural dweller, Age 18–45 yrs
Selection	Existing loan clients	By field staff of BASIX	By field staff of BASIX	By field staff of BASIX
Sum assured	1.5 times loan amount	Rs20,000–50,000 (~US$450–1,125)	Rs20,000–100,000 (~US$450–2,250)	Rs10000–100,000 (~US$225–2,250)
Term	Monthly, multiple terms until the full repayment of loan amount	5, 10 years	5, 10, 15, 20 years	5, 10, 15, 20 years
Premium	1.8% of the loan amount disbursed	Based on age of client and term (paid one time or annually)	Based on age of client and term (paid one time or annually)	Based on age of client and term (paid one time or annually)
Benefit	Sum assured on natural death	Sum assured on death; double the amount in case the death is accidental	Sum assured on natural death; return of premium on maturity	Sum assured + (6.5%*sum assured*no. of completed policy years) on natural death and maturity

Source: Discussion with senior staff of BASIX.

Table 6.6 Life insurance coverage by BASIX

Year	Number of policies	Sum assured (in Rs)	Premium collected (in Rs)
2000–1	1,475	22,125,000	—
2001–2	300	4,500,000	—
2002–3	3,180	48,916,250	48,366
2003–4	49,912	640,228,950	2,807,725
2004–5	75,229	973,391,434	3,341,072
2005–6 (till June 2006)	27,711	410,381,000	815,118

Source: BASIX's *MIS Reports*, 2001–6.

settled. While all the Credit Plus for all clients has grown tremendously over the years, the retail insurance business of clients and non-clients has been slow to increase. Out of the 27,711 policies insured during the first three quarters of the current year, only 1,936 are under the retail sales through corporate agency agreement (i.e. approx. 7 per cent of the total policies).

BASIX receives a commission of 36 per cent of the premium collected under the master policy agreement. Since the marginal cost at the field level for the insurance services under the master policy agreement is nominal, this has been a profitable proposition for the MFI. However, BASIX acknowledges that this cannot be said for the retail business under the corporate agency. So far no empirical study has been carried out to assess the costs associated with retail business of insurance; possibly the initial investments, additional paper work and compulsory training of field staff (which has a cost) might be the reasons for the low or non profitability of the retail segment of the business.

This has been a profitable proposition for AVIVA also. Against the cumulative premium collection of more than Rs7 million (US$0.16 million), only 225 claims have been settled so far amounting to a value of Rs3.2 million (US$73.3 thousand). Though AVIVA has put one full-time dedicated staff to manage its relationship with BASIX, the other costs are relatively very low.

A significant achievement under the partnership has been the development of MIS software for insurance products at BASIX. This software is very effective in generating the relevant reports in appropriate formats. AVIVA and BASIX also have plans for marketing this software on a commercial basis. However, both partners realize that there are some problems: BASIX is concerned about the time that claim settlement is taking and the number of claims rejected by AVIVA. Against the cumulative claims of 261 (until June 2005) reported and certified by BASIX, only 225 were settled. In order to resolve these issues, meetings are held every 6 months, and the presence of a dedicated relationship manager for BASIX also helps in sorting out matters.

Over the last three and half years, BASIX has covered the lives of all its clients. Through the corporate agency of AVIVA, it has also sold its products to rural non-credit clients. BASIX's partnership experience in the life insurance field has been instrumental in forging relationships with other insurance providers, such as Royal Sundaram General Insurance Company for the delivery of a livestock insurance product, and ICICI Lombard for the delivery of rainfall insurance. It also has plans to introduce health insurance coverage to its rural clients in the near future. It has already started negotiations with insurance companies to provide this service. As illustrated in Box 6.1, BASIX's clients have gradually started to use the insurance services with greater eagerness as they are starting to experience the benefits of coverage.

Self–Employed Women's Association (SEWA)

SEWA, which is AVIVA's largest partner in terms of number of policies administered, was registered as a trade union in 1972. SEWA's main goal is to organize women workers for full employment and self-reliance. SEWA Bank was created in 1974 to help provide financial services to SEWA members. In-house studies conducted in 1978 revealed that nearly 50 per cent of the borrowers were having problems in meeting their repayment obligations because of health reasons, signalling a need for financial services beyond savings and credit. Because most of these members were living in poverty in the urban slums of Ahmedabad city, their access to health services was severely constrained mainly because of lack of money to pay for it.

In response to this finding, SEWA attempted to provide health and life insurance derived from an internally mobilized and managed fund. They soon realized, however, that they lacked the necessary capacity and internal resources to provide adequate coverage to their members. In search of a more viable solution, they turned to the only life insurer at the time, Life Insurance Corporation of India, (LIC), and convinced them to provide coverage for their

---

Box 6.1 Case Study of Mr Madhusudhan Rao and Mrs Madhulata Rao

A resident of Nijampet village in Rangareddy district of Andhra Pradesh, a southern Indian state, Mr Madhusudhan Rao has been a client of BASIX for the last 4 years. He is a small farmer with land holding of around 8 acres. He also owns three cows, four buffaloes and two oxen. He has a family of four comprising of his wife, a son and a daughter. He was introduced to the concept of insurance when he first borrowed from BASIX to buy a buffalo, and the company required him to have insurance coverage not only for himself, but also for cattle. Initially not convinced with the idea of spending money for this purpose, he agreed to the proposition very reluctantly on persuasion from his wife. Unfortunately, his cattle died in a nearby river before the end of his loan cycle. If it hadn't been for the insurance coverage from Royal Sundaram Insurance Company, he would have been stretched to repay the borrowed amount.

This incident made him understand the benefits of insurance. Today, he has bought insurance coverage worth Rs50,000 (US$1,200) for himself and another insurance coverage worth Rs25,000 (US$600) for his wife. Apart from insuring lives, he has also insured the lives of all the cattle he owns, even though he does not have any debt. He has also bought medical insurance coverage for himself and his wife. The coverage of insurance is Rs25,000 (US$600). The outlook for all of the Rao family has changed since the first time he bought insurance coverage for himself and his cattle.

members. With great reluctance, and after much negotiation from both sides, LIC agreed to the partnership. Because of the absence of any other options, SEWA Bank remained solely with LIC until 1992 despite their inadequacy in meeting the insurance needs of SEWA's members, i.e. health, asset and life for family members.

In 1992, SEWA set up a partnership with United India Insurance Company (UIC) permitting them to provide an expanded insurance product, which included health as well as life insurance. At the same time, to focus more concretely on new product development, SEWA removed the insurance business completely from SEWA Bank and placed it in a separate wing of the organization, called Vimo SEWA. This separation propelled product innovation leading to the development of an integrated insurance package that today provides coverage against illness, death, asset loss and accident. SEWA accomplished this by expanding its partnership base to include various life and non-life insurance companies.

Over the years, SEWA has collaborated with LIC, AVIVA and Om Kotak Mahindra Life Insurance Company Limited (OLIC) for life insurance coverage and with UIC and ICICI Lombard for non-life coverage. However, in December 2004, in search of better products and services, SEWA switched partners to AVIVA as its main life insurance provider. With more than 500,000 members from the rural and social sector, SEWA was a 'prize catch' for AVIVA, one they grasped by agreeing to all of SEWA's requirements. AVIVA's flexibility effectively knocked out the competition, such as LIC, the current provider as well as other suitors (Max New York Life, TAT-AIG or ICICI Prudential). Details of Vimo SEWA's insurance products are provided in the Table 6.7.

The product offered by Vimo SEWA indicates that the insurance is heavily subsided. As shown in Table 6.8, despite the numbers that SEWA has enrolled, the premium charged is not adequate to cover the costs of the insurance company. As far as the life insurance is concerned, the insurance companies are hardly able to meet the costs of the claims from the premium collected from the clients. The situation is much worse in the non-life and health insurance where the insurance companies have incurred losses over the last 5-year period.

In addition, it is apparent from the case study in Box 6.2 that the effectiveness of the insurance services also needs to be examined. While the family of the deceased would have been much worse off in the absence of Vimo SEWA, the question about the efficacy of the insurance service remains.

Impact of linkage

As illustrations presented above indicate, linkages in the insurance industry in India appear to be making a difference on several levels. In particular, AVIVA Life Insurance Company's partnerships with several organizations have resulted in a significant impact on clients as well as its partners. AVIVA has discovered the untapped potential of the rural market through partnerships, and its success

Table 6.7 Vimo SEWA's insurance schemes

Risk covered	Scheme I	Scheme II	Scheme III
Members' insurance	Annual pre Rs100 (US$2.2); or FD of Rs1,000 (US$22.2)	Annual pre Rs225 (US$5); or FD of Rs2,500 (US$444)	Annual Pre Rs450 (US$10); or FD of Rs5,000 (US$110)
Natural death Accidental death	Rs3,000 (US$66.7) Rs40,000 (US$889)	Rs20,000 (US$444) Rs65,000 (US$1,444)	Rs20,000 (US$444) Rs65,000 (US$1,444)
Accidental death of spouse	Rs15,000 (US$333)	Rs15,000 (US$333)	Rs15,000 (US$333)
Hospitalization	Up to Rs2,000 (US$44.4)	Up to Rs5,500 (US$122)	Up to Rs10,000 (US$222)
House and asset insurance	Up to Rs5,000 (US$111)	Up to Rs10,000 (US$222)	Up to Rs20,000 (US$444)
Admin charges for SEWA	Rs25 (US$0.6)	Rs50 (US$1.1)	Rs100 (US$2.2)
Husband's insurance	Annual pre Rs55 (US$1.2); or FD of Rs650 (US$14.4)	Annual pre Rs150 (US$3.3); or FD of Rs1,800 (US$40)	Annual pre Rs325 (US$7.2); or FD of Rs4,000 (US$88.9)
Natural death Accidental death	Rs3,000 (US$66.7) Rs25,000 (US$556)	Rs20,000 (US$444) Rs50,000 (US$1,111)	Rs20,000 (US$444) Rs50,000 (US$1,111)
Hospitalization	Rs2,000 (US$44.4)	Rs5,500 (US$122)	Rs10,000 (US$222)
Admin charges for SEWA	Same as above	Same as above	Same as above
Joint insurance	Annual Pre Rs140 (US$3.1); or FD Rs650 (US$14.4)	Annual Pre Rs350 (US$7.8); or FD Rs4,200 (US$93)	Annual Pre Rs725 (US$3.1); or FD Rs8,800 (US$14.4)

Source: Discussion with Vimo SEWA staff.

along with the success of other private insurers has spurred IRDA to expand the rural initiative.

Impact on clients

The regulatory compliance requirement for the rural and social sector seemed to have been at least partly successful if Boxes 6.1 and 6.2 are any indication. Some of the visible impacts on the lives of clients include:

- *Access to a new financial service.* In the case studies presented in Boxes 6.1 and 6.2, insurance was a completely new service to the clients. These families would not have had access to such services considering the transaction costs (cost of travel, opportunity cost of time and lack of knowledge) involved.

Table 6.8 The insurance record of Vimo SEWA for the last 5 years

Year		No. of policies covered	Premium collected (Rs)	No. of claims settled	Amount settled (Rs)	Admin cost collected from clients (as part of premium) (Rs)
2001	Life	92,928	2,316,392	431	2,039,000	579,098
	Non-life	71,678	685,326	1,135	3,487,905	171,332
	Health	92,928	1,142,260	1,225	1,234,842	285,565
2002	Life	92,928	1,218,482	169	837,000	304,621
	Non-life	71,678	324,421	6	11,781	81,105
	Health	92,928	679,429	696	774,653	169,857
2003	Life	109,758	2,887,220	418	2,005,000	721,805
	Non-life	85,042	979,300	2,299	1,107,126	244,825
	Health	112,112	2,066,455	2,726	4,362,165	516,614
2004	Life	104,525	2,385,000	401	2,309,000	596,250
	Non-life	71,937	1,219,000	627	857,354	304,750
	Health	106,479	1,806,000	3,728	6,189,742	451,500
2005	Life	115,142	3,156,000	214	1,121,000	789,000
	Non-life	80,389	892,640	31	93,390	223,160
	Health	133,683	4,530,000	2,185	3,652,830	1,132,500

Source: Records of Vimo SEWA.

Box 6.2 Case of Janakiben Parmar

Janakiben Parmar was a rag picker and a member of SEWA since 1997. She was a resident of Asarwa slums in the Kuberpura Bhilwas locality of Ahmedabad city. After the death of her husband in 1990, Janakiben was the only breadwinner of the family. She had a fixed deposit account with the SEWA Bank, and through this account she had the benefit of insurance.

Unfortunately Janakiben passed away in June 2005 after a sudden illness. Her dependents received Rs5,000 (US$111) 35 days after her death, but it was not enough to cover the costs of her final medical treatment and last rites. Although she had purchased medical coverage with Vimo SEWA, her reimbursement claim of Rs3,000 (US$67) for expenses incurred at the government run hospital at the end of her illness, was denied since she spent less than 24 hours there, one of the minimum criteria for reimbursement set by the insurer. In the end, Janakiben's daughter, Pushpaben, had no choice but to borrow Rs6,000 (US$133) and use the remaining of Janakiben's lifetime savings Rs4,000 (US$89) to pay for the hospital expenses and her last rites ceremony. Despite getting the claim amount of Rs5,000 (US$111), Pushpaben and her sisters would need to work harder to repay their outstanding borrowings of Rs2,000 (US$44.40).

- *Learning about insurance.* As Box 6.1 shows, there is an increasing awareness among clients about insurance services.
- *Better coverage of risk.* With insurance coverage, clients are better positioned to face the vagaries of nature. This shows more in the case of livestock and weather insurance.

Impact on the linkage partner

The visible impacts of linkage on the partner organizations are:
- *Sound instrument for risk management.* With the lives of poor clients insured, the micro and collateral free loans of microfinance institutions do not face any risk because of uncertainty of the life of the client.
- *Improvement in systems.* As the micro insurance business of the organization grows, the need for better monitoring, information collection and reporting systems are clear. The insurance companies can achieve this through a good incentive mechanism.
- *Investment in human resources.* All the institutions regularly invest a significant amount of time and money in mandatory insurance training. IRDA regulations require a basic training (of 100 hours duration designed by IRDA and delivered by training institutes designated by IRDA) of staff involved in the marketing of insurance business. Such training benefits the MFI staff.
- *Improvement in bottom line.* Inadequate revenue sharing or poor incentive to the partner organization can cause a linkage arrangement to fail. The judicious design of revenue sharing means that partner organizations, apart from sharing their operational expenses, also add to their surpluses (or reduced deficit).

Impact on AVIVA

The initial response of insurers to the mandatory rural and social insurance coverage was of scepticism and withdrawal. Even without any infrastructure in rural areas, AVIVA is finding a foothold in this insurance market through innovative partnerships. Against the popular perception of such linkages as being loss-making, at least two of the three linkages of AVIVA have been profitable.

Impact on the regulatory environment

IRDA has been quite happy with the way things have developed up to this time. Buoyed by the response it has received so far, it has enhanced the coverage ceiling for policies from rural areas to 18 per cent of total policies in the sixth year of operation (IRDA circular to this effect came into force in May 2005). As the experience of AVIVA suggests, the whole business can be profitable to all the parties if the product is designed appropriately. With the apparent success of these linkages, all insurance companies are more optimistic about the rural market (The Hindu 2005).

Conclusion

While insurance is one of a suite of crucial financial products for poor rural people, access in the rural areas has always been a challenge. India has taken significant steps in the liberalization of its insurance sector in recent years; and has succeeded in making such services available to rural people. Insurance companies such as AVIVA saw the potential in this market and chose to explore the market through establishing appropriate linkages.

Although these linkages seem to be successful in meeting the dual role of enhancing the outreach of rural clients to insurance, as well as being a profitable proposition for the insuring companies and the linking organizations (with the exception of SEWA), challenges remain. The common problem shared by all the insurance companies is the lack of progressive and trustworthy partners in the rural areas. On the other hand, the common problem shared by all the linkage partners has been the delay in processing the claims and the lengthy and technically heavy documentation required.

On another level, there is a need to invest more in research and development related to new, more appropriate products for rural clients. It is apparent from the study on which this chapter is based that a good revenue sharing formula can provide a very strong incentive to partners. Insurance companies need to view this reality in a pragmatic framework. It is also apparent that there is a need to keep the products and process of insurance as simple as possible. A common but not agreed fact about the insurance companies has been to justify the investments being made in the rural sector. With the immediate return on investment in the rural market being less than the one earned from the urban market, the managers are often hard-pressed to justify the investment in the rural sector. AVIVA and its partners are leading, and it is hoped that other companies will catch up. There could be a fortune at the 'bottom of the pyramid' for the insurers while the lives of the poor would be significantly better as a result.

Further reading

Agarwala, A.N. (1961) Life Insurance in India: A Historical and Analytical Study, Allahabad, *Allahabad Law Journal Press*.

Asian Development Bank (2005) *Basic Statistics, Economic and Research Department*.

Bryson, J. (2005) *India Country Report,* Wachovia.

Murdoch, J. (2004) *Micro-Insurance: The Next Revolution,* New York University.

Ramesh, M. (2002) *Insurance: Rural India Beckons,* The Hindu Businessline.

Singh, R. (2004) *Life Insurance Market in India.*

SEWA (2004) *Annual Report.*

Websites

'Community approach for viable rural insurance', 4 July 2005, *The Hindu*.
http://www.hindu.com/2005/07/04/06hdline.htm
Indian insurance: at the crossroads, IRDA. http://www.irdaindia.org
Insurance in India (2005) http://www.tourindia.com
http://www.banknetindia.com/finance/ihist.htm.
http://www.basixindia.com/insurance.asp.
http://www.gtz.de/en/presse/8075.htm.

CHAPTER 7
Indonesia: a Regional Development Bank linked with village-based non-bank financial institutions

Iketut Budastra

Abstract

The case of financial linkages between the Regional Development Bank (BPD) and village credit institutions (LPDs) in the province of Bali demonstrates the impact of banking policies, regulation and supervision on the nature, and to a certain extent, the level of success, of formal and informal financial sector linkages. BPD, mandated by government decree, supervises and provides management training to LPDs in the province. Although other financial ties exist between the BPD and LPDs, the main purpose of the relationship appears to be the transfer of knowledge and assurance of good financial health. The author claims this relationship to be a success but cautions against certain rigidities of the model, e.g. restrictions on an LPD having saving accounts with other financial institutions.

Introduction

This chapter presents the major findings of a study of financial linkages between the Regional Development Bank (Bank Pembangunan Daerah Bali, or BPD) and Village Credit Institutions (Lembaga Perkreditan Desa, or LPD) in the province of Bali, Indonesia. This study addresses the main drivers, the challenges, and the costs and benefits of these linkage arrangements. Several sources of information were used, including relevant publications, reports, statistics from previous studies and in-depth interviews with selected stakeholders and LPDs.

BPD is a commercial bank with a regional development focus, owned jointly by the provincial and district governments. In this study it is referred to either as 'the provincial bank' or as 'the BPD'. LPDs are non-bank financial institutions with a village development focus, owned by customary villages (*desa adat*). The *desa adat* is an indigenous community sharing common traditions and customs and unified by a common temple in Bali.[1] The highest authority of the *desa adat* is the assembly of its members. It elects a leadership board and agrees upon the *adat* (customary law to be applied within the village). The Board takes decisions based on the applicable customary law. An LPD is embedded in a community that is regulated and socially integrated by its *adat*. Conceptually, the customary laws can be a powerful framework of social integration and control, including loyalty of members to LPDs. The central bank classifies the LPDs as one of a broader class of non-bank rural financial institutions established by provincial governments from the 1970s and referred to as Lembaga Dana dan Kredit Pedesaan, or LDKP (literally 'rural fund and credit institutions').

The LPDs were established as part of a 'second generation' of LDKPs following a 1984 directive from the Ministry of Home Affairs for the more widespread replication of this model. According to Steinwand (2001), LPDs resemble most closely the Badan Kredit Kecamatan (BKK) of Central Java, although with several modifications. It is owned by the community (rather than the provincial government), is a village institution (rather than a sub-district one) and is a financial intermediary (rather than simply a credit institution). The ownership is in line with the objective to empower the customary villages. Holloh (1994) regards the LPDs as the most recent form of community financial institution in Indonesia, possessing unique characteristics. He explains:

> "The unique character of the LPD lies in the fact that it is not related to the official village administration (desa dinas) but is an institutional element of the custom village (desa adat). The character of the desa adat as a democratic system regulated by customary law provides strong sociocultural bonds and effective control mechanisms. The LPD is not only the most recent but ... also the most democratic form of local finance in Indonesia"

Initially, the provincial government of Bali established 161 LPDs during a three-year pilot phase between March 1985 and March 1988. Their number increased rapidly during the following years. Compared with LDKPs in other provinces, the LPD system in Bali has shown an outstanding performance. LPDs hold a major proportion (more than 80 per cent) of the overall assets of the LDKP systems in Indonesia (Holloh, 2001). The apparent success of the LPDs may be attributed to a number of factors, internal and external, and including institutional settings, management, products offered, the regulatory and policy environment. Of particular significance are the sociocultural and economic conditions of Bali, described briefly in Box 7.1.

The institutions: the BPD and the LPDs

The provincial bank and the LPDs of Bali were initially established under the umbrella of provincial government regulations, as regional (local) enterprises. BPD Bali was established in 1965 and licensed as the regional development bank for Bali by the Ministry of Central Bank Affairs (predecessor of today's central bank) in the same year. Hence the provincial bank is supervised by the central bank under the banking act. The first LPDs were established in 1985 under provincial authority[3] but, unlike BPD, they are not subject to central government regulation, being neither regulated banks nor credit cooperative institutions[2]. BPD's mandate is to accelerate economic development in the

---

Box 7.1 The general condition of Bali Province

Bali is one of the most famous tourist destinations in Asia with beautiful beaches and landscapes, a tropical climate and a unique and living Hindu culture. Tourism has developed rapidly in the province since the 1960s. One of the smallest provinces in Indonesia with an area of only 5,600 km², Bali measures just 90 km along the north-south axis and less than 140 km from east to west. The population is dense with more than 500 persons per square kilometre, 3 million residents and 800 thousand households in 2003. The majority (more than 90 per cent) is Hindu, and there are thousands of Hindu temples in Bali, large and small.

According to the national socio-economic survey and the regional statistical bureau, Bali's economy was worth Rp16.5 trillion (US$1.9 billion), or 1.3 per cent of the national economy in 2000. Per capita income was slightly above Rp7 million (or about US$880) in 2003. However, the regional economy has experienced little growth in recent years (1 per cent per annum from 1997 to 2000 and 3 per cent from 2000 to 2003) and subsequent events have worsened the situation. Tourism plays an important role in the economy, in terms of incomes, employment and demand for local goods and services. In 2000, the trade, restaurant and hotel sector accounted for 24 per cent of employment and 33 per cent of regional gross domestic product. However, the tourist economy is vulnerable to international security shocks. Recent terrorist attacks, such as the World Trade Center tragedy and the Bali bombings, impacted the economy negatively. Thus, the occupancy rate of hotel rooms in Bali plunged from 60 per cent to below 10 per cent after the first local bombing in 2003.

---

province of Bali, and the LPD system's task is closely linked to that, specifically, to empower the customary villages. An LPD serves its community by providing convenient access to financial services as well as an income source to cover the ceremonial and maintenance expenditures of the *desa adat*'s temples.

The provincial government and the customary village jointly provide the initial capital of an LPD. The initial capital provided by government was Rp10 million (US$1,079) in 2002. A customary village is qualified for establishing an LPD when it has a written code of customary law and is judged to have sufficient economic potential. These qualifications must be confirmed by the district-level LPD Board. This is known by the acronym PLDPK, and comprises representatives from the government and BPD. The regulations have been amended several times. An important amendment increased LPDs' capital and upgraded their corporate status (from local government enterprise to limited company). Changes in regulations also addressed governance issues, such as establishment of LPD supervisory boards at village level and LPD centres at district level, the introduction of an insurance fund scheme, adoption of prudential banking principles, setting the maximum amounts an LPD can borrow, prohibiting equity investment and increasing minimum initial capital.

The architecture of the Indonesian banking system as envisioned by the central bank in the next 10 to 15 years (from 2004) is presented in Figure 7.1. The figure depicts the structure of the Indonesian banking system, consisting of four tiers, namely: international banks, national banks, banks with special focuses and banks with limited activities. Depending on their asset sizes, the commercial banks are distributed into one of the first three tiers while the 'rural' banks (BPRs, or Bank Perkreditan Rakyat) are members of the lowest (fourth) tier. BPD Bali is a small commercial bank with assets less than Rp3 trillion (US$320,863,580) in December 2003. This makes it a third tier bank (Bank Indonesia, 2004). Since they are not banks, the LPDs do not feature in the diagram. For comparison, the average assets of an LPD are comparable in size to those of regulated banks in the fourth tier.

Although it is a small bank at national level, BPD Bali is a large bank in Bali, accounting for 15 per cent, 23 per cent, and 15 per cent of overall bank assets, loans and savings, respectively, in Bali in 2003. The overall bank assets, bank loans and bank savings in Bali in the year were Rp17, 8, and 12 trillions, respectively. BPD has developed into a bank with headquarters and 46 branch and sub-branch offices across the nine districts of Bali. These offices are generally located in areas surrounding the districts' cities.

Bali's LPD system has experienced even greater institutional development than the BPD since its inception. Their number increased rapidly, except from 1996–2001 because of national economic crisis and greater emphasis on consolidation. In 1990, the assets of the LPD system were Rp375.3 billions while the assets of other LDKP systems ranged from Rp0.8 billions for the LKP system in Nusa Tenggara Barat to Rp67.9 billions for the BKK system in Central Java (Holloh, 2001). Recent statistics reflecting the institutional development of LPDs are given in Table 7.1, which shows that the number of LPDs substantially increased from 2001. Almost 1,300 LPDs were in operation in 2004, covering some 90 per cent of the customary villages in Bali. Thus, the objective 'one LPD for each *desa adat*' (as advised by the regulations) is nearly achievable as only a small proportion remains to be served. LPDs' assets also significantly increased during the period. The governance of the LPD system is further discussed in the section below.

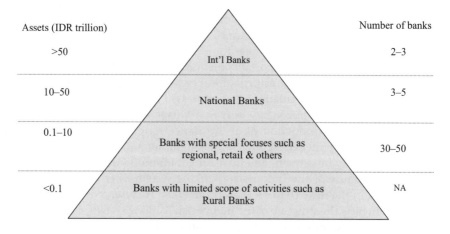

Figure 7.1 The envisioned structure of the Indonesian banking system

Table 7.1 Institutional development of the Balinese LPD system, 1999–2004

Year	Number of desa adat	Number of LPDs	Assets (Rp)[4]
1999	1,364	912	336,679
2000	1,371	926	500,786
2001	1,380	953	695,435
2002	1,392	1,152	840,143
2003	1,407	1,208	1,071,645
2004	1,427	1,296	1,346,238

Source: BPD Bali, Denpasar, 2000–2004.

Governance of the institutions

Governance quality is generally assessed in terms of transparency, accountability, delegation of authority, participation of stakeholders and compliance with regulations. A lack of functional differentiation among the key stakeholders may result in conflicts of interest, ineffective management and services, weak supervision and weak enforcement, dysfunctional interference by local officials and fraud. Provincial regulations specify the governance structure of the LPDs, as noted above. The owners, the management, the supervision, the technical assistance providers, and their responsibilities and rights are specified in the regulations. The governance structure of the LPDs, as specified in the 2002 provincial regulation for LPDs, is summarized in Figure 7.2.

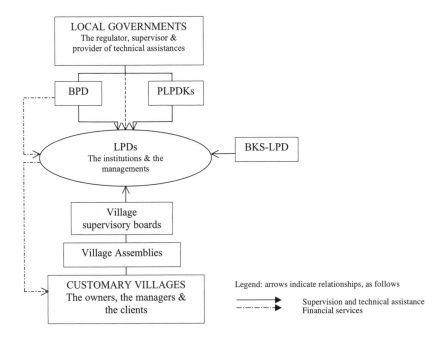

Figure 7.2 The structure of the LPD system's governance, 2002

Figure 7.2 depicts the governance of the LPD system. The provincial government delegates supervisory and technical assistance functions to the provincial bank along with PLPDKs. While BPD has carried out the function since the inception of the LPDs, the PLPDKs came into being with the 2002 regulation. The new regulation also suggests the establishment of an LPD association, BKS-LPD (Badan Kerjasama LPD). Except for the benefits of the management personnel, the regulation does not authorize BKS-LPD to play any function in the governance of the LPDs. How the supervisory and technical assistance functions are done is discussed later in the text. The village supervisory boards carry out daily supervision of their LPDs. The establishment of these boards is also advised by the new regulation, to give the villages an opportunity to effectively control the operations of their LPDs. As the management personnel, the village assemblies also choose the members of the boards from the village members. In other words, the villages (*desa adat*) function as the owners, managers, and village-level supervisors of the LPDs.

Thus, unlike the governance of parallel LDKP institutions in other provinces, which are fully or largely under the control of local governments, governance of the LPDs in Bali is apportioned between owners, regulators and operators. Elsewhere, community control is weak in the governance of village-based financial institutions, which although owned by communities are controlled by government officials (Holloh, 1994). Holloh claims that the effective control of the community in the governance of the LPD system is one of the determinants of the LPDs' success, relative to other village-based financial institutions in Indonesia.

However, the greater roles of the villages in the governance of the LPDs may create conflicts of interest. Our study found that there were cases of conflict of interest between management and village supervisory boards. The management at several LPDs visited for this study considered the role of village supervisory boards too dominant in the selection of management personnel and in other decisions. Loan disbursement to clients, inter-bank loan applications, business plans and reports all require board approval. Boards frequently interfere with loan disbursement processes, threatening management independence, the effective implementation of prudential lending principles and the operational efficiency of LPDs, because of high non-repayment rates. Management often faces great difficulties when new board members are appointed. New board members may have incomplete knowledge about matters of LPD management. For instance, a newly constituted Board can demand that the manager of a well-performing LPD be replaced. Such a replacement may be costly, harming the future of the LPD because the new manager may lack the necessary skills and experience.

With assistance from GTZ (Deutsche Gesellschaft für Technische Zusammenarbeit), the provincial government has attempted to set a standard qualification for suitable persons as managers of LPD-type institutions and has developed a training programme to certify them. However, individual villages may lack qualified persons ready and willing to take the position as LPD manager.

Persons with banking management skills and experience are generally rare in the villages, and those with the required skills and experience are not likely to take the position since the wages are very low. Therefore, replacement of a good LPD management should be prevented since failure cases of LPDs have resulted primarily from mismanagement, according to the supervisors from BPD and PLPDKs (informal interviews). The same was also reported as the reason for recent failures of several LPDs in Negara District (Openg, 2004).

Furthermore, recent policies of national decentralization giving greater authority to district governments may bring other problems. District governments in Bali may attempt to get greater control over the LPDs in their jurisdictions. For instance, the district of Denpasar City introduced its own regulation concerning the LPDs in its region, authorizing the district government as the principal regulator, the supervisor and the technical assistance provider of the LPDs. These authorities properly belong to the provincial government, under the provincial regulation (discussed above). A more important deviation is that the LPD association (BKS-LPD) assumes the supervisory and technical assistance functions delegated to the provincial bank and PLPDKs, under the provincial regulation. Thus, conflict can arise between the provincial government and district governments concerning their role with respect to LPDs. Such conflict may weaken the governance of LPDs and threaten their future performance.

Figure 7.2 also depicts the LPDs' financial services to clients and their financial linkage with BPD. The services of the LPDs are discussed further in the next section. Their financial linkage with the provincial bank includes saving and credit links. While it is compulsory for the LPDs to place their excess funds with BPD, it is optional for the LPDs to borrow from it. Instead, LPDs may choose to take loans from other financial and non-financial institutions. However, savings and credit links between the LPDs and the provincial bank are totally commercial and prudential. The 2002 provincial regulation requires LPDs to implement prudential banking principles. BPD is not responsible for bailing out failed LPDs, nor is it the lender of last resort. In case of LPD failures, the government generally serves as the lender of last resort. In this regard, an insurance mechanism was established to cover the bailout costs in case of an LPD failure.

The services and performance of the linked institutions

As a commercial bank (a *bank umum*), BPD can offer a wide range of financial services, from savings, credit, transfer/payment services to foreign exchange services, excluding insurance and pawnshop services to the general population (under the 1992 Banking Laws and as amended in 1998). However, savings and loan services are the core services and form the major income sources of BPD. The provincial bank's services are provided in branch offices, often far from clients' homes and businesses, especially those in remote rural areas. This 'in office' service strategy, on the one hand, and the fact that BPD's offices cluster around the cities, on the other, limits the rural outreach of its services. Links with the LPDs could perhaps help BPD to overcome this rural service problem. In this regard, the provincial bank has two relevant (micro) loan service products, known as PUNDI and KPKM. The former targets the business enterprises of the poor while the latter aims at the promotion of small and medium enterprises.

Under PUNDI and KPKM, loan transactions between BPD and LPDs are commercial. BPD charges a commercial interest rate and treats an LPD as proxy for a group of the targeted clients, for which the LPDs assume full responsibility as the borrower. The LPD, in turn, re-lends the funds to its clients, applying its own credit policies. Hence, the PUNDI and KPKM loans are sources of additional loanable funds for LPDs facing high growth of loan demand. In fact, however, only a few of the LPDs are liquidity-constrained. Most LPDs have excess liquidity and place funds with BPD. The extent to which the linkage between BPD and LPDs has improved rural access to financial services is a subject discussed in the following section.

As village non-bank financial institutions, LPDs only provide savings services and loan services to their customary village members. Savings products offered include passbook and term deposits. Loan products vary from one LPD to another and no standardization has been suggested by the supervisory board. But while there is scope for a variety of experiments in product development as between LPDs, there is no scope for competition between them. This is because clients have limited freedom to switch their custom from one LPD to another, given their allegiance to a particular *desa adat*. However, there is strong competition between any LPD and other financial institutions within its area of operation. For instance, there were 10 rural cooperatives and rural banks in the *desa adat* of one of the LPDs visited in this study.

Voluntary savings deposit accounts are the primary source of funds mobilized by the majority of the LPDs, while compulsory savings generally contribute less than 10 per cent of funds mobilized. At present, LPDs offer 9–10 per cent annual effective interest rates on passbook savings, and 9–16 per cent on term deposits, rates close to those of commercial banks. In determining interest rates, most LPDs react flexibly to local market conditions and their own need for funds.

Generally, an LPD offers a monthly credit (with 6 and 12-month terms) and a local specific loan product. An LPD with farmers as the core clients offers loans with seasonal terms, while an LPD with small industries and traders as the core clients has loans with daily or weekly terms. The sizes of loans and savings also vary, but the average is less than Rp5 million (US$627.75 in 2003). Interest rates of service products also vary, depending on the interest rates of comparable services offered by other financial institutions in the rural financial market, such as cooperatives and rural banks. Consumption loans are of some importance in larger LPDs. The present interest rates charged on monthly loans range from 2 per cent declining to 3 per cent flat per month. Seasonal loans (6 months) carry similar interest rates. Loans with daily instalments have most usually a 100-day term, with annual effective annual interest rates ranging from 36 to 72 per cent. LPDs emphasize service convenience by servicing at the client home or workplace, requiring minimum paperwork and collateral, and offering quick loan appraisal, generally 3 days or less. Data reflecting the loan and saving performance of the institutions are given in Tables 7.2 and 7.3.

Table 7.2 shows that BPD performed relatively well during 2000–3, mobilizing substantial proportions (11–16 per cent) of overall bank savings in Bali and from 16 to 23 per cent of overall bank loans. Furthermore, the share of BPD in the overall bank savings and loans steadily increased. The relatively high saving and loan shares of the provincial bank, along with its financial sustainability (discussed latter) suggest that it is an effective supplier of financial intermediation services. Perhaps befitting its role as the provincial development bank, it was more successful than the banking system as a whole in re-lending funds within the provincial economy. To some extent, BPD's links with the LPD system may contribute to the good savings performance of the bank (a topic discussed further later).

The LPD system also performed impressively with respect to volumes of loans and savings outstanding over the period 1999–2004 (Table 7.3).

Table 7.2 Loan and saving portfolios of BPD Bali, 2000–3

Year	Loans outstanding		Saving deposits	
	BPD Bali (Rp million)	As per cent of all banks in Bali	BPD Bali (Rp million)	As per cent of all banks in Bali
2000	63,1585	15.82	1,177,852	10.78
2001	1,012,427	16.67	1,715,191	13.39
2002	1,440,695	20.34	1,776,537	16.32
2003	1,845,852	22.69	1,826,212	15.33

Source: BPD Bali (2000; 2001; 2003).

Table 7.3 Lending and saving performance of the LPD system, 1999–2004

Year	Loan		Passbook saving		Term deposit	
	Amount (Rp million)	Borrowers (number)	Amount (Rp million)	Savers (number)	Amount (Rp million)	Savers (number)
1999	215,774	204,842	143,929	573,751	112,157	37,780
2000	355,092	218,632	227,820	626,576	164,873	50,204
2001	512,085	233,990	307,906	702,581	232,623	41,055
2002	638,206	270,321	346,676	781,759	283,529	44,880
2003	759,182	301,328	429,056	836,005	385,360	49,320
2004[1]	907,312	318,995	559,746	956,633	487,538	55,375

Source: BPD Bali (2003).
[1]Condition in September 2004.

Table 7.3 shows that loans advanced and the passbook and term deposits mobilized increased more than 70 per cent during the period. Similarly, the numbers of borrowers and savers also increased more than 30 per cent. Compared with the overall LDKP system in Indonesia, the LPD system was dominant, accounting for more than 70 per cent of savers, 75 per cent of savings deposit amounts, 41 per cent of borrowers and 64 per cent of loan amounts in 2000.

It is striking that the 1997 national economic crisis did not affect the savings and credit performance of the LPDs negatively. Rather, a substantial increase was also observed during 1996–8 (the period in which the economy experienced the banking crisis). The total value of loans outstanding increased 52 per cent, from Rp95,519 million in 1996 to Rp145,541 million in 1998; while the amounts of savings deposits increased 64 per cent, from Rp94,007 million to Rp154,346 million.

Thus, the crisis did not bring a significant negative effect to the overall LPDs' operations as the national crisis did not bring the tourism industries down. As noted above, Bali's economy is largely dependent on tourism. Contrarily, more recent bombings on the island negatively affected the local economy. Even so, the tourism industries' downturn might not significantly affect the performance of the LPDs since the business activities of their clients are generally not related to the tourism industries. The performance of individual LPDs is also influenced by internal factors. LPDs with larger assets, more developed service products and experienced management may perform better than LPDs with smaller assets, less developed service products and inexperienced management.

Financial sustainability of the institutions

BPD and the LPDs are financially sustainable institutions as their operations are profitable. Table 7.4 shows selected financial ratios. The returns on asset and equity (ROA and ROE) during 2000–3 were consistently higher than the central bank standards for 'healthy' regulated financial institutions. The central bank standards require a healthy bank to have ROA at least 1.125 per cent per annum and ROE at least 15 per cent per annum. LPDs typically maintained high loan to deposit ratios (LDR), at 90 per cent or above. The LPDs loan repayment rates were high, with 'non-collectible' loan rates much less than 5 per cent. Non-collectible loans here refer to the amounts of loan principal and interest declared uncollectible by the institutions.

The high achievement of the LPD system reflects the trust and support of the village communities besides the service and management quality. The importance of the community trust and support is obvious, considering the fact that several other financial institutions also operate in the rural financial market, such as Rural Banks and Cooperatives. The service and management quality are closely linked with the quality of supervision and technical assistance. In this regard, the role of BPD and the government (including village government) is

Table 7.4 The selected financial ratios of BPD Bali and the LPD system, 2000–3

Year	ROA	ROE	LDR	NCL
BPD				
2000	1.86	25.98	47.19	0.09
2001	3.44	46.04	55.16	0.02
2002	4.16	35.83	81.53	0.10
2003	4.37	29.61	83.21	0.33
LPD				
2000	7.31	56.37	90.00	1.69
2001	7.83	61.22	95.00	1.23
2002	7.96	52.75	101.00	1.13
2003	6.63	41.95	93.00	1.34

Source: BPD Bali (2000; 2001; 2002; 2003). Notes: NCL is the non-collectible loan rate, the amounts of loans (principal plus interest) that had been in arrears and declared uncollectible by the institutions.

crucial. Also, 'ownership' is among the major factors explaining the community's trust in and support for the LPDs.

Moreover, people may also feel obliged to save their funds with their LPDs and to borrow loans from them in order to promote the development of their own enterprises (LPDs) whose benefits are for the communities. The benefits include the retained profits, and the development funds of the customary villages. The regulation states that LPDs allocate 40–60 per cent of their profits for capital formation, 20 per cent for village development funds, and 5 per cent for social funds. The development funds are used by the village for financing the maintenance and ceremonial expenses of the customary village temples.

The socio-economic and demographic environment also plays a great role in the LPDs' apparent success. Bali has socio-economic-demographic and cultural characteristics (such as dense population, prosperous economy, and supportive social and cultural system) which are regarded as key determinants of successful rural banking. Moreover, customary villages in Bali have the power to demand and enforce their members' loyalty to LPDs, in terms of saving their funds and repaying their loans. The maintenance and ceremonial costs paid with the LPDs' profits give an economic incentive to the members to stay loyal to the LPDs, as described above. Unlike the parallel institutions in other provinces whose management personnel may be appointed by provincial government, LPDs are managed by member representatives chosen by the villages themselves. This democratic management further strengthens the loyalty of the members to LPDs. However, as noted above, individual LPDs may perform differently.

Since many of the LPDs have been operating for more than two decades and are performing well, the management of certain LPDs may have found that they needed to extend their service areas beyond the village they belong to, to achieve higher operational scale and operational efficiency. Apart from limiting the LPD's growth, the service area limitation makes it vulnerable against risks resulting from local casualties (such as natural disaster and harvest failures), which make the clients unable to meet their obligations to the LPD. The intention, however, is prevented by the regulation. It states that an LPD is to serve only the members of the customary village where it is located or belongs. As against this, the operational area limitation of individual LPDs can be regarded as one of the determining factors for the success of the LPDs. It ensures close identification with and support of *desa adat* and the members (noted above). Therefore, successful LPDs are trapped by the dilemma that the very thing that assures their success is also a barrier to their expansion beyond the boundaries of the *desa adat*, and hence a barrier to their achievement of economies of scale.

The linkage

The links between the provincial bank and the LPDs have existed since the inception of the LPDs and have become institutionalized with provincial government regulations. Under the 1988 regulation, the provincial Governor has responsibility to supervise the LPDs (although in practice this is delegated to BPD). BPD also provides technical assistance. BPD assigns two (full-time) officers in the headquarters and branch-based officers to carry out the supervisory and technical assistance responsibilities. The responsibilities include report review, field visit, collating data for the LPD system and training of LPD management. As the number of LPDs has greatly increased, the new (2002) regulation introduces the establishment of district centres for LPDs (the PLPDKs) to support BPD in carrying out its responsibilities effectively. In future, these centres will assume the supervisory and technical assistance responsibilities at district level.

For supervision purposes, individual LPDs have to submit their annual business plan (3 months prior to its implementation) and three periodic reports (monthly, three-monthly and annual) to BPD. The reports are also submitted to the village assembly and the (provincial/district) government through the PLPDKs. In addition to reviewing the reports, on-site supervisions in LPD offices are also conducted. For technical assistance purposes, BPD (along with PLPDKs) is responsible for the management training of the LPDs. At least one training session is organized per year. Under the 1988 regulation, 5 per cent of the profit covers the supervisory and technical assistance services. Under the 2002 regulation, a part of these supervisory and technical funds is saved for the insurance funds of LPDs. The LPDs submit the funds to BPD, which then distributes them to PLPDKs (50 per cent), district and provincial supervisory boards (32.5 per cent), LPD insurance funds (7.5 per cent), as well as retaining 10 per cent itself. As a percentage of the LPDs' profits the distribution of the supervisory and technical funds are: 2.5 per cent, 1.63 per cent, 0.38 per cent, 0.38 per cent and 0.5 per cent to PLPDKs, district and provincial supervisory boards, LPD insurance funds and BPD, respectively.

Holloh (2003) identified four kinds of linkage between superordinate and subordinate institutions. These are savings linkages, credit linkages, facilitation linkages, and capacity building and supervision linkages. The savings linkage occurs when the subordinate institution is assisted in managing excess liquidity by holding an account with the superordinate institution. The credit linkage occurs when the subordinate institution faces effective demand for credits exceeding its loanable funds, and/or when the subordinate institution channels loans from the superordinate institution to the clients. The facilitation linkage occurs when the subordinate institution facilitates the access of the superordinate institution to clients within its operational areas. For instance, as the subordinate institution does not offer a demand deposit or large-sized loan services, it facilities client access to services from the superordinate institution. Lastly, the capacity building and supervision linkage occurs when banks take on capacity building and/or supervision functions for the benefit of the subordinate. The supervision and technical assistance links between the provincial bank and the LPDs can be regarded as a 'capacity building and supervision' linkage.

Regulations also require each LPD to place its excess liquidity with the nearby branch offices of BPD. This is a 'saving linkage'. As to credit linkages, the regulation does not prohibit LPDs from taking loans from institutions other than BPD. In principle this enables LPDs to get loanable funds from various sources with the lowest costs possible, including from donors and government-subsidized credit schemes. However, LPDs, when in need of loans, often consider taking loans from the provincial bank if it is more convenient, especially considering their access to a concessional interest rate, discussed further below. With their current institutional status, operating under the provincial government regulation without any operational status recognized in the national legal framework, such as a saving and credit cooperative or a rural bank, LPDs have less chance of receiving loans or finance from a national bank or financial company, in cases where they need external funds. Although external funds are not an issue for most LPDs, considering the fact that the majority of them are in excess of funds, leaving the options open wide may be helpful for the future development of the LPD system.

The institutional status of LPDs has been an unresolved issue since the introduction of a 1988 national policy package for the banking sector. The failure of national authorities to resolve this problem, despite the passing of various deadlines for the LPDs (as for all LDKPs) to regularize their status, may suggest that there is resistance at provincial and local level to the national policy thrust. Governments argue the negative consequences for the future of the LPD system resulting from the new status, either as a rural bank or rural cooperative. This is because the national regulations have several elements contradictive of the provincial regulation, in terms of operational areas, supervision and tax policy, among others.

Individual LPDs can put excess funds with the provincial bank immediately after their establishment, but they have to show good performance for two consecutive years to be eligible for loans from BPD (BPD Director Decree No 0246.101.10.2003). Such loans are for additional loanable funds to 'well performing' LPDs, not bailout loans. Under the 1988 regulation, the provincial/

district government is responsible for bailing out a poorly performing LPD. The government is no longer responsible for bailing out problem LPDs since the introduction of the new (2002) regulation, which authorizes the establishment of an LPD insurance scheme (noted above). In practice, however, the supervisory boards encourage the management of the LPD and the respective village to solve the problem, before deciding to bail out a poorly performing LPD. In their attempts to solve liquidity problems resulting from poor management, frauds, or other issues, individual LPDs may make the management (including their relatives) responsible for fraud and misbehaviour. The case of the failure of Kapal LPD in 2000, where management was made responsible for the bailing out, illustrates this point (informal interview with the head of the village assembly). If there was no management fraud or misbehaviour, the village boards would ask the (wealthy) members of the villages to deposit more funds. If the management and the village boards could not solve the problems themselves, they would request government assistance. The government decision would depend on the recommendation of BPD and PLPDKs. Normally, only the viable ones are bailed out.

In response to the regulations and to promote the development of the LPDs, the provincial bank applies a special interest rate policy to the LPDs. The policy specifies that in dealings with LPDs, the provincial bank pays a higher interest rate on savings and charges a lower interest rate on credits than is applicable to the regular clients. BPD applies 6.5 per cent interest on savings and 14 per cent interest on loans in transactions with LPDs while applying 4–5 per cent and 14–18 per cent for comparable saving and loan services to the general clients, respectively. The special interest rate policy should give an incentive to an LPD to save its excess funds with and borrow from the provincial bank, rather than deal with other institutions. With a few exceptions, LPDs generally do so, and the extent of these links is discussed later. The special interest rate, however, is still within the range of commercial rates specified by the central bank for prudential purposes. Outside that rate range, bank savings are not eligible for the central bank's saving guarantee, and bank loans are qualified as risky. This is not an interest rate cap, but a measure to prevent the banking system from incurring problems arising from 'moral hazard' behaviour of bankers.

In summary, the linkage is essentially a simple (quasi-commercial) bilateral linkage, in operation since the inception of LPDs in 1985 and built into the design of the LPD system. The main driver is the government of Bali, which promotes the establishment of an LPD, provides the initial funds, and designs and introduced the provincial regulation and provincial government decrees that govern the linkage.

The extent of the supervisory and technical assistance linkage

In this linkage, the provincial bank provides supervision and technical assistance to the LPDs. The tasks include training the management of LPDs, reviewing their business plans and reports (noted above), field visits (for on-site supervision and technical assistance), and collating data from the LPD system (at provincial level). Training modules include skills to manage an LPD: LPD regulation, business planning, service product design, saving and loan management, financial management, bookkeeping and reporting, and risk management. BPD (and PLPDKs) organize training once a year, at least. Individual LPDs submit reports to the district branch offices of BPD. After reviewing them, the branch offices consolidate the reports and submit them to the headquarters office. During the review process, the officers of BPD may give advice and suggestions to LPD management, and if necessary, the officers visit LPD offices.

Considering the relatively high service performance of LPDs (discussed above) and the familiarity of the provincial bank officers with LPD management (noticed by this study in the field), the supervisory and technical assistance seems to be successful. Each LPD pays the costs of the supervisory and technical services with 5 per cent of its profits, referred to as the supervisory and technical assistance funds (noted above). The new (2002) regulation rules that 7.5 per cent of the funds are allocated for the LPD insurance funds. Therefore, the amounts of the funds would be dependent on the profitability of the LPDs. During the period of 1999–2003, the amounts of the supervisory and technical assistance funds were relatively large (Table 7.5) as the LPD system generated relatively large profits, comparable to 41 to 66 per cent of the BPD profits during the period. Table 7.5 indicates that the supervisory and technical assistance funds were 3 per cent of the overall LPD operational costs, up to 1 per cent of BPD's operational costs, and 2–5 per cent of BPD's labour costs, from 1999–2004. In addition, the amounts of the LPD supervisory and technical assistance funds steadily increased as the profits of the LPDs grew. The saving and credit linkage is discussed below.

The extent of the saving and credit linkage

The saving and credit linkage between BPD and the LPDs is reflected by the inter-bank savings and inter-bank loans of the LPDs for several reasons. First, by regulation (noted above), an LPD has to put its excess funds in BPD. Second, BPD treats individual LPDs as its special clients with a higher interest rate on savings and a lower interest rate on credits, relative to the general clients (noted

Table 7.5 LPD supervisory and technical assistance funds, 1999–2004

Year	Rp million	As a % of LPD operational costs	As a % of BPD operational costs	As a % of BPD labour costs
1999	1,355	2.98	0.43	2.31
2000	1,831	2.84	0.86	3.29
2001	2,719	2.88	0.91	3.89
2002	3,344	2.76	0.78	4.58
2003	3,552	2.56	0.99	4.39

Source: Calculated based on data provided by BPD Bali.

above). The transaction processes are quick and convenient. Third, the LPD/ BPD relationship has lasted since the inception of the LPDs, where the provincial bank serves as the supervisor and technical assistance provider to the LPDs (as noted above). The LPDs regard BPD as their father, in their words: 'BPD bapene LPD'. Therefore, they are generally loyal to BPD with respect to bank saving and credit services. The inter-bank savings and credits of LPD are reflected in Table 7.6.

Table 7.6 shows that the amounts of savings LPDs placed with banks and the amount of borrowing from BPD increased between 2000 and 2004. The savings placed by LPDs with BPD were quite substantial, much larger than the amounts of credits borrowed. LPDs' inter-bank savings was comparable to 16 to 28 per cent of the LPD system's assets, or 7 to 12 per cent of the amount of saving deposits mobilized by BPD during the same period. On the other hand, credit obtained by LPDs from banks was relatively small, far less than 1 per cent of the amount of BPD's loan outstandings.

Thus, the LPDs are net savers in the saving and credit linkages with BPD. The saving-credit discrepancy in the linkage mirrors the financial intermediation performance of the LPDs, which generally mobilize more savings than disbursed loans. This is a common feature among well-performing rural- and microfinance institutions, such as BRI (Bank Rakyat Indonesia) Units and others well known in the literature. The saving-credit discrepancies may result from limited investment opportunity and risk-averse investment behaviour of the clients, among others. Balinese communities generally see saving as the capital formation strategy and consider borrowing as the last resort. Hence, the linkage has opened the opportunity for the LPDs (and the villages) to earn income from their otherwise unproductive funds through the inter-bank markets. This improves the efficiency of the economy, in aggregate terms, apart from the benefits to the individuals and institutions concerned. Also, and importantly, the saving and credit linkages have provided a relatively large and reliable source of funds for the provincial bank while giving an effective and convenient liquidity management system to the LPDs. Individual LPDs can cost-effectively and conveniently save their excess funds with BPD or borrow from BPD should they need additional loanable funds.

However, a word of caution is necessary concerning the future of the saving and credit linkage. Opposition to these compulsory arrangements has begun to

Table 7.6 Inter-bank savings and loans of the LPD system, 2000–4

Year	Inter-bank savings		Inter-bank loans	
	Rp million	As % of assets	Rp million	As % of assets
2000	94,578	19	717	0.14
2001	114,133	16	2,194	0.32
2002	132,938	16	3,111	0.37
2003	216,343	20	3,531	0.33
2004	375,396	28	3,067	0.23

Source: Calculated from data provided by BPD Bali.

appear in the news media since 2000 (e.g. Antara, 2000). Many LPDs consider the restriction unfair, eliminating their opportunities for higher interest income. This may endanger the future of the financial linkage. One of the LPDs visited put a part of its excess funds into a cooperative set up by the LPD association (BKS–LPDs) as it offered higher interest rates and allowed withdrawals on Saturdays, when the BPD was closed. The consequences of the linkages to BPD and the LPDs (including the villages, as the owners and the clients) are discussed next.

Some assertions about the impacts of BPD–LPD linkages

This section briefly discusses the financial impacts of the linkage on the institutions, the LPDs and the provincial bank. Impacts on the customary village communities (as the owners and the clients of the LPDs) are also discussed. Results reported here are based on unpublished research by the writer and for reasons of space it is not possible to spell out the arguments or the data in detail. Conceptually, the LPDs and BPD should benefit from the linkage, as should the communities within which they operate. However, the costs and benefits were difficult to quantify accurately. In spite of the difficulties, the impacts of the linkage on the institutions and the communities were estimated, making use of data available (primarily from BPD) and the best judgments of the researcher. As the linkage started at the inception of the LPD system, impacts were assessed from 1985 to 2002. Costs were divided into three categories: establishment costs, supervisory and technical assistance, financial service costs and other institutional development costs. Measured benefits included the retained profits of LPDs, profits earned by BPD through access to the excess funds of the LPD system and the financial benefits received by communities from LPD profits. Estimation of the value to communities of having access to effective and convenient financial services was also attempted, using assumptions about the opportunity cost of funds placed with LPDs by communities and the costs of alternative sources of credit for village borrowers in the absence of the LPDs.

In terms of overall cumulative costs and benefits, the linkage reached its breakeven point in 1992 (year 8) if the net benefits of community access to LPD services are taken into account, or in 1999 (year 15) if they are not. This was in spite of the rapid and continued growth of the LPD system over the whole period, involving substantial establishment costs in each year. With net benefits of community access included, the benefit/cost ratio was 3.46 to 1 by 2003, and without them it was 1.42 to 1. In terms of costs and benefits applicable to particular categories of stakeholder, the linkage provided services to more than 7 million savers and more than 2 million borrowers. The value of this service access was calculated at Rp435 billion. The linkage brought about Rp197 billion retained profits to LPDs while giving Rp23 billion profits to BPD over the period of 1985–2003. Lastly, the linkage also contributed more than Rp82 billion to the villages' development and social funds in the same period. The provincial government's intention was to empower the customary villages in Bali through the development of the LPD system, and it succeeded in that the linkage benefited the parties involved and the benefits generated exceeded the costs.

Summary and conclusions

The linkage between the provincial bank and LPDs can be regarded as a simple bilateral one involving supervisory and technical assistance, and savings and credit services. BPD provides the supervisory and technical assistance necessary for the LPDs. They save excess funds with BPD and may borrow from the provincial bank. The links are generally commercial in that the LPDs pay commercial rates for services. The linkage was initiated by the provincial government of Bali to empower the customary villages, beginning in 1985. The government provides initial capital and the training of new LPD management. The villages also contribute to the initial capital. In addition to provision of financial services to the communities, the establishment of the LPDs is also to generate incomes for the villages to cover the maintenance and ceremonial expenditures of their common temples. These social benefits, in turn, contribute to the social cohesion of the communities concerned and motivate them to behave supportively and loyally to their LPDs.

The linkage has performed relatively well in terms of the performance of the institutions involved. Both institutions are financially healthy. The number of LPDs and their assets, savings, credits and clients significantly increased during 1999–2004. The amounts of the LPDs' savings with BPD and the amounts of credits borrowed from BPD also increased during the period. An increasing trend in the performance indicators of the institutions was also found earlier, including during 1996–8, the period of national economic crisis. Recent bombings (remembering that tourism is the major sector in the economy) only affected the economies of villages around the handicraft centres. Detailed estimates of the financial impacts of the linkage from 1985 to 2003 further confirmed that the linkage brought more benefits than costs to the parties involved, namely government, village communities, the LPDs and BPD.

The apparent success of these linkages is the result of several factors, including the institutional settings, the government's strong commitment and support, and village communities' positive participation and loyalty. In addition, credit must be given for the dedication, hard work, and accountability of management, the provincial bank's helpful supervision and technical assistance and financial services, and the supportive socio-economic and demographic conditions. These are factors internal to the institutions concerned, as well as external (or market environment) factors. These findings reflect the performance of the linkage between the LPDs (as a system) and BPD. Conceptually, the performance of the linkage between individual LPDs and BPD might vary from one another as their internal and external factors are not identical. For example, individual LPDs with larger assets, more developed service products, and experienced management tend to perform better than LPDs with smaller assets, less developed service products and inexperienced management. In fact, however, the study found that cases of non-performing LPDs were rare. For those few 'failure cases', misbehaviour of management personnel and village board members and a poor economic environment locally were among the primary causes.

In spite of the apparent success of these linkage arrangements, there are five issues considered important for further improvement. First, the growing opposition of individual LPDs to the restriction on inter-bank saving accounts, which requires LPDs to place their excess funds with BPD, may endanger the future of the financial service linkage. This is because many LPDs may decline to place their excess with BPD, and put them with other financial institutions best serving individual LPDs' needs.

Second, 'successful' LPDs may face a dilemma that the very thing that assures their success is also a barrier to their business expansion beyond the boundaries of the *desa adat*, and hence a barrier to their achievement of higher operational scale and efficiencies. However, among the organizational settings and governance structure of the LPDs often regarded as the determinants of the LPDs' relative success are that they are owned and managed by the *desa adat,* for the benefit of the members, and to serve the members only.

Third, related to the issue above, the LPDs have fewer chances to receive loans or finances from a national bank or financial company, in case they need external funds. This is the result of their current institutional status, operating under provincial government regulation without any status recognized in the national legal framework, such as a saving and credit cooperative or a rural bank. Although external funds are not an issue for many individual LPDs, they are for a few that face loan demands higher than their funding capacities. More importantly, leaving the option of getting external funds open may be helpful for future development of the LPD system.

Fourth is the current governance structure of individual LPDs which gives a dominant role to the village board in the selection of the LPD's manager. This may lead to misbehaviour of the board members and could potentially threaten the future performance of the LPDs.

Lastly, the greater power of district governments authorized by the (1992) national decentralization policy has resulted in a conflict of interest between the provincial government and district governments concerning their regulatory power over the LPDs. For example, the district of Denpasar City introduced its own regulation concerning the LPDs in its administrative jurisdiction, containing elements contradictive of the provincial one. Such governance restructuring may be counterproductive to the future performance of the LPDs.

Notes

1   The *Desa Adat* is not co-extensive with the *Desa Dinas*, the lowest unit of official administration in Indonesia. A *Desa Dinas* is generally larger than a *Desa Adat.*

2 Governor's Decree (No. 972/1984) confirmed by Provincial Government Regulation (No. 2/1988).
3 They are not subject to either the national Banking Laws (No. 7/1992 and No. 10/1998) or the Savings Cooperative Regulation (No. 9/1995).
4 The exchange rate for US$1 for the indicated years is as follows:
    31 Dec. 1999, Rp.7,006
    29 Dec. 2000, Rp. 9,679
    31 Dec. 2001, Rp. 10,409
    31 Dec. 2002, Rp. 8,975
    31 Dec. 2003, Rp. 8,447
    31 Dec. 2004, Rp. 9,258
    Source: Bank of Canada, www.bankofcanada.ca/cgi-bin/famecgi_fdps

References

Antara, (2000) 'LPD di Bali Tolak Setor Dana ke BPD', *Bali Post,* Denpasar.
Bank Indonesia, 2004. *The Indonesian Banking Architecture,* Bank of Indonesia, Jakarta.
Bank Pembangunan Daerah Bali (BPD) (2000) *Annual Report,* BPD, Denpasar: 28.
BPD (2001) *Annual Report,* BPD, Denpasar, 28.
BPD (2003) *Annual Report,* BPD, Denpasar, 28.
BPD (2003) LPD Consolidated Balance Sheets and Profit/Loss Report (unpublished).
BPD (2004) *Annual Report,* BPD, Denpasar.
Holloh, D. (1994) 'Community Financial Institutions in Bali, Some Empirical Findings', University of Cologne Working Paper No 1994-1, Cologne, 4..
Holloh, D. (2001) 'ProFI Microfinance Institutions Study', Denpasar, Bank Indonesia and GTZ-German Technical Assistance, 220.
Holloh, D. (2003) *Sustaining microfinance project (SMFP): World Bank Preparation Mission Report, September 8–26,* GTZ, Eschborn.
Openg, D. (2004) '15 LPD di Jembrana Sekarat', *Baliage,* Jembrana, Negara, Bali.
Pemerintah Bali (2003). Peraturan Daerah Provinsi Bali Nomor 8 Tahun 2002 Tentang Lembaga Perkreditan Desa (LPD) Disertai Keputusan Gubernur Bali. Bali, Indonesia, Biro Perekonomian dan Pembangunan Sekretariat Daerah Provinsi Bali.
Steinwand, D. (2001) *The Alchemy of Microfinance: The Evaluation of the Indonesian People's Credit Banks (BPR) from 1895 to 1999 and a Contemporary Analysis,* VWF, Berlin.

Websites

Bank of Canada, www.bankofcanada.ca/cgi-bin/famecgi_fdps
Bank Indonesia: www.bi.go.id/web

CHAPTER 8

The rich variety of microfinance linkages in Indonesia

John D. Conroy and Iketut Budastra

Abstract

Recognizing the particular richness of linkage arrangements available for study in Indonesia, the authors decided to conduct an overview study as part of the cross-country study of linkages implemented by the Food and Agriculture Organization (FAO) of the UN for the Ford Foundation. This overview provides a descriptive mapping of different linkage models that exist in Indonesia, and reflects on Indonesia's rich variety and wide range of financial institutions. The linkages are characterized by several small, regulated financial institutions engaging in chain relationships with major financial institutions and grassroots financial actors. Indonesia also has special apex institutions set up to create linkages, and linkages have an explicit role in a new 'banking architecture' being created by the central bank. The linkages are categorized based on a distinction between autonomous linkages and those occurring as the result of government or central bank initiative.

Introduction

Current and recent rural- and microfinance activities in Indonesia incorporate an array of institutional models bewildering to the newcomer in their variety and novelty. Activities range from profitable, regulated financial institutions operating at best practice levels to opportunistic and politically driven mass credit schemes. A number involve linkages between formal financial institutions and informal development financing institutions. However, a simple duality of formal and informal institutions will not suffice to describe the more complex reality of rural financial service provision in Indonesia. The country has many small, community-owned formal financial institutions that are subject to regulation. These have relatively few analogues in other financial systems, in terms of their small scale and strong local character. Many are engaged in linkages with major financial institutions and with grassroots financial actors. These small institutions occupying intermediate positions in the financial hierarchy are often involved in chain relationships, rather than simple linkages.

Status of financial institutions involved in linkages in Indonesia

A rich variety of financial institutions is involved in microfinance linkages in Indonesia. The linkage partners include regulated banks, community based financial institutions, savings and credit cooperatives, and unregulated financial institutions. The next section introduces these various institutions. Many of them originated during the period of the so-called 'New Order' government of President Suharto (1967–98), which used linkages as a policy instrument. These linkages, inspired by government programmes, remain an important feature of the Indonesian rural financial landscape today.

Regulated banks

Formal institutions regulated by Bank Indonesia (BI, the central bank) include the commercial banks. A sub-set of these consists of Regional Development Banks (BPDs) owned by provincial governments, which are of particular significance for linkages. While they act as bankers to their governments, the BPDs also perform some apex functions. BPDs act as wholesalers to convey loanable funds from governments and donor agencies to smaller linked financial institutions. Some BPDs also have responsibility for supervision of certain small formal financial institutions operating within their provinces. This is because these institutions (known collectively as the LDKPs) operate under provincial, rather than central bank regulations.

A second class of banks regulated by Bank Indonesia consists of small and locally based institutions known as Bank Perkreditan Rakyat (BPR) or 'rural bank'; and offers a more restricted range of services, compared with commercial banks. The banking Act of 1992 differentiates rural banks into two classes, namely: 'BPR non-BKD' and 'BPR-BKD' (Steinwand 2001; Robinson 2002). For simplicity, in this study the two categories of small bank institutions are simply called BPRs and BKDs.

BPRs have a special place in a new 'banking architecture' being constructed by the central bank, in that they are encouraged to enter into linkages with commercial banks. Linkages are thus an explicit element in national banking policy. Most BPRs are limited liability companies in private ownership, operated for profit. Originating from financial deregulation in the 1980s, the BPRs are an impressive example of the mobilization of private capital for microfinance. Some are in chains associated with commercial banks or NGOs. Others are registered as cooperatives, while some are organized on Islamic principles (BPR *Syariah*) and some are local government owned.

Badan Kredit Desa (BKDs) or village credit bodies date back to the late nineteenth century and were formed under Dutch colonial rule, making them pioneer MFIs. They are much smaller institutions than the BPRs. Since both categories are subject to the Banking Act, both are in principle regulated and supervised by Bank Indonesia. In practice, Bank Indonesia has delegated the task of supervising the BKDs to a major commercial bank, Bank BRI.

The LDKPs

Community-based non-bank financial institutions, known as LDKPs, were mentioned above in connection with the Provincial Development Banks (BPDs). The acronym LDKP is applied generically to a range of savings and credit institutions that exists in a number of provinces (Steinwand 2001; Robinson 2002). One set of these, the LPDs in Bali, are reviewed in Budastra's forthcoming study on financial linkages. The Banking Act of 1992 obliged the LDKPs either to upgrade themselves to the status of regulated BPRs by 1997 or to cease operating. A majority (including all the LPDs in Bali) have chosen not to come under the umbrella of central bank regulation, or have not satisfied the criteria. In a sense, they are 'unfinished business' left over from financial reforms of the 1980s.

Most of the LDKPs came into existence as local initiatives during the period from 1970 when, amid recovery from the economic chaos of the Sukarno years, Bank Indonesia authorized provincial governments to set up rural non-bank financial institutions. Significantly, these institutions benefited from being 'under the radar' of interest rate controls imposed upon the banking system at that time. Many of the more efficient LDKPs prospered while the banking system laboured under heavy regulation. The numbers of LDKPs are now declining, except in Bali where they flourish, 2,272 LDKPs were operating in mid-2000; serving more than 1.3 million borrowers. However, the number fell to around 1,620 by 2002. The financial strength of the Balinese institutions, together with the capacity of the Bali Provincial Government to protect them from closure by national authorities, seems likely to assure the LPDs' continuing operation for some time.

Both the BKD and LDKP systems are generally quite liquid, with savings and reserves adequate to finance lending and to permit significant deposits in the banking system. In terms of mean loan size, the LDKPs sit at roughly the same social level as the BKDs and on a very much lower level than the BPRs and the village-based 'units' of Bank BRI. Table 8.1 provides a comparison of the mean loan and deposit sizes for these institutions. The village 'units' of Bank BRI, a world-leading institution in 'micro-banking', are included in Table 8.1 for the purposes of comparison.

Table 8.1 Comparative account sizes: loans and deposits of regulated institutions

Institution	Loan accounts: numbers (million)	Mean balance outstanding per account (Rp. million/US$)	Deposit accounts: numbers (million)	Mean balance per account (Rp. million/US$)
BRI units	2.60	Rp2.55m/US$340	16.7	Rp0.65m/US$85
BPRs	1.68	Rp1.94m/US$260	4.6	Rp0.25m/US$33
BKDs	0.70	Rp0.22m/US$29	0.6	Rp0.05m/US$7
LDKPs	1.30	Rp0.28m/US$35	n.a	n.a

Sources: BI and BRI. Various dates during 2000. *Notes:* Data for BRI relate to the Kupedes (loan) and Simpedes (deposit) accounts. Term deposits are excluded. n.a, not applicable.

Table 8.1 has been compiled to indicate the levels at which the bank and non-bank microfinance institutions described above fit into the rural financial landscape. The data (for year 2000) are not recent, but their value lies in suggesting the relativities between institutions, which are unlikely to have changed. On the evidence, the BRI Units cater for clients with somewhat larger loan and deposit accounts than the BPRs, while the smaller institutions (BKDs and LDKPs) are operating at an entirely lower level. Thus if the BRI units are serving a clientele that is relatively well-off and the BPRs have a somewhat more modest constituency, the BKDs and LDKPs appear to serve a genuine microfinance market.

Savings and credit cooperatives

Savings and credit cooperatives are also significant linkage partners in modern Indonesia. Multi-purpose cooperatives were a primary instrument of state policy under Suharto's 'New Order' and independent cooperative initiatives were discouraged. In 1998 a new government removed the rural monopoly which the official cooperatives had enjoyed. Independent entities are now free to obtain licences to set up Kalimantan Sanggar Pusaka (Savings and Credit Cooperatives – KSPs) and to form cooperative networks. This offers opportunities for the emergence of new, poverty-focused, cooperative initiatives.

Some NGOs have taken advantage of the new situation to set up financial services cooperatives. Islamic self-help savings and loan groups (Baitul Mal Wat Tamwil – BMTs) are adopting the cooperative legal form, while a long-running Agriculture Ministry microfinance programme, the P4K (income-generating project for marginal farmers and the landless), is working towards having its self-help groups adopt cooperative status. The remaining savings and credit cooperative units (Unit Simpan Pinjam – USPs) dating from the Suharto era, are strategically located in rural areas and still have great potential for financial service provision. For this reason they are now receiving attention from PN Madani, a financial apex institution set up by the Government in 1999. PN Madani is creating linkages with both the USPs and the newly formed KSPs. It also encourages the emergence of effective secondary cooperative bodies. Both primary and secondary cooperatives are being tapped to act as executing agencies for credit provided by PN Madani.

MFIs, NGOs and self-help groups

Finally, the discussion turns to financial service organizations that are outside the scope of financial sector regulation, such as MFIs, NGOs and Self-Help Groups (SHGs). The Indonesian term *lembaga keuangan mikro*, commonly translated as 'microfinance institution', or MFI, refers in practice to a wide range of entities active in provision of financial services for their members. These include both regulated and informal entities. Many informal Indonesian 'MFIs' are the survivors of structures originally created for mass financial service initiatives taken by various ministries during the late 'New Order' period. While politically driven, these mass credit programmes have nonetheless left behind pockets of autonomous microfinance activity in various parts of Indonesia, sometimes preserving 'revolving funds' originally disbursed by government agencies and channelling institutions. These informal MFIs appear capable of benefiting from linkage relationships, but are constrained by lack of an appropriate legal status. There is a blurring of boundaries between such MFIs and self-help groups.

Self-help groups (SHGs) are completely informal organizations. Indonesian SHGs with savings and credit activities are often an outgrowth of *arisan*, a traditional group activity and the Indonesian version of the rotating savings and credit associations found in most developing countries. Many SHGs were founded by government and community organizations, and many are organized on *Syariah* principles. The microfinance umbrella group, the GEMA PKM, estimates that over 400 000 groups were formed during the 1990s in connection with some government programmes, involving perhaps 10 million individual members. If this is so, there was enormous outreach to the poor and very poor, even if many SHGs were short-lived. For the SHGs, as for the MFIs, there is scope for the better-managed survivors to benefit from having access to the newly available cooperative legal form.

Credit subsidies, politics and linkages

From references in the narrative above, it will be obvious that subsidized credit initiatives, often involving linkages, were an important element in 'New Order' economic policy and political control. Suharto's use of credit created by Bank Indonesia (so-called 'liquidity credits') demonstrated the absence of central bank independence. The Bank's involvement in protecting the interests of the government during the Asian economic crisis from 1997 contributed to enormous public debt, that continues to overshadow the Indonesian economy, and hampered the response to the crisis. However, this is not to say that the 'New Order' was completely resistant to reform. Financial liberalization, including the removal of interest rate caps, commenced during the 1980s, while efforts to wind back credit creation for subsidized lending commenced in the 1990s. The trauma of the financial crisis and the end of the 'New Order' government provided the catalyst for further reform, and linkages are used as a policy instrument. Box 8.1 describes attempts to remove Bank Indonesia from the sphere of 'policy lending' and the creation of a new vehicle, a state-owned entity known as PN Madani, for the purpose.

Linkage models found in Indonesia: a description

Table 8.2 maps all the major linkage models found in Indonesia. It is concerned with linkages of a purely financial nature, such as the flow of loanable funds between institutions as well as the mobilization of savings. It also distinguishes

---

Box 8.1 Bank Indonesia, PN Madani, and attempts to reform state-subsidized 'linkage' lending

Central bank subsidized credit was a policy and political instrument of the 'New Order' government (1967–98). Created 'off-budget', these credits were tools to secure industrial, agricultural and social objectives. For example, credit was used as instruments of income redistribution to support SMEs against the perceived power of big business. As a tool of political control, these off-budget resources were distributed so as to bestow rents, through mistargeting and misappropriation, upon functionaries and supporters of the government at every level down to the village. The primary instrument for achieving agricultural policy goals and distributing political patronage in rural areas was the officially sanctioned Village Cooperative Unit (KUD). State banks, including the retail branches of Bank BRI, also acted as channels for cheap credits. Thus financial 'linkages' were a tool of state policy as well as part of the apparatus of financial repression.

Continuing the financial sector liberalization process of the 1980s, a reform in 1990 reduced some of Bank Indonesia's subsidized credit programmes and halted others. Of those remaining, credits for food self-sufficiency, SMEs and cooperatives are of primary interest for the purposes of this study. Such credits continued to be made available to channelling institutions by the central bank for fixed terms, during which they were to be circulated to finance priority economic activities. Thus, at the commencement of the Asian financial crisis in mid-1997, a considerable volume of Bank Indonesia credit that had been channelled via linkage arrangements was still held on the balance sheets of banks. With the economic downturn, and as non-performing loans (NPL) mounted, the banks' capacity to recover payments from linkage partners and to meet obligations to BI was severely affected.

A new central banking law was enacted in 1999. BI's previous role as an 'agent of development', including credit creation for priority sectors, was abolished. The government issued debt instruments (known as SUP) to compensate Bank Indonesia for outstanding liquidity credits and transferred responsibility for their further management to certain state-owned enterprises (including PN Madani and Bank Mandiri). These entities are now responsible for securing repayment of credits held by channelling banks and for recirculating them, for purposes set by government, until their expiry dates. Credit subsidies were to continue, but to be time-bound, while their costs were to be taken into the national budget, rather than being funded off-budget by the central bank as in the past.

These procedures are an attempt to wind down the provision of credits for policy lending while dealing with the outstanding debts of the banking system to the central bank. It also serves to expose the subsidy costs of policy lending. One particular debt issue, amounting to Rp3.1 trillion and with a currency to 2009, was designated specifically for micro- and SME lending. This was earmarked for linkage lending, via a range of intermediary institutions. However, disbursement of this 'SUP No. 5' funding by PN Madani and other agencies has been slow while the process of strengthening BPRs and cooperatives to act as efficient linkage partners is said to be continuing. The system still contains significant elements of subsidy and the longer-term capacity of PN Madani to stand above politics remains to be seen. Moreover, despite efforts at reform in the central bank, in post-Suharto Indonesia line agencies of government continue to channel cheap loan funds appropriated in the national budget or obtained from off-budget sources. A variety of formal and informal financial institutions, often involved in linkage relationships, continues to be used for the purpose.

between cases where lending is funded by direct financial intermediation and others where lending via apex institutions, such as PN Madani, is funded by government appropriation of funds (as described in Box 8.1).

The following discussion differentiates between situations arising as the result of market forces ('commercial' relationships) and those which occur as the result of government initiative or central bank moral suasion ('sponsored' relationships). Thus, since the Asian financial crisis, many banks in Indonesia are undergoing rehabilitation under close supervision of BI, while others may seek the goodwill of regulatory authorities for a variety of reasons. Similarly, financial institutions owned by governments at the national, provincial or local levels have public service objectives beyond immediate profitability. It will be useful in observing the linkage relationships that have grown up in the financial system to consider how far these would arise without the influence of such non-market considerations, or without the intervention of apex institutions such as PN Madani.

Simple bilateral linkages

Simple bilateral linkages between commercial banks and BPRs are encouraged as an element in the new 'banking architecture'. At least two private commercial banks, Bank Niaga and Bank Danamon, have begun to initiate such relationships on a commercial basis, although this may also reflect central bank moral suasion directed to encouraging micro- and small business lending by the private commercial banks.

Another set of bilateral linkages is that between provincial government-owned commercial banks and locally based LDKPs. The BPDs (provincial development banks) are responsible for supervision of, and varying degrees of technical assistance to, the LDKPs. LDKPs hold accounts with their BPDs and resort to them for liquidity management as necessary. A similar relationship exists between Bank BRI and the BKDs. BRI branches have been delegated by the central bank to supervise and otherwise support BKDs, and receive financial compensation for doing so. BKDs deposit their excess liquidity with BRI and can borrow from the bank in the event of liquidity problems. Bilateral linkages also exist between BPRs and informal entities.

Simple bilateral linkages involving apex institutions

Simple bilateral linkages between apex institutions and other entities include those between PN Madani and Bank Mandiri on the one hand, and a variety of small-localized institutions with access to low-income people in the rural sector on the other. Both of these are state institutions with mandates for public service (although Bank Mandiri is now partly privatized). P N Madani is purely an apex institution, dealing only with financial institutions, whereas Bank Mandiri is a licensed financial institution, which deals with final borrowers, as well as operating in an apex-like fashion by creating linkages, as encouraged by the new financial architecture. Bank Mandiri appears unique among commercial banks in the extent to which it is incorporating the linkage mechanism into its growth strategy.

The microcredit intermediaries selected by PN Madani as its focus include mostly conventional BPRs but it has a special concern for *Syariah* BPRs and even has relationships with *Syariah* commercial banks. Madani makes working capital loans for their expansion, and subordinated loans to strengthen the capital base of selected institutions. PN Madani's 2003 Annual Report records it had working relationships with around 800 BPRs, either for financing or technical assistance. Via these latter institutions, PN Madani links with the BMT (Islamic self-help groups, many of which have assumed cooperative legal identities and which PN Madani aims to upgrade to BPR *Syariah* status. It also links with KSPs (savings and credit cooperatives) of which there are around 1,200 in operation. Madani deals with these via secondary cooperatives, which obtain capital injections and working capital loans. Services provided by PN Madani to its linkage partners include management consulting and technical services, training in the application of standardized systems and procedures, including IT services, and the placement of Madani advisory staff in selected institutions.

Bank Mandiri positions itself as an apex institution catering for the most bankable among the rural banks. Mandiri had established formal linkages with some 700 BPRs by mid-2004. It planned to reach 1,000 BPRs (almost half of the present total) by the end of 2004 and has ambitious targets for further expansion of outreach to what it believes will become a growth sector as part of the 'new architecture'. Aside from credit lines and access to programme financing, Mandiri also provides training and assists with the installation of a standard IT system. Mandiri sees this as promoting the government's objective of increasing the availability of financing for micro- and small business activity, and as providing an extension of the bank's own distribution network for its loan products. These include programme credits it is administering as part of former Bank Indonesia liquidity and SUP credits for micro- and small enterprise lending (Box 8.1). Bank Mandiri was responsible for a third of all lending to the BPR sector in mid-2004 (around US$21 million, as compared with PN Madani's US$4 million). The numbers are small still, and delays in disbursement of SUP funding have been a matter of public comment.

Linkage chains

In Indonesia, it is rather difficult to identify commercial chains, or linkages operating according to market principles but serving a low-income rural constituency. Rather, such chains appear to operate as a matter of public policy or are at least initiated or sponsored by government institutions. Thus the provincial development banks, BPDs, provide support to LDKPs and to provincial government-owned BPRs. Some of these, in turn, serve informal MFIs and community-based self-help groups. Here the relationships are often influenced

THE RICH VARIETY OF MICROFINANCE LINKAGES IN INDONESIA 141

Table 8.2 Modes of financial linkage between institutions

Sources of loanable funds, savings and capital flows	Modes of financial linkage between Indonesian financial institutions serving a poor and low-income rural clientele		
(i) flows are financed by direct financial intermediation, including mobilization of savings from subordinate entities.	**(i) Simple bilateral linkages**		
	O→ Commercial bank	O→ Rural bank (BPR)	Final borrowers
	O→ Commercial bank	O→ Non-bank financial institutions (LDKPs)	Final borrowers
	O→ Rural bank	O→ Self-help group	Final borrowers
(ii) flows are now (since 1999) backed by state debt, subsidies are transparent, and (in principle) subject to a hard budget constraint.	**(ii) Bilateral linkages (with apex institutions)**		
	O→ Apex institution	O→ BPR LDKP KSP	Final borrowers
(iii) flows financed by direct intermediation, including mobilization of savings from subordinate entities.	**(iii) Linkage chains**		
	O→ BPD	O→ BPR	O→ Self-help group → Final borrowers
	O→ BPD	O→ LDKP	O→ Self-help group → Final borrowers
	O→ Commercial bank	O→ DABANAS Foundation	O→ BPRs → Final borrowers

Sources of loanable funds, savings and capital flows	*Modes of financial linkage between Indonesian financial institutions serving a poor and low-income rural clientele*			
	(iv) Linkage chains (from apex institutions)			
	O→	O→	O→	Final borrowers
(iv) flows are now (since 1999) backed by state debt and subsidies are constrained by the state budget.	Apex institution	KSP(secondary) BPR KSP Syariah LDKP	KSP (primary) BMT	
	BRI	MFI/Koperasi		Self Help Groups
	Bank Mandiri	BPRS		SHGs
	(v) Agribusiness financing via non-financial entities			
(v) flows are commercial, delivered via non-financial intermediaries	O→	O→	O→	Final borrowers
	Venture capitalist	Agribusiness entity		(Producers)
	Commercial bank			

Source: Developed from case study field interviews.

by the disbursement of programme funding, for example, subsidies distributed in recent years to local governments to compensate for high fuel prices.

Another chain relationship is that deriving from the desire of commercial banks, members of the association of private commercial banks, PERBANAS, to access BPRs. The association has set up a foundation, known as DABANAS (National Private Commercial Bank Foundation), as an intermediary for this purpose. It receives a margin over the lending rate of the member banks for passing funds through to qualified BPRs. It is hard to see any motive for these transactions other than banks' need (for whatever reason) to comply with BI's 'credit policy', urging them to support sub-ordinate banks in the BPR sector. The foundation provides a means of doing this at minimal transaction cost. DABANAS itself had its origins in an earlier, mandatory policy by which commercial banks were obliged to devote a certain proportion of total lending to SME borrowers. The DABANAS structure is convenient for present purposes, even though there is no longer a formal requirement for banks to comply. Where a commercial bank has a commercial or strategic motive for linking with BPRs it is likely to want to do so directly, as with the cases of Bank Niaga and Bank Danamon, mentioned above (refer Table 8.2).

Linkage chains from apex institutions (see Table 8.2)

Such institutional chains are directly related to public policy goals. The Bank Mandiri linkages could also serve longer-term strategic interests of market positioning and market development. Thus Bank Mandiri has recently acquired the role as implementing agency of a bilateral aid project (surrendered by Bank Indonesia as a result of its loss of the 'agent of development' function). In this project, BPRs and other small financial institutions linked with Bank Mandiri will be executing banks, targeting groups of the poor in farming and fishing communities. This three link chain will prove profitable for Bank Mandiri if the lending is well executed and should give the opportunity for institutional learning and market development. Bank Mandiri is conscious of the value of Bank BRI's rural outreach for savings mobilization and of the contribution to BRI's group profit from rural- and micro-operations.

PN Madani's mandate is determined by public policy. It is mandated to continue with the policy lending funded by the former BI liquidity credits, while managing the transition to an accountable and transparent regime for such lending. PN Madani operates in a policy environment in which there is now greater consciousness of the distinction between 'micro' and 'small' enterprise and of the differing financial service needs of these two levels of economic activity. Partly as a means of addressing this issue, and partly for political ends, PN Madani has a brief for the support of Islamic financial institutions, especially those based in community and grass roots action. These *syariah* institutions do not require collateral for lending, as a matter of religious principle. Madani also has a special brief for the support of cooperative financial service institutions.

An agribusiness linkage (see Table 8.2)

PT HM Sampoerna is a company sourcing tobacco leaf from growers in NTB Province. Its relationship with growers provides an example of a commercial linkage relationship. Sampoerna assures supply by production contracts with growers. It acts as the financial intermediary in a linkage between the funding source (a venture capital financier) and the grower, as well as providing specialized inputs and being the final purchaser of the product.

Unfortunately, neither hard data on costs and returns nor details of contractual arrangements between the company and growers were available. Besides offering production loans, Sampoerna also finances investment in on-farm processing facilities. Calculating the real cost of credit supplied under this system and the distribution of benefits between the parties would require, apart from details of the nominal interest rate, the calculation of fair market prices for inputs and services supplied to growers and estimates of open market prices for leaf. Sampoerna itself purchases all inputs. It also grades the leaf delivered by contracted growers so that it is difficult to assure transparency in this critical aspect of the relationship. Nonetheless, this kind of linkage offers a model for a potentially sustainable microfinance linkage arrangement.

Conclusions

This study of the variety of linkage mechanisms observable in Indonesia suggests that good policy can exist and even flourish alongside bad. It suggests that commercial mechanisms can survive in a politicized lending environment, perhaps because the selective reach of politicized lending is likely to exclude many bankable micro-borrowers. Further, the study indicates that considerable demand for savings services exists, sufficient to permit the emergence of viable processes of financial intermediation within rural communities. Small and well-managed financial institutions, anchored in the communities they serve, operating within a supportive policy environment and subject to adequate regulation and supervision, are capable of extending financial services to previously excluded segments of the rural population.

The Bali BPD–LPDs linkage case study described in Chapter 7 suggests there is genuine utility in commercially motivated linkage arrangements for financial institutions in rural communities. The support of such linkages is central bank policy, embodied in its planning for a 'new banking architecture' for Indonesia. However, linkages are still employed extensively in Indonesia for the channelling of government programme credit, and such linkages continue to introduce significant elements of subsidy into rural- and micro-finance. This policy decision may make life difficult for good institutions attempting to survive in Indonesia's highly segmented rural financial market.

References

Robinson, M. (2002) *The Microfinance Revolution. Volume 2: Lessons from Indonesia,* The World Bank and Open Society Institute, Washington D.C.

Steinwand, D. (2001) *The Alchemy of Microfinance: Evolution of the Indonesian People's Credit Banks from 1895 to 1999, and a Contemporary Analysis,* VWF, Berlin.

CHAPTER 9

Self-reliance vs. donor dependence: linkages between banks and microfinance institutions in Mali

Hans Dieter Seibel

Abstract

Since the mid-1980s, the government-owned agricultural bank, Banque Nationale de Développement Agricole (BNDA), has been the main intermediary offering financial services to local microfinance institutions (MFIs). This chapter discusses and compares the financial linkages that BNDA has with two of the largest MFI networks in Mali. First it looks at the liquidity balancing linkages with Kafo Jiginew, a federation of regulated savings and credit cooperatives, which is based on self-reliance through savings mobilization, using bank linkages mainly for liquidity balancing. The second case describes BNDA's financial linkage with the CVECA-ON (Caisses Villageoises d'Epargne et de Crédit Autogerées-Office du Niger) network. This linkage is geared to credit expansion more than liquidity balancing, with a significantly lesser emphasis on savings mobilization. Given the striking difference in strategy between the two networks, the question is posed whether donor generosity leads to MFI complacency.

Introduction[1]

Over the last 20 years microfinance has evolved rapidly in Mali. As of 2003, the microfinance sector consisted of 41 networks with 752 local microfinance institutions (MFIs) and a total outreach of 614,000 clients. Since the mid-1980s, the government-owned agricultural bank, Banque Nationale de Développement Agricole (BNDA), has been the main intermediary offering financial services to MFIs. This chapter compares the financial linkages that BNDA has with two of the 41 MFIs networks in Mali: Kafo Jiginew, a federation of regulated savings and credit cooperatives based on self-reliance through savings, using bank linkages mainly for liquidity balancing; and Caisses Villageoises d'Epargne et de Crédit Autogerées-Office du Niger (CVECA-ON), a network of so-called village banks which has financed its expansion mainly from donor funds. Given the striking difference in strategy and dynamics between the two networks, the question is posed whether donor generosity leads to MFI complacency.

The financial sector and microfinance

Mali, with a population of 11.7m, 70 per cent rural, is located in the Sahel zone of West Africa. With a per capita income of US$245 and a Human Development Index rank of 174, it is among the poorest countries in the world, highly vulnerable to external impacts (IMF, 2003; Republic of Mali, 2004). Since the mid-1980s microfinance has evolved rapidly. The Parmec law, introduced in 1994, provides full recognition to financial cooperatives and renewable licensing to other types of microfinance institutions (MFIs) (Fruman and Seibel, 1995). Regulation applies to the whole sector and includes an interest rate ceiling of at present 27 per cent. Regulation and supervision are entrusted to a unit in the Ministry of Finance, the Cellule d'Appui et de Suivi des Systèmes Financiers Décentralisés (CAS/SFD). As of 2003 (Table 9.1), the microfinance sector comprised 41 networks with 752 local MFIs and a total membership of 614,000, covering close to one-third of all families in Mali. In December 2004 the sector's total assets amounted to €69m (US$93,398,803 million), total deposits of clients were €36m, and total loans outstanding €49m; the repayment rate was 94 per cent.

Table 9.1 Microfinance networks in Mali, Dec. 2003 (amounts in million Euro)

	Regulated (financial coops)	CVECA (village banks)	Solidarity credit	Total[1]
Number of networks	27	6	7	41
Number of unions/associations	15	14	7	37
Number of institutions	431	276	44	752
Number of authorized entities	431	14	7	452
Number of members	430,166	120,206	63,247	614,211
percent female	30	35	88	37
percent male	65	63	11	59
percent groups	5	3	1	4
Number of depositors	267,112	25,253	55,214	347,579
Total assets	56.31	6.37	5.82	68.98
Deposits	32.03	2.46	1.54	36.24
Capital (without grants)	10.52	1.59	2.74	15.04
Bank credit lines	12.30	1.84	0.88	15.02
Grants	1.36	0.36	0.65	2.45
Soft loans	0.11	0.13	0	0.24
Bank deposits	6.83	0.70	0.87	8.40
No. of loans outstanding	142,510	34,800	51,148	228,458
No. of disbursements in 2003	153,085	41,631	63,672	258,388
Loans outstanding	40.65	4.10	3.49	48.52
Amount disbursed in 2003	45.99	4.83	7.89	58.70
Repayment rate[2]	93.3	96.3	95.7	93.8

Source: Cellule d'Appui et de Suivi des Systèmes Financiers Décentralisés, *Rapport Annuel 2003.*

[1]Including Azaouad Finances S.A., not listed in the three preceding columns.

[2]Amount collected on due-date/loans outstanding.

The microfinance sector comprises three sub-sectors: cooperatives with 70 per cent of total outreach, village banks (*caisses villageoises* or CVECAs) with 20 per cent, and solidarity credit groups in the Grameen tradition with 10 per cent (Table 9.2). A major difference between these three subsectors is the emphasis placed on savings. In terms of total resources, savings represent 57 per cent of equity and liabilities among cooperatives, 39 per cent among village banks and 27 per cent among solidarity groups. The sector is highly concentrated: 88 per cent of all deposits and 84 per cent of all loans outstanding are in the cooperative subsector, and two-thirds of that in just two networks. The largest networks are Kafo Jiginew with 165,000 members and Nyesigiso with 127,500 members, accounting for almost half of the total microfinance client base.

Mali has a small banking sector of nine banks. BNDA, the agricultural development bank, has been the main bank providing financial services to MFIs through both forward linkages with MFIs and backward linkages with donor organizations (Samassékou, 2000). As a channelling bank for funds provided by Kreditanstalt fuer Wiederaufbau (KfW), the bank (BNDA, 2002) started refinancing a village banking network in the Dogon area in 1986, one of the poorest areas in Mali (Adler, 2001). Since 1994, BNDA has acted as an executing bank for donors, offering also loans from its own resources, in addition to deposit services. By 2003, BNDA disbursements and commitments had reached €5.6m and the loan portfolio stood at €4.65m (BNDA, 2004b). Its backward linkages with AFD (Agence Française de Développement) and KfW cover almost half (47.5 per cent) of its MFI portfolio; €1.75m were refinanced by AFD, €0.46m by KfW, totalling €2.2m. Non-financial support comprised funding for staff training and related forms of institution-building, provided by BNDA as a channelling agency on behalf of AFD (Table 9.3).

Table 9.2 Comparative data on three microfinance subsectors in Mali, Dec. 2003 (in per cent)

	Financial coops	CVECA	Solidarity credit	Total
Institutions	57	37	6	100
Members	70	20	10	100
Subsector				
% female	30	35	88	
% depositors	62	21	87	
% borrower	33	29	81	
Total assets	82	9	8	99
Deposits	88	7	4	99
Loans outstanding	84	9	7	100
Amount disbursed in 2003	78	8	13	99
Credit lines	82	12	6	100
Non-performing assets in %:				
2002	4.6	2.3	4.4	4.4
2003	6.7	4.2	3.7	6.2

Source: CAS/SFD 2004.

Table 9.3 Credit lines of BNDA to MFIs[1], 1997–2003 (in '000 Euro)

	Units*	1997	1998	1999	2000	2001	2002	2003
MFIs financed by AFD:	5	1,421	1,351	1,245	1,581	1,547	1,727	1,753
CVECA-Office du Niger	3	1,207	1,082	1,091	1,215	1,372	1,651	1,677
PAAF Bamako	1	137	172	154	229	175	76	76
PAF Mopti	1	76	96	0	137	0	0	0
MFIs financed by KfW:	5	721	998	637	518	337	838	457
CVECA-Pays Dogon	3	572	762	305	218	76	305	152
CVECA-Kita/Bafoulabé	2	149	236	332	300	261	534	305
Other MFIs:	12	994	1,020	1,965	1,649	1,953	2,757	2,352
Kafo Jiginew	1	762	762	1,524	1,067	1,067	915	1,677
Canef Bougouni	1	91	183	305	305	305	305	305
NEF Douentza	1	64	37	0	64	152	23	0
Pasacoop-San/Djenné	2	0	38	59	105	110	133	142
CMEC/SAN	1	0	0	0	32	90	0	76
Kondo Jigima	1	0	0	76	76	76	76	76
Others	5	76	0	0	0	152	1,305	76
Total	22	3,136	3,369	3,848	3,748	3,837	5,322	4,649

Source: Mission d'évaluation AFD/DEG, 2004
[1]Unions, associations or single-unit entities as legal borrowers.

BNDA's portfolio is highly concentrated. The two largest borrowers are Kafo Jiginew (Kafo) and CVECA-Office du Niger (one of the village bank networks), each with a credit ceiling of €1.68m. The financial linkages between BNDA and these two borrowers were selected as case studies for the Ford/FAO linkage study and are described in detail below.

BNDA has largely abandoned retail lending, which it found too risky, and is now mainly a wholesale and corporate lender. Only 2.9 per cent of its loans outstanding are invested in the microfinance sector (2003; down from 5.5 per cent in 2000) (Table 9.4). The main reason for the decline is not a lack of willingness of the Bank to lend but a lack of effective demand (i.e. by creditworthy MFIs). The number of loans to MFIs has also declined: from 70 to 56. With such a small share of the business with MFIs and an interest rate of 8 per cent (compared to a corporate rate of 15 per cent), its microfinance operations are closer to social than commercial lending. Furthermore, no information is available to ascertain whether BNDA is breaking even or making a loss on its MFI lending.

Risks are low and mitigated at three different levels: borrowers provide a guarantee deposit with their local MFI (e.g., in the case of Kafo Jiginew 10 per cent on smaller and 30 per cent on larger loans); in the case of commodity loans (cotton, rice), repayment to the bank is guaranteed through deductions at source by the respective parastatals; part of the portfolio is guaranteed by donors – a substitute for what is one of the core functions of banking: risk management.

Table 9.4 Disbursements and commitments of BNDA by borrower category, 2000–3, in per cent

Borrower	2000		2001		2002		2003	
category	Number	Amount	Number	Amount	Number	Amount	Number	Amount
Loans guaranteed by CA	79.6	27.8	87.2	52.7	85.0	31.0	84.5	35.2
Cooperatives sector	2.7	0.4	1.4	0.4	0.4	0.1	0.2	0.1
Individuals	11.6	1.0	7.1	1.0	10.2	1.3	10.2	1.1
Corporations	3.8	65.3	3.7	41.4	3.8	63.7	4.8	60.7
MFIs	2.2	5.5	0.6	4.5	0.6	3.8	0.3	2.9
Total %	99.9	100.0	100.0	100.0	100.0	99.9	100.1	100.0
Total (amount in million €)	3,213	69.6	7,163	85.5	11,649	141.0	17,135	190.6

Source: BNDA, 2004a.

Defaulting on loans provided by BNDA to MFIs is zero, compared to default rates of up to 50 per cent of retail loans in an earlier phase.

Since 1994, Banque Internationale pour le Mali (BIM), a commercial bank, has entered the market, concentrating on three major networks. It is prepared to lend more, but faces a shortage of effective demand. The banks have a highly effective system of loan protection, with a repayment rate of 100 per cent, shifting all risks to the networks. In 2003, Banque Malienne de Solidarité (2005), (BMS) designed as a bank for micro finance intermediaries, became operative, soon to be joined by a regional solidarity bank. It is expected that the increased supply of funds will not be matched by effective demand: the big cooperative networks adhere to a policy of self-reliance through deposit mobilization; most of the smaller networks and single units, with a shortage of loanable funds, are not creditworthy.

Quantitatively, the main overall function of financial linkages in Mali is liquidity balancing through deposits and borrowing. The MFIs need liquidity balancing over the course of the year, since their business is characterized by large seasonal fluctuations. Excess liquidity increases during the first half of the year and peaks in July, whereas liquidity shortages increase during the second half of the year and peak in December. The financial linkage with BNDA means that the MFI partners have access both to credit on demand and to a secure deposit house. This is exemplified by Kafo Jiginew, the largest network of financial cooperatives. Kafo uses BNDA credit lines mainly for liquidity balancing. A second linkage model is expansion of the portfolio through bank borrowing, historically backed by donor funds. This is most clearly exemplified by the village banking network CVECA-ON. As illustrated in the example below the CVECA financial linkage model is motivated more by access to credit for portfolio expansion, than it is for liquidity balancing.

Kafo Jiginew: Bank linkages for liquidity balancing

Origin and structure

Kafo Jiginew (literally 'federation of granaries') is a federation of savings and credit cooperatives in the south of Mali and the largest network of MFIs; it is not divided into unions or associations as separate legal entities. Its mission is 'to organize the poor population of Mali and to help them take control of their finances,' combining outreach to the poor with self-reliance and institutional sustainability. It was initiated in 1987 by CECCM, a consortium of European NGOs which continues to provide financial and technical assistance, in close cooperation with the Companie Malienne de Développement des Textiles (CMDT)[2], a parastatal organization (GECE, 2004). Since its inception Kafo Jiginew has received grants amounting to €2.33 million. The federation, with its seat in Koutiala in the cotton belt of Mali, comprises four regional offices, 129 cooperative MFIs with an additional 12 service units, a representative office in Bamako since 2001, and a central fund which may eventually be transformed into a finance company or a bank. Total staff is 162: 28 per cent in the head office and the remainder in the regional offices; 21 per cent are female.

Governance

The federation and each of the member-cooperatives, as autonomous MFIs, are regulated under the Parmec law and supervised by CAS/SFD; the regional offices have no legal status and no organs of governance. Each cooperative is owned by its members, with the general assembly as its ultimate decision-making body, a credit committee and a supervisory council. The regional offices are in charge of guidance and supervision, assessment of major loans, and reporting. The federation, which is owned by the cooperatives as shareholders, is in charge of overall strategy, training, consolidated reporting, supervision and the management of a central fund for liquidity exchange and refinancing. It has the right to open, suspend and close cooperatives. Its operational costs are borne by the member-cooperatives, which also contribute to a disaster relief fund.

Membership

Most cooperative members are cotton farmers in the area of CMDT. Since 1994, the onset of a general policy focus on financial cooperatives, it has spread slowly into other parts of the country including urban areas (as net depositors, accounting for 30 per cent of deposits and 18 per cent of loans outstanding as of June 2002), and diversified its membership to include craftsmen, small traders, and wage and salary earners. The predominance of cotton farmers means that the performance of the cooperatives is closely connected with the world market for cotton. As of December 2003, the 129 cooperatives of the federation had 165,000 members: 71 per cent male (mostly as heads of household), 25 per cent female and 4 per cent groups (down from 8 per cent in 2002). The groups usually have on average 30 members, mostly women who are too poor to qualify for regular membership. The loans obtained by the groups are on-lent to their members.

Interest rates

Interest rates on deposits[3] are as follows: savings deposits (also referred to as sight deposits) at 3 per cent per annum on amounts stable over at least 3 months, with a minimum of €1.50 in rural and €3.00 in urban areas; and 4 per cent on term deposits with a minimum of €38. There are four loan products: fertilizer loans of 4–6 months at a flat rate of 10 per cent, equivalent to around 25 per cent per annum; short-term loans of 3–6 months at 30 per cent per annum.; seasonal loans of 9 months at 24 per cent per annum; and equipment loans up to three years at 18 per cent per annum.

Basic data

By the end of 2003, there were 149,000 depositors (75 per cent male) and 94,000 borrowers (90 per cent male). Total consolidated assets amounted to €23.6m (an increase of 24 per cent over 2002), loans outstanding to €16.7m, 75 per cent in agriculture. The main source of funds are deposits of members, amounting to €12.2m; 78 per cent are savings deposits available for withdrawal at any time, 10 per cent term deposits and 12 per cent guarantee deposits. Guarantee deposits are collected at a rate of 10 per cent for loans up to €1,500 and 30 per cent for loans above. The loans-to-deposit ratio was 137 per cent. Next in importance are bank borrowing of €5.5m, grants of €1.9m and capital of €1.2m. The average cooperative thus had 1,280 members, among them 1,155 depositors and 730 borrowers, €183,000 in total assets, €130,000 in loans outstanding and €95,000 in deposits; or per member: total assets of €143, loans outstanding of €102 and deposits of €74.

Performance

Its consolidated performance as of 30 June 2002 was evaluated by PlaNet Finance (Table 9.5); it received a 'B' rating, which is remarkable given the difficult economic environment. From 2002 to 2003 performance has declined. This is attributed to a lack of rain in 2002, resulting in a decline in the production of cotton and grains by 25 per cent and 24 per cent, respectively; and the crisis in Côte d'Ivoire, which has closed an important market for Mali. From 2002 to 2003, the repayment rate fell from 95.2 per cent to 93.2 per cent. Short-term loans, accounting for 88 per cent of the portfolio in 2003 (85 per cent in 2002) declined slightly from 94.9 per cent in 2002 to 94.3 per cent in 2003. The biggest drop was among the medium-term loans, which accounted for 8 per cent in 2003 (14 per cent in 2002); the repayment rate fell from 96.6 per cent in 2002 to 80.6 per cent in 2003. Long-term loans, which accounted for 4 per cent

Table 9.5 Kafo Jiginew, consolidated data, 2002–3 (amounts in million Euro)

	2002	2003
Number of cooperatives	129	129
Number of members	144,742	164,596
per cent male	72	71
per cent female	20	25
per cent groups	8	4
Number of depositors	122,603	149,109
per cent male	75	75
Number of borrowers	77,135	93,904
per cent male	90	90
Total assets	19.02	23.58
Bank deposits	2.09	2.40
Loans outstanding	13.39	16.69
per cent agricultural	75	75
per cent short-term	85	88
per cent medium-term	14	8
per cent long-term	1	4
Deposits of clients	9.80	12.22
per cent savings deposits		78
per cent term deposits		10
per cent guarantee deposits		12
Bank borrowing	3.85	5.48
Donor funds (loans and grants)	1.71	1.86
Capital (without grants)	1.01	1.19
Repayment rate in per cent	95.1	93.2
Return on assets in percent	2.7	0.8
Return on equity	16.6	5.3
ROA calc. by PlaNet Finance	1.0	1.4
AROA (adjusted for subsidies)[1]	(1.6)	n.a.

Sources: Kafo Jiginew, 2004a,b,c,d.
[1]PlaNet Finance (2003).

of loans outstanding in 2003 (1 per cent in 2002) remained unaffected, at repayment rates of 100 per cent in both years. The loss ratio (overdue >1 year) in 2003 was 2.0 per cent, compared to 1.5 per cent in 2002. (Kafo Jiginew, 2004b: 22–3) The consolidated figures conceal that only 44.5 per cent of the cooperatives are profitable, while 55.5 per cent are loss-making. In 2004, with good rains and a record cotton harvest, Kafo Jiginew more than recovered.

Kafo Jiginew reports a return on assets of 2.7 per cent in 2002 and 0.8 per cent in 2003; and a return on equity of 16.6 per cent for 2002 and 5.3 per cent for 2003. Adjusted for subsidies as calculated by PlaNet Finance (2004), returns on assets were negative (–5.4 per cent in 2001, –1.6 per cent in 2002).

Types of linkages

All linkages are mediated by the federation through its central fund; there are no direct linkages between member-cooperatives and banks or donors. Kafo Jiginew borrows funds and on-lends them to the cooperatives. Each cooperative is autonomous in its lending decisions, using its own capital, deposits mobilized and funds borrowed from the federation. Linkages are purely financial, comprising bank deposits and bank borrowing. Bank deposits, part of which serve as a guarantee fund, constitute 54 per cent of bank borrowing as of December 2002 and 43 per cent as of Dec. 2003. These percentages vary widely over the year as bank borrowing, in contrast to deposits, is far more subject to seasonal fluctuations (see Figure 9.1). Kafo Jiginew receives 3 per cent per annum on its ordinary bank deposits (the bulk of its deposits) and 4.15 per cent on term deposits; it pays 8 per cent per annum on domestic bank borrowing and 6.5 per cent on the EIB (European Investment Bank) loan. Client deposits are its cheapest source of funds, averaging 1.5 per cent.

Institution-building through training of cooperative managers and board members is financed by AFD; the funds are channelled through BNDA. The banks provide no capacity-building to the MFIs and their networks.

Linkage partners

Kafo Jiginew has three major types of linkage partners, providing €7.34m in loanable funds at 31 December 2003): national banks provide about half of external funds, EIB and donor agencies about one-quarter each.

National bank borrowing constitutes 21 per cent of loans outstanding, international banks (EIB) 12 per cent, and donor agencies 11 per cent, together 44 per cent (Table 9.6). Over the two-year period 2002 and 2003, national bank borrowing increased by 88 per cent, similar to the rate of increase of the total portfolio, 85 per cent. Historically, BNDA was the first bank approached by Kafo Jiginew, followed later by BIM. In 2002 BIM was the main national lender, with €1.04m (guaranteed by ADA/Luxemburg at a charge of 2.5 per cent to Kafo Jiginew), compared to €0.81m from BNDA (guaranteed by AFD). In 2003 there were three national lenders: BNDA and BIM with almost equal amounts: €1.40m and €1.38m, respectively; and €0.70 from the newly established BMS. Almost two-thirds of national borrowing (63 per cent) in 2003 was credit lines of a

Table 9.6 Kafo Jiginew: external sources of funds, 31/12/2003 (amounts in million Euro)

Source of funds	Amount	%	% of loans outstanding
National banks	3.48	47	21
European Investment Bank	2.00	27	12
Donor agencies	1.86	25	11
Total	7.34	99	443

Source: Kafo Jiginew, 2004a,b.

similar magnitude from all three lenders; 22 per cent was short-term borrowing (up to one year) from BNDA; 15 per cent was medium-term borrowing from BIM (Table 9.7).

The EIB loan, granted in August 2002, is a five-year loan at 6.5 per cent interest, with the main purpose of refinancing seasonal input loans of 4–6 months, mainly for fertilizer. Between 2001 and 2002, it enabled Kafo Jiginew to almost double the volume of its input lending (from 12 per cent to 22 per cent). This loan represents a net expansion of the credit portfolio of Kafo Jiginew: deepening its services to its members rather than expanding outreach. At the same time, it involves a financial paradox: the largest long-term loan of Kafo Jiginew is mainly used for very short-term loans to clients.

The funds provided by donor agencies are for special projects, either directed at special target groups, such as women in a particular region, or at particular purposes. In most cases they use Kafo Jiginew as an organization to implement their own objectives.

Kafo Jiginew's financial strategy is explicitly geared to self-reliance: growth on the basis of deposits and own capital, which constituted 80 per cent of loans outstanding as of December 2003, rather than bank borrowing. International funds are mainly used for special programmes, with the exception of the EIB loan, which is being used to provide input loans to existing members.

Table 9.7 Kafo Jiginew: donor credit funds and bank borrowing, 2002–3 (in million Euro)

Bank	31/12/2002	31/12/2003
(i) National Banks		
BNDA credit line	0.66	0.64
BNDA short-term loan	0	0.76
BNDA medium-term loan	0.15	0
Total borrowing from BNDA at 8%	0.81	1.4
BIM credit line	0.62	0.84
BIM medium-term loan	0.42	.53
Total borrowing from BIM at 8%	1.04	1.38
BMS credit line	0	0.7
Total national banks	1.85	3.48
(ii) International banks		
EIB medium-term loan at 6.5%	2	2
Total bank borrowing	3.85	5.48
(iii) Donor credit funds		
SOS Faim Bruxelles at 0%	0.63	0.76
SNV/PDCD	0.18	0.19
FAO at 0%	0.05	0.05
P/CIF	0.68	0.68
ADA Luxemburg at 8%	0.03	0.03
SYCREF at 5%	0.15	0.15
Total donor credit funds	1.71	1.86
Grand total	5.56	7.34

Source: Jiginew, 2004a,b.

The main function of borrowing from national banks is liquidity balancing. 88 per cent of Kafo Jiginew's lending is short-term, i.e. less than one year (Table 9.5), with wide seasonal fluctuations as shown in Table 9.8. Cotton, the main commodity, is harvested during the first months of the year and sold in the following months; most loans are repaid towards the middle of the year, marking a low in loans outstanding. Planting is done towards the end of the year; the turn of the year thus marks a peak in loans outstanding. Year-end statistics, as they are commonly reported in annual reports, thus give a lop-side picture[4]. While the overall number of borrowers with loans outstanding increases substantially from year-end to year-end (72 per cent as of Dec. 2001, 35 per cent as of 2002, 22 per cent as of 2003), similarly the amounts of outstanding (55 per cent, 48 per cent and 25 per cent, respectively), this hides substantial drops in the middle of the year. As of 30 June 2002 the number of borrowers is down by 48 per cent compared to the preceding December, and in June 2003 by 36 per cent; similarly, the amount of loans outstanding is down by 22 per cent and 28 per cent, respectively. In contrast, deposits of members peak in the middle of the year after harvest and are lowest around the turn of the year. The increases of deposits in December 2002 and 2003 over the preceding June are 59 per cent and 21 per cent, respectively, while changes in June over the preceding December are −14.8 per cent and 3.3 per cent, respectively. Thus, in December 2001, 2002 and 2003 loans outstanding exceeded deposits by 20 per cent, 27 per cent and 27 per cent, respectively; while in June 2002 and 2003 they fell short by 62 per cent and 23 per cent, respectively. (Table 9.8; Figure 9.1)

How external resources contribute to liquidity balancing is shown in Table 9.9. In 2003, the year is clearly divided in two parts in terms of loans outstanding: January to July, with a volume varying between €8.23 and €12.45 and a low in May; and August to December, varying between €16.69 and €18.48, with a peak

Table 9.8 Semi-annual fluctuations in client loans, deposits and liquidity balances, 2001–3

	Dec. 2000	Dec. 2001	June 2002	Dec. 2002	June 2003	Dec. 2003
Number of borrowers	33, 217	57,171	29,522	77,025	49,679	93,904
% change over prev. Dec.		72.1	−48.4	34.7	−35.5	21.9
% change over prev. 6 months			−48.4	160.9	−35.5	89.0
Loans outstanding in €m	5.84	9.03	7.08	13.39	9.62	16.69
% change over prev. Dec.		54.5	−21.5	48.4	−28.1	24.6
% change over prev. 6 months			−21.5	89.0	−28.1	73.4
Deposits of clients in €m	5.95	7.23	11.50	9.80	11.83	12.22
% change over prev. Dec.		21.5	59.1	35.6	20.7	24.7
% change over prev. 6 months			59.1	−14.8	20.7	3.3
Excess of loans over dep. in €m	−0.11	1.80	−4.42	3.59	−2.20	4.47
Excess of loans over dep. in %	−1.8	19.9	−62.4	26.8	−22.9	26.8

Source: PlaNet Finance, 2004.

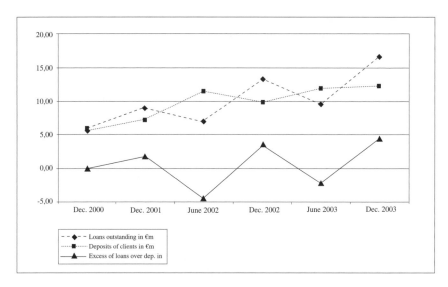

Figure 9.1 Semi-annual fluctuations in client loans, deposits and liquidity balances, 2001–3

in October and November; the highest monthly credit volume is €10.25m, or 125 per cent, above the lowest. During the first part of the year when the harvest is sold, credit needs are significantly lower, and deposits increase over the period. During the second part of the year, September to November, which is planting and growing season, there is a high demand for loans and a drop in savings. In December where harvesting starts, the loan volume is still high but declining already; at the same time there is a jump in deposits. On the whole fluctuations in deposits are much less than those in loans; the highest monthly deposit balance is only €2.3m or 24 per cent above the lowest, which is but a fraction of the credit differential. This shows that farmers prefer to do their own liquidity balancing mainly through loans and not through savings[5]. Note should be taken that there are annual variations in this cycle of up to two months.

The variation in external borrowing follows the variation in loans outstanding with a time difference of 1–2 months. The lowest level of external borrowing is during the first part of the year, particularly March to July; the highest level is reached in December and January; the highest monthly volume of borrowing is €3.6m or 95 per cent above the lowest, somewhat less than the differential in loans outstanding, indicating that a minor part of liquidity balancing is done from the network's own resources. As external borrowing is largely medium-term funds, short-term liquidity balancing is mostly done from domestic bank borrowing, which is mainly credit lines and short-term loans[6].

Non-financial transaction costs between Kafo Jiginew and its lenders are reportedly minimal. The domestic banks require documentation only at the time of negotiations. EIB demands minimal monthly reporting from Kafo Jiginew, requiring no changes to its existing reporting procedures.

Table 9.9 Kafo Jiginew, monthly variations in sources of funds, 2003 (in million Euro)

	Dec. 2000	Dec. 2001	June 2002	Dec. 2002	June 2003	Dec. 2003
Number of borrowers	33, 217	57,171	29,522	77,025	49,679	93,904
% change over prev. Dec.		72.1	−48.4	34.7	−35.5	21.9
% change over prev. 6 months			−48.4	160.9	−35.5	89.0
Loans outstanding in €m	5.84	9.03	7.08	13.39	9.62	16.69
% change over prev. Dec.		54.5	−21.5	48.4	−28.1	24.6
% change over prev. 6 months			−21.5	89.0	−28.1	73.4
Deposits of clients in €m	5.95	7.23	11.50	9.8	11.83	12.22
% change over prev. Dec.		21.5	59.1	35.6	20.7	24.7
% change over prev. 6 months			59.1	-14.8	20.7	3.3
Excess of loans over dep. in €m	−0.11	1.80	−4.42	3.59	−2.20	4.47
Excess of loans over dep. in %	−1.8	19.9	−6.4	26.8	−22.9	26.8

Source: Kafo Jiginew, 2004a,b,c,d.

Domestic vs external resources

It appears that more domestic bank resources are offered than Kafo Jiginew is willing or able to accept. As BIM reports a lack of demand from the networks it has been financing and a willingness to expand its lending, it appears that donor funds, which were of crucial importance in the start-up phase of microfinance in Mali, might now be distorting financial markets. This is an issue which requires further study, all the more as BMS has entered the market as the new bank for MFIs and as a new regional solidarity bank (BRS), with a branch expected in Mali, is being established to serve the same market. In light of the intent of Kafo Jiginew to convert its central fund into a bank or finance company, one may expect that there will be increasing competition and that the market for the commercial banks might be even more limited. One likely consequence is that the need for external liquidity will be greatly reduced. Will donors hear the message?

CVECA-Office du Niger: Bank linkages for financial deepening

The village banking system in Mali

CVECA-ON is one of six networks of so-called village banks (*caisses villageoises*) promoted by CIDR (Centre International de Développement et de Recherche), a French NGO[7]. Nationwide these comprise 276 units organized into 14 unions licensed under the Parmec law, with a total of 120,206 members. Ten unions belonging to the four older networks, self-managed and independent since 2001, are being refinanced by BNDA. Eight of these are being financed with resources provided by donors: €1.68m by AFD to three unions of CVECA-ON, €1.52m to three unions of CVECA-Pays Dogon and €3.05m to two unions of CVECA-Kita/Bafoulabé by KfW. The two unions of Pasacoop-San/Djenné are being refinanced by BNDA from its own resources with €1.42m. Credit lines comprise 45 per cent of loans outstanding, 75 per cent of deposits and 29 per cent of total assets of the six networks; adding soft loans from donors, the respective percentages are 48 per cent, 80 per cent and 31 per cent. External financing thus doubles the loan portfolio of the networks.

A network of village banks in the interior Niger Delta

CVECA-ON operates in the area of the Office du Niger (ON), a parastatal established in 1932 with the objective of irrigating 950,000 ha in an area called the interior Niger Delta; only 60,000 ha have been actually developed. ON was nationalized in 1961 and restructured in 1984 and 1994; its activities are now confined to water and agricultural input management. Since 1970, cotton has been replaced by paddy, supplemented by sugar cane and vegetables. Its area of operation comprises 208 villages with 240,000 inhabitants, organized in 152 community associations and 205 interest groups (MDR, 2001).

There are three networks of MFIs in the area: CVECA-ON with its seat in Niono and 51 village banks, the Fédération des Caisses Rurales Mutualistes du Delta (FCRMD) with its seat in Niono and 54 cooperatives, and Nyésigiso with its seat in Bamako and a total of 49 cooperatives, 12 of these in the area of the Office du Niger. They all function in similar ways and have about the same average number of members per unit. Their target population are the inhabitants of the operational area of the Office du Niger, who are paddy and vegetable farmers. There is no competition between the networks, as they have divided the market among them, with one unit per village. In 1996 a credit information system (*centrale des risques*) was established in the area by CVECA, FCRMD and BNDA, where all borrowers and their repayment performance are to be registered; this worked well for several years, but is now experiencing operational difficulties (Wonou and Biakité, 2004).

Origin and structure

CVECA-ON was established by CIDR as a project in 1994 when the Office du Niger was reorganized and divested of its credit function (CIDR, 2004). Since 2001 it has operated on its own as an autonomous organization, without any foreign staff. It comprises three unions and 51 village banks (December 2003, reduced to 50 in 2004) with 26,290 members, 63 per cent male, 35 per cent female and 3 per cent groups of mainly women; both husband and wife may be members. Only 44 per cent of the members are depositors, which means that more than half the members do not maintain a savings account, despite the fact that the area is rather well monetized; 38 per cent of the members are borrowers. CVECA-ON is a network, not a federation, in the sense that, unlike the three unions, it has no legal status but comprises an area under a technical assistance office, Centre d'Appui au Réseau des Caisses d'Epargne et de Crédit (CAREC), financed by the unions and village banks[8]. CAREC has a technical staff of five, who provide capacity-building, accounting and supervisory services.

Basic data

The network has consolidated total assets of €3.3m, a loan portfolio of €2.43m and bank deposits of €0.33m. Member deposits amount to €0.73m, capital and reserves to €0.86m and bank borrowing to €1.55m. The repayment rate in 2003 was 95 per cent, return on assets was 1.25 per cent (up from 0.37 per cent in 2002). The portfolio-at-risk ratio (>1 month) increased from around 2 per cent during 1999–2001 to 4.8 per cent in 2002 and 12.4 per cent in 2003.

The average village bank has 515 members, €63,300 in assets, €47,650 in loans outstanding, €14,300 in member deposits, €16,900 in capital and reserves, and €30,400 in bank borrowing. However, performance of the village banks varies widely. Seven are loss making and are likely to be closed; one of them has already been closed in 2004. This has affected the three unions unevenly[9]. CAREC functions as an effective supervisor: action is taken, remedial or terminal,

Table 9.10 CVECA-ON: basic data (amounts in million Euro)

	2001	2002	2003
Number of cooperatives	51	51	51
Number of unions	3	3	3
Number of members	23,689	25,175	26,290
per cent male			63
per cent female	32	32	35
per cent groups			3
Number of depositors	9,416	11,064	11,529
Number of borrowers	8,797	9,233	10,014
Total assets		3.09	3.23
Bank deposits		0.40	0.33
Net loans outstanding	2.08	2.28	2.43
Loans from internal funds in per cent	42	43	43
Loans from external funds in per cent	58	57	57
per cent agricultural			71
per cent short-term loans		90	88
Deposits of clients	0.74	0.74	0.73
per cent sight deposits		31	28
per cent term deposits		66	70
per cent other deposits		3	2
Bank borrowing		1.44	1.55
Soft loans		0.04	0.04
Capital and reserves		0.85	0.86
Repayment rate in per cent			96
Return on assets in per cent		0.37	1.25
Portfolio at risk (>1 month) in per cent	1.9	4.8	12.4

Source: CVECA-ON, 2004.

when village banks are not performing well. In July 2003, the time of disbursement of new loans, five village banks were excluded from refinancing, which led to considerable tension.

The agricultural cycle covers the period June to May: planting starts in June; October to December is harvest time; the produce is marketed during the following 4–5 months. The demand for credit fluctuates accordingly: starting in June, it is high during the second half of the year and decreases during the first half.

Linkages

Linkage partners

BNDA is the only banking partner of the CVECA-ON network. BNDA has backward linkages with AFD, which has provided the resources for a credit line of €1.68m in 2003 of which €1.39m were outstanding at the end of the year (Table 9.10, Agence Française de Développement, 2004). The credit line ceiling constitutes 69 per cent of the outstanding loan portfolio at year end; and 57 per cent of the end-of-year outstanding are actually financed from external resources (BNDA and donors).

In terms of forward linkages with CVECA-ON, bank linkages comprise bank deposits and borrowing. They are in the hands of the three unions, which in turn act as financiers of the village banks. Consolidated reporting is done by CAREC as a technical assistance office for the three unions; there is no federation and no central fund at network level. Loan negotiations are held at the branch in Niono and involve little time and costs. Relations are considered very satisfactory.

Financial products and interest rates

BNDA lends to the unions at 8 per cent per annum[10] 10 per cent of the loan amount has to be deposited as a guarantee fund; there is no other collateral. The unions lend to the village banks at 10 per cent. Interest rates vary between the village banks and are fixed annually by the general assembly. The village banks treat internal and borrowed funds separately, using different ledgers. Loans from internal resources (43 per cent of the portfolio) are mainly used for small trade, horticulture and livestock; they carry interest rates of 20–25 per cent. There are two types of loans refinanced by BNDA (57 per cent of the portfolio in 2003): input loans at a flat rate of 12 per cent per annum, and loans for planting paddy at 20–25 per cent. Penalties are stiff, at 1–3 per cent per day overdue. The village banks and their members are aware of the source of funds of their respective loans and are very much concerned about repaying their bank-refinanced loans on time lest they lose their creditworthiness. New loans are reportedly issued only after full repayment. Repayment to BNDA is thus on time at 100 per cent; the repayment problem is shifted to inside the network, as required by the logic of linkage banking. As the village banks and union do their job of repaying on time, so does BNDA with regard to disbursement: In contrast to the practice of agricultural development banks in many other countries, credit delivery by BNDA is reportedly on time.

BNDA, through its branch office in Niono, acts as the central fund for the village banks. Sight deposits are not remunerated. BNDA pays 3.5 per cent on deposits withdrawable at any time. It does not offer term deposit accounts; with their higher interest rate, they would reduce the narrow margin of BNDA even further. There are reportedly plans to limit the amount that any individual or union may deposit in a remunerated account.

The village banks offer three deposit products: unremunerated sight deposits, which are only safeguarded and not used as loanable funds; term deposits up to five years with interest rates of 5–10 per cent depending on the duration; and ROSCA (rotating savings and credit association) savings (*dépôt à terme pari*, DTP)[11] with interest rates of 3–5 per cent depending on the duration. CAREC estimates the average cost of internal funds at 4.9 per cent + 1 per cent savings mobilization costs, which is lower than the costs of borrowing from BNDA.

There are three functions of bank linkages of the CVECA-ON network: The first and main function is expansion of the portfolio; a second and minor function is liquidity balancing – the reverse of the order in Kafo Jiginew. In 2004, onlending funds through the network as a wholesaler has been added as a third function.

Portfolio expansion

The village banks were reportedly established in the expectation of refinancing by BNDA; the very first ones obtained their loans only two months after their establishment: 'Sans le refinancement les caisses n'existeraient pas' *(A. Cissé, CAREC, 2005)*. According to balance sheet data for 2003, borrowing from BNDA constitutes 64 per cent of loans outstanding, member deposits 30 per cent. The loan portfolio is divided according to source of funds (not shown on the balance sheet): loans from external funds (BNDA) account for 57 per cent, loans from internal funds for 43 per cent. In 2004 the loan portfolio reportedly grew by 59 per cent; 56 per cent of the 2004 portfolio is refinanced by BNDA. Bank borrowing thus more than doubles the portfolio of the village banks. Savings reportedly do not suffice to finance the growing demand, despite the seasonal nature of the loans. Why do the farmers not save up-front every year when they sell their crop instead of borrowing and repaying after the harvest? Is it because of the absence of an emphasis on savings and of appropriate savings products?

Most loans (88 per cent in 2003) are short-term, not exceeding one year. There is a shortage of funds for medium-term loans. CAREC is involved in negotiations with BNDA in Bamako for loans up to three years (e.g., for draught animals, carts, motor cultivators, rice hullers). Due to bad experience with three-year loans, BNDA is suggesting two years as a maximum period, a saving-for-credit product with a 24-months saving period followed by a 36-months loan period.

Liquidity balancing

Bank deposits are a mere 21 per cent of bank borrowing, compared to 44 per cent in Kafo Jiginew, indicating the limited importance of liquidity balancing in CVECA-ON (December 2003). However, monthly data on bank deposits and borrowing was not available to demonstrate this in full detail.

CVECA-ON as a wholesaler

In 2004 the gross loan portfolio grew by €1.5m from €2.6m to €4.1m. €0.9m of that amount are funds provided to CVECA-ON as a wholesaler to Fasojigi, an organization of paddy farmers in the area of the Office du Niger, assisted by the Cereal Marketing Assistance Program (PACCEM) and financed by the Canadian International Development Agency, (CIDA). The program has an ingenious structure, integrated into the village banking system: BNDA lends the resources to the three unions, which lend to 23 participating village banks These in turn lend, in legal terms, to Fasojigi, but disburse the loans to the 2,212 members of Fasojigi, who may or may not be members of a village bank. Fasojigi, to be eligible as a borrower, becomes a member of each of the 23 village banks involved. Fasojigi guarantees the repayment and has deposited a guarantee fund of €91,500 in the unions.

Institution-building in general and training of the staff of village banks and their unions was provided until 2001 by CIDR. Since then it has been provided by CAREC and fully paid for by AFD through BNDA, without any local contribution. BNDA also finances the audits of CAREC, the unions and the village banks, implemented by a private auditing firm, as well as the preparation of a business plan. Guidance by CIDR continues to be available from its representative office in Bamako. A visit to the German Raiffeisen banking system has been supported by GTZ. Capacity building is thus a function of donor support, not of bank linkages.

Self-reliance vs donor dependence

The different players in the Mali microfinance linkages have all benefited from the financial linkage. The managing director of CAREC, speaking on behalf of the village banks, states that: 'Our outreach is fully due to the availability of bank refinance'. For BNDA a major advantage of working through the village banking network has been that, in contrast to former schemes of retail lending with their high default rates, the bank is now experiencing full repayment on time. However, the number of MFI clients is negligible, and accounts for only 2.9 per cent of BNDA's disbursements. At the same time, from the viewpoint of the target population, the new credit discipline is increasingly reaching marginal clients who would previously have defaulted on individual loans from BNDA and become unbankable.

On the impact side three key effects are observed: There is a substantial increase in overall outreach; the credit portfolio is performing well; and there is an increased coverage of marginal clients. There are, however, a number of remaining challenges at the village bank level.

There is a striking difference between CVECA-ON, which links up with banks to expand its portfolio, and Kafo Jiginew, which uses bank funds mainly for liquidity balancing. What is the impact of this difference in strategies on growth in terms of savings mobilization and loans outstanding? Both networks operate in comparable environments; there is not much difference in terms of total assets per individual member (€143 in Kafo Jiginew, €123 in CVECA-ON); and both have access to banks. Is it because of the initial and continual availability of ample donor credit lines in the first case and a policy of self-reliance in the latter? If so, this hypothesis might explain the difference in terms of propensity to save: virtually all members (96 per cent) of the Kafo Jiginew cooperatives save, and they save significantly more (€74 per member) compared to the members of CVECA-ON, less than half of whom (44 per cent) have a savings account, with average savings per member of just €28 (Table 9.11). Moreover, the Kafo Jiginew cooperatives are far more dynamic than the CVECA-ON village banks in terms of growth of client deposits during 2001–3 (69 per cent vs –1 per cent) and growth of loans outstanding (85 per cent vs. 17 per cent). A sequel to our first question is thus: Does donor generosity lead to MFI complacency in terms of savings mobilization and a slow-down of growth?

Chao-Béroff (2003), *spiritus rector* of village banking in Mali through CIDR, raises the same issue by asking 'Mobilizing Rural Savings to Reinforce the MFI or to Reinforce the Client?' She tentatively concludes that there is a 'lack of incentive mechanisms and adapted products...the highest performing MFIs should be encouraged to develop and market (this type of savings). In rural areas, saving for productive self-financing has a future, especially as a financing mechanism for agricultural activities.' This is indeed the conclusion to be drawn from comparing the two networks.

Finally, it is interesting to reflect on the temporary versus permanent nature of these linkages. We may ask: After twenty years of bank linkages, 'will backward linkages with donors become superfluous, if not hazardous?' With BIM willing to lend more to MFIs but meeting a limited demand, and BMS newly entering the market as the designated bank of MFIs, are donor credit lines still needed to refinance BNDA? It appears that they have played an important role in the first stage of the evolution of microfinance in Mali. They may now be taken over by

Table 9.11 Bank borrowing and member deposits in Kafo Jiginew and CVECA-ON, 2003

	Kafo Jiginew	*CVECA-ON*
Bank borrowing in per cent of loans outstanding	33	57
Depositors in per cent of members	96	44
Deposits per MF unit in €	94,700	14,300
Deposits per member in €	74	28
Growth of client deposits, 2001–3, in per cent	69	−1
Growth of loans outstanding, 2001–3, in per cent	85	17

domestic banks, marking the second stage of evolution. Given the availability of additional loan funds from national banks in Mali and the risk of a devaluation, it is questionable whether hard currency loans, a substitute for domestic resources made attractive by a lower interest rate, are still good policy. The coming of the third, and ultimate, stage has already been announced: the establishment of a bank of its own by the largest network of MFIs, and thus the incorporation of linkages within that apex institution.

Notes

1 The study is based on field work in Mali during 17–26 January, 2005. Unless otherwise stated figures pertain to end-2003. Currency amounts are expressed in Euro, at a fixed exchange rate of FCFA 656.
2 CMDT covers a territory of 96,000 km², with 2.8 million inhabitants.
3 Average costs of deposits: 1.5%.
4 Similarly, the PlaNet Rating study of 2003, with last data for June 2002, gives a contrasting lopsided picture. The semi-annual data reported in Table 9.8 are taken from that study.
5 The rationale is psychological: 'Our loans we pay back; if we withdraw our savings, we waste our money'.
6 Monthly data are only reported for the total of external resources and not broken down by domestic and external borrowings.
7 CIDR maintains an office in Bamako, which continues to provide technical assistance to the networks after they have attained financial autonomy.
8 To cover the costs of CAREC the village banks have to pay €550,000 per annum, or €1,1000 each.
9 PAR (>3 months) of the three unions is 3.9% in Macina, 5.9% in Kalari and 2.5% in Kouroumari.
10 The CVECA networks are shareholders of BMS, which lends at 7%, but so far have remained loyal to BNDA.
11 *Pari* is the Bambara term for rotating savings and credit association or *tontine*, an indigenous informal financial institution. Traditionally, a *pari* is a system of regular standardized savings, with the total allocated to one member at a time in turn. One cycle usually covers as many time periods (e.g. days, weeks, months) as there are members; there is no interest payment. In the case of DTP, a person saves fixed amounts regularly in the village bank, mostly for a period of six months, after which he may withdraw the total, plus an interest margin. There are no doorstep services.

References

Adler, M. (2001) 'Village banks in Mali', in *D+C Development and Cooperation*. (1): 18–20.
Agence Française de Développement (AFD) (2004) *Rapport Annuel 2003*, Paris.
AFD/DEG, Mission d'évaluation Mali, unpublished report, 2004

Banque Malienne de Solidarité (2005) *Situation des emplois et des ressources au 31 Décembre 2004*, BNDA, Bamako.

Banque Nationale de Développement Agricole du Mali (BNDA) (2002) *Revue et bilan des actions de la BNDA en faveur de la microfinance au Mali (1998–2001)*, Bamako.

BNDA (2003) *Rapport Annuel 2002*, Bamako.

BNDA (2004a) *Rapport Annuel 2003*, Bamako.

BNDA (2004b) 'Octrois de crédit BNDA aux SFD, 1997–2003'. Mission d'évaluation AFD/DEG, Bamako.

Interview with A. Cissé, CAREC, January 2005

Cellule d'Appui et de Suivi des Systèmes Financiers Décentralisés (CAS/SFD) (2004) *Rapport Annuel 2003*, Bamako.

Chao-Béroff, R. (2003) 'Rural Savings Mobilization in West Africa: Guard against Shocks or Build an Asset Base', *MicroBanking Bulletin*: 16–17.

Centre International de Développement et de Recherche (CIDR) (2004) *Microfinance et Développement – Cellule Nationale de Diffusion et d'Appui des Systèmes Financiers Décentralisés au Mali*, Note de présentation, Bamako.

Réseau des Caisses Villageoises d'Épargne et de Crédit Autogérées en Zone Office du Niger (CVECA-ON) (2004) *Rapport Annuel d'Activités 2003*, Niono, Mali.

Fruman, C. and Seibel, H. D. (1995) *Stratégie Nationale de Diffusion des Réseaux Financiers Décentralisés au Mali*, GTZ, Eschborn.

Groupement Européen des Caisses d'Epargne, avec la Caisse Nationale des Caisses d'Epargne, France (GECE) (2004) *Evaluation du Plan d'Action National de la Micro Finance 1999–2002. Projet de Développement du Secteur Financier, Groupe Consultatif National pour la Microfinance*. Ministère de l'Economie et des Finances, Bamako.

International Monetary Fund (IMF) (2003) 'Mali: Poverty Reduction Strategy Paper', *Country Report 9*, Washington D.C.

Kafo Jiginew (2004a) *Rapport Annuel 2003*, Koutiala.

Kafo Jiginew (2004b) *Etude de Rentabilité des Caisses de Kafo Jiginew 2003*, Koutiala

Kafo Jiginew (2004c) *Rapport Annuel Inspection Générale 2003*, Koutiala

Kafo Jiginew (2004d) *Rapport sur l'Exploitation 2003*, Koutiala.

Ministère du Développement Rural (MDR) (2001) *Le nouvel Office du Niger*. Bamako, Éditions Jamana, 11–12, 5–6

Planet Finance (2003), PlaNet Rating Kafo Jiginew, http://www.planetrating.com/FR/rapport.php [accessed October 2007]

Republic of Mali (2004) *Report of the First Year of Implementation of the Poverty Reduction Strategic Paper (PRSP)*.

Samassékou, S. (2000) *Final Report of the Study on Intermediation between Banks and MFIs in Mali*. Weidemann Associates, Arlington VA, USA.

Wonou, C. and Diakite, B. (2004) *Plan de développement à moyen terme des CVECA Office du Niger (2004–2007)*, CAREC – Centre d'appui au réseau d'épargne et de credit, Niono.

CHAPTER 10

Partnership to expand sources of funds for rural microfinance in Peru: The case of Confianza

Janina León

Abstract

This study explores the way a regulated microfinance institution in Peru, Confianza, links to external partners to expand its sources of funds. The author discusses the impact of recent microfinance regulation on the opportunities for Confianza to diversify its sources of funds. The author states that, in the Peruvian context, regulation plays a significant role in the type and nature of financial linkages MFIs can engage in. Regulated MFIs, like Confianza, have greater access to funds from international investors, commercial banks and the government backed apex organization, COFIDE, than non-regulated NGOs. For purposes of comparison the author discusses briefly the challenges faced by ARARIWA, a non-regulated financial NGO, in obtaining funds on a sustained basis.

Introduction

While rural people need access to financial services, the supply of such services in rural areas is extremely limited due to the high costs and risks associated with providing them. In Peru, as well as in other countries, some local organizations are making great strides in expanding access to credit in remote areas due to their informational advantages and innovative lending practices and systems. However, their efforts are often constrained. Unable to mobilize deposits and access external funding on a sustained basis, especially through commercial channels, these organizations have limited resources from which to expand their outreach. Among their efforts to overcome these restrictions, some microfinance institutions (MFIs) have established linkages with the formal financial sector. The main objective of this study is to examine these financial linkages between different financial institutions and how far they helped to expand services provision in rural areas.

This study primarily explores the ways in which a regulated MFI, Confianza, has linked with external partners to expand its sources of funds. The case focuses on Confianza's organizational type, and, given its type, the potential to diversify sources of funds, operate efficiently and penetrate rural areas. The experience of another MFI, a non-regulated financial NGO, ARARIWA, is briefly presented for comparison purposes.

In the sections that follow a brief presentation of the context of Peru is presented, followed by a detailed description of the Peruvian financial system, identifying the main microfinance actors and products. The next section largely examines the experience of the regulated MFI, Confianza, including an analysis of its linkage types, motivations, mechanisms, their role in its institutional capacity strengthening and financial outcomes as well as its outreach performance. A summarized reference to the NGO Arariwa is included to compare both institutions in terms of their linkages impact on rural outreach. The chapter concludes with a presentation on the main lessons learnt, some reflections about possible trade-offs between organizational type and subsequent effects on rural penetration, and the need for further empirical research.

Country context

Peru is located in South America, next to the South Pacific Ocean and bordering Chile, Ecuador, Colombia, Brazil and Bolivia. Its wide geographical diversity allows it to have more than twenty microclimate areas, from temperate to dry desert near the coast, frigid and dry weather in the Andes Mountains, and tropical temperatures in the jungle. Peruvian natural resources include mineral and metal (copper, gold, zinc) reserves, ample coastal waters for fishing, and highlands for growing high quality coffee. Agriculture is very heterogeneous, including non-tradable peasant production and larger units producing for exports. The Peruvian economy is largely driven by exports of minerals, textiles, and agricultural products. Given this, the country's growth is heavily vulnerable to world price fluctuations in copper, zinc, gold, petroleum, coffee and oil, despite public policies to strengthen native industries.

Approximately 27 million people live in Peru (2005 estimate), largely descendents of Spanish settlers and native Inca and pre-Inca cultures. Due to high rural-urban migration that took place from the 1960s through to the 1980s, seven out of ten Peruvians live in urban areas. The population density is, on average, 20 people per square kilometre. The population is unevenly distributed, with overcrowding taking place in many urban centres, like Lima, while mountainous regions and jungle areas remain sparsely populated. Microenterprises have multiplied mostly in urban areas, becoming the main source of income for the labour force. For several decades, poverty has been spread along the country, with extreme poverty largely located in rural areas, mostly in the Trapecio Andino area.

Since the dramatic economic conditions of recession and hyperinflation of the 1980s, Peru has experienced a sustained period of macroeconomic growth and recovery during the 1990s and 2000s (see Figure 10.1). With a stable exchange rate, low inflation, low-risk premium on Peruvian bonds, prudent fiscal policies, and openness for trade, Peru has become an attractive place for

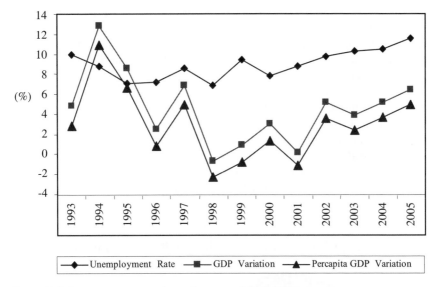

Figure 10.1 Peru: macroeconomic performance 1992–2005
Source: Author's elaboration, based on Banco Central de Reserva del Peru (2005) and Ministerio de Trabajo (2005), with unemployment data for Lima Metropolitana.

foreign investment (CIA Factbook, 2005; Banco Central de Reserva del Peru, 2005).

However, economic gains have not been shared by all segments of the population. Although formal employment increased in number during this period, underemployment and unemployment increased more. Statistics also show that approximately 50 per cent of the population has remained poor, with the poorest concentrated in rural areas (CIA Factbook, 2005; Banco Central de Reserva del Peru, 2005).

Financial system and microfinance in Peru

Financial services in Peru are provided by diverse institutions and agents in the market. By 2005, the Peruvian financial system consisted of 11 commercial banks, 38 regulated MFIs, four government apex and first-tier banks, 13 insurance companies, four pension fund firms and nine other financial institutions. The MFIs include 13 municipal banks (CMACs), 12 *cajas rurales* (CRACs) and 13 EDPYMEs (Entidad de Desarrollo de la Pequeña y Micro Empresa). All regulated financial institutions are under supervision of the Superintendencia de Banca y Seguros (SBS), following regulatory guidelines set by Basel and audited in compliance with internationally accepted auditing standards, having customer deposits backed by their common deposit insurance fund (Superintendencia de Banca y Seguros, 2005).

As expected, commercial banks have most of the market share in terms of loans and deposits (COFIDE, 2004). Based upon their loan portfolio, Figure 10.2 provides the market participation of regulated institutions: commercial banks count for around 80 per cent of the market, while MFI supply almost 10 per cent of total market when looking at loan portfolios. The picture changes, however, when looking at the sector by number of loan contracts institutions hold. In this way, commercial banks and MFIs serve 50 per cent and 25 per cent of the market, respectively. Thus, as one would expect, large loans are common among commercial bank clientele, while small loans are mostly issued by MFIs.

Commercial banks and MFIs target different loan clientele. As shown in Figure 10.3: commercial banks lend for business, housing and consumption, accounting for almost 75 per cent of their loan clientele. MFIs, on the other hand, primarily lend for microenterprise development and personal

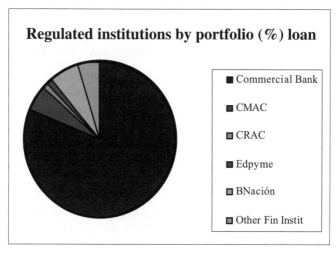

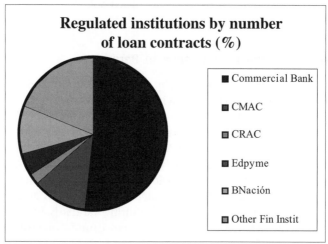

Figure 10.2 Regulated financial institutions and their loan market share

consumption, roughly 80 per cent of the loans they grant. Still commercial banks are the main suppliers of loans for business and microenterprise development in the market, in terms of loan volume.

Several regulatory and macroeconomic events have shaped the current MFI industry in Peru. In 1996, in an attempt to organize and manage a burgeoning microfinance sector, the Government of Peru (GoP) revised the banking laws to favor NGOs to become regulated MFIs, in essence requiring them to become private sector institutions, regulated and supervised by the SBS. The impetus for the new microfinance regulation, some believe, was that the government, wanting to support micro and small enterprises, felt that a well-managed microfinance sector could be a sustainable system to invest in these enterprises (Alvarado and Galarza, 2003; Leon, 2001). The Peruvian regulatory framework

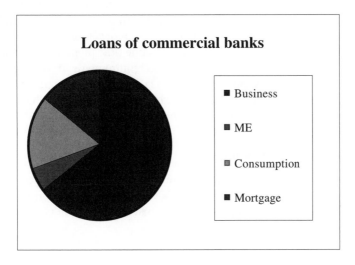

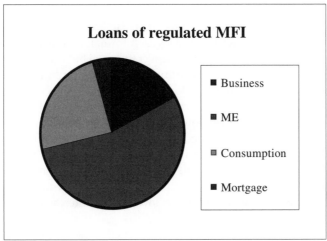

Figure 10.3 Regulated financial institutions by type of loan clientele

for formal microfinance institutions sets specific rules regarding key financial ratios and provisions, granting well performing MFIs the legal status to take deposits. However to date, none of the EDPYMEs have been awarded this privilege due to a rather conservative approach of the SBS regarding this segment of the MFI market (Interview with an SBS official, 2006).

Besides the formal institutions previously described, we find semiformal institutions and informal channels providing financial services, mostly loans (Trivelli et.al, 2004). Semi-formal institutions, such as savings and credit cooperatives are under direct or delegated supervision of SBS, while NGOs are not financially regulated. Specialized NGOs supply very small loans in rural and urban areas (Portocarrero et.al, 2002; Valdivia, 1995). The Consortium of Private Organizations to Promote the Development of Small and Micro Enterprises (COPEME) plays an informal supervisory role to its financial NGO members by monitoring their financial and institutional outcomes as well as by providing training, resources and advice on sector developments. This helps to organize the semiformal sector while at the same time prepares NGO members wanting to become formal MFIs to meet SBS requirements. Informal financial channels include input suppliers, commercial traders, moneylenders, *panderos* and *juntas* (Peruvian rotating savings and credit associations – ROSCAs), and other family networks, and operate without any supervision.

Financial linkages of Confianza

In this section, Confianza's financial linkages are reviewed. In particular, its linkage types and actors are presented as well as the motivation for creating financial linkages and the impact they have had on sustainability and outreach, in particular rural outreach.

Linkage types and actors

Two broad types of linkages are proposed: facilitating linkages and direct linkages. A facilitation linkage involves an informal institution engaged by a formal one to act on its behalf, while a direct financial linkage involves a formal institution helping an informal institution to diversify its funding sources and/ or balance its liquidity through bulk loans, lines of credit and savings instruments (Pagura and Kirsten, 2006). In this case, because Confianza developed multiple linkages, two more types are proposed here, related to their purpose and funding use: equity linkage and assistance linkage. Equity linkages involve a longer term engagement of the formal institution to the informal institution. In some cases, staff of the formal institution will serve on the board of the MFI it has invested in. An assistance linkage pertains to a formal institution, often non-financial, issuing a one-time grant or low to zero interest loan for specific technical assistance purposes.

Confianza has created linkages with several public and private sectors partners, both locally and internationally. Table 10.1 presents the multiple

---

Box 10.1 Confianza – Conquering formal microfinance market to persist serving rural outreach

Confianza is an EDPYME headquartered in Huancayo city located 300 km from Lima, in the middle of the Andes highlands. Huancayo is one of Peru's major commercial and agricultural centres, marketing and shipping wheat, corn, potatoes and barley to the rest of the country. Confianza has six branch offices, four located nearby Andean small cities and two in poor neighborhoods of Lima.

History and business environment preconditions

Confianza was created based upon the agricultural lending experience and resources of Separ, a rural NGO providing education and credit services to the poor. In 1998, following the SBS incentives, Separ transformed its five-year-old agricultural lending program into the regulated EDPYME Confianza, complying with the stricter SBS regulation rules for formal MFI (Pearce and Reinsch, 2005; interview with the CEO of Confianza, August 2005). By 1999, Confianza faced a severe delinquency crisis in which more than 50 per cent of their loan portfolio was at risk for default. In order to address the crisis Confianza knew it had to make some difficult operational and managerial decisions.

Strategies and financial linkages

By 2000, keeping basic institutional goals of sustainability and outreach, Confianza implemented an overall organizational reengineering, including changes in its institutional management, funding policies for liabilities and equity, and lending technology and client approach. New funding strategies involved seeking all possible external financial sources, whether local or international ones. Confianza partners are formal and semiformal local financial institutions, international banks and organizations, acting as lenders and shareholders. Non-financial links involve advocators, observers and international leaders, all as institutional friends. During the last six years, positive results include outstanding financial performance and increasing numbers of poor outreach, rural outreach, as shown in its annual reports.

---

financial linkages in which Confianza has been engaged. Establishing a range of partnerships has been an integral part of its strategic growth and development plans. These linkages have helped to maintain and even increase its rural outreach over the years.

It is evident that Confianza relies heavily on financial linkages to fund its loan activities since it is unable to mobilize deposits. Facilitating linkages have involved low financial resources from formal MFIs (e.g. Caja Municipal de Huancayo) and larger banks (e.g. Banco de Materiales) although these partnerships are short-lived. Direct linkages with formal institutions have been the dominant type of linkage used by Confianza, including commercial banks (e.g. Banco Wiese, Banco Continental, Interbank), public apexes (e.g. Cofide and Agrobanco) and other institutions (Foncodes), international organizations (e.g. Corporacion Andina de Fomento, CAF) and private socially motivated banks (e.g. OikoCredit, Hivos-Triodos). In addition, Confianza has created equity linkages with international investors (e.g. Interfin, Alterfin), as well as a small number of local investors, notably its parent NGO, SEPAR, and individuals. Technical assistance needs also induced Confianza to become partners with the Inter-American Development Bank (IADB).

Table 10.1 Confianza: linkage types and main partners, 2005

Type of linkages	Private sector	Public sector		
	Local institutions	International institutions	Apex and state-owned banks	Other public institutions
F: Facilitating	• Caja Municipal Huancayo, • EDPYME Raíz		• Banco de Materiales	Water and other public utilities (private) firms
D: Direct	• Banco Wiese, • Banco Continental • Interbank	• Corporacion Andina de Fomento CAF, • CreditoSud, • Oikocredit, • Hivos-Triodos Fonds, • Dexia, • Microvest, • LaCif', • Oikos, • Novib	• Cofide • Agrobanco	• Foncodes
E: Equity	• NGO Separ, • Notable local individuals	• Incofin • Volksvermogern • Fundación Gilles • Alterfin • SIDI • Folade • Novib, • Triodos	—	—
A: Assistance	—	• Interamerican Development Bank – Fomin	—	—

Source: MicroRate Report, December 2004; Confianza – Annual Memory (2004 and 2005).

Notably, Confianza has been particularly successful in solidifying partnerships with international financial investors and partners. The following is a description of its most salient partnerships:

TRIODOS

- An international funding organization, self-defined as socially responsible bank to the microfinance sector, values the professional provision of financial services to microentrepreneurs as key for local economic development in developing countries.
- Through different funds, TRIODOS provides equity and debt, as well as its expertise in sustainable banking, to microfinance institutions.
- In 2000, when contacted, TRIODOS considered Confianza too small for consideration. Instead, Confianza asked for 2-year period to show better

portfolio results. After this span and good results, TRIODOS visited Confianza in the field and by 2003 issued credit lines.
- Since that time, TRIODOS has renewed its credit lines to Confianza given its continual positive financial evaluations as reported by Microrate.

OIKOS

- OIKOS is a Dutch privately owned cooperative society that works with (church and church-organization) private investors to fund socially responsible investments.
- Its main mechanism of operation is issuing loans for development, mostly to microfinance institutions, but also to cooperatives and small and medium enterprises, to support projects with cooperative perspective, women's participation, environmental preservation and impact on community.
- Confianza contacted OIKOS in 2000 and obtained a US$150,000 first loan for focusing on rural women in the Peruvian highlands with poor financial access. Because of satisfactory outcomes, additional loans have been issued and paid in the following years, helping Confianza to establish itself as a regulated MFI.
- By 2004, OIKOS became a shareholder of Confianza, with an important equity participation.

NOVIB

- NOVIB is a Netherlands-based organization that partners and works with Oxfam International and has as its main goal to eradicate world poverty and exclusion. Beside advocacy and awareness campaigns, NOVIB supports local development projects initiated by private organizations in developing countries.
- In 2000, Confianza motivated NOVIB with its institutional outcomes regarding rural credit, women's involvement and work in the Peruvian central highlands. In 2001, after an in-field third-party consultation, NOVIB visited Confianza and issued a credit line for US$400 million.
- By 2002–3, and because of good results, NOVIB also funded impact and institutional strengthening studies for Confianza.
- *In 2004, on Confianza's invitation, NOVIB became shareholder for a period of six years.*

IADB – FOMIN

- As an investment fund of IADB, FOMIN is designed to channel donations and capital investment for private sector development, including development of micro and small micro-enterprises.
- The main FOMIN mechanism of operation is technical assistance by funding a group of projects for institutional development.

- In 2001, following an international competition, Confianza obtained a non-reimbursable technical aid grant for institutional strengthening, including activities of institutional technical assistance, training courses and software improvement.
- This FOMIN agreement contributed US$190 000 to the MFI while Confianza committed US$140 000 to the technical assistance project.

In conclusion, Confianza linkage strategy has been intense, generating a large, diversified set of formal and informal financial partner organizations. This has been a feature of this MFI general strategy for funding its financial activities. This overall strategy has allowed the MFI to overcome challenges of being legally allowed to mobilize deposits, which has impacted positively on its ability to attend to its non-conventional clientele in rural areas.

Linkage motivations

As mentioned in Box 10.1, Confianza established a range of financial linkages and partnerships in an effort to fund its ambitious, long-term growth plans. First, Confianza, in an effort to deal with a severe delinquency crisis in 1999 and to meet performance indicators set by the SBS, substantially reorganized itself, focusing on financial and operational sustainability. Faced with an inability to mobilize deposits on its own, Confianza soon realized that establishing sustained linkages with local and international partners was the only way that it could achieve its performance outcomes. By 2000, Confianza engaged itself in a very aggressive campaign within the country and abroad, to involve formal local and international institutions as partners to increase its funding resources. After five years we may conclude that these linkages have helped Confianza to become a competitive formal MFI, serving an increasing rural clientele.

Contracting mechanics

Confianza met many challenges in setting up appropriate contracts with its external partners, especially those abroad. To deal with the challenges head on, Confianza would often send its General Manager, Elizabeth Minaya, to work out the contracting issues in person. Almost all of Confianza's international investors are socially oriented banks, pursuing social goals of sustainable banking, poverty eradication, microenterprise development. In other words, Confianza and its partners have a shared vision which helps to negotiate fair contract terms in the end. The contracting process is relatively straightforward and is based upon Confianza's financial outcomes and outreach. First, Confianza applies for a first credit line with the objective of extending credit to the population that the investor is interested in targeting. The loan application review process ensues, which may include an in-field third party evaluation (as in the case of Novib). If accepted, Confianza works out the terms and conditions of the loan contract as well as the responsibilities of each party in the management of the loan. Typically, any risk from management is assumed by Confianza. The investor requires that an impact evaluation be conducted at the end of each debt cycle.

After full repayment, Confianza provides the investor with its portfolio and impact evaluation results. This is often followed by an in-country visit by the international partner to Confianza headquarters in Huancayo. In some cases, international investors make equity investments in Confianza. This was the case for Triodos and Oikos banks when they became shareholder investors in Confianza in 2003 and 2004 respectively. Under these equity linkages, institutional risks and profits are shared, in relation to the participation owned. By 2005, foreign shareholders held around 60 per cent of Confianza's equity, with no one partner possessing a dominant share.

A potential weakness in the direct and equity linkages is the conditions set by international partners in terms of lending to a specific target group or to operate in a certain manner. These conditions sometimes do not allow Confianza to make its own choices freely. Confianza has addressed this challenge to some degree by accessing funds through local, commercial providers. However, there are drawbacks to this approach because Peruvian commercial banks and apex organizations lend relatively small amounts for short periods of time. Thus, linkages with local providers have helped in funding their expansion issues, but have not had a significant impact on Confianza's rural outreach.

Its role in capacity building

It appears that financial linkages with a range of partners have helped Confianza achieve its outreach and growth targets. Significant organizational transformations have occurred mostly since 2000, after most linkages with foreign institutions were set.

One notorious characteristic that also helped was Confianza's effort in distancing itself from its past NGO-heritage, in terms of management. While competing with other formal MFIs and meeting the SBS requirements, Confianza had to enforce operational and financial efficiency in its institutional perspective. Such changes also involved policies for human capital improvement, incorporating more professionals onto the staff. Adjustments to the salary payments and incentives were also included.

Still, Confianza was committed to serving its rural clientele, as demonstrated by its target of maintaining at least 20 per cent of its loan portfolio for rural clients. Confianza knew that in order to meet this goal it would have to gain access to additional funds, locally and from abroad. Its outreach growth policy included the opening of new branches in rural and poor peri-urban areas of Lima. The financial linkages it established were instrumental in the organization achieving its targets.

Confianza has become an important MFI in the Peruvian market, including formal microfinance markets in rural and urban areas, and that is remarkable. Still some institutional problems are pending, and may be summarized as follows:

first, heavy dependence on one-person leadership for institutional policies, decisions, contacts, vision, and so on, with potential problems of delegation, and second, its investment in physical resources is still modest, with significantly low productivity of infrastructure, compared to other MFIs.

Financial outcomes

What are the main results of the overall strategy implemented by Confianza, more specifically after its engagement in multiple financial linkages over the last several years? Updated financial information provides interesting information on this question as presented in Table 10.2.

In terms of profitability, a low positive return on assets (ROA) and higher, but volatile return on equity (ROE) are observed, showing stable profitability of the MFI. During this period, Confianza has been financially self-sufficient, covering all of its financial costs. Still operational self-sufficiency problems have arisen after 2003, probably associated with new branches in further areas, including rural areas. By 2005 Confianza's overall operating expenses to outstanding portfolio ratio was 12.5 per cent, decreasing but still above the market average. Loan officer productivity has increased on average, becoming triple the value for 1999. Growth of the loan activity and number of clientele, improvements in the credit technology and better positioning in the market may explain these results. In terms of the portfolio quality, its portfolio at risk ratio is moderate (almost 5 per cent) and, at times, volatile. However, Confianza has decreased this ratio since 2004 and its portfolio write-offs are low and have been decreasing since 2003.

The performance indicators of Confianza's agricultural portfolio are presented in Table 10.3. Between 2000 and 2005, both the number of agricultural clients and the number of outstanding loans have multiplied five times, while the overall agricultural portfolio practically tripled. There is one remarkable difference between the evolution of the overall portfolio and the agricultural portfolio. The portfolio at-risk is slightly decreasing for the overall portfolio, but increasing for the agricultural portfolio, which explains a slightly higher default rate for agricultural loans as one would expect.

Outreach

It is well-known that Confianza has continued serving its rural clientele while expanding into new, urban markets. In diversifying its loan portfolio, coupled with a sound re-organization of its operational and managerial systems, Confianza has protected itself against default crises of the past. Finding financial backers with a shared outreach vision and strategy has been a key factor in this success.

In terms of economic activity, almost 50 per cent of the loans were for retail trade, 20 per cent for agriculture and 9 per cent for personal services; by gender, 46 per cent were issued for women. Confianza strategies included a minimum

Table 10.2 Confianza: key financial indicators, 1999–2005

June 1999–December 2005	1999	2000	2001	2002	2003	2004	2005
Sustainability/profitability							
Adjusted return on assets (%)[b]	−6.80%	5.10%	5.10%	3.50%	2.8%	0.95%	3.10%
Adjusted return on equity (%)[b]	−13.40%	18.50%	22.50%	18.70%	15.4%	5.39%	18.06%
Operational self-sufficiency (%)	NA	1.55	1.73	1.75	1.84	0.85	0.89
Financial self-sufficiency (%)	NA	1.22	1.35	1.22	1.24	1.23	1.49
Operational efficiency							
Operating expenses as % of portfolio	102.60%	19.70%	16.40%	15.90%	14.30%	13.76%	12.54%
Number of clients per loan officer[2]	172	328	383	378	416	372	626
Number of borrowers per staff [2]	NA	94	134	147	174	248	233
Portfolio quality							
Portfolio at risk > 30 days as % of portfolio[1]	NA	0.20%	4.50%	4.20%	3.40%	4.67%	2.63%
Write-offs as % of average gross portfolio	NA	1.10%	1.50%	0.90%	1.52%	1.29%	0.88%
Outreach							
Number of loans outstanding	686	2,473	3,650	5,290	10,411	17,131	37,575
Outstanding gross portfolio (US$)	391,000	1,495,083	2,699,332	4,407,154	7,967,678	13,468,588	21,533,771
Average outstanding loan size (US$)	570	608	695	833	765	786	573
Average loan size as % of GDP/per capita	28%	29%	34%	35%	37%	51.30%	38.33%
Exchange rate							
Nuevos soles/US$	3.33	3.52	3.44	3.51	3.46	3.28	3.463
Inflation	3.47	3.76	1.98	0.19	2.26	3.66	1.5

Sources: *CGAP (2005)*; MicroRate Report, *December 2004*; Confianza – Annual Report *2004 and 2005*. NA, no available data.
[1]Includes loan losses written off of Pampas Branch office as of 31 December 2004.
[2]Includes credit promoters and analysts.

Table 10.3 Confianza: indicators for its agricultural portfolio

June 1999–December 2005	1999	2000	2001	2002	2003	2004	2005
Number of active clients	682	631	671	2,148	3063	3,102	3,501
Number of active loans	791	1,085	1,300	2,195	3,011	2,952	3,253
Active portfolio (US$)	559,394	913,713	1,280,407	2,094,578	2,182,842	2,529,564	2,631,646
Average loan size (US$)	707	842	985	954	794	905	831
Portfolio at risk > 30 days[1]	NA	1.00%	3.30%	3.30%	10.28%	9.91%	9.53%
Agriculture as % of total portfolio	37%	34%	29%	26%	31%	21%	14%

[1]Includes loan losses written off from Pampas Branch office as of 31 December 2004.

Sources: *CGAP, 2005; MicroRate Report, December 2004; Confianza Annual Report 2004 and 2005.*

share (20 per cent) of agricultural loans in its total portfolio, and increasing penetration in other markets, included Lima. By 2004 average loan size was US$720 (and US$900 for agriculture), with more than 17,700 loans issued. By 2006, two Confianza branches were operating in a poor urban zone in Lima city, with a large presence of small retail microenterprises.

The accelerated growth of Confianza activity might be largely influenced not only by its new organizational changes but also by its linkages. Most of Confianza linkages are with international partners, who are mainly financial institutions with social perspectives. These international partners pursue the expansion of the financial supply in rural areas, peasants and women being their main constituencies.

The average loan size to per capita GDP has increased significantly, an indicator of the MFI market penetration, showing a slow but sure increase in Confianza's ability to penetrate the microfinance market. Larger penetration among clients and wider outreach may have contributed to these results. Also a significant number of old clients continue working with Confianza, partly as a consequence of an institutional fidelity programme. Still a couple of potential outreach problems may emerge: first, the vulnerability of willingness to pay from agricultural clients, a problem already experienced by Confianza in 1999 in some areas, although it appears that the internal policies that Confianza has set-up to minimize such systemic risks appear to be working. Another potential problem may have to do with the way in which the MFI deals with pressures to only court the most profitable clients, i.e. urban clients, in an effort to reduce risk and maintain sustainability. This may be less of a problem as the MFI is closely aligned with the vision of its parent-NGO, SEPAR, which is dedicated to serving rural clientele over the long-term.

Unintended consequences

As Confianza discovered, one does need to abandon one's commitment to serving rural clientele if one develops the right institutional policies and procedures. By diversifying its loan portfolio to include urban as well as rural clientele and by obtaining long-term debt and equity finance through linkages, Confianza is in a better position to serve farmers and other non-farm rural people on a sustained basis than it was in 1999. This may not have been the case if the organization decided to maintain its NGO status, rather than becoming an EDPYME. For comparison purposes only, the case of ARARIWA, an NGO, focusing on financial services and rural development, is presented in Box 10.2. It may be the case that the additional level of formality that Confianza has attained by becoming a registered EDPYME in Peru has allowed it to access funds with a range of local and international partners. ARARIWA, by contrast, has had difficulty accessing these same funds. Neither the local banks and apex organizations, nor most international investors, will lend to NGOs that are not registered as EDPYMES. This makes organizations like ARARIWA heavily dependent on grants and funds from donors.

Box 10.2 ARARIWA, an NGO for rural clientele

Brief reference

Located in the Peruvian highland Cuzco is a region with more than one million people, 54 per cent living in rural areas, with an illiteracy rate of 25 per cent. Taking advantage of its historical heritage, Cuzco has developed a vibrant tourism industry. Agriculture and locally processed products are the main economic activities of its people. Petroleum and gold, exploited by foreign firms, generate fiscal resources for the regional government.

Arariwa has operated in the region since 1985, pursuing the self-declared sustainable development of rural Cuzco by providing financial and non-financial services. Until 1994 in-kind donations from international donor agencies were its main resources. In 1999, under financial cooperation restrictions, Arariwa faced serious funding constraints. This external situation induced the NGO to make internal changes and review its organization and financial technology. The outcome of this review was the creation of the Unit of Microfinance. ARARIWA created a credit fund to pool financial resources and simplify management of its financial activities. Village banking is its predominant technology, with mid-term loans (US$50 to US$100), compulsory savings and compulsory non-financial services. Individual loans count for 15 per cent of portfolio, with larger amounts (around US$500), flexible terms and lower interest rates. With only one office, Arariwa supplies financial and non-financial (promotion, training and technical assistance) services with thirty mobile officials.

Outreach outcome

By 2005 Arariwa operated in ten Cuzco provinces, nine in rural areas, with more than 50 per cent of its population being agricultural workers and community peasants. Most of its clients are peasants, small and micro-enterprises, engaged through the village banking technology and group lending mechanisms. Women have been an important target for Arariwa, mainly those in rural areas.

Main financial linkages and contracting mechanisms

Since its inception Arariwa has relied heavily on international transfers from donors engaged with similar social perspectives on rural development. When started in 1985 the NGO engaged with donors seeking in-kind credit support. After generalized default problems from peasants and new trends in the international cooperation, by mid-1990 Arariwa moved towards seeking financial support to extend its credit schemes, courting new international donors with similar outreach goals. Financial constraints and growth plans induced the organization to seek funding from local financial institutions. However, to date, the lack of market valued collateral and non-regulated status have precluded ARARIWA from obtaining loans from the financial sector.

By 2005, more than 70 per cent of its debt finance came from one source, Plan International, an international donor that increased financial and other links with Arariwa over the years. Contrary to diversification, Arariwa has opted to 'put all its eggs in one basket', relying on one financial partner. For the time being it appears to be working. Since 2003, ARARIWA has borrowed US$450,000 with a zero interest rate for five years.

ARARIWA has minor funding partners through its linkage with a local NGO network PROMUC (Promoción de la Mujer y la Comunidad, that targets women economic participation), and another with ASDT and Inka (a Cuzco-based civil association), both counting for less than 10 per cent of its total funds.

ARARIWA's equity is largely composed of donation revenue. Donations were very large: 98 per cent in 2002, 82 per cent in 2005. Thus from the liability side, only one partner counts: Plan International, making the organization highly vulnerable to shifts in the donor's funding priorities and requirements.

Financial outcomes

ARARIWA claims a default rate of 0.6 per cent and a 100 per cent coverage of its costs. Since it is not regulated by the SBS and other regulation authorities, or a member of COPEME, the largest Peruvian NGO network, it is difficult to verify the reliability of these figures. It may be that the lack of officially recognized and accepted financial indicators has contributed to ARARIWA's difficulty in accessing commercial debt and equity finance. Recognizing this fact, ARARIWA asked Planet Rating (an international microfinance rating agency) to evaluate its financial and operational efficiency. The results were good, showing satisfactory outcomes. Even still, this report has had little impact on its ability to create financial linkages with external partners.

Conclusions

Serving non-conventional, rural, clientele, requires a large amount of financial resources for lending activities. Because MFIs face funding constraints more than other financial institutions, strategies to increase such resources in a sustainable manner help to facilitate growth and outreach objectives. Based upon two Peruvian experiences, the main inferences of this study on financial linkages are as follows:

- Because of limited equity and internal funding, external financial resources are crucial for MFIs to supply their financial services in sustainable terms. This is more urgent when outreach includes non-conventional clientele in rural areas.
- Organizational type appears to be a significant factor in an MFI's ability to access external funds and equity. Regulated MFIs have greater access to local and international investors.
- MFIs rely on linkages to fund their business growth and development objectives until they have received authorization from the banking authority to mobilize deposits. Trade-offs in time and costs may emerge when managing several linkages at the same time. Striking the right balance with a few good partners may be harder than it sounds.
- Financial linkages may have an impact on rural outreach if embedded into an overall institutional strategy of financial and operational sustainability, especially one that focuses on putting in the right mechanisms to deal with risks involved in lending for agriculture. Still these are not sufficient conditions because other determinants matter as well. Good management is also critical for incorporating more rural clientele in a sustainable manner. Effective management of external funding providers, who insist on delimiting specific outreach markets, will also affect the impact that financial linkages may have on rural outreach.

- Financial linkages facilitate increased financial activities of MFIs. Partnership with other MFIs and financial institutions in sustainable terms help the MFI to supply financial services in longer horizon while minimizing volatility risk of resources.
- Financial linkage conditions, amount and possible outreach may vary by type of partners engaged and the specific requirements and perspective of the MFIs. Other institutional conditions may also play a role in the success of the linkage.
- Financial linkages procure but do not guarantee obtaining large amounts of financial sources for lending and other services supplied to rural areas.
- The institutional framework matters for increasing financial funds to the MFI. Formal status reduces perception of the risk of entering into a contract with the MFI. Formal large financial institutions, local or international ones, prefer to do business with formal or regulated MFIs than those that are not. Formal status may appear to reduce asymmetric information problems from the MFI's point of view.
- Management best practices are also crucial to minimize risks and transaction costs in serving microenterprise and rural clientele in a sustainable manner.

References

Alvarado J. and Galarza, F. (2003) 'De ONG a EDPYME: algunos resultados del proceso', *Debate Agrario* 35: 65–104.

Banco Central de Reserva del Peru (2005) *Memoria Annual*, Lima.

CGAP (2005) *'Confianza in Peru overcomes adversity by diversifying loan portfolio'*, CGAP Agricultural Microfinance. Case Study 1.

COFIDE (2004) *Memoria anual*, Corporación Financiera del Desarrollo, Lima

León, J. (2001) *Cost Frontier Analysis of Efficiency: an application to the Peruvian Municipal Banks*, PhD Dissertation, The Ohio State University, Columbus.

Pagura, M. and Kirsten, M. (2006) 'Formal – informal financial linkages: lessons from developing countries', *Small Enterprise Development*, **17**(1), pp. 16–29.

Portocarrero, F. et al. (2002) *Microcredito en el Peru: quienes piden quienes dan*, Consorcio de Investigación Economica y Social, IEP, Lima.

Trivelli, C. et al. (2004) 'Mercado y gestion del microcredito en el Peru'. CIES, *Diagnostico y Propuesta*, 12.

Valdivia, M. (1995) 'Del Banco Agrario a las Cajas Rurales: pautas para la construcción de un nuevo sistema financiero rural', GRADE, *Notas para el debate* No. 13. Lima.

Websites

Confianza: www.edpymeConfianza.com.pe

SBS: www.sbs.gob.pe

CHAPTER 11
Financial linkages in the Philippines: constraints and success factors

Benjamin R. Quiñones, Jr

Abstract

The incidence of poverty and income inequality in the Philippines is among the highest in Asia. Microenterprises are the dominant source of employment and income for the majority of the population, but in the past an oppressive financial policy hindered the flow of small loans from formal banking institutions to micro-enterprises. This chapter examines the People's Credit and Finance Corporation (PCFC) and its linkages with downstream financial intermediaries as a successful strategy for improving the flow of financial services in the rural Philippines. It is based on an in-depth case study and is part of a global review on financial linkages conducted by the Food and Agriculture Organization (FAO) of the UN, thanks to funding from the Ford Foundation. The PCFC case was selected for this region because of its crucial role in mainstreaming microfinance in the country.

Introduction

The Philippines is an archipelago in the south-eastern part of Asia composed of 7,100 islands clustered around three major island groups: Luzon in the north, the Visayas in the centre, and Mindanao to the south. Its capital city, Manila, is located in Luzon. The Philippines has a population of approximately 86 million, 60 per cent of which resides in urban or urbanized areas, and which is growing at 1.9 per cent per year. The Philippines has one of the highest levels of income inequality in Asia, with the poorest 20 per cent of the population accounting for only 5 per cent of total income or consumption. The country's Gini concentration ratio has gone up from 0.47 in 1985 to 0.51 in 2000 (Reyes, 2002).

The incidence of poverty, measured in terms of the percentage of households unable to attain a minimum standard of living, has declined from 49.3 per cent of the total population in 1985 to 36.8 per cent in 1997, and increased slightly to 37.5 per cent in 1998 as a result of the Asian financial crisis. Poverty incidence was lowest in the National Capital Region (NCR) at 9 per cent, and much higher in less developed areas outside the NCR, such as the Autonomous Region for Muslim Mindanao (66 per cent) and the Bicol region (55 per cent). Poverty alleviation efforts in these areas, particularly in Mindanao, have been hampered by armed conflict between the government and rebel groups (Congressional Planning and Budget Department, House of Representatives, 2003).

This chapter is based on a case study (Quiñones, forthcoming) conducted for the global financial linkage study funded by the Ford Foundation and managed by the Food and Agriculture Organization (FAO) of the UN. The People's Credit and Finance Corporation (PCFC) in the Philippines was selected as one of the Asian case studies to illustrate financial linkages. This chapter examines the factors that constrained the development of microfinance in the Philippines, identifies drivers that contributed to overcoming the constraints (using PCFC as a case study), and evaluates how these drivers contributed to expanded access to financial services, as well as to the sustainability of microfinance institutions (MFIs).

Factors constraining the advance of microfinance

Repressive financial policy

The government's policy of providing subsidized credit to enhance the productivity of certain sectors, such as the small agricultural producers, severely hampered the growth of a microfinance industry in the Philippines. Private financial intermediaries (e.g. rural banks, cooperative banks, cooperatives) were used to channel subsidized credit from government programmes. According to the National Credit Council (NCC), 111 government-directed credit programmes, 13 of which were targeted at the poor, existed in 1995. An assessment by Callanta, et al. (1996) showed that these programmes were symbolic in nature and had limited outreach. The study found government credit programmes to be 'costly and unsustainable, leading to gross inefficiencies, financial market distortions and a weakening of private sector incentives to innovate.'

A similar conclusion was reached by the Philippine–German Project 'Linking Banks and Self-Help Groups in the Philippines' (PLBS). Among others, the PLBS found that government supported programmes failed since the accumulated loan arrears and loan losses made them costly and ineffective; the reliance on credit subsidies undermined the ability of banks to respond to changes in the rural financial market; and the lack of appropriate financial technology prevented financial intermediaries from overcoming the high transaction cost of lending to the rural poor. The PLBS project concluded that banks needed a conducive policy framework, appropriate and innovative financial technologies, and a well-trained and dedicated staff if they were to reach significant numbers of the poor in a sustainable way.

High transactions costs discourage banks from lending to the poor

Most commercial banks in the Philippines discriminate against small savers and rarely lend to the poor. This is because of the perception that lending to the poor is costly, a view reinforced by the costly experience of failed government credit programmes and the fact that small and medium enterprises (SMEs) have limited track records, inadequate financial records, and lack acceptable collateral and business plans.

The physical distribution of bank outlets further reflects the bias of the formal banking system in favour of the more developed and affluent areas. According to the central bank (BSP), the National Capital Region (NCR) had the highest density of banks in 2004 at 155 banks per city/municipality. This contrasts starkly with the national average bank density of five banks per municipality. In comparison, of the total 16 regions of the country, 9 regions classified as 'less developed' had the lowest bank density (1 or 2 banks per city/municipality).

The rise of the services sector

The flight of the poor from agriculture to the services sector also placed a constraint on the advance of microfinance. Traditionally, agriculture, forestry, and fishery (AFF) provided employment to the majority of the Philippine population, justifying the provision of subsidized agricultural credit to food crop producers. Since 1970, the AFF contribution to the economy has declined from one-third of the GDP in 1970 to 13.7 per cent in 2004, and its share in employment has dropped from 52.1 per cent in 1970 to 37.1 per cent in 2004. The import substitution industrialization (ISI) policy in the 1970s, poor fiscal management, high incidence of natural disasters, the El Niño phenomenon, and uncontrolled population growth particularly in the rural areas contributed to the decline in the AFF sector.

The decline of AFF's share in GDP caused average agriculture incomes to fall, with more and more farm households seeking supplementary employment and livelihoods in the services sector. As a result, the GDP share of the services sector rose from 38.6 per cent in 1970 to 53.2 per cent in 2004, and its share in employment increased from 30.9 per cent in 1970 to 47.5 per cent in 2004. On a positive note, this suggests a prominent role for the services sector in the country's fight against poverty. Since government was so focused on lending to the agricultural sector it missed the opportunity to finance the growth of the services sector.

Concentration of SMEs in low value-added activities

Despite their growing number and rise in economic importance, SMEs remain unattractive to commercial banks because, in addition to the perceived high transaction costs of lending, SMEs are involved by and large in low value-added undertakings. Over 50 per cent of SMEs were engaged in wholesale and retail trade in 2003, which includes the ubiquitous grocery stores, 'sari-sari' (variety) stores, market stalls, and food stores, while only 15 per cent were in the high value-added manufacturing sector.

However, SMEs are the biggest source of employment, contributing 67.9 per cent to the total employed in the formal sector in 2003. These figures do not even include unregistered microenterprises and off-farm income-generating activities, all operating in the informal or unregistered economy. SMEs lack access to bank credit, and did not benefit from the government's priority focus on agriculture. Access to financial services will increase the capacity of the SME sector to generate employment, including for those outside the formal economy.

Lack of technical know-how

Lending to the poor is complicated, and it often takes dedicated institutions such as rural banks and cooperatives to reach the small borrowers. However, the government introduced a group lending approach that required the formation of agricultural borrowers into groups for the purpose of facilitating the release of loans. Very little or no investment was made towards developing group cohesion and group recognition. Agricultural credit was a government instrument for stimulating food production rather than a means of supporting the small enterprises. Loans were collected at harvest time or upon the sale of farm produce, which made it difficult for the lender to collect since the borrower may already have spent a good part of the proceeds on meeting household needs or to pay other loans. The government's group lending experiment ended in failure as accumulated loan arrears rendered the system unsustainable. Around one-third of all rural and cooperative banks were closed down by the Central Bank of the Philippines in the late 1980s because of severe loan arrears.

The persistent failure in delivering credit to the poor in a sustainable way created the impression that banking with the poor was not feasible on a commercial basis. Without a government subsidy, the banking sector was not motivated at all to lend to the poor.

Negative attitude towards poverty lending

Two pioneering NGO MFIs (i.e. Ahon Sa Hirap, Inc. (ASHI) in Laguna, Southern Luzon; and the Negros Women for Tomorrow Foundation, Inc., in Bacolod, Western Visayas) experimented with Grameen Bank replicas as early as 1986. In those early years it was believed that Grameen replication was costly, heavily dependent on external grants, and not likely to achieve financial self-sufficiency.

Non-Grameen MFIs (i.e. NGOs, cooperatives, and rural banks) were not inclined to adopt the Grameen philosophy, and considered their own systems and procedure for delivering credit to the poor to be more suitable to the local environment. The credit unions were particularly critical of the compulsory savings scheme of Grameen since they underscored the effectiveness of their voluntary savings mobilization programmes. Although credit cooperatives and cooperative banks admitted the weaknesses in their collection performance, they were quick to point out the dependence of Grameen replicators on external grants, their limited outreach, and their lack of sustainability. It took over 10 years for the Philippine MFIs to overcome their scepticism and embark on their own modified models of the essential Grameen.

Factors contributing to the success of microfinance
Deregulated policy environment

In the early 1990s the government introduced a broad range of liberalization reforms in the trade, industrial, and financial sectors aimed at boosting investments, increasing export revenues, and enhancing macroeconomic stability. A landmark measure significantly advancing microfinance was the establishment of NCC in 1993. This was in response to a resolution by a consultative group comprising NGOs, people's organizations, academia, concerned government agencies and government financial institutions recommending the rationalization of all government-directed credit programmes to ensure that the poor will have greater access to credit.

With technical assistance from the USAID-funded Credit Policy Improvement Project (CPIP), the NCC formulated and adopted several critical credit policy reforms: (1) the National Strategy for Microfinance, 1997, provided for: (i) an enabling policy environment to facilitate the increased participation of the private sector in microfinance; (ii) a greater role of private MFIs in the provision of financial services; (iii) adoption of market-oriented interest rates on loans and deposits; and (iv) non-participation of government line agencies in the implementation of credit and guarantee programmes; (2) the Social Reform and Poverty Alleviation (SRPA) Act, 1997, rationalized government-directed credit and guarantee programmes, gave emphasis to savings mobilization, and provided capacity-building assistance to MFIs; (3) the Agricultural Fisheries Modernization (AFM) Act, 1997, consolidated government-directed programmes in the agriculture sector and specified the role of government financial institutions (GFIs) as wholesalers of funds; (4) the Barangay Microenterprise Business (BMB) Act, 1997, directed GFIs to set up a special wholesale credit window for accredited MFIs; (5) Executive Order (EO) 138, 1999, transferred the credit programmes of government line agencies to GFIs; and required GFIs to provide wholesale credit funds to avoid competition with MFIs; and (6) the General Banking (GB) Act with specific provisions on microfinance, 2000, recognized the peculiar characteristics of microfinance (e.g. non-collateralized lending) and the use of the household's cash flow as a basis for the design of microfinance products.

The GB Act recognizes that only institutions taking deposits from the general public and/or from its members are subject to prudential regulation and supervision. In the case of microfinance NGOs, the NGOs that collect savings beyond the compensating balance will attract the attention of Bangko Sentral ng Pilipinas (BSP) because they have infringed the Banking Act and will be sanctioned accordingly

These policy reforms reversed the provisions and effects of the repressive financial policy and ended government control of the credit market to the poor.

At the same time, they gave MFIs the means to deal effectively with SMEs, especially those operating in the informal economy.

The emergence of the People's Credit and Finance Corporation (PCFC)

This enactment of key policy measures paved the way for the development of financial linkages between PCFC and MFIs. Through the implementation of the Rural Microenterprise Finance Project (RMFP), PCFC was established in September 1994, and later registered in 1995 as a finance company with the Securities and Exchange Commission (SEC). Its initial capitalization was US$3.89 million, augmented by another US$2.2 million in 1998, all from the National Livelihood Support Fund (NLSF), a poverty-oriented funding facility administered by the Land Bank of the Philippines. RMFP was a loan facility from the Asian Development Bank (ADB) and the International Fund for Agricultural Development (IFAD) intended for financing the enterprises of poor households using the Grameen lending methodology. PCFC's intervention was deemed necessary since commercial banks were still reluctant to lend directly to microenterprises because of perceived costs.

From a slow start, PCFC operations picked up in the ensuing years. After 8 years of operation (1997–2004), PCFC has successfully introduced microfinance for the poor, via both formal and informal financial intermediaries in the Philippines. PCFC arrived at this juncture by developing several financial linkage models. At the start, PCFC developed linkages mainly with NGO Grameen replicators, but this changed with the adoption of a regulatory framework for microfinance standards of performance. Integration of these performance standards into the lending criteria of PCFC levelled off the playing field and gave all types of microfinance institutions (MFIs) equal opportunities to seek PCFC accreditation and access to its wholesale lending facility (see Box 11.1).

Using its institutional credit facility, PCFC extended capacity building support to eligible MFIs of any type to strengthen their organizational capabilities, develop their microfinance technologies, and upgrade the knowledge and skills of their staff. Consequently, PCFC succeeded in building linkages with rural banks, thrift banks, cooperatives, cooperative banks, and even lending investors.

Opening the playing field for new financial institutions

One of the remaining constraints for the advancement of microfinance in the Philippines was the lack of appropriate banking technology to reach the poor in a sustainable way. To address this problem, BSP issued Circular 273 series of 2001, which partially lifted the moratorium on the licensing of new thrift banks, rural banks, and cooperative banks. This circular provided the opportunity for NGO MFIs to transform into formal banking institutions and for existing banks to establish new thrift or rural banks. These were classified as microfinance-oriented banks (MOB) if at least 50 per cent of the bank's gross loan portfolio consists of microfinance loans. Any existing bank that engages in microfinance but whose microfinance portfolio is less than 50 per cent of its total gross loan portfolio is classified as bank engaged in microfinance operations (BEMO). The box below provides an overview of the types of intermediaries currently engaged in microfinance.

Institutional and financial linkages with PCFC

The liberalized policy environment gave MFIs the autonomy to design their own microfinance programmes. It remains management prerogative to set the appropriate lending rates and loans terms, to diversify the MFI's financial products and services, and adapt a given methodology to suit the clientele. Such variations may include group size, rules of loan release, meeting cycle, and the respective roles of clientele groups and centres. Linkages with PCFC provided

---

Box 11.1 Types of financial intermediaries currently engaged in microfinance

(i) Rural banks (RBs): private shareholding banks with minimum capitalization ranging from US$58,309 in less developed municipalities to US$5.83 million in the NCR. RBs were created by law primarily to meet the normal financial requirements of farmers, fishermen, as well as cooperatives, merchants, private and public employees. All capital stock of RBs must, by law, be fully owned by Filipino citizens.

(ii) Thrift banks (TBs): private shareholding banks with minimum capitalization ranging from US$1.17 million for those with head offices outside MetroManila, and US$7.29 million for those with head offices within MetroManila. The functions of TBs are similar to those of the commercial banks only in smaller scale. At least 40 per cent of the TB's voting stock is required by law to be owned by Filipino citizens.

(iii) Cooperative banks (Coop banks): banks established by primary and secondary/tertiary cooperatives for the purpose of providing financial and credit services to cooperatives. Minimum capitalization amounts to US$0.36 million for those established in MetroManila, US$0.18 million for Coop banks in other cities, and US$3.64 million for national Coop banks. The capital stock of Coop banks should be 100 per cent fully owned by Filipino citizens.

(iv) Cooperatives (coops): registered and supervised by the Cooperative Development Authority (CDA), the cooperative's primary objective is to provide goods and services to its members. The required minimum paid-up share capital amounts to US$36 per cooperative; Coops are classified in the BSP Manual of Regulations as non-bank financial intermediaries (NBFIs) although they are registered and supervised by the CDA. A credit union or credit cooperative is a type of cooperative that specializes in providing financial services to its members.

(v) Lending investors (LI): lending investors are financing companies established by 20 or more lenders. LIs borrow money for the purpose of re-lending or purchasing receivables or other obligations. The LIs minimum capital accounts range from US$0.91 million to US$5.47 million for an investment house. At least 60 per cent of the combined capital accounts should be owned by Filipino citizens.

Source: BSP Manual of Regulations for non-bank financial intermediaries, revised as of December 2003.

MFIs access to large amounts of long-term funds (i.e. total credit line of up to US$4.56 million), and allowed them to pursue outreach into new territories at low overhead cost and to on-lend without having to mobilize funds.

Adoption of appropriate lending methodology

PCFC's Rural Microenterprise Finance Project (RMFP) prescribed the Grameen methodology in delivering PCFC funds to the end users. Two PCFC credit channels reviewed for this study – the Centre for Agriculture and Rural Development (CARD) and the Producers Rural Banking Corporation (PRBC) – adopted the so-called Modified GBA (Refer to Box 11.2 and Table 11.2).

The negative attitude towards the Grameen methodology, or the so-called GBA was mainly the result of limited information about this approach. However, this negative perception changed after the Microcredit Summit in Washington, D.C. in February 1997, which created an awareness of Grameen. The success of CARD, a leading GB replicator in 1997 and the first to become operationally and financially self-sufficient, also inspired many MFIs to follow its example. The adoption of microfinance standards and PCFC's institutional credit line, which provided support to partner MFIs for staff training particularly in GBA, also contributed to the eventual buy-in. The capacity building played a crucial role in building up the organizational/operational capacity of partner MFIs to reach out to significant numbers of clients. It is worth noting that, as a result of PCFC's technical assistance in GBA replication, banks were starting to form groups without the assistance of NGOs, and that this has become the characteristic mode of operation of PCFC partner banks.

The PCFC linkage process

Once the key policy measures were enacted the financial linkage route was paved. PCFC could enter into linkages with a range of MFIs. PCFC has two

---

Box 11.2 Grameen versus modified GBA

Seibel (1999) summarized the 'good practices' and 'innovative practices' of GBA replicators in the Philippines. The three 'good practices', which constitute the hard core social capital of the original GBA, were: (i) high moral commitment of leaders, based on values enforced through training; (ii) peer selection and peer enforcement, precluding adverse selection and moral hazard; and (iii) credit discipline, including weekly installments; rigid insistence on timely repayment; and repeat loans of increasing amounts, contingent upon repayment performance. On the other hand, the 'innovative practices', which brought about the so-called Modified GBA, were: (i) local rural bank status; (ii) deposit mobilization from the poor and non-poor through differentiated products with attractive interest rates; (iii) demand-driven differentiated loan and microinsurance products that cover all costs and risks; and (iv) client differentiation through different sized loan and deposit products.

types of financial products that it can offer via MFIs (see Table 11.1 below for the terms and conditions of the products):

- Investment credit: a credit line for microfinance services to the poor; and
- Institutional credit: a loan facility to finance capability building activities as well as for expenditures or asset acquisitions related to the lending programme.

PCFC credit lines to accredited MFIs are for financing the microenterprises of poor households. 'Poor household' is defined according to the Social Reform and Poverty Alleviation Act. Loan sizes for borrowers organized in groups or centres start from US$54 and US$2,678 respectively. For individual borrowers, loan size may start at US$178. The client decides on the type of project to be undertaken with the programme partner advising in determining the viability of the project.

PCFC wholesales short-, medium-, and long-term loans to accredited MFIs. At present, these include the rural banks, cooperative banks, thrift banks, NGOs and cooperatives that implement credit programmes using any proven microfinance lending methodology to finance livelihood projects that can augment the income of targeted poor clients. Three major sets of criteria comprise the preconditions for PCFC linkage, and they apply to all types of MFIs. To qualify for accreditation and eligibility to avail of the PCFC credit line, the MFI must pass the institutional, financial and lending performance criteria as well as provide appropriate documentation.

Underlying the eligibility criteria is PCFC's aim of selecting from among the existing financial intermediaries those with a minimum experience in microenterprise lending, the appropriate operating systems and procedure, and the management and staff to run the programme. PCFC has opted to select the 'best of the crop' that could create the greatest impact in terms of reaching

Table 11.1 Terms and conditions of PCFC credit lines to microfinance institutions

	Investment credit	Institutional credit
Tenor	One year revolving credit lines via drawdowns	
Short	1 year	2 years
Medium	3 years	3 years
Long	4–7 years	4–7 years
Interest rate:	12% p.a.per annum + 1% service charge	3% p.a.per annum + 1% service charge
Credit line amt to MFIs	Based on evaluation/credit needs	Based on evaluation/credit needs
Sub-loans to end borrowers	Up to P150,000	Not applicable; loan is directly to MFI
Collateral	Mainly promissory notes of sub-borrower clients and underlying collateral	Assets to be acquired from loan proceeds, if any

Source: PCFC – *Annual Report*, 2003.

significant numbers of the poor sustainably. Institutions not presently accredited by PCFC can get accreditation in one of the following ways: They can send their staff to the training courses organized by PCFC accredited training centres. These courses build up the capacity of MFIs for successful microfinance practice. The second option is to link up with existing partner MFIs of PCFC. PCFC itself is encouraging regional Programme Partners Associations to extend their network by including not only existing but also potential programme partners.

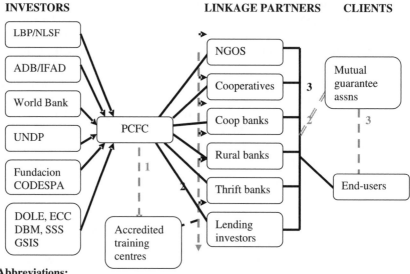

Abbreviations:
LBP/NLSF: Land Bank of Philippines/National Livelihood Support Fund
ADB/IFAD: Asian Development Bank/ International Fund for Agricultural Development
DOLE/ECC/DBM/SSS/GSIS: Dept of Labour/Employees Compensation Committee/Dept. Budget Management/Social Security System/Government Service Insurance Fund

———▶

(Funds flow 1) Investors enter into partnership with PCFC to implement microfinance programme.
(Funds flow 2) PCFC wholesales investment and institutional funds to MFI Programme Partners on a credit line basis. The MFI repays the loan and avails of fresh loans.
(Funds flow 3) The MFI releases loans to members/clients (end-users). The latter repays the loans to the MFI and avails of fresh loans.

— — —▶

(Service flow 1) Training on GBA/microfinance technology is provided by accredited training centres with support from PCFC. PCFC itself conducts training courses, refresher courses, and Lakbay Aral.
(Service flow 2) The MFI forms and strengthens Mutual Guarantee Groups. Through the weekly meetings, the MFI undertakes continuous group training (CGT) and values formation.
(Service flow 3) Centre coordinates activities of groups and promotes cooperation in managing the group fund need and controlled by members.

Figure 11.1 The PCFC linkage process.

The key actors in PCFC linkage are illustrated in Figure 11.1. It illustrates the financial linkage process by depicting the general flow of resources (both financial and technical assistance) from the investors to PCFC and down to the clients through the MFI-Linkage Partners. In 2004, PCFC had 6 investors, 199 partner MFIs, and 1.4 million active clients (see Table 11.2). PCFC wholesales the funds received from the investors to the MFIs who then retail to end-users with the assistance of mutual guarantee associations. To instil credit discipline and ensure collection of loans, the MFI enjoins the borrowers' mutual guarantee associations to enforce collective responsibility in loan recovery, or makes the borrowers individually responsible.

PCFC has accredited seven partner MFI training centres. Once the MFI training centres are accredited by PCFC the MFIs are eligible for institutional loan support from PCFC at the concessional interest rate of 3 per cent. PCFC allows the use of this loan for paying the salaries of MFI staff, the training costs, as well as the equipment required for upgrading of the MFI's operating systems.

Outcomes and impact

Outreach

The number of active clients served by PCFC grew from 217,240 in 1999 to nearly 1.4 million in 2004, implying a compound growth rate of 36.4 per cent per annum. The key reasons for the growth include: the increase in the number of partner MFIs, from 143 in 1998 to 199 in 2004; and the outreach expansion of the partner MFIs. PCFC's loan portfolio ballooned from US$19.64 million in 1999 to US$51.35 million in 2004.

Sustainability

The PCFC 2003 Annual Report stated that PCFC has already attained operational self-sufficiency of 110 per cent with financing as its main source of income. The average return of equity during the year was 4.7 per cent, and the income derived from operations could fully cover the cost of preferred dividends for the year.

A number of partner MFIs, particularly the mature ones, have also reached significant numbers of the poor and achieved operational self-sufficiency. A study by the Microfinance Council of the Philippines, Inc. (MCPI, 2003), of 14 MCPI members (13 of which were PCFC partners) revealed that all of them have achieved operational self-sufficiency; and three MFIs (two large and mature MFIs, and one small but mature MFI) have achieved financial self-sufficiency. An implication of this finding is that large MFIs have the advantage of scale economies, but it would take several years of 'maturing' (during which the MFI honed and adapted its microfinance technology to its environment) to capitalize on this advantage in order to reach financial self-sufficiency. On the other hand, small and medium MFIs can also achieve financial self-sufficiency provided they adopt a cost-effective lending methodology at the outset and go through the process of 'maturing' as well.

Penetration

PCFC and its partner MFIs managed to penetrate more developed areas much faster than poorer areas. The main reason for this was the existing banking infrastructure and the fact that new MFIs tended to start operations in areas where microfinance was already visible, i.e. new microfinance initiatives have sprung up in the same areas where CARD has achieved success.

As far as PCFC relationships with individual MFI's are concerned, Table 11.2 provides an overview of the outreach of two of PCFC's MFI clients, CARD-MRI (Centre for Agriculture and Rural Development – Mutually Reinforcing Institutions) and PRBC (Producers Rural Banking Corporation). Their outreach is presented in relation to the overall performance of all PCFC partner MFIs. As can be seen in the table, for 1998–1999, one-third of PCFC's total outreach was contributed by CARD-MRI (29.1 per cent) and PRBC (4.6 per cent), indicating the great weight carried by these MFIs in PCFC's overall performance (Table 11.2). In 2004, CARD's percentage share of the total PCFC outreach shrank to

Table 11.2 CARD-MRI and PRBC outreach in relation to total PCFC outreach

Type	Number of MFIs %		Outreach (active clients)		Loan portfolio (PHP million)	
	No.	% total	No.	% total	Amount	% total
Rural banks	83	41.7	468,672	33.5	1,358.96	47.2
Cooperatives	54	27.1	139,515	10.0	310.49	10.8
NGOs	34	17.2	624,499	44.7	795.32	27.6
Coop banks	24	12.0	138,455	9.9	329.33	11.4
Thrift banks	3	1.5	25,185	1.8	71.59	2.5
Lending investor	1	0.5	–	–	0	–
A. Total, 2004						
PCFC	199	100.0	1,396,326	100.0	2,877.78	100.0
CARD-MRI	2		112,174	8.0	678.3	23.6
PRBC	1		48,416	3.4	192.1	6.7
B. Total, past years						
PCFC, 1998	87	100.0	70,725	100	754.8	100
CARD-MRI, 1998	2		20,617	29.1	82.79	11.0
PRBC, 1999	1		2,919	4.6	7.45	1.0
C. Compounded annual growth rate %						
PCFC, 1998–2004			64.4		25.0	
CARD-MRI, 1998–2004			32.6		42.0	
PRBC, 1999–2004			59.7		91.5	

Sources: PCFC *Annual Reports* 2002, 2003 and 2004; CARD *Annual Reports* 2003 and 2004; Producers Rural Banking Corporation, 2005.

8 per cent and PRBC to 3.4 per cent as the portfolio of PCFC became larger and more diversified with the accreditation of new MFIs.

Also interesting is that PRBC's outreach grew at a faster pace compared to that of CARD-MRI's. The growth of PCFC's total outreach was powered both by horizontal expansion (i.e. increased number of partner MFIs) and by vertical expansion (i.e. increase in the number of active clients per MFI), especially through the fast-track approach of MFIs like PRBC in reaching out to significant numbers of the poor.

Conclusions

The future of PCFC linkages is very much contingent on the uptake by commercial banks and government financial institutions of the wholesale lending activity. Ideally, commercial banks should take over the role of PCFC as provider of wholesale funds to retail MFIs. Likewise, larger and matured MFIs that have reached financial sustainability could engage in wholesale lending themselves or franchise their microfinance business models and, henceforth, push outreach expansion to the less served areas in partnership with smaller MFIs as credit retailers.

But commercial banks may not yet see the situation as being ripe for their intervention. Some commercial banks have participated in the PCFC microfinance programme through their subsidiary thrift banks, but still their microfinance portfolio is negligible compared to their total portfolio. And while commercial banks may have funds for wholesale lending, the fact that the microfinance portfolio of the entire banking system constituted less than 2 per cent of the total bank resources indicates that the microfinance sector is not yet prepared to absorb substantial funds from commercial banks. PCFC has seen the need to consolidate its partner MFIs and further build up their capacity so that they may grow into Microfinance Mega Centres (MMCs), which might be more attractive for commercial banks and government financial institutions as channels of their wholesale funds.

In this light, three options are available for PCFC's future development: (i) increase the credit line of existing partners; (ii) consolidate partners into Microfinance Mega Centres (MMCs) clustered around a lead MFI, and build the capacity of MMCs as wholesale lenders of PCFC funds; and (iii) reorganize PCFC into a Credit Bureau for Microfinance. Option 1 has the least incremental impact on MFIs like CARD and PRBC – two partner conduits reviewed in this study to examine the linkages at the MFI level – as deposits of both MFIs have grown tremendously in recent years. Option 2, or Option 3, or both, would be highly beneficial to MFIs in general as these options will open new opportunities for outreach expansion in areas where there are few or no banks, and for upgrading microfinance lending systems to meet the financing requirements of small and medium enterprises (SMEs).

The above options are a means to an end, and PCFC is a means and not an end in itself. Whatever option PCFC takes in the future, if its moment of usefulness passes, that may dictate that it should close down. However, the emergence of new and especially commercial funding sources could be taken as vindication of the initial decision to set it up.

References

Callanta, R. (2000) Microfinance in the Philippines: battling the system in Remenyi, J. and Quiñones, B. Jr. (eds.) 2000, Microfinance and Poverty Alleviation: case studies from Asia and the Pacific, Wellington House, London.

Centre for Agriculture and Rural Development (2004) 'Client Empowerment – Our Mission, Our Commitment', *Annual Report*, Laguna.

Centre for Agriculture and Rural Development (2003) *Annual Report*, Laguna.

Congressional Planning and Budget Department, House of Representatives (2003) *Poverty Situation in the Philippines*, Policy Advisory (10).

International Fund for Agricultural Development (2003) 'Rural Micro-Enterprise Finance Project – Interim Evaluation Report', IFAD, Rome.

Microfinance Council of the Philippines Inc (2003) *Performance Monitoring Report*, Manila.

People's Credit and Finance Corporation (2002) *Annual Report*, Manila.

People's Credit and Finance Corporation (2003) *Annual Report*, Manila.

Producers Rural Banking Corporation (2005) *Producers Bulletin*, Series of January–March 2005 and May 2005.

Quiñones, B. Jr. and Seibel, H.D. (2000) *Social Capital in Microfinance, Montgomery.*

Reyes, C. (2002) *The Poverty Fight: Have We Made An Impact?, PIDS, 25th Anniversary Symposium Series on Perspective Papers.*

Websites

Bangko Sentral ng Pilipinas (2005) *Circulars* in BSP webpage: www.bsp.gopv.ph.

National Credit Council (1997). *National Strategy for Microfinance*, DOF webpage www.dof.gov.ph.

National Credit Council (1997) *Regulatory Framework for Microfinance*, DOF webpage.

CHAPTER 12

Extending the outreach of Rwandan People's Banks to the rural poor through village savings and credit associations

Chet Aeschliman, Fiacre Murekezi and Jean-Paul Ndoshoboye

Abstract

Over 65 per cent of Rwanda's rural population are poor and their principal activity is farming. Despite having the physical capacity and even the professional skills needed to undertake successful economic activities, this population completely lacks investment capital. CARE International based in Rwanda is improving this situation through its CLASSE-Intambwe methodology, which involves mobilizing rural poor into savings and credit associations and linking them to the vast network of people's banks that exist in the country. Although the 'linking' aspect is rather young, beginning only in late 2003, initial results are encouraging. Today, all 1,000 CARE-supported savings and credit associations have savings accounts in their respective people's bank, and many group members have opened personal, individual accounts, thus bringing many into the financial mainstream. This chapter explains the origins, mechanics and outcomes of this unique relationship.

Introduction

The Republic of Rwanda is a small, impoverished and land-locked highland country in Central Africa. It is surrounded by the Democratic Republic of Congo, Burundi, Tanzania and Uganda. Its total area is 26,338 km², of which 1,390 km² is composed of bodies of water. The country has an average altitude of about 2,750 m. Its main crops include beans, bananas and tea. Its population in 2003 was estimated to be 8,128,553, with a population density of 321 inhabitants/km², one of Africa's highest. The prevalence of HIV/AIDS increased substantially during the 1990s – partly because of war and genocide, the most profound national event in the past decade, from 1.3 per cent in rural areas in 1986 to 10.8 per cent at present.

Rwanda is now a trilingual country, where Kinrwanda is spoken by nearly everyone, with French being spoken mainly by the older generation, who were educated in pre-genocide Rwanda by its Belgian colonial masters and the national French-speaking school system following independence in 1962. English is spoken by those many Rwandans who grew up in exile in Uganda and returned after the genocide, thus explaining the mixture of French and English in this chapter.

Key players in Rwanda's financial sector

Rwanda's financial system is composed of the central bank Banque Nationale du Rwanda (BNR), plus 6 commercial banks, a network of 149 people's banks (*banques populaires*, essentially credit unions), a few (the exact number is unknown) rival networks of savings and credit cooperatives (COOPECs) and other multilateral financial institutions (MFIs), and a large number (perhaps thousands) of small 'savings and credit associations' (SCAs), essentially village banks, with linkages to the people's banks, the COOPECs, and sponsoring NGOs like CARE. The SCAs' linkage with the people's banks is, in fact, the subject of this chapter.

National microfinance policies and strategies

Since 1995, the period when banking activities resumed after the genocide, has been marked by reorganization of existing institutions that were decapitalized during the war. Because Rwanda's policy-makers agreed that microfinance constitutes an important part of the country's poverty reduction and economic development strategies, several MFIs were set up. Their creation, which was a good idea, derives from the fact that Rwanda is in general a very poor country, especially in rural areas, and that the majority of Rwandans have low incomes and do not have access to the classic financial system. However, a problem of lack of professionalism in existing financial and microfinance institutions and inadequate supervision increases their risk of failure and loss of customers' deposits.

As of 2002, as previously indicated, in an attempt to improve MFIs' operations, the BNR issued directives regarding the microfinance sector. The new regulations were welcomed by all actors and stakeholders. However, the new regulations – perhaps too hastily prepared – create some major difficulties for small MFIs, such as: a requirement to pay US$9,300 into a frozen account when applying for registration; the difficult (for barely literate people) format and timeframe required for submitting reports; and prudential ratios that are difficult to achieve (for example, the so-called 'creditworthiness' ratio: all MFIs must have equity capital equivalent to a minimum of 10 per cent of their assets).

As of 20 May 2005, a total of 206 MFIs had submitted applications to BNR to obtain registration (BNR, Banking Supervision Department). These included 148 people's banks and 58 other MFIs, of which around 40 are part of the Rwanda Microfinance Forum (RMF), whose principal mission is to lobby for, and build the capacity of, its member institutions. Of the total 206 institutions, 112 people's banks and nine other institutions have been approved. There are other institutions that have yet to request approval from the BNR. These are often hard to detect, often setting themselves up spontaneously without feasibility studies or market surveys, lacking effective management and control tools, lacking supervisory and technical support systems, and hence have a high risk of failure and, in fact, often disappear just as suddenly as they appeared.

Motivation for creating linkages

Over 65 per cent of Rwanda's rural population are poor and their principal activity is farming. However, their farms do not produce even sufficient food for family needs. The main reasons for such insufficiency are the vagaries of the weather, the ongoing subdivision of land into smaller and smaller units because of population pressure, soil degradation, non-use of agricultural inputs, and ineffective supervisory and advisory structures for rural producers and rural institutions. Despite having the physical capacity and even the professional skills needed to undertake successful economic activities, this population completely lacks investment capital.

Until recently, no financial or MFIs reached the poor for several reasons. Such people cannot provide material and financial guarantees, and in some cases are illiterate and therefore unable to write up their projects and plans, or even fill in loan application forms. The MFIs that finance this sector of the population are mainly the ones with a social vision that devote a great deal of time to mobilizing, training and educating their customers, such as CARE/Rwanda in the provinces of Umutara, Byumba and Kigali-Ngali.

The financial link, which aims to allow the rural population to have access to financial services, launches a dynamic development process in rural areas by enabling revitalization of the farming sector, and the freeing up and monetization of rural areas in general. Consequently, it opens up various economic opportunities within and beyond the farming sector that people may take advantage of. In this context, CARE/Rwanda, in its economic security programme, tries to help households, whose members belong to associations that are excluded from the classic financial system, to have easy and lasting access to rural financial services.

People's banks and savings and credit linkages

CARE/Rwanda has for several years been developing its CLASSE-Intambwe savings and loan methodology as part of its poverty reduction efforts among households in rural areas of Rwanda. CLASSE-Intambwe seems to be an appropriate response for mobilizing and structuring grassroots communities in order to unite efforts to fight poverty.

This approach focuses on:
- the economic security of the most marginalized households;
- HIV/AIDS and its consequences;
- access to basic education for the most marginalized sectors.

CARE/Rwanda has organized target households into self-help groups called 'savings and credit associations' (SCAs) or simply 'kitties', and helps them to start depositing weekly savings into an internal loan fund. CLASSE-Intambwe enables kitty members affiliated to it to accumulate savings and have regular access to funding from their 'kitties' and develop income generating activities (IGAs).

It turned out that the majority of the members of CLASSE-Intambwe associations wanted larger loans than their internal sources could provide. To resolve this problem, CARE/Rwanda made supplementary credit funds available to support these small entrepreneurs. These funds were entrusted to the various districts in the CLASSE project area, in compliance with national regulations in force at the time which stipulated that any intervention in a rural area had to be channelled through community development funds (FDC) managed by the districts.

The evaluation carried out at the end of the pilot phase of the CLASSE-Intambwe project concluded that the funds had not been well managed by the FDCs and that the target had not been achieved, despite the partnership that was set up for this purpose with the Épargne sans Frontières (Savings without Borders) Network (RESAFI), which provided external lending services. The balance remaining at the end of the project was used to strengthen the so-called 'inter-groupings', – i.e. regional, federative inter-group coordinating bodies – formed by a number of CLASSE-Intambwe member associations in a certain geographic locality.

Despite its limitations, and the errors noted during implementation of the pilot phase, the revised CLASSE-Intambwe methodology proved to be a distinct advantage for Rwanda with regard to mobilization of local savings and structuring of grassroots communities. This advantage warranted its being chosen as the preferred financial linkage between the people's banks (BPs), represented by the Union of People's Banks in Rwanda (UBPR) and the SCAs, and facilitated by CARE/Rwanda within the framework of the Expanding Competitive Client-Oriented Microfinance (ECOCOMF (Expanding Competitive Client-Oriented Microfinance) project and CLASSE-Intambwe.

The choice of the financial linkage between the people's banks and the SCAs was thus motivated by several considerations, including:

- The CLASSE-Intambwe methodology turned out to be a suitable, effective and efficient tool in the context of rural areas in Rwanda with regard to mobilization of local savings and social cohesion, which are two pivotal factors on which the link is built.
- The NBR's Regulation 06/2002 forbids any natural person who is not approved by the NBR from carrying out savings and credit activities. This regulation has enabled the bypassing of district authorities that initially proved incompetent to deal with financial management, and permitted the population to turn to people's banks, which are much more professionally managed. Because CARE has considerable experience worldwide in rural finance, its tendency and preference was to create its

own MFI network to provide the financial services. However, Regulation 06/2002, lack of project funding and practical considerations of long-term sustainability made it reconsider the alternative of partnership with existing financial institutions, i.e. the people's banks.

- The people's bank network broadly covers the entire country and has viable infrastructure even in rural areas. It is able to inspire confidence regarding the risk of theft, and above all the professional financial control exercised by the UBPR constitutes an additional guarantee in the public eye.

Individual people's banks and financial links with SCAs

Eleven people's banks, including six in the provinces of Byumba and Kigali-Ngali (Buliza, Buyoga, Kinihira, Muhura and Ngarama), operating in the area of the ECOCOMF project, and five people's banks in the province of Umutara (Kabarore, Matimba and Nyagatare) in the area of the CLASSE-Intambwe project, have financial linkages with SCAs via inter-groupings. The 11 banks, their location and a summary of SCA and inter-group linkages, are shown in the Table 12.1 below.

Linkage structure, management and operations

Management of the financial linkage is governed by a memorandum of understanding (MoU) between CARE International in Rwanda and the UBPR. This memorandum of understanding defines the responsibilities of each party involved. The operation of the financial linkage can be easily understood by examining the diagram on the following page (Figure 12.1).

The actors and their responsibilities in the linkage partnership are summarized as follows.

CARE/Rwanda

- Make available credit funds amounting to approximately US$90,000 to participating people's banks on behalf of associations brought together in their respective Inter-Group Bodies. Such funds are divided between six project partner people's banks. The portion allocated to each bank is paid into an account entitled 'CARE Credit Fund', which will be opened in each people's bank.
- Provide technical training in accordance with the requests and training needs of SCAs and Inter-Group partners.
- Train UBPR technicians and partner people's banks in CLASSE-Intambwe methodology.
- Work in close collaboration with Inter-Group Bodies to ensure that they comply with their contractual obligations, especially regarding the monitoring and recovery of loans granted to member associations.
- Assure that this agreement is ratified by participating Inter-Group Bodies.

Table 12.1 Saving and Credit Associations (SCAs) in the linkage with BPs through Inter-Group Coordinating Bodies (IG)

Province	District	Banque Populaire	Period With CARE (Months)	Project	Inter-Groupings	No. SCAs	No. SCAs Receiving Loans
Byumaba	Kinihira	Kinihira	5	Expanding Competitive Client-Oriented Microfinance Services in Rural Rwanda (ECOCOMF: 15 June 2003–15 June 2005).	IMAKIKI	152	28
Kisaro	Buyoga		5		IMAKIKI	156	39
Ngarama	Ngarama		5		CECANGAHU	126	16
Humure	Muhura		5		CACANGAHU	102	35
Kigali-Ngali	Rulindo	Rulindo	5		GOBOK ABAVANDIMWE	139	24
Buliza	Buliza		5		GOBOK ABAVANDIMWE	49	15
Umutara	Kahi	Kabarore	17	Strengthening New Community	I A B I K	12	12
Gabiro	Karangazi		17		IMPUDUGA	12	6
Muvumba	Rukomo		17		ISANGANO	9	8
Muvumba				DUKATAZE	8	8	8
Kabare		Nyagatare	3	Community Learning and Action for Saving Stimulation and Enhancement (CLASSE/INTAMBWE methodology)	URUKUNDO	28	2
Matimba			3		URUMULI	42	3
Kahi	Kabarore		3		TWISUNGANE	17	8
			3		UMUNYINYA	26	2
			3		TWIZIGAME	27	1
Bugaragara	Matimba		3		UMUGUZA	20	6
			3		URUGERO	23	3
			3		TUBEHAMWE	32	2
Umugi w'Umutara		Nyangatare	3		ISANGANO RY'UMUGI W'UMUTARA	35	8
Totals		11 BPs			19 Inter-Group briefings	1,006	226

Source: CARE/Rwanda, 2005.

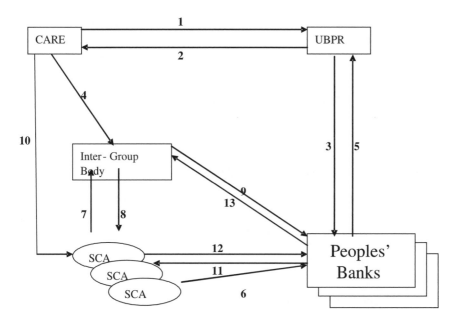

Nature of Responsibilities:
1. CARE provides UBPR with a revolving credit fund entitled 'CARE Credit Fund'
2. UBPR manages the 'CARE Credit Fund'
3. UBPR exercises financial control over the 'CARE Credit Fund' at the BP level
4. CARE supports the inter-group bodies through training
5. The BPs provide financial reports on the credit fund to UBPR
6. The SCA opens a term deposit account in its peoples' bank
7. The SCA submits a loan application dossier to its Inter-Group body
8. The Inter-Group body analyzes the SCA loan application
9. The Inter-Group body submits approved loan dossiers to the People's Bank
10. CARE organizes, structure and trains the SCAs
11. The BPs grant the loan from the Credit Fund to the SCAs
12. The SCAs repay their loans to the BPs
13. The BPs grant 30% of interest received on the Credit Fund to the Inter-Group Body

Figure 12.1 Linkage between savings and credit associations, inter-group bodies, individual people's banks and the Union of People's Banks in Rwanda

Inter-Group Bodies

- Analyse, sign and forward the projects and loan applications drawn up by SCAs to people's banks for their consideration.
- Monitor use of loans granted by people's banks to SCAs, ensuring that the proceeds are used for their declared purposes and that repayment schedules are respected.
- On behalf of the people's banks, ensure recovery of loans granted to member SCAs within the scope of the project.

- Promptly submit regular monthly reports to CARE regarding all microproject activities.
- Evaluate and examine the progress made by SCAs, and develop mechanisms and activities to support their strengthening.
- Submit monthly reports to women's councils and district authorities (Comité de Développement Communautaire (CDCs) and social affairs departments) on the state of progress of activities (for information purposes).

Union of People's Banks in Rwanda (UBPR)

- Monitor the management of CARE credit funds by people's banks.
- Supply CARE with a summary of the quarterly reports on loans granted and loan repayment status to associations by people's banks within the framework of the project.
- Assure that this agreement is ratified by each people's bank.

Partner People's Banks:

- Open term deposit accounts in the name of each prospective borrower SCA.
- Analyse and decide on SCAs' loan applications within the scope of this agreement within 15 days of receiving them from the Inter-Group Bodies.
- Prepare and sign loan contracts with SCAs.
- Release loans for the contracts signed.
- Monitor debtors and regularly inform Inter-Group Bodies about upcoming due dates (at least one week in advance) and overdue accounts. To this effect, the bank will prepare a report to be sent monthly to Inter-Group Bodies, the UBPR and to CARE/Rwanda.
- Introduce effective loan monitoring and recovery methods to the Inter-Group Bodies in order to improve their dealings with partner SCAs.
- Pay commissions to the Inter-Group Bodies in accordance with the terms laid down in the agreement.

CARE–UBPR loan policy

The intention is that the 'CARE credit fund' made available to the people's banks will be gradually replaced by the people's banks own funds at a level of 50 per cent at the end of the first year and 100 per cent after the second year, but only if an evaluation so recommends and all parties concerned agree. If need be, the funds may be transferred to other districts to re-create the same arrangements. Members of SCAs may also become members of a partner people's bank, on an associative or individual basis, if they so wish.

The sums borrowed must serve to strengthen and/or develop the SCA's economic activities. The activity should be profitable, have a distribution and sales market and generate sufficient revenues to pay back the principal and interest. Generally speaking, loan eligibility conditions are those applied by people's banks. This means that SCAs targeted by the ECOCOMF project should:

- be members of an operational Inter-Group Body and a CARE partner. This entails adopting the ROSCA system in accordance with the CLASSE–Intambwe model and being up to date with subscriptions;
- be an ordinary and active corporate member of the people's bank;
- give proof of irreproachable moral standards, notably regarding respect of previous commitments and have no prior history of unpaid loans;
- be made up of at least seven persons aged 18 years or over;
- be an SCA governed by current Rwandan legislation, recognized by the competent authorities and in compliance with their byelaws and internal regulations;
- present an economically viable project;
- provide a jointly and severally binding guarantee signed by all members, without exception, of the SCA requesting a loan.

The maximum amount of a loan is determined in accordance with the people's banks policies. For project partner SCAs, the maximum amount is set at US$930 for the first loan.

- Each SCA must constitute a mandatory term deposit that matures on the same date as the loan obtained from the people's bank. The interest accrued on the term deposit is paid on maturity and may be capitalized.
- All or part of the deposit may, if necessary, be used to cover unpaid loans after implementation of due diligence. Such deposit is seized 15 days after formal notice if no satisfactory response is forthcoming.
- When the loan is completely repaid, the savings plus accrued interest is returned to the SCA, which decides how it will be used.

Loan conditions are the same as those applied by the people's banks:

- The maximum repayment period is 12 months, with the possibility of a grace period, depending on the nature of the project to be financed.
- Accrued interest is paid with each loan instalment.
- The interest rate on loans corresponds to the current people's bank rate.

Remuneration of Inter-Group Body deposits

Each Inter-Group Body must also open a deposit account at the partner people's bank. For provision of technical assistance services (preliminary analysis of loan applications, monitoring of associations and loan recovery), Inter-Group Bodies will receive 30 per cent of the interest paid on loans granted to member associations, whatever the source of the funds used to finance the loan might be. A statement of the commission must be drawn up monthly and communicated to the Inter-Grouping, CARE and UBPR at the same time as the other reports. Commission is paid on each loan repayment.

Results and impact

CARE/Rwanda has worked extremely hard to organize SCAs and Inter-Group Coordinating Bodies in the three provinces where the CLASSE-Intambwe methodology is being used. In fact, as shown in the table above, just over 1,000 SCAs, supported by 19 Inter-Group Bodies, exist in this part of north-eastern Rwanda. With the size of groups reportedly being between 20 and 30 people, this means that somewhere between 20,000 and 30,000 rural poor have been mobilized by the three CARE projects. In principal, all groups now have savings accounts in their respective people's banks, and many group members have opened personal, individual accounts, thus bringing many into the financial mainstream.

The linkage's overall effect on bank membership, savings, loan and asset growth, as well as bank profitability, etc. is not clear, as shown in the statistical summary (see following page) of the three banks whose linkage operations with SCAs were researched.

Yet, if the banks can eventually serve a majority of the 20,000 to 30,000 and more new SCA members, and bring large numbers of them into the mainstream as individual bank members, then the methodology will clearly have been a success.

Less than a quarter of the SCAs have received loans so far, but repayment has been 100 per cent for these. Based on the sample of three people's banks, however, it would appear that the CLASSE-Intambwe group methodology is having a positive effect on the banks' overall repayment rates, as shown in Figure 12.2 below.

The following Table 12.2 shows the status of loans granted to SCAs with CARE's Credit Fund a little more than a year into the programme.

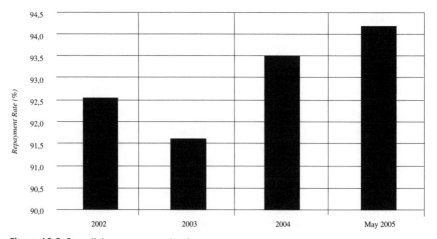

Figure 12.2 Overall loan repayment rates

Table 12.2 People's Bank–SCA loan summary as of 30/9/05[1]

People's Bank	Number of SCAs	Number of Loans	Total Amount Granted (US$)	Guarantee (25% block savings)	Capital Reimbursed	Outstanding Balance (US$)
Buliza	53	23	12,341	3,085	5,354	6,987
Humure	130	36	16,386	4,096	6,268	10,117
Kabarore	82	36	22,847	5,712	5,874	16,973
Karangazi	12	10	9,310	2,327	4,120	5,190
Kinihira	148	28	19,877	4,969	9,046	10,831
Kisaro	186	33	16,046	4,012	4,016	12,030
Matimba	70	27	19,923	4,981	4,216	15,707
Ngarama	97	31	19,023	4,756	6,845	12,178
Nyagatare	35	17	7,727	1,932	3,116	4,612
Rukomo	15	11	10,241	2,560	4,427	5,814
Rulindo	153	28	17,180	4,295	7,153	10,027
Total	981	280	170,901	42,725	60,434	110,467

Source: CARE/Rwanda, 2005.
[1]Exchange used 1US$=537 Rwandan French Francs.

On the People's Banks

The impact of the financial linkage on people's banks is not yet very discernable because the majority of SCAs are now taking out their first loan. Few have embarked on a second loan, taking into account that the maximum amount of the first loan is approximate US$930. In terms of absolute value, this amount is small compared to the maximum amount of credit granted by people's banks to private individuals.

Nevertheless, the partner people's banks have begun to experience an increase in their membership, and their aim of re-injecting the savings collected into the rural economic circuit is gradually taking shape and is actually being achieved. In addition, the material guarantee (collateral) requirement no longer hinders access to financial and non-financial services thanks to the spread of risk among SCA members. Consequently, their aim of reaching the poorest, and their plan to finance rural areas in order to contribute to poverty reduction, has a good chance of succeeding by means of this financial linkage.

Box 12.1 Example on savings and credit associations

The account given by the Duteraninkunga/Kibondo SCA in Umutara Province, with 25 members, of whom 19 are women and 5 are men, provides some insight into how their SCA's earnings increased. This association took out a loan of US$1,000 from the Kabarore people's bank which it invested in buying and reselling sorghum. After payment of the principal and interest, the remaining profit stood at US$400. The same association received a loan of US$280 which it used to buy a mobile phone to be hired out. A calling card purchased for roughly US$37 brings in average profits of US$20 per month. Many similar examples abound.

Another significant outcome is the professional training provided by CARE/ Rwanda to the personnel of partner people's banks. Such training, which aims to give them technical expertise, is likely to have a long-term positive impact regarding the future management of people's banks and in terms of innovation of products developed by them.

On savings and credit associations

The most notable impact is likely to be the strengthening of social capital arising from the additional revenues generated by the group loan received from the people's banks, which is allocated to various social purposes. The text to the right illustrates this.

The immediate outcome for SCAs also includes the growth of associations' revenues, thanks to the leverage provided by loans received, learning to set up small income-generating projects and securing of their assets.

On People's Bank members/customers

The impact of the financial link on customers is inextricably associated with the impact created by the local lending organization. In most cases, a loan taken out from a partner people's bank serves to strengthen the local organization. In accordance with their methodology, the sum received is redistributed among the members of the organization in the form of a loan, but at a higher rate of interest than that charged by the people's bank. In general, the internal rate of interest of the local organization is 10 per cent per month, while the lending rate at people's banks is approximately 1.1 per cent per month. However, the income growth of households that are members of associations affiliated to the link is quite remarkable, so much so that the loans and heavy interest charges are easily paid. Stories such as the following, 'I have a goat thanks to a loan received from the SCA. I can easily pay my children's school fees, I buy fashionable clothes, and I no longer ask my husband for money to buy salt...' were told to the researchers by nearly all the SCA members encountered.

In addition to income growth, establishment of the linkage also encourages the majority of association members to open bank accounts. Consequently, people no longer need to hoard their money and/or use it for unnecessary purposes. Security and planned spending are positive results arising from the linkage that benefit customers.

On the financial sector

The primary impact of the financial linkage on the Rwandan financial sector is 'integration' of the formal and informal financial sectors. The compartmentalization and imbalance between the formal and informal financial sectors in Rwanda truly hindered economic development. Therefore, establishment of a financial linkage between SCAs and BPs will obviously promote increased interaction between the two sectors.

The second impact of the financial linkage concerns the contribution of the financial sector to the national poverty reduction strategy. Indeed, financing of rural activities by the formal financial system will entail revitalization of farming, the freeing up of the farming sector driven by entrepreneurial spirit among rural dwellers and development of economies of scale. These new elements will undoubtedly have a positive impact on poverty reduction efforts in Rwanda.

Macro level impacts

Penetration of rural areas by the formal financial sector, with suitable financial conditions, thereby leads to an increase in the degree of monetization. Such increase facilitates exchange of goods and services, and as a spin-off, monetary circulation speeds up and macroeconomic advantages increase. Indeed, in the medium term, taking into account the economic context of Rwanda, success of the financial linkage between SCAs and people's banks, and/or with the financial sector in general, will encourage development of commercial centres in rural areas and lead to the creation of basic infrastructure (roads, schools, healthcare centres, etc.) and recreational facilities (sports fields, motels, cinemas, etc.). Such development of diversified economic activities will obviously lead to enrichment and development of the national economy, which is the ultimate indicator of a country's degree of development.

Conclusions and key lessons learned

The financial linkage being described was conceived as an attempt to trigger a dynamic process to integrate the rural population into the formal financial system, which obviously opens up more profitable economic opportunities than informal financing. How far has the programme gone towards achieving this objective?

While the programme is still in its early stages, the rapid progress and impressive achievements to date tend to confirm that it is an effective way to bring the rural poor into the financial mainstream. The financial linkage has facilitated and set in motion access by significant numbers of the poorest to financial services. It should be borne in mind that less than 2 per cent of CLASSE-Intambwe SCAs had a bank account before the linkage was set up, compared with a current level of approximately 90 per cent. It also should be noted that in addition to associations opening deposit accounts to benefit from loans from partner people's banks, association members also gradually are opening personal accounts to keep their own personal funds safe. Therefore, the financial linkage has definitely led to interactive stimulation between banks and rural populations.

In the 11 participating people's banks, approximately 25,000 rural poor have been organized into just less than a thousand SCAs supported by 19 Inter-Group coordinating bodies. Less than a quarter of the groups have now taken out loans from the CARE funding, and loan repayment, as seen above, remains at 100 per cent in this young programme. The programme is having a significant, but difficult to measure, effect on increasing people's banks' membership, savings, loans, assets and earnings. As previously noted, it also seems to be having a positive effect on overall repayment rates of the people's banks themselves, at least in the three banks chosen at random by the researchers conducting the study.

Another lesson that would seem clear from this experience is further confirmation, if it were needed, that the poor do not have great difficulty paying as high as 10 per cent interest per month on the subloans they received from the group loan provided by the people's banks. Clearly, timely access to credit is much more important to the poor than its cost. The problem of access to credit is rather a question of suitable services, geographic accessibility, recognition of customers and their needs and product flexibility, rather than the interest rate. It is well-intentioned, but misinformed, public servants that frequently raise the alarm that interest rates are too high to be affordable by the poor; whereas if the poor themselves are asked their opinion, it is access that matters to them.

Other reasons offered by various respondents for the perfect repayment rate for CLASSE-Intambwe associations include the following:

- The associations were initially intensively trained at grassroots level in the CLASSE-Intambwe credit approach and methodology.
- The risk of non-repayment is reduced because it is spread among several persons (the SCA members).
- The Inter-Group Bodies, which have greater knowledge of the SCAs and their members, play an import intermediary role between an association that is requesting a loan and the people's bank that is granting it.
- The local lending organization and the social fund (*ingoboka*) have a stabilizing influence on the incomes of the borrowing association's members. Therefore, loans are allocated to activities with high capital-intensive value that generate the most financial gains, since the profits to be spent on community investments are highly desired by all.

It is also important to point out that before embarking on the borrowing process, CLASSE-Intambwe SCAs all first of all had to set themselves a common goal. This is a key lesson because it indicates a certain mastery of strategic and operational planning by CLASSE-Intambwe associations.

Visits to villages having gone through this process are instructive, since it is impossible not to notice the change of habits and standard of living of CLASSE-Intambwe SCA members compared with their neighbours who are not members. CARE's experience in the field, backed up by many eyewitness accounts, has certainly proved this.

Need for additional research

While all this success early on is heartening, the programme needs to be monitored over the next few years to ascertain if it works as well once greater scale is attained. Some of the areas that need particular attention as the programme expands are perhaps the following:

- Gender breakdowns to distinguish behaviour.
- Monitor repayment of different types of loans.
- Cost the programme to enable calculations on becoming sustainable.

The last point is particularly important, because the current study made no attempt to look at costs versus benefits. Serving the remote, rural poor by linking their associations to professional financial service providers like Rwanda's people's banks seems an effective way of providing services and transitioning people into the financial mainstream. The question is, at what cost? The author of this chapter believes that, while such approaches will never be strictly sustainable, they are still worthwhile investments by development agencies because of the hundreds of thousands of poor that are lifted out of poverty and 'mainstreamed' by them. In theory, the investment need be made only once, and then the group coordinating bodies would presumably be phased out, as the population graduates out of poverty. Human nature being what it is, however, it is likely that once started, the IGs may well take on a life of their own, and not want to cease operations when their original goal is accomplished. If so, they will need to identify a new goal to achieve.

Preconditions for this type of financial linkage

Those wishing to emulate or adapt CARE's CLASSE-Intambwe methodology to affect poverty-reduction in their own countries should be aware of the preconditions necessary for it to work properly:

- There needs to be a wide network of rural-based financial service providers (credit unions, banks or MFIs, preferably, but perhaps NGOs as well to provide the professional financial services (term deposits and loans) that are the key to success. Said service providers should be no more than a day's walk from the ultimate borrowers.
- There must be a competent and sufficiently funded NGO or other organization capable of creating, nurturing, training and encouraging the institutional development of the village associations and the regional Inter-Group Bodies, who in addition must be capable of and willing to assist in loan follow-up and recovery.
- The legal and regulatory framework should encourage this type of approach, or at least not disallow it.

Further reading

Banque Nationale du Rwanda, *Rapports annuels 2001, 2002, 2003, 2004*, Kigali.
Kanimba, F. (2005) *Déclaration de la politique monétaire*, Kigali.

Minaloc, Rwandan Microfinance Forum and Aquadev (2003) *Analyse du cadre opérationnel du système financier au Rwanda. Cas de la microfinance*, Kigali.

Minecofin (2000) *Rwanda vision 2020*, Kigali.

Minecofin (2001) *Document de la stratégie de la réduction de la pauvreté*, Kigali

Minecofin (2002) *Indicateurs de développement du Rwanda*, Kigali.

Minecofin (2002) *Rwanda en chiffres*, Kigali.

Minecofin (2003) *Indicateurs de développement du Rwanda*, Kigali.

Minecofin (2003) *Rwanda en chiffres*, Kigali.

Minecofin (2004) *Politique nationale de micro finance*, Kigali.

Minecofin (2004) *Questionnaire unifié sur les indicateurs de base du Bien-être*, Kigali.

Minecofin (2004) *Rapport d'analyse des résultats*, Kigali.

Minecofin (2004) "Stratégie de réduction de la pauvreté", *Rapport annuel d'exécution*-version sommaire.

Minecofin (2005) *Stratégies nationales de micro finance: période 2006-2010*, Kigali.

Nzemen, M. (1999) "Faisabilité d'un système financier communautaire décentralisé au Rwanda", The World Bank.

Rwandan Microfinance Forum (2005), *Etude relative à la définition des mécanismes d'octroi de micro-crédits PADDEP*, Kigali.

Union of People's Banks in Rwanda (UBPR), *Rapports annuels 2002, 2003, 2004*, Kigali.

CHAPTER 13

Linking with savings and credit cooperatives to expand financial access in rural areas: a case study of CRDB Bank in Tanzania

Gerda Piprek

Abstract

The case study reviews CRDB Bank, the fifth largest commercial bank in Tanzania, and its desire to do 'something positive' about the majority of Tanzanians alienated from the commercial banking sector. Although this appears to be a story about CRDB's level of corporate social responsibility, it may have more to do with a smart, forward thinking bank strategizing to the deal with the inevitability of a saturated high-end, urban banking market. The author describes CRDB's strategy of linking with Savings and Credit Cooperatives (SACCOs) as a way to cost-effectively increase the supply of financial services in the rural countryside. Some of the findings from the study are that there must be the willingness and commitment from management to enter the lower-income market, to make a large upfront investment into the model and to have a long-term vision.

Introduction

This study aims to provide a description and critical review of Cooperative and Rural Development Bank Ltd (CRDB) and its microfinance linkage strategy with selected savings and credit cooperatives (SACCOs). CRDB is Tanzania's fifth-largest commercial bank. It was established in July 1996 and has launched its microfinance initiative in 2001. Since its inception, the microfinance unit in CRDB has grown rapidly and today serves more than 78 000 clients through 157 partner institutions.

The study is of particular interest given the challenges and importance of rural finance in Tanzania; the political and economic transformation which Tanzania has undergone over the past 10 to 12 years; the resulting transformation of the financial sector (including SACCOs); the highly successful transformation of CRDB from a state-owned to a privately owned commercial bank; and the nature and scope of the CRDB linkage model.

The study sets out to examine the main constraints to rural finance service provision in Tanzania, and aims to: identify the important preconditions for this type of linkage to emerge; identify key design factors of the linkage; evaluate the impact of the financial linkage at the institutional and client levels; and draw lessons learned for possible replication elsewhere.

Overview of Tanzania

Political overview

The period under Julius Nyerere – also known as 'Father of the Nation' – was characterized by a one-party state and the introduction of socialism. One-party rule came to an end in 1995 with the first democratic elections held in the country since the 1970s. President Makapa, elected in 1995, is heading the Tanzanian government today.

The Tanzanian population represents 130 indigenous tribes, and a small number (1 per cent of the population) of Asian, European and Arabian descendants. The main indigenous language is Kishwahili (Swahili), with English as a second official language. The historic Arabic influence remains in Tanzania through a strong Muslim following (35 per cent mainland and 99 per cent in Zanzibar).

Socio-economic review

Tanzania ranks as one of the poorest countries in the world. Despite various economic reforms and strong growth in GDP over the past 20 years, by March 2005, 60 per cent of the population was estimated to live on less than US$2 per day (http://microfinancegateway.org).

The structural adjustment process plunged Tanzania into a period of serious economic problems from 1992 to 1995, but the new government, which took control in 1995, adopted an economic recovery programme from 1995–1998, supported by the Enhanced Structural Adjustment Facility (ESAF) (DFID 2000). Continued donor assistance and the introduction of solid macroeconomic policies have resulted in an increase in industrial production and substantial growth of the mining sectors from 1995 onwards. The economy has been growing steadily since then and registered a GDP growth rate of 5.8 per cent in 2004 (CIA, 2005) with total GDP for 2004 estimated at close to US$24 billion. Inflation dropped from a high of 30 per cent in 1995 to 5.4 per cent in 2004.

An estimated 80 per cent of the population lives in rural areas, which is then also where the highest incidence of poverty is encountered (United Nations Development Programme, 2005). The population density and economic activity of the various regions differ tremendously, with the higher population density and the main economic activity being in the east (including the economic capital Dar es Salaam) and the northern border regions. In contrast, the central regions (including Dodoma) are sparsely populated and economic activity is limited, with even higher resulting poverty levels than elsewhere.

While improving, the infrastructure in rural areas remains poor. Markets for agricultural goods are underdeveloped or nonexistent and there is limited access to finance, particularly for subsistence farmers. This underscores the importance of poverty alleviation programmes and initiatives in rural areas. These include the development of rural farmers and associations, and improving access to financial services for the rural poor.

The financial sector in Tanzania

In 1991, the Government of Tanzania introduced financial sector reforms in line with the broader economic reform policy aimed at liberalization of the economy. The main goals of the financial sector reforms were to enable banks to operate on a commercial basis by allowing private ownership and decision-making on an institutional level. The key components of the reforms were: liberalization of interest rates; elimination of directed credit; restructuring of state-owned financial institutions (including CRDB); encouraging the entry of private ownership; and strengthening the regulatory and supervisory role of the Bank of Tanzania. In 1996, NBC was subdivided into a commercial bank, NBC, and the National Microfinance Bank (NMB), and CRDB was restructured and privatized.

The Cooperative Societies Act was also introduced in 1991. The Act created the legal framework for cooperatives to be established as privately owned equity-based institutions registered under the Ministry of Cooperatives and Marketing. The Act applies to all types of cooperatives, be that an agricultural production society or a SACCO. The main principle established by the Act was volunteerism and self-regulation.

However, despite these reforms, access to finance for poor Tanzanians – particularly in rural areas – remained limited. In 1996, the government, in collaboration with the donor community, initiated a microfinance policy formulation process that started with a national demand-side study. A draft National Microfinance Policy was discussed by stakeholders in 1999 and approved by the Government in 2001(Randhawa and Gallardo, 2003). The policy reflects the government's recognition of the microfinance sector as an integral part of the financial sector.

The policy led to the Microfinance Companies and Micro Credit Activities Regulations of 2004, which govern microfinance companies (under the supervisory authority of the Bank of Tanzania, as well as the Savings and Credit Cooperative Societies Regulations and Financial Cooperative Societies Regulations of 2004). The regulations on savings and credit cooperatives came into effect in March 2005 and stipulate that cooperatives with capital exceeding Tshs800 million (around US$755,572 in 2005), are subject to regulation and supervision by the Bank of Tanzania. Cooperatives with capital below this amount are subject to regulation and supervision by the Registrar of Cooperatives under the Ministry of Cooperatives and Marketing (http://www.bot-tz.org, accessed 2007).

The market place today

While much progress has been made in the reforms of the financial sector, it has been primarily mainstream banking which showed considerable progress. However, their clients represent less than 20 per cent of Tanzanians (Randhawa and Gallardo, 2003). In certain respects, the transformation process of the past 15 years has had a reverse impact on access to finance for the rural poor, as major banks restructured and consolidated their performance, in the process withdrawing to regional centres.

The Financial Sector Assessment Program of the IMF (2003) found that micro credit accounted for less than 5 per cent of all bank credit in Tanzania, or less than 0.4 per cent of GDP, around US$35.3 million, (Ingves, 2005). The main form of savings and credit for the rural poor are through Rotating Savings and Credit Schemes (ROSCAs or 'Upatus'). Other providers of microsavings facilities and microcredit to the poor are savings and credit cooperatives (SACAs), microfinance NGOs, the Post Office Bank and a few commercial banks.

- *SACCOs*. By January 2001, there were 646 registered SACCOs, of which 60 per cent were rural. The total shares and deposits of the 40 per cent urban SACCOs far outstripped that of the rural SACCOs (Randhawa and Gallardo, 2003). This demonstrates the extreme level of poverty of the rural poor, who mostly eke out an existence through smallholder farming or small/micro enterprises, whereas members of urban SACCOs are often salaried income earners. However, SACAs and SACCOs are often limited in terms of their capacity, access to capital, and outreach. There have also been weak linkages between the informal financial institutions and formal banking institutions.
- *NGOs*. The largest microfinance NGOs are the Mennonite Economic Development Association (MEDA), PRIDE-Tanzania, FINCA and the Presidential Trust Fund (PTF) which has been privatised as a microfinance NGO. However, most of the microfinance NGOs are heavily donor-dependent.
- *Commercial banks* with products and services targeted at the lower income segment include the National Microfinance Bank (NMB), CRDB, Akiba Commercial bank and some regional banks. NMB has then also engaged in 'linkages' with SACCOs, by providing loans and deposit facilities to SACCOs. Their focus has been primarily the small-scale sugarcane farmers.

The formal financial sector is generally reluctant to lend to donor-dependent NGOs. The main involvement of the commercial banks in microfinance is usually deposit-taking with a total deposit mobilization of about US$336 million in 2003, in contrast to US$12.5 million in microcredit.

Support to the informal sector: key players

The relevance of SACCOs among the poor, as well as their restraints, has been well recognized by the government and donors, and various initiatives have been launched to address these weaknesses and assist with capacity-building among SACCOs.

IFAD Rural Finance Support Programme (RFSP). RFSP, launched by IFAD in 2001, is a nine-year programme comprising of three phases, with the main aim of enhancing the capacity of the rural poor to mobilize savings and invest in viable income generating activities through the development of viable rural financial services (IFAD, 2004). The programme has three development components, namely: improvement of the managerial capacity and performance of grassroots microfinance institutions (MFIs); rural financial systems development; and empowerment of the rural poor. Capacity building includes the strengthening the linkages between the formal and informal sectors.

The programme was rolled out in three different geographic zones and targeted the poorest households and their financial institutions (SACCOs and SACAs serving them). Various forms of support has been offered to these SACCOs/SACAs, including training of staff, management and members; training-of-trainers; support in developing business plans; loans to SACCOs to increase their outreach, etc.

SELF. In 1999, the Small Entrepreneur Loan Facility (SELF) was launched by the Vice-President's Office, co-funded through a concessional loan from the African Development Bank (ADB). The main goal of the programme has been to improve access to finance for the rural poor by supporting microfinance intermediaries (including SACCOs) to improve their capacity and move towards sustainability. In the pilot phase the project covered six impoverished regions, namely Coast region, Morogoro, Dodoma, Singida, Mtwara and Lindi. In 2002 the project was extended to Unguja and the Pemba islands.

The project has three windows: lending (wholesale) microfinance institutions, for purposes of on-lending; capacity-building through training of key stakeholders and train-the-trainer; outreach (marketing) and monitoring of poverty impact of initiative. Lending is based on a rate between that of the Treasury Bills and the market rate, and in June 2005 was equal to 12 per cent plus a 2 per cent application fee. While the programme has made good progress, rollout has been slower than anticipated because of the high poverty levels within the target communities with limited viable economic activities, and the low existing skills level of MFIs.

SCCULT. The umbrella SACCO body, Savings and Credit Cooperative Union League of Tanzania (SCCULT), was reestablished in 1992. Membership is voluntary and appears to be predominantly urban-based. SCCULT provides various services to members through their regional field offices, such as training and a bookkeeping package, as well as access to funds for on-lending. Funds are raised through membership fees, some donor support and also through attracting member savings into a central fund. However, SCCULT's capacity seems to be limited and they are facing various challenges in obtaining sufficient funding for on-lending (IFAD, 2004).

CRDB Bank Ltd

The history of CRDB dates back to 1947, when the government established the Land Bank of Tanganyika (LBT), and is marked by a number of mergers and restructurings by the government in an attempt to mobilize credit for rural development and agricultural purposes.

CRDB was renamed CRDB Bank Ltd (1996) and the assets and liabilities of CRDB were transferred to CRDB Bank in 1996. Seven shareholders were elected to the board, with a further three members appointed by the DANIDA Trust Fund. DANIDA (Danish International Development Agency) has since been providing technical and managerial support, while pledging to continue its financial interests in CRDB Bank by owning a minimum of 20 per cent and a maximum of 30 per cent of the shares on a temporary basis (Table 13.1). As at June 2005, the paid-up capital of CRDB equalled US$10.9 million (Tshs12.3 billion), and CRDB has more than 11,000 shareholders (http://www.crdbbank.com).

Before becoming a commercial bank, CRDB had limited branches with staff moving around to serve clients. This changed when CRDB Bank Ltd was formed, and as at June 2005, CRDB had 35 branches, of which 7 are in Dar es Salaam and the rest in other regions.

CRDB and microfinance

Given the historic involvement of CRDB with rural areas and cooperatives, and the equity holding of DANIDA, CRDB's venture into microfinance seems an almost natural extension of its activities and a reflection of both its broader social goal and the strong emphasis on commercial banking practices adopted by the new CRDB Bank Ltd. However, CRDB could also have chosen to only remain in the 'safer' upper-end of the market, after the multitude of bad experiences with rural credit over the years.

Around 2000, CRDB realized that the institutional reforms it implemented following its restructuring had set it on a strategy which alienated the majority of Tanzanians – those earning less than US$221 (Tshs250,000) or approximately 6.8 million households (CRDB, 2004). The lower end of the market had become extremely impoverished following the structural economic crisis of the early

Table 13.1 Shareholding of CRDB Bank

Shareholders	% Equity
Private individuals	37.0
DANIDA investment fund	30.0
Cooperatives	14.0
Companies	10.2
Parastatals (NIC, PPF)	8.8

Source: www.crdb.com [accessed 2006].

1990s, while most players in the financial industry were targeting the increasingly saturated high end of the market.

The linkage model was selected, as it was found most appropriate given that it builds on the financial systems of the very communities it wishes to serve. The model was built on the following three assumptions:

- That a large number of community-based financial institutions already existed, and had the ability to act as intermediaries to mobilize deposits;
- That there was a large demand for financial services in rural areas and that the community-based institutions could meet this demand on a self-sustaining basis if they had the necessary capacity and access to capital;
- That both depth and breadth of outreach could be achieved in a self-sustainable manner through local financial intermediaries, which could provide a broad set of services through a large network to the currently under-serviced segment of the market.

The vision of CRDB is, then, to successfully serve the broader Tanzanian market, complementing traditional high-end commercial and retail banking with a focus on the lower end of the market, based fully on commercial principles. As CRDB also historically had a strong presence in the regions and a close relationship with agricultural cooperatives, extending this vision to include the rural poor seemed an easy fit with the organization's strengths and culture.

The first linkages were formalized in 2001 in four pilot regions. Towards the end of 2004, CRDB formalized the microfinance initiative and the CRDB Bank Microfinance Company Limited (hereafter referred to as the MFC) was registered as a separate company.

During the initial three-year pilot phase (2001–4), the Microfinance unit was operating as a division of CRDB Bank, and the costs associated with the initiative were not all ring-fenced. Staff were seconded from CRDB Bank Ltd and the unit was using CRDB Bank Ltd branch offices to conduct its work. The salaries of the managers of the microfinance unit, as well as certain overhead costs, were paid by CRDB Bank Ltd. Other direct expenses such as motor vehicles, stationery, and salaries of field officers, were paid for by the microfinance unit. Since the formation of the Microfinance Subsidy, CRDB (MFC), all costs are being accounted for and allocated to the MFC.

On-lending to the SACCOs has been funded by CRDB Bank (backed by the DANIDA guarantee) and by the deposits that the SACCOs have to place with the MFC as loan security (ranging from 10 per cent to 25 per cent of the loan amounts, depending on the MFI's performance record). With the Microfinance Unit becoming an independent registered company, it is envisaged that all funding will in future be based on the initial equity of CRDB Bank, deposits by linked SACCOs, and lending from external sources based on commercial principles.

Linkage between CRDB and SACCOs

The implementation of the proposed linkage strategy was carefully planned, while CRDB maintained flexibility and an openness to adjust the process as required. The process was not without its challenges, but the commitment and perseverance has yielded phenomenal results, with a total of 157 SACCOs linked in less than five years (some started from scratch by CRDB), representing a total clientele of 78,855 as at June 2005.

Piloting the initiative

In 2000, CRDB started negotiating with existing SACCOs and key players in the market, such as IFAD, on the formation of linkages with CRDB. CRDB also approached various community leaders and existing ROSCAs and SACAs. This presented a lengthy process of negotiation, where a team from CRDB spent much time in the selected regions.

The pilot process is described by the MFC management as one of collaboration, rather than a process of 'selection'. The pilot initially focused on four regions: Dodoma, Iringa, Mbeya and Morogoro. Contrary to the usual linkage model of first approaching the 'easy' areas, CRDB opted for these four regions exactly for the opposite reasons: these regions are some of the poorest in Tanzania, with low incomes, and few other financial intermediary initiatives prevalent. The rationale for selecting these 'difficult' regions was that, should they succeed in these areas, the other regions would be 'easy' and a sure success to follow.

In essence, the CRDB linkage model therefore has two options: firstly, identification and recruitment of existing SACCOs based on their potential and meeting the set criteria (below); secondly, to identify potential geographic areas that have no institution that delivers financial services. In these cases the MFC assists with the formation of a SACCO through mobilizing the community.

The selection of existing SACCOs is not based on historical performance, as most SACCOs had no records available and international standards could therefore not be used. Rather, SACCOs were selected based on the following:

- Commitment to learning;
- Commitment to make available time;
- Willingness to provide CRDB with required information;
- Experience with/prevalence of fraud;
- How the SACCOs were managing themselves and whether they were serious about what they were doing.

The process followed more from building relationships with the SACCOs over time and mutually negotiated agreements, than a quick assessment of SACCOs' historical performance. The initial assessments were undertaken through multiple field visits by CRDB microfinance staff. K-Rep was later engaged to further assist in the selection of the SACCOs and to assess future training needs of the SACCOs.

Profile of the 'linked' SACCOs

The nature of the linkage between the MFC and the SACCOs is manifold. Support ranges from assisting a community in the formation and registration of a SACCO, to capacity-building and ongoing technical assistance. The MFC provided the following support to SACCOs:

- Initial assistance
- Management and governance structure
- Systems and reporting
- Training and ongoing technical support and advice

Table 13.2 provides an overview of the SACCOs currently linked to the MFC. There are 157 linked SACCOs. Of these, 33 were formed by CRDB/the MFC while the remainder were already in existence and then linked up with the MFC. The majority (88) are located in rural areas, while the remainder are in urban areas or regional towns. This demonstrates the extent of outreach by the MFC into the very needy and underserved rural areas of Tanzania.

Various types of SACCOs exist and differ accordingly, depending on the membership profile and the products extended to the SACCO members. In essence, there are three broad categories of SACCOs:

- *Community-based SACCOs.* These SACCOs can be found in urban areas or regional towns, but are most frequently encountered on village level. A variety of group and individual loans can be found, including women's solidarity loans, business loans for individual members, or loans for small and micro enterprises;
- *Employee-based SACCOs.* These represent SACCOs where all the members are drawn from one employer and these SACCOs are generally located in urban areas or at regional level. Specific salary-based loans are extended which are often guaranteed by the employer.
- *Agricultural SACCOs.* To date these represent primarily small-scale cane growers in areas such as the Morogoro region. Both individual farmers and farmers' associations can be clients of the SACCO. Loans are extended for various purposes, including agricultural production loans.

Many SACCOs may have a combination of different clients, including women's solidarity groups, individual borrowers for small business purposes, individual salaried clients or farmers. The MFC does not encourage members to discriminate based on gender, but rather to welcome all potential clients who have a need for financial services and a good track record. However, the MFC does encourage SACCOs to extend loans to women's solidarity groups in an effort to deepen outreach to the very poor. The split among SACCO members in terms of gender is almost 50/50, with a slight bias towards women (Table 13.3), though this differs tremendously depending on the target clientele of the SACCO. The loans, in turn, tend to be biased towards men.

All SACCOs offer deposit-taking facilities, loans and certain transactional facilities (payment facilities, debit orders, stop orders, money transfers, etc.), but the operations of SACCOs and average deposit and loan sizes differ substantially

Table 13.2 Number of linked SACCOs per region

Regions	Dec-02	Dec-03	Dec-04	Jun-05
Dodoma	6	10	14	14
Iringa	10	16	20	22
Mbeya	7	11	17	23
Morogoro	9	12	16	19
DSM	0	18	22	27
Lindi	0	0	0	2
Mtwara	0	0	0	4
Tanga	0	0	0	4
Shinyanga	0	0	0	5
Mwanza	0	0	0	6
Kilimanjaro	0	0	10	15
Arusha	0	0	8	16
Total SACCOs	32	67	107	157

Profile of linked SACCOs as at June 2005

Formation: In existence pre CRDB 124
Formed by CRDB 33

Location/Nature: Peri-urban/Region 69
Rural 88

Source: CRDB Quarterly progress reports for microfinance activities (2000–4).

depending on the type of SACCO and its client profile. For example, the average deposit and loan size of the employee-based and urban/regional town SACCOs tend to be larger than those of community-based SACCOs, as the urban members generally have a higher income than on village level.

Similarly, the average loan and deposit of SACCOs with the MFC differs tremendously depending on the level of maturity of the SACCO and the number and type of members. The financial profiles of SACCOs are discussed later in the chapter.

Products and services offered to SACCOs and members

In addition to the technical support provided to SACCOs, the MFC provides various types of bank accounts and services to SACCOs, and some other services such as money transfers, insurance and the TemboCard to SACCO members.

On-lending to SACCOs

The MFC has a number of loan types available to SACCOs, depending on their financing needs. A SACCO must meet certain basic requirements to qualify for a loan. These requirements include audited accounts for the past three years; details of SACCO members, SACCO share capital, past performance report for individual borrowers, and so forth. SACCOs established by the MFC do not have to meet the initial requirement of audited financial statements, as these

Table 13.3 Number of SACCO members per region

Regions	Dec-02	Dec-03	Dec-04	Jun-05
Dodoma	2,025	5,284	7,957	9,434
Iringa	4,120	6,462	7,542	9,384
Mbeya	1,027	2,135	3,169	4,954
Morogoro	5,008	7,786	8,961	12,967
DSM	0	10,737	22,564	26,635
Lindi	0	0	0	559
Mtwara	0	0	0	1,190
Tanga	0	0	0	966
Shinyanga	0	0	0	680
Mwanza	0	0	0	946
Kilimanjaro	0	0	7,264	8,326
Arusha	0	0	2,355	2,814
Total Members	12,180	32,464	59,812	78,855
Gender of SACCO Members as at June 2005				
Male			38,430	
Female			39,825	

Source: CRDB Quarterly progress reports for microfinance activities, 2000–4.

SACCOs are well known to the MFC. The main qualifying criteria are the quality of SACCOs' portfolios, management capacity, profitability and portfolio at risk (PAR).

A SACCO can borrow up to 100 per cent of its arrears-free portfolio. For a first loan, the SACCO must also deposit 25 per cent of the loan amount ('lien') in cash at CRDB. For subsequent loans, the 'lien' could be adjusted downwards based on good loan performance and the loan size of the SACCO.

As at June 2005, the on-lending interest rate charged to SACCOs ranged from 12.5 per cent to 13.5 per cent, (set at 10 per cent above the savings rate of 2.5 per cent, plus a 1 per cent loan application fee which is equivalent to a commitment fee or loan processing fee. This percentage is applicable to the outstanding loan (declining balance approach). CRDB Bank's prime lending rate at the time was 19 per cent, and CRDB's cost of funds was reported as between 5 per cent and 6 per cent.

SACCOs' lending rates to individual members differ greatly, depending on the economic activity of the members and the borrowers, duration of the loan, collateral, competition from other lenders, start-up and administration costs, and so forth.

Loan surety and guarantees

There are different levels of surety in place – SACCO-member level, SACCO-MFC level, and MFC-CRDB level – to encourage a strong culture of loan repayment, mitigate risk to the MFC and to SACCOs, and to encourage the SACCOs and the MFC to extend outreach to lower income areas and for activities which are usually viewed as high risk (e.g. agricultural production loans). Firstly, an MFC loan to a SACCO is guaranteed as follows:

- The agreed 'lien' for the specific SACCO, over the fixed deposit account, with the coverage as specified in the partnership agreement (initially minimum 25 per cent of the loan amount).
- One hundred per cent of the arrears-free loan portfolio is pledged as guarantee.
- In addition to the above surety for individual SACCO loans, DANIDA has provided a blanket guarantee to CRDB Bank to encourage it to lend to the lower income groups. An amount of DKK12 million (US$1.96 million) has been deposited with CRDB Bank Limited, and CRDB Bank is allowed to issue loans to SACCOs (through the MFC) for up to 133.3 per cent of the guarantee fund. The fund therefore guarantees 75 per cent of the loans issued, while the SACCOs are required to provide for the remaining 25 per cent through the 'lien' deposited with the MFC. In the case of a default, CRDB must first recover the outstanding loan amount from the 'lien' deposited by the respective SACCO, before the DANIDA guarantee can be accessed.

    As at June 2005, the DANIDA guarantee fund had not been accessed and in theory should never be accessed as long as the initiative is well run.
- The Danish Private Agricultural Sector Support programme (PASS) provides a guarantee to the MFC for loans issued to finance SACCOs established by sugarcane growers, and the guarantee is structured in the same way as the DANIDA guarantee fund. The PASS guarantee was brought in when the DANIDA fund was exhausted due to the high volume of SACCO loan applications, but is limited to SACCOs focusing on small-scale sugarcane outgrowers.

Various other forms of surety or guarantees are also prevalent, based on the type of loan and/or SACCO:

(i)   *A group guarantee* from all the members on SACCO level (no monetary value).

(ii) *Tiered cross-guarantee.* This refers to loans by SACCOs to individuals, which are guaranteed by the group. These guarantees are often used for agricultural purposes, where an individual loan to a farmer is partially secured by the farmers' association's guarantee to purchase the farmer's produce.

(iii) *Employer guarantee loans.* There are two types of employer guarantee loans:

- A SACCO may have some members who are formally employed, and their loans are guaranteed through a salary-based deduction by the employer.

- In contrast, an 'employee-based' SACCO would have drawn all its members from one employer and the SACCO may receive a general guarantee from the employer for all its members. The guarantee is to the MFC, and stipulates that for the loans issued by the MFC, the employer is committed to effect salary deductions and deposit them in the SACCOs' account with the MFC. In this way, CRDB Bank forfeits the 25 per cent of the approved loan amount and the SACCO does not give any tangible security apart from the employer guarantee.

(iv)   *Women's groups*. SACCOs are encouraged to allow women's groups to operate at the SACCO level under group solidarity lending methodology.

Savings accounts for SACCOs are as follows.

The MFI Juhudi Account is the main account held by SACCOs at the MFC and has been specially designed for the linked SACCOs. A trademark account of K-Rep, 'Juhudi' means 'effort' or 'endeavour' and the savings account allows for multiple signatories and the withdrawal of funds on demand, with no withdrawal limit as long as the account is not overdrawn. Cheques can be used against the account and interest is earned on balances exceeding US$88.41 (Tshs100,000). As at June 2005, the interest rate was 2.5 per cent per annum.

An overdraft facility is also available on the Juhudi account. The facility normally includes term loans and lines of credit. These are handled on a case-by-case situation, as the MFC stated that it is difficult to monitor the overdraft facilities.

Fixed deposit accounts enable SACCOs to earn a higher interest rate than with the Juhudi account, and are normally used by SACCOs to deposit the mandatory 25 per cent of the approved loan amount as security for the loan. As at June 2005, the interest rate on fixed deposit accounts was 4.5 per cent per year.

Other products and services offered to SACCOs and their members are cash-taking facilities. MFC collects cash from the SACCOs for safe-keeping. To this end the MFC hires a vehicle and security from the regional CRDB branch.

Insurance services are offered by CRDB Bank Limited which is an agent for Royal Insurance. Thus the SACCOs secure their cash in custody, transit and teller cubicles against burglary through the CRDB Insurance agency.

Money transfer facilities are available to SACCO members through deposits made at any CRDB branch, or from the SACCO via the MFC to a CRDB branch.

TemboCard. CRDB Bank's TemboCard is also available at some SACCOs. There are two versions of the TemboCard: one is a debit card which allows clients to transact at CRDB and partner ATM's anywhere in the country. The other is a smartcard version, and is usually issued to rural SACCO members who do not have access to CRDB ATMs. The SACCOs have point-of-sale equipment which enables them to load value onto the account for a client. The clients generally use these smartcards for merchant-related purchases, such as paying for their agricultural inputs or stock.

Case studies of two SACCOs

The following case studies provide an in-depth view of the relationship of CRDB and two of its member SACCOs:

ROA Kiruvi SACCO

The ROA Kiruvi SACCO in Kilombero near Morogoro was established with the assistance of CRDB. Through educating and mobilizing the Kilombero community into forming the SACCO over a period of three months, ROA Kiruvi was registered as a SACCO in July 2001, and the Memorandum of Understanding (MOU) with CRDB was formalized by August 2001. At signing of the MOU, ROA Kiruvi SACCO had only 325 members. By June 2005, membership had grown to 1,717 members with member share capital of US$178,712.

In addition to assisting in the formation and registration of ROA Kiruvi, the MFC also provided support by providing front office equipment, training of 18 staff and management, and 538 members (June 2005). As at June 2005, the MFC has extended loans of US$2,016,251 (Tshs2,280 million) to Kiruvi, and held deposits of US$3 718 (Tshs 4,205 771).

The MFC also provides on-going technical and marketing support.

The membership profile of the 1,717 members of ROA comprises individuals, women's solidarity groups (about 10 members each) and institutions such as schools, churches and the local sugarcane farmers association (Table 13.4). Most of the individual clients are then also sugarcane farmers. While individual membership and loans have a strong male bias, the numbers of women benefiting through membership, deposits and loans are boosted significantly through the 53 solidarity women's groups, with an average of 10 members each.

Based on the loan volume reported below and the total number of loans disbursed, the average loans size appears to be about US$589. This is relatively high and probably influenced by the large number of annual agricultural loans. The women's solidarity group loans start off with a loan amount of maximum US$95 (TShs 100,000) per member, or just less than US$1,000 for a group of 10 women.

Table 13.4 ROA Kiruvi SACCO: membership and loan profile (June 2005)

	Membership profile		Loan profile with respect to member profile	
	Number of members	Percentage	Number of loans	TShs
Male	1,262	73%	2,826	68%
Female	380	22%	1,228	30%
Groups (women's solidarity)	53	3%	93	2%
Institutions	22	1%		0%
Total	1,717	100%	4,147	100%

Source: CRDB Quarterly progress reports for microfinance activities, 2000–4.

ROA Kiruvi has a variety of products, customized for their specific client profile. These include three forms of savings account:
* Regular savings account with interest at 3 per cent;
* Fixed deposit account with interest at 5 per cent; and
* Junior account for children's education with interest at 4 per cent.

Loan products include the following:
* Emergency loans at 5 per cent per month;
* Agricultural loans at 16 per cent per year;
* Business loans and development loans at 2 per cent per month; and
* Women's solidarity group loans at 2 per cent per month.

The portfolio is dominated by agricultural loans, reflecting the main economic activity in the area (sugar-cane farming) (Table 13.5). Women's loans were introduced more recently.

In addition to the savings and loan products offered by ROA Kiruvi SACCO, members can also hold CRDB's smartcard-based TemboCard. This enables members to make large payments to suppliers for business and agricultural purposes.

ROA Kiruvi SACCO has demonstrated phenomenal growth since its inception in 2000. Not only has membership and paid-up share capital grown tremendously, but cumulative loans of more than US$2.6 million have been disbursed with an outstanding loan portfolio of close to US$1.2 million (Table 13.6).

As at June 2005, ROA Kiruvi's repayment rate to CRDB has reportedly been 100 per cent. However, sugarcane farmers experienced some problems as a result of too much rain earlier in 2005, with the consequence that they were not able to meet their loan obligations on time. These loan obligations have been rescheduled based on an agreement between the SACCO and CRDB. It was the first time that this happened and has been a one-off within the MFC-SACCO linkage model (Table 13.7).

ROA Kiruvi SACCO aims to increase its membership to 3,000 members by 2006. It also wants to acquire its own premises and computerize all its operations. The main problems voiced by management were the lack of education of most of their members and staff, and the lack of title deeds among members (borrowers). The latter should improve with the recent changes in the Lands Act allowing for title deeds by individuals.

Table 13.5 ROA Kiruvi SACCO: loan profile by sector (June 2005)

	US$'000 (1:1110)	TShs '000	Percentage
Agriculture	2,182	2,422,144	82%
Trade	311	345,557	11%
Processing	63	70,390	3%
Emergency/Social	103	114,860	4%
Total	2,660	2,952,951	100%

Source: CRDB Quarterly progress reports for microfinance activities, 2000–4.

Table 13.6 ROA Kiruvi SACCO: financial performance as at June 2005 (US$)

US$ (1:1110)		06/2005
Fund mobilization	Paid-up shares	178,712
	Members deposits	48,999
	Total funds mobilized	227,711
Lending activities	Total loans disbursed	2,660,316
	Total capitalized interest	252,788
	Loan repayment (principal)	1,460,721
	Interest paid	253,766
	Total repayment	1,714,487
	Outstanding balance	1,199,595
Deposits with CRDB	MFI Juhudi account	3,789
	Deposit accounts	–
	Other	–
	Sub total	3,789
Deposits with other financial institutions	A/C NO. 1-NMB	13,761
	A/C NO. 2-CFP	180
	Sub total	13,941
	Total deposits	17,730
	Cash on hand	10,527
	Total cash balances	28,257
Loans from CRDB	Loan no. 1	5,405
	Loan no. 2	21,036
	Loan no. 3	125,739
	Loan no. 4	389,189
	Loan no. 5	45,045
	Loan no. 6	619,369
	Loan no. 7	90,090
	Loan no. 8	758,694
	Total CRDB Loans	2,054,568
Repayment of CRDB loans	1,219,539	
Balances of CRDB loans		835,029
Loans from other institutions	Loan no. 1	–
Total loan balances		835,029

Source: CRDB Quarterly progress reports for microfinance activities, 2000–4.

Table 13.7 ROA Kiruvi SACCO: quality of loan portfolio as at June 2005

	US$'000 (1:1110)	Tshs	Arrears (%)
Arrears free	1,096	1,216,944	100
Arrears > 30 days	3	2,781	0.2
Arrears > 60 days	0	0	0
Arrears > 90 days	1	959	0.1
Arrears > 180 days	0	0	0

Source: CRDB Quarterly progress reports for microfinance activities, 2000–4.

Kibaigwa SACCO

Kibaigwa SACCO, situated in a rural village about 50 km from Dodoma, was one of the first SACCOs to be formed by CRDB. Some of the members were members of a farmers' network (*Mtandao wa Vikundi vya Wakulima*) which spanned six villages. An MOU was signed with CRDB in 2001. Over the next three years, membership grew to 1,742 and the total client base to 2,174. Paid-up member share capital also increased from just over US$31,000 to US$310,343.

Support from the MFC included the provision of furniture, a safe and a counter, mobilization campaigns to attract members, stuff and management training, technical support, marketing and promotional advice.

The communities served by Kibaigwa are primarily dependent on agriculture and agricultural business and trade. Agricultural products produced in the area include groundnuts, maize, simsim and cow peas. As with ROA Kiruvi, membership is predominantly male, with individual female members representing about one quarter of all individual clients. However, in addition, they had 58 women's solidarity groups by December 2004, each with approximately ten members. Whereas ROA Kiruvi does not have any non-member clients, Kibaigwa has a substantial and growing number of non-member clients, totalling 432 or almost one-quarter of the total number of clients by December 2004 (Table 13.8). 'Non-members' do not hold shares in the SACCO but are merely clients of the SACCO.

Kibaigwa SACCO offers a variety of products to members, including savings accounts and loans. There are various types of loans available, such as agricultural loans (redeemable over eight months) and trade loans (redeemable over six months), both at an interest rate of 7 per cent per year. Loans for the purchase of agricultural equipment are also available, as well as emergency business loans. The latter has a maximum loan amount of US$5,746 (TShs 5 million). Social/emergency loans are available, with a maximum loan amount of approximately US$28 (Tshs 30,000), redeemable over three months. These social/emergency loans are common phenomena among Tanzanian NGOs, and enable the SACCOs to effectively compete with NGOs which offer solidarity group lending. In this instance, FINCA is active in the Kibaigwa SACCO area.

Table 13.8 Kibaigwa SACCO: membership profile

	12/2001	12/2002	12/2003	12/2004
No. of male members	378	477	945	1,272
No. of female members	106	144	286	412
Groups (women's solidarity)	25	34	46	58
Total no. of members	509	655	1,277	1,742
Non-member clients	8	42	309	432
Total no. of clients	517	697	1,586	2,174

Source: CRDB Quarterly progress reports for microfinance activities, 2000–4.

Agricultural-related loans initially represented more than 50 per cent of the total loan portfolio (2001). However, while the outstanding agricultural loan portfolio has been expanding rapidly from US$45,806 (Dec 2001) to almost US$700,000 by December 2004, the growth in trade-related loans has outstripped the agricultural loan portfolio, and the trade-related loan portfolio represented 53 per cent of the outstanding loan portfolio by December 2004 (more than US$800,000). This growth in trade-related loans reflects a deliberate strategy by Kibaigwa to diversify its loan portfolio. It also demonstrates the impact which Kibaigwa had on the communities, enabling individuals to start small businesses with the loans which they have received from Kibaigwa (Table 13.9).

In addition to the savings and loan products offered by Kibaigwa SACCO, members can also hold a CRDB smartcard-based TemboCard. This enables members to make large payments to suppliers for business and agricultural purposes.

Unlike ROA Kiruvi, which only holds loans and deposits from the MFC, Kibaigwa SACCO has deposits with NMB and loans from the SELF project. Though these deposit and loan amounts with other institutions are small, it demonstrates the ability of SACCOs to manage their own finances by using services from different institutions, depending on their needs at the time.

As reflected in Table 13.11, the growth of Kibaigwa SACCO has been almost exponential over the three years since it signed an MOU with CRDB. Not only did paid-up share capital increase tenfold, but members' deposits increased from US$6,447 to more than US$82,000, and outstanding loans to members from

Table 13.9 Kibaigwa SACCO: loan profile by sector

Total amount disbursed	12/2001	12/2002	12/2003	12/2004	% 12/2004
US$ (1:1110)	75,283	225,936	712,172	1,511,969	100
Agriculture	45,806	129,702	314,355	678,573	45
Trade	26,864	90,983	380,227	800,211	53
Processing	—	—	—	—	0
Social	2,613	5,250	17,590	33,185	2

Source: CRDB Quarterly progress reports for microfinance activities, 2000–4.

Table 13.10 Kibaigwa SACCO: quality of loan portfolio

US$ (1:1110)	12/2001	12/2002	12/2003	12/2004	% of 12/2004 Portfolio
Total Portfolio	57,631	115,067	343,070	700,771	100.0
Arrears free	55,442	108,980	329,710	698,492	99.7
Arrears >30 days	1,865	9	8,613	901	0.1
Arrears >60 days	324	234	2,811	243	0.0
Arrears >90 days	—	5,845	1,937	1,135	0.2
Arrears >180 days	—	—	—	—	0.0

Source: CRDB Quarterly progress reports for microfinance activities, 2000–4.

Table 13.11 Kibaigwa SACCO: financial performance

US$ (1:1110)		12/2001	12/2002	12/2003	12/2004
No. of members		509	655	1,277	1,742
Funds mobilization	Paid-up shares	31,405	43,439	137,904	310,343
	Members' deposit	6,447	22,393	65,737	82,682
	Total funds mobilized	37,852	65,832	203,641	393,025
Lending activities	Total loans disbursed	75,283	225,936	712,172	1,511,969
	Total capitalized interest	4,209	25,438	164,818	267,090
	Total repayment	21,861	136,306	369,103	811,198
	Interest paid	–	–	164,818	267,090
	Total repayment	–	–	533,921	1,078,288
	Outstanding balance	57,631	115,067	343,070	700,771
Deposits with CRDB	Juhudi account	–	1,061	509	73,308
	Deposit account	168	–	33,784	33,784
	Fixed deposit	5,743	13,514	22,760	324
	Sub-total	5,911	14,574	57,053	107,416
Deposits with other financial institutions	NMB DODOMA	–	–	90	90
Total deposits		5,911	14,574	57,143	107,506
	Cash on hand	–	–	-	52,446
	Total cash balances	–	–	57,143	159,952
Loans from CRDB	Loan no. 1	22,973	23	22,973	22,973
	Loan no. 2	–	54	54,054	54,054
	Loan no. 3	–	–	135,135	135,135
	Loan no. 4	–	–	–	350,450
	Sub-total	22,973	77	212,162	562,613
Repayment of CRDB loans		–	–	77,027	212,162
Balances of CRDB loans		–	–	135,135	350,450
Loans from other institutions	Loan no. 1: SELF	–	–	11,712	11,712
	Loan no. 2	–	–	–	63,063
	Sub total	–	–	11,712	74,775
Loan repayment to other institutions		–	–	8,784	36,937
Outstanding loans other institutions		–	–	2,928	37,838
Total outstanding loan balances		–	–	138,063	388,288

Source: CRDB Quarterly progress reports for microfinance activities, 2000–4.

US$57,631 to over US$700,000. At the time of writing, Kabaigwa's repayment performance to CRDB and SELF has reportedly been 100 per cent. As illustrated in Table 13.10, the loan repayment performance of members to Kibaigwa SACCO has also been strong, with less than 1 per cent of the outstanding loan portfolio in arrears.

Kibaigwa SACCO plans to expand to 19 villages, with a planned membership base of 5,000 over the next five years. They are also looking at expanding their products and services, including the development of a housing loan product. Kibaigwa would like to become a fully fledged cooperative bank and also serve other smaller SACCOs in the area. They are currently investigating the purchase of a four-wheel drive vehicle to assist them in their geographic expansion plans.

Performance of the linked SACCOs

The success of the SACCO linkage model has been phenomenal, as is illustrated in Tables 13.12 and 13.13 below. Considering the small number of staff employed at regional level to assist in forming and providing technical assistance to the SACCOs, CRDB certainly met its objectives of leveraging: as at June 2005 the average number of SACCOs serviced per regional staff member totalled 14, and the average number of SACCO members 5,632.

Paid-up share capital of SACCO members exceeded US$3.8 million by March 2005 and total funds mobilized by SACCOs (share capital and member savings) exceeded US$16 million, with deposits at 316 per cent of share capital. Of these, almost US$1.5 million has been deposited with the MFC and total loans of US$50 million have been made to SACCOs.

Major differences in performance exist between SACCOs formed by the MFC and those already previously in existence, with the former outperforming the latter. Firstly, this can be ascribed to the political basis on which many SACCOs were originally formed, with the result that in some instances the economic activities do not support the presence of viable and sustainable institutions. In contrast, the MFC focuses on the areas with an economic potential and with justifiable demand for financial services.

Secondly, the legacy of the poor history of the cooperative movement still exists among many Tanzanians. The absence of members' awareness, limited range of products and services, and historical poor governance are typical features of the existing SACCOs. People also remain reluctant to join and invest in these institutions. It often takes a long time for these existing SACCOs to adopt best practices, despite the numerous training programmes intended to build their capacity.

In contrast, where SACCOs are formed by the MFC, best practice is instituted from the beginning, and the MFC facilitates guidance on placement of quality

Table 13.12 CRDB (MFC) staff

	Dec-02	Dec-03	Dec-04	Jun-05
MFC Regional Staff	4	5	8	11
Average number of SACCOs per staff member	8	14	14	14
Average number of SACCO members per staff member	1,552	2,318	4,272	5,632

Source: CRDB, 2005.

Table 13.13 Consolidated performance of linked SACCOs

	Dec-02	Dec-03	Dec-04	Mar-05
Paid-up share capital	990,833	3,402,872	3,632,625	3,869,821
Member deposits	534,874	6,516,558	9,852,508	12,226,861
Total funds mobilized	1,525,708	9,919,429	13,485,133	16,096,681
Deposits with CRDB	472,781	804,235	2,037,383	1,450,032
Loans disbursed by SACCOS	4,773,713	25,862,155	42,170,552	50,798,363
CRDB loans to SACCOS	1,727,485	4,625,482	8,768,119	10,413,709
Member deposits as % of paid up share capital	54%	191%	271%	316%
Deposits with CRDB as % of funds mobilized by SACCOS	31%	8%	15%	9%
Deposits with CRDB as % of CRDB loans	27%	17%	23%	14%
CRDB Loans as % of paid-up share capital	174%	136%	241%	269%
Total SACCOs	32	67	107	157
Total members	12,180	32,464	59,812	78,855

Source: CRDB, 2005.

board members and professional staff who can deliver on members' expectations. This involvement by the MFC has generated confidence in the public and has resulted in rapid growth of the institutions.

Thirdly, the MFC facilitates the development of a wide range of products and services tailored to suit members'/client needs. Unlike the pricing strategies of traditional SACCOs, pricing guidelines by the MFC results in strong profits which, in turn, enables the payment of dividends to investors (members). This further serves to attract new investors while also setting the SACCOs on the path to financial sustainability.

Challenges facing the linkage model

While the linkage model has performed well, it is not without its challenges. Some of the key challenges mentioned are as follows.

From an MFC perspective

The challenges facing CRDB (MFC) are primarily, although not exclusively, from a legal/regulatory nature:

- The implementation of the 2005 Cooperative Law requires that MFIs conduct elections of new Board Members which will require on-going additional training of Board Members and professional staff. This will provide a challenge for the MFC to provide ongoing training with limited resources.

- The supervisory mechanisms in place for SACCOs remain weak, which places an ongoing burden on the MFC.
- The 2005 microfinance regulation does not make provision for wholesale funding to microfinance institutions and raises issues such as the loan concentration ratio which is limited to 1 per cent of the core capital and 3 per cent of fully secured loans. This may prove restrictive to entities such as the MFC.
- Furthermore, issues such as the establishment of microfinance subsidiaries by banks have not been provided for by the new regulations.
- The high initial cost of developing intermediaries because of the dispersion of the rural population and the lack of knowledge and experience in banking among the target population.
- The linked SACCOs have experienced growth of up to 4000 per cent in their assets and client deposits, and had to undergo drastic transformation and commercialization. This has in instances resulted in tension between the SACCOs and their clients, while confidence and monitoring is put to the test.

From a SACCO perspective

- Lack of education and skills among staff and clients.
- The on-going expansion and deepening of outreach into rural areas, has significantly increased the volume of transactions and appropriate MIS is an increasing challenge.
- Appropriate technology to reach an increasingly diverse set of customers.
- Appropriate strategies to achieve and maintain operational and financial sustainability over the long run.
- Developing the capacity to provide tailor-made products and conduct research and development.
- Government interference which forces SACCOs to grant credit only in specific geographical locations or for specific purposes could have various adverse implications for SACCOs and result in confusion relating to ownership and distort institutional development.
- The Government's intention to use SACCOs as a strategy for poverty reduction may jeopardize institutional best practices due to political pressure.

Competition

As SCCULT and SELF both provide training and access to credit for SACCOs, they effectively compete with CRDB, and some of CRDB's linked SACCOs also receive assistance and access loans from SELF and SCCULT. From a different perspective, these initiatives are supporting and complementing one another, and are all working towards the same goal of building the capacity of SACCOs and improving access to credit for the rural poor through on-lending to SACCOs.

What differentiates the MFC from SCCULT and SELF, is that the MFC is part of a private commercial banking group, and offers a much broader range of products and services to linked SACCOs and the SACCOs' clients, including deposit taking, cash handling, transactional facilities and the TemboCard. Furthermore, the MFC adheres to cooperative laws, insofar as they demand certificates for maximum liability issued by the Registrar when requesting a loan; and insists on SACCOs adhering to best practice.

The main competitors of CRDB in terms of broader commercial banking are commercial and microfinance institutions – and in particular NMB, which has also been targeting SACCOs, primarily in the cane-growing areas.

Another level of competition for CRDB are SACCOs not linked to CRDB, but operating in the same villages as linked SACCOs. These include independent SACCOs or those accessing services from any of the aforementioned players. They pose indirect competition for CRDB, as the SACCOs must compete for members within their particular communities.

Benefits of the linkage model to CRDB, SACCOs and clients

Benefits to CRDB

The immediate benefit to CRDB Bank is that the linkage model has enabled it to increase the outreach to previously underserved communities tremendously. While this model requires a larger upfront investment than the direct provision of services to low income markets, it should become self-sustainable over the long term and yield the following benefits:

- Leveraging: broad outreach has already been attained with a small number of staff. Once the SACCOs become profitable, the operating cost of the MFC relative to the number of clients reached (SACCO members), will be exceptionally low;
- The model enables CRDB to reach into distant geographical regions, as well as to service the very low-income groups. This can not easily and cost-effectively be achieved through other models;
- The linkage model has enabled CRDB to developing a strong position in the low income market – and particularly rural areas – which represents the majority of the Tanzanian market, and provides CRDB with a competitive edge over its competition which are primarily clamouring for the over-serviced higher income urban markets; and
- Over the long term, CRDB will also reap the financial benefits of investing in the SACCOs.

Benefits for linked institutions

The main benefits to the linked institutions are probably the credibility and legitimacy that they receive through their association with CRDB, the institutional capacity building and transformation, and then the improved efficiencies and (eventually) profitability. Through the support from and association with CRDB, the linked institutions have gained a new positive image in the market place. Communities regained confidence in SACCOs that client deposits would be safe with them, attracting newcomers to the market and attracting customers away from competition.

Profitability is further improved through the following factors.

- SACCOs have been able to expand their product range tremendously, attracting new members and increasing their customer base and the volume of their operations.
- Without the access to credit from CRDB, SACCOs would have remained cash-strapped and would not have been able to achieve the phenomenal growth witnessed of their loan portfolios.
- Improved operations, management and governance have led to newly gained efficiencies and improved loan performance.
- Through stronger internal controls and improved systems, loan performance has improved.
- Through access to interest-bearing deposit facilities, interest income has soared: A survey conducted in 2004 indicated that deposits with SACCOs increased 18.8 times since the institutions formalized the link with CRDB (MFC).

Benefits to clients

The main beneficiaries of the linkages are probably the end-clients or SACCO members.

- The main benefit of the CRDB linkage model is that SACCO members now have access to secure financial institutions thanks to the support provided by the MFC to the SACCOs.
- As owners of the SACCOs (as opposed to simply being clients of a large institution), the members can influence the strategy of the SACCOs:
  - Members therefore have greater security in having ongoing access to the SACCOs, as they are not dependent on the decisions and possible changes in strategy by a large formal institution;
  - The members decide on their product needs, ensuring that product development is a customized demand-driven approach; and
  - Members also have the potential financial benefit of sharing in dividends once the SACCO becomes profitable with the support of CRDB.
- With the support of the MFC, the SACCOs have been able to develop and provide their members with a variety of products and services. Two out of three SACCOs have introduced new products after linking with CRDB. These product offerings include:
  - Various types of safe, secure savings products with a positive interest rate;

- Access to affordable low-cost credit for a variety of needs, on suitable terms;
- Various types of payment and transactional facilities, including the TemboCard and business payment facilities;
- Ability to send or receive remittances to/from anywhere in Tanzania;
- A reduced need for cash, providing improved financial safety and security through the Tembocard – debit Card and Smart card version; and
- Access to their accounts countrywide through the Tembocard.
- All the above benefits are offered to members right at the doorstep, through CRDB's linkage with local village-level member-based institutions, even in areas traditionally neglected by financial institutions. In many instances, no SACCO or other form of access to finance existed in the villages, until CRDB facilitated the formation of such SACCOs.

As proof of the high perceived level of benefits offered by the CRDB-linked SACCOs, a study conducted by CRDB into the linkage model in October 2004 (CRDB, 2004), demonstrated that approximately 32 per cent of SACCO members defected from competitor institutions. This also displays the high level of confidence that members have in these linked institutions.

Impact of linkage

While no attempt has been made to quantify the impact of the CRDB/SACCO linkage model in this study, through observation and analysis of the performance of the MFC and the linked SACCOs, various current and potential dimensions of improved access to finance and more secure livelihoods can be derived. There is no doubt that the initiative has resulted in both improved breadth and depth of outreach – extending to rural areas and the poor – and as such has contributed to deepening the financial services in Tanzania, positively impacting on access to finance for many ordinary Tanzanians.

The number of SACCOs linked (157) in such a short period of time, and the number of members reached (78,855), speaks for itself in terms of the breadth of outreach. According to the survey conducted by CRDB on the linkage model (October, 2004), almost 40 per cent of members opened a savings account or applied for credit for the first time in their lives through the CRDB-linked SACCOs.

In effect, the injection of credit into these previously underserved markets has had a catalyst effect on the level of economic activity in communities. SACCOs report increased employment in communities – both directly with the SACCO as an employer, and indirectly through enabling individuals to start businesses and, at times, employ others.

One of the major impacts of the linkage model, is that on financial sector level. The development of this linkage model is an excellent example of closing the gap between the formal and the informal sector, as the informal sector (SACCOs) is gradually being integrated with the formal sector. This is an evolving process, and it can be expected that the SACCOs will become stronger and more sophisticated over time, further closing the gap by bringing their members even closer to the formal sector.

Through the MFC linkage model, CRDB has then also demonstrated to other commercial banks that it is possible to reach out to lower-income Tanzanians on a large scale and in a profitable manner. The opportunity is there. However, it does call for a long-term vision, the willingness to invest in the market, the ability to listen to the market and adjust the approach as required, and the dedication to follow through with the plan.

Conclusions and lessons learned

There are many potential lessons that can be derived from this study, some of which may be relevant to practitioners, others to donors or government. Many of these are indeed replicable in other institutions and/or countries in similar or even different circumstances:

- First and foremost, there must be the willingness and commitment from management to enter the lower-income market. In this particular instance, the role of DANIDA as guarantor, shareholder in CRDB, and part of the management team, certainly played a key role in setting CRDB on the path of targeting the lower income market. The initiative received broad support within CRDB, and, unlike many donor-supported initiatives, has been launched on commercial principles with MFC as an integral part of CRDB's business.
- While some may argue that such an initiative would not have been possible without the guarantee provided by DANIDA, to date the guarantee has been more symbolic and has played the role of motivator rather than as a financial catch net, as the guarantee has indeed not yet been accessed – the outcome of a well-managed initiative with a strong commercial focus, and various guarantees built into the system on different levels.
- One major requirement of this approach is the ability to make a large upfront investment into the model, and a long-term vision with the willingness to see this through. While many commercial banks or donors may have the means to do so, they should also have the dedication to stick to the programme over the medium to long-term, and should not be hampered by a short-term vision or a desire to reap immediate financial benefits. In the case of CRDB, their roots always have been in rural areas, and they had the support of one of their largest shareholders in the form of DANIDA. Whereas part of the management of CRDB was initially sceptical, they are now full of support given the strong performance of the linkage model, and having realized that it represents a good business opportunity for the bank.
- The challenge for many banks and donors is then not as much to obtain the required capital to invest in such a programme, but to spend it in the most appropriate manner. CRDB has demonstrated that a relatively small

capital investment in the actual SACCOs (such as equipment and strong rooms) may be necessary to get the SACCOs up and running in a professional manner. However, more importantly is the much larger investment that has to be made for a period of time in building the capacity of SACCO staff and management, and to develop an understanding of the approach and benefits among members and even the broader community.

- The support provided by other players in the market – notably IFAD and to a lesser extent also programmes such as SELF – of investing in the capacity-building of SACCOs, has also played a key role in preparing the market place. This linkage model therefore also demonstrates the benefits and synergies of introducing complementary initiatives.

- At the core of the SACCOs' success have been the strong market-driven approach and a willingness to collaborate with communities and existing SACCOs. Rather than adopting an approach of applying some international best practice in selecting the SACCOs to be linked, CRDB went to the villages and, together with the communities, developed a workable approach. Products are also not set from the top-down, but are developed on SACCO level, depending on the financing needs of the particular community. A truly demand-led approach.

- That said, CRDB has been tenacious in its application of basic commercial banking principles, when it came to issues such as managing the operations of the SACCOs, controls, loan repayment, reporting, and so forth.

- The end vision of the model is then to create self-sustaining profitable institutions, and to do so through a process of leveraging to achieve maximum outreach while containing institutions' (in this case CRDB) costs.

- It has also been (and still is) a learning process , with the model constantly being reassessed and improved to better meet the needs of SACCOs and their members, while improving performance and efficiencies.

- It should be noted that in the instance of CRDB, they have been a major player in rural areas – albeit it through various unsuccessful interventions – and there has therefore been a certain 'strategic fit' with CRDB's heritage and a renewed effort in accessing the rural (and agricultural) market. This has not altogether been virgin territory for CRDB.

- It is interesting to note that, apart from some expatriate managerial expertise on CRDB level and initial training by external experts in member-based institutions (paid for by DANIDA), the implementation of the linkage-model has by and large been done by local Tanzanians (including the management of MFC), working with local institutions and groups. This reflects a predominantly indigenous approach, with no high-cost expatriate salaries to be carried by the MFC for long-term implementation.

- The legal and regulatory framework was not ideal at the time that the initiative was launched: SACCOs fell under the Ministry of Cooperatives and Marketing with poor supervision and regulation, while banks were registered and regulated with the Bank of Tanzania; and commercial banks were (and still are) restricted in terms of the maximum value of loans to a single entity. However, a regulatory framework did exist which allowed for the legal existence of both SACCOs and microfinance institutions, and CRDB worked around the other shortcomings by, for example, implementing their own strict set of reporting criteria and controls.

- The MFC model has proven that the lack of confidence in institutions – in this instance, cooperatives – following previous bad experiences, can indeed be overcome if the strategy is well executed. The legacy of the past need not hamstring future initiatives.
- The volume of credit of a community is limited by the ability to mobilize savings – a big limitation in poor remote rural villages. The injection of capital into the community through effective provision of credit has a catalytic effect which benefits the broader community as a whole. It also helps smooth out the effects of seasonality, which often impacts an entire community because of overriding dependence on one or a few select commodities.
- The provision of a broader set of financial services is also limited by the capacity and skillset of the community. 'Injecting' skills into the community through training and support, benefits the members of the institution as well as the broader community directly through improved financial services, but also indirectly through increased capacity in the community as a whole. In this sense, it serves to empower communities to take better care of themselves.
- Success has a snowball effect, and as communities learn about the success of SACCOs in other communities, they become more open to engage in a similar process.
- The CRDB linkage model is a classical example of how the formal and informal sectors can be linked – despite various challenges – resulting in closer integration of the formal and informal sector, to the benefit of all parties. The success they have achieved will hopefully also act as a catalyst to inspire other institutions to follow suit.

References

Cooperative and Rural Development Bank (2004) *CRDB Bank in Nguzo: Changing Lives through Microfinance in Tanzania*, Arusha.

CRDB (MFC) (2000–4) 'Quarterly progress reports for microfinance activities', Arusha. Website: http://www.crdb.com

International Fund for Agricultural Development (IFAD) (2004) *Rural Financial Services Programme (RFSP), Phase I Implementation Review, 1: Final Main Report*, Rome.

Ingves, S. (2005) *Microfinance: A View from the Fund*, International Monetary Fund (IMF), Washington D.C.

Randhawa, B and Gallardo, J. (2003) *Microfinance Regulation in Tanzania: Implications for Development and Performance of the Industry*, The World Bank, Washington D.C.

United Nation Development Programme (2005) *Human Development Report*, UNDP, New York.

Websites

African Development Bank, http://www.afdb.org
Bank of Tanzania, http://www.bot-tz.org
CGAP Microfinance Gateway, http://microfinancegateway.org
CIA, http://www.odci.gov/cia/publications/factbook
DANIDA, http://www.um.dk
UNDP, http://hdr.undp.org

CHAPTER 14
Conclusions

In most parts of the world, rural areas are characterized by low population density and wide dispersion. Coupled with poor infrastructure and communication links, this makes provision of financial services prohibitively expensive. Low productivity in the agricultural sector, farmers' insufficient access to markets and market information and their often insufficient capacity and measures to manage risk resulting from unfavourable weather conditions, pests, diseases etc., furthermore turns agricultural lending into a highly risky business for financial institutions. In servicing the rural areas, financial institutions have limited opportunities to diversify loan portfolio risk as most of their clients need loans to invest in activities that are either directly or indirectly related to agriculture. In addition, financial services providers are faced with the seasonality issues that investing in agriculture presents. Liquidity management for the finance suppliers becomes increasingly challenging in rural markets, where loan turnover is much slower and loan size is much higher than in urban markets serving microentrepreneurs. They are also constrained by the population's low level of education and the shortage of well-trained people for their own institutional development. The list of problems and constraints can be made even longer.

Against this background, the challenges of providing financial services to the rural areas in a sustained manner seem daunting if not insurmountable. One way to address this difficult situation is through linking formal financial institutions to less formal ones. Formal financial institutions often offer a wide range of financial services, have extensive infrastructures and systems, have access to capital and have more opportunities to diversify their loan portfolio. However, they are often not interested in rural clients, lack the necessary skills to analyze their credit risks, are not familiar with local culture and market conditions, and have systems that are not flexible enough to enable them to innovate and improve their ways of delivering services. Informal financial institutions are closer to the rural population, are more flexible and innovative, and know local conditions well. Often, however, they can only offer a very limited range of financial services, lack the necessary infrastructure to serve a dispersed clientele, are faced with very concentrated portfolios, and have, at best, limited access to sufficient and adequate resources. Hence, on the surface, it appears that forming alliances between the formal and informal financial institutions could result in expanded access to financial services in rural areas.

This study was undertaken in an effort to learn more about formal-informal financial sector linkages and their impact on expanding the frontier in rural finance in Africa, Asia and Latin America. The financial linkages take many forms and no single circumstance is sufficient to explain the emergence of various types of linkages or the reasons why specific institutions enter into linkages. Some linkages are spontaneous and market driven, such as when a large urban commercial bank lends to a cooperative or NGO that specialises in rural lending. Other linkages are sponsored, such as when donors support the creation of wholesale apex institutions for lending to small rural retail institutions. Some linkages emerge out of compliance with regulations, such as when an insurance company links with rural microfinance institutions (MFIs) as a way to meet its quota of life insurance sales to rural customers. Sometimes small institutions seek linkages with larger ones to gain access to their more abundant resources and expertise, while larger institutions want to link with smaller ones that are closer to and more knowledgeable about the demands of a specific rural clientele for financial services. Some linkages are expected to be permanent because they serve the long-term business interests of both partners. Others, however, may experience a natural lifecycle in which they are designed, serve a purpose for a time, but then disappear because regulations, markets, institutions, or clients change.

Linkages can have positive outcomes at the level of both financial institutions and rural clients. Through linkages, financial institutions may be able to expand the scale and scope of their rural operations resulting in greater profits and better financial and institutional sustainability. New clients may be reached and existing clients may be offered a broader and/or cheaper range of financial products and services. Negative impacts can occur when subsidized new entrants crowd out established actors. Exclusive contract requirements within a linkage may also impede experimental linkages with other institutions that would generate new products and services.

This initial evidence indicates that the linkage between formal and informal financial institutions seem to afford both partners the opportunity to overcome a weakness in what they can achieve on their own. But does this initial appeal translate into anything sustainable and replicable? Although it is certainly too early to tell, financial linkages and alliances, while promising, are difficult to set up and manage, require strong less formal as well as formal institutions and seldom result in a significant expansion of financial services beyond credit.

In the following sections of the book we present a brief overview of the linkages reviewed, provide key observations drawn from the collection of the case studies, and offer recommendations on ways to foster financial sector linkages in rural finance. Readers should bear in mind that we did not review all types of formal-informal financial sector linkages in a given country, with the exception of Indonesia as presented in Chapter 8. Rather the intent was to identify and study in some detail cases that demonstrated success in expanding the supply of rural financial services. The selection process, as in any exercise of this nature, was less than perfect. We tried to cast the net wide using our formal and informal networks to identify cases that met our definition of success. Nevertheless, we may have missed some interesting cases and/or could not consider others because they were too young and just beginning to emerge[1]. That said, it would be erroneous to imply that we had ample cases from which to choose. In short, at the start of the study there were few partnerships between formal and informal financial institutions resulting in an increased supply of rural financial services[2].

Financial linkages overview[3]

In Table 14.1 we present an overview of the financial linkages reviewed, with an indication of the primary driver and motivation behind the partnership as well as a description of the main partners and other partners contributing to the implementation of the linkage[4].

We found that a diverse set of formal and informal financial actors engage in linkages for a variety of reasons, ranging from more commercial-oriented strategies of expanding services, penetrating markets, and diversifying sources of revenue and funds to more development-oriented strategies of increasing the rural poor's access to financial services. In the cases we studied both formal and informal actors drive the partnerships backing our complementarity hypothesis, that each actor possesses complementary characteristics which when joined, result in a synergistic effect. In our cases formal linkage actors consist of private and public commercial banks and second-tier apex organizations, a credit union, and an insurance company while informal actors range from self-help groups, village banks, savings and credit associations, financial NGOs, MFIs, and community banks. Non-financial actors, such as utility companies, mobile phone companies, money transfer firms, and government departments are also becoming important linkage partners.

Over the last several years many private banks and insurance companies have entered the microfinance market by establishing linkages with informal institutions. ICICI Bank, India's second largest commercial bank, partners with MFIs in unique ways to extend credit directly to Self Help Groups (SHGs) in rural areas (Harper and Singh, 2005). ICICI's preferred method is to use MFIs as facilitation agents to help screen and monitor SHG borrowers. ICICI reserves bulk lending for the best performing MFIs. AVIVA Life India, a leading global insurance company, uses MFIs to offer life insurance products to rural people by bundling life insurance to their loans. In limited cases, some MFIs even act as formal retail agents for the company, which allows them to offer life insurance products to individuals outside of their microfinance client base. In Tanzania, CRDB Bank Limited, a private bank, has aggressively entered the market by offering SACCOs a range of financial services including long and short-term loans and credit lines and various payment and transfer instruments. To do this

Table 14.1 Financial linkages overview

Country	Linkage	Main driver	Linkage motivation	Linkage partners	Other important partners
Bolivia	FADES with numerous financial and non-financial partners	FADES	Widen range of non-traditional financial services to current and new clients	Regulated credit union; Western Union; private pension fund administrator; power company; 3 mobile phone companies; 3 state programmes extending social benefits/services	Folade, an international NGO
Costa Rica	FINCA/Costa Rica with communal credit enterprises and financial NGOs	FINCA/Costa Rica national programme	Capacity building and fostering linkages of CCEs to formal financial market	Four financial NGOs regionally based; three commercial banks; one second-tier financial organization; 28 communal credit enterprises	Three state organizations, CODESPA, a Spanish NGO
Honduras	Covelo Holding Group with financial and non-financial partners	Covelo Foundation	Stengthen the capacity of linked financial and non-financial service organizations	Regulated MFI; one second-tier financial organization; private development finance organizations; international donors and investors	Financial Transactions Reports Analysis Centre (FINTRAC), Honduran Foundation for Agricultural Research, China/Taiwan Mission
India	ICICI Bank with microfinance institutions (MFIs) and self-help groups	ICICI Bank	Cultivate future market and meet regulatory requirement – sector targets	MFIs; self-help groups	CARE International project for 'accrediting' MFIs

Country					
India	AVIVA Life Insurance Company, Ltd. with rural and non-bank finance companies	Aviva Life	Cultivate future market and meet regulatory requirement – sector targets	MFIs; trade union	
Indonesia	Regional Development Bank (BPD) with village credit organizations (LPDs)	BPD, regional government	Monitor, supervise and strengthen the capacity of village credit associations	LPDs	BPD District Centres, LPD associations, village supervisory boards, village assemblies
Mali	Banque Nationale de Développement Agricole (BNDA) with MFIs	MFIs, donor community	Obtain credit for on-lending, liquidity balancing. Expand poor's access to financial services	BNDA	NGOs, donors, producer associations
Peru	Confianza with a range of bank and non-banking partners	Confianza	Expand sources of funds	Commercial banks; international investors; donors	
Philippines	PCFC with MFIs, rural banks	Donor/ government created apex organization	Expand poor's access to credit	MFIs; rural banks	Accredited training centres, accredited MFIs, donors
Rwanda	Union of People's Banks in Rwanda with savings and credit associations	CARE International	Expand rural poor's access to financial services	Local People's Banks; savings and credit associations	
Tanzania	CRDB Bank Ltd and savings and credit cooperatives	CRDB	Cost-effectively expand into rural market; increase rural poor's access to financial services	Savings and credit cooperatives	Danish Cooperation

Source: Individual case studies from linkage study.

Abbreviations: SACCO: Savings and Credit Cooperatives; PCFC: People's Credit and Finance Corporation; BPD/LPD: Indonesian Regional Development Bank and community-based nillage non-bank financial institutions; FADES: Fundación para Alternativas de Desarrollo; EDPYME: Entidad de desarrollo de la pequeña y micro-empresa.

the bank has set up a microfinance unit entirely dedicated to the development of this new market segment.

State-owned development banks continue to engage in partnerships, mainly by providing bulk loans to informal financial institutions. In Mali, the Banque Nationale de Développement Agricole (BNDA) has a long history of using bulk loans and lines of credit as well as savings accounts to help intermediaries like Kafo Jiginew, the largest network of savings and credit cooperatives, and CVECA-ON, a large village bank network, deal with cash flow variability and/or portfolio expansion. In Indonesia, the provincial bank in Bali, Bank Pembangunan Daerah (BPD) plays a significant parenting role for customary village banks (LPDs) by offering staff training as well as monitoring and supervision services, as mandated by the central banking authority. BPD also provides the LPDs with normal savings and loans services that help them manage their liquidity more effectively.

Public, private or community-owned apex organizations continue to play a significant role in expanding financial services in non-traditional markets through financial linkages. In the Philippines, the government-owned apex organization, PCFC, partners with numerous microfinance providers by offering wholesale credit and training. Through strict selection criteria backed by strong capacity-building mechanisms, PCFC has been instrumental in mainstreaming microfinance in the Philippines. In Honduras, a private first and second-tier organization, Covelo Foundation, offers bulk loans and lines of credit to MFIs and plays a significant role in strengthening its partner MFIs' internal systems and controls to improve self-regulation mechanisms. In Rwanda, the community owned apex, Union of People's Banks, through CARE's financial and technical assistance and its extensive network of People's Banks, is able to penetrate further into rural markets. For the first time, People's Banks are extending services to SHGs, a segment of the market that has proved to be surprisingly profitable.

Microfinance institutions and financial NGOs establish linkages with various actors in an effort to expand the scope and scale of their businesses, enabling them to survive in competitive, maturing microfinance markets. Fundación para Alternativas de Desarrollo (FADES), a non-regulated, non-government organization in Bolivia, created a number of strategic, inter-institutional linkages allowing them to offer their clients an array of services, such as deposit and money transfer facilities, bill payment and salary and pension contribution collections. In order to become less dependent on donor funds and conditions, FINCA/Costa Rica promoted the incorporation of each of its village banks in the late 1990s, paving the way for all units in the network to establish relationships with commercial banks and other non-bank financial companies. In Peru, Confianza, a regulated MFI, accesses lines of credit and bulk loans from commercial banks and donors as a way of increasing and diversifying its sources of funds.

Main study observations

Financial linkages are more commercial and strategic in their focus as compared to a more 'project-led' focus in the past

The linking of the formal and informal financial sectors is not new. In fact it was a major programmatic thrust of some development agencies, like GTZ, from the mid-1980s to the mid-1990s. The idea of linking informal self-help groups took hold during a regional workshop on 'Strengthening Institutional Credit Services to Low-income Groups,' in Nanjing, China in May 1986, which was organized by the Asia–Pacific Rural and Agricultural Credit Association (APRACA) and GTZ. Later that year APRACA decided to make 'linkage banking' its main programmatic thrust. Subsequently, with the financial and technical assistance of GTZ over a ten-year period, APRACA helped its partners to develop linkage banking programmes in Bangladesh, India, Indonesia, the Philippines and Thailand (Seibel, 2006). These efforts were backed up with GTZ's bilateral linkage banking projects in Indonesia, the Philippines and Thailand during the same period (APRACA–GTZ, 1997).

The linkage banking projects have had some notable successes in some places. For example, India, with its vast network of rural bank branches, has mainstreamed linkage banking on a national scale. Through the National Bank for Agricultural Development (NABARD), India has over 1.6 million self-help groups linked to 36,000 bank branches serving 24 million members, covering over 120 million people from the lowest income segments of the population (Seibel, 2006). However, as history has shown, these types of linkage banking programmes require a significant amount of financial and human resources, resources that are not readily available in most countries.

In contrast to past efforts, we found evidence that financial linkages and interactions between informal and formal financial institutions are more internally driven than the 'linkage banking' projects of the past. This is not a surprising finding given the paradigm shift in rural finance that has taken place over the last several decades, one that places emphasis on offering commercially viable financial services rather than subsidized interventions of the past.

Another factor explaining this trend appears to be a fundamental change in the way formal financial institutions view informal actors and vice versa. Formal financial institutions, spurred on by the recent good performance of informal financial institutions, see informal actors as important strategic partners for reaching new markets in a cost-effective manner. Several of the formal institutions reviewed in this study have made linking with informal actors an integral part of their outreach strategy. Similarly, informal financial institutions appear to be viewing formal financial institutions and other non-bank financial companies in a new light, recognizing the critical role that formal sector linkages can play in developing new lines of business and achieving sustainability. Under this backdrop and that of the push for more commercially oriented rural financial services provision, we are beginning to see more spontaneous and internally driven financial linkages, based on market principles. The following cases exemplify this 'market-based approach':

Formal institutions:

- Aviva Life Insurance Company and ICICI Bank. Faced with a priority sector mandate requiring that at least 40 per cent of all commercial banks and insurers' business target priority sectors, e.g. rural areas, small industries, exporting firms, housing and agriculture, Aviva Life and ICICI Bank turned to the local microfinance sector to reach into the rural market. What began for both of these companies as a way to meet priority sector targets soon became an important part of their long-term corporate strategy and vision.

- CRDB, Ltd. Responding to the president's call to extend banking services to all Tanzanians, especially in rural area, CRDB chose a business model of linking with rural savings and credit cooperatives (SACCOs) rather than serving this market directly. With a view to cultivating a future market, CRDB has dedicated significant resources to its partnership model.

- People's Bank Rwanda. Although the intention to link with self-help groups (SHGs) did not emerge from within, the People's Bank of Rwanda, encouraged by the impeccable repayment record of the groups and individuals, now sees SHGs as viable partners in expanding its services to new market segments it previously considered unprofitable.

Informal institutions:

- Fundación para alternativas de Desarrollo (FADES) a non-regulated NGO specializing in the supply of financial services, established strategic alliances with public and private organizations as a way to provide a number of additional services, such as bill payment, money transfers and deposit mobilization, to its target population in a cost-effective, sustainable manner. FADES has significantly increased and diversified its revenue base through the service fees earned from these alliances.

- BASIX, a non-bank finance company, in an effort to offer life insurance to its clients, established a strategic partnership with ICICI Prudential in early 2001. A year later BASIX shifted its insurance business to AVIVA Life, a more cost-effective and flexible partner, willing to experiment and pilot new products that better fit the needs of BASIX. Both partners have spoken highly of the experience of working together, expressing great satisfaction in the achievements they have made in providing health insurance to several thousand borrowers.

- Confianza, given its new status as a formally registered MFI in Peru, has established financial linkages with international and local (public and private) financial institutions to obtain competitively priced loans and lines of credit to meet its growing funding needs. This access coupled with a strategic re-orientation of its business operations and systems, has significantly impacted on the organization's development, from a client base of 900 in 1999 to approximately 38,000 in 2005.

A country's economic and financial system development affects the potential for establishing linkages

The development of a country's financial system dramatically affects the potential for financial linkages. In countries where both formal and informal organizations are weak, the potential for linking is extremely low. In contrast, in countries where formal and informal organizations are both strong the potential for linking is high. Conning and Kevane (2002) use the analogy of islands (institutions) linked with bridges (transactions), and indicate that: 'Where financial intermediation is more developed, a dense network of actual or potential bridges across islands will be in place'. They note that 'bridging the gaps' between the local, informal partners and the national, formal partners is something that will increasingly happen, as a country develops over time.

In Table 14.2 we rank the case countries by their human development index (HDI), an indicator of a country's overall level of development. Analysing the index ranking we see that the case countries fall broadly into three groups. For the purposes of this discussion let us call the first group (Costa Rica, Peru, and the Philippines) 'high development', the second group (Indonesia, Bolivia, Honduras and India) 'middle development', and the third group (Rwanda, Tanzania and Mali) 'low development'. As a measure of robustness of the banking sector we provide the Bank Capital to Asset Ratio. A higher ratio signals stronger financial institutions in a given country.

High income, stable growth, low rural population, and a robust banking sector characterize the 'high development' group. Countries in this group can be considered as having a well functioning formal financial sector and a small informal financial sector (Costa Rica) to larger informal sectors (Peru, Philippines). Countries in this grouping vary in their need and potential for linking. Costa Rica, with a well functioning banking sector and, a subsequent lack of informal actors, has less of a need for creating linkages in rural finance. The need and potential for financial sector linkages in Peru and the Philippines appears instead higher. In Peru, the recently enacted microfinance law has helped to organize the informal sector, having what appears to be a positive impact on the institutional capacity and performance of several MFIs in the country. Initial evidence from this study suggests that MFIs, given their new legal status, have been able to increase the number and types of financial sector linkages. However, financial linkages may not be able to overcome persistent risks and costs of serving the country's rural market, given its adverse geographical conditions, low rural population density, and, in some areas, poor economic opportunities. The Philippines, with a large rural market potential, coupled with high literacy rates, higher population density and a well-functioning banking sector, the country appears well suited for establishing a range of strategic partnerships to expand the supply of financial and other services in rural areas. Indeed, we are already seeing this happen, with the partnering of mobile telephone service providers linking with banks and others to expand telecommunication and other services in rural areas (Lyman, Ivatury, and Staschen, 2006).

Table 14.2 Case countries' socio-economic indicators

	2006	2005				Average annual growth rates 1999–2005		
	HDI ranking (life expectancy, literacy, real GDP at PPP)	Total population ('000)	Rural population (% of total)	Population density per square km	GNI per capita (US$)	GDP per capita (%)	Inflation rate (%)	Bank capital to asset ratio (%) (2006)
1. Costa Rica	4	4327	38	85	4590	2.5	10.5	74
2. Peru	82	27968	27	22	2610	2.1	2.6	56
3. Philippines	84	83054	37	279	1300	2.4	4.8	79
4. Indonesia	108	220558	52	122	720	2.5	10.1	48
5. Bolivia	115	9182	36	8	1010	0.9	2.8	78
6. Honduras	117	7205	54	64	1190	1.8	9.3	50
7. India	126	1094583	71	368	1280	4.3	4.1	34
8. Rwanda	158	9038	81	366	230	3.9	2.9	n.d.
9. Tanzania	162	38329	76	43	340	3.8	4.6	n.d.
10. Mali	175	13518	70	11	380	3.3	0.7	n.d.

Source: World Bank, 2006. n.d., no data available.

A larger portion of the total population in rural areas, higher population density (Indonesia and India), and emerging growth potential characterize the countries that fall into the 'middle development' group. With an expanded financial infrastructure, emerging to well operating informal actors, and steady growth, the countries in this group appear to be well suited for creating robust strategic partnerships in rural finance. However, caution is warranted. In some countries, government intervention, such as priority sector targets in India and mandated partnerships in Indonesia, and low capacity of MFIs, may truncate financial linkage potential. Establishing robust linkages may prove difficult, even in markets where both the formal and informal financial sectors are strong. This was the case in Bolivia where FADES, a well-established MFI, could not find a reliable formal partner for mobilizing deposits. Other factors such as size, differences in corporate culture and vision provoked the termination of this partnership in the end.

High percentage of total population in rural areas, lower total population density (excluding Rwanda), less developed formal, and in some cases, informal financial markets, characterize the third, 'low development', group. In short, there appear to be narrow opportunities to expand the supply of rural financial services through formal-informal sector linkages due to the limited number of actors operating in the countries. Although Mali and Tanzania have a more developed informal financial sector they, as with Rwanda, are limited by the number, strength, and openness of formal financial institutions. In these markets donors appear to play a bigger role in fostering formal–informal financial linkages.

Trade-offs exists between establishing a rural market presence on one's 'own accord' as compared to doing it through 'strategic linkages'

In this study we found that financial institutions wanting to establish a presence in rural areas continue to face formidable challenges. The high costs and risks of serving a rural clientele preclude many formal financial institutions from expanding into rural markets, even though they have the financial and human resources to reach a larger, more diverse clientele. On the other hand, informal financial institutions wanting to establish a presence in rural areas can take advantage of their proximity to overcome some of the challenges. Typically, however, informal institutions constrained by regulation (e.g. not allowed to take deposits) and other factors (e.g. inability to achieve economies of scale and scope) are only able to offer a narrow range of financial services, such as granting small, short-term loans.

Formal and informal financial institutions can overcome some of these costs and risks by strategically partnering with one another. However, there are several factors to consider when deciding to establish a rural market presence. The advantages and disadvantages of two ways of establishing a rural presence, i.e. by doing it on one's 'own accord' or by creating 'strategic linkages,' are reviewed

Table 14.3 Consideration factors for establishing a presence in rural areas

| Formal financial intermediaries | | | | Informal financial intermediaries | | | |
| On own accord | | By strategic linkages | | On own accord | | By strategic linkages | |
Advantages	Disadvantages	Advantages	Disadvantages	Advantages	Disadvantages	Advantages	Disadvantages
More control over screening and monitoring operations	Costly	Relatively quick to become operational	Limited number of reliable, competent partners	More control over terms and conditions of services rendered	Slow, arduous process to develop necessary capacity for offering full range of services	Relatively quick to become operational	May not have many private sector partners from which to choose
Able to monitor progress more quickly	Time consuming, slow process to expand branch network effectively	Cheaper, less capital-intensive investment required	Tricky to develop incentives to induce effective screening and monitoring actions of informal partners	Opportunity to grow with clients	Difficult to achieve economies of scale and scope	High potential to diversify sources of revenue	May run into difficulties in striking the right balance between outsourcing of services and those handled internally
	Increased staff and logistical management	Easier to dismantle if fails	Initial set-up costs high to establish partnership, and to align information systems and		Limited options to diversify portfolio risk; only operate in small geographic region	Can offer clients a broad range of services in a cost-effective way	Takes time to learn how to set-up and manage effective partnerships

| Formal financial intermediaries | | | | Informal financial intermediaries | | | |
| On own accord | | By strategic linkages | | On own accord | | By strategic linkages | |
Advantages	Disadvantages	Advantages	Disadvantages	Advantages	Disadvantages	Advantages	Disadvantages
	Limits to rural penetration, e.g. poor roads, electricity, communication links	High potential to cultivate future clients	Insufficient correspondent banking regulation limiting the nature of linkages		Can only offer clients a narrow range of services due to regulatory and other constraints	Good marketing tool to bring in new clients if other services are offered to general public	May lose clients to partnering organizations, especially those in the same line of business
		Demonstration of corporate social responsibility	May face high resistance from middle management responsibilities				

in Table 14.3, from both the formal and informal financial institutions' point of view.

Financial linkages demonstrate impact on rural client outreach, but seldom result in a significant expansion of rural financial services other than credit

It is important to recall our definition of a successful financial linkage as one that results in expanded access to financial services for new rural clients not traditionally served, broadens the variety of products and services offered, and/ or creates quality improvements of existing products/services through better terms and conditions. Without question the cases reviewed demonstrate success based on one or more of the success factors, mainly on expanding access to new rural clients. It is noteworthy that very few linkages resulted in new products and services other than credit. However, as shown in Table 14.4, some of the linkage cases are resulting in the expansion of 'non-traditional' services, including life insurance, bill payment, transfers and disbursements.

As shown in Table 14.5 the evidence is undeniable that linkage arrangements between formal and informal financial institutions expanded financial outreach, in terms of credit granted, into rural areas. In the Philippines, over a million clients have received loans from institutions linked to PCFC funding, of which more than 50 per cent went to partners operating in rural zones. In Rwanda, more than 20,000 smallholders and entrepreneurs living deep in the rugged countryside now access credit from the People's Banks on a regular basis through their savings and loan groups. In Tanzania, CRDB has reached close to 80,000 new rural clients through 157 SACCOs, by offering loans and deposit facilities.

Although we had difficulty obtaining substantial documentation on the impact of financial linkages resulting in product/service quality improvements, several informal organizations leveraged partnership experience to obtain better terms and conditions for the linked services. This was the case in both organizations reviewed in India. In addition, the 'leveraging of experience' was observed further down the financial continuum. In India many self-help group clients interviewed, encouraged by their linkage experiences, said that they now interact directly with other banks, negotiating better terms and conditions for the products and services received. In essence, they are playing one bank against another. Similarly in Rwanda, several group members leveraged their creditworthiness to open personal accounts with their local People's Bank to manage their personal and business finance matters.

We found some evidence on linkages that broadened the variety of products and services. In Bolivia, Costa Rica, Honduras and India well-established MFIs, with an explicit strategy of improving and expanding client services, are offering an array of integrated services. They have advanced well beyond simple direct financial linkages to interacting with a range of diverse actors to provide life, livestock, weather and health insurance, money transfer and bill payment as well as pension and salary payment services. For example, more than 200,000

Table 14.4 Typology of case study linkages

	Africa			Asia				LATIN AMERICA			
	Mali	Rwanda	Tanzania	India	India	Indonesia	Philippines	Bolivia	Costa Rica	Honduras	Peru
	BNDA and MFIs	People's banks and SHGs	CRDB Bank, SACCOs, community banks and NGOs	ICICI, MFIs and self-help groups	AVIVA Life and MFIs	BPD and LPDs	PCFC, rural banks and MFIs	FADES and various partners	FINCA/Costa Rica, commercial banks, MFIs	Covelo Foundation, MFIs and producer organizations	Confianza (EDPYME) partners
Direct financial linkages											
Bulk loans and credit lines	×	×	×	×		×	×	×	×	×	×
Savings	×		×			×			×	×	×
Facilitating linkages											
Credit				×							
Insurance					×						
Deposit mobilization			×					×			
Money transfers			×					×		×	
Payments			×					×	×	×	
Salary/pension disbursements								×			

Source: Financial linkages case studies, 2005–6.

Table 14.5 Expanded rural outreach through linkages

Country	Links	Date	Partners	Active clients	Loan portfolio (US$ '000)
Bolivia	FADES and various partners	Dec 2004	11	22,387	17,700
Costa Rica	FINCA/Costa Rica, commercial banks and MFIs	Apr 2005	230	7,200	675[1]
Honduras	Covelo Foundation with MFIs	Dec 2004	2	10,870	5,400
India – AVIVA	AVIVA Life with BASIX and SEWA Bank	Dec 2005	2	227,711	8,200
India – ICICI	ICICI with MFIs	Mar 2006	27	1,200,000	66,000
Indonesia	BPD with LPDs	Dec 2004	1,296	318,995	97,909
Mali	BNDA with cooperative network	Dec 2004	2	190,886	19,130
Peru	Confianza with commercial banks, public apex and international partners	Dec 2006	26	37,575	21,533
Philippines	PCFC with Rural Banks and MFIs	Dec 2004	199	1,396,326	51,350
Rwanda	People's Banks and Self Help Groups	Sep 2005	981	25,000	171
Tanzania	CRDB Ltd. linked with SACCOs	Jun 2005	157	78,855	n.d.

Source: Financial linkages case studies, 2005–6. n.d., no data available.
[1]Linked MFI member's equity.

clients now have access to life insurance products because of AVIVA's partnerships with several MFIs operating in rural India. In Bolivia, more than 25,000 former and new clients can transfer and receive money from Santa Cruz and can receive pension payments and pay electricity and phone bills in branches much closer to their homes. Many of these services are delivered to fill gaps in the market. It might be that other financial service providers, such as insurance companies or commercial banks, will directly service this rural market, once the MFI linkage has demonstrated that financial deepening is possible.

Partnerships with the formal sector enhances informal institutions' capacity

Through partnerships with formal sector actors informal institutions have improved their technical know-how in lending, insurance, MIS and management of external partners. Of the eleven cases reviewed, more than half had an explicit component to build the operational capacity of the informal actors. In the case of Rwanda, CARE International organizes and trains SHGs on savings and credit operations. In the Philippines PCFC, through its partnership with the large NGO, CARD, provides training to MFIs and others wanting to access wholesale funds but are unable to meet the necessary preconditions to do so. In Tanzania, CRDB tries to ensure the health of its partner clients by offering a training programme based on specific partner needs, such as MIS, portfolio management and loan appraisal. And in the cases of BPD–LPD linkage in Indonesia and the Covelo Group in Honduras, formal intermediaries act as mentors and supervisors to informal institutions. ICICI Bank, faced with a dearth of potential partners, struck a deal with an international NGO to provide training and technical assistance to MFIs to help build their capacity and bring them up to a level where the bank would consider them a viable partner. Through this partnership, the ICICI team was able to communicate their needs, effectively shaping the nature of the training provided to their future partners.

Nevertheless, none of the cases have included explicit assistance and/or training intended to help the less formal actors engage more effectively in the partnerships. We observed much experimentation and leveraging of learning (or 'learning by doing') by informal institutions to establish more suitable partnerships with commercial banks and insurers as was the case in India and Bolivia. Based on findings from this study, the Food and Agriculture Organization (FAO) and the Foundation for Development Cooperation (FDC), through its Banking with the Poor Network, developed a facilitation guide on establishing and maintaining financial sector partnerships. The organizations pilot-tested the guide during a workshop with 25 MFIs and several formal financial sector actors in India in December 2006. Since that time, FDC has conducted similar training in Sri Lanka and Indonesia and further refined the guide and plans to use it to promote partnerships in microfinance throughout the Asia-Pacific region.

The level of institutional development of informal financial actors determines the way in which they interact with formal financial actors. For example, more mature, well-established MFIs preferred bulk loans and equity investments to the facilitation of credit contracts on behalf of a formal bank. Typically, well-established MFIs are concerned with the threat of losing clients they have worked hard to cultivate. Less-established MFIs found instead that facilitating loans for banks afforded their organizations interesting opportunities for building internal loan management capacity without bearing all of the risk. When it pertains to expanding into non-traditional service offerings, like deposit mobilization, bill payment, transfers, and insurance, well-established informal financial institutions are more capable than young institutions in managing alliances with external partners.

Developing financial linkages and partnerships is not costless

Establishing and maintaining financial linkages takes time and money. Both partners incur costs in developing the linkage, but informal partners bear a heavier burden in relation to their cost structures. Typically, costs are related to the time and resources needed to negotiate partnerships, develop new systems and procedures, hire and train staff, purchase equipment and/or renovate office space and staff salaries, etc.

Adapting procedures and information systems to incorporate a new line of business is an arduous task for any business. Systems adjustment becomes more complex when the procedures and systems of one's business partners must be factored into the equation. This is especially true for business lines that are dependent on the sharing of information on a regular basis. The following cases exemplify the opportunities and challenges.

- FADES: Motivated to supply a wide-range of non-traditional financial services (remittances, bill payments, deposit mobilization, salary transfers, and pension fund disbursements) FADES sought strategic alliances with several partners (Western Union, a credit union, government, utility companies). Although conceptually valid, the organization soon realized the difficulties in adding and maintaining new lines of business with a range of partners. Each of the strategic alliances required programming and adaptation of the organization's software to handle the new service and to enable FADES' system to communicate with its partners' systems. In some instances, lack of compatibility forced FADES to run different programmes on more than one computer, which increased costs as antiquated hardware and software had to be updated to handle the new load. Additional costs were incurred in staff time to consolidate multiple systems in FADES' main business operating system at the end of each month.

- AVIVA Life focuses on 'process innovations' to drive down costs of its partnership model to a sustainable level. AVIVA worked with BASIX to develop a software programme that allowed the two organizations' systems to communicate and transfer data seamlessly. At the time of the study, the two organizations were planning to sell the programme to AVIVA's other partners.

In some markets donors and governments continue to attach conditions to their funding

Conditionalities embedded into the linkage contract, typically by the formal institution, are often binding on the informal partners. In the cases reviewed we observed that some MFIs were compelled to accept restrictive terms and conditions from funders. MFIs often do not have a choice but to accept these conditionalities, since their own regulatory status prevents them from accessing capital through deposit taking or straight loans. Such conditionalities included requirements on use of bulk loans, as in the case of a donor channelling funds through BNDA to the CVECAs for producer associations in Mali; PCFC, the government- owned apex requiring its MFI clients to use a preset lending methodology, the Grameen model; BPD, the provincial bank in Bali requiring its partner LPDs to save only with their bank; and FINCA/Costa Rica being pressured to accept requirements on interest rates, staffing and equipment purchase decisions. While well-established MFIs have come a long way in dealing with distorting conditions that limit their flexibility and growth, many still grapple with how to handle these more subtle issues. In the end it appears that frustration with these conditionalities has motivated many informal institutions to push for better terms and conditions, either with their current partners or with new ones. This was the case of the LPDs in Bali, which wanted to deposit their excess liquidity with other banks that offered better rates and conditions and more flexible hours of operation; stronger, well established MFIs in India negotiating bulk loans from ICICI rather than acting as facilitation agents; and FINCA/Costa Rica radically breaking away from the traditional institutional model by incorporating itself to achieve more flexibility in accessing 'condition free' sources of funding.

Conditionalities embedded in grant funding from donors and governments often result in unforeseen consequences, negatively impacting informal sector actors in the long-run. This was the case for FINCA/Costa Rica in which the organization linked with the Ministry of Agriculture to set up village banks in the Ministry's 'preferred' regions, but in which Finca had never worked. The government did not cover the technical assistance costs for setting up the new village banks, as previously agreed, and Finca was left responsible for finding loanable funds for them. In the end this was not a sustainable strategy and to this day the village banks from that region blame FINCA/Costa Rica, not the government, for being left behind. Another example comes from Mali, where BNDA, a government-owned agricultural bank, has been the main intermediary offering financial services to MFIs. BNDA is involved with two major linkage models: CVECA-ON, which links up with BNDA (and many donors) to expand its portfolio, and Kafo Jiginew, a network that expanded by relying on its own savings. Kafo Jiginew uses the BNDA linkage mainly for liquidity balancing. Both networks operate in comparable environments; there is not much difference in terms of total assets per individual member; and both have access to banks. However, virtually all members (96 per cent) of the Kafo Jiginew cooperatives save, and they save significantly more (US$90 per member) than the members of CVECA-ON, less than half of whom (44 per cent) have a savings account, with average savings per member of just US$32. Clearly the main difference is that CVECA-ON is highly dependent on donor funds while Kafo Jiginew is self-reliant. The unintended negative consequence of the Donor/BNDA/CVECA-ON linkage is that ongoing donor generosity may lead to MFI complacency.

Too early to tell if using agents to facilitate credit and insurance business is a promising strategy

We found that the more innovative and emerging linkages are those in which one partner acts on behalf of the other to perform various operations, including originating and servicing of loan contracts and insurance policies, processing bill payments, transferring funds, and disbursing salary payments and benefits. Only four of the cases involved this type of 'innovative facilitation' approach. And of the four, only two cases concerned the facilitation of credit and insurance. This is an important distinction given that the agency risks are higher when an institution hires a third-party to 'facilitate' credit and insurance contracts than when it outsources the straightforward processing of payments, transfers and disbursements. In short, it takes more time and skill to assess client risk and monitor client actions than it does to transact a one-time payment, transfer or disbursement.

The two cases, one involving credit and the other insurance, are from India. In these cases, ICICI Bank and AVIVA Life Insurance Company hired informal partners to act on their behalf to facilitate loan and insurance contracts. In the case of AVIVA Life, the agency risks are not an issue since the insurance contracts are bundled directly with the loans that the informal partner grants. As previously mentioned, AVIVA reserves the opportunity for its well-established MFI partners to retail insurance to non-clients. In these cases, the agency risks are higher. To address this, the MFI partners have to go through an extensive training and certification process with Aviva Life and the IRDA (Insurance Regulatory Development Authority) of India.

Regarding the second case, ICICI Bank has had a relatively successful experience of using MFI partners acting on behalf of ICICI Bank to originate and monitor loans. By March 2005 ICICI Bank was lending US$66 million to rural clients through 27 partner MFIs. This figure had ballooned to working with 102 MFI partners serving 3.2 million low-income clients by March 2006, already reaching about half of the 200–250 MFI partners the bank would like to partner with by 2010. A large part of its success was due to the approach of ensuring good behaviour by partner agents. To do this the bank instituted three different types of first-loss guarantees with MFIs. The first approach consists of requiring the MFI to place between 8 and 15 per cent of the total loaned in an escrow account which the MFI cannot touch until all loans have been repaid. The second approach is to give the MFI an overdraft limit with ICICI Bank up to the required guaranteed amount to which the MFI could draw upon to cover any losses. The third approach is for the MFI to use a third-party to put up a guarantee to cover any losses. Cashpor and SHARE, India's largest Grameen replicators, have used this approach with ICICI Bank through a guarantee received from the Grameen Foundation of the USA.

Although this model appeared to be working well for ICICI Bank at the time of this study, as of February 2007, the Reserve Bank of India (RBI) requested that ICICI Bank discontinue its partnership model with MFIs. It was concerned that the bank was not meeting the 'know your customer' requirements, since all direct client contact was undertaken with the MFIs and not by ICICI itself. As ICICI Bank is the largest player in the financing of MFIs, primarily through this partnership model, a severe liquidity crunch hit several MFIs abruptly. Young, emerging MFIs, who depended solely on funding from ICICI Bank, were hit hardest as they had not cultivated relationships with other banks in their area. Initial concerns about ICICI's decision and adverse impacts on the microfinance market (e.g. funds shortage, increased capital costs) were quelled when ICICI increased its lending to the informal sector through bulk loans (Business Standard, April 2007). This situation has positively affected the microfinance rating business in India as several MFIs, wanting to establish business with new commercial partners, have sought their services.

Banks and other non-bank firms are beginning to use commercial agents to expand access to 'non-traditional' financial services

We are beginning to see a trend by formal and informal banks towards building strategic alliances to offer non-traditional financial services. Two of the cases demonstrate this trend in practice. FADES, as previously mentioned, established several inter-institutional alliances to expand into new services, including bill payment, benefit disbursements, and transfers. In Tanzania, clients of linked SACCOs can obtain a debit card, allowing them to access any CRDB and partners' ATM in the country. Through the linkage SACCO clients can also transfer money anywhere in the country and make purchases with a limited number of input suppliers using their CRDB debit card.

Indeed, in the last three to four years we have witnessed banks and non-bank firms using commercial agents to 'facilitate' their business transactions, typically referred to as 'correspondent' or 'branchless' banking (Kumar et al., 2007; Lyman, Ivatury, and Staschen, 2006). In some markets, banks are utilizing grocery stores, petrol stations, lottery kiosks, pharmacies, post offices, MFIs, and NGOs to facilitate transactions where the business risks are lowest, such as account-opening, bill payments, collection services, government benefit and pension payments and transfers. Some models include the facilitation of 'limited' banking services (e.g. deposits and withdrawals to receiving and forwarding savings and credit account applications). Mobile phone network operators, with their wide and well-developed distribution channels, are also beginning to offer bank-like services to their subscribers, including transfer of airtime, deposit and withdrawal of funds, loan payments, and the purchase of goods at retail shops (Lyman, Ivatury, and Staschen, 2006).

Although not surprising, the most successful cases of correspondent and branchless banking are from emerging market countries, where the banking and telecommunication infrastructures are strongest. The most successful experiences to date are coming out of Brazil, India, Kenya, the Philippines, and South Africa. Although there is much optimism about the tremendous potential of emerging correspondent and branchless banking models to expand access to the unbanked, very few transformational models exist today (Porteous, 2006), especially with significant outreach in rural areas. Recent studies point to the following reasons why this is the case:

- uncertainties about pace and scale of operations and the viability of the low-end business models that require higher transaction volumes for survival;
- complex and ill-defined regulatory environments cross-cutting various regulatory domains, such as those regulating banking, telecommunications and information technology;

- technological sophistication of banking and other sectors weak or absent in most markets;
- increase of agent-related risks especially by those that are not prudentially regulated.

Therefore, from this research and the recent studies quoted above, it must be concluded that for the time being there is much more scope for formal and informal financial sector linkages to extend non-traditional services, such as bill payments, transfers, disbursements, pre-paid card purchases than for the facilitation of credit and insurance services, in which agency-related risks and complexity of contracting are greater.

Moving forward

Linkages between formal and informal financial institutions help expand financial services in rural areas. The eleven cases studies examined here offer a shopping bag full of options, from commercial banks using the infrastructure and local knowledge provided by MFIs to reach self-help groups, via MFIs seeking strategic alliances to offer non-traditional services to their clients (e.g. bill payments, transfers, deposits), to large international insurance companies gaining thousands of clients by linking their insurance products to every loan that an MFI makes. Clearly, linkages offer mutually beneficial solutions for both formal and informal financial institutions but, as is demonstrated in several of the cases, establishing and maintaining robust partnerships brings new challenges and risks.

The case studies were selected to ensure that we highlighted key examples from different continents and included a wide range of linkages. We see this study as an important first step in documenting the linkage options and lessons learned. It is our hope that each reader will adapt the knowledge gained from the cases to his or her context. Based on our experience we can make the following observations to help foster further reflection, debate and research on the potential role linkages play in expanding financial services at the frontier in rural finance.

Formal financial institutions

Given the continued development and success of the informal financial sectors in many countries we encourage commercial banks, insurance companies and other non-bank finance companies to consider linking with informal sector actors as a viable business model for a range of services, not just credit. As many of the cases have demonstrated, partnering with informal intermediaries, such as MFIs, SACCOs, self-help groups, village banks, etc., provides a lower cost way to expand outreach into peri-urban and rural markets.

Evaluating and selecting good partners is an important first step in building strong linkages with the informal sector. As we have seen in the cases presented in this book, institutional capacity of informal intermediaries varies widely across and within countries. Working through informal sector networks and associations of service providers can be an efficient way to learn about the capacity and interest of potential partners. It may be beneficial to seek assistance from third parties adept in microfinance training and technical assistance, including NGOs, donors, and government agencies, when faced with constraints to expand a partnership model on a wide scale due to poor capacity of informal partners.

Building alliances with non-traditional partners, especially those operating in rural areas, may not be welcomed by everyone. In many of the cases we found that seeking 'buy-in' at all levels is critically important. In some cases problems arose when the company tried to 'operationalize' the linkage model that middle management had not fully endorsed. Bringing in operational managers at the beginning of the process is critical; not only in terms of getting their buy-in, but, more importantly, to seek their technical input on the feasibility of the new line being considered.

Operationalizing the partnership model may prove challenging, especially when there is a large size and corporate culture difference between the two partners. Establishing a thorough communication plan within and across institutions appears to be key, as is hiring new staff with greater insight and experience about the informal financial sector. Indeed, this was the strategy of some of the formal actors, who hired microfinance professionals to help roll out their partnership programmes. Staff exchanges and business meetings with partner organizations are an excellent way to see the business model from their perspective.

Another way that formal actors can strengthen financial sector linkages is to actively participate in the dialogue and policy development of the informal financial sector. Promoting initiatives that will help to improve the transparency and assessment of local partners will be key, including liaising with objective rating agencies with standardized scoring and MFI networks and other professional associations that advocate self-reporting on key business indicators. These initiatives will, in the long-run, reduce the risks and costs of establishing strategic alliances with the informal sector.

Informal financial institutions

Partnering with a range of financial and non-financial actors to advance business and social objectives is becoming the norm in rural and microfinance. Although most partnerships are sought to broaden access to credit, we are beginning to see organizations use partnerships to expand into offering non-traditional services, including insurance, bill payment, transfers, deposit taking, and account-opening. Some informal organizations are seeing the benefits to their financial sustainability by diversifying revenue streams generated from additional services through these partnerships. However, there is a balance to strike between the number and quality of new services that an organization can offer and manage sustainably and the growth of its core business of credit delivery. Trying to offer too many new services at once without having the necessary systems, procedures, and staff in place to effectively manage them can be detrimental. Many complications can be avoided if operational procedures are outlined and communicated throughout the entire organization and systems are well tested and checked prior to the start of the new service.

Choosing the right partners is equally important for informal intermediaries as well as their formal counterparts. Formal banks and companies vary in their vision, financial health and strategy in partnering with the informal sector. Due diligence in exploring and comparing the benefits and costs of linking with potential partners is prudent. Clarity in knowing what your organization wants and needs from the partnership prior to engaging in a thorough search will typically result in a more fruitful exercise. Talking to similar organizations about their experience of engaging with the formal financial sector can also add benefit to the process.

In several of the cases presented in this book, informal organizations found it necessary to adapt and upgrade their management information systems to share information in a secure and real-time manner. In theory this sounds easier than we found in practice. The need to adapt MIS will depend on the nature of the service being provided and the willingness and capacity of the organizations partnering. New business models often require new information programmes. Some partners worked together to develop software programmes to allow the companies' systems to share information in real time.

Partnering with public sector entities will be distinctly different from partnering with the private sector. Discussions, negotiations and setting terms of the agreement most likely will be more complex and lengthy because of bureaucracy and transparency issues. One may expect more audits and higher reporting requirements and payments of fees and commissions are normal when partnering with the public sector. Sometimes alliances with the state have turned out to be more burdensome and counterproductive than originally perceived as government agencies have a tendency to use the partnership to advance a certain political purpose. As a general rule of thumb, engaging in strategic alliances with the state should only be considered when it is for the delivery of service, such as payment of a utility, disbursement of a benefit (pension, grants), and/or salary payments.

Policy makers

Ultimately, robust financial linkages depend on the business performance of the partners involved. Therefore, enacting policies and initiatives that promote the soundness of the financial sector, including informal actors, is the best point of departure. Indeed it is the role of the government to protect the financial system as a whole by overseeing the financial soundness and performance of formal financial sector institutions. With regard to the informal financial sector, promoting regulatory change that encourages the creation of new organizations and/or improves the performance of existing ones is recommended (Christen et al., 2003). As the enabling environment for financial systems development improves the scope for creating bridges and linkages between financial sector actors increases.

It is advisable to carefully consider policies that would foment linkages in banking, including those that would improve the payment systems and overall financial infrastructure in the country. Working with ministries in communication and information technology as well as designing suitable business contract laws will help to improve partnerships in rural finance. Credit bureaus and independent rating agencies that produce up-to-date, quality information on all financial intermediaries in the system would help foster partnerships.

Part of fostering an effective enabling environment involves avoiding common mistakes and tendencies seen often in development finance. For example, avoiding linkages that are promoted to channel government and/or donor programme credit is a good rule of thumb. Programmes that continue to introduce significant elements of subsidy into rural finance crowd out good organizations attempting to survive in highly fragmented rural markets and dilute good business practice incentives. Instead, one should promote initiatives geared at building the capacity of the informal sector to create commercially viable partnerships with the formal sector. This may be harder than it sounds since it is much easier to generate external resources that can show tangible impact in a relatively short amount of time. Unfortunately donors often seem more interested in knowing how many loans were granted to how many clients than in how much the local financial intermediaries have developed. Promoting professional excellence in rural and microfinance by supporting high quality professional training and academic instruction as well as professional associations and networks of informal financial organizations will strengthen the sector as whole, consequently making many actors more 'partnership worthy' with the formal sector.

In this study, we found that delegated monitoring and 'enforced mentoring linkages' may be counterproductive to the development of the local financial organizations, especially those that restrict formal financial sector engagement beyond transacting with the assigned 'mentor' partner. Although unintentional, this policy has resulted in the local intermediary not being able to choose the more appropriate bank to place its supplement funds, in terms of best interest rate, fees, hours of operations and location.

With respect to promoting regulation to handle new risks associated with correspondent and other branchless banking models, initial evidence suggests that making formal sector actors liable for the actions of their informal partners and maintaining the right to supervise informal agents as deemed necessary may itself be sufficient to deal with the new risks associated with these models (Lyman, Ivatury, and Staschen, 2006). For countries wanting to promote partnerships as a way to expand into new markets it may be advisable to promote those that are less risky and more straightforward (e.g. facilitation of payments, disbursements, transfers, etc.) than those that are more complex and involve more risk (e.g. screening and monitoring of loan and insurance contracts; account-opening based on client assessment, etc.). Governments should be cautious in letting non-banking firms offer financial services. A general rule of thumb is to only allow firms that demonstrate technical and financial strength, high liquidity and a reasonable level of transparency to provide bank-like services in a limited fashion (Lyman, Ivatury, and Staschen, 2006). Placing transaction limits on mobile phone network providers in the Philippines has worked well to date.

Donors and technical agencies

It is clear from these studies that donors and technical agencies, like the FAO and IFAD, have an important role to play in fostering linkages between formal and informal financial sectors in rural finance. Given our initial findings about financial linkages more focused attention and effort is needed to pilot and experiment in establishing financial linkages, especially in countries where the potential for linking is high. This could include the testing of different types of partnership models and analysing the costs and benefits of each type in various contexts. Experimenting with and analyzing the impacts of using advanced internet and telecommunication technology on the efficiency of partnerships could be considered.

Much more attention should be placed on developing partnerships and alliances that help to broaden the range of financial services in rural areas that go beyond credit, such as insurance, deposit, payments/disbursements and money transfer services. The services with the most potential for expansion appear to be transfers, payments and disbursements, and deposit mobilization, which, once the right systems and procedures are in place, are relatively easy to manage and involve little risk. Moreover, facilitating these services offers informal organizations new sources of revenue, which ultimately can affect their long-term financial and operational sustainability for the better. Nonetheless, caution is advised in expanding into too many new services all at once. As a couple of the organizations featured in this book discovered, there are managerial, operational and resource limitations that constrain the health of the partnerships, and often distract management away from their core area of business of credit delivery.

In tandem with experimentation, additional efforts are needed to build the capacity of informal organizations to enable them to actively engage in partnerships with formal sector actors. At a first level, capacity-building efforts could focus on strengthening capabilities in the organizations' core business. At a more advanced level capacity building assistance could focus on more specific nature of building robust partnerships to further the business development goals of the informal financial organizations, including how to select good partners, design appropriate linkage contracts, develop adequate procedures to handle the new line of business, hire new or train existing staff to manage and develop linkage partnerships, use cost-benefit methods to accurately assess the profitability of new services or products, and develop integrated MIS systems that account for new business as a result of linkages. Donors and technical agencies can play a key role in financing and fostering capacity-building efforts. Indeed, the FAO, through its collaboration with the Rural Agricultural Credit Associations in Africa, Asia and Latin America as well as its future planned work on enhancing small producer access to financial services, will use these case studies to build and adapt field activities, share information about and foster policy dialogue on financial sector linkages with its member countries.

Continued financial support for rigorous research on innovative financial linkages and partnerships for expanding the frontier in rural finance is recommended. Studies linked to financial linkage experiments and pilot projects, especially those focused on expanding financial service beyond credit, are in most demand.

Notes

1   Many of the new linkages involving branchless banking and the partnering of mobile telephone operators with banks were just beginning to emerge at the start of the study. See Lyman et. al (2006) for a review of costs and risks associated with branchless banking and the impact on expansion into new markets and Kumar et al. (2006) for an overview of correspondent banking in Brazil. To date, however, there is little empirical evidence on the models' impact on rural penetration.
2   At the time of this study, research on strategic alliances in microfinance was being conducted. See Green and Estévez (2005); Miller-Wise and Berry (2005); and Young (2006).
3   This section follows closely Pagura and Kirsten (2006).
4   Given that we were examining linkages between formal and informal financial institutions we did not study emerging models that have demonstrated potential in increasing the supply of rural financial services through agricultural value chains. These models include structured financial arrangements in which a third party, e.g. supermarkets, buyers, input suppliers, etc., vouches for an individual's creditworthiness, often a small holder vis-à-vis the bank in guaranteeing that they are a preferred supplier or buyer of the third party. For practical examples of these types of structured finance see Campion (2007), Gonzalez-Vega et al. (2006) and Matic et al. (2006).

References

APRACA–GTZ, (1997) *The Linkage Banking in Asia: the Assessment of Linkage Projects*, Volume 1, APRACA, Bangkok, Thailand.
Business Standard, India, April 2007.

Campion, A. (2007) 'Rural and agricultural finance: emerging practices from Peruvian financial institutions', *Enterprise Development and Microfinance*, 18 (2/3): 182–8.

Christen, R., Lyman, T. and Rosenberg, R. (2003) 'Guiding principles on regulation and supervision of microfinance', *CGAP Microfinance Consensus Guidelines*, Washington D.C.

Conning, J. and Kevane, M. (2002) 'Why isn't there more financial intermediation in developing countries', United Nations University, *WIDER Discussion Paper*, number 2002/28.

Green, D. and Estévez, I. (2005) 'Opening markets through strategic partnerships: the alliance between Ameen Sal and three Lebanese commercial banks', in *USAID microREPORT*, number 40.

Gonzalez-Vega, C. et al. (2006) 'Hortifruti in Central America: a case study about the influence of supermarkets on the development and evolution of creditworthiness among small and medium agricultural producers', *USAID microREPORT*, number 57.

Harper, M. and Singh, S.A. (2005) *Small Customers, Big Market: Commercial Banks in Microfinance*, TERI Press, New Delhi.

Kumar, A. et al. (2006) 'Expanding bank outreach through retail partnerships: correspondent banking in Brazil', *World Bank Working Paper*, number 85.

Lyman, T.R., Ivatury, G. and Staschen, S. (2006) 'Use of agents in branchless banking for the poor: rewards, risks, and regulation', *CGAP Focus Note*, number 38.

Matic, J. et al. (2006) 'Using value chain relationships to leverage bank lending: lessons from Croatia', *USAID microNOTE*, Washington D.C.

Miller-Wise, H. and Berry, J. (2005) 'Opening markets through competitive partnerships: the strategic alliance between FIE and Promujer', *USAID microREPORT*, number 23.

Pagura, M. and Kirsten, M. (2006) 'Formal-informal financial linkages: lessons from developing countries', *Small Enterprise Development*, *17* (1): 16–29.

Porteous, D. (2006) 'The enabling environment for mobile banking in Africa', report commissioned by the Department for International Development (DFID), London.

Seibel, H.D. (2006) 'From informal microfinance to linkage banking: putting theory into practice, and practice into theory', *European Dialogue*, 36: 49–60.

World Bank (2006) *World Development Indicators 2006*, International Bank for Reconstruction and Development/The World Bank, Washington D.C.

Young, R. (2005) 'Opening markets through strategic partnerships: the alliance between ICICI Bank and CASHPOR', *USAID microREPORT*, number 39.

INDEX

The following abbreviations are used in the Index:
fig = Figure; *n* = note; *tab* = Table